THE UNIVERSITY OF CHICAGO

THE

ESTAMENT OF SOLOMON

EDITED FROM MANUSCRIPTS
AT MOUNT ATHOS, BOLOGNA,
HOLKHAM HALL, JERUSALEM,
LONDON, MILAN, PARIS AND
VIENNA

WITH INTRODUCTION

A DISSERTATION
SUBMITTED TO THE FACULTY
OF THE
GRADUATE DIVINITY SCHOOL
IN CANDIDACY FOR THE DEGREE OF
DOCTOR OF PHILOSOPHY
(DEPARTMENT OF NEW TESTAMENT AND EARLY CHRISTIAN LITERATURE)

BY

CHESTER CHARLTON Mc COWN

LEIPZIG
J C HINRICHS'SCHE BUCHHANDLUNG
1922

Testament of Solomon.

= THE UNIVERSITY OF CHICAGO

THE
TESTAMENT OF SOLOMON

EDITED FROM MANUSCRIPTS
AT MOUNT ATHOS, BOLOGNA,
HOLKHAM HALL, JERUSALEM,
LONDON, MILAN, PARIS AND
VIENNA

WITH INTRODUCTION

A DISSERTATION
SUBMITTED TO THE FACULTY
OF THE
GRADUATE DIVINITY SCHOOL
IN CANDIDACY FOR THE DEGREE OF
DOCTOR OF PHILOSOPHY
(DEPARTMENT OF NEW TESTAMENT AND EARLY CHRISTIAN LITERATURE)

BY

CHESTER CHARLTON McCOWN

LEIPZIG
J. C HINRICHS'SCHE BUCHHANDLUNG
1922

Druck von August Pries in Leipzig

TO H. D. M.

WHOSE CONTINUED ASSISTANCE AND ENCOURAGEMENT

HAVE MADE THIS WORK POSSIBLE

Preface.

A new text of the *Testament of Solomon* has long been needed. Of the published texts, Fleck's was a careless and inaccurate transcription of a single manuscript, while Istrin's, which was indispensable for understanding the history of the work, is buried in Russian. Of unpublished manuscripts several were found which take us much nearer the original than did any of those already printed. Conybeare's investigation, while resulting in an excellent discussion and translation, labored under the disadvantage of depending upon Fleck, and, because of lack of fuller materials, could not avoid erroneous conclusions. In consequence of the paucity of materials there was a great variety of opinion as to the origin, character, and value of the document.

This edition cannot aspire to present all the materials nor to answer all the questions involved. It is hoped, however, that no accessible manuscripts have been missed, and that the materials available have been set forth in such a manner as to put scholars in possession of all data necessary for accurate conclusions.

When the task was begun, the intention was to edit the text of Fleck's manuscript with introduction, commentary, and translation; but as the number of manuscripts discovered increased, the commentary and translation were abandoned, since it was plain that the volume would be swollen beyond due proportions. The Introduction has in size far exceeded the writer's expectation and desire, and constitutes in part a commentary

The work here published has been under way for many years. Forced by ill health to leave the mission work in India

to which he had intended to give his life, the writer determined
to devote himself to New Testament study, to which he had
been especially attracted during his theological course under the
instruction of Professor D A Hayes of Garrett Biblical Institute
Directed by the *Expository Times* he went to Heidelberg to
work under Professor Adolf Deissmann. The latter with his
characteristic great-heartedness received the unknown student,
and after a few months suggested the *Testament* as a subject
worthy of investigation. Professor Albrecht Dieterich also pro-
mised to take an interest in the work. Upon Professor Deissmann's removal to Berlin and the untimely and lamented death
of Professor Dieterich the writer decided to go to Berlin There,
beside further guidance from the former and the inspiration of
the lectures of Professors Norden and von Wilamowitz-Moellen-
dorff, he had the highly prized advantage of suggestions from
Professor Hermann Diels, who read as much of the manuscript
as was then written

As it became necessary to return to America, the further
prosecution of the task was interrupted except for occasional
intervals during vacations until the writer had the good fortune
to remove to Chicago where, in time snatched from pedagogical
duties, the work was continued and practically completed under
the supervision of Professor E J Goodspeed. The manuscript
has since been read by Professors E. D Burton and H. Windisch.
Dr. Montague Rhodes James went through it very carefully and
made numerous suggestions which have been gladly used. At
an early stage of the work encouragement and direction were
thankfully received from the late Dr Eberhard Nestle, from
Professors von Dobschutz and E Kurz, and especially from
Dr. James These obligations are acknowledged, but not so fully
as they are felt, in the footnotes and bibliography.

In 1920—21 the writer was Thayer Fellow of the American
School of Oriental Research in Jerusalem. The manuscript was
put into the hands of the publisher as he was on his way to
Palestine. In browsing among the manuscripts of the Great
Greek Monastery in Jerusalem he had the good fortune to discover
two manuscripts, one of the *Testament*, one of the legend of

Solomon's dealings with the demons. Although the printing of the *Testament* has been delayed for various reasons, it was not possible to incorporate the results of the study of these manuscripts in the text. A collation of one, called MS N, and a copy of the other, called MS E, have been printed in the Appendix (see pp. 112—128 and 102*—120*) and a list of emendations suggested by MS N will be found on p 121*f

On the way to Palestine the writer passed through Milan and took occasion to visit its famous library and inspect the manuscript, Ambrosianus No 1030, in which fragments of the *Testament* are found, described below, pp 20f. Nothing new was discovered. The fragments seem to have been cut of some manuscript, perhaps for the sake of, what was on the *recto*, which, in the case of Uᴾ, contains rules for gematric prognostication. This fragment ends with the word ἡμέραν, p. 7*, l. 15. It follows the W text

For the patience and wisdom of the editor of the series, Professor Windisch, in dealing with many perplexing problems that have arisen and for the skill and carefulness of the publisher in overcoming the technical difficulties of a complicated critical apparatus the writer cannot express too high appreciation.

The task was practically completed at the beginning of the war. The course of events which has prevented publication until now has given further time for revision of the manuscript and, it is hoped, thus contributed to more careful conclusions

The work is given to the public with the hope that it may assist others, as it has the writer, to a better understanding of the devious ways of the ancient book maker and copyist and a better insight into the working of the popular mind in antiquity, and so advance the study of the *genus humanum*.

Berkeley, California Dec. 24., 1921.

Chester Charlton McCown.

.

Contents.

THE TESTAMENT OF SOLOMON.

INTRODUCTION.

I. GENERAL CHARACTER AND CONTENTS.

1. The *Testament of Solomon* is a combination of folktales and a magician's *vade-mecum* In its interpretations of Scripture and its legends of biblical personages it reminds one of the Haggadah. In its stories of demons and their activities it is similar to the *Arabian Nights* Its magical formulae and recipes relate it to the execration tablets, the amulets, and the magical papyri of antiquity, and to the medical recipe books of the Middle Ages. The same combination of naive popular science and laboriously learned philosophy runs indirectly into the Faust literature, and directly into the *Clavicula Salomonis*, the "Key of All Mysteries"[1]. It is a product of those three pseudo-sciences which have brought more disappointed hopes and abject terrors to mankind than any others astrology, demonology, and magic.

2. It is as a leaf from the common man's thinking that the *Testament* has its chief value. Its superstitious puerilities arouse intense interest, when one thinks of them as recording the hopes and fears of the vast majority of mankind. The "Meditations" of Marcus Aurelius and the "Confessions" of St. Augustine open the door to the innermost thoughts of two great personalities who have done much to mould the life of their own and all succeeding generations. Books like the *Testament* help one to understand the psychological reactions of the great shadowy

---

1 Cf. *infra*, p. 14 and n. 1.

army of men who followed these leaders afar off. They explain why the philosophical emperor, who had learned "not to give credit to what was said by miracle-workers and jugglers about incantations and the driving away of demons and such things"[1], should have allowed two lions to be cast into the Danube with elaborate ceremonies and costly sacrifices, in the vain hope of winning success for the Roman arms, and should have consulted the Chaldeans to cure Faustina's infatuation for a gladiator[2]. In spite of their absurdities demonology and magic had a tremendous hold upon the great body of mankind. The *Testament* is doubly welcome, since unfortunately we have too few first hand sources in this field[3].

3. The document also makes a contribution to a most important chapter in the early history of Christianity, coming as it probably does from the fourth century, or earlier, and embodying much older materials. One of the prominent motifs in the work is the conception of Christ as conqueror of demons The Christian compiler combines a simple, unhesitating faith in the efficacy of the pagan formulae he cites with an inconsistent trust in the superior power of *Christus invictus*. Dion Cassius ascribes the famous thunder storm that miraculously refreshed the Roman legions and discomfited their enemies during the Marcomannic war to the magic arts of an Egyptian sorcerer[4] The Christians claimed the marvel came in answer to the prayers of the 'Thundering Legion', and made the incident a powerful argument for the new faith[5]. Our author, combining the two contradictory points of view, stands as a representative of the great majority of the Christians of his time, to whom their faith

---

1 *Meditations* I 6.

2 Dill, *Roman Society from Nero to Marcus Aurelius*. London: Macmillan, 1905, pp. 446—450, Lucian, *Alexander* 48.

3 The *Test* in some measure fills the gap in our knowledge of ancient superstitions left by the missing books of Hippolytus' *Refutatio* (II and III).

4 *Hist.* LXXI 8.

5 Eusebius (*HE* v 5) quotes as his authority Claudius Apollinaris, who addressed an apology to Marcus Aurelius. Tertullian makes the same apologetic use of the story. Cf. the account of Dion with that of Xifilinus in *Dio Cassius Cocceianus* ed Bossewain, III 259 f.

was but another superstition superimposed upon the old. It was
impossible all at once to replace the old sensuous paganism
with a spiritual and ethical monotheism. During the long struggle
Christianity was fearfully debased and weakened. How much
of the old was carried over into the new religion the *Testament
of Solomon* helps one partly to realize

4. Another important service the *Testament* renders in that
it represents, so far as it is Jewish, "pre-Talmudic demonology"[1],
and one might add, Palestinian demonology. It is, to be sure,
much more than a Christian revision of a Jewish work. A pro-
fusion of both Christian and pagan ideas and materials are to
be found in it, and until these are indicated, the document must
be used with caution[2]. However, when once these elements are
eliminated, as they can be with some certainty, the *Test* comes
to be of real assistance in reconstructing the thought world of
the Palestinian Jew in the first century of our era, and it is,
therefore, important not only for the student of church history,
but for the New Testament and the Jewish scholar.

5. A complete table of contents is given at the end of this
section. The aim of the present paragraph is to call attention
to the main ideas that enter into the construction of the work
In the two chief recensions the story in brief is as follows. In
response to his prayers Solomon receives his famous magic ring,
in order that he may protect a favorite workman on the Temple,
who is being tormented by a demon. By means of the ring
the King calls the demon before him, learns the powers and
activities of all the demons, the formula, or angelic name, which
frustrates each, and in addition many secrets of nature and of
the future. The demons are used to perform various tasks in
connection with the building of the temple. The story ends
with an account of Solomon's fall because of his love for a
Shunamite girl, and of the consequent loss of his power over
the demons. This simple framework, without plot or progress
of thought, allows the introduction of a bizarré medley of stories

1 Dr. Kohler, art "Demonology" in *JE* IV 518 a.
2 V. *infra* III 12, a criticism of Ginzberg's use of the *Test.*

1*

about demons. The writer's chief interest is medico-magical.
He writes to make known to the world what the diseases and
ills are which demons bring to mankind, and how their male-
volent designs are to be frustrated. His angelology is only a
foil to his demonology, for God's messengers come to earth
solely for the purpose of counteracting demonic agency. The
motif of temple building, which introduces the story, is well-
maintained throughout, entering into almost every section. Yet,
while ostensibly primary, it is really subordinate, it is part of
the background against which the author can display his demonological knowledge. Another *motif* is the wisdom and glory
of Solomon. This also is kept continually in mind throughout
the entire narrative. In one brief section the demons are for
the moment entirely forgotten, while the magnificence of Solomon's buildings, the wealth of his treasury, and the homage
rendered him by other nations are described. Though the "Queen
of the South" is introduced as a sorceress ($\gamma \acute{o} \eta \varsigma$), it is without
a trace of the Jinn of the Bilkis legend. However, Solomon's
power is due to his ring, his wisdom and magnificence to what
the demons have taught him and done for him, and thus the
whole is brought within the writer's circle of ideas. Another
very natural interest betrays itself. No doubt many an in-
quiring mind had asked how the magicians came to know
the secret names and incantations by which the demons
could be laid. In a well known Egyptian legend, Isis, the
divine sorceress, wishes to learn the secret, allpowerful name
of Re. She causes him to be bitten by a serpent, and he
must reveal the name before she can cure him[1]. The question
which inspired the Egyptian story is more satisfactorily answered by the *Testament*. Solomon's magic ring forces the
revelations, and the wise king before his death writes all this
hidden lore in a "Testament", which is handed down to future
generations, that they may be able to escape the wiles of
their demonic tormentors. It is in this connection that the

---

1 Erman, *Handbook of the Egyptian Religion*, p. 154 ff. Unfortunately the
name is not pronounced aloud, and the reader never learns it.

motivation for the story of Solomon's fall is not unskillfully
supplied. According to one manuscript[1], a demon foretells the
sad end of the King's glory, and, when the prophecy is fulfilled,
the chastened monarch, satisfied of the truth of all that the
demons have told him, writes it down. Thus, with all its variety
of contents, the work is a real unity, owing to the writer's pre-
ponderating interest in magic and demonology[2].

6. The following inventory of the contents of the recensions
of the *Testament* is intended to show in the most concise manner
what the various forms of the work contain. By comparison
of the numbers in this list with those of the "Comparative Table"
opposite it will be plain at once what part of the total material
each manuscript contains. References to chapter and section
or to pages of the Greek text will, it is hoped, render the rapid
survey of the latter easier

The "Comparative Table" is intended to show the material
contained in each manuscript, and thus to illustrate the relations
of the manuscripts one to another The divisions of the manuscripts into families, or recensions, here adopted is supported by
other considerations, as will appear later. Yet the proof offered
by this table is so simple and decisive that further evidence is
hardly necessary.

In the table the figures at the left refer to the sectional
numbers in the conspectus of contents on the opposite page.
The letters, a, b, and c, used in the columns pretaining to the
manuscripts, stand for Recensions A, B, and C, and indicate that
the recension contains the material of the section in question.
Where one of the letters: d, h, i, l, p, etc., appears, it indicates
that in that section the manuscript shows material peculiar
to it. The cipher: o indicates that the section is wanting
through the carelessness of the scribe or accident to the manuscript, not by intentional omission on the part of the editor of
the recension.

---

1 P, XV 14 f., the only complete MS But see MS N in appendix.
2 Schurer, *GJV* III 419, is hardly right in calling the *Test* "Unterhaltungs-
literatur".

a) Prefatory matter (not originally part of *Test*)

1. Title
2 Doxology
3. David's sin with Bathsheba, D I 1—3 [1]
4. Failure of God's attempt to stop David, D I 4—6
5. Nathan's reproof of David, D I 7—11
6. Solomon's birth, reign, power, and wisdom, D I 12f
7. Solomon's prayer, command to build Temple, UVW[2], Prol. 1—5
8 Building of Temple, D II 1, cf. *Test* I 1

b) Testament proper, matter common to majority of MSS

9. The favorite slave, or chief architect, I 1; D II 2
10 His affliction by a vampire I 2[3], D II 2
11. Solomon's prayer about the matter, I 3, D II 3
12. Solomon examines the slave, I 3 f., D II 3f
13 Solomon's supplication for him, I 5, D II 5
14. The answer, a magic ring, I 6f., D II 6f.
15. The inscription on the ring (not original)[4]
16. Solomon gives the ring to the slave, I 8f, D II 8f
17. The capture of the demon, Ornias, I 10—14, D II 10—13.
18. Solomon examines Ornias, II 1—9, D III 1—4
19. Ornias fetches Beelzebul, who is examined, III 1—7[5]
20 Onoskelis summoned and examined, IV 1—12
21. Asmodaeus summoned and examined, V 1—5
22. Asmodaeus further examined, V 6—13[6]
23. Beelzebul re-examined, VI 1—11[7]
24. Lix Tetrax, VII 1—8[8]
25. The seven sister vices, VIII 1—12
26. Phonos, IX 1—7[9]

c) Testament proper continued in Recensions A and B

27. Punishment of Phonos, IX 8
28. Kyon, or Rhabdos, and the green stone, X 1—11
29. Leontophoron, XI 1—7

---

1 For compendia employed to indicate MSS see below, II.
2 U contains only a few lines in § 4 and again in Nos. 52 and 53.
3 About the middle of I 2 HI and PQ unite.
4 The inscription on the ring in HI and T is found also in an amulet in
V (Vr) not connected with the *Test*.   5 Q resumes in section 40 below

No.	D.	H.	I	L.	P.	Q.	S	T.	U	V.	W.	Migne col.	Text p.
		Rec A			Rec. B.		Rec. C.					Migne	Text

a) Prefatory matter (not originally part of *Test*)

No.	D.	H.	I	L.	P.	Q.	S	T.	U	V.	W.	Migne col.	Text p.
1.	d	h	1	o	b	b				c	c	1316A	98⁺ f.
2.		a	a		a	a						1316A	5*, 99*
3.	d												88*
4.	d												88*
5	d												89*
6.	d												89*
7.									c	c	c		78* f.
8.	d	a	a	l	b	b				c	c	1315A	90*

b) Testament proper, matter common to majority of MSS

No.	D.	H.	I	L.	P.	Q.	S	T.	U	V.	W.	Migne col.	Text p.
9.	d	a	a	l						c	c		5⁺ f., 90⁺
10.	d	a	a	l	b	b				c	c	1316A	6* f., 201
11.	d									c	c		8* f., 90*
12.	d	a	a	l	a	a				c	c	1316B	8* f., 90*
13	d	a	a	a	a	a				a	a	1317A	9* f., 90*
14	d	a	a	l	b	b				c	c	1317B	10*, 90*
15.		a	a	l	b	b	c	a		c	c	1317B	100* f
16.	d	a	a	l	a	a				a	a	1317B	11*, 90*
17.	d	a	a	l	a	a				a	a	1317C	11* ff, 90* f
18.	d	a	a	a	a	a				a	a	1317D	13*, 91*
19.		a	a	a	a	o				a	a	1320B	16*
20.		a	a	a	a	o				a	a	1320D	18*
21		a	a	a	a	o				a	a	1321C	21*
22		a	a	a	a	o				o	o	1321D	22*
23.		a	o	a	ap	o				o	o	1324C	25*
24.		a	o	a	a	o	c			ca	ca	1325C	28*
25.		a	o	a	a	o				a	a	1328B	31*
26		a	o	a	ap	o				a	a	1329B	35*

c) Testament proper continued in Recensions A and B

No.	D.	H.	I	L.	P.	Q.	S	T.	U	V.	W.	Migne col.	Text p.
27		a	o	a	a	o						1329B	37
28.		a	o	a	a	o						1332A	37
29.		a	o	a	a	o						1332C	39*

6 In V 12f. L has a different text. Sections 22 and 23 are wanting in VW, probably because of parablepsia. In V 8 MS I ends

7 In VI 3—9 P has its peculiar text

8 In VII 6 S has only a few lines of a magic formula in the form in which it appears in Rec C

9 In IX 7 P has a considerable interpolation.

---

1 MSS HL omit XIV 3—XVI 1.
2 In XVIII 4 P has an unique text. L breaks off at the end of XVIII 28.
3 In XIX P has numerous additions
4 MS Q reappears in XX 10. P often has a longer text than H.
5 In many sections H presents a highly abbreviated text, in XXVI 8—10
an inflated one. The B text is here probably better

No. D	Rec A H. I. L.	Rec. B. P. Q.	Rec. C. S T. U. V. W.	Migne col.	Text p.
30.	a o a	a o		1333 A	41*
31.	a o a	a o		1333 C	43*
32.	o o o	a o		1336 C	45*
33.	o o o	a o		1337 A	46*
34.	a o a	a o		1340 A	48*
35.	a o a	a o		1340 D	49*
36.	a o a	a o		1341 A	51*, 91*
37. d	a o o	p o		1348 A	59*
38.	a o o	p o		1348 A	59*
39.	a o o	p o		1348 B	60*
40. d	a o o	a a		1348 C	60*, 92*
41. d	a o o	p b		1348 D	64*, 94*
42. d	a o o	a a		1352 A	65*, 95*
43. d	a o o	a a		1353 D	69*, 95*
44. d	a o o	a a		1356 A	70*, 95*
45.	a o o	a a		1356 B	71*
46.	a o o	b b		1357 A	73*
47.	h o o	b b		1357 B	74*
48.	h o o				75*

d) Close of MS D

49 d				96*
50. d				96*

e) New material of Recension C

			Rec. C. S T. U. V. W.		Text p.
51			c c c c		77*
52.			c c c c		77*
53			c c c c		78*
54.			c o c c		83*
55.			c o c c		84*
56.			t o c c		84*
57.			c c		85*
58.			c c		87*
59.			c c		87*
60.			v		99*

6 Sections 52 and 53 are found in the *Clavicula Salomonis* in the same codex as L and Tᵒ, Harl. 5596, here called Tᵈ. MS U ends with X 11.

7 Sections 54—56 are found as an unrelated fragment in Harl. 5596, in this case called Tᵒ.

II. DESCRIPTION OF THE MANUSCRIPTS.

The manuscripts are here described in the briefest manner that seemed consistent with the desire to put the reader in possession of the main facts necessary to estimate their relative importance and their relationships. They are taken up in the order in which they appear in the foregoing table, that is, following the alphabetical order of the letters which have been chosen to symbolize them, which is also the order of priority in the development of the *Test*

> 1 D Dionysius monastery, Mt. Athos, No. 132, ff. 367ʳ—374ᵛ, XVI cent.; entitled περὶ τοῦ Σολομῶντος; published by Istrin, cf. Edition No. 4; collated by photograph[1], from which the title is missing, pages of *Test* deleted by transverse lines[2].

Istrin gives no description of the manuscript The photograph shows it to have been carefully and correctly written and well preserved, it seems to be in small format. The hand is heavy, round, and beautifully clear, with the customary ligatures and abbreviations. Orthography and punctuation (comma, question mark, and period) are exceptionally good. The iota subscript is lacking. The β is often written like an υ. In one instance an omitted word was added at the bottom of the page; in another the order of two clauses was reversed by putting the letter β before the first, α before the second[3]. Otherwise there are no important corrections or erasures. A later hand has added marginal notes giving some of the subjects mentioned in the text. The title given by Istrin appears to have been written above the ornamental head-piece, and only the lower part of the letter π appears in the photograph The Solomonic writing, which fills eight leaves, was wrongly bound. The leaves are in the order 367—371, 374, 373, 372. The page on which

---

1 Secured during the summer of 1914 through Dr. Heinrich Jantsch, Leipzig-Marienbrunn, by whose permission it is used.

2 It does not appear to be noticed by Lambros in his *Catalogue*.

3 κέκτημε occurs for κέκτημαι, I 10, σιτεῖα for σιτία II 2, 4, φησί is always written with the grave accent

the next selection begins appears to be 375. The writing covers only about two-thirds of f 374ᵛ, something having been erased from the remainder of the page. F. 366ᵛ contains the conclusion of a religious or ecclesiastical writing which I do not recognize[1]. On f 375ʳ begins a selection described in another hand as εἰς τοὺς αἱρετικούς, λόγ(οι) λδ´, φύλλα ε´[2]

    2. H Private library of the Earl of Leicester, Holkham Hall, Norfolk, England, No. 99, described in the catalogue as "Opuscula theologica varia, on paper, Quarto XV and XVI cent." The *Test* is of the XV cent., cm. 16×21.5; 35 ff, unnumbered, f. 1 *recto* and f. 35 *verso* blank, making 68 pages, entitled διήγησις περὶ τῆς διαθήκης σολομῶντος, etc.; well preserved, unpublished[3]

The writing is large, round, and clear, γ and ν, ε and σ may easily be confused. Ligatures and abbreviations are frequent, iotacism often appears; the iota subscript is rare. The punctuation, which is intelligently used, consists mainly of the period, placed sometimes higher, sometimes lower. Corrections and erasures are rare. It is the only manuscript which boasts rubrics placed before the chief divisions of the story. The title and the

---

1 The page begins, χαίρουσα παραστῆς, τὰς ἀιδίους | ἐκείνους (in -ας corr.) καὶ θείας ἐλλάμψεις πλου|σίως ἀεὶ δεχομένη . ., and ends, οὐ δὴ | καὶ ἡμεῖς μετρίως μὲν ἐνταῦθα, πλουσίως δὲ ἐκεῖ ταῖς σαῖς ὁσίαις εὐχαῖς ἐπι| τύχοιμεν χάριτι τοῦ Κ(υρίο)υ καὶ Θ(εο)ῦ καὶ σ(ωτῆ)ρ(ο)ς ἡμῶν Ἰ(ησο)ῖ Χ(ριστο)ῦ· ᾧ|πρέπει πᾶσα δόξα|τιμή, etc

2 It is called Ἔκθεσις κατ᾽ ἐπιτομὴν τοῦ τῶν Ἰακωβιτῶν|δόγματος καὶ τῶν ἄλλων ὧν ποιοῦσι παρὰ τὴν|ἐκκλησιαστικὴν καὶ ὀρθόδοξον πίστιν τε καὶ παρά|δοσιν· συγγραφεῖσα παρὰ δημητρίου μητροπο|λίτου κυζύκου· ἐκ προτροπῆ(ς) τοῦ φιλοχρίστου | κωνσταντίνου τοῦ πορφυρογεννήτου υἱοῦ λέον|τος τοῦ σοφοῦ· ἐν ᾗ καὶ περὶ τῶν χατζιτζαρίων· — | Inc · Ἐπειδή σου τὴν ὑπερφυῆ καὶ τῷ ὄντι βασιλικωτάτην φύσιν ἐξαιρετόν τι χρῆμα Θ(εὸ)ς τῷ κόσμῳ ἐδωρήσατο... the page ends with καὶ πρὸς τὸν τῶν Ἰακωβιτῶν διανέστησεν ἔλεγχον ὡς ἂν μὴ|καὶ οὗτοι διεστραμμένα καὶ βλάσφημα δόγματα.

3 Professor Deissmann very kindly made inquiries concerning the *Test* while lecturing in Cambridge in 1907. Dr. M. R. James informed him of the Holkham Hall MS, and later was so kind as to send me a copy of the first nineteen pages. In January, 1908, I went to Holkham and, through the generosity of the owner and the goodness of the librarian, Alexander I. Napier, Esq., was allowed to collate the MS in the library of the Hall. It is published by permission of the owner.

initial letters of the lesser sections are also in red. In XXII
10, 11 ς for σ has been mistaken for ι.

Aside from the *Test* the contents of the codex are theological and ecclesiastical. There is nothing to indicate its provenience except a tract copied in the same hand as the *Test*
and called in the catalogue "Johannes Canabutii magistri ad
principem Aeni et Samothraciae"[1] This seems to point to Greece.

> 3. I Bibliothèque Nationale, Paris, Supplément grec, No. 500,
> XVI cent., paper, cm 16×22, ff. 78—82; entitled σολο-
> μῶντος, etc, with διαϑήκη τοῦ added in a careless
> hand in the upper margin of the page; well preserved,
> published by Istrin, cf Edition No 4

The writing is fine, slender, and somewhat crowded, ligatures
are extremely frequent and intricate, abbreviations and compendia numerous. Iotacism is comparatively rare; Attic orthography appears occasionally, e. g., φρίττω (II 1), the iota subscript is wanting; the punctuation (comma and period), the
division of words, and the use of breathings and accents correct.
Corrections and erasures are very rare. Although a broad
margin has been left, marginal variants and glosses are wanting.
The title with a conventional ornamental head-piece above it,
the magical inscription of the ring, and occasional initial letters
of sections are rubricated

The codex contains a miscellaneous collection of classical,
philosophical, ethical, theological, and biblical writings, including
Ecclesiastes and Canticles, some of them unfinished. The *Test*
follows the two Solomonic works just mentioned. Unfortunately,
as with some of the other works, the copyist soon became
weary of the stories of the many demons and broke off in the
middle of a sentence and a column, when he had written about
one sixth of the *Test*.

The well known Greek scholar, Minoïdes Minas, whose name
appears on one of the fly leaves at the back, owned the codex,
and through his heirs it came into the Bibliothèque Nationale in

---

1 Johannes Canabutzes was a Graeco-Italian from Chios, first half of the
fifteenth century, Krumbacher, *BLg*.

1864. Minas had been under commission from the French go-
vernment to seek manuscripts in European Turkey, Asia Minor,
and especially at Mt. Athos. Where he acquired this one is
unknown Doubtless it was somewhere in the Levant[1].

4. L Harleian MSS, British Museum, No. 5596, 58 ff., paper,
   cm. 23×34, XV cent., described in the printed catalogue
   as "Geomantica, exorcismi, divinationes et huius modi,"
   with the addition in the written "Class-catalogue' of the
   words "quaedam Salomonis;" well preserved, unpublished. Four fragments are used as follows· 1) ff. 8ʳ—18ᵛ,
   the title, originally missing, supplied by a later hand
   in Latin "Quomodo Solomon aedificaturus templum
   cum spiritibus colloquitus fuit, et multa edoctus,"
   2) f. 7ʳ—7ᵛ, 3) f. 33ʳ, and 4) ff. 39ᵛ—41ʳ (On the last
   three fragments, which are designated by T, see below.)

The writing is low, broad, round, and heavy, it is somewhat
run together, yet it is regular, very clear, and not without
beauty. Abbreviations and ligatures are frequent, compendia
less so. Iotacism is not frequent. The iota subscript does not
appear. The comma (rather infrequent), the period, and, at the
end of the more important sections, a triple period make up
the punctuation. Erasures, corrections, and Greek glosses are
wanting. A later hand has added in Latin, besides the title,
occasional marginal notices and translations, and has marked by
a cross and circle those peculiar directions for the use of the
Test as a magical remedy for disease which render this MS
unique. The MS also has the distinction of being the only one
written in columns, two to the page. They are seven to eight
centimeters wide, and contain twenty lines. In fragment 1) no
colors are used except on the seal of Solomon. It is painted

1 In a personal letter, dated April 10, 1908, M. Omont very kindly gave
me information regarding the three MSS of the *Test* found in the Bib. Nat.
Regarding this one he says: "Suppl. gr. 500. Provient de Minoïde Mynas, no. 35
d'une list de ses manuscrits, mais sans qu'on puisse autrement préciser l'origine
orientale du volume." My wife copied the MS in Paris in 1907. I compared
the copy with the original then and again in Heidelberg, where it was sent
through the customary diplomatic channels to the University library for my use.

with silver over red, as are the titles of the sections in the
Clavicula (see below), and the numbers as well as the article (ὁ)
before each name in the list of fifty-one demons (Fragment 4).
The rather coarse, yellow paper of the codex is beginning to
decay. At one spot in the lower half of the inner column many
of the leaves have rubbed until a few letters have disappeared.

Harleian MS 5596 is entirely filled with magical, astrological, and demonological matter, evidently written by a mediaeval
magician for practical use in his profession. The largest part
(ff. 18 –44ʳ) is taken up by the Greek form of the *Clavicula
Salomonis*[1] In it Fragments 3) and 4), which appear respecti-
vely in Recensions A and C in other MSS of the *Test*, are
found. The first seven leaves of the codex contain various brief
magical, geomantical, and astrological excerpts and observations,
ending with Fragment 2), which is the second form of the
Onoskelis story, found in Recension C of the *Test*. Two other
of these excerpts bring this MS into relation with MS V, which
contains a copy of Recension C, viz, ἕτερα τοῦ Πυθαγόρου
ἡλιαδι (sic)[2], f. 5ᵛ, col. 2, and a "Pythagorean table," πλινθὴς
(sic) α³, f. 6ᵛ, col. 2, both also found in MS V. I have discovered only one other MS in which the *Clavicula* and the *Test*
appear together, and that is MS W, in which there are three
very badly written pages of the former and a complete copy

---

1 This well known magico-astrological work, though mediaeval in its
present form, is based on older materials. The Harleian MS contains the longest
Greek copy I have seen. The ὑγρομαντεία in Munich MS. 70, ff. 240—253 (cf.
CCAG VII 3, 3, f. 240), is well written, but shorter. *Paris graec.* 2419 (= MS W)
has, as remarked above, only a fragment, and that miserably written. It is to
this last that Reitzenstein refers in *Poim.* 187, n. 1 Other Greek MSS, known
to me only through catalogues, are Turin C VII 15, f. 75ᵛ (*CCAG* IV 16), called
ἑρμανεία; Mt Athos, Dionysios monastery, (Lambros, *Cat* I 400) No 3816,4
(282), f. 28ᵛ—37ʳ, entitled τὸ κληδὴν τῆς πάσης τέχνης τῆς ἱγρομαντίας,
. . . συντεθὲν παρὰ τοῦ Σολομῶντος, κ. τ λ Latin, French, Italian, and
English MSS of the *Clavicula* are numerous. Cf. the translation from Latin into
English by S. L. M Mathers, *Clavicula Salomonis*, London, 1889. Seligsohn in
JE, art. "Solomon, Apocryphal Works" (XI 447), accepts a Hebrew original.
He knows no Greek form.
2 MS V, f. 274 (cf. *CCAG* IV 41, Bon. Univ. 3632).
3 MS V, f. 274ᵛ, closing the ἐπιστολὴ Πυθαγόρου.

of Recension C of the latter. Fragment 1), or L, contains about two-thirds of the *Test*, ending in the middle of a column.

While on a brief visit to England in January and February, 1908, I undertook to go through all the Greek MSS of magical contents in the British Museum, as well as all the Solomonic literature in Latin, French, and English. In the course of the search I came across the Onoskelu story, then the longer fragment of the *Test* (L), and later the other pieces in the *Clavicula*. Unfortunately I have been able to get no light on the provenience of the codex. But it certainly has Italian relationships, since the "Pythagorean' letter and table are found in several other Italian MSS[1] besides V, and S of Vienna which is closely related to V[2].

> 5. P Bibliothèque Nationale, Anciens fonds grecs, No. 38 (Colbert 4895); XVI cent., paper, cm. 15.5×20.5; 24 ff. in three quaternions; well preserved, entitled διαϑήκη σολομῶντος, etc.; published by Fleck, reprinted in part by Furst, and entire by Migne; cf Editions Nos. 1, 2, and 3.

The manuscript has been carefully and intelligently written. The handwriting is somewhat unskilful and angular in appearance, but easily readable. The letters are ligatured as ordinarily in the sixteenth century, but compendia and abbreviations are rare, even such words as ϑεός and Ἱεροσόλυμα being often written out in full. Iotacism is very rare. The iota subscript, the accents, and the breathings are almost always correctly given. Unfortunately the punctuation, consisting of the comma, and the period at various heights, is most profusely employed and, as Furst says, "verstößt gegen jede auf bestimmte Grundsätze basierte Abzeichnung der Satzteile"[3].

Not only has the manuscript been carefully written, but part of it has also been through the hands of a corrector. A large number of letters which seemed uncertain to the co-

---

1 Cf. *CCAG* IV (codd. Ital.) 15 (Taurin. 5, f. 39ᵛ), 31 (Mutin. 11, f. 77), 53 (Neapol. 19, f. 44), 75 (Florent. = Laurent. 29, f. 38), also Milan (Ambros.) 1030, f. 247.   2 Cf. *CCAG* VI 33.   3 *Orient* V, col. 596 note.

pyist were marked with three dots, in other instances he left
part of a line vacant for the insertion of the proper words. Two
such cases occur on the first page, where blacker ink, smaller
and more crowded letters, and more numerous abbreviations[1]
show that the words were put in later[1]. In one case the corrector hit upon the right text, in the other he missed On f. 2r2
a similar blank was left, but the corrector was too uncertain to
put his conjecture in the text; it remains on the margin. Unfortunately he failed to go carefully through the entire manuscript, and not all of the uncertain places received his attention
Occasional corrections were made in the course of the writing[3]
Initial letters of sections are enlarged, and in two or three instances the closing lines of paragraphs have been left partly
blank No attempt has been made to rubricate or decorate the
manuscript. It contains only the *Test*.

As to the provenience of the codex little can be made out.
It belonged to the library of M. le President de Mesmes according to the catalogue printed by Montfaucon in 1739[4]. Henri
de Mesmes died in 1596, his son, Jean-Jaques, who inherited his
manuscripts, in 1642. In 1679 Colbert bought about 215 manuscripts from the Duchesse de Vivonne, great-granddaughter of
the former[5], among them the *Test*, as the list shows[6]. The
manuscripts of Colbert came into the *Bibliothèque du Roi* in 1732[7]
In the catalogue of the *Bibliothèque Royale* (later *Nationale*) of
1740[8] it is mentioned as "No. 38 olim Colbert" Back of the
library of de Mesmes it cannot be traced Above the beginning of the text on the first page is written "Codex Colb. 4895
Regius 2913 3", preceded by a short word ending in many
flourishes. Of this, to me illegible, part of the superscription

---

1 In I C. 3, 4
2 In C. I 9. Similar blanks are left in II 3, XXVI 3, 4. Marginal notes
are found in IV 5, V 19, VII 3, VIII 7, 0, 10, IX 6, XIII 2, 3, XVIII 27, 37,
XIX 1, XX 1.
3 Cf. XVIII 33, XXVI 2. The only serious omission due to carelessness
is in XXI 3 f   4 *Bib bib. mss*, II, p. 1327
5 Cf. Delisle, *Cab des msc*, I, pp. 469, 471, and Omont, *Inv.* IV, pp. XXI,
XXX.   6 It is *msc lat.* 9364 f. 11 in the *Bib. Nat.*   7 Delisle, *op. cit.* p. 439
8 *Cat codd mss bib reg*, voll. 1—4, Paris, 1739—1744.

M. Omont says. "'Cent': ce numero est une code d'inventaire des manuscrits de la duchesse de Vivonne, il provient très vraisemblablement des de Mesmes"[1]

This manuscript has been occasionally noticed by scholars Du Cange used it in his *Glossarium* published in 1688[2], referring to "Salomonis Testamentum ex Codd. Reg. 1843[3] et Colbert," and adding "vide notas nostras as Zonarae Annal p 83"[4]. In these *Notae*, published in 1687, he gives the title almost as in P with the remark, "legimus apographum ex Bibliotheca Thuanea." Either this is a slip of the memory, or else the "apographum" was merely a copy of the title. The library of Jaques August de Thou (died 1617) was sold in 1680, most of the ancient manuscripts being acquired by Colbert. But none of the printed catalogues of the library of de Thou show any copy of the *Test*[5].

Other references to the *Testament* are secondary and rest upon Du Cange[6] or Gaulmin, until finally Fleck came across the manuscript and published it in 1837. His edition[7] has been the basis of all subsequent labors upon this piece of Solomonic literature, until the publication of Istrin[8].

1 In the personal letter above referred to, p. 13, n. 1.

2 *Gloss. ad script. med. et infin. graec.* (Paris, 1688), II, col 32, in "Index Auctor. Graec. ined." 3 Now *Par. gr.* 2419, see below MS W.

4 *Zonarae Annalia* ed. Du Cangius, Parisiis 1686—7, 2 vols.

5 Cf. Delisle, Cab. des msc., I, p. 471, Omont, *Inv.* IV, p XXX, *Biographie Universelle* (Paris 1826), XLV, p. 505 and n 17, *Nouvelle Biographie Universelle* (Paris 1866), XLV, p. 229; Maichell, *Intro. ad hist. lit. de praecip. bibl. Paris*, p. 60. Concerning this M Omont, in the letter already mentioned, says "Bien que le ms. 38, comme vous le verrez provienne de De Mesmes et non de De Thou, je crois cependant que c'est lui auquel Du Cange fait allusion à la p. 9 des notes du t. II de Zonaras En tous cas, il n'y avait pas de ms. du Testament de Salomon dans le Catalogue imprimé au XVIIe siècle de la Bibliothèque de De Thou "

6 So the references by Hemsterhuis in *Thomas Magister* (Lugd. Bat. 1757), p. 636, and *Etymolog Mag.* (ed. Gaisford, Oxford 1848), p. 142, 7, depend upon the *Glossarium*. Fabricius reprinted the title from *Zonaras*. On a slip pasted on the inside of the cover of the codex one reads 'Testamentum Salomonis, Fictitium, non semel laudatum a Gaulminio in Notas ad Psellum de operat. Daemonum. 4895." This is a mistake. On Gaulmin's quotations see below on the use of MS W. 7 Edition No. 1, cf. *infra Intro* III 1.

8 Edition No 4, cf. *infra Intro* III 4.

6. Q Andreas Convent, Mt. Athos, No. 73, ff 11—15: XV
cent., published by Istrin, cf. Edition No. 4[1].

Although Istrin has given no description of the manuscript
or critical apparatus, it is evident from the number of omitted
letters which he has supplied in brackets, as well as from the
frequent longer lacunae that it was carelessly copied from a defective exemplar.

The manuscript contains only about one third of P, viz.,
the first ninety and the last two hundred thirty-seven lines,
cc. III 1—XX 9 being omitted. The omission occurs near the
bottom of f. 12[r], many pages, evidently, having dropped out of
its exemplar.

7. S Vienna, codex philos. graec. 108; paper, cm. 19×25;
XVI cent.; well preserved; the greater part unpublished.
Contains two unpublished fragments: 1) copies of the
twelve seals said in MSS VW to have been found on
the ring of Solomon, f. 361[v]; 2) one of the recipes found
in the same recension (VII 7), f. 167[v][2].

The codex contains much astrological matter, and many
Solomonic amulets and selections. It has a large number of
amulets like those in MS V, and long selections of magical
content written in the peculiar cryptography to be found in
that manuscript. They must, therefore, be of related origin,
S having been copied from V or its exemplar. I have not
learned anything concerning its provenience.

8 T British Museum, Harleian MS No. 5596, cf. supra,
No. 4.

This manuscript has already been fully described. A different letter, T, is used to designate the three fragments which are

---

1 I attempted to secure a photograph of this manuscript, as of MS D, but
none was sent No reason was given for the failure.

2 Cf. CCAG VI (Codd. Vindobon.), p. 1. Some of the Solomonic matter
is edited in the catalog. The names of the *decani* from ff. 357 ff. (p. 73 ff.), bear
practically no resemblance to those in the *Test* XVIII, yet the materials are
ultimately related; cf. *infra* p. 56. I studied the codex in Berlin, where it was
very kindly sent to the imperial library for my use.

not incorporated in the incomplete copy of the *Test* found in this manuscript, and which belong to different recensions.

T⁰ (or simple T) designates a fragment containing the variant story of Onoskelis (Rec. C, XI), and part of Solomon's conversation with Paltiel Tzamal (Rec. C, XII 1—4, and 6 — in part —). It begins without title in the middle of col 1 on f. 7ʳ, being separated from a magic formula which precedes it by a slight space, and ends in the middle of col. 2 on the *verso* of the same leaf. The remainder of the column is blank. The *Test* begins at the top of the next column, f. 8ʳⁱ.

Tʳ designates a fragment from the *Clavicula* containing a representation of a seal and inscription which, according to MSS HI, was that on Solomon's ring. The seal, an elongated six-sided figure containing ten circles and various magical characters with the word σαβαωϑ, takes up the greater part of the first column on the page (f 33ʳ), and following it are given certain instructions and the inscription (cf. infra p. 2/3.), which runs over into the second column, under the rubric περὶ τοῦ δακτυλιδίου. The *Test* in this manuscript (L), contains a somewhat different but closely related version of the inscription on the seal.

Tᵈ designates a section in the *Clavicula* which contains the list of fifty (or fifty-one) demons which makes up a considerable portion of the unique matter in Rec. C. It runs from f. 39ᵛⁱ (bottom) to f. 41ᵛⁱ (top), and bears the rubric, ἕτερα πράξης (sic) τῆς αὐτῆς The previous section has for its rubric, ἕτερα πράξης τοῦ καθρέπτου (modern Greek, *mirror*). It is an exorcism of a certain female demon and her people (ἡ κυρὰ βασίλισσα ἡ συμπίλια ὁμου με τοῦ λαοῦ της … ἐσύ καὶ οἱ ἄρχοντές σου) in order that they may perform certain services for the magician, particularly that they may answer truthfully any questions he may ask. It is written in very late Greek with an Italian flavor, much more modern than the already late Greek of the list of fifty demons. Tᵈ is followed by a list of the demons and angels that rule each hour of the day, and another of the ruling planets and the work proper to each hour of the day. Both of these subjects had already been covered more briefly in an earlier part of the *Clavicula*; that is, the writer is here adding to the *Clavicula* matter of various kinds that belongs to the same sort of magic, but was not found in his copy. The last two sections he probably found in another recension of the *Clavicula*, for they appear without great difference of text in the Munich codex[1]. The origin of the list of fifty demons will be discussed later[2]. The text of T^d covers about one fifth of Rec. C.

> 9. U Ambrosian library, Milan, No. 1030 (H 2 inf.), paper, cm. 16×226, ff. 1—378, XVI cent.; two fragments. 1) f. 233^v, (= U^d), 2) f. 252^v (= U^p).

As this manuscript is known to me only through the catalogue[3] and a photograph of the page on which Fragment 1) is found, a full description of it is impossible. As to the handwriting of the page photographed, however, and general contents, it closely resembles manuscripts V and W, discussions of which follow. It has two pages from the *Clavicula*[4], here called ὑγρομαντεία as in Munich MS No 70, the "Pythagorean" letter[5] and table found in Harl. MS No. 5596 and Bologna University MS 3632, and some astrological matter found in the Bologna manuscript[6].

The manuscript contains several unfinished fragments, some of them, like those from the *Test*, "transversis lineis deleta." I should judge that the scribe filled up odds and ends of time and space by copying little sections from other manuscripts. Thus he started in on the list of demons, and when he had reached the bottom of the page stopped. He probably had W or its exemplar before him, for he usually follows the W text.

U^d designates a fragment which, like T^d, contains the list of demons given in Rec C In this case, however, it is a mere fugitive fragment, with no relation to what precedes or follows, except as it is all of astrological character, and it does not com-

---

1 Cod. 70, ff. 243ᵣ—246ᵣ, ff. 240ᵣ—243ᵣ.   2 Cf. infra VII 12

3 *CCGBA*, II 1096. The photograph was obtained through Dr. H. Jantsch, as was that of MS D, cf *supra*, p. 10, n. 1.   4 Cf. *supra*, p. 14, n. 1.

5 Cf. *supra*, pp. 14, ns 2—3 Here it reads, πυθαγόρου ἡλιοδώρῳ χαίρειν πολλὰ παθὶν, κτλ.

6 περὶ τῶν ζ′ βατανῶν (sic), f. 250; περὶ βοτανῶν ιβ′ ζωδίων καὶ τῶν ζ′ πλανητῶν, f. 246ᵣ

plete the list, ending with § 11. It bears the title, *Δαίμων σφραγισάμενος ὑπὸ σαλυμῶνος τάδε εἶπε. Δαιμονίων δυνάμεις καὶ
ὀνόματα.*

Uᴾ I have chosen to designate a little fragment which begins
very abruptly in the middle of a sentence in § 5 of the "Prologue" to Recension C, with the words, *πρὸς αὐτόν· σολομὼν,
σολομὼν, κύριος ὁ θεός σου ἐρεῖ* The catalogue does not quote
farther, nor give the *explicit*.

10. V Bologna, Library of the University, MS No. 3632;
475 ff, paper, cm. 21.9×29.6; XV cent.; written by a
physician, John of Aιo (or the son of Aro, or Aron);
Test, entitled *Διαθήκη τοῦ σοφωτάτου σολομῶντος, κτλ*,
ff. 436ᵛ—441ᵛ; dated (f 441ᵛ) December 14, 1440[1].
Unpublished[2]

The codex is poorly preserved. The leather of the half-
leather binding is torn away, and the book is almost in pieces.
The rough, gray paper is becoming discolored, yet the writing
is distinct. One would not form a high estimate of the education
of Dr John from his handwriting, for it is loose, careless, and
irregular, and his lines run up hill. His spelling is equally unsatisfactory. No distinction is made between, *ει, η, ι, οι,* and *υ*,
between *α* and *ε*, or between *ο* and *ω* Often *β* and *υ*, occasionally *α* and *ει*[3] are interchanged. The accents are usually placed
on the right syllable, but no attention is paid to the distinction
between acute, grave, and circumflex, the last appearing even
on *ε*. The breathings also are interchanged The iota subscript
is wanting The punctuation, consisting of comma and period,
is in general not bad, but not entirely consistent. Abbreviations,
ligatures, and compendia are extremely frequent. Well known
words or forms are abbreviated by leaving off the last few

---

1 Cf. *CCAG* IV (codd. Ital. praeter Flor. etc.) 46. Olivieri, "Indice", 452.

2 Through the customary diplomatic channels the officials of the University Library at Heidelberg very kindly secured the loan of this MS for a period
of three months from February to May, 1908, and later the extension of the
time for three months more, transferring it also to Berlin, where I had gone for
the summer semester. This gave opportunity for a careful study of the whole codex.

3 Probably because the ligature for *ει* closely resembles a common form of *α*.

letters. The title, the subscription, and the initial letters of the chief sections are rubricated. Corrections, erasures, and marginal notes are wanting.

The contents of the codex are instructive both as to the medical practice and the religious beliefs of the Middle Ages, for they include all sorts of pseudo-scientific biological information, pages of medico-magical formulae, partly in cryptography [1], and long astrological treatises. The codex is rendered unique by its cryptography and by the large number of illustrations, poorly drawn and highly colored, including drawings of animals and plants, and magical and astrological figures.

The *Test* stands in gathering μ of the codex, being preceded by 1) $\lambda a \beta \acute{v} \varrho \iota \nu \vartheta o \varsigma \ \tau o \tilde{v} \ \sigma o \varphi o \tilde{v} \ \sigma o \lambda o \mu \tilde{\omega} \nu \tau o \varsigma$, f 435[r 2], and 2) $\pi \varepsilon \varrho \grave{\iota} \ \beta o \tau a \nu \tilde{\omega} \nu \ \tau \tilde{\omega} \nu \ \iota \beta' \ \zeta \omega \delta \acute{\iota} \omega \nu \ \dot{\varepsilon} \varrho \mu o \tilde{v} \ \tau o \tilde{v} \ \tau \varrho \iota \sigma \mu \varepsilon \gamma \acute{\iota} \sigma \tau o v \ \varkappa a \grave{\iota} \ \pi \varepsilon \varrho \grave{\iota} \ \beta o \tau a \nu \tilde{\omega} \nu \ \tau \tilde{\omega} \nu \ \zeta' \ \pi \lambda a \nu \acute{\eta} \tau \omega \nu$, f. 435[v 3]. Following the *Test* comes $\dot{o} \nu \varepsilon \iota \varrho \acute{o} \varkappa \varrho \iota \tau o \varsigma \ \dot{o} \ \sigma \eta \varrho \eta \mu$[4] $\varkappa a \grave{\iota} \ \ddot{\varepsilon} \tau \varepsilon \varrho o \varsigma \ \dot{o} \nu \varepsilon \iota \varrho \acute{o} \varkappa \varrho \iota \tau o \varsigma \ \varkappa a \iota \ \pi \acute{a} \lambda \iota \nu \ \ddot{\varepsilon} \tau \varepsilon \varrho o \varsigma \ \varkappa a \tau' \ \dot{a} \lambda \varphi \acute{a} \beta \eta \tau o \nu$. After the letter π of this third $\dot{o} \nu \varepsilon \iota \varrho \acute{o} \varkappa \varrho \iota \tau o \varsigma$ the codex ends (f. 475). Two further writings mentioned in the $\pi \acute{\iota} \nu a \xi$ (f 16[1]) are wanting; 1) $\varepsilon \dot{v} \chi \grave{\eta} \ \tau o \tilde{v} \ \dot{a} \gamma \acute{\iota} o v \ \varkappa v \pi \varrho \iota \acute{a} \nu o v \ \varkappa a \grave{\iota} \ \dot{\varepsilon} \tau \acute{\varepsilon} \varrho o v$ (sic) $\tau o \tilde{v} \ \dot{a} \gamma \acute{\iota} o v \ \gamma \varrho \iota \gamma o \varrho \acute{\iota} o v$, and 2) $\varkappa a \grave{\iota} \ \ddot{\varepsilon} \tau \varepsilon \varrho \varepsilon \varsigma \ \tau \acute{\varepsilon} \chi \nu a \iota \varsigma \ \tau o \tilde{v} \ \sigma o \lambda o \mu \tilde{\omega} \nu \tau o \varsigma$[5]. None of these items were originally in the $\pi \acute{\iota} \nu a \xi$, but the writings themselves are in the same hand as the greater part of the book. They evidently were not a part of the original plan of the copyist. The codex contains also the "Pythagorean" matter found in Harl 5596[6], but in this case the copyist saved himself trouble by pasting in six leaves, the first five of which, containing the "Pythagorean" letter, were written in another hand, Dr. John continuing on the sixth The titles of the

---

1 Cf. *infra*, p 23 and n. 1.

2 Cf. Berthelot, *Col. alch* I 156f, Texte grec I XX 39f (from MS 299, St. Mark's, Venice, f 102[v], XIV or XV cent.), I have found it also in Munich MS 395 (Hardt, IV 228), and Brit. Mus. Add. MS 34060, f. 162[v]. The Bologna MS lacks the text which in three different forms accompanies the *Labyrinth* in the above three MSS.

8 Cf. *CCAG* IV 134, VI 83, VII 29; Fr Boll in *N JBB kl Alt* XXI (1908), 110 n 2, see below p. 26 on MS W

4 See below on MS W, p 26, n. 2.   5 Was this the *Clavicula*?

6 Cf. *supra*, p. 14 and ns 2—3 and p. 20 and n. 5.

writings which were pasted in are an original part of the πίναξ, and therefore, probably of the plan. From the similarity of subject matter it is plain, I think, that T, U, and V are very closely related.

The *Test* covers the lower two thirds of f. 436ᵛ, on which it begins. After fifteen lines at the top of the succeeding page, all the remainder is occupied by the twelve seals which were engraved on Solomon's ring, with an additional circle in which the description of the seals given in the text is repeated[1]. The next six pages are written solid, the writing space averaging cm. 17.5×25. On f. 441ᵛ the first eleven centimeters of the writing space are occupied by a circular figure intended to represent a magic writing of Solomon which is mentioned in the text (Rec. C XIII 14), and bearing the superscription, αὗτ(η) ἡ βούλ(α) ἦν ἐφόρεσ(ε) σωλομὸν ἐπάνο τη σκευει αυτου. Beside it stands another, empty circle. There follow the concluding five lines of the *Test*, and then the subscription, consisting of seven lines, the first five of which are in the cryptographic character peculiar to this MS and Vienna 108

The subscription, reduced to ordinary characters, is given in the Text, p. 212. Lines five and six read, ἐγράφη παρ' ἐμοῦ Ἰω⟨αννου⟩ ἰατροῦ τοῦ αρο ἐν ἔτει ͵ςͳμθ' (ἰνδιχτιόνος) δ' ἐν μηνὶ Δεχε⟨μ⟩βρίῳ ιδ'. The name, Ἰωάννου is abbreviated to Ἰω, the remainder of the line up to and including αρο being in cryptographic characters On f 362ʳ the name is given again in cryptographic characters, this time spelled. out in full, as follows· ιοάνου ιατρου του αρου. On f. 327ʳ it is found again thus. ιοανου του αρό του ιατρου. There can be no doubt as to the reading of the characters, since by a combination of two lists of words and their equivalents in different parts of the codex a key is formed to the cryptography[2]. *Aro* I take as a place name, but am unable to locate it.

As to date there is no difficulty, since that part of the subscription exhibits only the common abbreviations The world

---

1 Called Vˢ in the apparatus crit., cf. p. 214
2 The writer has in preparation an article on this cryptography

year 6949 corresponds to 1440—1. The indiction, four, fits that
year according to the table given by Gardthausen. The date is,
therefore, December 14, 1440. On f. 269ᵛ (bottom) one reads
the date ͵ϛϡλθ′, and on f. 327ʳ after the name, ͵ϛϡνβ′; that is,
6939, or 1430—1, and 6952, or 1443—4 Although the meaning
of the accompanying notice is not clear to me, I take it for an
astronomical remark¹. That on f. 327ʳ has the appearance of
having been added to the page at the lower margin after the
original writing had been completed. As we have already seen,
the codex falls into two parts, the second beginning with gathering μ, f. 435, and there is no reason why the first part may
not have been written last, yet I incline to think the date was
added after the writing.

There are several other writings in the codex which in the
πίναξ are called πρᾶξις Σολομῶντος, all of them having to do
with magic. The references to Solomon, however, were added
after the first writing of the index, and it would seem that after
writing the latter part of the codex, the scribe came to the conclusion that Solomon was the great source of all magical science
and proceeded to give him due credit. The *Test* may well have
been the cause of this opinion.

Most of the writings marked πρᾶξις Σολομῶντος have no
relation to the ancient king, except that they are magical. However, on ff. 360—361 is a considerable collection of amulets,
two of which bear his name. In the one it is simply a part of
the incantation². The other, a circle four centimeters in dia-

----

1 The three notices read, after correction as to orthography, as follows
1) f. 327ʳ μνήσθητι, κύριε, τὴν ψυχὴν τοῦ δούλου σου Ἰωάνου τοῦ Ἀρὸ τοῦ
ἰατροῦ + (ἔτει) ͵ϛϡνβ′ (εἰσὶν) ὦ ⚹ ης τ(ους) ·) (· l. ὁ χρόνος εἰς τοὺς
ἰχθίας), at lower margin in faded ink ξβ′ ͵ϛϡξε′   2) f. 62ʳ: Ἰωάνου ἰατροῦ
τοῦ Ἀρὸν· ἡ μὲν ἡ χείρ ἡ γράψασα σίπεται τάφῳ, τὸ δὲ γραφὲν εἰς τοὺς
αἰῶνας μένει. + εβρετε βρεμα εκ θεου ελειι (l. εὕρεται βλέμμα ἐκ θεοῦ
ἐλεεινοῦ?) + Γαλήνου. 3) f 269ᵛ (not in cryptography) ἔτει ͵ϛϡλθ′ κύκλ⟨ου⟩
κγ′ (σελήνης) (ἡμέρα?) δ′ θεμελ⟨ίῳ⟩ ξ′ (ἰνδικτιῶν)ος θ′   Cf. Gardthausen,
Gr. Pal. II 495.

2 The same amulet is found in S (— Vind. phil. gr. 108), f. 361ʳ, on the
page preceding the copies of the twelve seals of Solomon (cf. supra p 15). The
amulet consists of a circle decorated within and without with magic signs and
containing the following ιωηλ βοηθει (within a triangle). ιδου σολομ(ον) υιος

meter, bears the title, $\tau o\tilde{v}\ \sigma o\lambda o\mu\tilde{\omega}\nu\tau o\varsigma\ \mu\varepsilon\gamma(\acute{a}\lambda o v)$, and it contains within it the inscription which, according to H and I, belongs on Solomon's magic seal, and which is given in the *Clavicula* in Harl. 5596 (= T r), and in a slightly different form in the *Test* in that manuscript (L). The Bologna version has been designated as V r [1].

As to the provenience of the codex I have been able to learn nothing more than has been already intimated. The cryptography of the manuscript is sufficiently like the stenography of Cod. Vat Graec 1809 to make one think of the monastery of Grottaferrata [2] as some way the source of Dr. John's knowledge of stenography. Yet the inference that he was connected with the monastery would be extremely uncertain. He may have gotten the stenography indirectly or even have developed it independently upon the basis of more ancient systems. That the manuscript is Italian in origin there can be no doubt.

11 W Bibliothèque Nationale, Paris, Anc. fonds grecs, No. 2419, XV cent. paper, cm 27×37, 342 ff., written by George Mediatēs. *Test* entitled $\delta\iota\alpha\vartheta\acute{\eta}x\eta\ \tau o\tilde{v}\ \sigma o\varphi\omega\tau\acute{a}\tau o v\ \sigma o\lambda o\mu\tilde{\omega}\nu\tau o\varsigma, x\tau\lambda.$, ff. 266ᵛ—270ᵛ. Well preserved. Unpublished [3].

The codex resembles very closely the foregoing. The writing is somewhat more regular and less hasty in most of the codex. Iotacisms are almost as numerous; doubled letters are almost always written singly, even where they belong to different words. As to all other points W is just a trifle better than V. W omits occasional phrases that are found in V, sometimes apparently through carelessness, sometimes because they were unintelligible.

As to contents again there is great similarity, but in W the

$\delta\alpha(\beta\iota)\delta\ \delta\varrho\alpha x o\nu\tau o\varsigma\ \gamma\lambda o\sigma(\sigma)\alpha\ \varepsilon\chi\omega\nu\ \beta\alpha\sigma\iota\lambda\varepsilon o\varsigma\ \varepsilon\gamma x\varepsilon\varphi\alpha\lambda o v$. Beneath is written the following prescription for the use of the amulet $\alpha v\tau(\eta)\ \eta\ \beta o v\lambda\alpha\ \gamma\varrho\alpha(\psi\varepsilon)$ $o\mu o\iota\omega\nu\ x\varrho o x o\nu\ x\alpha\iota\ x\eta\nu\alpha\beta\alpha\varrho\iota\ x\alpha\iota\ \mu\alpha\gamma\nu\eta\tau\eta\ x\alpha\iota\ \beta\alpha\sigma\tau\alpha\ \varepsilon\nu\vartheta\alpha\ \varepsilon\iota\sigma\iota\ \chi\varrho\iota\mu\alpha\tau\alpha\ (x\alpha\iota$ $\varepsilon\sigma\iota\ \alpha x\eta\nu\eta\tau o\varsigma$ add. Bol; more correct spelling adopted where MSS differed).

1 Cf. Text p 100*.   2 See M. Gitlbauer, *Überreste*, 1 Fasc. p. 3.

8 On this MS cf. Omont, *Inv*, II 256f. I copied the *Test* in Paris in May and June, 1907.

alchemistic and astronomical interests outweigh the biological and the magico-medical. Berthelot says of it, "Ce manuscrit in-folio . est des plus précieux pour l'histoire de l'Astronomie, de l'Astrologie, de l'Alchimie, et de la Magie au moyen âge; c'est une réunion indigeste de documents de dates diverses et parfois fort anciens, depuis l'Almageste de Ptolémée et les auteurs arabes jusqu'aux écrivains de la fin du moyen âge"[1]. The codex contains three pages from the *Clavicula*, and some "Hermetic" and "Pythagorean" writings. The fact which connects it most clearly and indubitably with Bologna 3632 is that the *Test* is immediately preceded by the Hermetic work on the planets and the twelve signs of the zodiac, and followed, though not immediately, by two of the "dream books" which also appear in the Italian manuscript[2]. The very position of the beginning of the *Test* on the page is the same in the two manuscripts. As in V, so in W, the *Test* begins about one third down the page, and at the bottom of the next page are found the large seals that in this recension belong on Solomon's ring. Either the one was copied from the other, or both followed very closely the same exemplar. The decision of this question can best be left to a later section (III 4) where the text will be discussed.

As to the provenience of the codex, M. Omont has given me the following information[3]: "Grec 2419 Provient du cardinal Nicolas Ridolfi († 1550), puis du maréchal Pierre Strozzi († 1558) et de Catherine de Medicis, après la mort de laquelle (1589), il resta sous scellés jusqu'à son entrée dans la bibliothèque du Roi en 1599. Au fol. 340ᵛ°, le bibliothécaire de Ridolfi, Matthieu Devaris, a écrit cette note sur l'origine du ms.: αὕτη ἡ μεγάλη βίβλος, ἣν ἐκόμισέ τις Ἕλλην ἐν Βαλνεαρίᾳ διατρίβοντι τῷ δεσπότῃ, περιέχει ἀστρονομικά τινα καὶ ἰατρικὰ καὶ ἄλλα διάφορα. Νο 35. [Deleted by a transverse line] Νο 44 vigesim. quart (Ce sont deux numéros successifs de la bibliothèque du Cardinal Ridolfi; s. e. *capsae*. τῷ δεσπότῃ désigne ici le maître de De-

---

1 *Col. alch.* I, Intro., I, 205; MS described, pp. 205—211.

2 Cf. *supra*, p. 22. The titles of the "dream books" as given by Omont (*loc. cit.*) are *Onenocrites Syrim* and *Manuelis Palaeologi oneirocrites*.

3 In the letter already referred to above, p. 13, n 1, p. 17, n 1.

varis, le cardinal Nicolas Ridolfi.)" W, then, like V, came from Italy.

The name of the writer was George Mediates (or, Meidiates), as appears from a subscription found on f 288 From a *Pascha-lion* on f. 275 running from 1462 to 1492 the conclusion is drawn that the codex was written about 1462.

The codex has been frequently used by scholars. Gaulmin in all probability took from its the excerpts he quoted in his notes on Psellus *de oper. daem*[1]. From it Du Cange prepared a very considerable list of chemical and astrological abbreviations and tachygraphic signs[2] In more recent times Berthelot has taken from it some important chapters in his *Collection des Anciens Alchimistes Grecs*, while Reitzenstein refers to it several times in his *Poimandres* Aside from Gaulmin I know of no publication which refers to the *Test.*

12 Βιβλιοϑήκη μόνης Κουτλουμουσίου, Χαρτ. 16. XVI (Φ. 431), .. 4 διαϑῆκαι Σολομῶντος. Ἅπαντα ἐν τῇ καϑωμιλημένῃ.

This reference is taken from Lambros' Catalogue of the MSS on Mt. Athos, No. 3221, p. 287. I attempted to secure a photograph, but was unsuccessful, and know only this reference to the manuscript.

13 While studying in Berlin, Paris, London, Heidelberg, Munich, and smaller places on the Continent, I made search for other manuscripts and for translations of the *Test*, but without success. None of the catalogues which I was able to consult gave indications of its presence in any form. Through the kindness of Dr A. F. R. Petsch, then professor in Heidelberg, and later in the University of Liverpool, inquiries were mady by friends of his in the libraries at St. Petersburg and Moscow, but without success. Dr. F. C Conybeare was so kind as to search in the Vatican Library. Though he was under the impression that a Latin manuscript was in existence[3], he was

---

1 See above, p. 17, ns. 6, 7.

2 *Gloss.*, "Notarum characteres, Notae aliae," coll. 19—22, in vol II.

3 At Florence; see the *Guardian*, Mar. 29, 1899, p. 442 Dr. Conybeare

unable to verify that supposition or to find any other manuscripts. No doubt such exist and will be found, but no others
are available at present [1]

III. MODERN EDITIONS, TRANSLATIONS, AND TREATISES.

1. Fabricius [2] deserves mention before all others, because he
first attempted a systematic collection of materials bearing on
the *Test.* As already indicated [3], he gathered his excerpts from
Gaulmin and Du Cange, whose quotations he prints in full with
some attempt at emendation.

2. Fleck rather inaccurately copied the *editio princeps* [4] from
MS P, mistaking many letters, and so causing himself and those
who have had to depend upon his edition much difficulty. He
evidently was not familiar with sixteenth century ligatures. While
it has not seemed necessary to note his misreadings in the
critical apparatus of the present edition, some of the more important have been included as samples of his errors [5].

3. Apparently the first scholar to concern himself with the
text which Fleck had printed was Bornemann. In 1843 and in
1846 he published conjectural emendations of the text, showing
no little ingenuity, and in some obvious cases finding the original, though missing it in every real difficulty, as is usual with
such conjectures. In 1844 he published a complete translation
in German [6], marked by the same learning and good sense shown
in his "Conjectanea".

4. Furst [7] was the next to deal with the *Test,* printing the
Greek text after Fleck, with a German translation, also in 1844.

---

was so kind also as to send me a reference to Chachanov's *History of Georgian
Literature* (I 170 ff.), where mention is made of Georgian manuscripts of the *Test.*
Unfortunately the work was to be found neither in Berlin, London, nor Chicago,
and I have not seen the pages in question.

1 The index to Omont, *Inv* refers to Anc. fonds grecs 2511 as having a
copy of the *Test,* but it is merely a copy of Prov. XXV 1—XXIX 29. Two
Jerusalem MSS discovered later are discussed in the appendix

2 Cf. Bibliogr. III 1.   3 Supra p. 17, n. 6, p. 27, ns. 1, 2; Bibliogr. IV.
4 Cf Bibliogr. I 1.   5 Cf. c. I 2, II 6, IV 4   6 Cf. Bibliogr. III 1 and II 1.
7 Cf. Bibliogr. I 2 and II 2.

The work, however, was not completed. Little attention was given to emending the text, but no small learning was expended on its proper translation and interpretation, though, rather strangely, the title is rendered "Bund", not "Testament", or "Vermachtniss."

5. In Migne's *Patrologia Graeca*[1] a reprint of the text from Fleck with a Latin translation was appended to Psellus, because of the fact that Gaulmin had quoted the *Test* in his *Notae* to Psellus' *de oper. daem* The reprint shows the usual additional typographical errors, but in a few cases Fleck's more obvious mistakes were corrected. The article in Migne's *Dictionaire des Apocryphs* (Bibliogr. III 3) adds nothing new.

6. Chronologically next in order is Dr. F. C. Conybeare's translation with introduction in the old *Jewish Quarterly Review*[2], which is marked by the famous rationalist's usual careful scholarship and independence of judgment. He did all one could do with Fleck's edition. However, I am inclined to differ from him on questions of date and origin

7. As a result of the publication of Conybeare's translation there appeared two brief articles in the *Manchester Guardian*[3], one by Dr. Montague Rhodes James, and the other by Dr. Conybeare, and a brief review in the *Theologische Literaturzeitung* by Schurei[4], who differed with Conybeare as to the Jewish origin of the *Test*.

8. In the same year that Dr. Conybeare's translation appeared, the Russian scholar, Istrin, presented the text of the fragmentary manuscripts which I have called I and Q, and of the interesting story called MS D[5] His introduction indicates the true relationship, as I believe, between D and the *Test*.

9 A brief notice of Istrin's publication and a review by Dr. E. Kurz appeared in the *Byzantinische Zeitschrift*[6]

10. Harnack has a brief notice in his *Altchristliche Literatur*[7], and Schurer a considerable one in his *Geschichte des judischen Volkes*, which includes a valuable collection of materials[8]. To

---

1 Cf. Bibliogr. I 3   2 *Ibid.* II 4 and III 4   3 *Ibid.* III 5 and 6.
4 *Ibid.* III 7.   5 *Ibid.* I 4 and III 8.   6 *Ibid.* III 9 and 10.
7 Vol. I 858.   8 *GJV* III 419f, *HJP* II III 154f.

Dr. Kohler's article in the *Jewish Encyclopedia*[1] I owe the interesting suggestion that the *Test* represents pre-Talmudic demonology. Other encyclopedia articles make no special contribution[2].

11. In Salzberger's dissertation on the *Salomosage* much space is dedicated to the *Test*[3] He accepts Conybeare's conclusions as to authorship and date, and accordingly takes the *Test* as representative of early Jewish-Christian demonology and folklore, making no attempt to distinguish Hellenistic elements. He has evidently used Conybeare's translation without reference to the Greek text[4].

12. Ginzberg's *Legends of the Jews*[5] contains a section devoted to the *Test*. It is a paraphrase and epitome rather than a translation, but follows the text of Fleck rather closely. One error is sufficiently serious to deserve mention: the aerial column of c. XXIV is confused with the cornerstone of c XXIII. As unfortunately the notes and references, which, according to the preface[6], were to have appeared in the last volume, are lacking, there is nothing to indicate the source from which the story was taken As a piece of entertaining writing the work may have a place, but it is a hindrance rather than a help to the study of ancient Jewish thinking because of its uncritical confusion of older and later materials. Ginzberg was not justified in using the *Test* without first sifting out the considerable non-Jewish elements more carefully than he does.

IV. THE TEXTUAL HISTORY OF THE *TESTAMENT*.

1. The manuscript families. — On the textual evidence alone, without reference to wider considerations of language and subject matter, which will be taken up later, the various

---

1 IV 518, art. „Demonology"   2 Cf. Bibliogr III 3 and 12.

8 Bibliogr. III 13.

4 This appears from his citing only Conybeare (p. 9, n 9) and from his use of *"Flasche"* for ἀσκός (p. 97), following Conybeare's "flask" in secs. 119—123, though the latter once has "leather flask" (119).

5 Bibliogr. II 5.   6 Vol. I XV.

MSS divide themselves into four clearly marked classes or recensions[1].

a) MS D differs from the rest in that it is not a "Testament." Of magico-medical formulae there are none. It is simply a biography of Solomon in which the demonological interest outweighs all others, quite closely resembling in many features the *Arabian Nights*. It clearly belongs to the "literature of entertainment," where Schurer wished to class the whole *Test*[2].

b) MSS H, I, and L (Rec A) stand very close together, H and I agreeing in a beginning which is entirely different from that in the other MSS, H and L (after I drops out) in the long omission, cc. XIV 3—XVI 1 L might deserve to be put by itself as a separate recension, for it has at a late period undergone a special revision. A magician has endeavored to make the work more useful for members of his profession by introducing directions for the use of the more important magical formulae in the cure of some disease, probably demon possession. He has also made some further changes in the opening sections. However, all these alterations, marked by modern Greek forms[3], are so easily detached from the remainder and affect it so little that there is no need to separate it from H and I as a textual witness

c) MSS P and Q (Rec. B), again, clearly stand together almost from beginning to end. The title and the opening sentences are good illustrations of their close similarity throughout. This recension, in P at least, is marked by two explanations of the writing of the *Test*[4], by a shorter beginning and ending, and by more extended accounts of many of the demons[5].

d) MSS V and W with the fragments S, T, and U group

---

1 The variety of recensions is not at all remarkable in popular literature such as this; cf. the remarks of Krumbacher, "Studien zur Legende des heil. Theodosius," in *Sitzungsber. d. bay. Akad. d. Wiss*, *philos., philol. u. hist. Cl.*, 1892, Heft II, p. 225.

2 Since this is not a *Test*, I have not called it a recension, but refer to it as MS D. See above, p. 5, n. 2.   3 Such as ἦτον ἕνας, I 1.

4 See XV 14 and XXVI 8; no great weight can be attached to this, since c. XV is wanting in HILQ by accident or scribal error.

5 See cc. XIX, XX, and XXVI.

themselves as an entirely different recension (C), which has undergone a thorough revision. The *Prologue*, as I have called it, in
order to bring the chapter and verse divisions into line with the
other recensions, and the altered title, but especially the entirely
different ending from IX 8 on are sufficient evidence. This recension is more interested in demonology as a means for reveal-
ing nature's treasures and mysteries than in its medical aspect
as emphasized in the original *Test* It is marked by scribal
omissions [1].

   2 The relationships and relative dates of the recensions. —
   a) MS D represents the story which formed the basis of
the *Test* The recensions have just been considered in what the
writer regards as their chronological order   It is inconceivable
that any one should take the *Test* as found in Recs. A, B, or C,
and, by eliminating all the magico-medical element and the
"testament" motif, reduce it to the simple tale of Solomon's birth
and greatness, his temple building and dealing with demons,
which appears in MS D. On the other hand, the very close
resemblances between MS D and Recs. A and B as to general
outline and even as to text in places, e. g , in the story of the
old man and his son, c. XXI, proves the closest possible relationship, and, therefore, the dependence of the *Test* upon the
story as found in MS D.

   Yet D in its present form cannot have been the basis of
the *Test*. It occasionally shows a fuller, secondary text, e. g.,
in the threat of the old man to cease working if Solomon did
not condemn his son (D IV 2) Especially is this true of D VII.
The question of c. VII 1, ἔστι καὶ ἕτερον δαιμόνιον; and its
answer, εἰσὶ μὲν πολλά, ὦ βασιλεῦ, after the statements of c.
III 4—8 that all the demons had been brought in and set to
work in the temple are manifestly a later addition. There is no
reason why c. VII should not have been put into the *Test* if it
had lain before its writer. It is evident, then, that MS D represents a revision of the work that formed the original of the *Test*.

─ ─ ─── ─   ─

   1 See cc. I 4, 11, 14, V, VI, etc. The language of C is more consistently
late than in any of the other recensions; see below, V 2.

The question as to whether cc. I, II, and VIII were part of this original is harder to answer. The editor of the *Test* could not well include cc. I and II in a "testament," which must have been written in the first person to have entirely consistent. The abrupt beginning of Rec. B is probably due to truncating the original story in order to eliminate these elements, which do not fit the new plan C VIII could easily have been put into the first person and left in the *Test*. Yet it seems entirely possible that it was in the original and was omitted by the editor of the *Test* merely because it did not interest him, or perhaps because it did not suit the pathos of the fall. It is not inconsistent with the remainder of D, but rather comes as a fitting conclusion to a narrative of which the account of the sin of David and the birth of Solomon was the beginning[1]. I am inclined, therefore, to regard D I—VI, VIII as the original basis for the *Test;* with certain changes which we cannot follow and the addition of c VII, D received its present form. The making of the *Test* was a much more complicated process.

b) Recensions A and B are both revisions of the original *Test* The question of priority in this case is much more difficult. It is plain that A is secondary at its beginning, because it is much fuller than B (c. I 1 f.). Again at its conclusion, A, here represented by H only, is much fuller, and probably represents an expansion (C. XXVI 8—10). In the main, however, A has the shorter text in so many places where B presents fuller information regarding the demons[2], that one cannot but conclude that Rec. A has the claim to priority in most cases, and is nearest the original *Test*[3].

c) Recension C is a revision of Recension B. The nature of the material in the added chapters of C, as well as the fact that in the fragments, especially in T, much of it occurs in, or in

---

1 The transposition of sentences in c VIII does not affect these conclusions, as it may have occured in the exemplar from which MS D was copied, or in the copying of D without touching the original. But see MS E in appendix

2 Cf., for example, VI 4 f., XVI 4 f., XVIII 42, XX 6, etc.-

3 Rec. A presents omissions due to careless copying or a defective exemplar; e g., XIV 3—XVI 1

connection with, the *Clavicula*, which is a mediaeval product,
establishes the character of this recension as secondary and late.
The interesting account in C XIII of the origin of a καινὴ διὰ-
θήκη which is to be given to the world as a deception and a
snare, while the true, original *Testament* is to be preserved in
one copy only until "the expected parousia of God," when it is
again to be spread abroad, is plainly intended to establish faith
in this recension as the real original article over against Rec. B,
which it was to supplant. The numerous agreements of B and C
prove that the latter was based upon the type of text found in
the former[1], yet in some cases C has a more primitive text
than the present MS representatives of B (MSS PQ) offer.

d) Illustration will serve to make the relationships of the
recensions clearer. A good example is to be found in c. III 7
Here Rec. A (HIL) gives a text which is entirely fitting and
intelligible. ἀπῄτουν δὲ τοῦτον ἀδιαλείπτως ἔγγυθέν μοι προ-
⟨σ⟩εδρεύειν. This became nonsense by misreading into ἀπάντων
δὲ τούτων οὐ διαλιπο⟨, as V shows (W omits this much). P,
wishing to leave nothing unintelligible, altered to ἅπαντες δὲ οἱ
δαίμονες ἔγγισθέν μου προεδρεύουσι, which in itself is good, but
does not fit the context which follows in § 8. Another example
of B's improvement upon a text which seemed unintelligible is
found in II 8, where both V and W, as W in the previous case,
omitted the difficult words. In c. XVIII 42 the editor of B ex-
pands a short section which in A merely closes the account of
the thirty-six *decani* into an entirely new narrative of Solomon's
treatment of demons in general. On the other hand, in the
latter part of the *Test*, where H alone represents Rec. A, there
are a number of sections in which the text of H is so brief as
to be almost unintelligible, and, as it seems to me, shows evidence of hasty abbreviation[2]. In these sections I have given B
the preference, as also in the conclusion (c. XXVI 7—8), where H
has an expanded text.

---

1 Examples may be found on almost any page; cf c. VII. This account
of the writing of a "New Testament" may be compared with IV Ezra XIV
26, 42, 45 f.
2 Cf. XXII 3, 11, XXIV and XXV *passim*.

3. The evolution of the Testament. summary of conclusions — A number of stories about Solomon in which demons played a large part were gathered into a tale, *d*, a revision of which lies before us in MS D[1]. Some one who was interested in the magical cure of diseases then conceived the idea of the *Test*, and decapitated the story of *d*, leaving it to begin abruptly as in Rec. B with the tale of a demon who plagued the King's favorite workman during the temple building. The editor added a more fitting conclusion in the story of Solomon's fall as found in Rec B The original *Test*, then, consisted of the beginning and ending as in Rec B (MSS PQ), but with the body of the work mainly as in Rec. A (MSS HIL)[2] The present beginning of Rec A resulted from an attempt to remove the abruptness of the first sentence, being constructed by piecing together from later sections items regarding the favorite workman. This redacteur also thought himself able to construct a conclusion with greater parenetic value. Rec. B is another independent working over of the original *Test*, with certain interesting additions Whereas redacteur A was mainly concerned with making the story read better, redacteur B was in possession of fuller knowledge regarding many of the demons mentioned, and accordingly added to or replaced several sections[3]. Finally a student of demonological literature with a theological and scientific bent discovered some fragments which he thought Solomonic and which appeared to him to have greater value than a good part of the *Test*. So taking Rec. B he constructed another *Test*, putting in a preface, or prologue, containing certain prayers of Solomon, removing the abruptness of the beginning much as redacteur A did, and replacing the latter two-thirds of the *Test* by his new material. In the story of Onoskelu (Rec. C XI) he

---

1 Istrin in his introduction to the MSS which he edited came to the same conclusions regarding the relation of MS D to the *Test* as those expressed above, and I am in part indebted to him for this theory, and especially for the discovery of MS D.

2 The text printed at the top of the page in this edition is an attempt to reconstruct this original *Test*.

3 These are printed in brackets thus ⌜ ⌝, or placed in the critical apparatus at the bottom of the page

presents a variant form of a tale which he allows to remain in
the earlier, unaltered part under the name of Onoskelis (c. IV)[1]
He seeks to give authority to his version by representing that
it was feared and secretly preserved at the request of a great
demon, Paltiel Tzamal, who wished to prevent the publication
of its great mysteries, and that the well known, current form of
the *Test* had been specially written for Hezekiah, thus utilizing
an early tradition[2]. MS L represents an interesting step in another direction, the attempt to make the work of greater practical value as a physician's *vade mecum*, or book of prescriptions.
Its reading with the proper rites would cure the possessed[3].

4. The textual value of the MSS and their use in reconstructing the text. — Although MS D represents the original
story from which the *Test* was evolved, it possesses no primary
textual value, since it is not the *Test*, and, though its contents
are similar, its text is rarely that of the *Test*. The attempt here
is to reconstruct the original *Test* out of which Recs A and B
have grown. MS D is printed separately at the end of the
volume

Our MSS of Rec. C come from a class of men of rather
low mentality and poor Greek education. The numerous omissions are textually of little moment, because the redacteur was
interested in different matters from the originator of the *Test*,
and the scribes were careless. Since, as we have already shown
above (IV 2 c, d), C is derived from B, their agreement can have
little weight *per se* against acceptable readings found in A alone
Where, however, Recs. A and C agree, they represent the original text. Without C it would have been much more difficult
to show that B was secondary While neither V nor W could
have been copied the one from the other[4], they may have come
from the same exemplar. Where it was unintelligible or corrupt,

---

1 In the critical apparatus to c. IV readings from c XI of C have been
distinguished by adding a superior letter o to the letters T, V, and W.

2 Rec. C XIII, cf. Josephus, *Hypomnesticon* c. 74, Suidas, s. v. Ἐζεκίας,
see below VIII 3c (3)   8 Cf. II 5, 6; IV 12; V 8, 9, 12 f.

4 I can find no words in W omitted by V which the scribe of W might
not have added by guess, while the reverse (words in V omitted by W) often

V sometimes reproduces conscientiously where W omits or emends, for W had the more intelligent copyist. Accordingly V has been given the greater weight except where mistakes appear to have arisen from carelessness or misunderstanding.

Rec. B represents a learned, and in MS P a very careful, revision[1]. Occasionally P alone preserves the true text owing to the greater intelligence with which it has been handled. Yet it must be used with great caution, since both redacteur B and scribe P have taken great liberties with the text in making additions, alterations, and omissions. Q shows more errors than P, but fewer intentional changes.

The MSS of Rec. A have been rather mechanically copied. In some instances the scribes have not taken the liberty to drop or emend what they could not understand, but have reproduced it letter for letter[2]. There are omissions due to carelessness, one so long as probably to have been caused by a missed or missing leaf in the exemplar. In general H appears to have suffered least from intentional revision, but to have been in less skilful hands than I[3] Both were conscientiously copied by scribes who knew little of magic. Therefore the better instructed L occasionally presents a preferable reading, although he was somewhat careless and illiterate and his practical directions often vitiate his text. In c. I I have followed MS I, since it alone preserves the first person, which the original *Test* ought to have shown throughout[4], and also since it appears to me, following

occurs, where other MSS make it possible to determine the true text, e g, IV 5 (φύσεως), II 9, IV 12 W omits by homoeoteleuton, IV 12, of intention, II 9, VIII 9, where the passage seemed unintelligible. Therefore V could not have copied from W But I do not believe W could have made out the true text from V's unwarranted expansion in II 6 (φοβούμενος ... προσψαῦσαι), nor is he likely to have omitted the right words in IX 9

1 In one case at least P omits a difficult passage where H and L are unintelligible, viz., V 7; it omits difficult lines in V 4, cf. VW; it makes a glaring omission by homoeoteleuton in XXI 3 f., and a minor one in IX 6.

2 Cf. II 2, 3 (HIL), 6 (H), V 6 (HL), XVIII 4 (HL).

3 Cf. XXII 7 and XXIV 3—5 (H), XIV 3—XVI 1 (HL). In V 4, 5, IX 6 H appears to have read ·/. (= ἐστίν) as j (= δέ).

4 L maintains the third person for Solomon consistently, I the first, the others vary, but in general begin with the third and change to the first.

a suggestion of Dr. Goodspeed, that H exhibits an attempt to make clearer the somewhat unusual language of I regarding the favorite slave. Here, however, as in the concluding sections, Rec. A shows signs of undue expansion, and in constructing the text of the *Test*, which always appears at the top of the page, I have followed Rec. B. Again, in certain sections toward the end, I have thought that Rec. A gave evidence of abridgment, and in these places, especially since the carelessly written H is here the only MS of Rec A, I have given Rec. B the preference[1]. In general, then, unless weighty reasons appeared to the contrary, H has been made the basis of this edition The rule adopted has been, 'When in doubt, follow H.'

In concluding this section it should be noted that we cannot claim to have the original *Test* in our reconstructed text. Such an admission would be called for on a priori grounds alone. But we have evidence on the subject, for, in the quotation from the *Test* which occurs in the *Dialogue of Timothy and Aquila*[2], the Jew insists that Solomon οὐκ ἔσφαξεν ἀλλὰ ἔθλασεν, while in the *Test* as we now have it, although the Shunamite says σφάξαι (MS H) or σύντριψον (MSS PQ)[3], Solomon merely says ἔθυσα (MS H) or ὅπερ καὶ ἐτέλεσα[4]. If we could find the original MS, many such differences would appear, but not enough to vitiate our general conclusions regarding the work[5]

V. LANGUAGE AND STYLE.

This section will be made quite brief, as the grammatical index will supplement it by presenting the evidence for the positions taken.

1 MS D. — As to language and style there are decided

---

1 Cf. *supra*, IV 2 b, d. MS N has valuable readings. See appendix.

2 *Antc. Oxon* Class Ser VIII 70, c XIII 6; cf. *infra*, VIII 3 d) (2) (e)

3 C XXVI 4   4 C. XXVI 5.

5 In general the effort has been made to print the text as the author may he supposed to have written it, following the ordinary practice of the early Christian centuries as to spelling and grammar. As to ν moveable the classical rule has been followed for the sake of simplicity

differences between the recensions. In this regard, as well as from the diplomatic standpoint, MS D is far superior to the rest An educated Greek has edited and written it. The outstanding inaccuracy in his grammar is the use of the nominative absolute, or rather *nominativus pendens*, not a serious blunder[1], which occurs a few times. Once ἅμα is used with τό and the infinitive[2] Otherwise tenses and cases are on the whole correctly used. The optative, subjunctive, imperative in both second and third person, and a future participle of purpose are found. Late forms and usages are rare. For the dative πρός with the accusative is frequent. In IV 9 οὐκέτι ἴδῃς is a (Homeric and) late usage, subjunctive for future, which has contributed to such a future as εἰσενέγκομεν in VI 2[3] βούλεσαι replaces βούλει in IV 11[4].

As to style, the constant use of the historical present and the occasional omission of λέγει or φησί after the name of the speaker in dialogue lends vivacity, while the conversations are short and to the point. The writer has a fairly large vocabulary, including a considerable number of particles. There is a heaping up of epithets and synonymous words when opportunity offers[5]. Specially noteworthy is the constant use of the circumstantial participle in various relations. The author is fond of dropping in a verb to separate the article and attributives from their noun[6] The use of βασιλεία == "Majesty," and κράτος == "Excellency" in direct address is Byzantine

2. Rec. C — This, the latest recension, is at the antipodes from MS D How far its present condition is due to scribal carelessness and ignorance we cannot say, but probably they are partly accountable for its very poor Greek Errors, such as the accusative for the dative, and late forms, such as -αν as ending of the accusative singular in the third declension with an analogous nominative, e g., σφραγῖδα, abound, and there are several Latinisms The first sentence is an unattachable genitive absolute. The editor was fond of compound tenses. As to style[7]

---

1 Cf. Moulton, *Proleg.* 69.   2 C III 5   3 Cf Dieterich, *Unters.* 243 ff.
4 *Ibid* 249.   5 C, I 2, 13; IV 6, 7, 9, 18
6 C. IV 2, VI 14, VII 2, 4, 5   7 See Prologue 1, 2, c. XIII 4, 12.

the additions show somewhat ambitious attempts at fine writing,
e. g., in the prayers of the Prologue and in the closing chapter.
The same trick appears as in D, of dropping the verb in between attributives and their nouns.

3. Rec. B — Rec. B is more correct as to grammar and
simpler as to style than Rec C Between A and B there is
little difference, but in its additions B, especially MS P, shows
a tendency to more "correct" usage, but also to compound
words, and in one instance it has a decided Latinism, $πρωτο-$
$μαίστωρ$[1].

4. Rec. A and the original *Testament* — The editorial additions to Rec A have some glaring errors, particularly in MS L,
but, if we may judge from this recension, the *Test* was originally
a very simple piece of writing in fairly correct Koinē Greek It
paid no attention to refinements of rhetoric or lexicography, but
told its story in a straightforward, paratactic style, such as one
might expect from a man of small education and mental ability
in recounting an interesting series of stories. On the whole the
grammar is that of the New Testament, with developments along
the lines taken by the Koinē such as would seem to point to a
period subsequent to the New Testament. The disappearance
of the optative, the aorist subjunctive for the future, the increase
in the use of prepositions and compound words, and the numerous locutions which are characterized by the Atticists as vulgar
constitute the evidence on this point. Real Semitisms do not
appear in the *Test* That the $καὶ ἐγένετο$ construction may be
called such I cannot believe[2] Another so-called Semitism, the
demonstrative repeating the relative, occurs, but it is a mere
blunder due to an attempt to repair a garbled passage[3]

5. Letter of Adarkes to Solomon. — The letter of the
Arabian King in c. XXII contains two peculiarities, the absence
of the name of the sender from the introductory formula and
in MS D the use of direct address, $βασιλεῦ Σολομῶν, χαίροις.$
Unfortunately the two treatises which have appeared on the

---

1 C. I 2   2 Contrast Conybeare, *JQR* XI 6, and Moulton, *Proleg* 16f.
3 C I 9, Rec C, cf Moulton, *op cit.* 94f.

subject of Greek letter formulae[1] do not carry the subject far
enough into the Byzantine period to aid us here, and the extant
letters have too often been handed down without the introductory formula[2].

So far as the evidence goes, the use of variations of the
customary formula, ὁ δεῖνα τῷ δεῖνι χαίρειν, does not mark any
particular era. The use of χαίροις with the vocative seems a
sign either of servility or of poor breeding, for three of the instances known to me from the papyri are from people of little
culture, while the ancients particularly reprobated the use of the
first person and direct address[3]. Perhaps the editor of D thought
such familiarity entirely legitimate between kings, or wished to
represent the Arabian king as inferior to Solomon[4].

To account for the absence of the senders's name three
theories are possible· either βασιλεὺς Ἀράβων Ἀδάρκης has fallen
out by haplography, or the MS D form was original and the
present text of A and B is a correction to the third person, or
the writer has used the form which was customary in copies of
letters[5]. Other evidence for the secondary character of the
present text of D seems too strong to allow the second alternative For the first speaks the fact that the MSS differ decidedly
as to the lines immediately preceding the letter. More decisive,
however, seems the consideration that such a writer could hardly
be expected to be precise as to letter formulae, particularly as
the identity of the sender is plainly indicated in the text.

Unfortunately in any case we reach the negative conclusion
that the peculiarities of the letter formulae give no aid in determining the date of the recensions.

---

1 Gerhard and Ziemann, see Bibliography IV *infra*.
2 See Hercher and Migne, *PG*.
3 Apollonius Dyscolus, *de const.* II 9, III 14, ed. Bekker, 112, l. 27—113,
l. 10, 232, ll. 18 ff.; Scholiast to Dionysius Thrax, 550, ll 14—23, ed. Hilgard.
Ziemann found six examples of χαίροις to which add *Ox P* 112 (I 177, III/IV
cent.) and the optative εἴης, Migne, *PG* 161, cols. 688, 692, 697, and nine
examples of χαῖρε to which add *Ox P* 1156 (VIII 258, III cent), *op cit.*, 295.
4 Ziemann, *op cit*, 296 f., suggests also the possibility of Latin influence.
5 Cf. Ziemann, *op. cit.*, 285 f., petitions and memorials give no precedent
for such a form, cf. *ibid*, 259—266

6. Is the *Testament* a translation? — Dr. M. Gaster argues that the *Test* is translated from Hebrew[1]. Such a view is naturally suggested by the large number of Hebrew names of angels and demons, to say nothing of the fact that Solomon, the great Jewish wise man, is the hero of the story. Dr Gaster finds evidence of translation in the expression τῷ ἀγγέλῳ τοῦ θεοῦ τῷ. καλουμένῳ Ἀφαρώφ, ὃ ἑρμηνεύεται Ῥαφαήλ, ... καταργοῦμαι[2]. He believes that we have here a misunderstanding of the word *Shem-ha-meforash, perush* having been taken to mean "interpretation." Aside from the precariousness of argument from a single case such as this, the decisive fact is that this expression is an editorial addition found only in MS P. HL present a shorter and simpler text, ὑπὸ τοῦ ἀγγέλου Ῥαφαήλ (καταργοῦμαι). There is no reason why HL should have omitted the phrases of P if they had stood in the original *Test*, for they are perfectly intelligible, with only an element of mystery in the word Ἀφαρώφ such as this sort of literature loves. The editor of Rec B contributed this out of his fund of magical knowledge[3].

As it seems to me, the strongest evidence for translation from a Semitic original is to be found in Rec. A in the list of *decani*, the thirty-six στοιχεῖα, where all from the twentieth on call themselves ῥύξ (H, XVIII 24—40), or ῥίξ (L, XVIII 24—28). This word surely is a transliteration of רוּחַ. But even such a transliteration does not prove that the whole *Test* was originally written in Hebrew or Aramaic. This particular section, which is plainly of Egyptian origin, has been partially revised by a Jew before it was taken over into the *Test*[4]

Another possible piece of evidence is to be found in the clause ἀπόγονος δέ εἰμι ἀρχαγγέλου τῆς δυνάμεως τοῦ Θεοῦ[5]. Ouriel is not the "power of God," as in Recs B and C, but the "light of God." It might be thought that originally נְבְרִיאֵל stood in the text and was translated by some one who failed to recognize it as a proper noun. The copyists, feeling the need of some name, have made various "corrections" Such a supposi-

---

1 "The Sword of Moses," *JAS* 1896 p. 155, 170.   2 C. XIII 6.
3 Cf. *infra* VII 11.   4 Cf. *infra* VII 5   5 C. II 4.

tion would be entirely probable if the language of the *Test*
elsewhere gave evidence of translation. It is more likely the
passage was written by one who knew no Hebrew.

7. Tentative conclusion. — It seems much more natural to
explain all apparent indications of Semitic origin as due to the
fact that the writer of the *Test* has used materials already translated from languages unfamiliar to him. Did the heathen compiler of the great Paris magic papyrus translate the biblical
material he used? Did the writers of the Synoptic Gospels translate their sources from Aramaic? No one so alleges. Our tentative conclusion, then, at this stage of the investigation, must
be that the native language of the writer of the *Test* was Greek.
So far a study of the language of the work has taken us. For
a more precise answer as to its origin we must analyze its chief
ideas and their sources.

VI. THE CHIEF IDEAS OF THE *TESTAMENT*

The *Test* is a collection of astrological, demonological, and
magical lore, brought together without any attempt at consistency. The writer attempts no science or philosophy of demonology; indeed he is a compiler rather than an author

1. Demonology [1]. No general statement is made as to the
origin of demons, and the data given in particular cases disagree.
Some are fallen angels [2], others are the offspring of angels and
the daughters of men [3] One is the spirit of a murdered giant,
one is perhaps born of a *bath qol* [4] They dwell in deserts,
tombs, precipices, caves, chasms, and at cross roads [5].

As to their nature certain intimations are given. Most of
them are embodied spirits. Of one this is distinctly stated [6],
while a number are minutely described, generally as griffins
combined of animals and birds, or of animals and man. One is
a wind merely, but when put into a sack he acts like a man [7].
They can, within limits, assume different forms [8] They are an-

1 Cf. Index II.   2 C. VI 2   3 C. V 3
4 C XVII 1, IV 8   5 C. IV 5; VIII 4   6 C IV 4
7 Cc. XXII, XXIII.   8 C IV 4; II 3.

thropomorphically conceived. Onoskelis quails before a threat-
ened beating[1], Asmodaeus is bound and beaten[2], Kunopegos
almost faints from thirst[3], Akephalos Daemon sees through his
breasts and is blinded when the seal is pressed upon him[4].
Some are female, and the writer probably thought it possible
for both males and females to have offspring[5] They have all
the physical as well as psychical passions of mankind.

Though they thus resemble human beings so closely, they
have a certain likeness also to the angels. They escape many
of the physical limitations of men, in that they may assume
various forms and are supernaturally crafty and powerful. They
know the future, and several of them tell Solomon of coming
events. How this is possible is explained by Ornias, who relates
that the demons fly up to the gates of heaven and overhear
the decisions announced to the great concourse of angels there;
then, coming down, they make use of their knowledge to injure
mankind. However, this foreknowledge is gained at great risk,
for, having no place to light at the gate of heaven, they become
weary and fall, and these falling demons are what men call
shooting stars[6].

No systematized demonic hierarchy is known. Beelzebul,
as chief of the whole tribe of demons[7], is summoned to assist
Solomon in dealing with them. He has a vicegerent, named
Abezethibou, like himself a fallen angel, who is the great spirit
of rebellion against God and the good. Beelzebul apparently
now rules upon earth and Abezethibou in Tartarus, though the
latter is "nourished in the Red Sea," where he was confined on
the overthrow of Pharaoh and his host[8] He is haled before
Solomon by Ephippas, not by Beelzebul, and may, therefore, be
thought of as independent of the latter[9] Beelzebul is plainly

---

1 C. IV 11.   2 C. V 6   3 C. XVI 5.   4 C. IX 3.
5 C. V 4; Rec. B certainly so thought, cf VI 6; XXII 20.
6 C. XX 14—17
7 Cc. III, VI.   Βεελζεβούλ, the form occurring in the majority of
N Γ MSS and adopted by Tischendorf, Nestle, and von Soden, is the form of
Recs. BC.   H has Βεελζεβουήλ, said by Legge to be the Coptic form (PSBA
XXIII 248)   8 Cc VI 3, XXV   9 Cc. VI 5, 6, XXIII 2, XXIV 1.

identified with the ἄρχων τῶν δαιμονίων of the Gospels[1], for he trembles before "Emmanuel of the Hellenists"[2]. But he is not "Lucifer, star of the morning"[3], his star is Ἑσπερία[4] Except in C III, where he is first summoned, and in C. VI, where he is examined, Beelzebul is a figurehead. Only Kunopegos, a sort of Poseidon, mentions the fact that he, with all the demons, is subject to Beelzebul's direction, and at intervals comes to land to consult him, it was on one of these trips that Beelzebul arrested him and brought him before Solomon[5].

Many interesting demonic figures appear, such as Ornias, Asmodaeus, Lix Tetrax, Pterodrakon, the dog Rhabdos, the three headed dragon called κορυφὴ δρακόντων, Leontophoron the demon of Gadara, three liliths, or Empusas, called Onoskelis, Enepsigos, and Obyzuth, seven stars that are κοσμοκράτορες τοῦ σκότους, and other thirty-six with the same high sounding title who are the *decani*. Limitation of space forbids their further discussion here. They cause all kinds of diseases and bodily defects, from seasickness to epilepsy, being particularly dangerous to women in childbirth and to infants. They destroy fields, flocks, houses, ships, and human lives, and will finally bring the end of the world[6]. The thirty-six *decani* are entirely of this sort[7]. Demons are sources also of moral evil, inspiring heresies, idolatry, lust, theft, envy, hatred, murder, war, and kindred evils The seven spirits who call themselves κοσμοκράτορες are of this kind[8] So far as the writer of the *Test* has thought the matter out, evil does not reside in the flesh, nor in matter, nor can it be ascribed to God; sins are the result of demonic incitement How or when the angels came to sin we are not told. In any case there is no real dualism in the *Test* Though Beelzebul rules "the spiritual hosts of wickedness," they and he are completely subject to God and to the divinely ordained means for their subjugation. Mention is made of demons in Tartarus, but no punishment for them seems to be known ex-

1 Cf. Mk III 22, — Mt XII 24, — Lk XI 16   2 C VI 8
3 Is XIV 12 AV; ἑωσφόρος ὁ πρωὶ ἀνατέλλων LXX.
4 C. VI 7.   5 C. XVI 3, 5.   6 Only in P VI 4, ἀπολῶ τὸν κόσμον
7 C XVIII   8 C VIII

cept that which Solomon and the magic revealed in the *Test* can inflict

2. Astrology. — A large proportion of the demons in the *Test* have some definite astrological relationship. Demons and men are said to reside in a star[1], or a sign of the zodiac[2], or a phase of the moon[3], and mortals seem to be particularly liable to injury from demons who are συναστροί with them, that is belong to the same star[4]. The author seems to think of the influence of the stars as wholly baleful. Asmodaeus says, "through the stars I ⌜scatter⌝ madness after women"[5], and that suggests the prevailing notion. There is, I believe, no reference to prediction by means of astrology.

One chapter (XVIII), a list of the thirty-six *decani*, is a piece of astrological material taken over bodily. In this case each δεκανός is thought of as a demon causing certain diseases, which are recorded, and the means for counteracting them are detailed. Here the astrological entity does not *belong* to the demon, or the demon to it, but *is* the demon. On the other hand one may doubt whether the stars are thought of as living beings, for in XX 17 it is said, "the stars are founded in the firmament" so that they cannot fall. It would seem that astrological influences are operative, not of themselves, but through the demons that "dwell" in each star or sign. In other words, the astral deities of paganism have become demons[6]. It is interesting to note also that the pillar of cloud of the ancient Israelites is transferred to the heavens, for, as Dr. James has pointed out[7], the pillar suspended in air[8] is the Milky Way.

3. Angelology[9]. — The angelology of the *Test* is entirely undeveloped. Aside from Michael and Raphael no angels appear as actual actors. Numerous angel names, including many that are familiar and many not elsewhere discovered, are scattered

---

1 Cc V 4, VI 7, VII 6, *et passim*. λείμαι and όδεύω are the verbs used. ἄστρον seems to mean any astrological entity An astrological papyrus fragment at Munich has points of affinity with the *Test*, see *Archiv f. Pap.-Forschung* I (1900—1) 492 ff.   2 C II 2.   3 C. IV 9.   4 C. IV 6.   5 C V 8

6 Cf. the attempt to combine the polytheistic and polydaemonistic viewpoints in VII 6.   7 Cf. Bibliogr III 5.   8 C. XXIV 5.   9 See Index II

through the book, but they are charms rather than designations
of real beings. They are given solely for their apotropaic value.
Considering the fact, however, that the two great archangels do
actually appear, it is likely that the author believed in the actual
existence of great numbers of angels, just as he did of demons,
and thought that each appeared, when his name was called, to
subdue the demon subject to him[1]. Aside from the use of the
word ἀρχάγγελος there is no allusion to an angelic hierarchy.

4. Magic and Medicine. — The prime interest of the writer
of the *Test* was medical For him demons were what bacilli
are to the modern physician, and his magical recipes and angel
names are his pharmacopoeia. The one case where he embarks
upon a piece of magical mysticism only serves to emphasize
this fact For when, at Solomon's request that he speak περὶ
τῶν ἐπουρανίων, Beelzebul tells him the recipe whereby he may
see the heavenly dragons circling 'round and hauling the chariot
of the sun[2], he is at once rebuked and silenced. Evidently this
was forbidden magic, although it might well be true. There is
likewise a story of obtaining wealth through a demon[3], but such
suggestions bear fruit only for the beautifying of the temple[4]
Such use of demons is evidently dangerous.

As in his demonology, so also in his magic the author combined various and inconsistent views. He has full confidence in
the power of the magic name, which, in most cases, is an angel
name. To subjugate Onoskelis Solomon "spoke the name of the
Holy One of Israel"[5]. Men are led astray, says Asmodaeus,
"because they do not know the names of the angels which are
ordained over us"[6]. In the original *Test* Ephesia grammata are
infrequent, except in the list of the thrity-six *decani*[7]. Here
there appear some well known angel names, a few that are possibly real names, but not a few ὀνόματα ἄσημα in the best
manner of the magic papyri and "Gnostic" amulets. Since these
voces mysticae are less numerous in the former part of the

---

1 As Raphael does, II 7 f. Ct. *Test Dan* VI 1. 2 C. VI 10f.
3 C. IV 7. 4 C. X 5—9 5 C. IV 12. 6 C. V 5, cf. XXVI 8 H.
7 C. XVIII, esp. secs. 15 f., 21, 29, 32; cf also VII 6, likewise a piece of
unregenerate Hellenistic magic.

section, it would appear that a Jewish editor had undertaken
the task of removing the heathen elements, but had become
weary before he was done.

Likewise there appear the well-known apotropaic materials,
such as iron, lead, wood from a wrecked ship, spittle, certain
organs of animals, and kinds of plants[1], and the common magical devices, such as the use of the cause to cure the ill, i. e.,
the name of the demon to drive the demon away or a fishbone
to cure a person who has swallowed one[2], the drinking of po-
tions or sprinkling them about, and the writing of amulets or
hanging them in the house[3]. Surely these methods of aversion
are fundamentally inconsistent with monotheism and with the
view that the angels are appointed to frustrate the demons. The
ring of Solomon differs only in that it was probably thought to
contain the ineffable name[4]

5. Solomon. — Few figures have bulked larger in the folklore of Jews, Mohammedans, and Christians than Solomon. In
the *Test* he is already the wise man and magician *par excellence*,
the favorite of God, endowed by him with divine σοφία, which
includes insight into the crafty wiles of his demonic captives.
He uses the demons for one purpose only, to assist in building
and beautifying the great Temple at Jerusalem, this labor being
the usual form of punishment adopted for them. Solomon's
glory, the visit and gifts of the Queen of Sheba, and the gifts
of other kings are described in some detail; but all this is only
temporary, for the wise king, deceived by Eros, held by the
bonds of Artemis as the demons prophesied[5], is eventually led

---

1 See II 6, V 12, IV 8, XVIII 28, VII 3, V 9t., 13, VI 10, XVIII 20, 33.
I am much in doubt whether the means used by Raphael in II 8 to subdue
Ornias is the application of parts of the κήτη θαλάσσης (as with Asmodaeus of
the fish), or the casting of the μοῖρα (in astrological fashion?), or both as in the
restored text. I do not find μοῖραν ῥίπτειν in Vettius Valens as an astrological phrase, but Dr. Conybeare so understands it (*JQR* XI 18 and n. 2).

2 C. XVIII 35.   3 Cf. c. XVIII.

4 Cf. *infra* VII 14. Cf. Charles' interesting view that the sealing of the
144,000 in Rev VII 4—8 was to secure them against demonic attack (*Studies in
the Apocalypse*, 1913, pp. 118—32).

5 C. VIII 9, 11. That Solomon was not regarded as a model of perfection
is indicated by the statement that the murder of his brothers was caused by Ἀπάτη

by the Shunamite to sacrifice locusts to the gods of the Jebu-
sites, and thus loses all his power. How soon he dies is not
indicated, but at his death, convinced by the fulfilment of their
prophecies that all the demons had said was true, he writes the
Test and leaves it to the Children of Israel.

The chief part of Solomon's magical equipment is his ring,
which is given to him by Michael at God's command in answer
to the king's prayer[1]. Either in his own hand, or that of his
best beloved servant, or even the demon Ornias it at once subdues every demon. The editors have removed the original
statement as to the inscription, if there was one[2]. What became
of the ring after Solomon's fall is not stated.

Several features of the Solomonic legend receive their first
known literary expression in the *Test* To quote Salzberger,
„Immerhin wird es hier zum ersten Male ausgesprochen, daß Sal
Geister beim Tempelbau verwendet habe und daß er, durch die
Liebe zu einer Jebusiterin in heidnischen Kult verstrickt, der
Macht uber die Geister verlustig gegangen und ihnen zum Ge-
spött geworden sei. Zu beachten ist auch, daß die „Konigin
des Sudens" bereits als eine Zauberin ($\gamma \acute{o}\eta\varsigma$) auftritt"[3].

6 Apocalyptic element. — The apocalyptic element in the
Test is very slight[4] Certain prophecies by the demons and their
speedy and exact fulfilment are related in order to prove the
trustworthiness of the demons' revelations in general, and, in
particular, of their statements regarding their own activities and
the means for their frustration[5]. In some cases these prophecies
extend far beyond Solomon's time, particularly in certain references to Christ as one who will subdue individual demons[6].
The only section which may be called measurably apocalyptic

---

1 C. I 5—7.   2 Cf. *infra* VII 14.   3 *Salomosage* 11.

4 Dr. James, *TS* II 29 *The Testament of Abraham*, says, "The names 'Testament' and 'Apocalypse' are convertible terms. In the case of the Apocalypses
of Adam, Moses, and Isaiah we have positive evidence of this fact, and it is
known that most, if not all, extant 'Testaments' have a large Apocalyptic element The Testaments of Job and Solomon come nearest to transgressing this
rule, but even they do not actually transgress it."

5 Cc. V 5; VI 3, 5; VIII 11; XII 4.   6 Cc. XI 6; XII 3.
UNT 9 McCown.   4

in tone[1] is found in that part of the *Test* which is preserved only in MS P, and, therefore, while there is no doubt that the original *Test* had a prophecy in this place, it seems very likely that it resembled the one in V 5, and contained at least no such detailed reference to Christ as is now there found[2].

Did the writer of the *Test*, then, know nothing of the apocalyptic hopes of Judaism and Christianity? At best these hopes had little meaning for him. He makes no reference to that element in Apocalyptic for which we would most naturally look, the expectation of the final overthrow and eternal binding of Beelzebul and his hosts[3] Aside from a single mention of the συντέλεια[4], the writer has his eyes on his muckrake and sees no happier future for the world than in the continued use of his wretched recipes.

7. Jesus Christ — One of the outstanding inconsistencies of the *Test* is its introduction of Christ as the "angel" who subdues certain demons Whether these passages are Christian interpolations in a Jewish document will be discussed later[5]. We are now concerned with the religious standpoint of the writer who gave the *Test* its present form[6].

It is probable that VI 8 contains a reference to Christ. Certainly Rec B so understood it, and the phrase παρὰ δὲ Ἕλλησιν Ἐμμανουήλ is natural from the pen of a Christian who was without knowledge of Hebrew, but familiar with the use of the term Immanuel in Christian circles, as in XI 6. Yet the text is so corrupt and the MSS agree so little that the meaning cannot be certainly made out The garbled allusion to the "place of a skull" and "the wood" in XII 3 is so unintelligible as to afford no light on the author's views, but is plainly of Christian origin.

Unmistakable is the reference in c. XI to the incident of the Gadarene demoniac who had a legion of devils. But what is the meaning of ἐν τρισὶ χαρακτῆρσι κατάγεται περιηχούμενος,

---

1 C. XV 8—12.   2 Cf. *infra* VII 11.
3 Jub X 8, I En X 6, 12, XIV 5; XVI 6, Mt XXV 41   4 C. XXV 8
5 Cf. *infra* VII 11.
6 With this discussion cf. Conybeare in *JQR* XI 5—12.

in section 6? P probably understood it to refer to $\chi\mu\delta'$ ($= 644$), the numerical value of Ἐμμανουήλ, already introduced in VI 8 and XI 6[1]. Can the three characters mean the trinity? In XVII 4 is mentioned ὁ μέλλων κατελθεῖν σωτήρ. Οὗ τὸ στοι-χεῖον ἐν τῷ μετώπῳ may be a reminiscence of Apoc XXII 4, καὶ τὸ ὄνομα αὐτοῦ ἐπὶ τῶν μετώπων αὐτῶν. The sign is the cross, as the next line shows, not a number as Conybeare con-cluded fiom P's frequent introduction of $\chi\mu\delta'$[2]. Another distinc-tively Christian passage is much milder in the A form than in Rec B, which, as Conybeare points out, is distinctively patri-passian in character[3] Rec A mentions the virgin birth, an adoration by angels, and the crucifixion The allusions to the permanent immaculacy of the Virgin and to the victory of Christ over Satan in the Temptation in XV 1 0f. cannot be used to define the position of the originator of the *Test*[4].

Dr. Conybeare's characterization of the Christianity of the *Test* as "equivocal" is far more true of the original than it was of Rec B, which he had before him[5]. The nature of the writer's faith can be better understood after an investigation of the sources and relationships of his subject matter, to which we now turn.

VII. THE SOURCES AND RELATIONSHIPS OF THE SUBJECT MATTER.

1 Syncretism of the *Testament* — To set forth what the present writer has collected for the purpose of interpreting the *Test* and determining its sources and relationships would require a large volume. Yet what has been gathered has only touched the fringe of that great body of material bearing on magic, demonology, astrology, and kindred superstitions which has recently appeared, much of it since this work was first under-

---

1 So Conybeare understood, *op. cit.* 28, n. 6.

2 *Op cit.* 34, § 71. Diog. Laert 6. 102 uses στοιχεῖον foi "sign" oi the zodiac. 8 C. XXII 20, Conybeare *op. cit.* 11.

4 Cf *supra* sec 6, *infra* VII 11. 5 *JQR* XLI 11

taken[1] The purpose is to introduce here only what is absolutely germain to the subject of the section. One point is clear beyond cavil· Like other magic the *Test* is thoroughly eclectic. It borrows and combines elements, often contradictory, from all the nations that contributed to the civilization ab out the eastern Mediterranean, without any apparent consciousness of their sources. The whole course of the succeeding discussion will offer illustrations of this patent fact

2. The universal human element. — In one direction caution is necessary, perhaps especially in the realm of comparative magical and mythological study. Similarities are not always an evidence of borrowing. Take an example from the story of Lix Tetrax. As the demon in the form of a sand storm whirl-wind approaches Solomon, he lays it by spitting on the ground[2] In a modern Bengali charm for a whirl-wind exactly the same means is used to stay the demon[3]. Did the *Test* borrow from India or the Bengali from the *Test?* Manifestly neither. Spitting is almost universally apotropaic[4] And what is more natural than that spittle should magically lay a dust storm. So in many instances from widely separated localities the human mind under similar circumstances has reached similar conclusions With this caution in mind we can proceed to notice the instances of real borrowing.

3. Assyrian and Babylonian influence. — The great civilization on the Euphrates deeply affected Hellenistic, Jewish, and Christian demonological and magical beliefs. Babylonia is one of the few countries in which theology and demonology, religion and "her bastard daughter, magic," seem from the first to have gone hand in hand[5] There are no indications that the official cultus ever regarded magic as alien Rather, the exorcism of

1 See, for example, *ERE*, arts "Ancestor Worship," "Baalzebub," "Birth", "Charms and Amulets," "Cross," "Demons and Spirits," "Disease and Medicine," "Divination," "Evil Eye," "Keres," and the literature there referred to

2 C. VII 3.

3 In a little collection of charms sent the author by former pupils, Babu Probodh Chandra Mallik and Babu Shusil Chandra Karuli. One must spit on his own breast, however.   4 Cf. Conybeare, *op cit.* 23, n. 3

5 Farnell, *Greece and Babylonia*, 300 f.

countless demons seems to have been one of the regular duties
of the priesthood, and, to judge from the relative proportion of
magical texts among those that have been preserved, one of the
most important duties[1]. Nowhere do we find a ranker growth
of demonological beliefs than in Babylonia. Every possible ill
or accident that could happen, "a toothache, a headache, a
broken bone, a raging fever, an outburst of anger, of jealousy, of
incomprehensible disease"[2], all were ascribed to demonic agency,
and were to be averted or cured by means of incantations.

This is precisely the atmosphere of the *Test*. But it is also
that of Hellenistic superstition[3], and such a general similarity
of tone proves no direct relationship between the *Test* and the
Euphrates valley Can we find more definite evidence of dependence?

A peculiar resemblance appears between one class of Babylonian demons and a figure in the *Test*. the *ašakku marsu* and
Ephippas, the wind demon of Arabia. Since the similarity is
somewhat vague, I call attention to it with some hesitation.
Ephippas is an early morning blast of wind that kills man and
beast[4], or, according to MS D, "uproots houses and trees and
hills, and destroys men"[5]. The *ašakku marsu* is „der Dämon
der auszehrenden Krankheit" according to Jastrow[6], but Sayce[7]
and Thompson[8] render the word "fever" The following from
Thompson's translation of the *Ašakku* series shows interesting
similarities with Ephippas' activities:

---

1 Zimmern, *Bab. Hymnen*, 13, cf. Jastrow, *Rel. Bab. Ass.*, 253—93, Germ.,
I 273—392, Rogers, *Rel. Bab. Ass.* 144—159; Weber, *Dämonenbeschwörungen*
The chief part of the hymns that have been preserved consists of incantations.
2 Rogers, *op. cit.* 145.   3 Cf. *infra* VII 7.
4 C. XXII 2 f.   5 MS D VI 1
6 *Rel. Bab. Ass* I 348 ff.; he is uncertain as to what disease is meant
7 *Hibbert Lect.* 1887, 477, Sayce translates thus "The plague-demon burns
up the land like fire. The plague-demon like the fever (*ašakku*) attacks a man.
The plague-demon in the desert like a cloud of dust makes his way. The plague-
demon like a foe takes captive a man. The plague-demon like a flame con-
sumes a man. The plague-demon, though he hath neither hands nor feet (cf.
Ephippas), ever goes round and round. The plague-demon like destruction cuts
down the sick man."
8 *Devils and Evil Spirits* II 31. Cf. Rogers, *Rel. Bab. Ass* 147

> . . . . . . the evil Fiend,
> The roaming windblast . . . . [1]
> The evil Spirit which in the street creates a storm wind .   [2]
> The evil Fever hath come like a deluge, and
> Girt with dread brilliance it filleth the broad earth,
> Enveloped in terror it casteth fear abroad,
> It roameth through the street, it is let loose in the road . . . [3]
> An evil ghost(?) hath assailed the land,
> And perturbed the people of the land above and below
> A pestilence, a plague that giveth the land no rest,
> Hath cast desolation upon it.
> The great Demon, Spirit, and Fiend, which roameth the broad places for men,
> The angry, quaking storm [which if one] seeth
> He turneth not nor looketh back again . . . . . [4]
> Fever (*ašakku*) hath blown upon a man as the wind-blast[5].

That this is the closest parallel between the *Test* and Assyro-Babylonian demonology is significant. Granting that Babylonian, or, at least, Semitic superstition may have contributed to the figure of Ephippas, we still can assert only that the *Test* rests ultimately upon that great mass of Sumerian-Semitic beliefs of which we have the earliest and fullest illustrations from the Babylonian tablets, but not that it has borrowed directly[6].

4. Iranian influence. — To Mazdaism is to be ascribed the questionable honor, not of introducing demonology and angelology into Judaism[7], but of decidedly directing its development[8]. The *Test* has not been so deeply affected as has the New Testament Apocalypse, for example, in its war between Michael and the Dragon[9], nor even as Paul[10], for there is no dualism in our text. Its writer knows Beelzebul only as "ruler of the

---

1 *Op. cit.* 5.   2 *Ibid.* 9   3 *Ibid.* 11   4 *Ibid.* 13

5 *Ibid.* 31. It is, perhaps, worthy of note that Ephippas is caught in an ἀσκός, a sack. However silly it may seem, is it not possible that a popular etymology connected *ašakku* and ἀσκός ?

6 The lilith, who appears in three forms (cf. *supra* p. 45), is an international figure, and, therefore, no evidence of Babylonian influence

7 So Perles, *Bousset's Rel. des Judentums*, p 36

8 Moulton, *Early Zoroastrianism* 304 ff., 325 ff., *HDB* IV 991 f., Mills, *Zarathuštra* 436, Bousset, *Rel. des Jud* 387, Clemen, *Prim. Christ.* III ff. = *Religionsgesch Erkl* 85 ff, where earlier literature is cited. See particularly Grünbaum, "Beitrage" in *ZDMG* XXXI, 256, Dibelius, *Geisterwelt*, 183 ff., 190 ff.

9 Cf. Moulton, *HDB* IV 992.   10 ὁ θεὸς τοῦ αἰῶνος τούτου, 2 Co IV, 4.

demons"[1]. He has no doubt that God can empower Solomon
or any one who knows the angelic names to frustrate and bind
any and all demons. The archangels, though their names appear,
never are grouped together as seven, and the one group of
seven demons has no Parsi coloring[2] Yet one cannot read the
Persian sacred writings without being struck by the *Test*[3] And,
furthermore, the *Test* has adopted one Mazdian demon, Aēšma
daēva, or Asmodaeus[4], very much in his Magian character.
Plainly the demon of the *Test* is the same as that of Tobit[5],
but the writer did not have Tobit before him or he would not
have used the heart and gall, instead of the heart and liver, of
the fish as his φάρμακα. His additional details, such as the name
of the fish, γλάνος, show that, while he may have had the story
of Tobit in his mind, he was drawing upon the developing Jewish
folklore which had its fount in the original source and eventua-
ted in the Talmudic Asmodaeus[6].

In another direction we naturally look for Persian influence
to manifest itself, namely on the Solomonic legend The Mohammedans identified Solomon with Yima, the Jamshīd of Firdausi,
because he had taken over so many traits of the Persian hero,

---

1 C. II 9   2 C. VIII, cf. *infra* VII 6, p 60

3 See the *Vendîdâd*, the "anti-demoniac law," (Moulton, *Early Rel. Poetry
of Persia*, 12), esp. the incantations of Fargards XIX and XX, and the account
in XXII of Angra Mainyu's creation of 99, 999 diseases (*SBE* IV 203—235),
and Darmesteter's discussion, *ibid*. LXXXV—XCV

4 Moulton, *Early Rel Poetry of Persia* 68f, accepts the derivation from
Aēšma Daēva, as does Stave, *JE* I 220f., and Marshall, *HDB* I 172. Ginzberg,
JE II 219, though admitting the identity, denies the derivation, cf Clemen,
Prim. Christ. 112, n 7 = *Rel.-Gesch. Erkl.* 86, n. 7. Moulton's theory that
Tobit is a Magian legend revamped by a Jew in its present form (*Early Zoroast*
246—253) is accepted by Simpson, Charles' *Apoc and Pseudep of the OT* I 185f
On the influence of the Ahikar cycle see J Rendell Harris, "The Double Text
of Tobit," *AJT* III (1899) 541—554, and Clemen, *loc cit*, who quotes Fries,
ZNTW 1905 168, which I have not at hand

5 *Test* V, Tob III 8, 17; V 7f, VI 13—17, VIII 2f.

6 A. is more plainly the "wrath demon" in the *Test* than in Tob There
is no reference to Egypt in the *Test*, cf Tob VIII 3 Is the uncertain phrase
πλήρης ὁδοὺς πικρίας (*Test* V 13) an attempt to render the "wounding spear"
of Aēšma (Y I 32)? Cf *SBE* IV p. LXVII, *JE* II 217f

particularly his renown as a builder[1]. The Talmudic story of
Solomon combines elements from the legends of Takhma Urupa,
who made Ahriman his horse until his wife betrayed him[2], of
Yima, the prosperous king and great builder, who, like Takhma
Urupa, "ruled over the Daēvas and men, the Yātus and Pairikas,"
but sinned and fell before the usurping Azhi Dahāka[3], and of
Thraētaona, the first healer, the inventor of magic, the fiend-
smiter[4]. In the *Test*, however, we catch the story midway in
its development. There has arisen, as yet, no demonic being
to depose the king, and the *Test* lacks, therefore, the most
characteristic detail which the Talmud borrowed from Persia[5].

The evidence, then, justifies the conclusion that Persian influences are at work upon the folklore from which the *Test*
drew its inspiration, and have affected our text in part directly,
in part through Tobit and, no doubt, other Apocrypha. Yet the
Test cannot come from circles where, as in Babylon, for example,
Magian influence was dominant.

5. Egyptian elements. — Egypt is pre-eminently the land
of magic, but not of demonology[6]. Her "Book of the Dead"
almost from its inception had the purpose of magically insuring
the happiness of the dead in the hereafter, and the ancient in-
habitants of the Nile valley were so much concerned with the
future life that their magical texts gave little attention to avert-

---

1 Salzberger, *Salomosage* 5, *SBE* IV 18, n. 3

2 *Yt* XIX 29 (*SBE* XXIII 292 f.; cf *ibid* 252, n. 1).

3 *Yt* XIX 31—38 (*ibid.* 293—295, 297, and n. 5).   4 *Vend* XX (*SBE* IV 219).

5 The legends of the *Shahnāmeh* (cf. Atkinson, 5—34, the only version of
Firdausi available to me) with the allusions in the *Dādīstān-ī-Dīnāk* (XXXIX
16 f., *SBE* XVIII 127 f.), *Bundahish* XXIII 1 (*SBE* V 87), and elsewhere throw
much light on the references in the earlier literature, but they have probably
been influenced in their turn by the developed Jewish and Musulman tales, cf.
Darmesteter, *Le Zend Avesta* II 624, cited by Moulton, *Early Zoroast.* 150. *Bundahish* XXXIV 4 f. (*SBE* V 149 f.) is particularly interesting because it brings
Dahāk into connection with Scorpio, much as the *Test* connects certain demons
and zodiacal signs. Cf. a closer parallel to Solomon and Asmodaeus in King
Mukunda and the hunchback in the *Pañchatantra* (Benfey II 124—127, cf. I 129 f.).

6 Cf. *ERE* IV 584—590, 749—753 (Foucart), III 430—433 (Naville),
Wiedemann, *Mag. und Zaub* ; Breasted, *RTAE* 281 f., 296, *et pas.*, Erman, *Äg
Rel* , c VI, 148—164.

ing ill from the living. Yet enough has been preserved to show
that the fear of evil spirits, especially the ghosts of the dead,
was abroad here as in Babylonia and Persia, even thought the
official texts reflect but little of it. Egyptian demonology is so
lacking in definite color and in general so much like that of
Babylonia and Greece that one can hardly hope to show from
this side any distinctive Egyptian traits in the *Test*. In the
times when the *Test* was written it was of the variegated mix-
ture that we call Hellenistic [1]

When we turn to astrology, however, the case is different,
for one of the longest sections in the *Test*, that having to do
with the thirty-six *decani* [2], is distinctly Egyptian. It has been
generally accepted since Letronne that astrology is not, as the
ancients supposed, of Egyptian origin, but rather that Babylonia
was its native land [3]. As Boll, however, has shown [4], having
been adopted by the Egyptian priesthood and actively practised
by them, it came to be so thoroughly at home and so mixed
with Egyptian elements as to be really native, "in ihrer *Eigenart*
autochthon, wenn auch in allem rein agyptischen Inhalt von sehr
spatem Ursprung" [5]. Particularly is this true of the *decani*. They
were originally, not Babylonian [6], but Egyptian divisions of the
equator [7], which were given an astrological significance. "Nur
diese (the Egyptian astrology) hat die 36 Dekane personifiziert
alle andere Dekandarstellungen in Indien oder bei den Arabern
gehen darauf in letzter Linie zuruck," says Boll [8]. This sentence
is especially noteworthy for our purpose, for the *Test* has fully
personified the *decani*.

Various lists of *decani* have come down to us [9]. With

---

1 Erman, *op. cit.* 227 ff.   2 C XVIII.

3 M. Letronne, *Sur l'Origine du Zodiaque Grec*, Paris 1849, esp. p. 2
Cf. Riess, in *Pauly-Wissowa* II 1808, art. "Astrologie", Cumont, *Or. Rel.* 133 f.,
163; *Astrol.* 74 ff.   4 *Sphaera* 372 f.   5 *Ibid.* 373.

6 Bouché-Leclerq, *Astrol Gr.* 215—240.

7 Boll, *op. cit.* 316, 336, n. 2.   8 *Ibid.* 216 f.

9 See the comparative table in Bouché-Leclerq, *op. cit.* 232 f., and that in
Budge, *Gods of the Egyptians* II 304—308, also articles by G. Daressy, *Annales du
Service des Ant. de l'Égypt*, I 79—90, III 175, 236—9, X 21 ff, 180 ff., by Ahmed
bey Kamal, *ibid.* IX 192.

these the names in the *Test* do not at all agree, but seem rather
for the most part to be Hebrew, or, perhaps, mock Hebrew[1].
Yet the *Test's* account of the activities of these siderial spirits
is not original invention, for, at the beginning, the two chief
lists, one given by Pitra from a Moscow and a Vienna MS[2],
and one given by Kroll from another Vienna MS[3], agree with
the *Test* in certain essential particulars. The names in Vind. 108
and its fellow, Par. 2419, do not correspond with any other list,
just as those of the *Test* do not. The peculiarity of the names
in the last, therefore, need not trouble us. That the activities
ascribed to the several decans should not agree in all the lists
is not strange, in view of the confusion in the Egyptian lists[4]
While there is much closer resemblance between Pitra's and
Kroll's documents than between either of them and the *Test*,
still they differ in many important particulars. They all agree
on the fundamental proposition, which Celsus described as an
Egyptian belief, that the decans rule diseases, each of a certain
part of the body[5]. In the case of the first decan all three agree
that it is the head, although the *Test* adds κροταφούς, which
M-V puts under the second. Vind. 108 has πάθη ὀφθαλμῶν
under the second decan, while the *Test* has it unter the third
Under the third both M-V and Vind. 108 have among other
things toothache. All three agree that the fourth decan rules
diseases of the throat From this point on there are still fewer
similarities between the three accounts, yet these we have indi-

---

1 The allusion of Origen, *contra Cels.* VI 30, to οἱ ἑπτὰ ἄρχοντες δαίμονες is not applicable to the *decani* There is, to be sure, an Antiochus excerpt which mentions the ζ' δεκανῶν σχῆμα (Boll, *Sphaera* 57), but this either
means the Pleiades, or, as seems to me more probable, it is a mistake for the
seven planets (cf. *ibid* 280), which are sometimes connected with the thirty-six
decani (*ibid* 302). See Bouché-Leclerq, *Astrol Gr* 224—230.

2 *Analecta* V, 2, 285, from Mosquensis 415 and Vindobon Medic. 23,
ol. 50, referred to as M-V.

3 *CCAG* VI 73—78, from Vind, Graec. 108 (= MS S, cf. *supra* II 7,
p. 18) with the seals for each decan, there is also given a parallel list of names
from Par. 2419 (= MS W, cf. *supra* II 11, p. 26)

4 Cf. Bouché-Leclerq, *op. cit.* 230, n 3

5 *Contra Cels.* VIII 58. Cf. Bouché-Leclercq, *loc. cit.*, quotation from Fir-
micus, and ch. XV, "La Médicine Astrol.," pp. 517—542

cated are more than fortuitous. They evidently rest upon a
common tradition. But M-V has for the first few names the
Hellenistic transliteration of the old Egyptian names[1], and therefore serves to connect this common tradition with Egypt.

We are safe, then, in concluding that this chapter of the
Test comes from Egyptian sources, presenting probably a
Jewish revision of a list of *decani*. The editor has made it more
nearly monotheistic than the other accounts mentioned above,
in regarding the decans as demons who cause disease, rather
than deities who "rule" (κυριεύει) or cure (ἰᾶται) the parts affected. Yet he has failed to purge out all the heathen elements,
such as the amulets and *voces mysticae*[2] Other evidence of
Egyptian influence I am unable to find

6. Jewish elements and relationships. — a) That Judaism is
one main source of the *Test* is apparent on every page The
background, the plot, and the principal characters are Jewish.
Solomon, wise man, builder, and glorious king, the Queen of
Sheba, and the Shunamite girl[3] are all familiar Old Testament
figures, though sometimes presented here in strange connections
In pre-Christian times Solomon was already on the way to become a magician, both in the canonical books and in the Apocrypha[4] Josephus shows this conception of the king gradually
developing, his exorcisms and the remedial or magical plants
he had recommended being already in practical use by Jewish
magicians[5]. His ring, his power over demons, and his use of
them on the Temple become commonplaces of Jewish legendary
lore. His glory and his fall are put in telling contrast by the
editors of the Old Testament as they are by the *Test*.

b) The angelology and demonology of the *Test* are
practically those of the Apocrypha and Pseudepigrapha. Our
text contains the view, based upon Gen VI 1—4 and found
in Ethiopic Enoch VI—VII, XV—XVI and Jubilees VII 21 ff.,
X 5, that the angels who fell and their offspring became

---

1 Bouché-Leclercq, *Astrol gr.* 232f., Budge, *Gods* II 304—308, beginning
with No. 27, p 307.   2 Cf *supra* VI 4

3 Cant VI 12, VII 1.   4 See fuller discussion below, VIII 1 a), b)
5 *Ant* VIII 25, quoted below VIII 1 d)

demons[1], but much of it seems rather to follow the belief found in the Similitudes (I En XXXVII—L XXI; cf. Charles, *Enoch* p. 107) that demons have existed since the creation. The Pseudo-Philonic Jewish work *de antiquitatibus biblicis*, dating from the latter part of the first century A. D., in its *citharismus regis Dauid contra daemonium Saulis*, unites this view with another found in the *Test* as to the origin of certain demons. According to a badly tangled passage Onoskelis is born of an echo. In the *Citharismus* David addresses the demon thus

> Et factum est tunc nomen in compaginatione extensionis quod appellatum est superius caelum . . (There follows a reference to the creation of the earth but not of animals and man.) Et post haec facta est tribus spirituum vestrorum. Et nunc molesta esse noli, tanquam secunda creatura, si quominus, memorare Tartari in quo ambulas Aut non audire .   Aut immemores quoniam de resultatione in chaomate nata est vestra creatura.

Less apposite is a parallel Dr. James notes from Dieterich, *Abraxas*, p. 17, γελάσαντος δὲ τοῦ θεοῦ ἐγεννήθησαν θεοὶ ἑπτά[1].

In spite of great differences in detail the general manner in which each demon's work is described in I En LXIX 1—12[3] may well have contributed to the demon portraits in the *Test* The section on the seven κοσμοκράτορες (c. VII) is based upon exactly the same conceptions of evil and of demons as the list of seven vices in Test. Reuben III 3—6; yet the lists do not agree except that the third in each has to do with μάχη, apparently a mere coincidence. Jub X 7—9, which tells how God commanded the angels to imprison nine tenths of the evil spirits in "the place of condemnation", and left one tenth free under

---

1 See above VI 1. Cf. Grunbaum, "Beiträge," *ZDMG* XXXI 225.

2 Dr. James printed the *Citharismus* with three other Pseudo-Philonic fragments in *TS* II 3, *Apocrypha Anecdota*, Cambridge, 1893, without being aware of their origin. Dr L. Cohn called attention to the source in *JQR* X (1898) 277—332 in an article entitled "An Apocryphal Work Ascribed to Philo of Alexandria." The text I have quoted Dr. James communicated in a letter of July 8, 1916, after making a further collation of MSS. James and Cohn agree as to the date. See below VIII 1 c) for the concluding sentence of the so-called song.

8 From the "Apocalypse of Noah." One might think the *Test* depended particularly upon this work, were it not that the rest of the sections Charles ascribes to it (*Enoch*, pp. 24 f.) do not at all agree with the *Test*, e. g. as to sorcery and witchcraft, I En VIII, IX.

command of Mastema, explains the statement of Beelzebul in
Test VI 3 that his second in command rules his race in Tartarus Not only its demonology in general but certain particular figures of our text are well known in Jewish mind. Tobit
has made Asmodaeus at home in the Jewish folklore. The lilith
also came to belong to Judaism as it did to other nations.

Judaism, however, gave more attention to angels than to
demons. While here the *Test* differs in emphasis, the view point
. is the same. Among the Jews as in our text exorcism was one
of the chief means of healing, so much so that in antiquity the
Jew became almost as famous for magical arts as the Chaldean.
"The Graeco-Roman world regarded the Jews as a race of magicians"[1]. Angel names, of which so many occur in the Pseudepigrapha, were often used in incantations The Jews were
fully persuaded of the power of the "name"[2], and they also
thought of the angels as specially commissioned to protect the
righteous from the machinations of demons

There are thus many similarities between the *Test* and
Jewish folklore and superstition of the beginning of the Christian
era. But that our document is dependent in a literary way
upon the Apocrypha or Pseudepigrapha does not at all appear.
I have discovered but two quotations from Jewish literature, one
the passage touching the corner stone[3], the other the phrase
τὴν τῶν σῶν θρόνων πάρεδρον σοφίαν[4], taken from the Wisdom
of Solomon, and a possible allusion to the same book[5]. In the
passages describing Solomon's glory and the Temple, where one
would expect quotation, there is only a free development of
the biblical accounts[6]. One might mention elements of Jewish
thinking which are absent from the *Test*, such as the coming
of the Messiah to destroy all the demons[7] We must, then,

---

1 Ludwig Blau, *JE* VIII 255f., art. "Magic." He says, *ibid.* 255, "The
frequency of allusions to it in the Bible indicates that the practice of magic
was common throughout ancient Israel." Cf. his *Altjud Zauberwesen*, one of
the classics on the subject, also Bousset, *Rel. Jud.* 391 and Schurer *GJV* III 408f.
2 Heitmuller, *Im Namen Jesu* 176—80.
3 C. XXIII 4; Ps CXVIII 22, Mt XXI 42 and parallels, I Pt II 6
4 C. III 5; Sap IX 4. 5 C. V 3; Sap VII 1
6 C XIX, XXI. 7 Cf. I En LXIX 27.

conclude that, while the writer of our document operated with much the same beliefs as the Apocryphal and Pseudepigraphic writers, he is not in a literary way dependent upon any Jewish literature. On the other hand so many traits connect him with the rabbinical writings that we must suppose him to live during or after the first century of the Christian era.

c) Turning to the Talmud we find parallels to many of our stories[1] The account of Benaiah's capture of Asmodaeus by the use of a magic ring and chain, a bundle of wool, and a skin of wine[2] reminds one of the slave's capture of Ornias (I 10—14) and again of Ephippas (XXII 9—16), for the ring is used in both cases. It is pressed upon Ornias and seals Ephippas in his sack, while in the rabbinic legend Benaiah cries to Asmodaeus, "The name of the Lord is upon thee." Ephippas is caught in the sack instead of by drinking wine from it. Asmodaeus shows a knowledge of the future and laughs at men's foolish plans, just as Ornias does[3] The idea that the demons know the future is found elsewhere in the Talmud In *Hagiga* 16a the collocation of ideas is much the same as in the *Test.* "The rabbans taught: The demons possess six characteristics, three like the ministering angels, and three like the sons of men. Three like the ministering angels· they have wings like the ministering angels and they fly from one end of the world to the other like the ministering angels and they know what is determined for the future (מה שעתיד להיות) like the ministering angels. They know! Do you come to that opinion? Rather they hear it from behind the curtain like the ministering angels. Three like the sons of men they eat and drink like the sons of men, they propagate themselves like the sons of men, and they die like the sons of men"[4]. The *Aboth* of R. Nathan

---

1 Ginzberg, *Legends* IV 165—9

2 *Gittin* 68a; Ginzberg, *loc. cit.*; *JE* XI 443f.

3 C XX 6—18, cf a story of the angel of death related by Biechei, *Transcendentale, Magie und magische Heilarten im Talmud*, Wien 1850, p. 58f., from Suca 53a.

4 Goldschmidt III 2 839, Streane, 92, cf. *Test* XX 16 for "hearing behind the curtain "

adds. "Many say: They change their appearance according to
every form as they wish, and they see and are not seen"[1]
This passage is instructive in that it describes the demonology
of the *Test* and reduces it to a system which apparently our
writer was not able to construct

d) While, however, there are many resemblances between
Jewish angelology, demonology, magic, and mythology and the
Test, it must not forthwith be taken as proved that it is a Jewish
work. It certainly was not a product of rabbinic Judaism such
as is seen in the Babylonian Talmud, and later Jewish specu-
lation. Samael appears only in MS D, the angel of death, Malak
ha-Moweth, of the Zohar and Qelippoth not at all[2] Asmodaeus
is an entirely different character, his place being taken by
Ornias and the New Testament Beelzebul[3].

The mists of Jewish tradition come to surround Solomon
with a halo which only begins to appear in the *Test*[4]. Among
the many later traits not found in our document, one which
might easily have been used is the statement in Targum Shem
Esther that "Solomon ruled over the wild beasts, over the birds
of heaven, and over the creeping beasts of the earth, as well
as over the devils, the spirits of the night, and he understood
the language of all these according as it is written, 'and he
talked with the trees,'" instead of 'of the trees,' I Kg IV 33[5]

One of the most decisive illustrations of the difference
between the *Test* and later Judaism is the account of the fall
of Solomon. The subject was one which the Jewish theologians
in the early Christian centuries discussed with some heat[6]. The
Test in its attitude stands midway between the Tannaim and
the Amoraim, in that, while Solomon falls, it is under the
pressure of a passion which seems not to be regarded as ille-

1 A. Wunsch, "Die Zahlenspruche in Talmud u Midrasch", *ZDMG* LXVI
416 f.; *Aboth di R. Nathan* 37 3   2 Cf. Meyer, *Qabbalah* 430 f, 432—7

3 See Grunbaum's characterization of the Talmudic Asmodaeus in *ZDMG*
XXXI 216, following *Git* 68 a, b, and *Pes* 110 a

4 Cf. Eisenmenger, *Entd. Jud.* I 441, Faerber, *K. Sal.*, Salzberger, *Salomosage*; *JE* XI 438 ff., 448.

5 Salzberger, *op. cit.* 93 f, from f. 440, ed. David p. 8.

6 Faerber, *K. Sal.* 4—19, Salzberger, *Salomosage* 12 f.

gitimate, and his worship of idols was not conscious and
brazen, but consisted merely in crushing certain locusts before
idols, for he "did not consider the blood of the locusts"[1]
This charitable estimate quite befits a writer who wished his
work accepted as a valuable medical treatise from Solomon's
own hand   That in the *Test* Asmodaeus has nothing to do
with the king's fall at once differentiates the work from the
Talmud and proves that it had no close connection with those
popular cycles of Solomonic myth from which the rabbis probably drew their stories. Moreover, in the *Test* there is, on the
one hand, no hint that the king lost his throne along with his
power over the demons, and, on the other, no restoration of his
power, while the ring, which is the chief means by which he
gains his power over the demons, is not indispensible, as it is
in the Talmudic legends[2]. The connection of a Shunamite girl
with Solomon's fall is unique. It must have been suggested by
the name in Cant VI 12; VII 1, and it would seem to hint at an
interpretation of Canticles otherwise unknown to me[3], and entirely

---

1 C. XXVI 5. The *Test* takes the attitude of the Half-Tannaites, Faerber,
op. cit. 8 f

2 See *Gittin* 68 a, b. Salzberger, *op. cit.* 115 is hardly justified in making
the *Test* present a later development of the ring legend than the Talmud, if that
is what he means   Josephus (*Ant* VIII 2 5) presupposes a ring of Solomon.
The often published passage from the great Paris magical papyrus (Suppl.
grec 574) is no doubt borrowed from Jewish, not Christian magicians. Dieterich
believes the section cannot be earlier than the time of Eupolemus, and probably
comes from the Essenes (*Abraxas* 142 ff., *Leid. pap.* 780 ff)   In any case this
papyrus, written in the III or IV cent. A. D., but embodying much older
material, stands beside Josephus as a witness to the prominence of Solomon and
his ring in magic during the earliest centuries of the Christian era.   No satisfactory explanation of the clause ὁρκίζω σε κατὰ τῆς σφραγῖδος ἧς ἔθετο
Σολομὼν ἐπὶ τὴν γλῶσσαν τοῦ Ἰερημίου καὶ ἐλάλησεν (ll. 3039 f.) has been
advanced. Professor Deissman (*Licht* 187, n 15, *LAE* 257, n. 10) thinks it
may allude to some legend connected with LXX Jer I 6—10. Is it not more
likely that the name Jeremiah is a mistake for some demon or dragon name that
has been misread?   In one of the phylacteria of the Bologna MS which contains the *Test* is the line ἰδοὺ Σ. υἱὸς Δαβὶδ δράκοντος γλῶσσαν ἔχων βασιλέως ἐγκέφαλιν (cf. *supra* II, p. 24, n. 2)   One can go no farther than to suggest
the possibility of a connection. I can discover no Essenic material in the *Test*,
unless indefinite prescriptions of "cleanness" can be supposed to be such (VI 10,
XIII 2).   3 See my article in *Jl. Palest. Or Soc.*, I 116—121.

contradictory to that which became customary in Jewish and Christian circles.

A comparison of the *Test*, then, with Jewish thought in the same field confirms the statement which Dr Kohler makes, that our document is pre-Talmudic[1]. It is, moreover, closer to the Palestinian than to the Babylonian Talmud[2]. If Loewe is right in his contention that it was Galilean, not Judean, rabbis who believed in demonology and magic[3], we have just the line of tradition we should expect in a Christian work, which would be connected with Palestine rather than Babylon, and with Galilee rather than Judea.

e) One offshoot of Jewish magic remains to be considered. Perhaps the most interesting and valuable of recent publications in this field is Montgomery's *Aramaic Incantation Texts from Nippur*, inscriptions from a series of magic bowls in rabbinic Aramaic, Syriac, and Mandaic, intended to protect the houses and families of the clients, and dating from the sixth century A. D. Some are distinctly heathen, all are decidedly eclectic, mingling Babylonian, Jewish, and Hellenistic elements, but the majority show Jewish influence and were prepared for Jews. Strangely enough, in view of the place of origin, Persian demonology has left no trace, but "Egypto-Hellenistic magic is one of the prime sources of our texts"[4] How is the *Test* related to this remarkable series of incantations?

In many respects the similarity is great. We find the same kind of angel names ending in -el[5], the same trust in their efficacy[6], and the same conception of demons as the causes of ills and diseases of all sorts The sealing of demons is mentioned in most of the texts[7], and Solomon's seal is referred to in some[8] In a related text Grunbaum found the phrase "jinn of Solomon"[9]

---

1 Cf *supra* I 4.

2 Grünbaum (*ZDMG* XXXI 215) and Perles (*Bousset's Rel. d. Jud.* 35 f.) call attention to the difference. The *Test* comes nearer to the soberer views of the former, as is natural in a Christian work, which would not show direct Babylonian influence. 3 *ERE* IV 612f. 4 *Op. cit* 115, cf. 116

5 *Ibid.* 96 ff.; see review by the writer, *AJT* XIX (1915) 292 ff

6 *Ibid.* 56 ff., 111. 7 Cf *ibid.* 127, 133, 165, 191, 231 f

8 *Ibid.* 170, 173, 232, 248. 9 *Ibid.* 80, גינא דשלמיה

On the other hand there are decided differences. The magician is not concerned with individual demons or angels Personal names of demons are few, rather they are addressed as classes, "Demons and Devils and Satans and Liliths"[1], while the angels, even more than in the *Test*, come to be mere charms, not personalities. The black art is personified, and "the Curse and the Vow, and Arts and Practices" are adjured[2] Certain familiar names appear which the *Test* lacks, for example, Metatron[3], Abraxas[4], and Hermes[5]. Rather more of plainly Hellenistic magic enters into the Aramaic texts; for example, Zeus and Okeanos[6] Heathen deities appear more distinctly Sames, Sin, Bel, and Nirig[7]. The charms are much more elaborate than any in the *Test*

From this hasty comparison it is evident that Montgomery's texts and ours belong to the same world, that of syncretistic Hellenism, but not to the same part of that world, nor to the same era. The *Test* comes from an earlier, or at least a less highly developed stage in the history of magic, and, strange as it may appear, shows really less of Hellenistic influence on its magic, if not on its demonology, than do the Semitic texts.

7. Hellenistic elements and relationships. — No one familiar with the magic papyri can fail to identify the *Test* as a Hellenistic work. Upon the basis of primitive Greek and Roman animism the popular mind had constructed by the time of the early Empire a magic that borrowed from all the races, Babylonian, Persian, Indian, Jewish, and Egyptian, that had contributed to its civilization, and yet was thoroughly naturalized[8] It is in this world that the *Test* belongs

---

1 *Ibid.* 225; cf. 68. Such summaries are frequent and long, cf. pp 188f, 218. The magician wishes to include all possible evil spirits.

2 *Ibid.* 237, *et passim.*   8 *Ibid* 207, cf. 98, 113.

4 *Ibid* 148, 196, 232, cf. 57.   5 *Ibid.* 147, 196, 207, cf. 123, 113

6 *Ibid.* 197, cf. 113.   7 *Ibid* 238, in a heathen charm, cf. 70f.

8 Cf art. "Demons and Evil Spirits (Greek)" in *ERE* IV 590—4 by A C. Pearson and art. "Dämonen u. Dämonische" in *Realenc.* IV 408—19 by J. Weiss, with bibliographies.

Onoskelis is no doubt, the well known Greek female demon, although the manner of her birth can be paralleled from both Greek and Jewish sources[1]. Enepsigos is probably Hekate[2] One demon I have identified with Lix Tetrax, two of the original *Ephesia grammata*, in part because, while the name is corrupted, it is in the *Test* connected with a wind as it is in a Cretan tablet of the fourth century B. C.[3] In any case the section is Hellenistic, as the charm βουλταλά· θαλάλ· μελχάλ· shows, the demon also cures fever, a heathen, not a Jewish or Christian idea. Kynopegos may be identified with Poseidon[4]. Akephalos Daemon appears in the magic papyri[5]. The idea of demons as the cause of disease was familiar to the Greek mind, for the' Κῆρες were the ancient Greek form of microbe[6]. The similarity of views on this subject among men widely separated in time and place is illustrated by the fact that Plato, Apuleius, and the Talmud all agree in regarding demons as partly human, partly supernatural in their nature[7]

The magic of the *Test* is not outwardly so different from that of the magic papyri, and the writer was familiar with the praxis of the latter, as VI 10 and XVIII show. But ὀνόματα ἄσημα rarely appear, and when they do they are an evidence that the section in which they occur has come from Hellenism; nor do the incantations and amulets have the elaborateness that characterizes them in the papyri. The angel, a messenger of God, is the agent of healing and protection. No black magic, nor *defixiones* appear. The *Test*, then, differs from the magic papyri chiefly in that it is the work of a Christian using heathen

---

1 C. IV Cf. Roscher, *Lexicon*, s v. Ὀνόσκελις; J. Harrison *Proleg.* 202 f., Gruppe, *Gr. Myth.* 1306 and n. 17, 769, Lucian *ver hist* II 46, *supra* VI 1, VII 6 h.   2 She is a moon goddess, called μυριώνυμος, and has three forms.

3 Ziebarth in *NGG* 1899, 131, Wunsch, *Rh Mus.* LV (1900) 73ff. The writer is preparing an article in defense of this identification.   4 C. XVI

5 Lond. P 46 145ff, *Gr. Pap Br. Mus.* I 69f, Deissmann, *Licht* 194, *LAE* 139 Of course the headless ghost is an international figure (cf. Washington Irving's *Legend of Sleepy Hollow*), but allusions to fire and lightning in both accounts make the identification certain.

6 Harrison, *Proleg* 163ff, Bouché-Leclerq, *Astrol. Gr.* 24 n 1.

7 *Sympos.* 202 e, Apuleius *de Socr.* XIII. Cf. *supra* VII 6.

materials rather than that of a heathen working on Jewish or Christian matter

The passages in the papyri which mention Solomon merely show that his fame as a magician was spreading beyond the limits of Judaism and Christianity[1]. One is inclined to think that some legend of Solomon's dealing with demons is back of the line that speaks of Solomon's laying his seal on the tongue of Jeremiah[2]

8. Christian elements and relationships.

a) Relation to the New Testament. — The thought of our text regarding Christ has already been sufficiently discussed[3]. As to demonology the New Testament is not sufficiently detailed to permit a comparison of individual figures except in the case of Beelzebul, who is a purely New Testament character, so far as our knowledge goes, and who has been fully adopted into our text[4] In general it is quite evident that Paul and the writers of the Synoptic Gospels believed in demonic activities, such as are described in the *Test*[5]. They differ in the essential point that Christ's is the only name to use in exorcism, and, according to Luke, it could safely be invoked only by real Christians[6], all magic books were to be burned[7].

New Testament language has been adopted by our writer in the phrases στοιχεῖα κοσμοκράτορες τοῦ σκότους, applied to the seven spirits of evil[8], or στοιχεῖα οἱ κοσμοκράτορες τοῦ σκότους ⟨τοῦ αἰῶνος⟩ τούτου applied to the thirty-six *decani*[9], and ἀρχαὶ καὶ ἐξουσίαι καὶ δυνάμεις as designations of angelic beings[10]. Dr. Conybeare has collected and discussed a considerable number of words and phrases common to our text and

---

1 Par MP 850, 853, 3040.

2 Cf. Deissmann, *opp citt* 184, 252, Dieterich, *Abraxas* 139, cf. *supra* p. 64, n. 2.   3 Cf *supra* V 7.   4 Cf. *supra* VI 1 and p 44, n. 7.

5 Dibelius, *Geisterwelt*, 37—114.

6 Mk IX 38 ff., Lk IX 49 f., Ac XIX 13—17.

7 Ac XIX 19.   8 C. VIII 2.

9 C XVIII 2, combining Gal IV 3, 9; Col II 8, 20 with Eph VI 12. MS P omits τοῦ αἰῶνος as do the best witnesses in Eph VI 12.

10 C. XX 15, Eph. I 21, Col I 16; II 15 and I Pt III 22 are combined, but MS P, putting κοσμοκράτορες for δυνάμεις has the order of Eph VI 12.

the New Testament[1]. He comes to the conclusion, with which
we must on the whole agree, that the similarity of phrase is
due to common environment. "Paul merely glances at a system
of belief which the *Testament* sets before us in lengthy detail"[2].
But the environment of our writer includes the New Testament.
Not as if he had first hand acquaintance with it. That is ex-
cluded by those passages which deal with its incidents or ideas.
When he describes the "Gadarene" demon, Leontophoron, he
refers only to the outstanding features of the story which any
one would remember who had heard it read or told[3]. Likewise
in mentioning Jesus he alludes only to characteristic features of
Christian doctrine which would impress themselves on a hearer
who was δεισιδαιμονέστερος. The story of the rejected corner-
stone, combining as it does Ps CXVIII 22 and Is XXVIII 16
after the manner of I Pt II 6f.[4], but referring them to an actual
stone, reads like anti-Christian polemic from the Jewish side
Certainly our writer was not familiar with the Christian application of these verses, if he was a Christian.

After weighing the evidence one is driven to the conclusion
that the author of the *Test* had the same relation to the New
Testament that we have found him sustaining to the Old Testament and the apocryphal literature. All this constitutes part of
the background of his thinking, and he had a superficial knowledge of it derived from hearing it read in the Sabbath worship,
or mentioned in sermons and discussions; an occasional phrase
or quotation sticks in his mind, or he may borrow from other
better instructed magicians; but he is not working with copies
of any of this literature before him. He composes freely without
literary trammels It is auricular knowledge with an absence
of literary dependence rather than a very early date which
makes the *Test* at once like and unlike the New Testament[5].

1 *JQR* XI 5 f.   2 *Ibid* 6   3 C IX, cf. *supra* VI 7, p. 50
4 C. XXII 7 f., XXIII 2—4. Cf. Mt XXI 42 and parallels, see above VII 6,
p 61 f., also IX 2 and n. 16, p. 102
5 Cf. Conybeare, *JQR* XI 10, "The allusion [to the miracle of Gadara] is
not of such a kind as to involve our Gospel text in its present form, but rather
reflects the oral tradition which went before it."

b) Relation to the early Church. — To what class of Christians would such a work as the *Test* appeal? One would expect to find much Gnostic material in such a work, especially, in view of the fact that so many so-called "Gnostic amulets" have been preserved, many of them coupling the name of Solomon with Abraxas and similar words of power[1]. In fact, Dr. Conybeare concludes, "It is probable .. that the *Testament* was the favourite book of the Ophiani, or of some analogous sect which combined a belief in Emmanuel with a mass of pre-existent Jewish superstitions"[2] With this we cannot agree.

The passage on which Dr. Conybeare seems to base this judgment appears to me directly to contradict it. The seven ruling demons, faith in whom Origen ascribed to the Ophiani[3], are, to be sure, just the sort of beings in which the author of the *Test* believes. But these seven, which with the "mother" play so important a part in Gnosticism[4], are certainly the seven planets In the *Test* the only group of seven which appears is to be identified with the Pleiades[5], they have none of the characteristics of the Gnostic seven[6], nor is there any "mother" mentioned with them Sophia is personified in Proverbs and Wisdom as in the *Test* long before her appropriation by Gnosticism.

The prohibition of the invocation of angels' names "um irgend eine Sache" in the *Second Book of Jeû*[7] is a direct attack upon such practices as the *Test* sought to further. A similar condemnation of heathen magic and astrology appears in *Pistis Sophia*[8],

---

1 In the British Museum is a bronze nail with the inscription, ABARAXAS ASTRAEL IAO SABAO (drawing of a serpent) SOLOMONO, cf. H. B. Walters, *Cat. of the Bronzes in the Br. Mus , Greek, Roman, and Etruscan*, p. 370, No 3194 Henzen, *Bull. d. Inst. di Corr. Arch* 1849 p. 11 cites from a magic nail the inscription, AO SABAO SOLOMONO. Wessely, *Eph. Gram* 22, 202, cites ιαο σολομων σαβαο from Montfaucon *Tab* 164.   2 *Op c.t.* 14

3 *Contra Cels.* VI 30, Conybeare, *JQR* XI 13

4 Cf Bousset, *Hauptprobl.* c I, pp. 9–58

5 So Bousset, *op. cit.* 21 n. 4, decides; as does also Conybeare himself, *op. cit.* 24 n. 2, though suggesting the planets as an alternative.

6 Cf Bousset, *op cit* 27   7 Schmidt, *K-Gn Schriften*, 305, 30†.

8 *Ibid.* pp. 15—18, 167

but, as Dieterich pointed out, the Gnostic insisted he had the key to the true science[1], and it was this that gave Gnostic amulets such tremendous vogue. Now one of the striking facts about the original *Test* is that, outside the chapter on the thirty-six decani (XVIII), which, as we have seen, is of Egyptian origin[2], it contains practically none of the names which are commonly found on Gnostic amulets, or are regarded as characteristic of Gnosticism, such names as Abraxas and Ialdaboth The distinctly Gnostic elements belong to sections which have been assigned on other grounds to the later recensions[3].

The one piece of cosmic mysticism occurring in the *Test*, the directions for seeing "the heavenly dragons dragging the chariot of the sun"[4], presents a contrast to *Pistis Sophia* c 136, which describes the sun as a great dragon with his tail in his mouth[5] The words and phrases in the list of the *decani*[6] which have a Gnostic sound may be in part really of Gnostic origin, for example, ἰαέ· ἰεώ· υἱοὶ Σαβαώθ[7], κάλλιόν ἐστι Σολομῶν ἕνδεκα πατέρων[8], ἰοῦδα ζιζαβοῦ[9]. Some, perhaps all, are borrowed by Gnosticism and the *Test* from the same sources, Judaism, heathenism, and Christianity[10]. None of the characteristic features of the Gnostic systems, such as dualism, emanations, syzygies, and mystic names being found in the *Test*, and there being so few allusions of any kind to Gnostic language, the conclusion must be that our text has not come under Gnostic influence.

One story in the *Test* brings it into touch with Ethiopia From Ethiopia comes a story of Solomon's fall which closely parallels that in the *Test*. In the Talmud it is Asmodaeus who temporarily deposes the King by seizing his ring. In this Ethiopian legend Pharaoh's daughter seduces him. She urges him to worship her idols, he refuses. She entices him until finally he promises on oath that he will do whatever she wishes Then

---

1 *Abraxas*, 151 f and n. 2. 2 Cf *supra* VII 5
3 Cf. *infra* VII 11 and 12. 4 C. VI 19.
5 Schmidt, *K-Gn. Schriften* 233 18 f. 6 C. XVIII
7 *Ibid.* § 16. 8 *Ibid.* § 18, P only 9 *Ibid.* § 21
10 E g., Σαβαώθ, Ἀδωναί; cf. § 17

she ties a thread across the middle of the door of the temple
of her gods (that is, across the door half way up), brings three
locusts, sets them in the temple of her gods, and says to him,
"Come to me stooping so as not to break the woolen thread,
kill these locusts before me, and twist their necks." When he
complies, she says to him, "From now on I will do thy will,
since thou hast made offering to my gods and hast prayed to
them." The writer, moved by the same apologetic tendency as
in the *Test*, explains that he acted thus on account of his oath
in order that he might not perjure himself, although he knew
that it was a sin to enter the idol temple[1].

The parallels between this legend and that in the *Test* are
too striking to be overlooked Furthermore, Ethiopic magic and
demonology as a whole are much like those of the *Test*. "Very
great importance is attached in (Ethiopic) magic spells to the
knowledge of names and the power resident in them; and in
this potent element of the magician's art Jewish, Christian, and
pagan ideas curiously meet ...   In Abyssinia, Biblical sacred
names, together with a large number of fanciful appellations
much resembling those in the Jewish Kabbala, were magically
pronounced for the purpose of warding off the power of demons
and all kinds of diseases"[2]. The use of slips of paper as amulets to be tied to the person or wall[3], the prominence of Michael, the use of angelic names against demons and diseases[4],
the lilith-like Werzelya[5], and the power of Solomon over demons
almost make the impression that it is the *Test* which Margoliouth
is describing[6]. Remembering also the similarity of the *Test* and
Ethiopic Enoch one might be led to the conclusion that the

1 Prof Di Carl Bezold, *Kebra Nagast, Die Herrlichkeit der Könige, nach
den HSS. in Berlin, London, Oxford, and Paris*, c. 64, in *Abh. der philos-philol.
Klasse der königl bayer. Ak d Wiss* 23. Bd , 1 Abt., München 1905, 60f
Salzberger, *Salomosage* 96, says the same story is found in Kisā'ī, cf *infia*
§ 9, p. 80.

2 G. Margoliouth, "The Use of Charms and Amulets in Ethiopia," *ExT*
XXI 9 (June 1910) 403.   3 *Ibid*. 404. Cf. *Test* XVIII 22—42.   4 *Loc cit*.

5 Montgomery (*AITN* 261 f.) gives several parallels to the story of Christ's
meeting with a lilith. In Canaan *Aberglaube* 27 f the story is told of Solomon.

6 *Op cit* 405

Test must have come from the land from which the Ethiopic church received its legends, that is, from Egypt.

Lest one should infer too much, it is to be noted that legends similar to those in our text are to be found in other parts of the Christian world. Dr. Conybeare has discovered a parallel to the story of the corner stone which human agency could not lift[1] in life of St. Nino, the mother of the Georgian church[2]. In the Georgian life of the saint and the Armenian history of the Georgians is a story of a cedar column, the seventh and last necessary to the erection of the first church in the newly converted kingdom, which the king and all his people were unable to move, but which, in the early morning, after the defeat of the hosts of evil by St. Nino's prayers, is moved by invisible hands to the base prepared for it[3]. In Rufinus' *Ecclesiastical History* the same story is told of the "Iberians" and their king, but the miracle is heightened by leaving the pillar suspended above its base[4]. One might think of a combination of the stories of the corner stone and the aerial column in this last legend, but the connection is very tenuous

Dr. James writes to me: "I would add two more references to your bit of *testimonia* In the Syriac *Obsequies of the Virgin*, Wright, *Contributions to the Apocryphal Literature of the NT,* 1865, p. 42, is the story of the old man and his son [*Test* XX] — the end of it only, and in different guise, but unmistakably the same tale It is from a fifth century MS (see p. 12). Also in a tract called *Inventiones Nominum* which I printed in *Journal of Theological Studies*, 1903, p. 224, § 27, is, 'Tres sunt Orniae. . Tercius est Ornias princeps demoniorum.' In one MS this is emended to 'Ornias princeps Lacedaemoniorum' in allusion to I Macc. XII 7, but I feel sure it *is* an emendation. It is interesting to find an allusion in Latin."

Returning from these excursions to outlying fields of Christian thought and life we find every reason for believing

---

1 *Test* XXII 7, XXIII.   2 *Guardian,* Mar 29, 1899, 442

8 *Stud. Bibl.* V (1908) 38—41, and 83 f., edited by Miss Wardrop and Dr Conybeare. The accounts are full of wild stories of demons and exorcisms.

4 *Ibid.* 60, *Eccl. hist.* I x, Migne, *PL* XXI 482.

that the *Test* belongs in the ordinary current of Christian faith
and practice. From Paul on down the church fathers believed
in the real existence and the dangerous powers of demons[1]
"Aus dem tiefsten Gefühl heraus, von der Hilflosigkeit und
niedergedruckten Stimmung, wie dieser Glaube sie erzeugt hatte,
eine Rettung gefunden zu haben, schreibt ein Christ des II. Jahrh.
(Clemens Alex., Theodoti Exc. 71, 72) die Worte: 'Verschieden-
artig sind die Gestirne und ihre Kräfte, heilsame, schädliche,
rechte, linke .. Von diesem Widerstreit und Kampf der Kräfte
rettet uns der Herr und gibt uns Frieden vor dem Kampfe der
Kräfte und der Engel, den die einen für, die anderen wider uns
führen'"[2] Origen also seems to believe fully in the "powerful
names" known by "the Egyptians, or by the Magi among the
Persians, or by the Indian philosophers called Brahmans," as
he does in the power of the name of God and of Jesus and of
angel names[3]. That Christians practise sorcery or exorcism
by demonic names he indignantly denies, it is the name of
Jesus which drives out demons. Jesus has freed the Christian
from all superstitious fears[4].

   If such was the case with the leaders in the Christian
church, how can we expect that the rank and file of their fol-
lowers should fully grasp and consistently apply the one great
idea in which Christian magic differed from heathen, that
Christ's was the sole name of power to use for all purposes of
healing and protection? The newly converted idolater cannot
at once rise to the full heights of Christian spirituality[5] The
ancient church replaced the heathen deities with the crucifix

---

   1 Cf. von Dobschütz, *ERE* III 413—30, art. "Charms and Amulets
(Christian)," very strangely H. L. Pass, *ibid.* IV 578—83, art. "Demons and Evil
Spirits (Christian)" treats only of angels, but see now VIII 277f., art. "Magic."
See also Heitmüller, *Im Namen Jesu*, 291—5   2 Wendland, *Kultur* 81.
   3 *Contra Cels.* I 24f. cf. V 45. οὕτως οὐ τὰ σημαινόμενα κατὰ τῶν
πραγμάτων ἀλλ᾽ αἱ τῶν φωνῶν ποιότητες ‛αὶ ἰδιότητες ἔχουσί τι δυνατὸν ἐν
αὐταῖς πρὸς τάδε τινὰ ἢ τάδε. I 25 20, *KV Com.* II 76.   4 *Ibid.* VIII 57ᵗ
   5 Experience as a missionary in India has vividly impressed upon the
writer's mind the difficulties which converts to Christianity have in acquiring
its point of view. But modern western Christianity is not without illustrations
of the same problem.

and the images of the saints and madonna, and the old abra-
dacadabra with angel names[1]. At a very early time on Christian amulets the Lord's Prayer, verses from the Psalms, and
other familiar passages replaced the heathen myths and incantations[2]. Similarly the writer of the *Test* is making a brave,
though but partially successful, attempt to put Christian (i. e,
Jewish and Christian) ideas in the place of heathen. This whole
movement is most illuminatingly set forth in an excerpt quoted
by F. C. Burkitt from the Syriac homily *De magis, incantoribus,
et divinis,* in which "the writer complains that his fellow-Chris-
tians, even the clergy, resorted to Magicians *and Jews* He
says (col. 395) 'Instead of the blessings of the Saints, lo, they
carry about the incantations of the magicians, and instead of
the holy cross, lo, they carry the books of devils ... One
carries it on his head, and another round his neck, and a child,
who knows nothing at all, carries about devils' names and comes
(to church)... Polluted and abominable priests take refuge
in the names of demons .."[3] Magic grew in power in the
church, especially from the fourth century on, and was officially
recognized in the sixth and seventh[4] Our text is a document of
this progressive paganizing of official Christianity rather than
the product of some obscure heretical sect.

c) Relation to mediaeval Christianity. — That the *Test*
belongs to orthodox Christianity is further demonstrated when
one turns to study the preservation of the ideas for which it
stands in the European world. Illustrations are too numerous
to present in detail. The Queen of Sheba will serve as one.
Kraus has collected many references of Byzantine writers to the
fabled queen, which show that in using her the *Test* was following, or inaugurating, Christian tradition[5].

---

1 Cf. Heitmuller, *Im Namen Jesu,* 252f.
2 Cf. Deissmann, *Licht,* 24, 167, 297, *LAE* 39, 232, 415 ff.
3 In *PSBA* XXIII (1901) 77f. The homily is "ascribed in MSS to S.
Ephraim and edited as his by Lamy (vol. II, col 393—426), but ... in my
opinion is more likely to be the work of Isaac of Antioch (*circ.* 450 A. D.)"
4 Cf. von Dobschutz, *ERE* III 414.
5 "Die Konigin von Saba in den byz Chroniken," *BZ* XI (1902) 120ff.,
cf Nestle, *BZ* XIII (1904) 492f.

As to Solomon there was in the beginning some difference of opinion among Christian writers. Early anti-Jewish polemics, like the *Dialogue of Timothy and Aquila*, for example [1], find Solomon used to offset the claims of Jesus. Not only did their Jewish opponents apply many a Messianic passage to the wise son of David, but they made the claim that he had anticipated and excelled Jesus in his power over demons, thus undermining the Christian argument that Jesus was the Messiah because he had broken the power of Satan, and weakening the Christian appeal to a world that was languishing under the oppressive fear of demonic activities. To offset this Jewish claim these Christian writers bitterly attacked the memory of the wise king, maintaining that his was only a temporary victory over the demons, who overcame him at the end of his life. Leontius of Constantinople argues at some length that Christ's greatness is manifest in his power over demons while he was here on earth. In the midst of his description of the cure of the Gadarene demoniac he abruptly turns the request of the "Legion" to enter the swine to account in this fashion: Τίνι εἶπεν ὁ λεγεὼν τῶν δαιμόνων· Εἰ ἐκβάλῃς ἡμᾶς, ἐπίστρεψον ἡμῖν εἰς τὴν ἀγέλην τῶν χοίρων εἰσελθεῖν; Σολομῶντι, τῷ τὰ Ἱεροσόλυμα κτίσαντι, ἢ τῷ Δεσπότῃ Χριστῷ, τῷ τὰ σύμπαντα ἐν τῇ χειρὶ βαστάζοντι, Ἀλλ' ἐροῦσιν εὐθέως οἱ φιλοδαίμονες Ἰουδαῖοι· Τί οὖν, ὁ Σολομῶν οὐκ ἐδεσπότευσε τῶν δαιμόνων, οὐχὶ πάντας ὑφ᾽ ἓν ὡς ἕνα συνέκλεισεν, οὐχὶ μέχρι τῆς σήμερον τοῦτον δεδοίκασιν; Ἀλλ᾽ ὦ Ἰουδαῖοι μαγγανοδαίμονες, μάτην ταῦτα προβάλλεσθε· μόνος γὰρ ὁ Δεσπότης Χριστὸς κραταιῶς τὸν ἰσχυρὸν ἔδησε, καὶ τὰ σκεύη αὐτοῦ διήρπασε Σολομῶν γάρ, οὐ μόνον οὐκ ἐδέσποσε τῶν δαιμόνων βασιλικῶς, ἀλλὰ καὶ ὑπ᾽ αὐτῶν ἐδεσποτεύθη πρὸς τὰ τέλη καταφθαρείς ἀγαπήσας γὰρ τὸν τῆς πολυγαμίας ἔρωτα, τῇ τοῦ διαβόλου μαστροπότητι δελεασθείς, ... ἐρρύπωσε τὸν τῆς θεογνωσίας θάλαμον. ... Πῶς οὖν δαιμόνων δεσπότης, ὁ τῶν δαιμόνων δοῦλος; [2]

---

1 Cf. *infra* p. 103 f.

2 From the homily *In mediam Pentecosten*, Migne, *PG* 86, col. 1980, According to Loofs, *Das Leben usw. des Leont. v. Byz.*, summarized by Krumbacher, *BLg* p. 54 f., this Leontius was a Constantinopolitan presbyter who lived

Similarly in the *Disputatio* of Pseudo-Gregentius, in reply to the claim of Herban the Jew that Solomon had ruled all the demons the archbishop replies. Σολομῶν ἐταπείνωσε δαίμονας, οὐκ οἶδας τί διαγορεύεις. πρὸς καιρὸν μὲν ἠσφαλίσατο τούτους ἐν τοῖς ἀγγείοις καὶ σφραγίσας κατέχωσεν ἀλλά γε τὸ τηνικαῦτά μοι σκόπει, ὅτι νητῶς καταπολεμηθεὶς ὑπ᾽ αὐτῶν τῶν δαιμόνων καὶ ἡττηθεὶς περὶ σωτηρίαν αὐτοῦ ἐκινδύνευσεν, ὡς ἡ γραφὴ μαρτυρεῖ[1].

The original *Test* shows no suspicion of a conflict of claims between Solomon and Christ, but in c. XV 10—12 Rec B (MS P) attempts to combine the Jewish and Christian viewpoints. As to the glorious king's sad end, these early fathers think of him as falling a prey to the demons through the seduction of women, or vice versa. But the majority of Christian writers, like Josephus[2], ascribe his fall into idolatry to his love for women without the interposition of demonic agency[3]. The *Test* in one place takes the former view[4], but in the closing chapter apparently the latter. Here again our text shows its early date.

The conception of Solomon as a great magician who was powerful over demons and disease is witnessed to by scores of amulets and incantations, and especially by such books as the *Clavicula*[5] Many of the demons of the *Test* lived on. Asmo-

about 485—542. Cf Gelzer, *Leont v. Byz.*, etc, and *Hist. Ztschr.* LXI (1899) 1—32, Fabricius, *Bib Graec.* VIII 319 ff.

1 Migne, *PG* 86, col. 644 A. Gregentius was bishop of the Homerite church in Taphar in southern Arabia in the early part of the sixth cent The *Disputatio* is not authentic, but may contain historical materials. Cf Smith and Wace, *DCB*, Krumbacher, *BLg* 59, Bardenhewer, *Patrol.* 477 The mention of ἀγγεῖα makes connection between the Arabic type of tradition and the *Test*, cf. XV 9, XVIII 43, XXV 7, where the word is found only in MS P, and XVI 7, where Recs. A and B both should probably have it, though A reads φυλακήν.

2 *Ant* VIII 7 5 cf. 1 Kg XI 43.

8 Georgius Syncellus, P 181, V 145, B 341, Georgius Hamart, *Chron.* II 43 (Migne *PG* 110, 252—64), Glycas, *Ann.*, Migne *PG* 158 353 f.; Joseph *Hypomn.* 74, (Migne *PG* 106 89 D). 4 C VIII 8, 10

5 Solomonic amulets can be found in many museums as well as in a large number of mediaeval MSS. They occur in Syriac, Arabic, and Hebrew, and in Latin, Greek, and modern European languages, e g, Sachau, *Verz. Syr HSS Berlin* I 367, No. 101, f. 54 b Sol. on horseback attacking Asmodaeus,

daeus goes through many transformations[1]. Obyzut appears in
the Abyzu of Pradel's *Griechische und suditalienische Gebete*,
while Ornias appears in the same documents[2]. Gaulmin and
Migne were right in bringing the *Test* and Psellus together. The
great Byzantine's περὶ ἐνεργείας δαιμόνων διάλογος is but the
effort of a master mind to systematizise the ideas which the
Test merely registers. Withal, this whole complex of Byzantine
demonology and magic makes the impression of being a more
highly developed form of the conceptions with which our text
is operating. The roots of the tree run back to the Sumerians,
the Babylonians, the Iranians, and the Pelasgians, the *Test* stands
for the blossom, Psellus gives us the ripened fruit dissected and
analyzed.

9. Relation to Arabian folklore — Arabic literature, since
it is especially rich in demon lore and Solomonic myth, invites
particular comparison with the *Test*. In general Arabian beliefs
and practices in the field of demonology and magic are not
essentially different from those of our text except in one feature
which Islam inherited from heathenism, the idea of the Jinn,

Schwab, *Dict* 421, "ΣΦΡΑΓΙΣ ΘΕΟΥ, sur une hématite figurant un Salomon
à cheval, perçant de sa lance un ennemi terrassé, avec la legende ΣΟΛΩΜΩΝ,
au Cabinet des Medailles et Antiques de la Bibliothèque Nat. Il 3039" The late
Prof Nestle wrote me of a Sol on horseback as an amulet against *malocchio*,
published by Bienkowski in *Eranos Vindobonensis*, 1893, 288. Amulets in MSS
are well illustrated by those in *cod Bonon. univ.* 3632, cf. *supra* p 24. Cf.
Heim "Incantamenta magica," in *Jbb. für class Philol. Sup.* XIX (1893) pp. 463
—576, Nos 56 = 169, 61, 62, 236, 237, and Sorlin Dorigny, "Sal als Reiter,"
in *Rev. des Études Grecs* IV (1891) 217—296 The pilgrim of Bordeaux in the
IV cent. was shown the "crypta ubi S. daemones torquebat," Schürer *GJV*
III 418, from Tobler, *Palaest. descript.* (1869) 3, Pal. Pil. Text Soc., *Bordeaux
Pilg.* 20 Dr. Conybeare drew my attention to Gamurrini's ed of St. Silvia's
Peregrinatio (IV cent), according to which the ring was kept in the Church of
St James (p. 96 and 95 n 2). The tradition was that Vespasian took it to
Rome, whence Constantine returned it (*ibid.* 96 n. 3), cf. Petri diaconi *liber de
locis sanctis, ibid.* 117, see Pal Pil. Text Soc., *The Pilgrimage of S. Silvia to
the Holy Places,* 64 and 125.

1 As Markolf, Morolf, Kitovras, Saturn; cf. Fr. Vogt, *Die deutschen
Dichtungen von Sal u. Markolf*, I, J M Kemble, *The Anglo-Saxon Dialogue of
Sol. and Saturn.*

2 Cf Index I, s. v "Damonen," and Reitzenstein, *Poim.* 297 ff.

which are often kindly and beneficent creatures[1]. In our writer's
mind there is properly no place for any good among demons,
although he is once or twice betrayed by his pagan materials
into referring to their healing powers. The wild exuberance of
Arab fancy as we see it in the *Thousand and One Nights* is
another mark of differentiation.

The Quran and even more the *Arabian Nights* have made
all the world familiar with Solomon's authority over the Jinn
and with the latter's terrible forms and powers. In the Quran
are allusions to the fallen angels, Hārūt and Mārūt[2], and to the
devils who were subject to Solomon, some as builders, and
others bound in fetters[3]. In the *Nights* we find full accounts
of how Solomon placed rebellious Jinn in bottles, or in cucu-
bites of copper, poured lead over them, and sealed them with
his ring[4], with tales of their later escape from these prisons[5].

According to the Quran the Jinn are not allowed to listen
at the gates of heaven, but God has placed the stars there as
weapons for the angels to throw at them if they make the
attempt. In the *Nights* the Jinniyah Maymunah "made for the
firmament, thinking to listen by stealth to the converse of the
angels," and when she ascended "skywards till she drew near
the heaven of the world, the lowest of the heavens," she found
an Ifrit there before her[6]. In another story "Allah suffered his
angelic host to shoot down the Ifrit with a shooting star[7].

---

1 Cf. Wellhausen's account of primitive Arabic beliefs, *Reste* 148—67, and
Canaan, *Aberglaube* 6—27, for modern demonology; also *Encycl. of Islam*, I 1045 f.,
art "Djinn," by D. B. Macdonald.

2 Sura II 97 ff., *SBE* VI (Quran I) 14, Sale *ad loc* quotes the legend
substantially as told in Midrash Yalkut c 44, see St Clair-Tisdall and Muir,
Sources of Islam, 30 f., and Weil, *Bibl. Leg.* 208 ff Zohra resembles Shunamite
in her activities.

3 Sura XXXVIII 35 ff, *SBE* IX (II) 179, cf. Sale, *ad loc.*; XXVII 7, *SBE*
IX (II) 101. 4 Lane-Poole III 110 f., Burton VI 84, Nights 566 f

5 Burton VI 85. The most famous is that of the "Fisherman and the
Jinn," Burton I 38, cf. MacDonald's transcription from Galland's MS in *Or
Stud. Th. Noldeke gewidmet*, also separately published. 6 Burton III 223 f.

7 Burton, I 224, Night 22, cf. Quran, Sura XXXVII 6—9, *SBE* IX (II)
168, III 31, *ibid.* VI (I) 50 and n. 2, LXVII 5, *ibid* IX (II) 293; LXXII 8 f.,
ibid. 305, Burton VI 100, Night 571, VIII 293, Night 870

The likeness and unlikeness of the conceptions in the *Test* are apparent.

Salzberger's dissertation on the *Salomosage*, although it does not reach the fall of the king, presents a rich collection of legends, particularly with regard to his relations to the demons. He gathers them under four rubrics, the punishment of the demons, their appearance before Solomon, the description of certain individuals, especially Sahr, and Solomon's ring[1]. Two descriptions of the appearance of the devils as they are marshalled before the king are given from three Berlin MSS of Kisa'i. The portrayal of demonic forms as given "nach dem korrecteren und vollstandigeren Text der dritten Berliner Handschrift des Kisa'i"[2] would seem most strikingly like that in the *Test*, were it not that the other two MSS give in a longer and shorter form descriptions which are still more similar[3]. Solomon inquires from the demons, just as in the *Test*, what their activities are, and, having learned, chains them so they may injure mankind no more. The ring, as in the *Test*, is brought down from heaven, and by its aid Solomon becomes master of the demons.

Yet, with all these close resemblances, there are also great differences between the *Test* and the Arabic legends. All the Jewish stories of Solomon's glory and wisdom, his wonderful ring, the building of the Temple by the aid of the demons, and his dealings with the queen of Sheba have grown marvellously under the fructifying fancy of the Arabs. Beside the marvels of the Quran and its commentaries, and especially the *Arabian Nights* the *Test* is dull and tame[4] Most of the features in which we found Jewish legend to have evolved beyond the *Test* are to be found in still more highly developed form among the Arabs, for example, Solomon's power over the animals is greatly extended[5];

---

1 (1) *op. cit.* 98 f., 113 ff., (2) 99—112, (3) 112—115; (4) 115—29

2 *Ibid* 99, Mg. 40, f. 72 b

3 *Ibid.* 105 ff., Pm. 627, 1. 160 a f. gives the longer form, which most resembles the *Test*, Spr. 86, f. 226 a ff the shorter.

4 Cf, for example, Lane-Poole, III 51 f., 110 f., 239, 317, 329, 454.

5 In the Quran he knows the language of the birds, Sura XXVII 16, *SBE* IX (II) 100.

Saḫr is the Talmudic Asmodaeus, but worse; Iblis, the devil, whose refusal to worship Adam leads to his fall[1], is not, like Beelzebul in the *Test*, subject to Solomon, but carries a step farther that independence and insolence which Asmodaeus shows in the Jewish legends, the king's fall has quite a different aspect in the Quran[2].

The ring also, as Salzberger shows, develops a new character in Arabic legend different from that which it has in the *Test*, evolving along the lines suggested by the Talmudic story of Asmodaeus' theft of it[3]. Kisa'i is the first to describe it fully[4] It is so glorious that no one can look at it without repeating the Moslem creed, and has four considerable legends engraved upon it[5]. It is either brought by Gabriel, or of itself comes from the throne of God and appears upon Solomon's hand

Solomon's fall according to Kisa'i was due to conscious or unconscious idolworship, which, if I understand Salzberger, was connected with the sacrifice of locusts[6]. This tradition, then, connects the *Test* on the one hand with Ethiopia, and on the other with Arabia. Since Ethiopia was closely connected with Arabia in Christian history, we have probably to think of a Palestinian Jewish tradition which never found its way to Babylon, nor, so far as I know, into official Palestinian Jewish literature, but passed by way of the Jewish colonies in southern Arabia into Ethiopian and Mohammedan legend, and directly from Palestinian Judaism into our Christian work, for we cannot suppose that the *Test* arose in Arabia. This being so, one of the links that would connect our text with Egypt is broken.

These examples are sufficient to illustrate both the likeness and the unlikeness of the *Test* to Arabic literature. They show how Arabic legend, where it resembles our work, has developed its

1 Sura II 33f., VII 19ff., XV 30ff, XVII 63f, XVIII 47ff., XXXVIII 75ff., *ibid.* VI (I) 5, 138f, 246f., IX (II) 8, 20, 181

2 Sura XXXVIII 33f., *ibid.* IX (II) 178 and n. 2.

3 *Salomosage* 115—9.   4 *Ibid*, from Mq. 40 f. 70b—72b.

5 In the *Nights* an oath by the names on Solomon's ring is peculiarly powerful, Burton III 224f, Night 177, cf. VII 317 n

6 *Op. cit.* 96, refers to Pm. 627, f. 151b—155a.

ideas farther and in a different manner, and how in many particulars it rests upon the sort of Jewish tradition seen in the
Talmud.

10 Unique matter in Recension A — Having studied the
material relationships of the *Test* as a whole we now undertake
the same task for the individual recensions. As Rec. A is
nearest the original, it has little matter that calls for comment
Its expansions are of a purely narrative sort[1]. MS L alone has
undergone a considerable revision by a mediaeval magician, who
added nothing new, but merely mutilated the document. The
single addition of importance in this recension is the inscription
on the ring[2].

11. Unique matter in Recension B. — The peculiarities of
Rec B, and particularly of MS P, the only complete MS of this
recension, consist in the main of unimportant interpolations and
alterations. There are, however, a few additions of moment.
These may be classed under four heads: (1) those which show
familiarity with demonological tradition, e g , the reference to
the ghosts of the giants[3], to the female demon Obyzuth as
$\pi\nu\varepsilon\tilde{\nu}\mu\alpha$ $\mu\nu\varrho\iota\acute{\omega}\nu\nu\mu\sigma\nu$ $\varkappa\alpha\grave{\iota}$ $\pi\sigma\lambda\acute{\nu}\mu\sigma\varrho\varphi\sigma\nu$ [4], and to Enepsigos, another
female demon, as $\mu\nu\varrho\iota\acute{\omega}\nu\nu\mu\sigma\varsigma$ [5], the allusion to a cycle of legend
regarding $\mathring{E}\lambda\beta\sigma\nu\varrho\iota\omega\nu$ and $\sigma\mathring{\iota}$ $\mathring{\varepsilon}\pi\tau\grave{\alpha}$ $\delta\alpha\acute{\iota}\mu\sigma\nu\varepsilon\varsigma$ [6], the added charms
in XVIII 23, 27 f., further information regarding Abezethibu[7];
(2) those which are Gnostic in character; e. g., the allusions to
the eleven fathers and the eleventh aeon[8]; (3) those which have
a cabalistic tendency; e. g, the introduction of Apharoph for
Raphael, of $\chi\mu\delta'$ for Emmanuel, and of $\chi\mu'$ for Raphael[9], and

---

1 Cf. c I I f and XXVI 8—10   2 Cf infra VII 14.   3 C. XVII 1.

4 C XIII 3, cf. $\mathring{E}\varkappa\acute{\alpha}\tau\eta$ $\mu\nu\varrho\iota\acute{\omega}\nu\nu\mu\varepsilon$ Par MP 2745, Orph. Hymn. *passim*,
$\mathring{E}\varkappa$ $\pi\sigma\lambda\nu\acute{\omega}\nu\nu\mu\varepsilon$ Par MP 2815, her many names are given in *cod Par*. 2316,
f. 432, cf Reitzenstein, *Poim*. 299 (one is $\mathring{A}\beta\iota\zeta\acute{\alpha}$), Pradel, *Gr. Geb*. 23 (275)
($\mathring{A}\beta\nu\zeta\sigma\tilde{\nu}$), Montgomery, *AITN* 260 (No 42), 262, Gaster in *Folklore* XI 133,
Avezuha, $\pi\sigma\lambda\nu\acute{\omega}\nu\nu\mu\varepsilon$ is frequent   For $\pi\sigma\lambda\acute{\nu}\mu\sigma\varrho\varphi\sigma\varsigma$ cf. Par MP 2726, 2799, of
Hekate and Selene; *cod. Par*. 2316 f. 318ᵛ (Reitzenstein, *Poim*. 297) $\Sigma\tau\varrho\alpha\gamma\gamma\alpha\lambda\iota\grave{\alpha}$
$\pi\sigma\lambda\acute{\nu}\mu\sigma\varrho\varphi\varepsilon$.   5 C. XV 2   6 C. IX 7.

7 C. XXV 1—5, possibly omitted by accident from Rec. A. See also additions in VI 4   8 C XVIII 18, 31.

9 C XIII 6, XV 11. See other additions in XVIII 3, 23, XXII 8, XXIII 4

(4) those which show familiarity with Christianity. Additions are found in every section that refers to Christ; viz., VI 8, XI, XII 3, XVII 4, and XXII 20. The additions in the first three passages are not important. The remaining two, however, seem to be due to an attempt to make the Christianity of the *Test* less "equivocal," since in XVII 4 the "becoming man" of the Savior is mentioned, and in XXII 20 the one to be born of a virgin and crucified is called ὁ μονάρχης θεός These additions lead to the belief that in XV 10f, where Rec. A is wanting by accident, the positive Christian ideas advanced, viz., that it is the son of God who is to be stretched on the tree, that his mother is never to know man, and that he is especially fit to receive dominion over all the demons because he overcame the devil (διάβολος rarely occurs in the *Test*) are probably the work of the B redacteur. This conclusion is supported by the fact that the *Test* elsewhere makes no attempt at systematic thought or generalization. At any rate we cannot definitely claim these ideas for the original writer, and must conclude that B is not only much better instructed in the faith, but also later.

12. Unique matter in Recension C — Rec C deserves a special investigation of much greater proportions than can be given here, in order to determine its sources and relationships. As we have already seen, its language is late, and the codices in which it is found as well as its unique material relate it to the *Clavicula* [1]

Many problems I must leave to others. Why is Beelzebul called Eltzianphiel [2]? What is the meaning of Onoskelu's birth ἀπὸ φωνῆς βηρσαβεὲ ἱππικῆς χρηματικῆς [3]? Whence comes the idea of the bird that flies over God's head? One of the most interesting and baffling sections is that which we have called the "Prologue". In spite of defective grammar the editor has

---

1 Cf *supra* II 4, IV 2 c   2 Rec C XI 1, cf Τζιανφιέλ, X 1

3 *Ibid.* XI 6. Dr James writes, "I am clear that χρηματικῆς has something to do with χρεμετίζειν, *neighing of horse*, and I compare Jer V 8, ἵπποι θηλυμανεῖς ἐγενήθησαν, ἕκαστος ἐπὶ γυναῖκα τοῦ πλησίον ἐχρεμέτιζον. When David sinned with Bathsheba, βηρσαβεέ, he was a ἵππος θηλυμανής See *Test* V 8, θηλυμανεία.

been able to select from some source certain high sounding
prayers, which, I think, have no parallels in the LXX, the New
Testament, or the early fathers. Possibly he borrowed from
some, to him well known, liturgy.

The magical cup and table in c. XI 7 ff are related to the
"marvelous cup of crystal middlemost of which was the figure
of a lion faced by a kneeling man grasping a bow with arrow
drawn to the very head, together with the food-tray of Sulay-
man, the son of David" in the story of "Sinbad the Seaman
and Sinbad the Landsman" from the *Arabian Nights*[1]. The
added magical formulae connect this recension more closely
than the others to the magical literature of the Middle Ages on
the one hand, and to the magical papyri on the other. The
word Agla (XIII 6), which by *notarikon* stands for "thou art
mighty forever, O Lord," indicates dependence upon Jewish
cabalism, and probably a relatively late date, for the word is
not in the magic papyri, so far as I can discover, but is a
favorite in the Middle Ages[2].

The magical recipe of c. IX 9f and the list of fifty demons
in c. X have many marks which show that they are later than
the original *Test* and have arisen in a different circle. The list
is not concerned solely or primarily with the cure of diseases;
it relates the powers, some good, some evil, of each demon, and
implies that these powers are under the control of him who
knows the demon's seal. Furthermore, each demon rules a
certain number of inferiors. These ideas are to be found, on
the one hand, in Gnosticism, which details the number of
spirits ruled by each ἄρχων[3], and, on the other, in mediaeval

---

1 Seventh Voyage in the Calcutta edition, Burton VI 80.

2 The word is an acrostic from the first four words of the second blessing
of the Shemoneh 'Esreh אתה גבור לעלם אדני. Since this liturgy and also the
practice of *notarikon* are early, one can argue as to date only on general probabilities, cf *JE* I 235, IX 270—82, Schwab, *Dict* s. v. אגלא. It occurs often in
Horst, *Zauberbib.*, I 127, II 90, 103, 121, 123 ff., etc ; in Mather's *Key*, p. 7, in
Harl. MS 5596 (cf. *supra* II 4) f. 30ᵃ¹ in an incantation to secure treasure
ὁρκίζω ὑμᾶς, δαίμονες, εἰς τὰ ὀνόματα τοῦ θεοῦ τὸ τετραγράμματον ὅπερ
ἐστὶν ἀγλα· ἀγλαατά· ἀγλαί· ἀγλαώρ, also f. 30bᵃ, 32bᵃ, often in Latin
Clavicula. 3 Cf. p. 85, n. 2.

magic[1]. The resemblance between c. X and the language of *Pistis Sophia* regarding the five ἄρχοντες and the ψῆφοι and σφραγῖδες of the thirteenth αἰών[2], and the various χαρακτῆρες, σφραγῖδες, and lists of names in chapters 5—40 and 45—52 in the *First Book of Jeu*[3] is most striking. Furthermore, there are close resemblances between the magical figures of the Coptic papyri, the *Clavicula*, both Latin and Greek, and the unique sections of this recension.

We cannot attempt to trace the connecting links between these widely separated branches of magic, which, no doubt, go back to a common source in Hellenistic syncretism. The facts presented are an interesting illustration of the wide wanderings of superstitions, and the tenacity with which they maintain their forms in their migrations.

13 Unique matter in MS D. — On internal grounds and by comparison with Recs. A and B we have decided that MS D c I—VI and VIII present in general the form of the original story of Solomon out of which the *Test* was developed[1]. From what sources did this legend come? As it now stands, it is quite plainly a Christian redaction of Jewish *midrashim* regarding Solomon, Palestinian, perhaps Galilean, in origin, rather than Babylonian[5]. That the legend of c. I is ultimately Jewish is suggested by Nathan's stopping to bury a dead countryman, a trait borrowed from Magianism[6] Traces of later influences are to be found in c. VII[7]. The story of Solomon's flying through the air appears in Jewish mythology, where he is said to have ridden on an eagle[8], but in Mohammedan legend, according to the Quran on a wind[9], and in the

---

1 Cf. Trinity Col (Cambridge) MS 1404 in French; Harl. (Br. Mus.) 6483, which contains "all the names, orders, and offices of all the spirits Sol ever conversed with" (f. 1)   2 Cc. 138 ff., Schmidt, *K-Gn. Schr.* 235 ff

3 *Ibid.* 260—97, 308—29.   4 Cf. *supra* IV 2   5 Ct. *supra* VII 6 *d*), p 64 f.

6 Cf Tob I 19, II 3 ff. Dr James points out to me that the story is found in Ps.-Epiphanius, *Vitae Prophetarum*, see ed. Schermann (Teubner 1907), pp. 4, 54, 89, Migne, *PG* 43, col. 425, and thinks this is its probable source. For D it would then be indirectly Jewish, I suppose Calish, *JE* IX 176, says the rabbis are practically silent as to Nathan.   7 Cf. *supra* IV 2.

8 Grünbaum, *ZDMG* XXXI 23.

9 Suras XXXI 81, XXXIV 11, XXXVII 35, *SBE* IX (II) 52, 151, 179.

Arabian Nights on a magic carpet[1]. If the story originally
referred to Asmodaeus' usurpation of the throne, then we have
also Jewish sources. This chapter, then, would seem to be an
addition from a Jewish-Mohammedan type of tradition. All the
remainder of this version we have already traced to Jewish
sources[2].

From considerations of textual and literary criticism we
concluded that D in its present form was late, but that its
archetype (*d*) was the starting point for the *Test*[3]. From its
language and style we concluded that it was Byzantine[4]. Our
conclusions based upon a study of its subject matter accord
with this and take us one step further: an originally Jewish
document or cycle of legends has been thoroughly worked over
by an educated Christian in early Byzantine times. Since there
are no Christian elements in those parts of *d* which were taken
over into the *Test*, and the quality of the Christianity in Rec A
is much poorer than in D, it is natural to conclude that *d* had
nothing Christian in it when it was transformed into the *Test*.

14. Solomon's seal — The origin of the seals supposedly
engraved on the ring of Solomon is of subordinate importance,
since they are in any case secondary additions in our MSS.
The simplest form is that found in Rec B, which attempts no
reproduction, but merely says the inscription was a pentagram.
Since this is the western type of the tradition, it cannot have
been original[5].

Rec A presents an interesting formula consisting for the
most part of unintelligible words and containing those combi-
nations of vowels so common in Hellenistic magic. MS L alone
reproduces the seal with the legend in the form of a circle, the
formula appearing around the circumference, while the interior
contains magic signs. In the manuscript in which L is found,
Harl 5596, the *Clavicula* contains a seal of different shape on

---

1 Burton III 267.   **2** *Supra* VII 6.   **3** *Supra* IV 1, 2, 3.   **4** *Supra* V 1.
5 Cf. *JE* XI 438 ff., 448, Grunbaum, *Neue Beiträge z. sem. Sagenkunde* 251.
The text of the inscriptions as given in our MSS will be found below, p. 100f.
Canaan, *Aberglaube*, p. 112f., *et passim*, gives the seal of Solomon as usually
the sixpointed star among modern Arabs, but also the five.

which the same legend was to be written   In Bologna University-
sity MS No. 3632 (V of the *Test*) there is found among many
such "pentacles" a circle inscribed τοῦ σολομῶντος μεγάλου,
within which is written the same legend. No doubt the editor
of Rec. A got his seal from some such collection. The wording
of the inscription would seem to link it to the older amulets
and magic papyri, but in any case it is younger than the *Test*,
which shows little trace of such influence.

In Rec. C twelve large seals are found, the first a rectangle
with various transverse lines and magic sings, the remaining
eleven round and also containing various mystical symbols   In
the fifth and the ninth are figures that look like the signs for
Virgo and Scorpio, in the seventh for Aquarius, in the eighth for
Pisces; the third, fourth, and fifth contain among others modi-
fications of the Christian monogram ☧. The fact that these
same seals are found in a Vienna MS which does not contain
the *Test* is, I think, indicative of their origin. We must conclude that the original *Test* contained no description or reproduction of the seal.

15. Summary and conclusions. — If our previous conclusions
are correct, the original Jewish stem of the present *Test* consisted
of the narrative parts of chapters I, II, XX, XXII, XXIII, and
XXIV, i. e, of those parts which are common to the *Test* and
MS D. Upon this parent stem have been grafted (1) certain
sections which describe the demons more fully, (2) two brief
references to the work as a *Test*, which give it the name (XV
13f., XXVI 8), other considerable sections containing demonic
prophecies whose later fulfilment is represented as constituting
the basis for Solomon's faith in their testimony, and which,
therefore, are intended to validate the work to the public (XII 4,
XV 12ff, XX 21)[1], and (4) additions made merely for the story's
sake or intended to link the parts of the story together (VI 3,
5f., XIX, XXI, XXII 7f., 17).

In this division of the *Introduction* we have given attention
mainly to the origin of the first of these four classes of additions,

1 Note also the late (P) addition XV 8—11

which includes the demonological, astrological, and magical
elements in the work[1], additions marked by the questions τίς
εἶ σύ; τίς καλεῖσαι, ποίῳ ζῳδίῳ κεῖσαι, ποίῳ ἀγγέλῳ καταργεῖσαι; It is for the sake of answering these questions that the
Test was written. As we have seen, the material for the answers has been drawn through Judaism from Babylonia in Ephippas (XXII) and possibly in the lilith-like Obyzuth (XIII) and from
Persia in Asmodaeus (V), from Hellenistic Egypt come the
decani although the section has been much altered by Jewish
or Christian revisers (XVIII); from Hellenistic Greek mythology
come Onoskelis (IV), Lix Tetrax (VII), Akephalos Daemon (IX),
Enepsigos (= Hekate, XV), Kunopegos (= Poseidon, XVI), and
possibly the dog, Rhabdos (X, = ? Cerberus) and Pterodrakon
(XIV = ? Typhon)[2], from Hellenistic mysticism the recipe for
a cosmic revelation (VI 10f.); from (perhaps Galilean) Jewish
sources come the seven κοσμοκράτορες[3], the giant, Machthon[4],
the demon of the Red Sea, Abezethibou (XXV), and probably
the Shunamite (XXVI), from Christian, or Jewish-Christian sources
in part, come Beelzebul (III, VI 1—9), Leontophoron, the demon
of Gadara (XI), and perhaps the demon of epilepsy called
κορυφὴ δρακόντων, beside the charms which include some
allusion to Christ (XV 10f., XVII 4).

What sort of a man could have held such inconsistent and
ill-digested views drawn from all these diverse sources He
cannot have been a heathen for he knows Judaism and Christian-
ty, the Old Testament and the New too well. He cannot have
been a Jew because of the Christian elements Dr Conybeare
suggests that we have here as in the *Testaments of the Twelve
Patriarchs*, "a Christian recension of a Jewish book"[5] Although
I cannot agree with Schurer that there are no Jewish passages
in the book[6], Dr. Conybeare's hypothesis does not seem to

---

1 MS D shows that some of this was in the original story, *d.*

2 Azazel, the serpent tempter of Eve, has human hands and feet in the
Apoc. of Abraham XXIII, Bonwetsch p. 33, cf Hughes, *Ethus Jew. Apoc*, 211.

3 C. VIII, it has some Hellenistic and Christian additions.

4 Is he a Titan rather than one of the Nephilim?

5 *JQR* XI 13f   6 *Th Litztg.* 1899 110.

meet the facts in the case. There is too much Christian material in the *Test.* Particularly is it to be noted that, in both places where the word *testament* occurs (XV 14, XXVI 8), it is closely connected with passages which are Christian in tone; c. XV 10f. in the form in which we have it is the most characteristically Christian section in the entire work; c XXVI 8 in Rec. B, which we believe to represent the original here, is less markedly so than is MS H with its reference to the "Jews," and yet we have discovered that the whole of the last chapter is based on a legend which otherwise comes to us from a Christian source. Moreover, the demonology of the work, which so much resembles that of the New Testament and the pseudepigrapha which were accepted in the Christian church, and the language with its resemblances to that of the New Testament even in passages where there is no quotation or direct allusion point to a Christian origin. The absence too of smaller inconsistencies from the narrative, especially of Rec. A, the impossibility of finding the joints in the mending, point to unity of authorship for the *Test* as such. We conclude, then, that while the original story *d* was probably Jewish, the demonological document which first called itself a *Testament,* best represented in Rec A, was a Christian work

The man who composed our *Test* bears no distinctive marks of any heterodox circle, yet he was no thorough-going Christian. He was above all a magician, and it is as such that he collected this bizarre potpourri of fragments from almost every nation that had contributed to Mediterranean civilization. He must have been a Greek Christian, familiar, perhaps from childhood, with the language of the Septuagint and New Testament, familiar also with many legends of Jewish origin, but entirely familiar too with the demonology and magic of the heathen world, to which he belonged almost as truly as he did to Christianity. For him Christ is not yet master of the whole world; nevertheless, Christ's is a name to conjure with, and, when he is at a loss for a powerful angel name, the new savior comes into the exorcism He is a half-hearted Christian in a world where Christianity is not yet the conquering religion. This is the more

evident when one compares Recs. B and C, which introduce
elements which reveal the period when Christianity had con-
quered, and was absorbing its former foes and their superstitions.

VIII. THE TESTAMENT IN LITERATURE AND HISTORY.

1. Solomonic books of healing and magic among the Jews. —

a) The literary starting point for all the later legends regarding Solomon's wisdom is to be found in III Reg III. Here, as
Benzinger points out, it is the judicial wisdom of the ruler that
is in the writer's mind[1]. In c. V 9—14, on the other hand, it
is "religiose Lebensweisheit"[2] Furthermore, Benzinger believes
that in comparing Solomon's wisdom with that of the children
of the East and the wisdom of the Egyptians the writer intended
to imply that Solomon knew magic and astrology, for these
ancients were famous for such knowledge, as the records of the
Exodus, for example, testify. How far back may we place this
earliest reference to Solomon's magical knowledge? The verses
in question can hardly belong to the earlier sources of the Books
of Kings as Kautzsch seems to imply[3], but rather to the final
redaction of the book[4]. The least that one can say is that it
must date before the Septuagint translation. More than two
centuries, therefore, before Christ, in the leading circles of
Palestinian Judaism, Solomon is already a magician. The interpolator of the passage may not have thought of him as the
author of magical books, but surely many readers would understand from the allusion to the wisdom of the ancients and Egypt
that ᾠδαί meant, not psalms, but *carmina*, incantations, and that
the discourses ὑπὲρ τῶν ξύλων must include their medical, or
what amounted to the same thing, their magical uses[5].

---

1 *Könige*, p 23 f., on I Kg V 9—14

2 I Kg V 9—14 (Heb), IV 29—34 (Eng).

3 According to markings adopted in *Heil. Schr. des AT*.

4 So Benzinger, *loc cit* Stade and Schwally in Haupt's polychrome Hebrew
Bible color it as a "non-Deuteronomic addition of unknown origin" Cf. Steuernagel, *Einl. AT* 356, and *ZATW* 1910 70, whose suggestions require a very
late date.

5 Cf Salzberger, *Salomosage*, 5 ff., for an analysis of the biblical passage.

b) The next reference to Solomon's magical powers, in Wisdom VII 17—22, makes no allusion to writings; indeed the context does not call for it. But it does plainly involve the ascription to the supposed writer of knowledge of astrology, of the nature of beasts and spirits, as well as of men, of the ἐνέρ- γεια στοιχείων, the διαφοραὶ φυτῶν, and the δυνάμεις ῥιζῶν, of "all things that are either secret or manifest"[1]. The Wisdom of Solomon, then, is a witness to the acceptance of the legend of Solomon's astrological, demonological, and magical accomplish- ments in Alexandrian Judaism in the first century B. C, and, let it be noted, by a thoroughly educated and highly cultured Jew of the Dispersion

c) A still further allusion to Solomon's authority over de- mons is found in Pseudo-Philo, *de antiquitatibus biblicis*, in *Ci- tharismus regis David contra daemonium Saulis*, which we have already quoted. The lines which concern us here should run, according to Dr. James, as follows: Arguet autem te metra nova unde natus sum de quo nascetur post tempus de lateribus meis qui vos domabit. Dr. James says, "In this last sentence it seems at first sight as though we had a prophecy of Messiah, and a possible Christian touch. But a little consideration will show, I think, that the 'vanquisher of demons' who is to spring from David is not Messiah, but Solomon the king of Genies, the wi- zard whose spells produced such marked effects in the time of Josephus, the hero, too, of the *Testament of Solomon*, where he figures almost solely as the restrainer and chastiser of mischie- vous spirits"[2].

d) The next mention of Solomon's power as a magician is the decisive one, without which one might doubt the interpre- tations adopted above. There can be no doubt as to Josephus' meaning on the whole when he relates the following: ⟨44⟩ συνε- τάξατο δὲ καὶ βιβλία [περὶ] ῴδῶν καὶ μελῶν πέντε πρὸς τοῖς χιλίοις, καὶ παραβολῶν καὶ εἰκόνων βίβλους τρισχιλίας· καθ᾽

---

1 Following the translations by Siegfried in Kautzsch, *APAT* I 490, and Holmes in Charles, *APOT* I 546.

2 *TS* II 3 (1893) *Apoc. Anec.* 183ff., cf. *supra* VII 6 b), and p. 60 n 2.

ἕκαστον γὰρ εἶδος δένδρου παραβολὴν εἶπεν, ἀφ᾽ ὑσσώπου ἕως
κέδρου. τὸν αὐτὸν δὲ τρόπον καὶ περὶ κτηνῶν καὶ τῶν τ᾽ ἐπιγείων ἁπάντων ζῴων καὶ τῶν νηκτῶν καὶ τῶν ἀερίων· οὐδεμίαν
γὰρ τούτων φύσιν ἠγνόησεν οὐδὲ παρῆλθεν ἀνεξέταστον, ἀλλ᾽
ἐν πάσαις ἐφιλοσόφησε καὶ τὴν ἐπιστήμην τῶν ἐν αὐταῖς ἰδιω-
μάτων ἄκραν ἐπεδείξατο. ⟨45⟩ παρέσχε δ᾽ αὐτῷ μαθεῖν ὁ θεὸς
καὶ τὴν κατὰ τῶν δαιμόνων τέχνην εἰς ὠφέλειαν καὶ θεραπείαν
τοῖς ἀνθρώποις. ἐπῳδάς τε συνταξάμενος αἷς παρηγορεῖται τὰ
νοσήματα, τρόπους ἐξορκώσεων κατέλιπεν, οἷς ἐνδούμενα τὰ δαιμόνια ὡς μηκέτ᾽ ἐπανελθεῖν ἐκδιώκουσι. ⟨46⟩ καὶ αὕτη μέχρι
νῦν παρ᾽ ἡμῖν ἡ θεραπεία πλεῖστον ἰσχύει· ἱστόρησα γάρ τινα
Ἐλεάζαρον τῶν ὁμοφύλων, Οὐεσπασιανοῦ παρόντος καὶ τῶν
υἱῶν αὐτοῦ καὶ χιλιάρχων καὶ ἄλλου στρατιωτικοῦ πλήθους,
τοὺς ὑπὸ τῶν δαιμονίων λαμβανομένους ἀπολύοντα τούτων.
ὁ δὲ τῆς θεραπείας τρόπος τοιοῦτος ἦν. ⟨47⟩ προσφέρων ταῖς
ῥισὶ τοῦ δαιμονιζομένου τὸν δακτύλιον, ἔχοντα ὑπὸ τῇ σφραγῖδι
ῥίζαν ἐξ ὧν ὑπέδειξε Σολομών, ἔπειτ᾽ ἐξεῖλκεν ὀσφρομένῳ διὰ
τῶν μυκτήρων τὸ δαιμόνιον, καὶ πέσοντος εὐθὺς τἀνθρώπου
μηκέτ᾽ εἰς αὐτὸν ἐπανήξειν ὥρκου, Σολομῶνός τε μεμνημένος
καὶ τὰς ἐπῳδάς, ἃς συνέθηκεν ἐκεῖνος, ἐπιλέγων .... ⟨49⟩ γινο-
μένου δὲ τούτου σαφὴς ἡ Σολομῶνος καθίστατο σύνεσις καὶ
σοφία .. [1]

We have quoted the passage at length, because we believe
that, having it before the eye and remembering the previous
Jewish allusions to Solomonic incantations, one cannot but accept
Albrecht Dieterich's conclusion that Josephus means to imply
that books were in circulation under Solomon's name which
gave the magical, or medicinal, virtues of plants after the plan
of the works later written by Pamphilus and called εἰκόνες κατὰ
στοιχεῖον [2]. And surely the ἐπῳδαί had long ago been written
down.

 e) The Mishna says that Hezekiah hid the "book of recipes"[3],

1 *Ant* VIII 44—49 (Naber) = VIII 2 5.
2 *Abraxas* 142 f, *Leid. Pap* 780 ff
3 In the Gemara, *Berakoth* 10 a (Goldziher I 35), *Pesachim* 56 a (*ibid* II 520).
גנז ספר רפואות. רפואה means *Heilung*, in the plural *Arzeneien, Heilmittel*, Levy-
Fleischer, s v, cf. Jer XXX 13. See also A. Wünsch, *ZDMG* LXVI (1912) 414

which, according to Maimonides and Rashi meant a book which Solomon had written, Maimonides holding that it was a book of magic [1], Rashi that the evil consisted in its leading men not to pray to God for their healing [2] Otherwise rabbinic literature does not refer to such Solomonic works, evidently this sort of tradition was avoided in official Judaism.

f) After Talmudic times I know of no reference to such books until we reach the Jews of the Middle Ages. In fact Moses takes the place of Solomon in Jewish literature and becomes the representative wise man, as Solomon does for the Christians [3] Steinschneider gives citations from writers of the twelfth and following centuries who look upon Solomon as the source of all wisdom, including medicine, magic, and astrology [4]. In particular, Sheintob ben Isaac of Tortosa (1260) in his paraphrase of Zahravi's *Tasrif*, called ספר השמות (XI cent.) [5], gives "eine Schilderung der Weisheit Salomo's (namentlich in der Naturkunde), unter dessen Namen in Zahrawi ein Verband (רטיה) erwähnt werde, der auf weißer Marmortafel an der Wand seines Palastes eingegraben war, wie verschiedene Rezepte (נוסהאות ופורקחות)), die von den Spateren (האחרונים) erläutert worden; Scheintob hat 'hier in Marseille' den Christen mehr davon erläutert, als er in Zahrawi fand" [6]. We have here possible the contract with the demons [7], and certainly the magical recipes said to have been written on the temple gates [8] Steinschneider

---

1 Surenhusius, *Mishna* II 149, *de Paschati* IV 9. Maimonides says, "Haec Mishna est ex Tosaphta, quam exponam propter utilitatem illius; ספר רפואות *liber medicinae*, erat liber qui tractabat de medicis quibus se sanare non permittebat Lex, uti sunt ejusmodi res quae proponebantur per figuras, erant enim Astrologiae periti nonnulli quorum dicto homines faciebant suo tempore imagines ac figuras quasdam, qui aliquibus damnnm (sic) vel utilitatem adferebant, haec autem figura in lingua Graeca vocabatur τέλεσμα ... Prolixius esse volui in hisce, eo quod mibi exposuerant, quod Shelomo composuisset librum medicinae

2 Grunbaum, *ZDMG* XXXI 200

3 Kohler in *JE* IV 518, cf. Gaster, *Sword of Moses*.

4 *Hebr. Ubers.* 936, ns. 225 and 226; 849 f.

5 *Ibid.* 740 ff. Zahravi is called Açararius, Azaravi, etc

6 *Ibid.* 743   Is Scheintob borrowing from the Christian tradition, or vice versa? See below VIII 3 b) (2).

7 Cf *infra* VIII 3 d) 2) (d).   8 Cf. *infra* VIII 3 c) 2)

is only partly right in trying to relieve his compatriots of the
responsibility for the ascription of such works to Solomon[1]. The
Christians, however, developed the tradition far more than did
the Jews from whom they received it.

2 Solomonic books among the Arabs. — A single reference
in the Quran and the comments thereon show that among the
Jews of Mohammed's time magical books of Solomon were
known. Sura II 95ff. reads: "And when there came unto them
a prophet from God confirming that *scripture* which was with
them, some of those to whom the scriptures were given cast
the book of God behind their backs as if they knew it not. and
they follow *the device* which the devils devised against the kingdom of Solomon, and Solomon was not an unbeliever, but the
devils believed not, they taught men sorcery." The context
supports Sale's interpretation drawn from Yahya and Jallalo'ddin,
that this device against the kingdom of Solomon consisted in
the devils' attempt to blacken the character of Solomon by
writing books of sorcery, hiding them under his throne, and
after his death pretending he had had in them the recipes by
which he obtained his power[2].

3. Among Christians —

a) The power of Salomonic exorcisms. — One line of Christian tradition goes back to Josephus and follows him more or
less closely, recounting merely the power of the exorcisms he
had composed. Origen, who writes "a Salomone scriptis adjura-
tionibus solent daemones adjurari. Sed ipsi qui utuntur adjura-
tionibus illis, aliquoties nec idoneis constitutis libris utuntur:
quibusdam autem et de Hebraeo acceptis adjurant daemonia,"
may be merely paraphrasing Josephus, or he may have had
personal knowledge of Solomonic works[3]. The first I have discovered to quote Josephus expressly is Georgius Monachus

---

1 *Op. cit.* 936. An interesting reference to Jewish magic, Burton, *Nights*
II 234.

2 Cf. Sale *ad loc* Palmer's note, *SBE* VI (Qu II) 14, does not so well
explain the passage, which is concerned solely with books.

3 *In Mattheum comm ser.* (tract. 33) 110, Migne *PG* 13, 1757, in discussion
of Mt XXVI 63.

(c 850)[1], who is followed by Cedrenus (c. 1100)[2], Zonaras (c. 1150)[3], and Glycas (after 1150)[4].

b) Solomon the ultimate source of medical wisdom. — Other Christian writers start from the Old Testament notices of Solomon's wisdom, developing the tradition in various directions. In the first place, according to Theodoret (386/393—458), he was wiser than the most famous wise men to whom the Hellenistic world looked back. In his *Quaestiones in III Reg*, Qu. X he asks, Πῶς νοητέον τὸ "Ἐπλήθυνεν (cod. α, ἐπληθύνθη) ἡ σοφία Σολομῶντος ὑπὲρ τὴν φρόνησιν πάντων τῶν υἱῶν ἀρχαίων, καὶ ὑπὲρ πάντας φρονίμους Αἰγύπτου," He answers, Ἐκ παραλλήλου δεῖξαι αὐτοῦ τὴν σοφίαν ὁ ἱστοριογράφος ἠθέλησεν. Τούτου χάριν καὶ τῶν πάλαι γεγενημένων σοφῶν ἀορίστως ἐμνήσθη ... Τούτους, φησίν, ἅπαντας ὁ Σολομῶν ἀπέκρυψεν, ἅτε δὴ θεόθεν τῆς σοφίας τὸ δῶρον δεξάμενος[5]. Procopius of Gaza, without acknowledging his debt, quotes Theodoret almost word for word[6]. Georgius Monachus[7] and after him Georgius Cedrenus[8] give a slightly different version of Theodoret, adding also a part of Theodoret's *Quaest. XVIII.*

In the second place Theodoret represents the wise king as the source from which the ancients derived their knowledge of medicine He asks, Πῶς νοητέον τὸ "Ἐλάλησε περὶ τῶν ξύλων ....", and answers, Καὶ τὰς φύσεις, καὶ τὰς δυνάμεις, καὶ τῶν βοτανῶν, καὶ τῶν δένδρων, καὶ μέντοι καὶ τῶν ἀλόγων ζῴων πεφυσιολογηκέναι αὐτὸν εἴρηκεν ἐντεῦθεν οἶμαι καὶ τὰς ἰατρικὰς βίβλους συγγεγραφότας ἐρανίσασθαι πάμπολλα .... καὶ τοῦδε τοῦ ζῴου τόδε τὸ μόριον τίνος πάθους ἀλεξιφάρμακον· οἷον ἡ τῆς ὑαίνης χολή, ἢ τὸ λεόντειον στέαρ, ἢ τὸ ταύ-

---

1 Or Hamartolos, *Chron* II 42 4, Migne *PG* 110 249 C, cf Krumbacher, *BLg* 352—8.

2 Migne, *PG* 121 156 Bf. and 196 CD, cf Krumbacher, *BLg* 368 f., Gelzer, *Sext Jul Afr* II 1 357—84

3 *Ann.* II 8, Migne, *PG* 134 168 B, cf Roger Bacon, *Opera inedita*, ed Brewer London 1859, vol I, App. p. 526.

4 Migne *PG* 158 349 C, cf. Krumbacher, *BLg* 380—5

5 Migne, *PG* 80 676 AB

6 *Com ad III Reg.* II 45, Migne, *PG* 87 1 1152.

7 *Chron.* II 42 1 f, Migne, *PG* 110 249 A.   8 Migne, *PG* 121 197 Df.

ρειον αἷμα, ἢ τῶν ἐχνιδῶν αἱ σάρκες. Περὶ τούτων γὰρ οἱ σο-
φοὶ τῶν ἰατρῶν συγγεγράφασιν, ἐκ τῶν Σολομῶντι συγγεγραμ-
μένων εἰληφότες τῶν πρώτων τὰς ἀφορμάς[1]. Procopius of
Gaza quotes Theodoret as far as πάμπολλα[2]. Anastasius Sinaites repeats both question and answer almost word for word[3].
So far as I have discovered, no others use the first part of the
reply ending with πάμπολλα, but Georgius Monachus, Cedrenus,
and Glycas weave into their account of Hezekiah's suppression
of Solomon's books the sentence, ἀφ' ὧν οἱ τῶν Ἑλλήνων
ἰατροσοφισταὶ σφετερισάμενοι καὶ τὰς ἀφορμὰς εἰληφότες τὰς
οἰκείας συνεστήσαντο τέχνας, or its equivalent[4].

c) Hezekiah's suppression of Solomon's books.

1) Origin of the legend. — The question naturally arose as
to what had become of all the proverbs, odes, and scientific
writings of Solomon. So far as the sources show, this question
was first raised and answered by Hippolytus in his commentary on Canticles, portions of which are preserved in Armenian,
Syriac, Slavic[5], and Georgian[6]. The last mentioned version
contains a discussion, the essence of which has been handed
down also in a quotation or summary found in the *Quaestiones*
of Anastasius Sinaites.

In *Quaest* XLI Anastasius collects several ancient references
to Solomon's books and wisdom. Beginning with an unacknow-
ledged quotation from Theodoret[7], he reproduces Sap VII
16—21 and III Reg IV 26—29, and then adds the following:

---

1 *In III Reg. Quaest.* XVIII, Migne, *PG* 80 681 AB   Does Jerome have
this tradition in mind? Cf. *Quaest. Hebr in libr III Reg.* (Migne, *PL* 23 1365 C)·
Disputavit enim de naturis lignorum, jumentorum, reptilium, et piscium, de vi
videlicet et naturis illorum . . . .

2 *Com ad III Reg* IV 33; Migne, *PG* 87 · 1 1153

3 *Quaest.* XLI; cf. *infra* p 97 n 1. It is the first part of the ἀπόκρισις and
immediately follows a quotation from Θεοδωρήτου ἐπισκόπου Κύρου, which
stands at the end of *Quaest.* 40.

4 *Chron* II 42 4 (Migne *PG* 110, 249 B) for G. Monachus, Migne, *PG* 121
200 B, 224 C for Cedrenus, Glycas (*ibid.* 158 348 D) has, τὰς τοῦ Σ. βίβλους,
ἀφ' ὧν καὶ οἱ τῶν ἰατρῶν παῖδες ἀφορμὰς ἔλαβον.

5 Bonwetsch, *KVCom* I 343—74.

6 Bonwetsch, *Hippolyts Kom. z. Hohelied* in *TU* NF VIII (23) H 2, 22 t.

7 Cf. *supra* n. 3

Ἱππολύτου ἐκ τοῦ εἰς τὸ ᾆσμα ᾀσμάτων. Καὶ ποῦ πᾶσα ἡ
πλουσία αὕτη γνῶσις, ποῦ δὲ τὰ μυστήρια ταῦτα, καὶ ποῦ αἱ
βίβλοι; ἀναφέρονται γὰρ μόναι αἱ παροιμίαι καὶ ἡ σοφία καὶ ὁ
ἐκκλησιαστὴς καὶ τὸ ᾆσμα τῶν ᾀσμάτων. τί οὖν; ψεύδεται ἡ
γραφή, μὴ γένοιτο. ἀλλὰ πολλὴ μέν τις ὕλη γεγένηται τῶν
γραμμάτων, ὡς δηλοῖ τὸ λέγειν ᾆσμα ᾀσμάτων· σημαίνει γὰρ
ὅτι ὅσα περιεῖχον αἱ πεντακισχίλιαι ᾠδαὶ ἐν τῷ ἑνὶ διηγήσατο.
ἐν δὲ ταῖς ἡμέραις Ἐζεκίου τὰ μὲν τῶν βιβλίων ἐξελέγησαν, τὰ
δὲ καὶ περιώφθησαν . . .[1] Perhaps Jerome has this in mind
when he says, Aiunt Hebraei cum inter cetera scripta Salomonis
quae antiquata sunt, nec in memoria duraverunt, et hic liber
[Eccl] obliterandus videretur ... ex hoc uno capitulo [XII]
meruisse auctoritatem[2].

That general encyclopedia, the *Hypomnesticon*, written by
the otherwise unknown Josephus Christianus, mentions πεντακι-
σχιλίας παροιμίας written by Solomon among the books referred
to in the Scriptures but not now found[3]. Michael Glycas gives
a badly garbled account of it all, making Hezekiah's revision
fall after the Exile and Ezra's labors, and naming ὁ σοφώτατος
Ψέλλος as his authority, evidently by mistake[4]

2) The writings on the temple gate. — In view of Hezekiah's iconoclastic zeal as to the brazen serpent, it was inevitable
that some one should suggest that he had also suppressed the
magical writings of Solomon. Two Christian writers present an
independent tradition, somewhat like that of Sheintob already
mentioned[5]. Georgius Syncellus (c. 800) in his ἐκλογὴ χρονο-

1 *KVCom* I 343, Migne, *PG* 89 589, cf *supra* p 96 n 6 Anastasius' floruit
is placed by Krumbacher (*BLg* 64 ff.) between 640 and 700 The *Quaestiones* in
their present form are not original, but that does not affect our material, for it
is all quoted 2 *Com in Eccl* XII 13 f

3 Cap. 120, *PG* 106 124 A. The date of the *Hypomnesticon* is still un-
settled. Schurer, *GJV* III 420, refers to Gutschmidt, *Kleine Schriften* V 618, who
places it in the tenth century, and the "more accurate researches" of Diekamp,
Hippolytus von Theben (1898) 145—151, who decides for 800 at the latest, possibly a much earlier date. To the writer it appears that aside from certain
evident interpolations it may belong to the fifth century.

4 *PG* 158 349 A, cf. 122, 537, 540 for Psellus' opinion

5 Cf. *supra* p. 93. The story in Ez VIII 7—11 does not appear to have
played any part in these speculations

γραφίας, when speaking of Solomon's reign, merely describes most concisely his wisdom and fall; when he comes to Hezekiah, after expanding IV Reg XVIII 4, he adds, Ἐζεκίας μὲν οὖν ὁ βασιλεὺς Ἰούδα μετὰ τὸ κατασκάψαι τὰ εἰδωλεῖα καὶ τὰ ἄλση ἐκκόψαι καὶ τὸν χαλκοῦν ὄφιν ἐξαλεῖψαι τοὺς εὑρισκομένους εἰδωλολατροῦντας ἐξ Ἰουδαίων ἐθανάτου. τοσοῦτον γὰρ τῇ εἰδωλολατρείᾳ συνείχοντο ὥστε τῶν θυρωμάτων ὄπισθεν ζωγραφεῖν τὰ βδελύγματα τῶν ἐθνῶν καὶ προσκυνεῖν αὐτοῖς, καὶ ἵνα παρ᾽ Ἐζεκίου ψηλαφᾶν πεμπομένων κρύβοιντο ἀνοιγομένων τῶν θυρῶν. ἦν δὲ καὶ Σολομῶντος γραφή τις ἐγκεκολαμμένη τῇ πύλῃ τοῦ ναοῦ παντὸς νοσήματος ἄκος περιέχουσα, ᾗ προσέχων ὁ λαὸς καὶ τὰς θεραπείας νομιζόμενος ἔχειν κατεφρόνει τοῦ θεοῦ· διὸ καὶ ταύτην Ἐζεκίας ἐξεκόλαψεν ἵνα πάσχοντες τῷ θεῷ προσέχωσιν [1] Suidas abbreviates the account and puts βίβλος ἰαμάτων for γραφή [2].

3) Solomon's magical books suppressed ' — Turning to Anastasius Sinaites again we make the interesting discovery that he ascribes the account of the reforming activity of Hezekiah to Eusebius. The final section in *Quaest.* XII runs as follows. Εὐσεβίου Παμφίλου ἐκ τῆς ἀρχαιολογικῆς ἱστορίας. Τὰς δὲ βίβλους τοῦ Σολομῶντος, τὰς περὶ τῶν παραβολῶν καὶ ᾠδῶν, ἐν αἷς περὶ φυτῶν καὶ παντοίων ζώων φυσιολογήσας, χερσαίων, πετεινῶν τε καὶ νηττῶν, καὶ ἰαμάτων πάθους παντός, γραφείσας αὐτῷ, ἀφανεῖς ἐποίησεν Ἐζεκίας, διὰ τὸ τὰς θεραπείας τῶν νοσημάτων ἔνθεν κομίζεσθαι τὸν λαόν, καὶ περιορᾶν αἰτεῖν, καὶ παρορᾶν ἐντεῦθεν παρὰ θεῷ τὰς ἰάσεις [3].

The *Hypomnesticon* of Josephus, which in chapter 120, as we have seen, tells of Hezekiah's revision of Solomon's proverbs, says in c. 74, εἰσὶ δὲ καὶ ἕτεροι πλεῖστοι λόγοι, οὓς ἀπέκρυψεν ὁ εὐσεβὴς βασιλεὺς Ἐζεκίας, οὐδὲν ὄφελος ἐπὶ πολλοῖς εὑρίσκεσθαι λόγοις [4].

The account given by Georgius Monachus of Solomon's wisdom combines part of the Eusebian quotation with express

---

1 B 376 f, P 200, V 160 See Gelzer, *Sext Jul. Afr.* II 176—249, Krumbacher, *BLg* 339 ff.   2 *Lex.* s. v. Ἐζεκίας   8 *PG* 89 592 Df ; cf. *supra* p. 96 f
4 *PG* 106 89 C. C. 74, which is in a part of the work that recounts the deeds of Old Testament characters, is itself a record of the reign of Solomon.

indication of its origin, with extracts from Theodoret and Flavius Josephus, as we have seen[1]. Georgius Cedrenus practically repeats Monachus, but with the addition of a clause βιβλίον Σολομῶντος ἰαματήριον παντὸς πάθους ἐγκεκολαμμένον, apparently borrowed from Syncellus or Suidas; he mentions no authority[2]. Glycas presents on the whole an independent account of Solomon's wisdom and literary activities, but like Anastasius, he appeals to the authority of Eusebius; he says, τὰς τοῦ Σολομῶντος βίβλους, ἀφ᾽ ὧν καὶ οἱ τῶν ἰατρῶν παῖδες τὰς ἀφορμὰς ἔλαβον .... παρὰ δὲ Ἐζεκίου κεκαῦσθαί φησιν ὁ πολυμαθὴς καὶ πολυΐστωρ Εὐσέβιος[3].

Is this appeal to the authority of Eusebius deceptive? We may not be sure of the date of the *Quaestiones* of Anastasius in their present form, but, whoever the writer of *Quaest.* XII is, he quotes accurately from Theodoret, and from a lost work of Hippolytus. Is not the presumption in favor of accepting his testimony regarding Eusebius, and supposing that he is quoting from some lost work of the great historian[4]? That Eusebius should make such a statement cannot seem at all strange in view of the reference by Origen to "a Salomone scriptis adjurantionibus"[5]

4) One further reference to the tradition that Hezekiah took summary measures with Solomon's medico-magical writings is of particular interest to us, since it is found in Rec. C of the *Test* (c. XIII 1—12) and, indeed, forms its *raison d'être*. If this

I discover no marks to indicate its date, the quotation above is more closely related to Glycas than Georgius Monachus, yet the similarity may be due merely to likeness of literary method.

1 *Chron.* II 42 4), *PG* 110 249 B, sec 273 B, cf. *supra* p. 96.
2 *PG* 121 200 B, 224 C Both Monachus and Cedrenus mention the suppression of the books in their accounts of Solomon and again under Hezekiah.
3 *PG* 158 348 Df.
4 Although no "archaeological history" by Eusebius is known to historians of Christian literature, Bonwetsch, in his chapter on "Die vornicanische Litt. in altslav HSS." in Harnack, *Altchr. Lit.* I 900, mentions a Russian MS in the Synodal library at Moscow (cod. 339 [1001] 4⁰ s, 17, f. 310) which has "Eusebeios(?) Pamphilos, aus der Archaeologie(?)," and strangely enough it begins, "Das Buch aber des Salomo, welches von den Sprichwortern handelt." It at least has some mention of Solomon. 5 See above, VIII 3a), p. 94

legend was already found in Eusebius, as it was in the Mishna,
there were plenty of channels through which redacteur C might
have obtained it. Yet the mention of „burning" *and* "hiding"
(c. XIII 4, 8f) suggests that Rec. C comes from the time of
Cedrenus and Glycas, for the earlier writers do not use the word
κατακαύειν.

d) Solomonic books of incantations in the Middle Ages. —

1) Solomonic books of magic and astrology found in mediaeval manuscripts — In spite of these records of the sad fate
of Solomon's medico-magical literary efforts, such books continued to flourish The long lists given by M Seligsohn in his
article, "Solomon-Apocryphal Works", in the *Jewish Encyclopedia* is by no means exhaustive. Indeed Solomon's reputation
became such that any thing connected with magic or astrology
or science might be ascribed to him[1]. The most popular of
the works which are consistently handed down under his name
is the *Clavicula*, or Ὑγρομαντεία, as some of the Greek copies
have it The two are not exactly the same, but along with the
Sepher Raziel[2], the *Semiphoras*[3], and others of the sort, are of a
well marked type. They consist mainly of prayers and incantations intended to accomplish various purposes, usually by
commanding demonic aid. The prayers are usually interlarded
with barbaric names, and there are many pentacles, or magical
drawings, each of which gives power over the demon to which
it belongs, or serves as an amulet for some specific purpose
Lists of the angels and demons who rule the days and hours
are given

None of these works is like the *Test*. It is much older in
language than any of the Greek works of this sort, and differs
from them all as to purpose, for, aside from Rec C, which has

---

1 See above II 4, 8, 10, 11, pp. 13 and p n. 1. 18f., 21ff, 25ff. Professor
von Dobschutz in a personal note first called my attention to the fact that in
the Ambrosiana the *Physiologus* of Aristotle is ascribed to Solomon, *Cat Codd,
Gr. Bibl Ambr.* I 104, cod 89, 183. In Lambros, *Cat. of the MSS on Mt. Athos*
are illustrations of this, see Pinax A; s. v. Σολομωνική On the *Clavicula* cf.
Reitzenstein, *Poim.* 186f., and Steinschneider, *Heb Üb.* 938.

2 See Steinschneider, *op. cit.* 937   3 Scheibel, *Das Kloster* III, 289 ff.

drawn upon them in part, the *Test* is interested in the demons
primarily as the causes of disease. The writer wishes to disclose
their nature, relationships, and activities for the same reason that
a doctor studies diseases, that he may counteract them. These
other books are technical works for the professional astrologer
and magician, not concerned with the cure of diseases, in fact
rarely showing any medical interest, but anxious rather to show
how the demons may be used to gain wealth, power, and happiness. The list of fifty demons in Rec. C (c. X) is characteristic of this type of literature. With it compare the list of
thirty-six *decani* in Recs. A and B (XVIII) to gain a sharp def-
inition of the contrast. When, therefore, the Christian writers
refer to a Solomonic "book of healing" they are not thinking
of the *Clavicula*, nor of any of the similar works. The *Test* is
the one Solomonic work which fits the term. Having thus
cleared the way, we are ready to consider the evidence that
goes to show that such a book was actually in use during the
Middle Ages.

2) Literary references to contemporaneous Solomonic medical works.

(a) The citations above which mention medico-magical books
of Solomon might be supposed not to imply first hand knowledge of any such works. There are others, however, which
show that they were well known. Following the brief quotation
given above[1] the *Hypomnesticon* continues, τοὺς δὲ δαιμόνων
ἐκφευκτικούς, καὶ παθῶν ἰατρικούς, καὶ κλεπτῶν φωρατικοὺς
[λόγους] οἱ τῶν Ἰουδαίων ἀγύρται παρ᾽ ἑαυτοῖς φυλάσσουσιν
ἐπιμελέστατα, τῶν πιστῶν τῆς ἁγίας ἐκκλησίας τούτοις οὐ κεχρε-
μένων διὰ τὸ τῇ Χριστοῦ πίστει καθοσιοῦν ἑαυτοὺς δεδιδάχθαι.
The man who wrote this is not depending upon what he has
read, but describes what he knows of personal observation.
There is no reason why such a sentence could not have been
written in the fifth century.

(b) The next allusion is equally direct and unambiguous.
Nicetas Acominatus, or Choniates, who was a high official at

1 See above VIII 3c) 3), p. 98.

the Byzantine court about 1200 and wrote his *History* from
personal recollections[1], knew an interpreter and sycophant at
the court, Aaron by name, who was also a magician. He relates
of him, ἑάλω δὲ καὶ βίβλον Σολομώντειον ἀνελίττων ἥτις ἀνα-
πτυσσομένη τε καὶ διερχομένη κατὰ λεγεῶνας συλλέγει καὶ παρί-
στησι τὰ δαιμόνια συχνάκις ἀναπυνθανόμενα, ἐφ᾽ ὅτῳ προσκέ-
κληνται· καὶ τὸ ἐπιταττόμενον ἐπισπεύδοντα περατοῦν, καὶ
προθύμως δρῶντο τὸ κελευόμενον[2] This describes accurately
parts of the Ὑγρομαντεία and the Latin *Clavicula*, as well as
the new material in Rec. C. The list of fifty demons (c X) is
intended to accomplish just the end of calling in certain demons
and the hosts they command, while Paltiel Tzamal uses almost
the language of Nicetas in describing the obedience Solomon
may expect[3]. It is no doubt a book of this sort, not the *Test*,
which Aaron used, for no mention is made of healing

   (c) Michael Glycas, in the passage already referred to[4], has
a description of Solomon's magical books which we have reserved for separate discussion, because in it he takes a path of
his own. His statement is as follows: ἐφυσιολόγησε δὲ Σολομῶν
καὶ περὶ λίθων .... ἀλλὰ καὶ περὶ δαιμόνων ἐτέθη βιβλίον
αὐτοῦ, ὅπως τε κατάγονται, καὶ ἐν οἷοις εἴδεσι φαίνονται, φύσεις
δὲ τούτων καὶ ἰδιότητας ἔγραψε, πῶς τε δεσμοῦνται καὶ πῶς
ἐμφιλοχωροῦντες ἀπολύονται. ὅθεν ἔργα τούτοις ἀχθοφόρα ἐπέ-
ταττεν, ὑλοτομεῖν τε, ὡς λόγος, ἠνάγκαζε, καὶ κατωμαδὸν τὰ
ἄχθη φέρειν παρεβιάζετο, ᾠδηκότα τε σπλάγχνα ἢ ἐπῳδαῖς ἢ
βοτάναις περιτιθεὶς ἐθεράπευσεν. ἀλλ᾽ ὅ γε θεῖος Ἐζεκίας θεῷ
ἑαυτὸν ἀνατιθεὶς καὶ πάντα τῆς ἐκεῖθεν προνοίας ἐξαρτήσας
τῶν ὑπὲρ φύσιν τῷ Σολομῶντι φιλοσοφηθέντων ὠλιγώρησεν.
This βιβλίον περὶ δαιμόνων is the *Test* in everything but name.
The latter is throughout concerned with bringing down demons;
their forms, natures, and peculiarities are most carefully described.
One of the chief purposes of the work is to tell how they are
discovered in their lurking places and bound or destroyed.
A special feature is the labor to which each demon is con-

---

1 Krumbacher, *BLg* 281—6.   2 Migne, *PG* 139 489 A (= P 95)
3 Rec. C XII 4 f.   4 Cf. *supra* p. 95 and p. 96 n. 4, Migne, *PG* 158 349 B.

demned, one of the most striking instances being that of Leontophoron, who is sentenced to the task of cutting wood for the
Temple[1]. Cures by the means Glycas mentions are to be found[2].
One cannot avoid the conclusion that it is the *Test* which is
here described, either from Glycas' own knowledge, or after
some popular account[3]. That he does not name the title need
not trouble us[4].

(d) The next allusion is dubious. In the *Decretum Gelasia-
num* mention is made of a *Salomonis interdictio*, or as the later
texts have it *contradictio*[5]. In the *Decretum* in the next line as
a separate item and in the *Collectio Herovalliana* in the same
and the following lines mention is made of *phylacteria*, which
contain the names, not of angels, but of demons. In pseudo-
Isidor, *de Muneris*, a line intervenes between the *contradictio*
and *phylacteria*. Probably, therefore, the two are distinct works,
and the second is no doubt the *Clavicula*, which is characterized
by seals and amulets. We must at least postulate the possibility
that the *interdictio* is the *Test*, since in this sort of literature
there is a tendency to assimilate titles[6]. It is entirely possible,
however, that the *Test* never became sufficiently known in the
West to call for a pronouncement against it.

(e) The most important notice we have reserved to the last.
In the *Dialogue of Timothy and Aquila* the Christian says,
Γνῶθι δὲ Ἰουδαῖε, ὅτι [Σολομῶν] προσεκύνησεν, καὶ ἀκρίδα
ἔσφαξεν τοῖς γλυπτοῖς. The Jew replies, οὐκ ἔσφαξεν ἀλλὰ
ἔθλασεν ἐν τῇ χειρὶ ἀκουσίως ταῦτα δὲ οὐ περιέχει ἡ βίβλος
τῶν βασιλέων, ἀλλ' ἐν τῇ διαθήκῃ αὐτοῦ γέγραπται. The Christian accepts the correction ἐν τούτῳ γὰρ ἔστην πιστοποιῶν,
ὅτι οὐκ ἐν χειρὶ ἱστοριογράφου ἐφανερώθη τοῦτο, ἀλλ' ἐκ τοῦ

---

1 C. XI 7   2 C XVIII 29, 15, etc

8 Glycas names Psellus as authority for the "contemning" of the books of
Solomon, probably he means Eusebius, cf. *supra* p. 97 and n. 4   In this
account Glycas is true to the character Krumbacher (*BLg* 380—5) gives him as
being a popular, rather than a learned, writer.   4 See below (e).

5 Cf. E. von Dobschütz, "Das Decretum Gel. etc.." TU (1912) 13, ll. 332—5,
84, ll. 112 f., 74, ll 242—5, cf. p. 319.

6 See James in *TS* II 2 p 9 on the convertibility of the titles "testament"
and "apocalypse"

στόματος αὐτοῦ τοῦ σολομῶντος ἐγνώθη τοῦτο[1]. This allusion is of value, not only for the sake of the help is gives us in dating the *Test*, as we shall see in the next section of our discussion, but also because the title appears here[2], and from the reference to the locusts we can be sure beyond a doubt that it is our *Test* to which reference is made; we also see that the *Test* was held in high honor in Christian circles.

(f) Summary. the Christian use of the *Testament*. — One might expect to find more allusions to the *Test* in early Christian literature and more evidence of its use. But it was one of those books which circulated among the people without attracting literary attention. Moreover, it represents a passing, though very important, phase of theological development. As the world became more and more Christianized, it could not but prove unsatisfactory to Christian thinking, even in the revised form of Rec. B, and it had no vital attraction which could overcome the fatal weakness of its inconsistent combination of paganism and Christianity. The allusions to it in *Timothy and Aquila*, in the *Hypomnesticon*, and in Glycas are all we could rightly expect in view of its character[3].

---

1 F. C. Conybeare, *Anecdota Oxon.* Classical sei. VIII 70

2 In connection with the title διαθήκη it should be noted that magical literature is perfectly familiar with a *covenant* which S. made with the demons, cf. Schlumberger in *Rev. des Ét. Gr.* V (1892) 87 διαθήκην ἣν ἔθεντο [δαίμονες] ἐπὶ μεγάλου Σολομῶνος καὶ Μιχαήλου τοῦ ἀρχαγγέλου, the same is quoted by Wessely, *Wiener Studien* VIII (1886) 179, see *Atti e Memorie della RR. Deputazioni di Storia per le provincie dell' Emilia*, N. S, vol. V, Part I, Modena 1880, p. 177, Pellichioni, "Un filaterio esorcistico", it was copied by Amati from a gold plate in a dealers shop, and is now lost. Vasiljev, *Anecdota*, 332, has a reference to their oath. Bezold, *ZA* XX 3—4 (Aug. 1907) pp. 405 f, gives "Eine arab. Zauberformel gegen Epilepsie," from the margin of ff. 24b—27a of cod. (113) Sachau 199 (Konigl. Bibl. Berlin) which mentions the contract between Solomon and the devils. Strangely Furst translated the title *Bund Salomos*, cf *supra* p. 28 f.

3 One gathers a wrong impression from Di. Conybeare's note (*JQR* XI 32, n. 6 to § 65) to c. XV 8—11. "This prophecy roughly corresponds to the one which Lactantius, *Instit. Div*, lib. iv. c. 18, quotes from an apocryphal *Book of Solomon*" Even more misleading is another statement (*ibid.* 11) "The apocryphal Book of Solomon, used by Lactantius in his *Institutions*, was so far Christian as to speak both of the birth from a virgin of Emmanuel and of the crucifixion" But the passage he evidently refers to (c 18 32 f, Vienna *Corpus* XIX 359 f.) is

IX. THE DATE OF THE *TESTAMENT* AND ITS RECENSIONS.

1. Previous opinions as to date. — Having studied our document on the linguistic and material sides and investigated its
sources and relationships, we are prepared to attempt to date it.
It will be an advantage first to summarize previous opinion on
this point.

a) Fleck regarded the *Test* as a Byzantine work belonging
to the Middle Ages, but advanced no arguments to substantiate
his conclusion[1]. Likewise Istrin, who discovered MS D and recognized it as the basis of the *Test*, regarded the latter as belonging to the Middle Ages (c. 1200), though containing pre-
Christian elements[2].

b) Bornemann concluded that it belonged to the early fourth
century, since its demonology resembled that of Lactantius in
his *Institutions*[3]. Toy accepts this verdict without investigation[4].
Harnack merely refers to the *Test* in this fashion: "Verschiedene
'Testamente', so das des Salomo, deren Alter nicht zu bestim-
men ist, und die vielleicht gar nicht in die ersten Jahrh. gehoren"[5].
Schurer makes no attempt to fix the date, but thinks the passage
from Leontius is especially to be considered in this connection[6].

c) After careful investigation Dr Conybeare concludes, "It
is impossible to say when and where the Christian elements
present in the *Testament* were worked into it, but the stress

---

only a loose epitome of III Reg IX 6—9a, with the addition of the phrase "et
persecuti sunt regem suum dilectissimum et cruciauerunt illum in humilitate
magna" (*ibid.* p. 360, II. 32 ff.). It may well come from some Christian apo-
cryphon (as Roensch supposed) which summarized O. T. history, or even from
a *Book of Solomon*, but it can hardly have any connection with the *Test. In
humilitate magna* does not necessarily imply the virgin birth, while *in ultionem
sanctae crucis* (*ibid.* p. 359, l. 10) presents an anti-Semitism to which our document has no parallel

1 "Est hoc monumentum *Byzantinum* . . . . Per mediam vero, quae dicitur,
aetatem hic liber late sparsus in mythologiae Salomoneae fonte est habitus."
Quoted from Fleck's preface in Migne, *PG* 122, 1315.

2 *Gr. Spiski Zab. Sol.*, 18 f.

3 In introduction to his translation, cf. Bibliography II 1

4 *JE* XI 448 f, art "Sol, Testament of" He evidently knows nothing of
Conybeare's work on the *Test.*   5 *Gesch. altchr. Litt.* I 858.

6 *GJV* III 419, cf. *supra* VII 8 c), p 76.

laid on the name Emmanuel and on its numerical value, on the writing of the name on the forehead, the use of the word ταυυ-σθείς, the patripassian conceptions, all have a very archaic air, and seem to belong to about 100 A. D." "In its original [Jewish] form" it may be "the very collection of incantations which, according to Josephus, was composed and bequeathed by Solomon"[1]. Kohler accepts Conybeare's results and, as we have already seen, regards our document as representing pre-Talmudic demonology[2]. Salzberger adopts the views of Kohler and Conybeare[3].

2 Conclusions. — Which of these dates can we adopt? Unfortunately there are in the work no historical allusions which can aid us. Yet one piece of external evidence immediately proves the late date adopted by Fleck and Istrin untenable, I mean, of course, the mention of the *Test* in the *Dialogue of Timothy and Aquila*[4] Conybeare's manuscript of the *Dialogue* belongs to the twelfth century, and he says of the work, "The title affixed to TA describes the debate as having taken place in the days of Archbishop Cyril, and to this date belong the allusions to the Trinity in foll. 75 v⁰, 101 v⁰, 103 r⁰ But this title really no more than marks the time at which the work assumed its present form." The materials are in part much older[5]. Since, however, we have no way of proving that the allusion to the *Test* belongs to the older stratum, our *terminus ad quem* must be set about the time of Cyril (died 444), that is at 400.

As to the *terminus a quo* we must conclude that it is 100 A D, at which date Dr. Conybeare would place the *Test*, regarding the Jewish original as still earlier. But what Conybeare regards as the "Jewish original" was a book of incantations, while we have found the original to be only a story containing no exorcisms, as MS D shows, and the *Test* as such to have been a Christian work[6]. The book which Eleazar in Josephus' story

1 *JQR* XI 12   2 *JE* IV 578, art. "Demonology."   3 *Salomosage* 10.
4 Cf. *supra* VIII 3d) 2) (e), p. 103.
5 *Op cit* XI, XXXIV, cf. also LVI n. 2.
6 Cf. *supra* VII 15, p. 87 ff., VII 13, p 85, IV 2, p. 32.

used may be represented by the *Hygromanteia*, or *Clavicula*, it cannot have been the *Test*, for a Jew would not have used such a Christian work, nor is it likely to have been written so early

Can we now date our document more precisely within the limits 100—400 A. D.? We are left to depend upon general considerations of language and subject matter. In view of the lateness of our manuscripts we cannot be absolutely sure of the linguistic evidence, but, as we have seen, it seems to point to a time when the Koinê was in full sway, after the New Testament was written[1], which merely confirms the general conclusion we have already reached

As to the type of thought and the materials entering into the work, we come to conclusions differing from Conybeare's. The items upon which he most relies are found to belong to a secondary recension. The relation to the New Testament we have explained, by supposing the *Test* to depend, not upon pre-Gospel Synoptic tradition, but upon imperfect, perhaps auricular, knowledge of the written Gospels[2]. The allusion to the corner stone[3], which might seem to imply a date before the idea of Christ as the corner-stone became common Christian property, proves nothing, for in the fourth and the sixth century we have the application of the same Old Testament passages to an actual corner stone[4]. Rec. B belongs to the time when Christianity was conquering the world, but the original *Test* to the age of Alexander Severus and his *lararium* with Apollonius, Christ, Abraham, and Orpheus on an equal footing[5]. As Conybeare well shows, its demonology is much like that which Celsus and Origen described[6]. As it appears to the writer, without attempting to be too precise, the conditions of language and

---

1 Cf. *supra* V 4, p. 40

2 See quotations above, IX 1 c), p. 106 n. 1, and VII 11, p. 82 f., 8 a), p. 68.

3 C. XXII 7 f , XXIII 2—4, cf. *supra* VII 8 a), p. 68.

4 Nestle, *ExT* XIV (1903) 528, "The Stone which the Builders Rejected," quoting the Pilgrim of Bordeaux and Antonius of Piacenza from "Itinera Hierosolymitana," ed P Geyer, in vol. XXXVIII of the *Vienna Corpus*, pp. 23, 173.

5 Cf. *supra* VII 15, p. 87   6 *JQR* XI 7 ff., 12 ff.

and subject matter are best met by supposing the *Test* to have
been written early in the third century.

3 Date of the original Jewish ground work. — Josephus
shows that ideas of Solomon's character and his dealings with
demons such as are found in *d* (the prototype of MS D and the
Test) were common among the Jews already in the first century
A. D, although they do not appear in the Talmud until the
third century[1] Therefore *d* may be as early as the first century of the Christian era At present our data allow no more
precise date.

4. Date of the Recensions. — Rec. A, which differs but
little from the original, probably underwent trifling changes with
every transcription. The concluding sections (XXVI 8—10) belong to Byzantine times. For MS L the same man was probably editor and copyist, in mediaeval times Rec. B may well
belong to the fourth or fifth century, when Christianity was
conscious of her conquest of the world, and her theology was
being carefully formulated. Rec. C, although probably containing very old material, presents also much that smacks of the
Middle Ages, and is apparently not much older than the manuscripts that preserve it[2]. It may well belong to the twelfth or
thirteenth century.

X. AUTHORSHIP AND PROVENIENCE.

1 Authorship Opinions. — As to the kind of individual
who wrote the *Test* there are at least four possibilities: he may
have been either a Jew or a Christian; if a Jew, either Aramaic
or Greek speaking, if a Christian, either Jewish or Greek in
origin. Gaster believes that originally the *Test* was written in
Aramaic[3]. Harnack[4], Conybeare, and Kohler[5] think it to be

---

1 Salzberger, *Salomosage* 92 f
2 Cf *supra* VII 12, p 83 and VIII 3 c) 4), p. 99.
3 *JAS* 1896 p. 155, 170.
4 *Gesch altchr Lit.* I 858; it is included under "die von den Christen an-
geeignete und z. Th. bearbeitete judische Litteratur."
5 See IX 1 b), c) p. 105 and ns. 1 f., p. 106.

a Christian revision of a Jewish work. Toy concludes, "the author of the *Testament* is a Greek speaking Jewish Christian"[1]. Schürer held it to be the work of a Christian with "no Jewish places" in it[2].

2 Authorship Conclusions. — We have found Gaster's assumption of an Aramaic original untenable[3]. Our new materials render the opinion that the *Test* was originally Jewish likewise impossible. Only the ground work, *d*, which was not a "testament", and certain of the materials were Jewish[4]. Was the author, then, a Christian of Jewish or Gentile origin? A final answer can hardly be given. On the one hand, the abundance of Jewish material and the Jewish trust in angel names, on the other the plainly Christian and heathen elements worked into the warp and woof of the document point in opposite directions. However, if the date for which we have just argued is correct, there is no reason why a Greek Christian should not have written the whole work, for he would be heir of both Jewish and Gentile materials and much more likely than a Jewish Christian to combine them in his faith[5] In the third century also Christian Jews would be few. The probabilities, therefore, are in favor of Greek Christian authorship

3. Provenience. — So far as I am aware, no one has attempted to decide from what part of the ancient world the *Test* came — perhaps wisely, for no certain conclusion can be reached. Three regions suggest themselves Palestine, Egypt, and the province of Asia. Much is in favor of the first, particularly if one think of Galilee, where Judaism and Hellenism were in the closest contact, and where Christianity took its rise and won its first conquests[6]. Again, as we have seen, some of the materials come from Egypt, and some appear in Ethiopia, which was Christianized from

---

1 *JE* XI 449.   2 *Th Litztg.* XXIV (1898) 4, col. 110.

3 See above V 6f, p. 42f.   4 See above IX 2 and n. 6, p. 106.

5 See Deissmann's argument regarding the archangel inscription at Miletus, *Licht* 333f, *LAE* 453ff.

6 See above VII 6e), p 65f

Egypt[1], while the only early literary allusion to the work by
name is Egyptian[2]. One would think that the sand storm
demon, Lix Tetrax, had originated in a land like Palestine or
Egypt, where such storms were familiar phenomena[3]. Yet from
Ac XIX 19 we see that "Asia" was probably as much a center
of magic as Agypt, and if its climate had permitted, we
should no doubt have an abundance of magical papyri from
that region also.

Against Palestine is the fact that its popular Christianity
was no doubt Aramaic rather than Greek speaking, while the
Test, which is not the work of a leader in the church but of
some uninstructed individual, is nevertheless thoroughly Greek
in its language and much of its material. Against Egypt the
strongest argument is the absence of Gnostic influence and
of specific resemblances to the magic papyri. Against Ephesus
or some part of "Asia" no decisive objections appear[4]. In its
favor are the only two geographical terms in the document,
Lydia and Olympus[5] The very fact that the sand storm
receives as its name two of the *Ephesia grammata* points —
very weakly, to be sure — in the same direction. Like Egypt,
Asia was a meeting place for all the currents of ancient
thought.

We are dealing only with probabilities; in a work that borrows so impartially from all lands, no marks are decisive. As it
seems to the writer, the probabilities are to be ranged in ascen-
ding order, Galilee, Egypt, Asia Farther one cannot go until
more light is thrown upon the whole subject of demonology,
magic, and astrology, as well as on Christian origins

---

1 Harnack, *Mission and Expansion* II 179, but see above VII 8b), p. 68f,
VII 9, p. 70

2 *Dial of Tim and Aquila*, see above VIII 3d) 2) (e), p. 103f and IX 2,
p. 106   3 C. VII.

4 Perhaps because Asian magic material is scant. Gnosticism was there,
but less vigorous. The Milesian inscription offers a point of contact.

5 That is, outside Palestine, c. VIII 4, Olympus might point to Greece,
but other reason sare lacking. Where is the "great mountain"? Is it Hermon?
Cf. I En VI 4, Montgomery, *AITN* 126.

4 Provenience of the recensions. — As to the place of origin of Recs. A and B I see no possibility of arriving at a conclusion, unless Rec. B may be thought of as western on account of its western form of Solomon's seal, the pentegram [1]. The manuscripts of Rec. C are so thoroughly Italian that one is tempted to suppose the recension originated in Greek-speaking southern Italy. MS D is, as we have seen, Byzantine in origin [2], but whether from Asia Minor or Europe one cannot say.

---

1 See above VII 14, p. 86   2 See above V 1, p. 38f.

APPENDIX.

A. Manuskript N with a list of variant readings.

N. Library of the Greek Patriarchate, Jerusalem, Sancti Saba, No. 422, XV or XVI cent., paper, cm. 11×15; beginning and end of codex lacking; as recently numbered, ff. 49ʳ—93ᵛ. Catalogue, vol. B, p. 541 [1]:

This manuscript I discovered while spending the winter of 1920—21 in Jerusalem as fellow of the American School of Oriental Research. I had called for the codex to examine the imperfect copy of the *Narratio Iosephi* with which it begins, but in leaving it through came suddenly upon the familiar matter of the *Test.* As the first page of the latter is wanting, the title did not get into the catalogue. Indeed the codex is so abominably written that a number of its selections are not mentioned.

As now bound sheets α—ε contain the *Narratio Iosephi*, beginning with c. I 4 [2]. Then begins a new subject and a new numbering, in a smaller but similar hand. Of this sheet α and two leaves of β remain. With sheet γ the second page of the *Test.* begins and it ends on f. 5ᵛ of sheet η F. 88 I found folded into the latter part of the codex The missing first page evidently was the last of sheet β and in rebinding was lost.

The learned author of the catalogue remarks that the copy of the *Narratio Iosephi* is λίαν ἀνορθόγραφον. It is even more

1 Ἱεροσολυμιτικὴ βιβλιοθήκη, ἤτοι κατάλογος τῶν ἐν ταῖς βιβλιοθήκαις τοῦ ἁγιοτάτου ἀποστολικοῦ θρόνου τῶν Ἱεροσολύμων ... κωδίκων ... ὑπὸ Α. Παπαδοπούλου Κεραμέως. 4 vols. Petrograd 1899.

2 Tischendorf, *Evangelia apocrypha.* ed alt. Leipzig, 1876, p. 461.

true of the *Test*. The copyist either understood Greek very imperfectly, or, what is more likely, had before him a manuscript which he read with the greatest difficulty, but which he tried to copy accurately. The result is a manuscript which often makes no sense at all. Not only are there occasional mistakes of haplography and dittography and constant iotacism, but cases and endings are constantly confused, words are wrongly combined and divided, and all rules of accentuation are repeatedly broken Worst of all, ν is added to almost any word ending in a vowel and even introduced within words.

Nevertheless, since we already have excellent manuscripts of the *Test*, this one proves to have considerable value, for, aside from the missing first page, it contains a complete text of Rec B. It adds another witness to the long section cc. XIV 3—XVI 1, which is wanting in all manuscripts but P. It has the longer form of P in cc IX 7, XI 6, XIII 3, 6, XVI 4 f., XVII 1, 4, XVIII 4, 18, 23, 27 f., 31, 42 f., XX 4, 6, 8 (in part), 13, 15, XXII 3, 8, 11, 20, XXIII 4 (in part), XXIV 3 ff., and XXV. N follows P in every one of the four instances where it introduces a numerical equi-,valent for a sacred name (VI 8, XI 6, XIII 6, XV 11), and in all the passages where P improves the theology of the *Test*, especially XIII 3, XVII 4, and XXII 20. This is sufficient to prove that it belongs to the B recension

However, in a considerable number of instances N does not support P. In a very few cases N follows Q against P, e. g. XX 13. In a number of places it supports C against B, e. g. V 4 f. In VII 5 it follows C in a few words which P omits. It often confirms the text of A, e. g. II 3, III 5, XXII 11, 12, but especially in c. XVIII, where it repeats the peculiar word ῥίξ, or ῥύξ, though often corrupting it. In VI 4—9, where P makes numerous additions for the purpose of reconstructing the theology and perfecting the demonology of the section, N follows the A recension in the main   It is certainly much nearer the original than P, but in some expressions, such as πευτηκή, οὖ καὶ ψῆφος χμδ and τὶς τῶν καλῶς ζώντων, it prepares the way for P. In II 8, also, it seems a step nearer the original than P and in passages like II 1 and 3 (καὶ λεβόμενος) it suggests

the error which led to diverse corruptions in the different recensions

The most important contribution made by the manuscript
to the text of the *Test* is in the concluding sections. Here H
seems so prolix that I had lost faith in it and chosen the B text
as nearer the original. Manuscript N, however, coincides with H
in part and thus shows that P and Q represent an unduly abbreviated text. In this and a few other instances, where the
textual evidence was evenly balanced, N has served as additional
weight to tip the scales in favor of a reading I had put into the
margin or has suggested a new reading. These emendations will
be found on page 121*.

Manuscript N makes certain additions of its own, e. g. in
XVIII 16, 22, and XXVI 5. None of them are such as to indicate
additional knowledge in matters demonological or magical. The
only one of any considerable size or interest is in c. XVIII, where
each of the thirty-six decani is equated with ten days of a Coptic month[1]. The copyists have not understood the intention of
the interpolator and have confused and corrupted his statements,
but it is quite easy to reconstruct the entire scheme. This matter
adds another connection between the *Test* and Egypt, but since
there is not the slightest trace of it in any of the other manuscripts,
it is quite impossible to suppose that the original *Test* contained
it. It rather shows what we might have expected had the *Test*
come from Egypt.

The chief textual fruits of the discovery of manuscript N,
then, are the list of emendations already mentioned and the con-
firmation of the strange word ῥύξ in c. XVIII But the greatest
value of the manuscript lies in its corroboration of the general
scheme of recensions and manuscript relationships already adopted. The fact that it fits in so well goes far to support the confidence that any subsequent discoveries will not invalidate the
conclusions reached in the *Introduction*.

The list of variant readings appended will illustrate the
character of the manuscript and give the basis for the emenda-

---

1 See *Intro*, above pp. 57 ff.

tions suggested. Variations merely of spelling, order, and stere-
otyped phrases, such as *καὶ εἶπον*, have been passed by. Only
where they confirmed some disputed reading or were different
enough to be of value in determining manuscript relationships
have they been noted. Otherwise it would have been necessary
to print the entire manuscript. Even the orthography has been
corrected when it was too misleading. Except where some other
manuscript is specifically indicated, N has been collated with P

Lectiones variae ex MS N (= Sancti Saba 422)
cum Rec B comparatae.

Incipit MS N (f. 49ʳ) c. I 5, p. 10*, l. 1 *τῆς ψυχῆς* (+ *αὐτοῦ*) *ἐξομολο-*
γούμενος νυκτὸς κ. ἡμέρας cum rec. B   **2** *μοι* B, om. N   **3** *ἐξουσιά-*
σει N | § 6. *ἐγένετο* — N   **4** *με* — N | *προσέρχεστε καθ᾽ ἑκάστην ἡμέ-*
ραν καὶ ἐδόθη   **5** *χάρις* B, — N   § 7. **7** *Σολ. βασιλεὺς υἱοῦ* | **8**. *ἦν*
9 *τά τε . . . αρσ. κ οἰκοδ. τὸν ναὸν τοῦ κυρίου ἐν τῇ σφραγίδι ταύτῃ* (om
glos. de anuli signo) § 8. p. 11*, l. 1 *γενομ. πάλιν ἐδοξ.* ll. 2—5 *ἐκάλεσεν*
τὸ παιδάριον ὁ σολ. κ. ἔδωκεν αὐτὸν τὸν δακτυλίδιον καὶ φήσας αὐτὸν ἐὰν
ἡμέραν ἐπιστῇ τὸ . . . δακ. (f. 49ᵛ) *ὃ ἔλαβον παρὰ κυρίου κ. Μιχαὴλ τοῦ ἀρχ*
καὶ λαμβάννοι ὁ πεδάριον τὸ δακ. κ. φάσας τὸ χαλεπὸν δαιμόνιον ῥήψας
τὸ δακ. ἐποί τοῦ στήθος αὐτοῦ τοῦ δαιμονίου λέγων δεῦρο   **6** *παραγενοῦ* |
καὶ μηδὲν διαλογιζόμενος τὸ μέλλο σοι φράσε   § 10. p. 12*, **1** *φλέγον*
§ 11. l **3** *τὰ ῥηθέντα* | *βασ. Σολ.*   **4** *ἐπὶ τοῦ στήθους τ. δαίμονος*   **5** *καὶ*
. . . Σολ. — N | § 12 *καὶ εἶπεν ὁ δ. τὸ πεδάριον*   **6** *πεποίηκας*   **7 8** *καὶ*
δώσω (f. 50ʳ) *σοι τὸ ἀργ. . . . γῆς καὶ μὴ ἀπ. με* cum A   § 13. l. 10 *ἰσδραήλ*
(sic passim) | *μὴ σου ἀνάξωμεν* | *σε ἀγάγω*   § 14 l 12 *χαίρον κ ἀγαλόμενος*
κ. εἶπε τῷ βασιλεῖ· βασ. Σολ   p 13*, l **1** *ἡμῖν δέσποτα* | *πρὸς τ. θυρῶν.*
τ. βασ. σου δεόμενος κ. κραυγάζων   **3** *μὴ αὐτὸν ἀπαγάγῃς με π σολομὸν*
С. II. *ἀκ. ταῦτα ὁ βασ Σολ*   **6** *αὐτοῦ ἐκ. ἐξῆλθεν εἰς τὰ πρ. τῆς βα-*
σιλείας αὐτοῦ κ. εἶδον   **8** *καλ.* — N | § 2. *κ. εἶπεν αὐτὸν ὁ βασ. σολ.*
(f. 50ᵛ) | *εἰς ποῖον ζῴδιον οἰκεῖσαι; κ. εἶπεν*   p. 14*, l. 1 *δι᾽ ἐπιθυμιῶν*
τῶν γυναίων ἐπὶ γῆν παρθένον τὸν ζῴδιον κεκληκότας   **3** § 3 *εἰς* — N |
μεταβαλλόμενος, ποτὲ μὲν ὃς ἄνθρωπος ἔχων ἐπιθυμίαν ἐνὶ πέδον θηλυκὸν
εὔκοσμον ἁπτόμενος· ἀλγῶσιν πάνυ   **5** *πάλιν* — N   **6** *ποτέ . .* (cum HI)
ἐνφαίνομαι ὑπὸ πάντων τῶν σι δαιμονίων καὶ)εβόμενος (1 *κελευόμενος*)
§ 4 l. **7** *τῆς . . . ἀρχαγγ. μιχαήλ. κ εἶπεν ὁ βασιλεὺς σολομὸν ὑπὸ ποίου*
ἀγγέλου καταργεῖσαι; ὑπὸ οὐρειὴλ ἀρχαγγέλου τῆς δυνάμεως τοῦ θεοῦ
§ 5. p. 15*, l. 1 *τῆς* (f 51ʳ   **3** *γιαλὸν* | § 6. *τὸ σήνδιριν προσφαῦσαι καὶ*
ἐφήμισε μιν   **5** *ἐάσομεν· ἀναφέρο καγώ σοι*   § 7. l. 6 *ηὐξάμην . . . μοι·*
ἐπαρεκάλεσε τ. ἀρχ. Οὐ. τοῦ ἐλθ   § 8. l. 8 *κῆτος ἐκ. τ. θαλ.* etc. c. B
p. 16*, l 2 *κακείνη οὗτος* etc cum textu, *μεγ κ. θρασύ*   **3** *κόψαι* | *τελεῖν*
§ 9. l. **4** *κύριον τ. θ. . . . γῆς σαβαώθ*   **5** *παρεῖναι τ. Ὁ σὺν τῇ μοίρᾳ*
7 *ὧδε* — N | *πάντων τῶν*

C III. βελζεβούλ constanter scr. N | Βεελ. τὸν ἄρχοντα τῶν δαιμονίων
11 σύ μοι φῆς p. 17*, § 4. l. 1 ὡς etc. c. textu, μεγάλως 3 πρὸς σολο-
μῶντα | § 5. ὁ δὲ εἶδεν ὁ βασ. σολ. 4 τ. θεὸν c. textu 5 θεός: + τοῦ
. . . γῆς c. L | Σολ., f. 52ʳ | τὸν σὸν θρόνον 6 εἰς ἐμὲ — N
9 § 7. ἀπήτουν . . . φαντ· ἅπαντα ἐγὼ ποιῶ ἀδιαλ. καὶ ἐμφανιζόμενος
ἕκαστος τὴν ἐργασίαν αὐτοῦ
        C. IV. l. 4 εἴη ἔστι ἐν ἐμῖν θηλεῖαι   5 εἶναι, ὦ δεσπότης, ἐβουλ.
6 ἐδειξέ μοι ἐν τάχει ἤνεγκε ἐνμπροστεν μοῦ | καὶ ἔχουσα περκαλὴν
7 δέμας δεπειε | εὐχρόστου   8 § 3 αὐτῆς , . . αὐτῇ αὐτοι ἔφη (bis) ἐγὼ
σολ.   § 4. 9 ἠνοσκαιλεῖ | σεσομεπεποιημένον   p. 19*, § 5. l. 2 εἰς ἔγ-
γονος σκολεικοιάζο αὐτ.   3 μοι ἔστιν | φράγγες   § 6. l. 4 με εἶναι
(— νομιζ)   5 μελαχο. | μου   6 λαθρέως κ. φανερὰ   7 βλάπτοι
7 s. κακουργοῖ   9 πορίζουσι   p 20*, § 8. l 1 αὐτὸν (f. 53ʳ) ποθ. γεννᾶται.
ὁ δὲ   2 φωνῆς ἀκερέου τ κ. σῆχον ἀν(θρώπ)ου μολήβου   3 § 9. δὲ ἐγὼ
πρὸς αὐτὴν· ποῖον ἄστρον   4 πανσέληνον ἄστρον   5 πλέον διωδειὸν.
καὶ εἶπον ἐγὼ σολ εἰς αὐτὴν ποῖος ἄγγελος καταργεῖ σε. κ. εἶπε· ἐσὺ
βασιλεύς   6 § 11. εἰς φλέβην   7 στρατ. φωνήσας πρὸς αὐτὴν ξίφει κροῦσαι. ὁ δὲ εἶπεν· λέγω σοι, βασ, ὑπό   § 12. l. 9 τὸ ὄνομα ἁγίου ἰωὴλ
10 διὸ ι. A | αὐτὴν — N | εἰς . . . καν om. c W
        C. V. p. 21*, l. 4 δαίμονα . . πονηρὸν — N   § 2 6 ἀπειλ βλ. βλέψας
πρός με κ. ἔφη· τίς ἦν καὶ αὐτῶν   7 § 3. οὗτος τετ. οὗτος (f. 53ᵛ) ἀπο-
κρίθη   9 ὁ υἱὸς ἧς ἄν., ἐγὼ   11 γηγενὴ | § 4. καὶ νῦν τό   p. 22*,
l. 1 φωλεύη ἐν τῷ οὐρανὸν c. C   1 s. διὰ τὸν δρακόντων παῖδας   3 καὶ
ὁ τοῦ θεοῦ πατρὸς ὁ θρόνος ἐστὶν καὶ τὸ ἀξ. μέχρι τὴν σήμερον ἐν τῷ οὐρ.
5 § 5. ἐρωτᾶν, κ. σοῦ γὰρ τὸ β. διαρ. ἐν κ. etc. c. textu   6 προσχωρήσει
καὶ   7 βασ. ἡμ. ἔχεις cum C | ἔχομεν τινα θροπότιταν etc. c. A   § 6
l. 11 δεσ αὐτ. (f. 54ʳ) καὶ ἐκελ. αὐτὸν ἐκήζεσται κ. ἀπολογεῖσθαι τίς καὶ κ.
ἐκηζεσται τί ἐστιν   § 7. p 23*, l. 1 καλ. παρὰ βροτοῖς εἰ δὲ μὴ παρὰ κα-
κούργων ἀν(θρώ)πων etc. c. textu   § 8. l 4 διὰ τῶν ἐπὶ πλεῖστον ἄστρων
καὶ τριγαμήας κ. ὡς ἑπτὰ καὶ ἐφορ. κ. δαμάζω   § 9. N c. P sed scr. ποῖον
ἄγγελον, om τοῦ θρόνου   ll. 9—10 ἐπὶ . . κἀπν· ὃ λέγεται γλαναῖος ὁ
ἐπὶ μερικῶν ἀνθράκων (f. 54ᵛ) καπν. ἢ κάλαμος στύρακος ὑποκαιόντων ἀσμό-
διον   § 10. p. 24*, l. 1 (fin.) ὃς στὸ ὄνομα κεκλ. κλάνος   2 ποτ. τῆ(ς)
συρίας εὖρ διότι κακεῖνα τὰ μέρη ἐζήλωσα πάντοτε κατοικὴν καὶ ἐν π(ᾶν)
τῷ κόσμῳ πλὴν οὐκ ἤμην, κύριέ μου   § 11 l. 6 δεσμεύσαντος   7 ἀληθής
ἐστιν | ἀξιῶ δέ σε. ἕνα με κατ. bis | μὴ με κατ. bis   § 12. l. 9 σίδηρον φο-
ρέσας ἀλλὰ . . . ποιήσας (f. 55ʳ)   10 ἀνατρ. τ. ποσίν σοι εἰς ὑπουργίαν τοῦ
ναοῦ τῆς οἰκοδομῆς   11 ὑδρίας δέκα δοθῆναι αὐτὸν   p. 25*, l. 1 αὐτὸν
2 s. τὸ δαιμόνιον ἀσμόδιος   § 13. l. 4 σοφίαν ταύτην τ δουλ. σου | χολὴν
καὶ κάλαμμα στύρακος λύων ὑποκαίων   6 ἡ φωνὴ ὀδῦς πικρίας
        C VI. 1 9 προσκ. τῆς ἐνδοξότερον καὶ ἐπηρώτησα αὐτ λέγων· ὁ δὲ
βελζεβουὴλ   10 ἄρχης   11 μόνομαν ὑπολελειφθέν   12 οὐράνιος — N
8 § 3. καὶ μετ᾽ ἐμὲ δεύτερος λέγε θὰν ἤγουν δεύτερος θεός   4 καρτῶ τὰ
ἐν ταρτάρῳ δεσμὰ cum A   p. 26*, l 2 ἐλ. καὶ εἰς θρίαμος | §§ 4—9. N
cum A | § 4 τί ἐστιν ἡ πραξίς σου   4 τοὺς δαίμονας | ἀνθρόπων
5 εἰς ἐπιθυμίας ἐγύρω | ἐν πολ. ἐγύρας   6 ἀποστέλω | ἐπάγω — N
§ 5. l 7 s. θν . . γένο(ς) σου τὸν . . . τρεφόμενος c. I.   8 ἐγὼ αὐτὸν οὐκ

ἐνέγγον πρὸς (— σε) c. L   9 ἐφῆπας κἀκεῖνος δέσμω δὲ θεὶς αὐτὸς ἀπὸ
τὸν βυθὸν τῆς θαλάσσης   § 6. l. 10 ἐκεῖνος ὁ υἱός σοι   11 τῆς θαλ. τῆς
ἐρ   12 οὐ γὰρ   p. 27*, l. 1, § 7. ἡ δὲ εἶπον αὐτόν σὺ δὲ ποῖον ἄστρον
οἰκεῖσαι   2 ἑσπέρειον   § 8 l. 8 φράσον | ποῖων ἀγγέλων | τοῦ ἁγίου
ὑμίου ὀνόματος τοῦ παντ. θ. καλούμενον παρὰ ἀνθρώποις ἑβραιστὶ πεντηκὴ
οὖ καὶ ψῆφος χμδ. ἔστιν δὲ νόητον ἑλληνιστὶ ἐμ, τὸν δεδοκόταρομέον ἐὰν
δὲ μή τις τῶν καλῶν ζωόντων ὁρκίσει τὸν ἐλεθεῖ τὸ μέγα ὄνομαν τοῦ θεοῦ
τῆς δυν (f. 56ᵛ)   § 9. 1 9 ἐν … αὐτὸν — N | ἠλάλαξαν φωνὴν πάντες
οἱ δαιμ διὰ τ. βασ. αὐτῶν c. B¯   § 10. l. 11 αὐτὸν ἐπηρώτησα | βούλει
ἀφ. λαβεῖν   12 τὴν c. A | ἔφη … βασ.   13 θαλασσίους   p. 28*, l. 2 οἰκ.
ἐρ. etc. N c. P   3 ἡμέρας | τοὺς (1°)

C. VII l. 8 πρὸ … μου: πρός με   13 ἐπὶ πολλῆς ἀναστάντα με
πτῆσε   p. 29*, l. 2 αὔβρα ἐκείνη   § 4. 5 κἀγὼ f. 57ᵛ   § 5. l. 9 στρόφους .. ἀγροὺς στρωφώνο κ. πῦρ αὐτὸν εἰποῇ στῆον κ. ἐν πυρὶ ἀγρ.
10 οἴκους ἐνμπυρίζω καὶ κατάγω   11 ὑποδύων ἡμέρας (— εἰς … καὶ)
§ 6. p 30*, l. 1 ποῖον ἄστρον οἰκεῖσαι   2 τοῦ ἐν τοῦ νότοι εὐ⟨ρι⟩σκόμενος
4 εἰδόντα πολλοὶ τῶν ἀνθρ. ἔχοντο εἰς τὸ μηηρητέον   5 βούλ΄ τἄλλα·
θαλλάλ¯ μελχαλ¯   § 7. l. 8 ἡμιτριταῖος παύεται   9 καταχ.   10 ζαζαὴλ

P. 31*. c. VIII. l. 4 τὸ δόντα μοι τοιαύτην ἐξ.   6 ἦλθον πρός με
συνπλεκόμενα, ἔμορφα τὸ εἴδει   § 2 1 8 ἔθαι (- μασα in fine pag.) f. 58ᵛ
εἰ δὲ ὁμοθυμαδὸν εἶπον μιᾷ φωνῇ ἔφησαν   9 τὰ λγ¯ στοιχεῖα οἱ κοσμο-
κράτορες τοὺς σκότους | § 3. καὶ εἰσὶν οἱ πρῶτοι | ἐγώ εἰμι ὁ vel ἡ statim
om N   p. 32*, l. 1 κλοθὸν ἢ ἔστι μαχία | τετάρτη λεγομένη   2 ἡ δύ-
ναμις   4 § 4. θεὰ   6 § 5. αὐτὸν   7 ἀρξ. ἀπὸ τῆς πρώτης   8 πλέκω
(bis) λέγω αὐτὰ ὧδε κακεῖς ἐρέσεις ἐρεθίζω   9 ἀγγ. τὸν κατ με λαμεχελαλ
10 ἐρήσις ῥήδον   11 τοῦ τόπου — N   p. 33*, l. 1 βαρηχηαὴλ   § 7.
l. 2 καὶ πάντα π μαχ.   μάχην ἐστὶν τὸ ὄνομά μου | εὐσχ. περιεξ. εὔχη
μόνος ἡσχῆσε κ. περησχοιθέναι ποιῶ   § 8. l. 5 μερίζω χωρίζω (— ἀπομερ.)
8 βαλθηούχ | ordinem sectionum habet N ut A   p. 34*, l. 3 ῥηδῆλ |
§ 10. δύναμις καλοῦμαι τυρ ἀνιστῶ   5 καθὲ παρέχων   7 ὅτε ἐκελείστων
ἀρτ. δεσμῆς ἡ δὲ ἀκ. μελλήσει]   8 ὡς φιλ. — N | ἐμοὶ δὲ κατα ἀντῆς
ἐποιθειμοιαν τη⟨ς⟩ σοφίας   10 ἴχνος αὐτῆς   11 ἐπειδὴ σύντομαι ἐκελ ¯
12 κ ἔτ. .. πεντ ἐπεὶ διακοσίας πηχῶων πεντ τὸ μῆκος   p. 35¯, l. 1 ἔφησα
.. καὶ δεινῶς γογγήσε τὰ κελεστέντα αὐτ κατ.

C IX l. 3 N post θεὸν (mss. CP) add. τοῦ οὐρανοῦ καὶ τῆς γῆς | ἔτ.
δαίμον   4 ἂν μὲν· ὡς ἔχων   § 2 l. 5 ἰδὸν αὐτὸν εἶπον c W | λέγει
… καλ. τί λέγεις   6 καλοῦμαι — N | ἐμαυτὸν   7 ποιήσασθαι. περι-
ποιῆσαι   8 ποιῆσαι τὴν αὐτὴν ἔχω | οἶαν ὡς· ἔνηαν   § 3. l. 11 ἐγόγ-
γυζεν | οἴμοι ἡμῖν   p. 36*, l. 2, § 5. ἡδονῇ. ἀδόδειν | ἤκοισε θέλω δὲ
3 ἡ μὴ φωνὴ ἡμῖν   4 βοβοὶ   5 γιν δ. ἡμ.   7 § 6. ἀωρίαις | πλεῖον
πορεύομαι καὶ τὸ   12 ἐκποιῶν   p. 37*, l. 1, § 7. N cum P, … οὐδὲ γὰρ
οὔπω, . ἐπευχόντων αὐτὸν … ἐλθὼν εἶπον τὸν ἴδιον ὄνομαν   § 8.
l 2 μεχρίου πάλιν ἀνάξω πρός με

C X l. 4 ἦλθε πρός με κύων. τὸ σχ. μεγ   7 §. 2. γενόμενος | ἀθέ-
σματα   9 ἀθέσματα   10 κατασχῶν   p. 38*, l. 8, § 3 τοὺς φρενεῖν ἀνθρώποις τοὺς τῶν ἐμῶν   8 § 5. τὸν λίθον πρ. μεταλευόμενον   12 § 6. ὃς
δ΄ ἂν ἐπιστρέψῃς καὶ δείξῃ σου   18 τὸ δακτυλίδιον   14 ἄγαγέ μοι ὧδε

τὸν δαίμοναν | § 7. καὶ ἔδειξεν αὐτὸν ὁ δαίμων τὸν (bis) πϱ. λ.   16 ἤνεγκεν
§ 8. ll. 17 ss. cum. P. τὰ δύο .   (— ὁμοίως) .. τηϱεῖται ... λαμπάδας πυ-
ϱὸς .   παϱαπέμποι .. τεχν.   p. 39*, l. 9, § 9 ἦϱον | πετάλου   4 ἀνα-
φωϱέσιν | ἦν δὲ ὁ λιϑ. ἐκεῖνος ὥσπεϱ κεϱασίου τοῦ ϑυσιαστηϱίου ὁμοιού-
μενον   § 11 l. 9 καταϱγεῖσαι | βάϱη ἐὼν
     C XI l. 11 πϱός με λέοντος etc. cum P   12 πν. εἰμὶ πν(εύμα)τι μηδ.
§ 2. l. 13 ἐγὼ δὲ ἐν πᾶσι   p. 40*, l 1 κατάκειμε | ἐφόϱμομεν   3 § 3 ἐκ-
βάλω   4 δεικτηκὸν (f. 63ᵛ) δέ εἰμι | ὑπ' ἐμὲ λεγεῶν   6 § 4. τί σου ἡ
ἐϱγασία καὶ τί τὸ ὄνομά σοι | λεοντόφϱον   7 § 5. πῶς οὖν καταϱγεῖς
8 ἔχεις   11 § 6. εἰς τὸ μέγαν ὂν τ ϑ. σαβαὼϑ   12 καταϱγῇ μὲν τὰ τῆς
δυνάμεώς σου   11 ἔχων πολλὰ παϑῶν   p. 41*, l. 2 κατὰ τοῦ — N   3 κα-
καταϱγοῦσα   § 7. l. 5 αὐτὸν δὲ τὸν λεοντόφϱονα   6 εἰς ἀπόκαψιν
     C. XII. l. 8 ἦλϑε πϱός με δϱακόντων τϱικέφ. φοβεϱοχϑϱῶς   § 2.
l 10 τϱικέφαλον καὶ τϱίβολον   11 νήπια | ἐπιδένω καὶ κουφένω κ. πάλιν
ἐν τῇ τϱ μου κεφ, ὑπόδυνα κ τύπτω   13 τὸ εἰκ. — N | κ τϱίζ. — N
p. 42*, l. 2, § 3 σιωμένης | η πϱοωϱιστον   § 4. l 7 ἀνάγω | ἔσω — N
'Αϱαβίας ÷ ὅστις καὶ ἀσκὸν ἐκεῖσε καὶ καταβληϑεὶς κοσμηστὴ ἀπὸ τῆς 'Αϱ
12 § 6. τί ἐστιν τὸ ὄνομά σου   13 πληϑουϱ | ναὸν, εἶχεν γὰϱ χ α
     C XIII p. 43*, l. 1 καὶ πϱὸς τῷ κυϱίῳ τῷ ϑεῷ ἰσδϱαὴλ ἐκελ. | ἦλϑε
πϱός με   2 καὶ αὐτὸν λυσίτϱιχον   § 2. l. 4 ἡ δὲ .. σύ — N   5 μα-
ϑεῖν . ὄντα καὶ ἔφη· ἄκουσον τὰ κατ' ἐμέ   6 ταμή σου   7 πϱοσκα-
ϑεῖσας   8 μαϑεὶς   § 3 l. 9 κ. ἐλέγξαι αὐτ. P — N   10 τίς εἶ σύ
λέγε μοι παϱὰ τοῖς ἀν(ϑϱώπ)οις πῶς καλεῖσαι | ὀβϱήζϑγελαοιϑ.   11 κα-
ϑεύδομαι | κόσμον. ÷ ἐπὶ ταῖς νύκταις   12 ἀποστοχαζόμενος p. 44*, l. 1 λίαν
αναχώϱισας | κ. νῦν με εἶναι μὲν εἰμίν | δεκτηκὰ μέϱη | οὐκ ἐποίησας
— N   § 4 l 4 στόματα χαλινοδεσμία   § 6 l. 8 ποῖον ἄγγελον   9 (— ὑπὸ)
τὸν ἄγγελον τ ϑ τὸν καλούμενον βαϱαφάν, .   ὁ κ νῦν καταϱγούμενος εἰς
τ. ἄπαν χ ἐὰν   καὶ ἐπιγινώσκει γ ἐπιγϱάψει τότε etc.   § 7. l 12 ἔμ-
πϱοσϑεν — N   p 45*, l. 1 βλέπουσιν καὶ   2 δύναμιν καὶ (f. 67ʳ) κϱα-
τέωσιν τὴν δεδομένην μοι παϱὰ
     C. XIV 3, l 11 πολλαῖς — N   12 ἐμόϱφοις | τοῦ ξείλου (f. 67ᵛ)
τούτου   13 § 4. ἀπέϱμε   14 ἐβάσταζεν ἡ ἐφόϱησα]   15 ἔϱος   16 τὴν
γυναῖκαν ἐκείνην   p. 46*, l. 1, § 5. ϑέλεισον | μονον — N   .2 καταϱο-
σόμενα   4 συγγενέσϑαι   § 6 l 7 ἅπεϱ ἅπτην   10 ποῖον ἄγγελον κατ-
αϱγείη σε   12 βαζαζόϑ
     C XV 3, l. 15 ἦλϑε πϱός με γύνη   § 2. l. 19 ἐνείψυχος   § 3. l 21 με-
ταβ. καὶ γίνομαι ὡς   22 καὶ γίνομαι — N   § 4. l. 24 εἰς τὴν σελ.   § 5.
l 26 ἕτεϱον δὲ παλ. παϱ' αὐτὸν κατάγομεν κ. φαιν.   p. 47*, l. 5, § 7. αὐτὴν ἀλείσεσιν τϱεῖς κ κατεδεσμείσας μὲ τὴν ἄλλησον καὶ σφϱαγισάμενος τῇ
σφϱαγίδην   § 8 l. 9 συνλευσϑ σκελευϑήσεται   § 9. l. 13 κατακλεῖς
§ 10 l 16 πολλοῖς καιϱοῖς   17 ὅμοιος ὡς ἐν σειεῖ ὑμῆ ὁ πάντα ἡμᾶς κατ.
§ 13. l. 25 ἀποασεβῶν   p. 48ˡ, l. 3, § 15. παϱαδωϑῆναι
     C. XVI. l. 5 καὶ ... δαιμ. — N   8 ἀποδεχ. χϱυσίον κ. ἀϱγύϱιον
ἐτοιοῦτον εἰμὶ | τὰ ἀλόμενα τ. ὕδατος   10 § 2. εἰς κῦμα μέγαν   14 οὕ-
τως .   σωματ οὐ γὰϱ εἰμὶ ἐπιϑυμῶ σώματος   § 3. l 16 ἄϱχων τῶν δαιμόνων ζεῖ καὶ βασιλεύει εἰς   18 σκέψιν (f 71ʳ) τινὰ ζῆν   p. 49*, l. 1, § 4.
δόξαν καὶ — N   4 ὄνομα ἀλ. νατῆα· ἀποστ. δὲ   10 § 6. 'Ιαμέϑ μηδσϑαι

C. XVII 1. 15 ἦλθε ὀμβρός μου   16 χεροσπάθην χαλκὴν   p. 50*, l. 1 ὁ
2 πνεῦμα γίγαντος   8 τῶν ὀνομάτων γιγ.   § 3, l. 9 κατατρώγει   § 4.
12f. ὁ μελ. σωτὴρ καλεῖσθαι παρ᾽ ἀν(θρώπ)οις   14 ἐπιστρέψῃ ἡττήσει
16 § 5, ἀπέκλεισα

C XVIII, l. 1f. ἦλθον ὀμπρός μου λς πνεύματα   4 θεριοπω.. σφηγγό-
σωμα, πυροειδῆ, τυποσώματα, βοωπρόσωπα, ἀθεοπρόσωπα, πτηνοπρόσωπα
§ 2. 1 7 τοῦ κοσμοκράτορος | τοῦ αἰῶνος   § 3. 1 8 ἀλλ᾽ οὐδὲ κατακλ.
ἡμῖν   p. 52*, l. 1f. pro ἐγὼ ... Ῥύαξ praebet N φαρμουθίον καλοῦμαι. ad
marg. adscr. ἀπὸ κριον πρώτο⟨υ ἕως⟩ δεκά⟨του⟩   3 κροτ. οκηλέβω | ἐγκλ
Ῥ. ἰγῶ κλήροσι ἄκας   § 6. 1 4 φαρμουθῆ κριοῦ. ὁ δευτ. ἔφη· β ā (l. ἀπὸ)
ι ā ξ ως κ· ἐγὼ δευτ καὶ βαρ.   6 ἐγκλ Βαρ — N   7 § 7. φαρμουθῆ
κριοῦ γ ἀπὸ κ ἕως λ. ὁ τρίτος | ἀρατοήλ   8 καὶ σφόδρα βλάπτω | ἀρα-
τοσαήλ   10 § 8. πάχο ταύρου ἀπὸ πρώτου ἕως δεκάτου | ῥοπεῖ | λῆμα
κ. συνοχᾶς κ. συνδονᾶς ἐκπέμπων   12 § 9. πάχο ταυρίου β ἕως κ   13 κη-
ριξουδάλ | καὶ σφηνόσια (f. 74ʳ) κορῶ ἐπιτελῶ | ἐὰν   ἀναχωρῶ — N
p. 53, l. 2, § 10. πάχο ταύρου γ· ἕως κ | σφοδραήλ | παρίσθμια Ρ, παρ-
θεμμια   3 ὄπισθ. Ρ, πιστότερον | βαηλ   4 σφοδραήλ | § 11 παύνι
διδίμου ū· ἕως (κ eras) ā   5 σφαδορ   6 ἐπιπήξω   7 σφαδορ | § 12 παύνι
διδίμου ἕως κ   9 βελζεβουλ

§ 13 1 10 παύνι διδίμου γ ἕως η᾽ κ ἕως λ | ουρταήλ   11 ἰὰθ
σαβάθ | κουρταήλ   12 § 14 ἐπιφημῆ (f. 74ᵛ) καρκίνου β | μεταθι
14 § 15 ἐποιφημη καρκίνου ἀπὸ β ἕως ἰα καὶ η κ | ἐντέκατος | καιι-
κοταήλ   16 κ. τ τ ὀν. (Ρ) — N   p. 54ʳ, l. 2 πλύνας δάφνας   3 § 16.
ἐπηφημὶ καρκίνου γ· ἀπὸ κ ἕως τὸν λ   4 σαφθορωθαήλ | ἐκβάλω   6 ἰαέ
. Σαβ — N, v infra | ἃς φορέσει ἐπὶ τ. τρ η κ. τὰς πρὸ τ. οὖς εἴθη | post
ἀναχωρῶ add. τὴν μέθην διαλύω. μεσόργεον λέοντος ū ἀπὸ πρώτου ἕως δέκα
ἄκουσον, βασιλεῖ σο⟨λο⟩μόν, τὰ ὀνόματα ὅπου θέλῃ φορέεει ὁποῖός ἐστιν
τῶν ἀγγέλων τὰ ὀνόματα· ἰαεω· ἰελεω· ἰωελέτ· σαβαῶν ἠθωθ βαέ (om N
supra l. 6)

8 § 17 βωθο(πο eras) θήλ   9 ἀθοναθθ...βωθωθήλ. | § 18. μεσορείον
λέοντος β· ἀπὸ ā ἕως η κ   10 Δερ. καλ. — N   11 ἐπάγω ἐκπιῶν, ὄνομα
δέ μοι ροκλίδ   12 ὅτι κολεῖ καλλιῶ ἐστιν   13 § 19 μεσόριον λέοντος γ ἀπὸ
εἰκουστοῦ λ   14 κωμετήλ   p. 55*, l. 1 κουμεταήλ | § 20. θὼθ πάρθη
ἀπὸ ā ἕως δεκάτου   3 πυρετ(ῆς) ἐνάτης   4 ἐπιέχριε τὸν τράχηλον κ.
λέγων τὴν σπονδὴν ταύτην   5 ἀναχωρῆ ἀπὸ τοῦ πλάσματος (f. 76ʳ) τοῦ
θεοῖ τοῦ ὑψίστου τὸν θρόνον ἀναχωρεῖ ἀπὸ ... θεοῦ

7 § 21 θὼθ πάρθη β ἀπὸ ἰα ἕως κ | ἐροπαήλ   8 σπασμοὺς   9 ὅπου
δ᾽ ἂν εὕρω   10 εἰς τοῦ οὖς τοῦ σπάχωντος εἰς τὸ δεξιὸν ἐκ τρίτου τ. ὁν
ταῦτα· ἰουδαρζῆ· βαβυννηδονηδέ   11 § 22 ὁ ὀγδη κ. δερ. παρθένου γ ἀπὸ
εἰκοστὸν πρῶτον ἕως λ ὀγδο καὶ   12 βολδομιχ   p. 56*, l. 2 τούτου Ρ.
+ ὀρκίζω σε βολομοχ χανης (l κατὰ τῆς) δυναστείας αὐτῶν ἀναχώρισον ἀπὸ
τοῦ οἴκου τούτου | § 23. ζηγός ā ἀπὸ ā ἕως ῑ   3 ἐγώ, κ(ύρι)ε σολομῶν,
καλ. ῥουξ μαδέρον | χαρτ. ἀβηβηλίου σφηνειραφαήλ· ἀναχωρῖν με δούρον
4 § 24. φανόφ ζηγὸς β ἀπὸ ἡ (l. οἱ?) κα ἕως λ   5 κήρηξ νουθάθ   6 φο-

νουβωήλ　7 (f. 77ʳ) § 25. φαωφῆ ζηγὸς $\overline{β}$ ἀπὸ η $\overline{κα}$ ἕως $\overline{λ}$　　8 γράφει
· ϱοϱιξ, ὃ οὐσ(οσο)λάϑ(?) κ περιάψη

10 § 26. om. N　　12 § 27. ἀϑοὺϱ σκοϱπήος $\overline{β}$ ἀπὸ $\overline{ια}$ ἕως η $\overline{κ}$· ο η·
$\overline{κ}$· $\overline{γ}$· ἐγώ, κήϱιξ σολομόν, καλ. ἐφϑάδα　p 57*, l 1 ἐ⟨ν⟩λάμνο κασσιτηϱῶ
| ἐφϑαδὰ | τ. ἰοχ. — N　　2 § 28 ἀϑοῦϱ σκοϱπίο ν$\overline{γ}$ ἀπὸ η $\overline{κα}$ ἕως $\overline{λ}$ ὁ η
$\overline{κδ}$ ἔφη· ἐγώ, κήϱιξ σολ, ἀκτόμεν καλ.　　4 ὕλο | ἀϱν μαϱμαϱώϑ, ἀκτόμε
διωξ　5 § 29 χοίαν τοξότης $\overline{α}$ ἕως $\overline{ι}$　| ἐγώ, κήϱιξ σολ, καλ. ἀνατϱέϑ
7 ἀϱ χαϱ. ἀποδιώξων ἀνατϱέϑ | § 30. χοιακον τοξότου $\overline{β}$ ἀπὸ η $\overline{ϱη}$ ἕως
$\overline{λ}$, ὁ η $\overline{κϛ}$ καὶ ἕτεϱα δέκατος ἐγώ, κήϱιξ σολ, καὶ ἐνόϑ.　9 ἀλλαζολ ..
ἐνϑϑ καὶ γϱάψει χαϱτ　10 § 31 χήακι τοξότης $\overline{γ}$ ἀπὸ $\overline{κβ}$. $\overline{λ}$· οη $\overline{κϛ}$
ἔφη ἐγώ κήϱιξ σολ, ὤφϑη καλ.　11 ὑπατικοὺς | αἰμ ἐνμωϱϱαγκὰς φιλῶ
12 ἐῶν P (1°) ἐώλ, (2°) ἐῶ | ἀξηωφήϑ | δὸς πίει τοῦ πάσχοντος

14 § 32. τίβη ἐγοκέϱον κέϱατον· οη $\overline{κη}$ ἔφη· ἐγώ, κήϱιξ σολ, ἅϱπας καλ.
15 γϱάψει εἰς φύλον δαφνις κόκο φνῆ δίσμος (+ μῶς eras) καὶ　16 § 33.
τοβηέϑ κέϱατος $\overline{β}$ $\overline{γ}$ ἀπὸ $\overline{ιβ}$ εἰκοστὸς οη $\overline{κϑ}$ ἔφη· ἐγώ, κήϱιξ σολ.. καλ. (no-
men om)　p. 58*, l. 1 σε κανοστιϱ　2 μαϱμαϱώϑ | § 34. πο $\overline{β}$ (1 τοβ)
ἐγόκαιϱος τω $\overline{γ}$ ἀπὸ εἰκοστοῦ πϱώτου ἕως $\overline{λ}$. ὁ $\overline{λ}$ ἔφη· ἐγώ, κήϱιξ σολ., καλ.
ἡφησικεϱάϑ　8 ποιῶ τοῖς ἀνϑϱώποις　5 βοηϑεῖτε, φεύγω καὶ ἀναχωϱῶ
καὶ ἀναπληϱῶν ἡμεϱῶν ἑπτά | § 35. μεσει δϱηχόου $\overline{α}$ ἀπὸ $\overline{α}$ ἕως $\overline{ϛ}$, ὁ $\overline{λα}$
ἔφη· ἐγώ, κήϱιξ σολ., καλ. ἀλλεβωϱίϑ　7 νυκτὸς φαγήσας καὶ ὀστίον ἀπὸ
8 § 36. μεσει· χηϱῆ δϱηχώου $\overline{β}$ ἀπὸ $\overline{α}$ ἕως $\overline{λ}$, ὁ $\overline{λβ}$ ἔφη· ἐγώ, κήϱιξ σολ., καλ.
ἰχϑήος　10 § 37. μεση δϱηχώου $\overline{β}$ $\overline{γ}$ ἀπὸ $\overline{κα}$ ἕως $\overline{λ}$, ὁ τϱιασκοστὸς τϱίτος ἔφη·
ἐγώ, κήϱιξ σολ, καὶ ἀγωχώνηον　11 σπαϱγάνοις κατὰ φάϱαγγι　12 κούϱ-
γος· οὔϱγος· ϱογος· ὁος ὅς

14 § 38. φαμενόϑ ἰχϑήος ἀπὸ $\overline{α}$ ἕως $\overline{ι}$, ὁ τϱιακ τεταϱ ἔφη· ἐγώ, κήϱιξ
σολ., καλ. ϱηξ (nomen om)　15 α $\overline{η}$ β　16 § 39. φαμενόϑ ἰχϑήος $\overline{β}$ ἀπὸ $\overline{ια}$
ἕως $\overline{κ}$, ὁ τϱ. πέπτος ἔφη· ἐγώ (bis), κήϱηξ σολ, καὶ ϱὶξ φηνόϑ　18 § 40.
φαμενόϑ ἰχϑηος $\overline{γ}$ ἀπὸ $\overline{κα}$· $\overline{λ}$ ὁ τϱ ἰκ. ἔφη ἐγώ· κήϱιξ σολ, καὶ βιανακήϑ
p. 59*, l. 2 ἐπήφϑονον　3 μηλτον· ἀϱϑουνα· ἐνᾶϑ　6 ὑδϱοφονεῖν | § 42.
N cum P, atque § 43, sed post κατέκλεισα add. ἄλλους δὲ εἰς ἀγγεῖα ἀπέκλεισα, et in § 44 ὑελῶν pro φιάλῳ, et τόπους εἰτήμασα .. κλιϑεῖναι

C. XIX N cum P. § 1 σολ. ὁ βασ. | παντὸς ἀνϑϱώπου τοῦ ὑπὸ
— ὅλον　§ 2 πᾶς τῶν βασιλέων τ. γ. πάσης | ϑεωϱεῖν | δοϑ. ἡμῖν
ἐπϱοσφέϱασι δόϱα, χϱυσ κ ἀϱγ. πολύ | κ πολ κ διαφ ἐκόμιζον πϱοσφοϱὰς
εἰς τὸν ναὸν κιϱίου τοῦ ϑεοῦ χαλκ τε καὶ | ξύλα σεπτὰ πϱοσφέϱομεν εἰς
p. 60*, § 3. ἐν οἷς — N | σάβα ἡ βασ. | ἐδόξαζον τὸν ϑεὸν

C. XX 1. 7 γέϱας μου | λέγε . ἔφη ὁ γέϱων λίγων　§ 2 1 6 πϱο-
σωπ .. μοι: πϱός σε εἰμι ἐκοδήσον με　§ 3 1 12 ἐλϑόντος ἐπηϱώτησα
τὸν νέον ἀληϑῶς οὕτως ἔχει　§ 4. 1. 18 om. πατέϱα　14 om. ἐπιπε-
πλησμένος et π(ατέ)ϱια　βασιλεῦς　15 ἀϑέσμιτα　p 61*, l 1, § 5 οὖν
| ἀκ. τοῦ νέου　3 ἀλλ᾽ εἶπεν· οὐχὶ ἀλλὰ ϑανατωϑήτω

§ 6 πϱεσβύτην | τ. δαίμονα ἐλϑε͂ν καὶ ἀνήγγειλέν μοι καὶ λέγοντά
μοι οὕτως· ἐγώ δὲ σολ. (+ ἀκούσας ταῦτα eras) ἐϑυμ. λίαν διὰ | εἰπέ μοι,

ὦ κατάρατε　§ 7.] 9 ἔτι τρεῖς | τελευτήσει　10 ἀνελεῖ | § 8 ταῦτα
οὕτως ἔχει (f. 72ʳ) ὁ δὲ ἔφη· ἀληθῶς ταῦτα　§ 9. l. 12 ἐλθ. τ. γηρ (μεταστῆναι eras) εἰς τὸ μέσον μετὰ καὶ τοῦ　13 φιλίαν τρ. ἅμα καὶ εἰς τὸν
τροφὴν αὐτ. παρασχόμε　§ 10 l. 14 τὸν νέον τ. υἱόν σου καὶ ἐπιμελοῦμαι
αὐτοῦ　15 οἱ δὲ προσκυν.　p. 62*, l 5, § 12 ὠπτάμεθα | ἀπὸ τ ϑ
6 § 13. εἰς τὸ ὀν. τ τεϑ (c. Q) ὥστε φαίνεσθαι | ἐπὶ τοῖς ἀν(θρώπ)οις
(— φύσεως)　§ 14] 9 ἐν　10 ἐν μέσῳ | μιγεντο　§ 15. cum P |
ὡς ἄτον μὴ | — ἀτονοῦμεν　§ 16. p. 63*, l. 2 δοκοῦσιν οἱ ἄνθρωποι καὶ
θεαροῦντες ἡμᾶς ὅτι ἄστερες ἐπίπτονσιν　3 § 17 οὐ οὕτως δὲ　4 ἀλλὰ
ἐκπίπτομεν ἐπὶ (ex ἀπὸ corr.) τὴν γῆν διὰ　5 πολλῇ　6 πόλεις πολλοὺς
§ 19 l.11 οὐκ ... πενθοῦντα ἔμελλον ἐπερωτᾶν αὐτὸν καὶ ἐλθον πρός
με ὁ ἄν(θρωπ)ος κατὰ πένθος καὶ μελλανόμενος τὸ πρόσωπον καὶ πλή-
τον ἑαυτοῦ τὸ σῶμα　§ 20. l. 14 παρακαθέζομαι | ἡμέραι　§ 21.
] 16 Ἰσραήλ

C. XXI l. 1 δοξάζουσα καὶ αὐτὴ τὸν　2 ἣν εἰκοδόμουν τετελειομένον
ἔδωκε σίκλον χρυσίου κ. ἀργ. κ χαλκοῦ ἐκλεκτοῦ μυρ　3 § 2. εἶδε | τὰς
ἀναφόρας　5 λίθους τοὺς τιμίους ὥσπερ λυχνοὺς ἀστραπτ　6 λυχνικοῦ
λίθον　7 § 3 κριθειδανόμενο　8 λησειδόντων | πλόκην περιπλεμένην
9 στάδιον δεκάξι ταύρους　10 § 4. N cum C　12 καὶ . γῆς P — N
C XXII p 65*, l. 1 ἀπεστ δὲ μὲ ὁ βασ. ἀράβων ὀνόματι ἀρδάκης |
ἡ δὲ ... οὕτως — N　2 βασιλεῦ σολομῶν τοῦ ἰῆλ, ἰδοὺ ἠκουσ πάντα περὶ
σου καὶ παν τὰ πέρατα, etc cum Q　§ 4. l 14 εἰρηνεύσεις πᾶσαν ἀραβίαν
| ταύτην τὴν δικαιοσ　p 66*, l 1 § 5. ὑποτεταγμένοι ὑπαρχίαν ἀπολέσις
2 καὶ πᾶσα ἡ γῆ μου — N

4 § 6 ἀκούσας καὶ ἀναγνοὺς　5 πτύξας αὐτὴν　6 § 7 καὶ . .
συνεπλ. — N　7 ἀκρογων μέγας ἐκλεκτὸς (— κείμενος) | ὅντινα βάλομεν
εἰς　§ 8 l. 10 οἱ συνπουργῶν τὸν λίθον ἐπὶ τὸ αὐτὸν ὅτε ἀνάγη τὸν λίθον
ἐπὶ τὸ αὐτὸ καὶ ἱθῆναι αὐτὸν ἐπὶ τὸ πτερυγ　12 τ θεματ αὐτῷ — N
ἐκεῖνος πάνυ — N | § 9. μνησθεὶς γνοῦς N　13 ἀρδάκου　14 τὴν |
μετά σε　15 § 10. ἐπὶ τοῦ　16 πνέει — N　§ 11 p 67*, l 3 κ σφραγ.
τ. δακτ cum H | ἐπίσαξω και. τὴν καμ. κ θέσε τ. ἀσκὸν ἐπὶ τὴν καμ. κο-
μίσεις ἐνϑ | τάξεται | θησαυροὺς μὴ ἀπο ἀλύσεις

§ 12.] 5 Τότε τοῦτον N | τὰ τελεσμένα | καὶ　ἀσκὸν — N
7 ἥκιστ. καὶ ἆρα δυνατόν τ πν τ πον. συλ | § 13 καὶ ὄρθρου mecum
8 ἐνωπ. . πνοῆς καθῦς τ. ἀσκὸν . . ἐπεφ. τὸ στόμα τοῦ ἀσκοῦ τῶ δακτυλίδιον　10 τοῦ δακτ . . στόμα P — N　11 § 14. σταθεὶς εὐθέως
p 68*, l. 1 § 15. κ. οὕτως ἐπέμενέν ὁ　2 πλέον ἐν τ χώρᾳ ἐκ.　3 § 16
ἐπέσαξεν τὴν καμ ὁ παῖς κ ἐπέθηκεν τ. ἀσκ. ἐπὶ τ. καμ.　5 καὶ εὐφ
ἐδόξαζον

§ 17. l. 9 με　§ 18 l 13 πεφυσημένος　§ 19 l. 15 εἰμι ὁ λεγ ἐφήπ.
πας　p 69*, l 1, § 20 ναί, κῆρι σολομῶν βασιλεῖ, ἐφιπτ | σταυρωϑ.
(f. 88ʳ) ἐπὶ ξύλον, ὁ καὶ προσκυνήσαντες ἄγγελον ἀρχάγγελον

C XXIII. εἶπον ἐγὼ σολομῶν βασ πρὸς αὐτόν　5 μεφέρειν | ἔπητα
ἀλλα　§ 2 l. 10 στήσεις | βούλει + κῆρη βασ σολ.　11 § 3. ἵνα ἀνα-
γάγει σε κ. φυσηθεὶς ὁ ἀσκ ἐκ τοῦτο κ. ὑποδέδοκεν τὸν λίθον p 70*, l 1
ἔθετο ἐπάνω εἰς τὰς γονίας τοῦ ναοῦ　§ 4 l. 3 ἡ ῥίθεισα | κ τὰ λοιπὰ
τοῦτον οὐκ ἔστιν ἄλλον ἀλλήνα τοῦ θεοῦ τὸ θέλημαν κατισχύσαι etc cum P

C XXIV, § 4 p 71*, l. 2 ὁ κίονας ὑπερμεγέθη σπόδρα διὰ τὸν ἀέρα
4 βαστάζοντα — N

C XXV. βασιλεὺς σολ. (f 89ᵛ) | τὸν ἕτερον δαίμοναν τὸν ἀν ἐλθὸν
8 καὶ σὺ τίς εἶ κ. τί σου   § 2. 10 ἀβεζεβιθοῦ | καὶ ἥμουν πότε μὲν καθε-
ζόμενος   12 § 3 πνεῦμα περοτὸν ἐπιβ.   13 ss. ἐγώ .. καρδίαν ἐγώ
εἰμι ὁ σκληρύνας τὴν καρδίαν φαραῶν καὶ τῶν θεραπόντων αὐτοῦ κατὰ τὸν
μονισὴν τὸν ἰσραηλίτον   § 4 ἐγὼ ἐκεῖνος ὃ ἐπικ. .. οἱ μαχόμενοι (f. 90ʳ)
τῷ βασιλεῖ ἐγύπτου   p 72*, § 6 l 4, ἐποίησα καταδιῶξαι ὀπίσω τὸν υἱὸν
ἰσραὴλ καὶ ἐγένετο ἐν τῷ ἐγγύζειν αὐτοὺς ἐν τῇ ἐρυθρᾷ θαλ. διέρηξεν ὁ θεὸς
τὴν θάλασσαν καὶ διεπέρασεν τοὺς υἱοὺς ἰ(σρα)ὴλ   6 τότε . . . ἐκεῖ παρη-
μῶν   7—10 § 7. καὶ διεγένετο καὶ ἐκάλυψεν καὶ ἔμειναν   11—14 § 8.
ἀλλὰ παραμέναι αὐτοὺς βαστάζον τὸν κίονα ἥγουν τὸν στεῖλον ὃν ἐκ τῆς
ἐρυθρᾶς θαλάσσης ἐκόμισαν καὶ ὤμοσαν . . . ὁ θεὸς τοῦ ἰηλ ὃς παρεδ.
ἡμᾶς ἀποχειρό σου οὐ . τοῦτον ἐπὶ τῆς γῆς . . . § 9   τὸν (f. 91ʳ)
θεὸν τοῦ οὐνῦῦ καὶ τῆς γῆς καὶ . . κυρίου μετὰ πάσην εὐπρεπίαν καὶ ἐμ-
νήσε(ην) ἐν . . .

C XXVI. l 1, p 73* τῆς βασιλείας μου ἐ γυνέκες καὶ ἄλλες πολλὰς¹
μοι γυνέκες οὐκ   2 πορεύθει   3 ἐκεῖ ἐκ τὸ βασίλειον αὐτοῦ   4 ἐβουλ.
δοξάσε αὐτ. πρὸς   § 2 l 5 μοι | σομανήτην   6 μολόχου   7 ἀγα-
πᾶς   8 τὸν μέγαν θεὸν (f 91ᵛ) τὸν καλούμενον ρ. κ. μ ἐὰν ἀγαπᾶς τὴν
παρθένον

τίς δὲ ἔστιν ἡ ὑποθ τοῦτο με ἀνάγασε προσκυνεῖσε καὶ ποιῆσαι, § 4.¹
. ὁμοιωθῇς τοῖς ἔθ[ν]εσιν τῶν .   ἡμ ἐμὴ πνθ οὐδαμῶς θύσω θεοὺς
ἀλλ καὶ παρεβίασε hoc a loco cum H

N cum H comp 12 Σολ + τοῦ βασιλέως ἰηλ ἀνάγκασε αὐτὸν προσκυνῆσαι τοῖς θεοῖς ἡμῶν καὶ ἐαν μὴ βουληθῇ ἐπακοῦσαί σου   12 αὐτῷ ın αἱ
τῶν corr N   13 ὁμ τοῖς θεοῖς ἡμῶν καὶ τῷ | καὶ αὐτὰς σφάξαι ὑπὸ τὰς
χεῖρας σου καὶ λεγον ἐν ὀνόματί σου ραφα κ μολόχ p 74* pro sec. 5 praebet
ms N textum hunc ἐγὼ παρενόχλουν τοῖς (ἰ)εβουσαίοις διὰ τὸ ἀγ τ. παρθένον ταύτην τὴν ὡραίαν εἰς ὑπερβολὴν καὶ καλὴν τὴν ὄψιν σφόδρα καὶ
εἶναι αἶνις(?) ἀγαθὴν ἐνόπιόν μου   καὶ εἶπεν πρός με· ἀθέσμιτός μου ἐστὴ,
βασιλεῦ, καὶ κοιμηθῆναι μετὰ μοῦ ἔθνη ἀλλοτριῶ   ἀλλὰ προσκύνησον τοῖς
θεοῖς τοῦ πατρός μου καὶ ἰδοὺ καὶ ἐγὼ δούλ(η) ἐνόπιόν σου   Ἐν δὲ τὸ τι-
στεῖναι μη ἐπεκαθήσαν μη δι᾽ ὕλης τῆς νυκτὸς λέγων πῶς λαλεῖς ἀγαπᾶν
με καὶ οὐκ ἀκούεις τῆς φωνῆς τῆς δούλη(ς) σου   Εἰ γοῖν βούλη προσκυνῆσαι τοῖς θεοῖς τοῦ πατρός μου, μὴ ἔστω σοι σχολιὸν τοῦτον   λάβε δὲ ἐν τῇ
χειρί σου ἀκρίδες ε̄ καὶ ἄρρας σφάξον ὅπως (f 92ᵛ) λήψεις με εἰς γυνα-
καν· καὶ ἔσομαι ἐγὼ καὶ ὁ λαός μου μετὰ σοῦ   ἐγὼ δὲ ὁ τάλας ὡς διετέ-
λος (sic) καὶ οὐδὲν ὁρμησα τῆς ἀκρίδος τὸ αἷμα καὶ σφάξας εἰς τὰς χεῖρας μου ἐν ὀνόματι μολὸχ καὶ ραφᾶ εἰπὼν καὶ ἔλαβα τὴν γυναῖκαν καὶ ἠγον
αὐτὴν εἰς τὸν οἶκον τ βασ μου

p 74*. § 6 N cum P. ἐξ οὗ . . Μολοχ καὶ ἐν τῷ εἶναι με ἐν αὐτῇ
ἠνέγγασεν ἡ γυνὴ ἐκείνη οἰκοδομῆσαι ναοὺς τοῖς βαὰλ καὶ ἦρα ἐγὼ τὸν ρα-
φὰν κ τὸν μολόχ

§ 7. N cum H. πάνη — N | αὐτὴν + καὶ ἀπέστη τὸ πνεῦμα ἀπ᾽
αὐτοῦ διὰ τὸ πορευθῆναι με ὀπίσο τῆς ἀθεμίας μου | καὶ ἐσκοτίσθη τὸ

πν μου καὶ ἐσκορπίσθην τὸ σπέρμα μου κ ἐδοθ. τῷ δούλῳ μου ἱεροβάμ
δέκα σκῆπτρα. τὰ δὲ δύο σκῆπτρα ἀπομείναντες πρός με διὰ δᾱδ τὸ πνᾱ
(l. τὸν πῤᾱ) μου· διὰ τοῦτο ἐλέησεν ὁ θεὸς καὶ τὰ δύο σκῆπτρα ἴασε τὸ
πεδίον μου τούτων σινηκαν παριθέντα (sic) μοι ὑπὸ τῶν δαιμ καὶ ἐμνήσθην
ὅτι ὅσα εἶπον ἀληθῶς εἶπον· ἔφησα γάρ μοι περὶ τούτων· ὑπὸ τ χεῖρας μου
δισάτει τελευτῆσαι καὶ ἐκλείπη ἐκ προσώπου τοῦ (ἡλίου)

§§ 8 et 9. N cum H. τοῖς ῑηλ καὶ ἀφῆλαν αὐτὴν εἰς μνημ. ὅτι προ
τελ. μου μακαριούσε με ὥστε οὖν φυλαχθῆναι τὴν διαθήκην μου πρὸς ἡμᾶς
(p. 75*) μυστ. μεγ (f. 93ᵛ) κατὰ παντό, ἀκαθάρτου πνς ὥστε γινώσκειν
ὑμᾶς | ἰσραήλ ἱποτάξε ἐπ᾽ ἐμὲ πάντα τὰ δαιμ. ὥστε εἶναι σφραγῖδα |
ταῦτα οὖν   δακτ τοῦ θεοῦ (§ 9) — N | προσετέθει πρὸς τοὺς πῤᾱς |
ἐν ἱλῆμ — N | οὗ ὑπὸ θρόνου ad finem om. N, sed add. ᾧ πρέπει τιμὴ καὶ
προσκύνησις εἰς τοὺς αἰῶνας τῶν αἰώνων ἀμήν

B. Manuscript E.

A Narrative Concerning Solomon the Prophet

E. Library of the Greek Patriarchate, Jerusalem, Sancti
Saba, No. 290, XVIII cent, paper, cm. 17×21,7; 204 ff.,
unpublished   Catalogue, vol B, p. 415

The first one hundred thirty-eight leaves of the manuscript
were written by Gerasimos, a monk from Chios in 1719 at the
μόνη τοῦ ἁγίου ἐνδόξου προφήτου Ἠλίου τοῦ Θεσβίτου (f. 48ˣ and
139ᵛ), probably, therefore, at Mar Elias near Jerusalem. The
"Narrative Concerning Solomon", however, is in a section of the
book which was written by other, and it would appear to me
somewhat older hands, although nearly every work in this latter
part of the codex is strongly marked by modern Greek forms

The "narrative", found on ff 177ᵛ—191ˣ, is in a clear strong
hand, comparatively easy to read. It is not free from errors, but
is immeasurably superior to MS N, to those of Rec C, or even
to L. It is unique in that it is not merely marked by occasional
late Greek forms, as are several of the others, but is entirely
written in Modern Greek of a style much more colloquial than
modern newspaper Greek   Aside from its relation to the *Test*,
it has some value as a sample of colloquial Greek of the XVII
or XVIII century

Its nearest relative is MS D   In other words it is not a
"testament" at all, but a story.   Certain sections read like a

paraphrase of MS D into Modern Greek. Indeed, it occasionally
uses the very phrases of D, for example in D c IV 6—9, 13 f., 16[1].
Moreover it follows the outline of MS D, beginning with the story
of David's sin, and then recounting the beginning of the building
of the Temple, the favorite slave's difficulty, the capture of Ornias, the sending of Ornias and the slave to capture the demons,
and their work upon the temple[2] All of D cc. IV—VII 3 is
repeated in E, often almost word for word[3]. From this point
on, however, E parts company with all the other accounts. It
tells how Samael was examined and replies and is set to work
in exactly the manner of the *Test*[4]. Then it goes on to narrate
how, after the Temple was finished, Solomon shut all the demons
up in vessels, how the Temple was dedicated, how later the
Chaldeans came and released the demons, and how later still
Jesus came and by the cross overcame them all, adding that this
was the symbol engraved on Solomon's ring and that anyone
who properly uses this sacred symbol may escape all their
attacks[5]

The differences between E and D go still farther than this
conclusion. The resemblance between the introductory sections
telling of Solomon's parentage is after all superficial. The account of the devil's frustration of Nathan's attempt to forestall
David's sin (D c. I 4—6) is entirely lacking in E and the account
of Nathan's parable and David's repentance is quite different[6].
When (D c. III 4) Ornias and the slave are sent to bring in the
other demons, they bring Beelzebul, who is examined as in the
Test. Here MS E uses material from the accounts of both Beelzebul and Asmodaeus, in something like this order, *Test* cc. III 6,
IV 1—3 a, V 8f. VI 4, 7f., 9 (part). Then it resumes the matter
and order of D (c. III 8)[7]

There are fewer resemblances in language between E and
the *Test* than between D and E, and yet in the account of Beelzebul the same words are often used and the likenesses are such

---

1 E, c. V 3—6, 8 ff.   2 E, c. I—IV 1, 12.   3 E, c. V—IX 4.
4 E, c. IX 7—10.   5 E, cc. X—XII.   6 E, c. I 6—9·
7 C. IV 11 ff.

as very strongly to suggest some kind of literary dependence. This is particularly true if one omits the account of Onoskelis and Asmodaeus from the *Test*, an account which breaks into the very middle of the examination of Beelzebul (cc. III 7—VI 1a). On other grounds also this appears like an interpolation, for only in . these chapters does Beelzebul figure prominently.

Just how it comes about that some traits which plainly belong to Asmodaeus are ascribed to Beelzebul it is difficult to explain. That Raphael and the gall of a fish called γλιανός belong to Asmodaeus cannot be disputed[1]. It is plain also that the writer of E is combining two accounts from the fact that in two separate places he introduces the means by which the demon is to be laid[2]. He must have known two descriptions of the chief demon and he preferred the name Beelzebul because of its use in the Gospels. MS E is more definitely Christian than any other of these documents.

We have in our manuscripts a "synoptic problem" rendered even more complicated by the discovery of E. The resemblances in phrasing and in order are too close to permit of an oral theory, but on the other hand, the differences are such as to preclude the conclusion that the *Test* was derived directly from either D or E or either of them from the other. Rather we must go back to an original "narrative", *d* which included a brief account of Solomon's parentage, the building of the Temple, the capture of Ornias, the use of demons in the building, the incident of the father and son, the gifts from foreign monarchs, the letter of the Arabian king, the capture of Ephippas, and the placing of the cornerstone and the aerial column. This *d* possibly had also some reference to Samael, for he appears in both E and D. Both the introductory account of Solomon's birth and the concluding reference to Samael where developed differently in the two editions.

E steps in to make the connection between *d* and the *Test*. In c. XVII is a nameless demon whose "work" is exactly that of Samael in E and who is frustrated in the same way, by the

---

1 E, c IV 7.   2 E, c. IV 7 and 9.

sign of the cross[1]. The demon is, moreover, "shut up ... like the other demons" (XVII 5), an idea especially prominent in E[2] As the *Test*, which was *ex hypothese* written by Solomon, could not tell of the future escape of the demons from their vessels, the writer had a demon foretell it and the power of the coming Son of the Virgin to overcome them again (XV 8—12), all of which is given in much fuller detail in E. The relations may be explained by supposing E to be based upon *e*, a manuscript derived from *d* and forming the original also from which the *Test* was developed. E, of course, represents a considerable expansion of *e*. A great deal of liberty must be allowed to editors and copyists in such literature as this This will explain changes and omissions of all kinds. The use of various sources is also to be expected. In one passage E mentions Jeremiah, Baruch, and Abimelek, and evidently depends on the *Paralipomena of Jeremiah*[3].

In the transcripton of E which follows[4] I have tried to be as faithful to the manuscript as possible, only correcting obvious errors and not trying even to introduce consistency

---

1 E, c IX 8f   2 E, c X 2.   3 E, c. XI 1f   4 See pp 102*—120*

BIBLIOGRAPHY.

I. Editions and reprints

1 Fleck, Dr. F. F,, Wissenschaftliche Reise durch das südliche Deutschland, Italien, Sicilien und Frankreich, II 3, Anecdota maximam partem sacra Leipz 1837, pp. 113—40. (= Fl) MS P only

2. Furst, J., Der Orient, 5. Jahrgang, 1844, 7. Jahrgang, 1846, Literaturblatt, Sp. 593, 663, 714, 741 Incomplete. (= Fu) Reprint of Fleck

3. Migne, Abbé J. P., Patrologia graeca, vol. 122, Paris 1864, coll. 1315—58. Reprint of Fleck. (= Mg)

4 Istrin, V M., Griečeski spiski zabesania Solomona (Greek Manuscripts of the Testament of Solomon) Odessa 1898, 50 pp [1] Printed also in the Year-book of the historical-philosophical Society at the Imperial Newrussian University (at Odessa) VII, Byzantine Division IV (Odessa 1899), pp 49—98. (Russian) Contains MSS D, I, and Q. (= Is)

II. Translations.

1 Bornemann, Dr. Friedrich August, Zeitschrift für die historische Theologie herausg. von Dr. C. F. Illgen, vol. XIV, Leipzig 1844, part 3, pp 9—56 German. (= Bn)

2 Furst, J., Der Orient 1844, 1846. Cf. *supra*, Edition 2. German Incomplete (= Futr)

3 Migne, Abbé J P, Patrologia graeca, vol 122, cf. *supra*, Edition 3 Latin. (= Mgtr)

4 Conybeare, F C "The Testament of Solomon", Jewish Quarterly Review XI (No 41), London October 1898, pp. 15—45 English (= Crtr)

5. Ginzberg, Louis, The Legends of the Jews, translated from the German manuscript by Henrietta Szold, 4 vols Philadelphia 1913, vol IV Bible Times and Characters from Joshua to Esther, pp. 150 ff.

---

1) This was very kindly sent to me by the author, whose address I owed to Prof. E. Kurz.

III. Treatises and discussions.

1. Fabricius, Johannes Albert, Codex pseudepigraphicus veteris testamenti, Hamburg 1713, I 1036 ff.
2. Bornemann, Dr. Friedrich August, "Conjectanea in Salomonis Testamentum", in Biblische Studien von Geistlichen des Konigreichs Sachsen herausg von Dr Kauffer, 2. Jahrgang, Dresden u. Leipzig 1843, pp. 43—60, 4. Jahrgang, 1846, pp 28—69 (= Bncn)
3. Migne, Abbé, Dictionaire des Apocryphes, vol. II (= Enc theol., vol, XLI), Paris 1853, pp. 839 ff
4. Conybeare, F. C, Introduction to translation 4, above II 4
5. James, M R., in the Guardian, vol. 54, pt I, No. 2780, London March 15, 1899, p 367
6. Conybeare, F. C., *ibid.*, March 29, 1899, p. 442
7. Schurer, E, Theol. Literaturzeitung, 1899, 110, review of Conybeare's translation and the introduction thereto
8. Istrin, V. M., introduction to text, above Bibliography I 4
9. Krumbacher, K , Byz Ztschr. VII (1900), p 634
10. Kurz, E., *ibid.* X, p. 238
11. Schurer, E., Geschichte des judischen Volkes, 4. Aufl , Leipzig 1909 III 419 ff. (= *JGV*) = The History of the Jewish People in the Time of Jesus Christ, New York 1891, II l. c. 153 ff. (= *HJP*)
12. Toy, C. H , Jewish Encyclopedia, New York 1907, XI 448, art. "Solomon, Testament of"
13. Kohler, K., Jewish Encyclopedia IV 518, in art "Demonology"
14. Salzberger, Georg, Die Salomosage in der semitischen Literatur ein Beitrag zur vergleichenden Sagenkunde I. Teil Salomo bis zur Hohe seines Ruhmes, Diss. Heidelberg, Berlin 1907, pp 9—12, 94—97, 99

IV. General Bibliography (including Abbreviations).

These lists include not only works referred to, but also a few others to which the writer has been especially indebted.

1 Dictionaries, encyclopedias, periodicals, and collections.

AJT = American Journal of Theology, Chicago 1897 ff.

Anecdota Oxoniensia, Classical Series, Part VIII, Oxford 1898. F C. Conybeare, The Dialogues of Athanasius and Zacchaeus and of Timothy and Aquila

Archiv fur Papyrusforschung, ed. by Ulrich Wilcken, Leipzig 1900 ff

B = Corpus Scriptorum Historiae Byzantinae, editio emendatior et copiosior consilio B. G. Niebuhrii instituta, auctoritate Academiae Litterarum Regiae Borussicae continuata, Bonnae 1828—1878

Biographie universelle, Paris 1826

BZ = Byzantinische Zeitschrift, hersg. von Karl Krumbacher, Leipzig 1892 ff.

CCAG = Catalogus codicum astrologorum graecorum, 7 vols, Bruxelles 1896—1908

CCGBA = Catalogus codicum graecorum bibliothecae Ambrosianae digesserunt Aemidius Martini et Dominicus Bassi, Mediolan. 1906

Catalogus codicum mss. bibliothecae regine, 4 vols,, Paris 1739—44

Encyclopaedia of Islam, a dictionary of the geography, the ethnography and biography of the Muhammadan peoples, ed. by M. Th. Houtsma, T. W. Arnold, R. Basset and R Hartmann, vol. I A—D, Leyden-London 1913

ERE = Encyclopedia of Religion and Ethics, ed. by James Hastings, Edinburgh 1908, 8 vols. up to 1916

ExT = The Expository Times, ed. by James Hastings, Edinburgh 1889ff.

Folklore, a quarterly Review of myth, tradition, institution and custom London 1890ff

Griechische Urkunden aus dem Berliner Museum, hersg. von Wilcken, Krebs und Viereck, Berlin 1892ff.

HDB = Dictionary of the Bible, ed. by James Hastings, 5 vols., Edinburgh 1898—1904

Jahrbucher fur klassische Philologie, ed by Alfred Fleckeisen, 43 vols, Leipzig 1855—97

JAS = Journal of the Royal Asiatic Society, London 1834ff

JE = The Jewish Encyclopedia, ed Isidore Singer, 12 vols., New York 1907—

JQR = Jewish Quarterly Review, First Series, ed. by L. Abrahams and C J. Montefiore, 50 vols., London 1888—1908

KVCom = Die griechischen christlichen Schriftsteller der ersten drei Jahrhunderte hersg v. der Kirchenväter-Commission der konigl Preußischen Ak. der Wissenschaften, Leipzig 1897ff

Migne, J. P, *PG* = Patrologiae cursus completus, Series Graeca, Paris 1857—65

Migne, J P, *PL* = Patrologiae cursus completus, Series Latina, Paris 1844—90

NGG = Nachrichten der konigl Gesellschaft der Wissenschaften zu Gottingen, Berlin 1860ff

N Jbb kl Alt = Neue Jahrbucher fur das klassische Altertum, Leipzig 1898ff.

Nouvelle Biographie universelle, Paris 1866

Der Orient, ed by J. Furst 1840ff.

Orientalische Studien Th Noldeke gewidmet, ed Carl Bezold, Gießen 1906

P = Corpus byzantinae historiae, ed Labbaeus, 43 parts, Paris 1648—1711, 1819

Palestine Pilgrims' Text Society, vol. I, Itinerary from Bordeaux to Jerusalem, Bordeaux Pilgrim, trans by A Stewart, London 1896

Palestine Pilgrims' Text Society, vol, I, The Pilgrimage of S. Silvia of Aquitania to the Holy Places, tr by John H. Bernard, London 1896

Pauly-Wissowa = Paulys Realencyclopadie der class. Altertumswissenschaft, hersg. von G Wissowa, Stuttgart 1894ff.

PSBA = Proceedings of the Society of Biblical Archaeology, London 1879ff.

Realenc. = Herzog-Hauck, Realencyclopädie fur protestantische Theologie u. Kirche, 24 vols., Leipzig 1896—1913

Religionsgeschichtliche Versuche u. Vorarbeiten, hersg. v A Dieterich u. R. Wunsch, Gießen 1903ff

Revue des études grecs, Paris 1888 ff.

Rh Mus = Rheinisches Museum, Leipzig 1833 ff.

SBE = Sacred Books of the East, ed. by F Max Muller, 50 vols. 1879—1894

Sophocles, E. A, A Greek dictionary of the Roman and Byzantine periods[3], Boston 1888

Studia Biblica et Ecclesiastica, Essays chiefly in biblical and patristic criticism by members of the University of Oxford, Oxford 1885 ff.

Studi Italiani di filolog classica, Firenze-Roma 1893 ff

TL = Theologische Literaturzeitung, Leipzig 1876 ff.

Thuanus, Catalog bibliothecae Thuanae a Petro et Jac Puteanis etc, Paris 1679

TS = Texts and Studies, ed. by J. Armitage Robinson, Cambridge 1893 ff.

TU = Texte u Untersuchungen, ed. by Adolf Harnack, Leipzig 1883 ff.

V = Bibliotheca Veterum Patrum Antiquorumque Scriptorum Eccl. ed. A. Gallandius, 14 vols and app., Venice 1765— 81, 2 ed. 1788

Vienna Corpus = Corpus scriptorum ecclesiasticorum Latinorum, Vindobon. 1866 ff.

ZA = Zeitschrift fur Assyriologie, ed. by Carl Bezold, Straßburg 1886 ff

ZATW = Zeitschrift fur die alttestamentliche Wissenschaft, ed. by D. Bernhard Stade, Gießen 1881 ff.

ZDMG = Zeitschrift der deutschen morgenlandischen Gesellschaft, Leipzig 1847 ff

ZNTW = Zeitschrift fur die neutestamentliche Wissenschaft, ed. by E Preuschen Gießen 1900 ff.

2. Modern Authors

Atkinson, James, see Sháh Námeh

Bardenhewer, Otto, Patrologie[3], Freiburg im Breisgau 1910

Benfey, Theodor, Pañtschatantra funf Bucher indischer Fabeln, etc, 1859

Benzinger, I., Die Bucher der Konige, Kurzer Handcommentar zum Alten Test. hersg. v D Karl Marti, IX Freiburg i B. 1899

Berthelot, M., and Ruelle, C E., Collection des anciens alchimistes grecs 2 vols, Paris 1887—88

Blaß, Fr., Grammatik des nt. Griechisch[2], Gottingen 1902, the same, 3 ed.

Blaß, Fr, Hermeneutik u. Kritik, Paläographie, Buchwesen u. Handschriftenkunde, in einleitenden u. Hilfsdisziplinen, vol. I of Muller's Handbuch de kl. Altertumswissenschaft

Blau, Ludwig, Das altjudische Zauberwesen (Jahresbericht der Landes-Rabbinerschule in Budapest, 1897—98). Budapest 1898

Boll, Franz, Sphaera neue griechische Texte u. Untersuchungen zur Geschicht der Sternbilder, Leipzig 1903

Bonwetsch, G. Nathanael, Die Apocalypse Abrahams, Das Testament der vierzi[Martyrer, Leipzig 1897, in Studien zur Geschichte der Theol u. der Kirche hersg. von N Bonwetsch u. R. Seeberg

Bonwetsch, G Nathanael, Hippolytus, *KVCom I*, Leipzig 1897

Bonwetsch, G Nathanael, Hippolyts Kom. z. Hohelied auf Grund von N. Marr Ausgabe des grusinischen Textes = *TU* XXIII (NF VIII) 2

Bouché Leclerq, A., L'Astrologie grecque, Paris 1899

Bousset, Wilhelm, Hauptprobleme der Gnosis,Gottingen 1907

Bousset, Wilhelm, Die Religion des Judentums im neutestamentlichen Zeitalter², Berlin 1906

Breasted, James Henry, *RTAE* = Development of Religion and Thought in Ancient Egypt, Morse Lectures, New York 1912

Budge, E. A. Wallis, The Gods of the Egyptians or Studies in Egyptian mythology, 2 vols , Chicago 1904

Burton, Richard F., A Plain and Literal Translation of the Arabian Nights' Entertainment, now entitled The book of the Thousand Nights and a Night, with introduction, explanatory notes on the manners and customs ot Moslem men and a terminal essay upon the history of the Nights. Printed by the Burton Club for private subscribers only, Bagdad ed. limited to one thousand numbered sets of which this is number 410, [1885—87]

Canaan, T., Dr. med., Aberglaube u. Volksmedicin im Lande der Bibel, Hamburg, 1914, in Abh. des Hamb Kolonialinstituts, Bd XX, Reihe B Volkerkunde, Kulturgesch. u Sprachen, Band 12

Chachanov, A. S., Očerki po Istorii Gruzinskoi Slovesnosti, Mosco 1895

Charles, R. H., The Book of Enoch, transl. from Professor Dillmann's Ethiopic Text, etc , Oxford 1893

' Charles R. H., *APOT* = The Apocrypha and Pseudepigrapha of the Old Testament, etc. 2 vols., Oxford 1913

Clemen, Carl, Religionsgeschichtliche Erklarung des Neuen Testaments die Abhangigkeit des altesten Christentums von nichtjudischen Religionen u. philosophischen Systemen, Gießen 1909 = Primitive Christanity and its Non-Jewish Sources, transl. by Robert G. Nisbet, Edinburgh 1912

Conway, Moncure Daniel, Solomon and Solomonic Literature, London-Chicago 1899

Conybeare, Frederic C., cf. Dial Tim. and Aquila, in Anecdota Oxon.

Conybeare, Frederic C., "The Testament of Solomon", JQR XI (1898) 1—45

Cumont, Frank, The Oriental Religions in Roman Paganism, Chicago 1911

Cumont, Frank, Astrology and Religion among the Greeks and Romans, New York and London 1912

Deißmann, Adolf, Bible Studies, Edinburgh 1901

Deißmann, Adolf, *Licht* vom Osten, Tubingen 1908 = *LAE* = Light from the Ancient East, New York and London 1910

Delisle, Leop , Le cabinet des msc de la bibliothèque imperiale, Paris 1868

Dibelius, Martin, Die Geisterwelt im Glauben des Paulus, Gottingen 1909

Dieterich, Albrecht, Abraxas Studien zur Religionsgeschichte des spatern Altertums, Leipzig 1891

Dieterich, Albrecht, *Leid Pap* = Papyrus Magica Musei Lugdunensis Batavi quam C. Leemans edidit, etc , in Fleckeisen's Jahrbucher, Suppl XVI, Leipzig 1887, pp 747—829

Dieterich, Karl, *Unters* = Untersuchungen zur Geschichte der griechischen Sprache von der hellenistischen Zeit bis zum 10. Jahrh. n Chr , Byzantinisches Archiv als Eiganzung der Byzantinischen Zeitschrift, Heft 1, Leipzig 1898

Du Cange, Carolo du Fresne, Glossarium ad scriptores mediae et infimae Grae-
    citatis, etc , Lugduni 1688, effigies recens, Vratislaviae 1891, 2 vols. in one
Eisenmenger, Entdecktes Judentum, 2 vols , Konigsberg 1711
Erman, Adolf, Die agyptische Religion, Handbucher der konigl Museen zu
    Berlin, Berlin 1905 = A Handbook of Egyptian Religion, London 1907
Fabricius, Ioh Alb., Bibliotheca Graeca, etc., 12 vols , Hamburg 1790—1809
Fabricius, Ioh. Alb , Codex pseudepigraphicus vet test. (Bibl III 1)
Faerber, R , König Salomo in der Tradition ein hist.-krit. Beitrag zur Geschichte
    der Haggada, der Tanaiten u Amoraer, Teil I. Diss. Straßburg, Vienna 1902
Farnell, Lewis Richard, Greece and Babylonia, a comparative sketch of Meso-
    potamian, Anatolian, and Hellenic religions, Edinburgh 1911
Gannurini, Iob F , S. Hilarii tractatus de mysteriis et hymni et S. Silviae Aqui-
    tanae perigrinatio ad loca sancta, Petri diaconi liber de locis sanctis, Romae
    1887
Gardthausen, Viktor Emil, Griechische Palaeographie[2], 2 vols., Leipzig 1911
    —13
Gaster, M., Sword of Moses, London 1896, printed separately and in Journal of
    the Royal Asiatic Society, January, 1896, pp 144—198, April, pp I—XXXV
Gelzer, Heinrich, Sextus Julius Africanus u die byzantinische Chronographie,
    Leipzig 1880—85
Gerhard, G A , Untersuchungen zur Gesch des griechischen Briefes, I Heft,
    Die Anfangsformel, Inaugural-Diss. Heidelberg, Tubingen 1903, also in Philo-
    logus LXIV (NF XV) 1905
Ginzberg, Louis, Legends of the Jews, trans from the German manuscript by
    Henrietta Szold, 4 vols., Philadelphia 1909—13
Gitlbauer, M., Studien zur griechischen Tachygraphie, Berlin 1903
Giltbauer, M., Die Überreste griechischer Tachygraphie in Codex Vat. Graec
    1809, in Denkschr. der kaiserl Ak der Wissenschaften, Philos.-hist Cl ,
    I Fasc vol XXVIII Vienna 1878, 2 Abt 1—110, Plates I—XIV, 2 Fasc.
    Vienna 1884, 2 Abt. 1—48, Plates I—XXVIII. Also published separately
Goldschmidt, Lazarus, B Tal = Der babylonische Talmud, etc ; (Heb & Ger-
    man) Berlin 1897
Grunbaum, Max, Beitrage zur semitischen Sagenkunde, in *ZDMG XXXI*
Grunbaum, Max, Neue Beitrage zur semitischen Sagenkunde, Leiden 1893
Gruppe, Otto Friedrich, Griechische Mythologie u. Religionsgeschichte, Munchen
    1906, in Muller's Handbuch der kl Altertumswissenschaft V 2
Gutschmid, Hermann Alfred, Freiherr von, Kleine Schriften hersg v Franz Ruhl,
    5 vols., Leipzig 1889—1894
Hardt, J , Catalogus codicum mss bibliothecae regiae Bavariae, 5 vols , Monac.
    1806—12
Harnack, Adolf, Geschichte der Altchristlichen Litteratur bis Eusebius, 2 vols.,
    Leipzig 1893
Harnack, Adolf, The Mission and Expansion of Christianity in the First Three
    Centuries[2], 2 vols , New York 1908
Harrison, Jane Ellen, Prolegomena to the Study of Greek Religion[2], Cam-
    bridge 1908

Heitmuller, Wilhelm, Im Namen Jesu, eine sprach- u. religionsgeschichtliche Untersuchung zum Neuen Testament, speziell zur altchristlichen Taufe, Gottingen 1903

Hemsterhuis, Thomas Magister, Ludg. Bat. 1757

Hercher, Rudolf, Epistolographi Graeci, Paris 1873

Horst, G C., Zauberbibliothek, 6 vols, Mainz 1821—26

Hughes, H. Maldewyn, Ethics of Jewish Apocryphal Literature, London n. d.

James, Montague Rhodes, The Testament of Abraham, TS II 2

James, Montague Rhodes, Apocrypha Anecdota, TS II 3

Jannaris, A. N., Historical Greek Grammar, etc., London 1897

Jastrow, M., Jr., Die Religion Babyloniens u Assyriens, 2 vols in 3, Gießen 1905, 1912, sometimes referred to as German edition of The Religion of Babylonia and Assyria, Boston 1898

Kautzsch, E., Die Heilige Schrift des Alten Testaments, 2 vols., Tubingen 1909—10

Kautzsch, E., APAT = Die Apocryphen u. Pseudepigraphen des Alten Testaments, 2 vols., Tubingen 1900

Kemble, J M., The Anglo-Saxon Dialogue of Salomon and Saturn, London 1848

Kenyon, F. G., GrPBMus = Greek Papyri in the British Museum 5 vols., London 1893—1917

King, Charles William, The Gnostics and their Remains, Ancient and Mediaeval, London 1864

Krumbacher, Karl, BLg = Geschichte der Byzantinischen Literatur, von Justinian bis zum Ende des ostromischen Reiches², Munchen 1897, in Muller's Handbuch der kl. Altertumswissenschaft IX, 1

Krumbacher, Karl, Studien zur Legende des heil. Theodosius, in Sitzungsber. d. bay Akad d Wiss., Philos, philol u hist. Cl., 1892, Heft 2, p. 225ff

Lambros, Spyr. C., Catalogue of the Greek Manuscripts on Mount Athos, 2 vols., Cambridge 1895, 1900

Lane-Poole, The Thousand and One Nights . . transl. by Edward William Lane, ed. by Stanley Lane-Poole, 1859

Letronne, M, Sur l'origine du zodiaque grec, etc, Paris 1840

Levy-Fleischer, Levy, Jacob, and Fleischer, Heinrich Leberecht, Neuhebraisches u. Chaldaisches Worterbuch uber d Talmudim u Midraschim, Leipzig 1876—89

Maichell, D, Introductio ad hist. liter de praecip bibliothecis Parisiensibus, 2 vols, Cantab. 1721

Mathers, S. L. M., The Key of Solomon the King, trans and ed., London 1889

Meyer, Isaak, Qabbalah The philosophic writings of Solomon ben Yehuda ibn Gebirol, etc., Philadelphia 1888

Mills, Lawrence H, Zaraθustra, Philo, the Achaemenids and Israel, Chicago 1906

Montfaucon, Bernard de, Bibliotheca bibliothecarum mss. nov., 2 vols., Paris 1739

Montgomery, James A, AITN = Aramaic Incantation Texts from Nippur, University of Pennsylvania, The Museum, Publications of the Babylonian Section III, Philadelphia 1913

Moulton, James Hope, Early Religious Poetry of Persia, Cambridge 1911

Moulton, James Hope, Early Zoroastrianism, Hibbert Lectures 1912, London 1913

Moulton, James Hope, *Proleg* = A Grammar of New Testament Greek, Vol I Prolegomena, Edinburgh 1906

Naber, Samuel Adrian, Flavii Iosephi opera omnia post Im Bekkerum recogn, 6 vols, Leipzig 1888—1896

Olivieri, "Indice dei codici greci delle bibliotheche Universitaria e Communale di Bologna", in Studi Ital. di filol. class. III 1895

Omont, Henri, Inventaire sommaire des msc. grecs de la bibliothèque nationale, 4 vols, Paris 1886—98

Perles, Felix, Bousset's Religion des Judentums im nt. Zeitalter kritisch untersucht, Berlin 1903

Pitra, Johannes Baptista Cardinalis, Analecta sacra et classica spicilegio solesmensi, 5 vols., Parisiis 1876—82

Pradel, Fritz, Griechische u süditalienische Gebete, Beschworungen u. Rezepte des Mittelalters, in "Rel.-gesch Versuche u Vorarbeiten" III 1907, 253—403, also separately paged

Reitzenstein, R., Poimandres, Studien zur griechisch-ägyptischen u. fruhchristlichen Literatur, Leipzig 1904

Rogers, Robert William, The Religion of Babylonia and Assyria especially in its relation to Israel, New York-Cincinnati 1908

Roscher, W. H., *Lexicon* = Ausfuhrliches Lexikon der griech. u. rom. Mythologie, 3 vols in 6, Leipzig 1884—1900

Sachau, Karl Eduard, Verzeichnis der syr Haudschriften der konigl. Bibliothek zu Berlin, Berlin 1899

St Claire-Tisdall, W., Sources of Islam, A Persian treatise, translated and abridged by Sir William Muir, Edinburgh 1901

Sale, George, The Koran, commonly called the Alkoran of Mohammed, translated into English from the original Arabic, with explanatory notes taken from the most approved commentators, to which is prefixed a preliminary discourse, London n. d.

Salzberger, Georg, Die Salomosage in der semitischen Literatur Ein Beitrag zur vergleichenden Sagenkunde, I Teil Salomo bis zur Hohe seines Ruhmes, Diss. Heidelberg, Berlin 1907

Sayce, A H, Hibbert Lectures 1887, Lectures on the Origin and growth of Religion as illustrated by the religion of the ancient Babylonians⁴, London 1897

Scheibel, J, Das Kloster, etc., 12 vols., Stuttgart 1845—49

Schlumberger, G., Sillographie de l'empire byzantine, Paris 1884

Schmidt, Carl, Gnostische Schriften in koptischer Sprache aus dem codex Brucianus hersg, etc, in *TU* VIII (1892) Heft 1/2

Schmidt, Carl, Koptisch-Gnostische Schriften, I. Band, *KVCom* XIII, Leipzig 1905

Schurer, Emil, *GJV* = Geschichte des judischen Volkes im Zeitalter Jesu Christi, 3 vols, Leipzig 1901—11 = *HJP* = A history of the Jewish People in the Time of Jesus Christ, 2nd and rev. ed, 5 vols., New York 1891

Schwab, Moyse, *Voc. Ang.* — Vocabulaire de l'angelologie d'après les mss. hebreux de la Bib. Nat., extrait des mémoires présentés par divers savants à l'Académie des inscriptions et belles-lettres, 1ère Série, tome X, 2e partie, Paris 1897

Smith, William and Wace, Henry, *DCB* = Dictionary of Christian Biography, Literature, Sects and Doctrines, etc, 4 vols, Boston 1887—1897

Stade, Bernhard and Schwally, Friedrich, The book of Kings. critical ed. of the Hebrew text printed in colors, etc., Leipzig 1904, in "The sacred books of the Old Testament", ed by Paul Haupt, Part 9

Steinschneider, Moritz, Die hebraischen Übersetzungen des Mittelalters u. die Juden als Dolmetscher, Berlin 1893

Steuernagel, Carl, Lehrbuch der Einleitung in das Alte Testament, etc., Tubingen 1912

Streane, A. W, חגיגה, a Translation of the treatise Chagigah from the Babylonian Talmud, Cambridge 1891

Surenhusius, G, Mishna sive totius Hebraeorum juris, ritum, etc., 6 vols. in 3, Amstel. 1698—1703

Tamborñino, Julius, De antiquorum daemonismo, in "Relig-gesch. Versuche u. Vorarb." 1908—09, Heft 3

Thompson, R. Campbell, The Devils and Evil Spirits of Babylonia, etc., 2 vols., London 1903—04 (Luzac's "Semitic Text and Translation Series" XIV and XV)

Thompson, R Campbell, Semitic Magic its origins and development, London 1908

Thumb, A., Die griechische Sprache im Zeitalter des Hellenismus, Straßburg 1901

Thumb, A., Handbuch der neugr. Volkssprache², Straßburg 1910

Vasiljev, Alex., Anecdota Graeco-Byzantina, ed. by S A Sokolovsky, 1893

Vogt, Fr., Die deutschen Dichtungen von Salomon u. Markolf, Halle 1880

Walters, H B., Catalogue of the Bronzes in the British Museum, London 1899

Wardrop, Margery, "Life of St. Nino", in Studia Biblica V 1908

Weber, Otto, Damonenbeschworungen bei den Babyloniern u. Assyrern, in "Der Alte Orient", VII 4, Leipzig 1906

Weil, G, The Bible, the Koran, and the Talmud, or Biblical Legends of the Mussulmans, compiled from Arabic sources, and compared with Jewish traditions, transl from the German, London 1846

Wellhausen, J, Reste arabischen Heidentums gesammelt u erlautert², Berlin 1897

Wendland, Paul, Die Hellenistisch-romische Kultur in ihrer Beziehung zu Judentum u. Christentum, Tubingen 1907, in Handbuch zum Neuen Testament I 2

Wessely, Carl, Ephesia grammata, Jahresber. des Franz-Joseph-Gymnasiums in Wien 1886

Wessely, Carl, Griechische Zauberpapyri von Paris u. London, in Denkschriften der kaiserl. Ak der Wissenschaften, philos-hist. Classe, vol XXXVI Part 2, Wien, 1888, pp. 27—208

Wessely, Carl, Neue griechische Zauberpapyri, in Denkschriften der kaiserl. Ak.
    d. Wiss., philos.-hist. Cl., vol. XLII, Part II, Wien 1894
Wiedemann, K. Alfred, Magie u. Zauberei im alten Agypten, in "Der alte
    Orient" VI 4, Leipzig 1905
Wunsch, R., Antike Fluchtafeln, in Lietzmann's "Kleine Texte fur theologische
    Vorlesungen u. Übungen", 20, Bonn 1907
Wunsch, R, Sethianische Verfluchungstafeln aus Rom, Leipzig 1898
Ziemann, F., De epistularum graecarum formulis sollemnibus (Diss. phil. Ha-
    lenses XVIII), 1911
Zimmern, Heinrich, Babylonische Hymnen u. Gebete in Auswahl, in 'Der alte
    Orient" VII 3, Leipzig 1905

ΔΙΑΘΗΚΗ ΣΟΛΟΜΩΝΤΟΣ

TEXTS

WITH

CRITICAL APPARATUS

Sigla et compendia in apparatu critico et in textu adhibita

Uncis rotundis ( ) circumduxi vocabula vel litteras, quae in codice compendio
scripta sunt, velut ($\hbar\mu\dot{\epsilon}\varrho\alpha$) = ð.

Uncis rotundis ( ) in apparatu critico circumdedi numeros sectionum interpreta-
tionis a Conybeare scriptae.

Uncis fractis ⟨ ⟩ circumdedi ea quae in codice perierunt vel a scriptore omissa sunt

Uncum fractum < post vocabulum posui cuius terminatio a scribente omissa est

His signis ⌐¬ inclusi lectiones in suspicionem vocatas, ubicumque errorem primarium vel interpolationem praesuppono.

Asteriscu * in textu apparatuque insignivi manuscriptorum editionumque initium
et paginarum numeros

+ vel add. = addit, addunt	i. q. = idem quod
— vel om. = omittit, omittunt	l. = lege(ndum) vel linea
cf. = confere(ndum)	leg. = legit, -unt
cod(d). = codex, codices	MS (ms) = codex manuscriptus
conj. = conjicit, -unt (quidam scriptores recentiores)	MSS (mss.) = codices manuscripti
	n. = nota
cor(r) = corrigit, -unt	pr. = praemittit, -unt
ego = proponit editor	rec. = recensio
exp = explicit, -unt	s., ss. = sequens, sequentes
f., ff. = folium, folia	tr. = transpone(ndum), -it, -unt
inc. = incipit, -iunt	v = vide(ntur)
ins = insere, -it	

A = Rec A, i. q., MSS HIL	I = Bib Nat., Suppl. grec cod. 500, cf. supra p 12
B = Rec. B, i. q., MSS PQ(N)	
C = Rec. C, i q., MSS STUVW	L = Harl. cod. 5596, cf. supra p. 13
Cᵒ = narratio altera de Onoskelu ex rec C	N = Monasterii Sancti Saba (Hierosol.) cod. 422, cf. App. infra p. 112
D = Dionysii monasterii (Athos) cod. 132, cf. supra p. 10	P = Bib. Nat., Anc fonds grec, cod. 38, cf. supra p. 15
E = Monasterii Sancti Saba (Hierosol) cod. 290, cf. App. infra p. 125	Q = Andreae monasterii cod. 73, cf supra p 18
H = Holkham Hall, cod. 99, cf. p. 11	S = Vind. Phil -graec. cod. 108, cf. p. 18

1 **

T = Harl. cod. 5596 fragmenta, cf. p 18

U = Bib. Ambros. cod. 1030, cf. p. 20

V = Bib. Bonon. Acad. cod. 3632, cf. p 21

W = Bib. Nat., Anc. fonds grec, cod. 2419, cf. p. 25

c = corrector

d = de li daemonis, C^d, cf. supra p. 19

o = narratio alt. de Onoskelu, C^o, cf. p. 19

r = phylacterium, H^r, L^r, C^r, cf. pp. 19, 25, et n. 1

s = descriptio altera de XII signis, cf. p. 23 et n. 1

Bn = Bornemann, versio, cf Bibliographiam

Bncn = Bornemann, "Conjectanea"

Cr = Conybeare

Fl = Fleck

Fu = Furst

Is = Istrin

Mg = Migne

tr = versio, velut Mgtr = versio in Migne, *Patrologia graeca*, vol. 122

ΔΙΑΘΗΚΗ ΣΟΛΟΜΩΝΤΟΣ

HIPQ Εὐλογητὸς εἶ, κύριε ὁ θεός, ὁ δοὺς τῷ Σολομῶντι τὴν
ἐξουσίαν ταύτην· σοὶ δόξα καὶ κράτος εἰς τοὺς αἰῶνας· ἀμήν

PQ I. Καὶ ἰδοὺ οἰκοδομουμένου τοῦ ναοῦ πόλεως Ἱερουσαλὴμ

5 HI I Καὶ ἰδοὺ ἀνοικοδομουμένης τῆς Ἱερουσαλὴμ καὶ ἐργαζομένων τῶν τεχνιτῶν, ἓν παιδίον ἔχων προθυμίαν μεγίστην ἐπὶ τὴν
τοῦ ναοῦ οἰκοδομήν, ὃς ἐποίει τοὺς τεχνίτας προθυμοτέρους πρὸς ἐρ-

L I. Βουλόμενος ὁ Σολομῶν υἱὸς Δαυεὶδ ἀνακτίσαι καὶ οἰκοδομῆσαι τὴν Σιών, κελεύσας κατὰ τόπον καὶ κατὰ χώραν τοῦ συναχ-
10 θῆναι τεχνίτας ἄνδρας τοῦ ἐργάζεσθαι εἰς τὸν ναὸν τοῦ θεοῦ, μέσον
δὲ τῶν τεχνιτῶν ἦτον ἕνας νέος πολλὰ ἄξιος καὶ πολλὴν προθυμίαν
ἔχων κατὰ τῆς οἰκοδομῆς τοῦ θείου ναοῦ· διὸ καὶ ἀπὸ τοῦ βασιλέως

VW I. Ἐργαζομένων δὲ τῶν τεχνιτῶν εἰς τὴν τοῦ ναοῦ οἰκοδομὴν ἦν τις ἐκεῖσε παῖς νέος ἄλκιμος σφόδρα καὶ ἀρχιτεχνίτης, ὃν
15 ἠγάπα ὁ βασιλεὺς πάνυ διὰ τὸ εἶναι αὐτὸν φρένιμον καὶ ἐπιεική.

Titulum primarium eruere non possum v. conspectum titulorum codd. mss
infra, pp. 98* s Benedictionem vel doxologiam scr. mss HIPQ, app crit. v
infra, p 99*.

Parallela ad c. I cf. infra in ms. D II 1—18.

MSS PQ — Rec. B c. 1, l. 4 inc. ms. P in f. 1ʳ, Fl p 113, Mg col. 1316,
ms. Q in f. 11¹, Is p. 29. (2) ⟨Κ⟩αὶ Is (Q) | οἰκονομουμένου P | Ἰεροσολύ-
μων P, Ἰεροσολὴμ Q

MSS HI — Rec A c. I, l. 5 inc ms. H in f. 1¹, ms I in f. 78ʳ   6 ἦν
γὰρ παιδίον ἓν ἔχων H | ἔχον Is (p 29 n. 1) | ἐπὶ τὴν οἰκ. τ. ναοῦ H |
ῖ ὃς . . ἐργασίαν I, καὶ ἦν διάγων ὥστε ποιοῦν τ. τεχ πρὸς τὴν ἐργ.
προθύμως H

MS L c I, l 8 inc. ms L in f. 8¹ col. 1

MSS VW — Rec C c. 1, l. 18 inc. hae lineae ms V in f. 436ᵛ, ms W in
f. 266ᵛ fin. initium mss. VW v. infra, Rec. C, p 76⁺   14 ἦν δέ τις V
15 ἀγαπᾶ V | ἐπιεική V, ἐπιοικὴν W

PQ καὶ ἐργαζομένων τῶν τεχνιτῶν ἐν αὐτῷ, 2. ἤρχετο ὁ Ὀρνίας τὸ
δαιμονικὸν κατὰ ἡλίου δυσμὰς καὶ * ἐλάμβανε τὸ ἥμισυ τοῦ μισθοῦ

HI γασίαν, καὶ οἱ ἀκούοντες ἔχαιρον πάντες ἐπὶ τῇ τοῦ παιδὸς
προθυμίᾳ. ἦν δὲ ἀγαπώμενος ἄγαν παρ᾽ ἐμοῦ Σολομῶντος, καὶ
5 ἐλάμβανε παρὰ πάντας τοὺς τεχνίτας διπλοῦν τὸν μισθὸν καὶ
τὰ σιτίδια διπλᾶ· καὶ ἐπέμενον χαίρων καὶ εὐφραινόμενος ἐγὼ
Σολομῶν καὶ εὐλογῶν τὸν θεὸν ἐπὶ τῇ τοῦ ναοῦ οἰκοδομῇ.

2 Φθονήσαντος δὲ τοῦ δαίμονος ἐπὶ τὴν τοῦ παιδὸς προθυμίαν, ἤρχετο καθ᾽ ἑκάστην ἡμέραν ὁ δαίμων καὶ * ἐλάμβανε
10 τὸ ἥμισυ κτλ.

L πολλὰ ἦν ἀγαπώμενος, καὶ τὰ σιτία καὶ τὸν μισθὸν διπλοῦν
ἐλάμβανεν ὑπὲρ πάντας τοὺς τεχνίτας· καὶ ἔχαιρεν ὁ βασιλεὺς
ἐπὶ τὴν τοῦ παιδὸς προθυμίαν.
2. Φθονηθεὶς δὲ ὁ νεώτερος ὑπὸ τοῦ δαίμονος, ἤρχετο ἀόρατος

15 VW ἔπεμπε δὲ αὐτὸν ἀπὸ τῆς τραπέζης αὐτοῦ βρώματα καθ᾽
ἑκάστην ὁ * βασιλεὺς καί ἐν τῷ δείπνῳ ἀπεδίδου αὐτὸν τὸν
μισθὸν ἐπὶ τὸ διπλάσιον.
2. Τοῦτο δὲ τὸ παιδάριον περὶ ἡλίου δυσμὰς ἐπιέζετο ὑπὸ χαλε-
ποῦ δαίμονος Ὀρνίου λεγομένου. ἐλάμβανε δὲ τὸ τοιοῦτον δαιμόνιον

MSS PQ = Rec. B. 1 τεχνιτῶν ἐν αὐτῷ Q· τεχν, ἐν αὐτοὺς P, τεχ. ἐν
αὐτοῖ, Fl, τεχ, ἐν αὐτοῖς BnMgtr | § 2. ἤρχετο ego ἔρχεται (Fl) in ἤρχεται
cor. P°, (ἔ)ρχετο Is(Q) 2 δαιμονικὸν B: in δαιμόνιον corr. P°Fl | δυσμᾶς Q,
pr τας P, δεσμὰς (δυσμὰς) Fl
*MSS HIPQ = Recc. AB. 2 τ. μισθοῦ — λ

MSS III = Rec A. 3 οἱ . . . προθυμίᾳ I· τοὺς ἀκούοντας ὥστε χαίρειν
πάντας ἐπὶ τὴν τ. π. προθυμίαν H 4 δὲ καὶ I | ἠγαπιμένος H | ἄγαν I
λίαν H | παρ᾽ ἐμοῦ I. ὑπὸ τοῦ H 5 διπλὸν I 6 σιτίδια conj Diels:
σιτείδια I, σιτήδια Is, στατίδια Fl | ἐπέμενον ego· ἐπέμενεν H, ἤμουν I |
καὶ . . Σολ. H 7 τὴν τ. ν οἰκοδομὴν H
§ 2. 8 ἐπὶ — H 9 ἡμέραν ὁ δαιμ. — H | * cf textum rec B, l 2
10 post ἥμισυ textus recensionis A cum rec B includitui

MS L 11 πολλὰ ἦν ego πολλὴν ms 12 ἔχαιρον ms

MSS VW = Rec. C. 15. 16 αὐτὸν mss | αὐτῷ 16 * W f. 267¹
§ 2. 19 δαίμονος δαιμονίου V | Ὀρν. λεγ. ὀνόματι Ὀρνίου V

HIPQ ⌐τοῦ πρωτομαΐστορος παιδαρίου ὄντος⌐ καὶ τὰ ἥμισυ σιτία. ⸉
καὶ ἐθήλαζε τὸν ἀντίχειρον τῆς δεξιᾶς αὐτοῦ χειρὸς * ἐφ᾽ ἑκάστην ἡμέραν. καὶ ἐλεπτύνετο τὸ παιδίον ὅπερ ἦν ἀγαπώμενον
ὑπ᾽ ἐμοῦ σφόδρα.

5 L καὶ ἐλάμβανε τὸ ἥμισυ τῶν μισθῶν τοῦ παιδὸς ὅτι ἄρα ἐπι-
δίδοντο αὐτῷ καθ᾽ ἑκάστην ἑσπέραν. μετὰ τὸ ἀποδιδόναι καὶ
ἀφεθῆναι τοῦ ἔργου ἤρχετον τὸ πονηρὸν πνεῦμα καὶ [ἠλάλαζε·
εἶτα λέγει ὁ ἀναγινώσκων ἐκ τρίτου μεγαλόφωνος ἐπάνω τοῦ *
ὀχλουμένου· εἶτα] ἐλάμβανε τὸν τοῦ παιδὸς δεξιᾶς χειρὸς δάκτυ-
10 λον καὶ ἐβύζανεν αὐτόν. *

VW τὸ ἥμισυ μέρος τοῦ μισθοῦ αὐτοῦ ὃν ἐλάμβανε παρὰ τοῦ
βασιλέως καθεμίαν ἡμέραν. καὶ οὐ μόνον τοῦτο ἐποίει ἀλλ᾽ ἔτεμε
καὶ τὸν δάκτυλον τῆς δεξιᾶς αὐτοῦ χειρὸς καὶ ἐξεθήλαζε τὸν
ἀντίχειρον τοσοῦτον ὥστε τὸ παιδάριον ἀσθενεῖν καθ᾽ ἑκάστην
15 ἡμέραν καὶ λεπτύνεσθαι.

MSS HIPQ ‒ Recc AB   1 τοῦ . ὄντος om A, 1 fortasse ἑνὸς τῶν
παιδαρίων μου, cf. D II 2 | πρωτομαΐστόρου Q | παιδαρίου ὄντος Q, conj.
Bn· παιδαρίου, οὕτως P | ⸲. τὰ ἥμ. σιτ. B: τῶν σιτείων αὐτοῦ I. τοῦ σιτείου
αὐτοῦ H | * H f. 1ᵛ 2 τ. ἀντίχειρα . . χειρὸς ἐθήλαζεν B | ἐθήλαζεν
ἐν I per geminationem | * I f 78ᵛ | ἐφ᾽ HQ: ἀφ᾽ P | ἐφ᾽ ἑκάστην ἡμέ-
ραν H: ‒ I, ἐφ᾽ ἑκάστης ἡμέρας PQ   3 παιδίον A παιδάριον B | ὅπερ
. αὐτῷ (§ 3, p. 8*, 1 2)· ‒ Q   4 ὑπ᾽ (ὑπὲρ H) ἐμοῦ σφόδρα A παρὰ τοῦ
βασιλέως πάνυ P

MS L.   5 τὸ μισθίον ms | ὅτι ego: εἴτι ms, 1. forte ἅτινα | ἐπιδίδον
τὸ ms.   6 ἑκάστη ἑσπέρα ms.   8 * f. 8ʳ 2   10 ἐβύζανεν, in marg. lat. scr.
man rec sugebat | * a sect. 3 ms I cum rec A (mss HI) includitur, cf
p 8*, 1 1

MSS VW ‒ Rec. C   11 ὃν. δ mss.   12 καθεμίαν ego καθὴν vel
καθεμ- mss. l. fortasse καθ᾽ ἑκάστην   13 καὶ (1°) ‒ V | δάκτυλον ... το-
σοῦτον: δεξιὸν δακτ. ἤγουν τὸν ἀντίχειραν, καὶ ἐξεθήλ. W | καὶ (2°) ‒ V
14 ἀσθενεῖ V | καὶ ante καθ᾽ ponit V

HILPQ 3. Ἐγὼ δὲ Σολομῶν ἐν μιᾷ τῶν ἡμερῶν ἀνα-
κρίνας τὸ παιδάριον εἶπον αὐτῷ· »οὐχὶ ὑπὲρ πάντας
τοὺς τεχνίτας τοὺς ἐργαζομένους ἐν τῷ ναῷ τοῦ θεοῦ
σὲ ἠγάπησα καὶ ἐπεδίδουν σοι ἐν διπλῷ τὸν μισθὸν

5   VW 3. Καὶ δὴ ἐν μιᾷ τῶν ἡμερῶν ὁ βασιλεὺς Σολομῶν
⟨ἰδὼν⟩ καὶ ⟨ἐκπετάσας⟩ τὰς χεῖρας εἰς τὸν οὐρανὸν εἶπεν· »θεὲ
θεῶν καὶ μόνε βασιλεῦ βασιλέων, ἀποκάλυψόν μοι τὴν τοῦ παιδὸς πᾶσαν βάσανον διὰ τὸ ὄνομά σου τὸ φοβερὸν καὶ πανάγιον.«
ἦλθε δὲ φωνὴ λέγουσα· »πρόσειπε εἰς τὸ δεξιὸν οὖς τοῦ παιδὸς
10 τάδε· »δαφνών· μαγατά· παλιπούλ«· ἔγγραφον δὲ ποίησον ἐν
ἀγεννήτῳ χάρτῃ ταῦτα· *** καὶ παραδοὺς πυρὶ ὑποκάπνισον
αὐτῷ, ἔχων δὲ καὶ βοτάνην τὴν λεγομένην κισσὸν καὶ λίθον
ἰασαφήτην ἐν τῇ χειρί σου· καὶ ἐν πέμπτῃ ὥρᾳ τῆς νυκτὸς ἐρώ-
τησον τὸν παῖδαν, καὶ ἀναγγελεῖ σοι ἅπαντα.« ταῦτα ἀκούσα.
15 Σολομῶν καὶ ποιήσας ἀπαραλλάκτως ἠρώτησε τὸν παῖδαν. *

MSS HILPQ = Recc AB. § 3. (3) **1** ὁ δὲ βασιλεὺς σολομῶν LP |
ἐν: καλέσας P | ἐν ... ἡμερῶν ὁρῶν τὸν νεώτερον ὃν ἠγάπα ὁ βασιλεὺς
σφόδρα ἐν ἀθυμίᾳ κατίσχον σκυθρωπάζων καὶ τῇ ὄψει παρελαγμένος ἐκάλεσεν
αὐτὸν L | ἀνακρίνας ... αὐτῷ A   τὸν παῖδα ἐπηρώτησεν αὐτὸν λέγων P,
καὶ ἀνακριν. οὕτως εἰπών· τί ὅτι σὺ λυπούμενον βλέπω σε L   **2** ὑπὲρ A:
παρὰ B   **3** τ. ἐργαζ. .. θεοῦ — L | ἐργαζ. ... ναῷ in spatio puro a
prim. man. relicto adscr Pᵍ   **4** ἀγαπῶ B, ποθῶ L | καὶ διπλὰ τὰ μισθία
καὶ τὰ σιτία ἐπιδίδωσι L | κ. ἐπεδίδου(⟨ν⟩ James) σὺ (l, σοι) H, κ. δίδωμί
σοι J, διδούς σοι P (-σοι) Q | ἐν διπλῷ IB: διπλοῦν H | τοὺς μισθοὺς B

MSS VW = Rec. C § 3. **6** ἰδών, ἐκπετάσας supplevit James   **7** βασιλεὺς τῶν βασ., ἀποκαλ. με πᾶσαν βασ. τὴν τ. παιδ. V   **9** καὶ ταῦτα εἰπὼν
ἦλθε φωνὴ κτλ. W | παιδός: παιδάριον V   **10** ἔγγραφον W | * V f. 437ʳ
11 χάρτην mss. | *** omitto sigilla magica mihi insensibilia   **12** κισσὸν
ego: κύσαν mss.   **13** ἰασαμφήτην V, l ἰάσπιδα? | ἐν πέμπτῃ ... νυκτὸς W
τῆς νυκτὸς ὥρᾳ ζ̄ V   **14** ἀνάγκελή V, ἀνηγγέλη W   **15** * a sect 4 mss
VW (rec. C) cum recc AB includuntur

ιὶ τὰ σιτία· καὶ πῶς ἐφ᾿ ἑκάστην * ἡμέραν λεπτύνῃ;‹ 4. τὸ δὲ
αιδίον εἶπεν· »δέομαί σου, βασιλεῦ, ἄκουσόν μου τὰ συμβάντα
ιι. μετὰ τὸ ἀπολυθῆναι ἡμᾶς ἐκ τοῦ ἔργου τοῦ ναοῦ τοῦ θεοῦ
τὰ ἡλίου δυσμὰς ἐν τῷ ἀναπαύεσθαί * με, ἔρχεται πονηρὸν
ιμόνιον * καὶ ἀφαιρεῖ ἀπ᾿ ἐμοῦ τὸ ἥμισυ τοῦ μισθοῦ μου
ιὶ τὸ ἥμισυ τῶν σιτίων μου, καὶ λαμβάνει μου τὴν δεξιὰν χεῖρα καὶ
ηλάζει μου τὸν ἀντίχειρον. καὶ ἰδοὺ * θλιβομένης μου τῆς
υχῆς τὸ σῶμά μου λεπτύνεται καθ᾿ ἑκάστην ἡμέραν.

5. Καὶ ταῦτα ἀκούσας ἐγὼ ὁ βασιλεὺς Σολομῶν εἰσῆλθον εἰς

MSS HILPQ = Recc. AB. 1 σιτία IB: συτίδια H, + διπλάσιον B | κ.
ἧς σὺ δὲ L, καὶ — P | ἐφ᾿ ἑκάστης ἡμέρας (τε P) ραὶ ὥρας B | " Mg
|17 | λεπτύνῃ P: λεπτύνης A (-εις) Q
MSS HILPQVW = Recc. ABC. § 4. (4) l. 1 τὸ δὲ (καὶ τὸ I) παιδίον
l. τὸ δὲ παιδάριον B, ὁ δὲ νεότερος L, ὁ δὲ W, ἡ δὲ V 2 εἶπεν HIVW
η πρὸς τὸν βασιλέα B, ὑπολαβὼν τῷ βασιλεῖ λέγει L, pr. ἡσυχῇ καὶ πραεία
ι φωνῇ C | δέομαι . . μοι ὅγουσον, ὦ θεῖε βασιλεῦ C | βασιλεῦ — L
. δέσποτα HI | μου A — PC, δὴ Q | τὰ συμβάντα μοι A: τὰ συμβ. τῷ
ῇ παιδαρίῳ Q, pr. καὶ ἐρῶσι (l σοι) πάντα I, + ραὶ ἐρῶσιν πάντα H + ὁ
ιγόμενος καὶ στιγνάζοντα L, + rubricam ἀπόκρισις τοῦ παιδὸς πρὸς σολο-
ᾶντα περὶ τοῦ δαίμονος τοῦ ὀρνίαν H | post τὰ συμβ in spatio puro mi-
ᵒre a man prim. relicto (om. μοι) adscr. καὶ ὅσα ἔχει τὸ παιδάριον Pᶜ 3 μετὰ
ῃν ἀπόλυσιν ἡμῶν HI | ἡμᾶς + πόντας B | ἐκ ἀπὸ B, — C | τῆς
ηγασίας H | τὸν τοῦ ναοῦ ἔργον (— τοῦ θεοῦ) L | τοῖ θεοῖ τῶν ναῶν V |
ῦ (3°) — W 4 καὶ μετὰ HI | δυσμὰς Q | ἐν μετὰ H, — V | ἐν
. με· καὶ ὀψίας γενομένης L | ἀναπαυθῆναι HI | ' H f. 2ʳ | μοι P |
έρχεται V | πον δαιμ. LC. πον. (-ῶν H) πνεῦμα HI, ἓν τῶν πονηρῶι
ιμονίων (-όνων Q) B 5 ' P f. 1ᵛ | καὶ ἀφαιρ. . . ἀντίχειρον (l. 7)
ιὶ τὰ ἥμισυ τῶν μισθὸν μου λαμβάνων καὶ μετὰ ταῦτα θυλάζοντά μοι (in
arg. lat. scr. man. rec. θηλάζοντα, sugendum) τὸν δάντιλον τῆς δεξιᾶς χειρὸς
ος πρωί L | ἀφαιρεῖται HI, διαφερητε (l. διαφαιρεῖται) V | ἀπ᾿ ἐμοῦ — C
καὶ (1°) . . . μου καὶ τὰ ἥμισυ σιτία B | καὶ (2°) . . χεῖρα. εἶτα λαμβ
ιὶ τ. δεξ μου χεῖρα B, — C | ϰ θηλαζ θηλαζ. δὲ (— V) καὶ λαμβ 7 τὸν
ντίχειρά μου B, τὸν τῆς δεξιᾶς μου χειρὸς (+ τὸν V) ἀντίχειραν C | καὶ
οὐ· ἐκ δὲ τοῦ φοβοῦ L | * L f 8ᵛ¹ | θλιβ . . ψυχῆς LC· θλιβ. τ ψυχ.
ου HI, θλιβομένη μου ἡ ψυχή B, + οὕτως W, + καὶ οὗτος V, + οὕτω B |
ου — LC 8 λεπτ.· — H, λεπτίνεσθαι C | καθ᾿· ἐφ᾿ I | ἡμέραν + ὡς
ιᾶς, δέσποτα, καὶ οὐκ ἔχω πον δρᾶσαι καὶ ἀποστὰν (sic) ἀπ᾿ ἐμοῦ τὸ πο-
ιρὸν καὶ κάκιστον δαιμόνιον, τοιούτως (ω supra o scr prim. man.) πάσχον-
ος) L
§ 5. (5) l. 9 Καὶ — LC | ἐγὼ — L | ὁ β. Σολ IL· Σολ. ὁ βασ. H,
βασ. — BC | εἰσῆλθα Q, εἰσῆλθε I, ἦλθον HI | ἐν τῷ ναῷ C | εἰς
. . αὐτῷ (p. 10, l. 2), ἐκ τὸν ναὸν τοῦ θεοῦ εἰς τὸν οἶκον αὐτοῦ· ἐν ῦπη
ιλλ⟨ῇ⟩ καὶ ἐξ ὅλης τῆς ψυχῆς ἐξομολογούμενος ραὶ προσευχόμενος L

τὸν ναὸν τοῦ θεοῦ καὶ ἐδεήθην ἐξ ὅλης μου τῆς ψυχῆς ἐξομολογούμενος αὐτῷ νύκτα καὶ ἡμέραν ὅπως παραδοθῇ ὁ δαίμων
εἰς τὰς χεῖράς μου καὶ ἐξουσιάσω αὐτόν. 6 καὶ ἐγένετο ἐν τῷ
προσεύχεσθαί με πρὸς τὸν θεὸν τοῦ οὐρανοῦ καὶ τῆς γῆς ἐδόθη
5 μοι * παρὰ κυρίου Σαβαὼθ διὰ Μιχαὴλ τοῦ ἀρχαγγέλου δακτυλίδιον ἔχον σφραγῖδα γλυφῆς λίθου τιμίου· 7. καὶ εἶπέ μοι·
›λάβε, Σολομῶν υἱὸς Δαυείδ, δῶρον ὃ ἀπέστειλέ σοι κύριος ὁ
θεὸς ὁ ὕψιστος Σαβαώθ, καὶ συγκλείσεις πάντα τὰ δαιμόνια
τά τε θηλυκὰ καὶ ἀρσενικὰ κἀ · δι' αὐτῶν οἰκοδομήσεις
10 τὴν Ἱερουσαλὴμ ἐν τῷ τὴν σφραγῖδα ταύτην σε φέρειν τοῦ
θεοῦ.‹

MSS HILPQVW — Recc. ABC. 1 καὶ — V | ἐδεήθην C | μου — A
| τῆς — IW | ἐξομολ. αὐτῷ (τὸν θεὸν H, — L.) W τῷ θεῷ καὶ ἐξομολ·
γούμην αὐτῷ C, — B 2 νύκταν κ. ἡμερ. HL, νύκτα κ. ἡμέρα I, νυκτὸς κ.
ἡμέρας B, νυκτὸς κ. ἡμέρος V, compendiis scr. W | ὅπως πῶς Q | παρα-
δώσει κύριος ὁ θεὸς τὸ δαιμόνιον εἰς κτλ. L | παραδοθῇ παραδοθεῖν H,
+ μοι B, + με V 3 τὰς — P | μου αὐτοῦ L, — Q | ἐξουσιάζω Q,
ἐπεξουσιάσει L | § 6. καὶ: κ om. W in literis rubricandis | ἐγένετο: ἐν τὸ
γένετο H 4 με om. sed προσεύχεσθαί scr. I, μοι P, αὐτὸν L, + καθ'
ἑκάστην ἡμέραν καὶ νύκταν C | πρὸς τὸν θεὸν HI τὸν κύριον L, τῷ θεῷ C,
— B | τοῦ .... γῆς ILC: — B, κ. τ. γῆς — H, + μετὰ συντετριμμένης καρ-
δίας ἐξ ὅλης τῆς ψυχῆς αὐτοῦ L 5 μοι αὐτῷ L | * I f. 79ʳ | παρὰ
κυρ. Σαβ. — L, + χάρις B | διὰ ... Ἱερουσαλὴμ (l. 9 f) σφραγῆς ὑπὸ μιχαὴλ
τοῦ ἀρχαγγέλου· λέγων· ποίει οὕτως σολομῶν καὶ δῶς αὐτῷ τὸ δακτυλίδιον
τιμιώτερον εἰσὶν λίθου τιμίου L, add. L glossam de anuli signo, v. infra, p. 100*
et fig. p. 101* | ἀρχαγγ αὐτοῦ P | δακτύλιον C 6 ἔχον IQBn. ἔχων HPW,
ἔχω V | σφραγῖδας W, compendio scr. forte idem V | γλυφῆς κολαστὴν I
| λίθον τιμίου λίθιδος τιμὴν C, pr ἐκ B, add glossam de anuli signo HI, v.
infra, p. 100* | § 7. μοι μου P, με Q 7 Σολ. + βασιλεῦ P, βασιλεὺς Q |
υἱὲ VW | δῶρον — HI | δ HIP: ὃν Q, ὕπερ Q | ἀποστέλλει I, ἀπέστιλάν
σι V | ὁ θεὸς HB: — IC | κυρ. Σαβ. ὑψ. Ἰσραὴλ C 8 ὁ ὑψ. — Q |
καὶ συγκλ.. ἵνα συγκλείσις C | πάντας τοὺς δαίμονας Q | δαιμ. τῆς γῆς P
9 τά τε ... ἀρσεν. (ἄσερν. H) HI: τὰ ἀρσηνηκὰ κ. θυλικὰ V, — W,
ἄρσενα κ θήλεα B 9 καὶ δεῖ μετ' αὐτῶν ἀνοικοδομῆσαι P | Q
f. 11ᵛ | δι'. μετ' Q | ἀνοικοδομήσεις QV 10 τὴν Ἱερουσ. ναὸν κυ-
ρίου τοῦ θεοῦ σου, add. glossam de anuli signo C, v infra, p. 101* | ἐν
. . θεοῦ ego: τὴν σφραγῖδα ταύτην σε φέριν τοῦ θεοῦ I, φέρειν σε τ.
σφρ. ταυτ. τ. θ. (add. glossam de anuli signo, v. infra, p. 100*) B, τῇ σφρα-
γίδῃ ταύτῃ ἣ ἔδωκέ σοι ὁ θεός H, ἐν δὲ τὸ τὴν σφρ. ταυτ. φορεῖν cum
sequentibus conjuncta C, λαβὼν ὁ σολομῶν τὴν σφρ cum sequentibus con
juncta L

8. *Καὶ περιχαρὴς γενόμενος ὕμνουν καὶ ἐδόξαζον τὸν θεὸν τοῦ οὐρανοῦ καὶ τῆς γῆς· καὶ τῇ ἐπαύριον ἐκέλευσα ἐλθεῖν πρός με τὸ παιδίον καὶ ἀπέδωκα αὐτῷ τὴν σφραγῖδα,* 9. *καὶ εἶπον αὐτῷ· ›ἐν ᾗ ἂν ὥρᾳ ἐπιστῇ σοι τὸ δαιμόνιον ῥῖψον τὸ δακτυλίδιον τοῦτο εἰς τὸ στῆθος τοῦ δαίμονος λέγων αὐτῷ· ›δεῦρο καλεῖ σε* * *ὁ Σολομῶν,‹ καὶ δρομαίως παραγίνου πρός με μηδὲν λογισάμενος ὧν μέλλει σοι φοβῆσαι.‹*

10 *Καὶ ἰδοὺ κατὰ τὴν εἰθισμένην ὥραν ἦλθεν ὁ Ὀρνίας τὸ*

MSS HILPQVW = Recc. ABC   § 8 (6) l 1 *Καὶ — LV* | περιχ. . ἐπαυρ· εἰχαριστήσας κύριον τὸν θεὸν τ. οὐρ. εἴτις (l. ὃστις) εἰσακούει τὴν δέησιν καὶ προσευχὴν τῶν προσευχομένων καὶ τὸ ζητούμενον, οὐκ ἔστιν ὡς (ἔστιν ἕως) L | γενομ.: + ἐγὼ σολομῶν B, + (ὁ βασιλεὺς H) ἐπὶ τοῦτο (τοῦτον H) πάλιν HI | κ. ἐδόξ. — HI | τὸν — P | τοῦ θεοῦ V   2 τοῦ ... γῆς — HI | παύριον W | ἐκέλ. ἐλθ (ἐωσθὴν H, l ἐπελθεῖν?) .. παιδ.(l 3) HI: ἐκελ. τὸν παῖδαν (τὸ παιδάριον V) VW, ἐκάλεσα τὸ παῖδα (τὸν L) BL   3 καὶ — L | ἀπέδωτο L, ἐπέδωκα P | αὐτῷ: — L, αὐτ̣ὸν W | τὴν σφραγῖδα A: τὸ δακτυλίδιον B, τὸ δακτύλιον (·ἱῳ V) VW, + ταύτην I, + τοῦ θεοῦ L | § 9 κ εἶπον αὐτῷ IPW (αὐτὸν) H (εἶπεν) L — Q, κ. φῆσας αὐτῷ V, + λάβε τοῦτο καὶ L   4 ἐν ... δαίμονος (l. 5). πορεύου ἐπὶ τὸ ἔργῳ σου· μετὰ δὲ ἀφεθῆναι τοῦ ἔργου καὶ ἐσπέρα(ν) ἤδη γενέσθαι καὶ ἐλθόν‹τος› τοῦ πονηροῦ πνεύματος ὅπως ποιῆσαι τὸ πρότερον· ῥῆψε τὸ δακτυλίδιον ἐπάνω τούτου L | ἐν ια ὥρ < V | ὥραν H | ἐπιστῇ σοι: ἐπιστήσει H, ἐπεστή σοι I, ἔλθῃ πρὸς σὲ B, σοι — C | ῥῖψ .. δαιμ. H (ῥ. τουτ. τ. δακτ.. δαιμονίου) Q: (εἰς τὸ m mg sin) στηθ. τ. δαιμονίου ῥ. τουτ τ δακτ. P, ῥ αὐτῷ ἐπὶ τ. στ. τ. δαιμ (+ τὸ δακτ. V) δ καὶ ἔλαβον τοῦτο παρὰ θεοῦ Σαβαὼθ C, ῥ. τ. δακτ τουτ. δ ἔλαβον παρα κυριου σαβαὼθ καὶ ῥίψον αὐτὸ εἰς τ. στηθ. τ δαίμονος I   5 λέγων αὐτῷ HC. καὶ εἰπὲ αὐτῷ IB, εἶτα εἰπέ L, + ἐπ' ὀνόματι (·τος Q) τοῦ θεοῦ B   6 * P f. 2ʳ | δ· — C, + βασιλεὺς B | Σολ.: + ἐν ὀνόματι κυρίου τοῦ θεοῦ παντοκράτορος (— καὶ ... φοβῆσαι) L | δρομαῖος P, δρομαίος I | παραγίνου V, ἔρχοι B | δραμὼν παραγ. πρός με δρομαίως ἐπειπὼν ›καὶ ταῦτα πρὸς τὸν δαίμοναν φαθαλά πιστηφούμ (πιστιροίμ V)· ἀλακαρτανάκ· C | μηδὲν ... φοβ (l. 7) (pr καὶ) C: μὴ διαλογιζόμενος ἃ μέλλει σοι λέγειν I, καὶ μὴ ἀμελήσεις εἰς ἄπερ (f. 3ʳ) μέλλει σοι λέγειν H, μηδὲν δειλιάσας (δειλιάζων Q) ἢ (μὴ δὲ P) φοβηθεὶς (·ῆς P) ἐν ᾧ μέλλεις ἀκούειν παρὰ (ὑπὸ P) τοῦ δαίμονος. (7) καὶ λαβὼν τὸ παιδάριον τὸ δακτυλίδιον ἀπῆλθεν B

§ 10. l. 8 Pro § 10 habet L hoc λαβὼν δὲ ὁ νεανίας τὸ δακτυλίδιον πορευθῇς ἐπὶ τοῦ θείου ἔργου· ἐργαζόμενος εἶτα ἑσπέρα γενέσθαι καὶ ἐκ τοῦ ἔργου σχολάσαντες ἦλθον πάντες οἱ τεχνῆτ(αι)· ἐπὶ τὰς κατοικείας αὐτῶν· ἦλθε δὲ καὶ ὁ νέος ἐπὶ τὴν κατοικείαν αὐτοῦ, καὶ ἐλθὼν ὁ πονηρὸτ(α-τος) δαίμων καθὼς τὸ σύνηθες, τούτου | εἰθισμ Kurz ἤθισμ. BC Is, ὁρισμ HI | εἰσῆλθεν VW

χαλεπὸν δαιμόνιον ὡς πῦρ φλεγόμενον ὥστε λαβεῖν κατὰ τὸ
οὔνηθες τὸν μισθὸν τοῦ παιδαρίου. 11. τὸ δὲ παιδάριον κατὰ
τὸ ῥηθὲν αὐτῷ παρὰ τοῦ Σολομῶντος ἔρριψε τὸ δακτυλίδιον
ἐπὶ τὸ στῆθος τοῦ δαίμονος λέγων αὐτῷ· »δεῦρο καλεῖ σε ὁ
5 Σολομῶν,« καὶ ἀπῄει δρομαίως πρὸς τὸν Σολομῶντα. 12. ὁ δὲ
δαίμων ἐκραύγασε λέγων τῷ παιδαρίῳ· »τί τοῦτο ἐποίησας;
λάβε τὸ δακτυλίδιον καὶ ἐπίδος αὐτὸ πρὸς Σολομῶντα, κἀγώ
σοι δώσω τὸ ἀργύριον καὶ τὸ χρυσίον πάσης τῆς γῆς· μόνον μή
με ἀπαγάγῃς πρὸς Σολομῶντα.« 13. καὶ εἶπεν αὐτῷ τὸ παι-
10 δάριον »ζῇ κύριος ὁ θεὸς τοῦ Ἰσραήλ, οὐ μή σε ἀνέξομαι ἐὰν
μὴ ἀπαγάγω σε πρὸς Σολομῶντα« 14. * καὶ ἦλθε τὸ παιδάριον
καὶ εἶπε τῷ Σολομῶντι· »βασιλεῦ Σολομῶν, ἤγαγόν σοι τὸν

MSS HILPQVW = Recc ABC   **1** φλέγων HI | ὥστε .   Σολ. (l. 7)
— Q | ὅπως τε λάβῃ P | κατὰ τ συνηθ.: — P, post παιδάριου ponit C
2 § 11 τὸ . . δαίμονος ἐν τῷ ἅμα ῥήψας τὴν σφραγίδα αὐτοῦ ἄνω τού-
τον L | κατὰ .   Σολ. — C, cf not. ad l. 5   **3** τὸ ῥηθὲν τὸ ῥη-
θὲντ < H, τὸ ῥηθέντι I, τῷ ῥηφθέντι Is, τὸ προσταχθὲν P | αὐτῷ. αὐ-
τοῦ H, — P | Σολ H· βασιλέως Σ. I, βασιλέως P | τὸ δακτ. τὴν σφρα-
γίδαν C   **4** ἐπὶ παρά H | δαιμονίου P | λεγ. αὐτ. I καὶ λεγ. αὐτὸ H,
εἶτα λέγ < L, καὶ εἶπεν PVW | ὁ: — C, + βασιλεὺς P   **5** Σολ.· + ἐν
τῷ ὀνόματι κυρίου τοῦ θεοῦ παντοκράτορος L, + ἐπεῖπεν δὲ καὶ τὰ ῥηθέντα
ὀνόματα C | καὶ ... Σολομῶντα: — LC | ἀπῄει Kurz ἀπολεῖ HI, ἄπιει Is,
ἀπῆγε P, ἀπήγαγε Buen | τὸν — I | Σολ. HI· βασιλέα P | § 12. Pro
§ 12 habet L hoc· ἀκούσας (f. 9ʳ¹) ταῦτα ὁ δαίμων βρυχιζόμενος λέγ(ει) τίς
ἐστὶν οὗτος ὁ σολομῶν   **6** ἐκραύγασε IP: ἐκραύγαξεν H, ἀνεκραξεν C |
λεγ. τ. παιδ. I λέγων παιδάριον PVW, τ. παιδ. — H | ἐποίησας. + πρὸς
με P   **7** δακτύλιον W | κ. ἐπιδ. αὐτὸ (αὐτὸν H) HI — BC | πρὸς Σολ.:
IVW πρ. τὸν Σ. H, ἀπ᾽ ἐμοῦ P | κἀγώ σοι δώσω HI κἀγὼ ἀποδώσω P,
ἐγώ σοι δώσω Q, καὶ δώσω σοι C   **8** τὸ ἀργ. κ. — B | πάσης — B |
μόνον· ἐὰν W, + λάβε τοῦτο ἀπ᾽ ἐμοῦ καὶ B | μή: μοι B   **9** ἀγάγῃς VW
 | ἀπάγῃς με B | Σολομῶνα P   § 13. (8) Pro § 13 habet L hoc: καὶ ὁ
νεανίας ἔλθε καὶ εἶδε | καὶ . . παιδ. HI (— αὐτῷ) V, τὸ δὲ παιδ. λέγει
(εἶπε W) πρὸς τὸν δαίμονα BW   **10** τοῦ: — HW, μου V | Ἰσρ. — H |
σε: — W, σου Q | ἐὰν ... Σολ. ἀλλὰ δεῦρο ἐλθέ P, ἀλλὰ δεῦρο ἀκολουθῇ
μοι Q   **11** σε ἀγάγω C | § 14. Pro § 14 habet L· ὁ δὲ ἀκόλουθος γενό-
μενος ὁ δαίμων ἦλθε ἐπὶ τὴν βασιλικὴν οἰκίαν | * H f. 3ᵛ | hic scr H
rubricam hanc ἔλευσις τοῦ χαλεποῦ δαίμον(ος) ὀρνίαν πρὸς σολομῶν(τα) |
ἦλθε. ἐλθὼν (ἐλθὸν P) δρομαίως B   **12** καὶ εἶπε HIC: χαίρων (χαῖρον P)
πρὸς τὸν βασιλέα λέγων (λέγον P) B, pr. πρὸς τὸν Σολομῶντα χαῖρον (-ων W)
βαστῶν (καὶ βαστάζων W) τὸν δαίμοναν C | τῷ Σολομῶντι H. τῷ βασιλεῖ I,
— BC | βασ Σολ IC — HB | σοι HI: — BC

δαίμονα καθὼς ἐνετείλω μοι, καὶ ἰδοὺ στήκει πρὸ τῶν πυλῶν
ἔξω δεδεμένος καὶ κράζων μεγάλῃ τῇ φωνῇ διδόναι μοι τὸ ἀργύριον καὶ τὸ χρυσίον πάσης τῆς γῆς τοῦ μή με ἀπαγαγεῖν αὐτὸν πρός σέ.«

5   II. Καὶ ταῦτα ἀκούσας ἐγὼ Σολομῶν ἀναστὰς ἀπὸ τοῦ θρόνου μου εἶδον τὸν δαίμονα φρίσσοντα καὶ τρέμοντα καὶ εἶπον
αὐτῷ· »τίς εἶ σύ, ⌜καὶ τίς ἡ κλῆσίς σου;⌝« ὁ δαίμων εἶπεν· »Ὀρνίας
καλοῦμαι.« 2. καὶ εἶπον αὐτῷ· * »λέγε μοι ἐν ποίῳ ζῳδίῳ κεῖσαι.« καὶ ἀποκριθεὶς ὁ δαίμων λέγει· »Ὑδροχόῳ· * καὶ τοὺς ἐν

MSS HILPQVW —· Recc. ABC   1 καθ᾽ ἐνετ   βασιλεῦ, ὡς ἐκέλευσας B |
μη (l. μοι) ἐνετ V | μοι· + δέσποτα BC | στηχ HI: στήκεται B, ἡστίκη V
ἡστήκει W | πρὸ IB πρὸς H, παρὰ C | τ. πυλ. I: τὸν πυλῶνα H, τῶν
θυρῶν (+ τῆς αὐλῆς B) τῆς βασιλείας σοι BC   2 ἔξω HI: — BC |
δεδεμ. κ. κραζ. I (— καὶ) H   δεόμενον κραυγάζει VW, κράζων κ. δεό-
μενος P, κραυγάζων κ. δεόμενος Q | φώνην μεγάλην H | διδοὺς
P | μοι IQ: ἐμοὶ P, με C, — H | τὸ ἀργ . . . χρυσ. HB. τ. χρ. κ
τ. ἀργ. IW, τὸ χρ κ πάντας τοὺς θησαυροὺς V   3 πάσης HIW· — BV
τοῦ . . σε — VW | τοῦ IB καὶ H | με — B | ἀπαγ. με I |
ἀγαγεῖν P

C. II   parallela v. infra in MS D III 1—10   (9) 1 5 Καὶ ταῦτα ... τρέμοντα. ἰδὼν δὲ ὁ σολομῶν τὴν τοιούτην ἐκπετάσας τὰς χεῖρας αὐτοῦ εἰς τὸν
οὐρανόν· εὐχαριστήσας κύριον τὸν θεὸν οὐρανοῦ καὶ γῆς ποιήτην τὸν τὰ
πάντα κτήσαντα· καὶ δύναται ὅτι ποιήματα καὶ κτήματα αὐτοῦ εἰσὶν τὰ
πάντα L | Καὶ HB: — IC | ἀκ. ταυτ. — B | ἐγὼ HI — BC | Σολ.
HIB — C, pr. ὁ H | ἀναστ. HI. ἀνέστη B, ἀνέστην C | ἀπὸ. εἰπὸ V,
ἐπὶ W   6 μον. αὐτοῦ B, + καὶ ἐξῆλθεν ἔξω εἰς τὰ πρόθυρα τῆς αὐλῆς
τῶν βασιλείων αὐτοῦ καὶ P, + καὶ ἐξῆλθεν (ἔξω ... καλοῦμαι, 1. 8, omissis) Q,
+ καὶ ἐξῆλθον εἰς τὰ πρόθυρα τὰ βασιλικὰ καὶ C | εἶδον: ἐθεώρει P·
φρίττοντα I, φρίττων H | τρέμων H | * P f. 2ᵛ | καὶ (2°) εἶτα L | εἶ-
πον HIW: λέγει LPV   7 αὐτῷ IP αὐτὸν HC, — L | τίς εἶ σύ AP: — C,
+ καὶ πόθεν εἶ L | κ. τίς ... σου A — P, τίς καλεῖ W (·ῆς) V | ὁ δαιμ.
εἶπεν· ὁ δὲ ἔφη PC | ἐγὼ Ὀρν. P   8 καλ. PC καλοῦμεν L, — HI | § 2
(10) κ. εἶπον αὐτ. ego κ. εἶπ< αὐτῷ ὁ βασιλεύς V, κ. εἶπον W, εἶπον οὖν αὐτῷ I,
ἐγὼ δὲ αὐτὸν λέγων H, εἶπε δὲ ὁ σολομῶν L, ὁ δὲ (καὶ ὁ P) σολ λέγει B |
* Mg 1320 | μοι· + οὖν VW, + ὦ δαίμων B | ἐν C· — AB | ποίῳ ζῳό
κεις. P. ποίων ζῳδίων κεισ. Q, πρὶν ἐξωδιάσω (ἐξάδιώκο H, ἐξεδιώκω L) σε A,
+ λέγε μοι ποῦ ἀγωνίζεσε L   9 καὶ ... λέγει· ν. ἀπεκρίθη τὸ δαιμόνιον
καὶ εἶπεν C, λέγει δὲ L, ὁ δὲ εἶπεν B | λέγει H· — I: | Ὑδροχόῳ κ τοὺς·
— LVW per homoeoarcton | ἰδροχοχρῶς, ἰδροχόῳ (p. 14, l 1) H, ἰδρουχρῶς,
ὑδροχρόῳ (p 14, 1. 1) I, υδρωχρόῳ L, compendio scr W | * I f 80ʳ | τῶν
κειμένων Q, ἐν Ὑδροχόῳ — PQ

Ὑδροχόῳ κειμένους δι' ἐπιθυμίαν τῶν γυναίων ἐπὶ τὴν Παρθένον ζῴδιον κεκληκότας ἀποπνίγω. 3 εἰμὶ δὲ καὶ ὑπνοτικόν,
εἰς τρεῖς μορφὰς μεταβαλλόμενος, ποτὲ * μὲν ὡς ἄνθρωπος ἔχων
ἐπιθυμίαν εἴδους παιδίων θηλυκῶν ἀνήβων, καὶ ἁπτομένου μου
5 ἀλγῶσι πάνυ. ποτὲ δὲ ὑπόπτερος γίνομαι ἐπὶ τοὺς οὐρανίους
τόπους. ποτὲ δὲ ὄψιν λέοντος ἐμφαίνω. 4. ἀπόγονος δέ εἰμι *
ἀρχαγγέλου τῆς δυνάμεως τοῦ θεοῦ, καταργοῦμαι δὲ ὑπὸ Οὐριὴλ
τοῦ ἀρχαγγέλου.« 5. ὅτε δὲ ἤκουσα ἐγὼ Σολομῶν τὸ ὄνομα τοῦ
ἀρχαγγέλου ηὐξάμην καὶ ἐδόξασα τὸν θεὸν τοῦ οὐρανοῦ καὶ τῆς

MSS HILPQVW = Recc. ABC. 1 κειμένους HP   κειμένος I, κεῖμαι C,
καιομένους conj. Cr   δι' ... κεκληκ. ego (τῶν γονέων monuit Diels, γυναικῶν vel γυναίων »certe recte« James): δι' ἐπιθ. τῶν γονέων ἐπὶ τι (τὴν W)
παρθένῳ ζῳδίῳ (ζῴδιον W) κεκληκότα Η, δι' ἐπιθυμιῶν τὸν λόγον (-ων Η)
ἐπὶ τὴν παρθένον (-ων Η) τὸ (τὴν L, ὅτι Η) ἐξόδιον (ἐξῳδίων Η) κεκληκότος
(κεκληκῶ L) Α, δι' ἐπιθυμιῶν γυναίων (γυναικῶν Q) ἐπὶ τὴν παρθένων (spatium purum minus reliquit P) τῷ ζῳδίῳ κέκληται B, τῷ ζῳδ. κεκλ pro glossa
marg. habet Cr   2 ἀποπν. BW: εἰπεπνήγω V, ἐπάγω A, pr. τούτους B |
§ 3. εἰμὶ .., ὑπνοτ.· — Λ | εἰμὶ εἰ μὴ PQV Fl | ὑπνατικόν P, ὑπνοτι-
κῶν Q, ὑπνοτιλός monuit Diels, forte recte   3 εἰς B — C, καὶ εἰς τοῦτο A
| μεταβαλ Α μεταβάλλομαι B, μεταλαμβανόμενος C | ποτὲ μὲν· ὁπό-
ταν B | * H f. 4ʳ | ὡς: ὅς V, οἱ B | ἄνθρωποι B | ἔχων (+ τὴν W)
.. ἀνηβ. C· ἔχων ἔτι (ἔτει Η, ἐπὶ L) εἰμὶ (ἡμεῖν Η, — L) ἐνι τα δον (μετὰ
δῶν L) θυλικὸν (-ῶν L) εὔοσμον (εἰμι L) Α, ἔρχωνται εἰς ἐπιθυμίας (-ίαν Q)
γυναικῶν ἐγὼ μεταμορφοῦμαι εἰς (ὡς Q) θῆλυ εὔκοσμον B   4 καὶ — C |
ἁπτ μον B: ἀπὸ ὅμουν V, ἀπὸ ὦμον W, δι' αὐτῶν Η, δι' αὐτόν l. fortasse
ἀπ' ἐμοῦ, vel ἀπ' ὤμων, vel ἀπομνώμενοι   5 ἀλγ. πάνυ HIV: ἀλγῶ σοι
π. W, οἱ ἄνθρωποι καθ' ὕπνον ἐμπαίζω αὐτοῖς (αὐτούς Q) B | πάνυ — L
| δὲ — Q, + πάλιν B | ὑποπτ.: γυνπότερον C | γίνομαι HIQ | ἐπί: ὑπὸ B,
πρὸς W | ἐπὶ .. τοπ.: καὶ τ. ἐπουρανίους ἐπὶ εἰσέρχομαι τοπ L   6 τοπ.
κόλπους W | ποτὲ (δὲ — Η) ... ἐμφ. HI πότε δὲ καὶ ὡς λέων (λέοντας Q)
B, πότε μὲν ὄψει (καὶ πότε ὄψιν W) λέοντος ἐπιφέρομαι C, add. glossam mar-
ginaliam in textum insertam· ὑπὸ πάντων (+ δὲ L) τῶν δαιμονίων (δαιμόνων Η) λαβόμενος A, quam in καὶ (— Q) κελεύομαι ὑπὸ πάντων τῶν δαιμό-
νων corrigere voluit B | § 4. ἀπογ.   . θεοῦ H (— ἀρχαγγ.) l — C | δὲ
— P | * L f. 9ʳ² 7 ἀρχ.   θεοῦ · L, pr. τοῦ Q, ἀρχ. Οὐριὴλ etc. P |
καταργ.... ἀρχαγγ. I (— δὲ) Η — P | δὲ — Q | Οὐριὴλ τ. ἀρχ. ego·
Μιχ. τ. ἀρχ. A, + τῆς δυνάμεως τοῦ θεοῦ (supra omissa) L, τ. ἀρχ. Οὐριὴλ
τ. δυν. τ. θεοῦ Q, τ. δυν. τ. θεοῦ οὐρουὴλ τοῦ (bis V) ἀρχαγγέλου C
8 § 5. (11) ὅτε (ὅταν Ι) .. Σολ. HI· ἐγὼ (+ δὲ P) Σ. ἀκούσας B, ἐγὼ δὲ
ἀκούσας ὁ Σ. C. πότε οὖν Σ. L | τὸ ὀν. τ. ἀρχ. IBC — HL, + μιχαὴλ l·
9 ηὐξάμ. A, εὐξάμενος BC | καὶ — LB | ἐδοξ HIB: δοξάσας C. — L | τ.
θεὸν· pr. κύριον Q, + καὶ κύριον P | τὸν ... γῆς: τὸ ὄνομα τοῦ κυρίου C,
τὸν θεὸν τὸν δόντα μοι τὴν χάριν ταύτην· καὶ εἶδα πνεύματα ἀσώματα· εἰς
σχῆμα μεταβαλλόμενα σεσωματωμένα L

γῆς, καὶ σφραγίσας αὐτὸν ἔταξα εἰς τὴν ἐργασίαν τῆς λιθοτο-
μίας, τοῦ τέμνειν λίθους τοῦ ναοῦ ἀρθέντας διὰ θαλάσσης Ἀραβίας τοὺς κειμένους παρὰ αἰγιαλόν. 6. φοβουμένου δὲ αὐτοῦ τοῦ
σιδήρου προσψαῦσαι ἔφη μοι· »δέομαί σου, βασιλεῦ Σολομῶν, *
ἔασόν με ἐν ἀνέσει εἶναι, κἀγώ σοι ἀναγαγῶ πάντας τοὺς δαίμονας.« 7. μὴ θέλοντος δὲ αὐτοῦ ὑποταγῆναί μοι, ηὐξάμην τὸν
ἀρχάγγελον Οὐριὴλ ἐλθεῖν μοι εἰς βοήθειαν· καὶ εὐθέως * εἶδον
τὸν ἀρχάγγελον Οὐριὴλ ἐκ τοῦ οὐρανοῦ κατερχόμενον πρός με.
8. καὶ ἐκέλευσε ἀνελθεῖν ἐκ τῆς θαλάσσης κήτη καὶ ἐξήρανεν

MSS HILPQVW = Recc. ABC. 1 σφραγίσαν H | αὐτὸν + μετὰ
δακτυλιδίου εἶτα λαμβάνει ὁ ἀναγινώσκων μεθ᾽ ἑτέρων λίθων βαρυτάτων καὶ
ἐπιθένεν ἐπάνω τοῦ ὀχλουμένου ἕως βοῆσαι· ὅταν βοήσει ὁ ὀχλούμενος· ὑπό-
ταξον τὸ πνεῦμα τὸ ἀκάθαρτον τοῦ ἐξελθεῖν· καὶ εἶπεν αὐτῷ ἔξελθε ἀπὸ
ὀνόματι τοῦ ἐπουρανίου βασιλέως θεοῦ ἡμῶν· καὶ τῆς σφραγίδος τῆς δωθήσης
τῷ βασιλεῖ σολομῶν⟨τι⟩· καὶ σφραγίσας αὐτὸν L | ἔταξα + αὐτὸν C |
τὴν — LC | τῆς — L] λιθοτόμου C 2 τοῦ τεμ. ... ναοῦ — L |
τέμνειν HIP τεμεῖν W, τέμνει V, κόπτειν Q | τοὺς λιθ. P | τ. ναοῦ ἐν
τῷ ναῷ B, — C | ἀρθέντ HI (-τος) L ἀχθέντας B, τοὺς συναχθέντας VW |
διὰ ὑπὸ L | Ἀραβ. BC ἀρράβω L, ἀνάγων H, ἀναλαβὼν I 3 τοὺς ..
αἰγιαλ — C] ἀγιαλλόν Q | § 6 φοβ. δὲ αὐτ H(L) φοβούμενος δὲ αὐ-
τὸς W (αὐτοὺς) I (— αὐτὸς) P, ἐφοβεῖτο οὖν Q | φοβουμ ... προσψαυσ
φοβούμενος δὲ αὐτό⟨ς⟩· τὴν ἀπόφασιν τοῦ βασιλέως περὶ τὸν λήθ⟨ων⟩ ἥνα
μὴ πρὸς ψαῦσι τὸ σύδῖρον φοβούμενος V, φοβουμένος δὲ αὐτοῦ· λάβε ὁ ἀναγινώσκων σίδηρον (in marg. lat. signum O+ scr man rec.) ἄλυσσον ἐπίθες ἐπὶ
τοῦ ὀχλουμένου τῷ τραχείλω καὶ δῆσον σφόδρα ἕως οὗ βοήσει· φοβουμένου
δὲ αὐτοῦ etc. L | τοῦ σιδήρου A. τὸ σιδήρω W, τὸν σίδηρον B 4 προσ-
ψαῦσαι LQW· οὐ προσάψωμαι I, οὐ προσψαύσω μεν H, post πρὸς spatio
puro VI litt. relicto ad marg. sin. man. prim. scr. πάντ < ἢ πρὸς ταῦτα P,
quod Fl τραυτὸν εἶπός ταῦτα legit | ἔφη μοι L (μιν) H καὶ λέγει μοι P,
λέγει Q, ἔφη ὁ δαίμων W, ὁ δέμων ἔφη V, ἔφη ὁ ὀρνίας I | σου σοι W
| Λ f. 9ᵛ¹ 5 με. μοι W, — L | ἐν ἀνεσ. IL: ἔναι ἔσοι H, ἄνετον BC |
εἶναι. ἦν αα H, + μοι L, + με B | ἀναγαγῶ IP. ἀνάγω in ἀνάγ corr. H,
ἀγαγῶ C, ἄγω L, εὐαγγέλω Q | πάντα τὰ δαιμόνια BC 6 § 7. μὴ ..
μοι. καὶ μὴ θέλοντα (-τες W) ὑποταγῆναι cum δαιμόνια conjuncta C | θέ-
λων A | αὐτοῦ: αὐτοὺς HL, αἶτὸς I | ὑποταγὸν μοι L | ηὐξαμ.. βοηθ.
ηὐξαμ· pr. ἐγὼ δὲ C, εὐξάμενος B, εἶξαμ V | ηὔξαμ ...βοηθ ηὐξάμην
τὸν θεὸν καὶ κατελθὼν τὸν ἀρχάγγελον οὐρουέλ ὑποταγήν μοι· εἰς βοή-
θειαν L | τὸ ἀρχάγγελον V, τοῦ ἀρχαγγέλου B 7 οὐρουὴλ IW | ἐλθεῖν
pr. τοῦ C, συνελθεῖν B | μοι HLQ με P, — IC | * P f. 3ʳ 8 τ. ἀρχ.
Οὐρ.: αὐτὸν C | οὐρουὴλ IC, οὐρουὲλ L | τῶν σὐρανῶν B | ἐρχόμενον C
| πρὸς με — L 9 § 8. (12) ἐκελ. ΙΒ· ἐκέλευσα C, ἐκάλεσεν HI, + ὁ ἄγ-
γελος B | ἀνελθ. (καὶ ἦλθον L) . ρήτη Λ κήτη (κῆτον W) θαλλάσης ἐλ-
θεῖν ἐκ τῆς ἀρύσσου BC | καὶ ... μέριδα A. — BC | ἐξῆρεν H

αὐτῶν τὴν μερίδα ⌜καὶ ἔρριψεν αὐτοῦ τὴν μοῖραν⌝ ἐπὶ τῆς γῆς,
κἀκείνως καὶ οὕτως ὑπέταξε τὸν δαίμονα τὸν Ὀρνίαν τὸν μέγαν
τοῦ κόπτειν λίθους καὶ συντελεῖν εἰς τὴν οἰκοδομὴν τοῦ ναοῦ
ὃν ᾠκοδόμουν ἐγὼ Σολομῶν. 9. καὶ πάλιν ἐδόξασα τὸν θεὸν
5 τοῦ οὐρανοῦ καὶ τῆς γῆς καὶ ἐκέλευσα περιέναι τὸν Ὀρνίαν εἰς
τὴν μοῖραν αὐτοῦ καὶ ἔδωκα αὐτῷ τὴν σφραγῖδα λέγων· ⟩ἄπελθε
καὶ ἄγαγέ μοι ὧδε τὸν ἄρχοντα τῶν δαιμονίων.⟨

III. Ὁ δὲ Ὀρνίας λαβὼν τὸ δακτυλίδιον ἀπῆλθε πρὸς τὸν
Βεελ*ζεβοὺλ καί ἔφη αὐτῷ· ⟩δεῦρο καλεῖ σε ὁ Σολομῶν⟨ 2. ὁ
10 δὲ Βεελζεβοὺλ λέγει αὐτῷ· ⟩λέγε μοι, * τίς ἐστιν οὗτος ὁ Σολομῶν ὃν σὺ λέγεις;⟨ 3. ὁ δὲ Ὀρνίας ἔρριψε τὸ δακτυλίδιον εἰς
τὸ στῆθος τοῦ Βεελζεβοὺλ λέγων· ⟩καλεῖ σε Σολομῶν ὁ βασι-

MSS HILPQVW ⟶ Recc. ABC. 1 αὐτὸν L | μερίδαν H, μεριπα L |
καὶ .. μοῖραν B — A | ἔρριψεν αὐτὸν C | τὴν μοῖραν ... συντελεῖν (l 3)
— C 2 κάκείνως κ. οὕτως ego: κακείνως κ. οὗτος H, κἀκεῖνος κ. οὗτος I
καὶ οὕτως L, καὶ Q, κἀκείνη et postea spatium purum VII litt. habet P, ⟩καὶ
οὕτως scheint Glossen⟨ Diels | ὑπίταξε· ὑπέταξα I, ἐκέλευσεν Q, + τὸ δαι-
μόνιον τὸ μέγα καὶ ἐκέλευσεν P | τ. Ὀρ. τ μεγ. HL. tr I, τὸν μέγαν καὶ
θρασὺν (θρασὺ Q) τ Ὀρν B 3 τοῦ — L | τοὺς λίθους P | καὶ .. Σολ.·
πρὸς τὸν ναόν B | συντελῶν L | εἰς LV 4 ὃν A ἦν C | Σολ. pr.
βασιλεὺ(ς) H, βασιλεύς V | § 9. καὶ πάλιν — γῆς — C | πάλιν. οὕτως
ἐγὼ Σολ. B | ἐδόξασαν L 5 τῆς — Q | γῆς: + ποιήτην B | ἐκέλευσα
.. δαιμονίων (l. 7) ἐκέλευσα τὸν ὀρνίαν συναπήνε μοι τὸν ἄρχονταν τῶν
δαιμονίων καὶ δέδοκα αὐτὸν, τὴν σφραγίδαν W | ἐκέλευσεν P | περιέναι
(περιεῖναι L) ... τὴν (— L) μοιρ. αὐτ. (αὐτὸν I, αὐτῶν H) A τὸν Ὀ παρῆ
ναι μη σὺν τῖ μύρα αὐτοῦ V, ἐλθεῖν τὸν Ὀ. σὺν τῇ μοίρᾳ αὐτοῦ B 6 ἔδω
κεν H, δέδωκα CL | αὐτῷ. αὐτὸν C, αὐτοῦ LB | τὸ σφραγίδιον B | λέγων·
φήσαν αὐτόν V, καὶ εἶπον I 7 καὶ — L | ἀναγαγέ I | ὧδε ὦ I | τ
δαιμ.: pr. πάντων I, + πάντων P, λαβεῖν ἀπὸ τῆς βασιλείας μου Q

C. III. MSS HILPVW — Recc. ABC. (13) c. III—XX 9 Ὁ δὲ ... γι
νέσθαι om. Q 8 δακτύλιον C 9 constanter sci. βελζεβουὴλ H, βεελζε
βουέλ L | βεζεελθεουλ in βεελζεβουλ con. V | * H f. 5ˣ | Βεελζ.: + τὸ
ἔχοντα τὴν βασιλείαν ἐπὶ τῶν δαιμόνων P, ὃς ἦν ἔξαρχος τῶν δαιμονίων C
add. insuper ἔχων το τὸ βασιλεῖ ἂν τω V | καὶ — P | ἔφη αὐτῷ IPC
λέγει HL, + αὐτὸν H, + ὁ (— V) ὀρνίας C | ὁ (1°) HI — LPC
§ 2. 10 λέγει αὐτῷ (— αὐτ. H) A: ἀκούσας ἔφη αὐτῷ P, ἀκούσας εἶπεν C
| λέγε IPC· εἶπέ H, ἀνήγγελέ L | * L f. 9ᵛ² | τίς· τί H, pr. τί ἐστὶν L
οὗτος AP αὐτὸς C | ὃν. ὧν I | σὺ. + μοι C 11 λέγεις φῆς μοι P
§ 3. τὸ δακτύλιον V, τῷ δακτυλλίῳ W | εἰς AP. ἐπὶ C 12 τω σθῆθος V
τὸ στήθει W | βελζεβοὺλ W, βελζεβουὴλ V | λέγων λέγει αὐτῷ H
+ αὐτῷ I | λέγων ... βασιλ. — L | δεῦρο καλεῖ HI | καλεῖς (— σε)
| Σολ. ὁ βασ. PV (pr. ὁ) I: βασ· σολ H (pr. ὁ) W

λεύς.« 4. * καὶ ἀνέκραξεν ὁ Βεελζεβοὺλ ὡς ἀπὸ πυρὸς φλογὸς
καιομένης μεγάλης καὶ ἀναστὰς ἠκολούθησεν αὐτῷ μετὰ βίας
καὶ ἦλθε πρός με. 5. καὶ ὡς εἶδον ἐγὼ τὸν ἄρχοντα τῶν δαιμονίων ἐρχόμενον, ἐδόξασα τὸν θεὸν καὶ εἶπον· * »εὐλογητὸς
εἶ, κύριε ὁ θεὸς ὁ παντακράτωρ ὁ δοὺς τῷ παιδί σου Σολομῶντι
τὴν τῶν σῶν θρόνων πάρεδρον σοφίαν καὶ ὑποτάξας εἰς ἐμὲ
πᾶσαν τὴν τῶν δαιμόνων δύναμιν.« 6. καὶ ἐπηρώτησα αὐτὸν
καὶ * εἶπον »λέγε μοι, τίς εἶ σύ; ὁ δαίμων * ἔφη: »ἐγώ εἰμι
Βεελζεβοὺλ τῶν δαιμονίων ὁ ἔξαρχος.« 7. ἀπῄτουν δὲ τοῦτον
ἀδιαλείπτως ἐγγύθεν μοι προσεδρεύειν καὶ ἐμφανίζειν μοι τὴν
κατὰ τῶν δαιμόνων φαντασίαν. αὐτὸς δέ μοι ἐπηγγείλατο πάντα

MSS HILPVW — Recc. ABC. 1 § 4. ᵏ V f. 438ʳ | κ. ἀνεκ HI εἶτα
κράξας L, ἀνεκ. δὲ PC | ὁ Βεελζ.: τὸ δαιμόνιον φωνὴν μεγάλην L, + φωνῇ
μεγάλῃ P | ὡς ... μεγαλ. L (— μεγαλ.) H. καὶ ἔῤῥιψε φλόγα πυρὸς καιο-
μένην μεγάλην P, λέγων ταῦτα· ὡς ἀπὸ πυρὸς φλογὸς καιομένης μοι μεγάλης C, ὡς ἀπ' φλογὸς καιόμενος Ι, add. rubricam ἡ ἔλευσις βελζεβούλ πρὸς
σολομῶντα H 2 ἠκολ. αὐτῷ Ι (αὐτὸν) Η. ἠκολουθ < αὐτῶ L, ἠκολούθει
τῷ ὁρνίᾳ PC | μετὰ βίας — P 3 καὶ ... με — C | καὶ — L | ἦλθε
IP: ἀπῆλθεν HL | με I: τὸν σολομῶντα HL, σολομῶνα P | § 5. (14) κ. ὡς
εἶδον H (— ὡς) I ὡς δὲ εἶδον P, καὶ (+ ὡς V) ἰδὼν δὲ C, ἰδὼν δὲ L | ἐγὼ
HIC: — P, ὁ σολ. L, + σολ. HI 4 ἐρχομ· — P, + πρός με HI, + τὸν
βεελζεβοὺλ C, + καὶ Ι | ἐδόξασε L | κύριον τ. θεὸν τοῦ οὐρανοῦ καὶ γῆς
ποιήτην P | εἶπεν L | * P f 3ᵛ 5 εἶ, κύριε. κύριος IL | θεός. + τοῦ
οὐρανοῦ καὶ τῆς γῆς L | δοὺς ... σοφ καὶ — I | σου — C 6 τῶν σ.
θρόνων HW τὸν σὸν θρόνον L, τὸ σὸν θρον- V, τῶν σοφῶν P 7 πᾶσαν
— H | τ. δαιμ. A. τοῦ διαβόλου PC | τ. δυν. τ. διαβ. P | § 6 (15) κ.
ἐπηρωτ. HI (ex -ωτητα corr.) Pᶜ. ἐπηρωτ. δὲ C, κ. ἐπηρώτησεν H | * I f. 81¹
| αὐτῶν H, αὐτὴν V 8 κ. εἶπον PC (— καὶ) H — I, λέγων L | * W
f. 268ʳ | λέγε μοι — L | μοι — P | τίς εἶ σύ. τίς εἰσὶν L | σύ — PW
| ὁ δαίμων· καὶ H | * H f. 5ᵛ | ἔφη· »ἐγώ· λέγει· ἐγὼ I, λέγω H 9 Βεελζ.
pr ὁ IL, + ὁ PV | δαιμ· δαιμόνων HI, + πάντων W | ὁ — LPW | ἔξαρ-
γος· ἄρχων V, ἀρχή H | § 7. ἀπητ. .. προσεδ. ego ἀπητ. ... ἀδιαλυπ.
(-λήπτως Is, -λειπτως Kurz) ἐγγυθὲν μοι προσεδρεύειν I, ἀπήπην ... ἀδιαλήπτως
ἐγγυθέν μοι προσεδρεύιν H, ἀπῄτουν δὲ οὖτον ἀδιαλήπτως προσεδρεύειν ἐγ-
γιθέν μοι L, ἀπάντ(ων) δὲ τούτ(ων) οὐ διαλιπο < ἐγκηθέν μοι προσεδρέ-
βειν V, (ἀπητ.... ἀδιαλ. — W) ἐνγγκιστά μου προσεβρεύειν (β forte ιν ὁ corr.)
W, ἄπαντες δὲ οἱ δαίμονες ἐγγιστέν μου προσεδρεύουσι P 10 ἐμφανίζει LW,
ἐφανίζει V, ἐμφανίζω P | μοι — IP | τ. κατὰ (μετὰ L) τ. δαιμ. φαντ. A:
ἑκάστου δαίμονος τ. φαντ P, ἑνὸς ἑκάστου δαίμονος φαντασίας C 11 αὐτ.
.. ἐπηγγ. (ἐπειγγειλε L) .. πνευμ AP. ἐπηγγ. μοι δὲ αὐτ. παντ. τ. δαιμόνια C

C. III, 5 Sap. IX 4
UNT. 9 McCown   2*

τὰ ἀκάθαρτα πνεύματα ἀγαγεῖν πρός με δέσμια. καὶ ἐγὼ πάλιν
ἐδόξασα * τὸν θεὸν τοῦ οὐρανοῦ καὶ τῆς γῆς εὐχαριστῶν αὐτῷ
πάντοτε.

IV. Ἐπυθόμην δὲ τοῦ δαίμονος εἰ ἔστι δαιμόνων θήλεια.
5 τοῦ δὲ φήσαντος εἶναι ἐβουλόμην εἰδέναι. 2. καὶ ἀπελθὼν ὁ
Βεελζεβοὺλ ἔδειξέ μοι τὴν Ὀνοσκελίδα μορφὴν ἔχουσαν περικαλλῆ,
⌜καὶ δέμας γυναικὸς εὐχρώτου, κνήμας δὲ ἡμιόνου.⌝ 3. ἐλθούσης
δὲ αὐτῆς πρός με εἶπον * αὐτῇ· »λέγε μοι σὺ τίς εἶ.« 4. ἡ δὲ
ἔφη· »ἐγὼ Ὀνοσκελὶς καλοῦμαι, πνεῦμα σεσωματοποιημένον *
10 φωλεῦον ἐπὶ τῆς γῆς· ἐν σπηλαίοις μὲν ἔχω τὴν κατοίκησιν,

MSS HILPVW = Recc. ABC. 1 ἀγαγῶν L | πρός με· μαι W | δεσμ.
ἀγ. με V | δεσμ. LPV. δίσμοια H (δέσμια conj. James), δεδεμένα I, — W |
ἐγὼ PC — A 2 * L f. 10ʳ¹ | τοῦ... γῆς τὸν παντοκράτορα σαβαὼθ L |
εὐχ. αὐτ παντ. H (παντα <) V· καὶ εὐχαριστῶ αὐτ. παντ. P, — ILW
C. IV. MSS HILPVWTᵒVᵒWᵒGlm = Recc. ABCCᵒ, cf. infra Rec. C XI
1—6, supra *Intro*, IV 1d), 2c), pp. 31—33 l. 4 (16) Ἐπυθ. δὲ. pr. εἶτα L,
+ ἐγὼ C | δὲ — P | τοῦ δαιμ pr παρὰ P, pr. καὶ ἠρώτησα τὸν δαίμονα
βεελζεβοὺλ I | δαιμ. — H | ἐπυθ. δὲ τ. δαιμ. ἐρωτηθεὶς δὲ ὁ βεελζεβοὺλ
(ἐπερώτησα δὲ ἐγὼ τὸν β. Wᵒ) ὃς ἰντζανφιὲλ (ἐλτζιανφηὲλ Vᵒ) καλεῖται παρ'
ἐμοῦ (ὃς ... ἐμοῦ. ὁ καὶ τζιανφιὲλ Tᵒ) Cᵒ | εἰ εἶσιν Vᵒ | εἰ — Tᵒ | δαιμ.
θηλ. ego δαιμ. θυλια ἔγγιος I, θύλιαν H, θήλεα ἔγγιος ἡμὴν L, ἐν αὐτοῖς
θήλειαι P, καὶ θήλεα (θήλεα Tᵒ) δαιμόνια Cᵒ (— καὶ) CGlm 5 τοῦ· τού-
του LTᵒ | δὲ + μοι PCWᵒ | ἐβουλόμην. pr καγὼ W, κἀγὼ εἶπον· ἤθε-
λον P | εἰδέναι APᵀ· ἰδεῖν CCᵒGlm | § 2 ὁ — PV | ὁ Βεελξ ACᵀ |
τοιοῦτος Wᵒ, ὅτι οὗτος Vᵒ, ὅτι οὕτως Tᵒ | — Glm | + ταχὺ P 6 ἐδείξ. μοι A
ἤνεγκέ μοι Tᵒ, ἤνεγκε πρός με P, ἤνεγκε ἔμπροσθέν μου CVᵒWᵒGlm | Ὀνοσκ.
AP ὀνοσκελοῖν WCᵒGlm (-λοῖ V), + καλουμένην TᵒWᵒ (-ενη) Vᵒ | ἔχουσα
HLTᵒVVᵒ | περικαλλῆ Kurz περικαλὴ HIPIs, -αλὴν WWᵒGlm (sic), περιπερ-
καλὴ L 7 καὶ ... ἡμιον. — A, add. rubric. ἔλευσις τῆς ὀνοσκελίδας πρὸς
σολομῶντα H | δέμας ego δέμαν V, δέρμα W James, δεσμὰ P, σῶμαν Cᵒ |
κνημ. δὲ ἡιον. Wᵒ (μιάονου) W (ἡμιῶν) VVᵒ μνήμος δὲ ἡμίονος Tᵒ, καὶ κερα-
τίζουσα τὴν κεφαλὴν P | κνήμην Glm | § 3. (17) Glm deest 8 δὲ — Tᵒ
| πρός με IL (μεν) H· καὶ ἰδὸν W, — PVCᵒ | εἶπον AW ἔφην PCᵒ, ἔφι V
| * Mg 1321 | αὐτὴν LWCᵒ | λίγε μοι· λέγων VᵒWᵒ | σὺ — P | τίς εἶ
σύ H | § 4. ἡ δὲ ἔφη ἐκείνη εἶπιν L 9 ἔφη: pr. μοι PC, + μοι VᵒWᵒ,
ἔφην W | ἐγὼ ἐ I, ἐγὼ Is. | Ὀνοσ⸍ P. ὀνοσκελὴς Vᵒ, -λ(ῆς) V, ὀνοσκε-
λίδα A, ὀνοσκελοῖ TᵒWWᵒ | σεσωματωπ. Wᵒ, σεσῶματοπηεμίνω Vᵒ, σεσω-
ματωπεποιημίνον P, σεσωματωμίνον πεποιημένον HL, σεσωματωμένον ITᵒ,
πεποιημένον W (-μένω) V, σεβωματω(?) πεποι .Fl | * H f. 6ʳ 10 φωλεῦον
P φολεύων HWᵒ, φολεύω LCTᵒVᵒ, φολέον I, + δὲ TᵒVᵒ | ἐν σπηλαίοις ἐπὶ
τῆς γῆς L | ἐν . κατοικ. I (ἔχον) H σπήλαιον οἰκῶ (οἶκον V) (ἐν σπη-
λαίοις Tᵒ) ἔνθα χρυσίον κεῖται CCᵒ, σπήλαιον μοι γρύσιον ἔνθα γεῖμαι P |
μὲν — L

ἔχω δὲ πολυποίκιλον τρόπον. 5. ποτὲ μὲν ἄνθρωπον * πνίγω,
ποτὲ δὲ ἀπὸ τῆς φύσεως σκολιάζω αὐτούς. * τὰ δὲ πλεῖστά
ἐστί μοι οἰκητήρια κρημνοὶ σπήλαια φάραγγες. 6. πολλάκις δὲ
καὶ συγγίνομαι τοῖς ἀνθρώποις ὡς γυναῖκα εἶναί με νομίζοντες,
πρὸ πάντων δὲ τοῖς μελιχρόοις ὅτι οὗτοι συναστροί μού εἰσιν,
καὶ γὰρ * τὸ ἄστρον μου οὗτοι λάθρα ** καὶ φανερῶς προσκυνοῦσι καὶ οὐκ οἴδασιν ὅτι ἑαυτοὺς βλάπτουσι καὶ πλεῖόν με κα-
κοῦργον εἶναι ἐρεθίζουσιν· 7. θέλουσι γὰρ διὰ τῆς μνήμης χρύ-
σιον πορίζειν. ἐγὼ δὲ παρέχω ὀλίγον τοῖς καλῶς με προσκυνοῦσιν.‹

MSS HILPVWT°V°W° = Recc. ABCC°.　1 ἔχω· ἔχων H | πολυπ. τροπ,
APC° καὶ πολυποίκιλα τρόπαια (forte ex τρόπα coir) C | § 5. μὲν HIPT°·
δὲ LCV°W° | ἀνθρώπους PCC° | δι' ἀγχόνης πνίγω ἀνθρώπους C | * P
f. 4ʳ | πνίγω· + δι' ἀγχόνης P, + ὡς δι' ἀγχόνης V°W°　2 αὐτοὺς ὑπὸ T°
· | τῆς — H | φύσεως: — W, + εἰς ἀγκῶνας P, ἐπὶ ἐγκύων(ων) CT°, (-όνωι)
W°, ἐπὶ ἐγκώνω V° | σκολιάζω LT°· σκελιάζω HIIs, σκωλιάζω V°, σκολιά-
ζων V, σχολιάζων WW°, σκωλήρια (ad marg.), φωλείω (in textu P) | αἱ-
τούς — P | * T° f. 7ʳ² | τὰ δὲ HP — ICC°, τοὺς δὲ L | πλειστ.. οἰκητ.
πλ. ἴσταμαι οἰκητήριον H, πλείστους ἔτεσιν οἰκητήρια L, πλεῖστα μοι οἰκητήρια εἶαι P (— εἶαι) T°, πλεῖστα δέ ἐστίν μοι οἰκητήρια κεκριμμένα VW.
πλεῖστα μοι δὲ ἔσται οἰκητήρια W°, πλ. ἔσται (in ἔστη corr.?) μη οἰκητήρια V°,
πολλάκις δὲ οἰκῶ I　3 κρημν. σπηλ. φαραγγ. P κρύμνοις σπήλαιον
φάραγγες H, ἔχω κρήμνους καὶ σπηλαίοις φάραγγες L, ἐν κρυμνοῖς ἐι
σπηλαίοις ἐν φαράγγοις I, σπήλαια καὶ κρήμνους καὶ φάραγκαι C, — C°
4 § 6. καὶ — HL | γύνη P | εἶναι με νομ. (l. νομίζουσι?) H νομ με
εἶναι I, ἦμαι νομ. L, με εἶναι CC°, δοκοῦσα εἶναι I　5 πρὸ παντ. ILPC
πρὸς πάντα H, πρὸ (πρὸς T°W°) δὲ τῶν ἄλλων C° | τοῖς μελιχ. P. τοὺς
μελιχρόους CV°W°, τοὺς μελαχρόους HT°, τοὺς μελανοχρόους L (ex μελαχρο
corr.) I, τοὺς μελαντοχρόους (in textu, μελιχρόους ad marg.) Is | ὅτι — L | ὅτι
οὗτοι HI: οὗτοι γὰρ PCC°, + καὶ CW°, + μου καὶ V° | συναστ μού εἰσιν ILT°W°
εἰσιν συν. μου H | μου μοι P, — CV°　6 καὶ　　ἀστρ. κ. τὸ ἄστρο T°
| γὰρ — L | * I f. 81ᵛ | προσκ λαθ. κ ἐναργέως (φανερὸς V) CW° |
λαθ προσκ. οὗτοι T° | ** L f 10ʳ² | φανερὰ HL　7 καὶ οὐκ .. προσκ-
κυν. (l. 9f) — C° | οὐκ οἶδ ὅτι — I | ὅτι — L | ἑαυτῶς C, αὐτοὺς P |
βλαπτ. AP: ἀπατῶνται C | καὶ πλεῖον ... προσκυν. (l. 9s.) — I | πλεῖον ..
ἐρεθ· πλ .. ρεθήζουσιν H, πλείων μεν κακοῦργος εἶναι ρεθίζουσιν L, πλεῖον
με κακουργεῖν ἐρεθίζουσι P, πλημελῶς κακούργους ἐρεθίζουσα C　8 § 7. θελ
PV. θέλουσα W, θέλοντες HL | γὰρ — L | διὰ .. χρυσίον αὐτοὺς μνή-
μην τοῦ χρυσίου L　9 πορίζ. HLP. πορίζεσθαι C | ἐγὼ　　προσρ. HP.
ἐγὼ γὰρ παρέχων ὀλ. τοῖς καλεῖς· μὲν προσ. L, τούς τε παρέχειν ὀλίγοις,
τοῖς καὶ καλουμένοις, προσκ. W, τῆς τε δὲ παρέχιν ὀλήγης τῆς κεκαλουμένης
προσκυνοῦση V

8. Ἐπηρώτησα δὲ αὐτὴν πόθεν γεννᾶται. ἡ δὲ εἶπεν· ›ἀπὸ
φωνῆς ἀκαίρου τῆς καλουμένης ἤχου οὐρανοῦ ⌜μολύβδου φωνὴ·
ἀφέντος⌝ ἐν ὕλῃ ἐγεννήθην.‹ 9. εἶπον δὲ αὐτῇ· ›ἐν ποίῳ ἄστρῳ
διέρχῃ;‹ ἡ δὲ εἶπεν· ›ἐν πανσελήνῳ, διότι καὶ ἐν σελήνῃ τὸ
5 πλείονα ὁδεύω.‹ 10. ἐγὼ δὲ εἶπον· ›ποῖος ἄγγελός ἐστιν ὁ κα
ταργῶν σε;‹ ἡ δὲ ἔφη· ›ὁ καὶ ἐν σοί, βασιλεῦ.‹ 11. κἀγὼ εἰς
χλεύην αὐτὰ λογισάμενος ἐκέλευσα στρατιώτην κροῦσαι αὐτήν.
ἡ δὲ ἀνακράξασα εἶπεν· ⌜›λέγω σοι, βασιλεῦ, ἐγώ, ὑπὸ τῆς δε
δομένης σοι σοφίας τοῦ θεοῦ.‹ 12. καὶ εἶπον τὸ ὄνομα τοῖ
10 Ἁγίου Ἰσραὴλ καὶ⌝ ἐκέλευσα αὐτὴν νήθειν τὴν κάνναβιν * εἰς τὸ

MSS HILPVWTᵒVᵒWᵒ = Recc. ABCCᵒ. § 8 (18) 1 ἐπερώτων L | δὲ
— H | αὐτὴν: αὐτοὺς C, + ἐγώ (κἀγώ P) Σολομῶν PCCᵒ | γεννᾶται A
γεννάσε Tᵒ, γενναστ < Vᵒ, γενᾶσται V, γενᾶσθαι WWᵒ, γεννᾷσα (σα transversa
linea del.) P | εἶπεν ATᵒ: μοι ἔφη P (ἔφησε) C, ἔφη μοι Vᵒ, ἔφη Wᵒ
2 ἀκαίρου .. οὐραν.. ἀκαιρ. τ. καλ. ἐγχοανῆς C, ἀκροατῆς καλουμένης (·με-
νου L) ἤχου οὐ(ρα)νοῦ A, ἀκαίρου τοῦ καλουμένου ἤχου ἀν(θρώπ)ου P, βηρ-
σαβεὲλ (βειρσαβεέ Vᵒ, βηρωβεέ Tᵒ) ἱππικῆς (+ καὶ VᵒWᵒ) χρηματικῆς Cᵒ,
explicit narratio parallela codd. mss. TᵒVᵒWᵒ | μολύβδου μολύγδον H, βολβίτον
conj. Cr, μολίβδους Bncn | φωνῆς HL | ἀφέντος P ἀφέντες C, ἀφιέντες A
3 ἐν ὕλῃ· ἐκήνη V, ἐκείνοι W | § 9 (19) εἶπον HI· ἔφησα C, ἔφη LP ||
δὲ. δ' ἐγώ P, + ἐγώ W, αὐτὴ L | ἐν — PC | δ' ἐν ἄστρῳ: ἐκ
τῶν ἄστρων L   4 δὲ· + μοι P | ἐν (1ᵒ): — PC | πανσελ. ILP: πάντι
σελήνῳ H, π(ανσέλη)ος C, + ἄστρῳ P | διὸ I | διότι . σελήνη — C
per homoeoteleuton | ἐν σελήνῃ I ἐν σελήνῳ HL, ἡ σελήνη P   5 πλείω I |
ὁδεύω W: ὁδέβω V, ὁδεύων H, ὁδεύει P, ποιῶ καὶ ὁδεύω L | § 10. ἐγὼ δὲ
— W | εἶπον HIW. λέγω PL, + δὲ W, + αὐτὴν LW, + πρὸς αὐτὴν P ||
ἔφη δὲ ἐγὼ αὐτὴν V | καὶ ποῖος ἐστιν ὁ ἄγγελος ὁ P | ποῖος· pr. καὶ L
| ἐστιν: δ' ἐς H, — C | ὁ — H | καταργῶ V   6 ἡ δὲ HIPW: ὁ δὲ L,
καὶ V | ἔφη HLV. εἶπε PW, λέγει I, + μοι P | ὁ καὶ ... κἀγώ — L |
ὁ — H | καὶ — PC | βασιλ. W: βασιλεὺς V, βασιλεύσῃ I, βασιλεύειν C,
βασιλεύων P   § 11. 7 χλεύην ILPW: χλέβην H, χλέβη I | αὐτὰ IL
αὐτῶν H, — PC | στρατιώτας C   8 λέγω: ἐγώ P | βασιλεὺς V, βασιλεὺς
σολομῶν L | ἐγώ I: κἀγὼ HL, — PC | ὑπὸ· ἀπὸ C | ὑπὸ τῆς: ἀπάτης L,
9 σοι. ης V, — L | τοῦ: ἐκ C | § 12. κ. εἶπον ego· κ. ὑπὸ P, εἶπον HIC,
ἢ L, ὑπὸ (in textu, εἶπον ad marg.) Is | τὸ ὄνομα — P   10 ἁγίου
Ἰ(σρα)ὴλ A ἀγγέλου Ἰωὴλ PC, ἁγίου Ἰωὴλ Is | (20) καὶ C: ἐγὼ δὲ P,
διὸ A | ἐκέλευσα. ἐκάλεσα C | νήθειν νήθῃ V, + κλώθειν W, ἠδυνή-
θειν H | τὴν κάνναβιν Bncn: τ κάναβιν LP, τ. κανάβην IW, τ(ὴν) κανάβῃ V,
ἐν τῇ κανάβῃ H | * L f. 10ᵛ¹ | εἰς ... κάνναβιν (p. 21, l. 3): εἶτα λαβὼν
σχοινίον δήσας τοῦ ὀχλουμένου ἀσφαλῶς L, — W | τὰ σχοινία HV· ›ασχι-
νί(αν) I, τὰς σχοινίας Is, τὰς σχοίνους P

σχοινία τοῦ ἔργου τοῦ ναοῦ τοῦ θεοῦ. καὶ οὕτως σφραγισθὲν
καὶ δεθὲν κατηργήθη ὥστε ἱστάναι νύκτα καὶ ἡμέραν νήθειν τὴν
κάνναβιν

V Καὶ ἐκέλευσα * ἀχθῆναί μοι ἕτερον δαίμονα· καὶ ἤγαγέ
μοι Ἀσμοδαῖον τὸν πονηρὰν δαίμονα δεδεμένον. 2. καὶ ἐπηρώτησα αὐτόν· »σὺ τίς εἶ;« ὁ δὲ ἀπειλητικὸν βλέμμα ῥίψας
λέγει »σὺ δὲ τίς εἶ;« 3. καὶ εἶπον αὐτῷ· »οὕτως τετιμωρημένος
ἀποκρίνῃ;« ὁ δὲ τῷ αὐτῷ βλέμματι προσχὼν εἶπέ μοι· »πῶς
ἔχω σοι ἀποκριθῆναι; σὺ μὲν υἱὸς ἀνθρώπου εἶ, κἀγὼ ἀγγέλου,
καὶ διὰ θυγατρὸς ἀνθρώπου ἐγεννήθην, * ὥστε οὐδὲν ὑπερή-
φανον ῥῆμα οὐρανίου γένους πρὸς γηγενῆ. 4 τὸ ἄστρον μου

MSS HILPVW = Recc ABC   1 τ. ἔργ τ. ν : ἐν τῷ ἔργῳ τοῦ κτίσμα-
τος P | τοῦ ναοῦ τοῦ θεοῦ τὸ ἔργων V | οὕτως P ls: οὗτος HI | σφραγ. H.
σφραγιστ(εν) V, σφραγίσας IP   2 καὶ δεθὲν ego ∕ δοθὲν V, κ διωθὲν H,
κ. δῆσας αὐτὴν P, — I | κατηργ HIV ἐκατηργ P, + τὸ δαιμόνιον V |
ἐστι̇νε V, ἰστασθαι in ἱστάναι corr. P | νύκτα κ. ἡμ ν τ κανάβειν IV,
νυκτὸς ∕ ἡμέρας) τ καναβ. P, νήθιν τ κανάβειν ἡμέραν κ νύκταν II
3 κάνναβιν FIMg
   C V. MSS HILPVW = Recc ABC   4 (21) Καὶ (1°) τότε L | * H
f. 7ʳ, P f. 4ᵛ | ἕτ. δαιμ. HW. pr. καὶ W, ἕτ. δαιμόνιον PVIs, ἕτερα δαιμό-
νια IL, add. rubric. ἔλευσις ἀσμοδίου πρὸς σολομῶν⟨τα⟩ H | κ ἤγ μοι
— L | ἤγαγε .. δεδεμ HI (— ἤγ μοι) L. εὐθέως μοι προῆλθεν ὁ δαίμων
ἀσμόδιος (ex -αιος corr) δεδεμένος P, ἔστιν ἐνταῦθα C   5 § 2. ἐπηρώτων C
6 δὲ — H | ἀπειλ βλ ῥιψ. ego ἀπολυτικὸν βλέμα ῥίψας H (ῥιψ. προε-
πιστρέψας πρός με) L, ἀπηλικὸν ὄμ⟨μ⟩α ῥίψας C, βλοσυρὸν βλέμα βλέψας
IBIs (βλέμμα Kurz), μετὰ θυμοῦ καὶ ὀργῆς ἐμβλέψας με P   7 λέγει HI.
ἔφη PC — L | σὺ   αὐτῷ — A | δὲ — L   § 3. αὐτὸν C | οὕτως
PW οὗτος V, καὶ οὗτος A | τετιμ. P τετιμωρημένα C, τετηρημένος IL
(-ωμενος) H   8 ἀποκρ APV ὑπεκρίθην W, + μοι P, + λέγ ⟨ L | δὲ
+ πάλιν H | τῷ   προσχ. τῶ αὐτῶ βλέμμα προσχ I, τὸ αὐτὸ βλέματι H,
τὸ (— V) αὐτοῦ βλέμματι προσχῶν W (πρόσσχήν) V, μετ᾽ ὀργῆς P | εἶπε HI.
ἔφη C, λέγει P | μοι — C | πῶς. pι ἀλλὰ PC   9 ἔχω — P | ἀπο-
κριθῶ P | μὲν: γὰρ P, + γὰρ C | ἀνθρ υἱὸς P | εἶ — LC | κἀγὼ A
ἐγὼ δὲ PC | ἀγγέλου G ἀγγέλου σπορὰ P, ἄγγελός εἰμι (ἤμην H) A
10 καὶ IL — HP | καὶ ... γηγενῆ (I. 11) — C | θυγ ἀνθρ. IP, θυγα-
τέρων ἀνθρώπων HL | ἐγενν LP. ἐγεννήθης I (pr σὺ) H | * I f. 82ᵛ |
ὥστε ILP. ὅτε H | οὐδὲν — L   11 γηγενῆ L γηγενήν I, γαγενάν l. Is
errore, γηγενουν vel -ους H, γηγενεῖς P (in textu) Is | § 4 τὸ pr διὸ καὶ P,
pι τὸ δὲ C

   V 3. Sap VII 1   Gen VI 1—4

ἐν οὐρανῷ φωλεύει καὶ οἱ ἄνθρωποί με καλοῦσιν ἅμαξαν, οἱ δὲ
τὸν δρακοντόποδα· διὰ τοῦτο καὶ μικρότερα ἄστρα συμπάρεισι
τῷ ἐμῷ ἄστρῳ, καὶ γὰρ τοῦ πατρός μου τὸ ἀξίωμα καὶ ὁ θρόνος μέχρι σήμερον ἐν τῷ οὐρανῷ ἐστιν. 5. πολλὰ δὲ μή με
5 ἐρώτα, Σολομῶν, καὶ * γὰρ τὸ βασίλειόν σου διαρραγήσεται ἐν
καιρῷ καὶ αὕτη σου ἡ δόξα πρόσκαιρός ἐστι καὶ ὀλίγον * χρόνον
βασανίσαι ἡμᾶς ἔχεις, καὶ πάλιν νομὴν ἔχωμεν * ἐπ᾽ ἀνθρωπότητα ὥστε σέβεσθαι ἡμᾶς ὡς θεούς, μὴ γινωσκόντων τῶν ἀνθρώπων τὰ ὀνόματα τῶν καθ᾽ ἡμῶν τεταγμένων ἀγγέλλων.ι
10 6. Ἐγὼ δὲ Σολομῶν ἀκούσας ταῦτα ἐπιμελέστερον αὐτὸν
δεσμεύσας ἐκέλευσα ῥαβδίζεσθαι καὶ ἀπολογηθῆναι τίς καλεῖται
καὶ τίς ἡ ἐργασία αὐτοῦ. 7. ὁ δαίμων εἶπεν· »ἐγὼ Ἀσμοδαῖος

MSS HILPVW = Recc ABC. 1 φωλεύει IPC φολεύειν H, πολιτεύει L,
φωτεύει FILs | φολεύῃ ἐν τῷ οὐ(ρα)νῷ C | καὶ HIV. δ W, + αὐτὸ P·
οἱ ἄνδρες καὶ πᾶς ἄν(θρωπ)ος με L | οἱ (1°) — P | με A. — PW, ειμ(ε) V
| καλοῦσιν· λέγουσιν P | ἅμαξα V | τὸν — IW 2 δρακοντ. HIC: δρα-
κοντόπαιδα LP | διὰ ... ἄστρῳ. πλησιάζομαι σὺν τῷ ἄστρῳ αὐτοῦ P |
συμπάρεισι IL· συμπάρην H, παρίστανται C 3 τ. ἐ. ἀστ. C: τὸ ἐμὸν
ἄστρον A | καὶ γὰρ .. ἐστιν· P, καὶ ὁ τοῦ πατρὸς θρόνος ἐστὶν τὸ
ἀξίωμα ἐν οὐρανῷ C | γὰρ IL: — H | μου HL — I | θρόνον H, + μου L
4 μέχρι + τῇ H | μεχ. σημ. — I | τῷ — I | ἐστιν: δὲ H | § 5. πολ.
δὲ: καὶ πολ. P | μή με I: μὴ μεμε L, μοι μὴ P, μοι H, μὴ C 5 ἐρώτα
PC. ἐπερώτα (-ωτᾶς L) A | Σολ A — PC | κ. γὰρ A: ὅτι καὶ P | *H
f. 7ᵛ | γὰρ — C | σου τ. βασ. PC | διαρ. ἐν καιρ. ILC: ἐν καιρ. διαραγ. H,
πρὸς χρόνους μικροὺς διαρήγνυται (διαρρ. Pᶜ) P 6 αὕτη .. δόξα ILC.
ἡ δόξα σου αὕτη H | προσκ ἐστιν ἡ δόξα σου P | προσκ. ἐστι· πρὸς και-
ρὸν εἰσὶν L, προσκ. δὲ H, ἀποχωρίσει C | ὀλ. χρ. ὀλίγα P | * L f. 10ᵛ²
7 βασ. ἡμ. ἔχεις C. ἡμ. τυραννήσεις P, βασ. με ἔχεις A | νομὰν V | ἔχω
μεν HL. ἔχομεν (post ἀνθρωπ·) I. ἔξομεν P, εὕρομεν V, εὕρωμεν W | * V
f. 438ᵛ | ἐπ᾽ A τίς P, πρὸς C, + τὴν PC 8 θεοὺς + ὄντας PV, ὂν
τες W | γινώσκοντα H, -οντες W, -οντος V | τῶν: τὸν H, — L 9 τὸ
— L | καθ᾽ ἡμῶν HIV: καθεμίνων L, μεθ᾽ ἡμῶν W, καθ᾽ ἡμᾶς P

§ 6. MSS HILP = Recc AB (22) c V, 6—VI, 10 ἐγὼ δὲ ... τοῦ ἡλίου
om. C (= VW) per homoeoarcton 10 ταῦτα ἀκ. P | αὐτ. δεσμ. HL· αὐτ
ἐδέσμευσα καὶ I, δεσμ. αὐτ. P, + καὶ πάλιν περισφι(γ)ξον αὐτοῦ τοῦ ὀχλοι-
μένου τὰς χεῖρας καὶ ἐξόρκισον αὐτοῦ τοῦ ἐξελθεῖν· καὶ τύψας τῇ κεφαλῇ
τοῦ ὀχλουμένου μετὰ καλάμου καὶ μετὰ ἀρτίκου λέγει ἔξελθε πονηρὸν δαιμόνιον ἐπ᾽ ὀνόματι τοῦ κ(υρίο)υ καὶ τοῦ παιδὸς σολομῶντος· καὶ L 11 ῥαβδ·
αὐτὸν ῥαντίς. H, αὐτὸν ὀργίζεσθαι L, μαστίζεσθαι βουνεύροις P | ἀπολο-
γεῖσθαι P | τίς: πῶς I | καλεῖ σε (1 καλεῖσαι) H 12 αὐτοῦ — H
§ 7 ὁ δὲ ἔφη μοι P

C V 7 cf Tob. III 8, VI 14†

καλοῦμαι ⌐περιϰλυτός· οἰδαίνομαι⌐ ϰαϰουργίαν ἀνϑρώπων ἐν ὅλῳ
τῷ ϰόσμῳ. νεονύμφων ἐπίβουλός εἰμι· παρϑένων ϰάλλος ἀφανίζω ϰαὶ ϰαρδίας ἀλλοιῶ.«   8. ἔφην δὲ αὐτῷ· * »μόνη αὕτη σου
ἡ ἐργασία;« * ὁ δὲ πάλιν λέγει· »διὰ τῶν ἄστρων ⌐στρώνω
5 ϑηλυμανίας ϰαὶ ἔπειτα εἰς τριϰυμίας⌐ ϰαὶ ἕως ἑπτὰ ἐφόνευσα.«
* 9. ϰαὶ οὕτως ὥρϰισα αὐτὸν τὸ ὄνομα ϰυρίου Σαβαώϑ· »φοβή-
ϑητι, Ἀσμοδαῖε, τὸν ϑεὸν ϰαὶ εἰπέ μοι ἐν ποίῳ ἀγγέλῳ ϰαταρ-
γῆσαι« ὁ δαίμων λέγει· »Ῥαφαὴλ ὁ παρεστὼς ἐνώπιον τοῦ
ϑεοῦ· διώϰει δέ με ϰαὶ ἧπαρ μετὰ χολῆς ἰχϑύος ἐπὶ ϰροϰίνων
10 ἀνϑράϰων ϰαπνιζόμενον.«   10. ἐπηρώτησα πάλιν αὐτὸν λέγων·
»μὴ ϰρύψῃς ἀπ᾽ ἐμοῦ ῥῆμα, ὅτι ἐγώ εἰμι Σολομῶν υἱὸς Δαυείδ,

MSS HILP — Recc. AB   1 ϰαλοῦ I | τεριϰλυτός ego. περίϰριτος I,
περύϰριτος H, περιϰρίτην L, παρὰ βροτοῖς P, 1 forte περιϰριτός (ἰ. q περὶ
et ϰριτός), excellentissimus⌐ | οἰδαίνομαι ego εἰ
δαὶ νε μαι H, εἰδένεμαι ϰαὶ L ἠδύνομαι I | ϰαϰουργίας I | ἐν .. ϰόσμῳ
ante περιϰλυτός ponit I   2 νεονυμφ .. παρϑ· ϰαὶ ἡ ἐργασία μου ἐστὶ τὸ
τοὺς νεονύμφους ἐπιβουλεύειν μὴ συμμιγῆναι, ϰαὶ παντελῶς ἀποχωρίζω διὰ
πολλῶν (f. 5ʳ) συμφορῶν, ϰαὶ γυναιϰῶν παρϑ P | ἐπίβολος I | παρϑ
παρνα, ϑ supra π et ο supra α (2°) scr. H | ϰάλλος P: ϰάλος HII, ϰαλῶς L
| ϰαὶ — I | 8 § 8. (23) ἔφη H | δὲ δ᾽ ἐγώ P | ἔφην δὲ αὐτῷ. ϰαὶ πάλιν
εἶπον L | * hic explicit pagina non omnino scripta cod ms I
MSS HLP — Recc. AB.   8 ϰαὶ μόνη L μόνων H | αὕτη .. ἐργ: σου
ἡ ἐργ. ἔστιν αὕτη P   4 L f. 11ʳ¹ | πάλιν — P | λέγει P: λέγων H,
ἔφη L, + μοι P | διὰ τῶν .. ἐφόνευσα. περιφέρω ἀνϑρώπους εἰς λύσσαν
(Mg 1324) ϰαὶ εἰς ὄρεξιν, ἔχον(τες) τὰς γυναῖϰας αὐτῶν πάλιν εἰς ἑτέρας ἑτέρων ἀπέρχεσϑαι ἐν νυϰτὶ ϰαὶ ἡμέρᾳ, ὥστε ϰαὶ τὴν ἁμαρτίαν ἐπιτελεῖν ϰαὶ εἰς
φόνους ἐμπλαϰήσεσϑαι P | στρώνω ego: ἴστρον I, — H, cf. Dieterich, Unters.
p. 220, 230f., l. fortasse οἴστρω⁹   5 ϑυλιμανίας L, — H   6 * H f 8ʳ |
§ 9 (24) ϰαί . . αὐτὸν· ὥρισα δὲ αὐτῷ P | τῷ ὀνόματι L | φοβηϑ.: λέγων
pr. P, add. L   7 τ. ϑεὸν ἀσμοδαῖε P | ἐν — P | ἐϰ ποίου ἀγγέλου L |
ϰαταργῇ σύ P   8 ὁ δαιμ. λεγ. ὁ δὲ ἔφη P | λέγων H | διὰ ῥαφαὴλ τοῦ
ἀρχαγγέλου τοῦ παρεστῶτος ἐνώπιον τοῦ ϑρόνου τοῦ ϑεοῦ P | παρεστιϰὸς L
9 με δὲ H | ϰαὶ — P | ἰχϑύος ἧπαρ ϰαὶ χολὴ P | ἧπαρ — L | (με)τὰ
χολῆς L. σὺν χολὴν H | ἐπὶ ϰορϰίνων ἀνϑρ. ϰαπν. II, ϰαπνιζόμενος ἐπὶ
ϰορϰίνου ἀνϑρ. L, ἐπὶ μυριϰίνῳ ἄνϑραϰι ἐπιϰαπνιζόμενα P, + ϰαὶ λαβὼν ϰαὶ
λαβὼν (sic) ὁ ἀναγινώσϰων τὴν ἁγίαν διαϑήϰην ταύτην· ἰχϑύος χολὴν ϰαπνί-
σας (III litt. perierunt, fortasse ὑπὸ vel τὸν) ὀχλούμενον λέγ(ων)· διώϰει σε
ῥαφαὴλ ὁ παρεστιϰὸς ἐνώπιον τοῦ ϑεοῦ· λέγ(ε) τοῦτο τρεῖς ϰαὶ ἄρξου L
10 § 10 ἐπερώτων δὲ αὐτὸν L | πάλιν ἐγώ P | λέγων H λέγω L, — P
11 ὅτι ... Δαυείδ. ὅτι ἐγὼ ἔλαβα ἐξεσίαν τοῦ χειρῶσαι πάντας τοὺς δαίμονας L, + βασιλέως Ἰ(σρα)ὴλ P

C. V 9: cf. Tob VI 17f., VIII 2f

καὶ εἰπέ μοι τὸ ὄνομα τοῦ ἰχθύος οὗ σὺ σέβῃ.« ὁ δὲ λέγει· »τὸ
ὄνομα κέκληται γλάνις· ἐν τοῖς ποταμοῖς τῶν Ἀσσυρίων εὑρί-
σκεται· μόνος γὰρ ἐκεῖ γεννᾶται, ὅτι κἀγὼ ἐν τοῖς μέρεσιν ἐκείνοις εὑρίσκομαι.« 11. καὶ λέγω αὐτῷ· »οὐδὲν ἕτερον παρά σου,
5 Ἀσμοδαῖε;« καὶ εἰπέ μοι »ἐπίσταται ἡ δύναμις τοῦ θεοῦ τοῦ διὰ
τῆς αὐτοῦ σφραγῖδος δεσμεύσαντός με ἀλύτοις δεσμοῖς ὅτι ἅπερ
σοι εἶπον ἀληθῆ εἰσιν. ἀξιῶ δέ σε, βασιλεῦ Σολομῶν, μή με
κατακρίνῃς εἰς ὕδωρ.« 12. ἐγὼ δὲ μειδιάσας εἶπον· »ζῇ κύριος ὁ
θεὸς τῶν πατέρων μου * σίδηρα ἔχεις φορέσαι καὶ πηλὸν ποιή-
10 σεις εἰς ὅλην τὴν σκευὴν τοῦ ναοῦ ἀνατρίβων τὴν χορηγίαν τῆς κώ-
μης « καὶ ἐκέλευσα γενέσθαι ὑδρίας δέκα καὶ περιχώννυσθαι αὐτόν.

MSS HLP = Recc AB. 1 οὐ σὺ σέβῃ. οὐ οὐ σεύει H, οὐ σέβῃς L, ᾧ σὺ
σέβῃ | ὁ δὲ λέγει H, ὁ δὲ ἔφη P, — L | τ. ὀν. κεκλ. γλάνις· τὸ ὀν καίκητε-
γλάνος H, ὀνόματι γλάνος P, λέγεται ὁ ἰχθὺς· γλαύρος L 2 γλάνις vel
γλανίς conj Bncn | εὑρισκ ἐν τ ποτ. ἀσσυρίας P | τοῖς — H | τῶν — H |
* L f. 11ˣ² 3 μόνος .. γενν. H: μόνοις ἐν τοῖς ὕδασι ἐκείνοις γενᾶται L,
— P | ὅτι κἀγὼ H· ὅτι ἐγὼ L, διότι καὶ P | ἐν τ. μερ. ἐκ.. ἐν ταῖς μέρε-
σιν ἐκείναις H, ἐν ἐκείναις ταῖς ἡμέραις L, εἰς ἐκεῖνα τὰ μέρη P 4 εὑρισ
HL: καταπεριπολεύω P | § 11 (25) κ. λέγω αὐτῷ (αὐτὸ) H. ἐγὼ δὲ λέγω
πρὸς αὐτὸν P, ὁ δὲ σολομῶν L | ἕτερον HP ἑτέρῳ L, ἕταιρον vel ἔτυμον
conj. Bncn | σου HL: σοι P 5 Ἀσμοδ. HLBncn· ἀσμοδίῳ P | κ. εἶπε
HL: ὁ δὲ ἔφη P | μοι — L | ἐπίσταμαι L, ἐπίστασαι H | τοῦ διὰ ...
δεσμ. H: διὰ τ. σφρ. αὐτοῦ δεσμ. L, τοῦ διὰ τῆς ἐκείνου σφρ δεσμεύσας P,
ἡ διὰ ... δεσμεύσασα Crtr 6 με — H | * H f. 8ᵛ 7 σοι P James: συ
HL | εἴπω H | εἶπον σοι P | εἴσιν P: εἶναι HL | ἀξιῶ δέ σε H. ἀξιῶ
σε δὲ L, δέομαί σου P | σοὶ βασ. L 8 § 12. μειδιάσας HP. θαυμάσας L
ζῇ . φορέσαι κύριος ὁ θεὸς τῶν πατ. μου ποίησον σίδηρον ὥσπερ μανιά-
κην καὶ βαλὼν τοῦ ὀχλουμένου εἰς τὸν τράχηλον αὐτοῦ καὶ ἀναγινώσκων τὴν
ἄνων (1 ἄνω) ταύτην διαθήκην· εἶτα λέγει ὁ ἀναγινώσκων· ὅτι σίδηρα ἔχει.
φορέσε (1 -σαι) L 9 * P f. 5ᵛ | ἔχεις φορ. H· φορέσω σε P | καὶ: pr.
ἀλλὰ P | supra τὸν πηλὸν adscr ποιήσεις P 10 εἰς: ἐφ᾽ H | κατα-
σκευὴν P | ἀνατρίβουν L | τ. χορ. τ. κωμ. H: τ. χορ. τοῦ ναοῦ L, τοῖς
ποσί σου P, 1 fortasse τ. χορ. ταῖς κόμαις? 11 κ ἐκελ: ἐκελ. δὲ L | γε-
νέσθαι H: ἀχθῆναι L, δοθῆναι αὐτῷ P | δέκα ὑδρ. φέρειν ὕδωρ P | καὶ
. αὐτόν — P | περιχωναιαθαι H | αὐτὸν: + καὶ λαβὼν ὁ ἀναγι-
νώσκων ἐκ τῶν τεσσάρων γονιῶν τοῦ ναοῦ· τοῦ δεσποτικοῦ χωριγην (f. 11ᵛⁱ)
ἐκ τῆς ἐπικειμένης ὕλης καὶ τύχους (1. τείχους) καὶ τρίψας αὐτὸν καὶ ποιήσας
ψηλόν· εἶτα λαβὼν ὑδρίας δέκα γεμᾶται ἐπὶ τὴν χωρηγίαν καὶ σταλάξας ἀπὸ
ἑκάστης ὑδρίας καὶ πηλὸν χρίσας ἐπὶ τὸ μέτοπον τοῦ ὀχλουμένου καὶ τὸν
πόγωνα καὶ τῶν δύο ὀτίων· εἶτα ἀπογυμνώσας τὸν ὀχλούμενον καὶ ἀνατρίψας
αὐτοῦ ὅλον τῷ σῶμα μετὰ τῆς χωριγίας ἀπὸ τοῦ ἀμφαλοῖ καὶ ἄνω εἶτα ὁ
ἀναγινώσκων πάλιν τὴν ἄνω ταύτην διαθήκην L.

καὶ δεινῶς στενάξας ὁ δαίμων τὰ κελευσθέντα αὐτὸν κατειρ-
γάζετο. τοῦτο δὲ ἐποίησε διότι καὶ τὸ προγνωστικὸν εἶχεν ὁ
Ἀσμοδαῖος. 13. καὶ ἐδόξασα τὸν θεὸν ἐγὼ Σολομῶν τὸν δόντα
μοι τὴν ἐξουσίαν ταύτην· τὸ δὲ ἧπαρ τοῦ ἰχθύος καὶ τὴν χολὴν
μετὰ κλάσματος ⌈στύρακος λευκοῦ ὑπέκαιον τὸν Ἀσμοδαῖον⌉ διὰ
τὸ εἶναι αὐτὸν δυνατόν, καὶ κατηργεῖτο αὐτοῦ ἡ φωνὴ ⌈καὶ
πλήρης ὁδοὺς πικρίας.⌉

VI. Καὶ ἐκέλευσα πάλιν παραστῆναι ἔμπροσθέν μου τὸν
Βεελζεβοὺλ καὶ προσκαθίσας ἔδοξέ μοι ἐπερωτῆσαι αὐτόν· »διὰ
τί σὺ μόνος ἄρχων τῶν δαιμόνων;« 2. ὁ δὲ λέγει μοι· »διὰ
τὸ μόνον με ὑπολειφθῆναι τῶν οὐρανίων ἀγγέλων. ἐγὼ γὰρ
ἤμην ἐν πρώτοις οὐράνιος ἄγγελος ὁ προσαγορευόμενος Βεελζεβούλ. 3. καὶ μετ' ἐμοῦ δεύτερος ⌈ἄθεος ὃν ἐπέταμε⌉ ὁ θεός, καὶ
νῦν κατακλεισθεὶς ὧδε ⌈κρατεῖ τὸ⌉ ἐν Ταρτάρῳ τῷ δεσμῷ ἐμοῦ

MSS HLP — Recc. AB. **1** δεινῶς πικρῶς H | αὐτὸν L· μοι P, — H |
ἀπειργ. LP. κατηρτίζετο H   **2** δὲ — L | ἐποίησε HLBn ἐποίησα P |
διότι ὅτι L | καὶ — H | τὸ προγν. εἶχεν H· προγινώσκων· εἶχεν L, τὰ
μέλλοντα ᾔδει προγνωστικὸς ὤν, τὸ χαλεπὸν δαιμόνιον P | ὁ — H   **3 § 13**
καὶ — L | ἐγὼ σολ. ἐδόξ. τ. θ. τοῦ οὐρανοῦ κ. τῆς γῆς H | ὁ σολ. L
| ἐξουσ. ταυτ. HL. σοφίαν τοῦ δούλου αὐτοῦ P. + ἵνα ὑπογνῶσι ἡμῖν οἱ
δαίμονες L | χόλην αὐτοῦ P   **5** μετὰ .. ὑπέκαιον· μ. κλασ. σωρακλώου
vel στυρακ) εἶπεν καὶ H, μ. κλάστομα· συρωκλωκοῦ καὶ εἶπον L, μ. καλα-
λίου στύρακος λύων ὑπέκαιον P | λευκοῦ ego· 1. forte λωτοῦ | τῷ ἀσομο-
λῳ H   **6** καὶ P — HL | κατηργεῖτο P, κατήργηται H, κατηργειτον L
| ἡ ... πικρίας (— καὶ) H: ἡ φ. κ. πλήροις ὁδοῦ πικ. L, ἡ φόρην ὃς πι-
ρία P, ἡ ἀφόρητος πικρία Pᶜ (ad marg.)

C. VI.   MSS HLP — Recc. AB. (26)   **8** παραστῆσαι H | ἔμπρ μου· μοι
μπρ. P   **9** Βεελζ.. + τὸν ἄρχοντα τῶν δαιμονίων P | προσκ. ... αὐτὸν
HL· ἐπικαθήσας ἐπὶ βήματος ἐνδοξοτέρου ἔφην αὐτῷ P, + καὶ εἶπον αὐ-
όν H   **10** ἄρχων ἄρχης H | **§ 2** λέγει HL· ἔφη P   **11** τὸ. τὸν L |
πελήφθην H, ὑπέληφθα L | ἀγγελ. + τῶν κατελθόντων P   **12** ἤμην P.
μὶν H, εἰμὶ L | ἐν πρωτ. ἐν πρότης HL, ἐν τῷ πρώτῳ οὐρανῷ P | οὐ-
άνιος H· οὐρανοῦ L, πρῶτος P | ἄγγελος HP   μὴ L

§ 3. MS P textum alium praebet hunc καὶ νῦν κρατῶ πάντων τῶν ἐν
ᾧ ταρτάρῳ δεσμῶν (δεσμένων Fl, δεδεμένων Mg). ἔχω δὲ καὶ γόνον καὶ
ἐμπολεύει ἐν τῇ ἐρυθρᾷ θαλάσσῃ, καὶ ὡς ἴδιον τινὰ καιρὸν ἐπανέρχεται
πρός με ὑποτασσόμενος, καὶ τὰ ἑαυτοῦ ἔργα πρός με ἀνακαλύπτει, καὶ στη-
ίζω αὐτὸν ἐγὼ
MSS HL — Rec A. **1. 13, § 3** ἄθεος ὃν ἐπέταμε ego   ἀθάε ἐπὶ τομὴν H,
θαὶ, ἐπὶ τὸ μὴν L | ὁ — L   **14** κατὰ κλειθεὶς L | κρατεῖ τὸ ego:
κρατεῖτε H   κρατῶ τε L; 1. forte κρατῶ τὸ? | ἐν τῷ ταρτάρῳ δεσμῷ L

γένος· καὶ τρέφεται ἐν τῇ Ἐρυθρᾷ θαλάσσῃ· ὃς ἐν καιρῷ ἰδίῳ
ἐλεύσεται εἰς θρίαμβον.« 4. καὶ εἶπον αὐτῷ· »τίνες εἰσὶν αἱ
πράξεις σου;« καὶ εἶπέ μοι· »κἀγὼ καθαιρῶ διὰ τυράννων καὶ
τὰ δαιμόνια ποιῶ παρὰ ἀνθρώποις σέβεσθαι καὶ τοὺς ἁγίους καὶ
5 τοὺς ἐκλεκτοὺς ἱερεῖς εἰς ἐπιθυμίαν ἐγείρω. ** καὶ φθόνους ἐν
πόλεσι καὶ φόνους ἀποτελῶ καὶ πολέμους ἐπάγω.« 5. καὶ εἶπα
αὐτῷ· »προσένεγκέ μοι τὸν ἐν τῇ Ἐρυθρᾷ θαλάσσῃ ὃν εἶπας
τρεφόμενον.« ὁ δὲ λέγει »οὐκ ἀνενέγκω πρός σε οὐδένα. ἐλεύσεται δέ τις ὀνόματι Ἐφιππᾶς ὃς ἐκεῖνον δεσμεύσει καὶ ἀναγάγει
10 ἐκ τοῦ βυθοῦ.« 6. καὶ εἶπον αὐτῷ· »λέγε μοι πῶς ἐκεῖνός ἐστιν
ἐν τῷ βυθῷ τῆς Ἐρυθρᾶς θαλάσσης καὶ τί τὸ ὄνομα αὐτοῦ.«
ὁ δὲ ἔφη· »μή με ἐρωτᾷς· οὐ δύνασαι παρ᾽ ἐμοῦ μαθεῖν, αὐτὸς
γὰρ ἐλεύσεται πρός σε διὰ τὸ καὶ ἐμὲ πρός σε εἶναι«.

MSS HL = Rec. A   1 γένους I | Ἐρυθ. — H | ὃς ὡς HL

§ 4 MS P. (27) ἐγὼ σολομῶν ἔφην πρὸς αὐτὸν λέγων· βεελζεβούλ, τις
(f. 6ʳ) ἐστὶν ἡ πρᾶξις σου, ὁ δὲ λέγει· ἐγὼ βασιλεῖς ἀπολῶ· συμμαχῶ μετὰ
ἀλλοφύλων τυράννων· καὶ τοὺς ἐμοὺς δαίμονας ἐπιβάλλω πρὸς τοὺς ἀνθρώπους ἵνα εἰς αὐτοὺς πιστεύωσι καὶ ἀπόλλωνται· καὶ τοὺς ἐκλεκτοὺς δούλους
τοῦ θεοῦ, ἢ ἱερεῖς καὶ πίστους ἀνθρώπους εἰς ἐπιθυμίας ἁμαρτιῶν πονηρῶν
καὶ αἱρέσεων κακῶν καὶ ἔργων παρανόμων διεγείρω, καὶ ὑπακούουσί μοι, καὶ
εἰς ἀπόλειαν φέρω αὐτούς. καὶ φθόνους καὶ φόνους καὶ πολέμους καὶ ἀρρε-
νοβατίας καὶ ἕτερα κακὰ τοῖς ἀνθρώποις ἐνεργῶ, καὶ ἀπολῶ τὸν κόσμον.
§ 5. (28) εἶπον οὖν αὐτῷ· προσάγαγέ μοι τὸν σὸν γόνον ὅνπερ λέγεις ὅτι
ἐστὶν ἐν· τῇ θαλάσσῃ τῇ ἐρυθρᾷ. ὁ δὲ λέγει· ἐγὼ αὐτὸν οὐ φέρω πρός σε·
ἐλεύσεται δὲ πρός με ἕτερος δαίμων ὀνόματι ἐφιππᾶς, (Mg 1325) αὐτὸν
δεσμεύσω καὶ αὐτὸς ἐκ τοῦ βυθοῦ ἀναγάγει πρός με. § 6. ἐγὼ δὲ λέγω πρὸς
αὐτόν· πῶς ἔστιν ὁ υἱός σου ἐν τῷ βυθῷ τῆς (FIMg, τοῖς MS) θαλάσσης καὶ
τί τὸ ὄνομα αὐτοῦ; ὁ δὲ ἔφη· μή με ἐπερωτᾷς, οὐ γὰρ δυνήσῃ παρ᾽ ἐμοὶ μα-
θεῖν· αὐτὸς γὰρ ἐλεύσεται πρὸς σὲ δι᾽ ἐμοῦ κελεύσματος καὶ εἴποι σοι φανερῶς.
MSS HL = Rec. A. 1 2, § 4. αὐτῷ: αὐτὸν H   3 καθαιρῷ ego: κα-
θαίρω HL | τύραννον H   4 τὰ δαιμόνια H, τοὺς δαίμονας L | σεβ. π
ἀνθρ. L   5 * H f 9ᵛ | ἐγύρω L, ἔγειρον H | ** L f. 12ᵣⁱ   6 φόνον ἐν πολ.
κ. φθόνους L | ἀποτελῶν κ. πολ. ἐπάγω H, ἀποστελῶ ἐν πολέμοις· ἐπάγω
καὶ πόνους καὶ οὐκ ἔστιν τοῖς ἀνθρώποις· οὐδὲν καλὸν οὐ (1. 8) δύναμαι·
ποιῆσαι αὐτῷ L | § 5. κ. εἶπα αὐτῷ H. ὁ δὲ βασιλεὺς λέγει L   7 τὸν
. . . τρεφομ.. τὸν . . . ὡς εἶπας τρεφομένας H, ὃν εἶπας γένους τὸ ἐν τῇ ἐρ
θαλ. τρεφομένους L   8 οὐκ (ἀνέγκω) . οὐδ. H. ἐγὼ αὐτῶ οὐκ ἀνενέγκω·
πρὸς σὲ L   9 Ἐφιππᾶς (cf. P): ἔφιππος H, ἐφηπτας L | ὃς ἐκεῖνον ego·
ὡς ἐκεῖνος HL | δεσμ. καὶ H: δεσμεύσας L | ἀνάγει L   10 § 6 αὐτὸν H
11 τῷ . . θαλ L· τῇ ἐρυθρᾷ θαλάσσῃ H | τί — L   12 παρ᾽ H: περὶ L
13 τὸ ego τοῦτο HL

7. Εἶπον δὲ αὐτῷ· »λέγε μοι ἐν ποίῳ ἄστρῳ προσοικεῖσαι.«
ὁ δὲ λέγει· »τὸ καλούμενον παρὰ ἀνθρώποις Ἑσπερία.« 8. ἐγὼ
δὲ λέγω· »φράσον μοι ὑπὸ ποίου ἀγγέλου καταργεῖσαι.« ὁ δὲ *
ἔφη· * »ὑπὸ τοῦ παντοκράτορος θεοῦ· καλεῖται δὲ παρ' Ἑβραίοις
Πατικῆ, ὁ ἀφ' ὕψους κατελθών· ἔστι δὲ τῶν Ἑλληνιστῶν Ἐμμανουήλ, οὗ δέδοικα τρέμων. ἐάν τίς με ὁρκίσῃ τὸ Ἐλωί, μέγα
ὄνομα τῆς δυνάμεως αὐτοῦ, ἀφανὴς γίνομαι.« 9. ἐγὼ δὲ Σολομῶν ἀκούσας ταῦτα ἐκέλευσα αὐτὸν Θηβαῖα μάρμαρα πρίζειν.
ἐν δὲ τῷ ἄρξασθαι πρίζειν αὐτὸν ἠλάλαζον ὅλα τὰ δαιμόνια
μεγάλῃ τῇ φωνῇ διὰ τὸν βασιλέα Βεελζεβούλ· 10. ἐγὼ δὲ Σολομῶν ἐπηρώτων αὐτὸν λέγων· »εἰ βούλει ἄφεσιν λαβεῖν, διήγησαί
μοι περὶ τῶν ἐπουρανίων.« ἔφη δὲ ὁ Βεελζεβούλ· »ἄκουσον,
βασιλεῦ· ἐὰν θυμιάσῃς στακτὴν καὶ λίβανον καὶ βολβοὺς θαλάσ-

§ 7 sectionem hanc om. ms. P.   § 8. (29) MS P. ἐγὼ πρὸς αὐτὸν λεγω
λέγε μοι ὑπὸ ποίου ἀγγέλου καταργῇ σύ. ὁ δὲ ἔφη· ὑπὸ ἁγίου καὶ τιμίου
ὀνόματος τοῖ παντοκράτορος θεοῦ, τῷ καλουμένῳ παρ' Ἑβραίοις πευστικῷ,
οὗ ἡ ψῆφος χμδ'· παρὰ δὲ Ἕλλησι ἐμμανουήλ· καὶ ἐάν τις τῶν Ῥομαίων ὁρκίσῃ με τὸ μέγα ὄνομα τῆς δυνάμεως ἐλεῆθ ἀφανὴς (f. 6ᵛ) γίνομαι   § 9. (30)
ἐγὼ σολομῶν ταῦτα ἀκούσας ἐξεπλάγην καὶ ἐκέλευσα αὐτὸν πρίζειν μάρμαρα
θηβαῖα. ἐν δὲ τῷ ἄρξασθαι αὐτὸν πρίζειν τὰ μάρμαρα οἱ ἕτεροι δαίμονες
ἀνεκραύγασαν φωνὴν μεγάλην, ἀλαλάζοντες διὰ τὸν βασιλέα αὐτῶν βεελζεβούλ.   § 10. textum similiorem habent cod. mss. HLP.

MSS HL = Rec. A.   1 § 7. προσοικεῖσαι L· καλεῖσαι H   2 ὁ δὲ . .
Ἑσπερ. H: — L | § 8: ἐγὼ ego· ὁ HL   3 φράσον ego· φφρασον H, φράσω L
| ποίων ἀγγέλων H | * H f. 10ʳ   4 * L f. 12ʳ² [τοῦ L. — H | κα-
λεῖται ego. καλοῦμαι HL   5 πατικῆ H, πατηκεῖ L | ὁ (James, οὐ ms.) ·
Ἐμμαν. H: παρὰ δὲ ἕλληνας ἐμμανουήλ καὶ ἀφ' ὕψους κατελθεῖν L   6 οὐ
δέδηκα τρεμ. H, οὐδὲ διατρέμων L | τίς με: τοῖς μοι H | τις ὁρκ. με L |
τῷ ἐλωῖθ H, ἐν τῷ ἐλωῖ L   7 γένομαι L, ἐγένομαι H | § 9. Σολ. — L
8 αὐτὸν H τοῦτον L | Θηβαῖα H: βριβαῖα L   9 ἐν ... αὐτὸν (αὐ-
τός) H. εἶτα ὁ ἀναγινώσκων· ἐγγίσας τοῦ ὀχλουμένου ἐπὶ τοῦ στήθους
λέγων ἐκ τρίτου μεγαλοφώνος L | ἠλάλαζαν H | ὅλα — L   10 φωνῇ·
λέγων L

MSS HLP = Recc. AB.   l. 10 §. 10 (31) ἐγὼ δὲ HP: ἀκούσας ταῦτα ὁ L
11 ἐπηρώτησα P | αὐτ. πάλιν λεγ. L | βούλει HL θέλεις P | ἀφ. λαβ..
ἄφεσιν λαβῶν L, ἀφ ἐκροῖν (l. ἔχειν) H, λαβεῖν ἄνεσιν P | διήγησόν L
12 περὶ P: τὴν A | ἔφη .. Βεελζ: ἔφη ὁ βασιλεὺς H, ἐφοβήθη δὲ ὁ βεελζ
καὶ εἶκεν L, λέγει δὲ βεελζ. P | ἄκουσον, βασ. P — H, ἀκ. βασιλεῦ καὶ
λαβῶν ὁ ἀναγινώσκων· νάρσιν· καὶ κρόκον καὶ καπνίσας τὸν (f 12ᵛ¹) ὀχ-
λούμενον· καὶ λέγει ὁ βεελζεβουλ L   13 βολβ. θαλ: β. θαλασσίους P
βόλους θαλ A

σης, νάρδον τε καὶ κρόκον, καὶ λύχνους ἅψῃς ἑπτὰ ἐν σεισμῷ,
οἰκίαν ἐρείσεις. ἐὰν δὲ * καθαρὸς ὢν ἅψῃς ὄρθρου ἐν ἡλίῳ
ἡμέρας, ὄψεις τοὺς δράκοντας τοὺς ἐπουρανίους πῶς εἰλοῦνται
καὶ σύρουσι τὰ ἅρμα τοῦ ἡλίου.« 11. ἐγὼ δὲ Σολομῶν ἀκούσας
5 ταῦτα ἐπετίμησα αὐτὸν καὶ εἶπον· »σιώπησαι καὶ πρίζε τὰ μάρμαρα καθὼς προσέταξά σοι.«

VII. Καὶ εὐλογήσας τὸν θεὸν ἐγὼ Σολομῶν ἐκέλευσα παρεῖναί μοι ἕτερον δαίμονα· καὶ ἦλθε πρὸ προσώπου μου καὶ ἦν
τὸ πρόσωπον ἐπιφέρων ἐν τῷ ἀέρι ἄνω ὑψηλὸν καὶ τὸ ὑπόλει-
10 πον τοῦ σώματος εἰλούμενον ὡσεὶ κοχλίας. 2. καὶ ἔρρηξε στρα-
τιώτας οὐκ ὀλίγους καὶ ἤγειρε * καὶ λάβρον κονιορτὸν ἀπὸ τῆς
γῆς καὶ ἀνέφερεν ἄνω καὶ πολλὰ ἔρριπτεν ἐπὶ τὸ ἐμὲ θαμβεῖσθαι,
καὶ εἶπον· ⌜»τίνα ἔχω ἐρωτῆσαι;« ἕως ἐπὶ πολύ. 3. καὶ ἀναστάν-

MSS HLP = Recc. AB. 1 νάρδιν L | ἀνάψῃς L | ἐν σεισμῷ. — H,
ἐν εἱρμῷ conj. dubitantei Cr   2 οἰκ. ἐρεισ. P· οὖν καὶ ἂν ὡρίσῃς H, οὐ-
κεῖαν ὀρώσεις L | δὲ — L | * H f. 10ᵛ | καθ. ὢν P: καθαρὸν A | ἀνά-
ψῃς L   3 ἡμέρας ego ἐνημεραν H, ἡμέρα L, ἡμ (compendia mihi inenoda-
bilia), 1. fortasse ἡμέρα vel ἡμερῶν P, ἡμένου (ἡμετέρου, ἡμετέρῳ?) Fl | pro
ἐν ἡλ. ἡμ. 1. ἐν ὕλῃ ἐνήμενος(?), cf. Test. XII Patr., Levi XVIII 3 | ὄψοι P
| τοὺς (1°)· τότε P | δράκοντας HP διακόνους L | οὐρανίους P   4 σύ-
ρουσι HP ἐσυρνουσι L | ἡλίου LP: θεοῦ H, forte recte
MSS HLPVW = Recc. ABC. § 11. (32) 4 ἐγὼ HPC: ὁ L | ἐγὼ .. ἀκουσ.
bis scr V | ταῦτα ... σοι — C | ἐπετίμησεν L, ἐπε-
τίμουν H | κ. εἶπον »σιωπ. καὶ ego: κ. ἐσιώπα καὶ ἐλάλουν αὐτὸν H, σιω-
πῆσαι καὶ L, κ. εἶπον, σιώπα μοι ἕως τούτου καὶ P   6 καθὼς προσετ. σοι
καλὸς προέταξά σοι· λέγε ὁ σολομῶν L, ὡς προσετ σοι P, κατὰ τὸ ὁρι-
σθὲν σοι H
C. VII. MSS HLPVW = Recc. ABC   7 Καὶ εἶτα L | Καὶ ... θεὸν
bis scr V, + τοῦ οὐρανοῦ B | ἐγὼ Σολ.. — L, + καὶ H | τότε ἐκέλευσεν L
| παρεῖναι: περίνε L   8 ἕτερα δαιμόνια καὶ ἦλθον ἕτερον δαιμόνιον ἐπὶ
προσώπου L | κ. ἦν . ἐπιφερ. A. ὃς ἦν ἐπιφ. τ. προσ. P, ὅπερ ἦν (— V)
ἡμιπρόσωπον C   9 ἐν . ὑψηλὸν P (— ἄνω) C· ἐν τῷ ἀρενόψει H, τὸ
ἄρενω· ὄψιν L | τὸ λοῖπον σῶμα L | ὑπόλοιπον HC 10 σώ-
ματος H. πνεύματος PC | ὡσεὶ κοχ. P· ὡς εἰ κόχλον H, ὡς κοχλύος L, ὡς
κοχλίας C | § 2 ἔρρηξε ... ὀλιγ. A. ὀλίγους διέρρηξεν PC   11 κ. ἤγειρε
κ. λαβ. κον ego κ. εἴγειρεν κ. λαῦρον οὐκ ὀνιορτὸν H, κ. ἴγειρεν δὲ καὶ
λαύραν καὶ (— V) κον. C, ἤγειρε δὲ καὶ φοβερὸν κον. P | ἀπὸ HC: ἐπὶ LP
| πολλὰ A: πάλιν PC   12 ἐν τῷ θαυμάσθαι με L, ἐν τῷ ἐμὲ θαμβηθῆ-
ναι C | ἐμὲ: ἡμᾶς P | θαμβῆσαι P   13 καὶ .. ἐρωτῆσαι — C | κ. εἶ-
πον H. κ. εἶπεν P, — L | ἐρωτίσω H | ἕως ... μου ego. καὶ δὴ ὃς ἐπὶ
πολὴ ἀνείσταντά με V, κ δὴ ὡς ἐπὶ πολὺ ἀναστάντος μοι W, ἐώω· ἐπὶ πολὺ
καὶ ἀν. μου H, ἕως ἐπὶ πολλῇ· καὶ ἀν. μου L, ὡς ἐπὶ πολύ, καὶ ἀναστάντα
με [in textu, κ(αὶ) ἀναστὰς ad marg.] P

τος μου ἔπτυσα¹ χαμαὶ * κατ' ἐκεῖνον τὸν τόπον καὶ ἐσφράγισα
τῷ δακτυλιδίῳ τοῦ θεοῦ, καὶ οὕτως ἔστη ἡ αὔρα. τότε ἠρώτησα αὐτὸν λέγων· »σὺ τίς εἶ;« καὶ οὕτως κονιορτὸν τινάξας
ἀπεκρίθη μοι· »τί θέλεις, βασιλεῦ Σολομῶν;« 4. ἀπεκρίθην δὲ
αὐτῷ· »εἰπέ μοι τί λέγεις κἀγώ σε ἐρωτᾶν θέλω.« οὕτως δὲ εὐχαριστῶ τῷ θεῷ τῷ σοφίσαντί με πρὸς τὰς βουλὰς αὐτῶν ἀπο-
κρίνεσθαι. ἔφη δέ μοι ὁ δαίμων· »ἐγὼ καλοῦμαι Διξ Τέτραξ.«
5. εἶπον δὲ αὐτῷ· »τίς ἡ πρᾶξίς σου;« ἔφη δέ· »ἀνθρώπους
σκορπίζω καὶ στρόφους ποιῶ καὶ πῦρ ἅπτω καὶ ἀγροὺς ἐμπυρίζω
καὶ οἴκους καταργῶ. ἐπὶ πλεῖστον δὲ ἔχω τὴν πρᾶξιν ἐν θέρει.
ἐὰν δὲ καιρὸν εὕρω, ὑποδύνω εἰς γωνίας τοίχων νύκτα καὶ ἡμέ-
ραν· ἤδη γὰρ γόνος εἰμὶ τοῦ μεγάλου.« 6. εἶπον * δὲ αὐτῷ·

MSS HLPVW = Recc. ABC.   **1** § 3. ἔπτυσα C (ad marg) P: πτύσας A,
πτύσαι P (in textu) | * H f. 11ʳ | κατ' . . θεοῦ H καὶ κατ' ... τὸ
δακτυλίδιον τ. θ. L, κατ' ἐκεῖνον τοῦ τόπον καὶ ... θεοῦ (in textu) P (— τοῦ
θεοῦ) V, χαμαὶ κατ' ἐκεῖνον τοῦ τ⟨ό⟩π⟨ον⟩ κ⟨αὶ⟩ ἐ P (ad marg.), καὶ ἐσφρ. τ
δακτ. κατ' ἐκεῖνον τοῦ τόπου W   **2** οὕτως PC. οὗτος A | ἔστη C: ἔστην (ex
ἔστιν corr.) P, ἐστὶν L, ἔσται H | αὔρα LP: λαύρα C, λαύρα τοῦ δαίμονος
σιωπᾶν H, + ἐκείνη LC | τότε κἀγὼ H | ἐπηρώτησα C   **3** τίς εἶ σὺ H |
κ οὕτως L. ↙ οὗτος H, κ τούτῳ (τοῦτο V) πάλιν C, ἄρα (αὔρα conj. Fl)
οὕτω πάλιν P | τινάξας AP. τὴν ἄξαν C, ῥίψας W   **4** μοι· + ὁ δαίμων
καὶ εἶπεν L | τί με.θέλεις ἐπερωτᾶν C | βασ. Σολ.· — L, add. rubric.
ἀπόκρησις τοῦ δαίμονος ἠλλξ πρὸς σολομ(ῶν) H | § 4. ἀπεκρίθην ... ἀπο-
κρίνεσθαι — H | ἀπεκριθ. . . οὕτως δὲ· ἐγὼ δὲ εἶπον L | ἀπεκρ. δὲ αὐτ.
(— δὲ) P (+ λέγων) V· καὶ εἶπον W   **5** τί ἂν λέγῃς C | δὲ. τ(οὺς) C
6 τοῦ θεοῦ W | τὸ σοφήσαντος V, τοῦ φήσαντος W | αὐτῶν P αὐτοῦ C,
ἡμῶν L | ἀποκρίνεσθαι P: ἃς ἀποκρ. μοι L, τοῦ ἀποκριθῆναί μοι C
7 (33) δέ LPC; — H | μοι LP. — HC | ὁ δαιμ. A. τὸ πνεῦμα C, — P |
καλοῦμαι AC· εἰμι P | Διξ Τέτραξ (nomina duo celeberrimarum literiarum
Ephesiarum) ego: ἡ λιξ τέφρας H, εἰς λἐξ· τεφράσθαι (cum sequentibus
ἀνθρώπων — conjunctum) L, θλιξ τέφρας C, τὸ πνεῦμα τῆς τέφρας (τέφραν
falso Fl) PFlMgtrCrtr   **8** § 5 εἶπον δε .. ἔφη δὲ — A | εἶπον δὲ αὐτῷ
PV: καὶ ἐπηρώτησα αὐτὸν W | ἔφη δέ C: ἡ δὲ ἔφη P | ἀν(θρώπ)ων L
9 σκορπίζω C: σκοτίζω AP | καὶ στροφ. ... ἅπτω· — P, + ἀπιστίω (l.
ἀπίστως) C | ἀγροὺς· + πυρὶ A   **10** καταργῶ PC: ϰατάγω A | ἐπὶ
πλεῖστον P· κατὰ πλίστην H, κατὰ πληθὴν L, τὰ πλεῖστα C | δὲ PW
— AV | θέρην L   **11** ἐὰν AC: ὅταν P | καιρὸν ϰερῶ V | ὑποδύνω
HC: ὑποδύνομαι P, τόπον (f. 13ᵣ¹) παιδινὸν L, τοίχων HC· τυχᾶκ L, τριχῶν P,
τειχῶν Fl | νυκτὸς καὶ ἡμέρας PV, ἡμέρας καὶ νυκτὸς W   **12** ἤδη ..
μεγάλου PC. καὶ γὰρ συγγενῆς εἰμι τοῦ (— L) μεγάλου δαίμονος A |
§ 6. * W f 268ᵛ | καὶ εἶπον αὐτὸν A | δὲ C: οὖν P | αἰτῶν V

»ἐν ποίῳ ἄστρῳ κεῖσαι;« ὁ δὲ εἶπεν· »εἰς αὐτὸ τὸ ἄκρον τοῦ
κέρατος τῆς σελήνης τὸ ἐν τῷ νότῳ εὑρισκόμενον ἐκεῖ μου τὸ
ἄστρον. διότι τὰ σφάλματα τοῦ ἡμιτριταίου προσετάχθην ἀνι-
μᾶσθαι. διὰ τοῦτο ἰδόντες πολλοὶ τῶν ἀνθρώπων εὔχονται εἰς
5 τὸν ἡμιτριταῖον ἐν τοῖς τρισὶν ὀνόμασι τούτοις· »βουλταλά·
θαλλάλ· μελχάλ« καὶ ἰῶμαι αὐτούς.« 7. εἶπον δὲ αὐτῷ ἐγὼ
Σολομῶν· »ὅτε οὖν θέλεις κακουργεῖν, ἐν τίνι καταργεῖσαι;«
ⸯὁ δὲ ἔφη· »ἐν τῷ ἀγγέλῳ ᾧ καὶ ὁ ἡμιτριταῖος * παύεται.«
ἐπηρώτησα δὲ αὐτόν· »ἐν ποίῳ ὀνόματι καταργεῖσαι;« ὁ δὲ εἶπεν·
10 »ἐν τῷ ὀνόματι τοῦ ἀρχαγγέλου Ἀζαήλ.«ⸯ 8. καὶ ἐπεσφράγισα

MSS HLPVW = Recc ABC. 1 ἐν — P | σὺ κεῖσαι H, συνοικῆσαι L
| εἶπεν LW· ἔφη PV, λέγει H | εἰς ... σελ. τὸ scr. posteaque supra εἰς scr.
ἐν et ιν αὐτῷ τῷ ἄκρῳ τ. κ τ. σ. τῷ corr. Pᶜ | αὐτὸ HP· — LC 2 κέρα
τος τ σελ. PC· καιράτου τῆς γῆς H, κέρκου τῆς ☽ (= γῆς) L | τὸ .. εὑ
ρισκ. ego· τῷ ἐν τ. ν. εὑρισκομένῳ BC, τὸν ἐν τὸ τόπω εὑρισκομένους H, ἐν
τόπω εὑρισκόμενος L | ἐκεῖ μου. ἐκείνου L | μου HC μοι ἐστὶ P 3 τὰ
σφαλμ τ ἡμ. προσετ. P (— τὰ) V σφαλ. τ. ἡμ. εἰμὶ ἐγὼ καὶ προετάχθην W,
τὰ ἡμετέρα τριταίει (ἡμέτερα τριταία L) σφαλ. προστάτης (-την H) A |
σφαλμ· σπάσματα conj. Cr 4 ἰδόντες .. ἡμιτριταῖον PC· εἶδον πολλοὺς
τῶν ἐθνῶν ἔχοντα πρός με τριταῖον (-αίων H) A 5 * Mg 1328 | ἐν ...
τούτοις P· ἐν τούτοις τῆς τριαὶν H, ἐν τούτοις τρισὶν ὀνόμασιν L, ἐν τοῖς δυ
αὶν ὀνόμασιν τούτοις ἢ καὶ τρισὶν ἅτινα εἰσὶν ταῦτα W, (— ἅτινα εἰσὶν) V |
βουλ ... μελχάλ P βουλ· ταλ· θαλάλ· H, βουλ· ταγιθαμαν· μελχαγ rubric
scr. W, βουλ· ταγιθαμάν· μελχαγι V, καὶ κράτει τοὺς δύο δατύλους τοῦ
ὀχλουμένου καὶ εἰπὲ οὕτως εἰς τὸ δεξιὸν ὠτίον ἑπτάκις· βουϲται. θαλάλ· L
| ιν cod. ms. Vindobon. phil.-graec. no. 108, f. 167ᵛ (S) scriptum est incanta-
mentum hoc. ὁ μιτριτεος (l. ἡμιτριταῖος) ⟨κατά⟩ργηται ἐν τὸ ὀνόματι ⟨το⟩ῖ
⟨ἀ⟩ρχαγγέλου ἀζαζηηλ· τὸν βουλ· τὸν τἀγηθαμαν· τὸν μελχαγι (literae in
uncis fractis inclusae compendiis cryptographicis scriptae sunt) 6 αὐτοὺς AP·
τούτους C | § 7. εἶπον APW. ἔφη K | δὲ· οὖν PC· — A
7 Σολ. πρὸς αὐτὸν H | ὅτε HP ὅταν LC | οὖν — L | θέλεις HP
θέλει L, ἔλθῃς C | κακουργεῖν ... καταργεῖσαι ego· κακουργεῖν, ἐν τίνι
κακουργεῖς PC, καταργῇ πῶς καταργῆσαι ἢ καὶ τοῦ μητριταίου παύεται H,
τίς καταργήσοισε· καὶ τὸν τριταῖον ἐν ποίῳ ἀγγέλῳ καταργῆσαι θέλει με L
8 ὁ δὲ ... καταργεῖσαι (l. 9). — A | δέ μοι P | ᾧ P· ὁ C | ἡμιτριταῖος
W· μιτριτέος V, τριταῖος P | * P f. 7ᵛ | ἐπαναπαύεται P 9 αὐτόν.
αὐτῷ V, + καὶ εἶπον P | ποίῳ δέ P | καταργ. — P | ὁ δὲ εἶπεν C. καὶ
εἶπεν μοι A, ὁ δὲ ἔφη P 10 ἐν τῷ ὀνομ. C — P | ἐν τῷ ἀρχαγγέλῳ A
| Ἀζαήλ AP· ἀζαζήλ C, ἀζαζηηλ S (v. supra) | § 8. κ. ἐπεσφρα.. κ. ἐπισο
σογραφίσασα H, εἶτα ἐσφράγησα L, κ. ἐσφράγισα C, κ. ἐπεκαλεσάμην τὸν ἀρ
χάγγελον ἀζαηλ, καὶ ἐπεσφραγ. P

τὸν δαίμονα καὶ ἐκέλευσα αὐτὸν λίθους ἀρπάζειν καὶ εἰς τὰ
ὑψηλὰ τοῦ ναοῦ ἀκοντίζειν * τοῖς τεχνίταις· καὶ ἀναγκαζόμενον
τὸ δαιμόνιον τὰ προστεταγμένα αὐτῷ ἐποίει.

VIII. Κἀγὼ δὲ πάλιν ἐδόξασα τὸ θεὸν τὸν δόντα μοι τὴν
ἐξουσίαν ταύτην καὶ ἐκέλευσα ἄλλον δαίμονα παρεῖναί μοι.
* καὶ ἦλθον πνεύματα ἑπτὰ συνδεδεμένα καὶ συμπεπλεγμένα,
εὔμορφα τῷ εἴδει καὶ εὔσχημα. 2. ἐγὼ δὲ Σολομῶν ἰδὼν αὐτὰ
ἐθαύμασα καὶ ἐπηρώτησα αὐτά· »τίνες ἐστε;« οἱ δὲ εἶπον· »ἡμεῖς
ἐσμεν στοιχεῖα κοσμοκράτορες τοῦ σκότους.« 3. καὶ φησιν ὁ
πρῶτος· »ἐγώ εἰμι ἡ Ἀπάτη « ὁ δεύτερος· »ἐγώ εἰμι ἡ Ἔρις «

MSS HLPVW = Recc. ABC. 1 τ. δαίμονα C τὸ δαιμόνων H, αὐτῷ L,
τὸν ἄγγελον scr. P, mox ἄγγελον transversa linea deleto δαίμονα scr. prim. man.
| ἐκελ. αὐτόν. προσέταξε τοῦτο L | λίθους μεγάλους PC | ἀπάζειν H |
ἀρπάζειν λίθους καὶ εἰς τὰ ὑψηλὰ μέρη τοῦ τείχους ἀκοντήζει L 2 τ ναοῦ
— C | * L f. 13ʳ² | τ. τεχν. P: τοὺς τεχνίτας AC, ÷ κελεύσας τὸν ὀχλού-
μενον ἐπιτιθέναι· ἐν τῷ ὄμω αὐτοῦ λίθους μέγας: εἶτα ὁ ἀναγινώσκων ἐπίθ-
θες αὐτῷ φέρειν· ἔνδω τοῦ ναοῦ· ἀπ᾿ ἔξωμεν L | ἀναγκαζόμενος ὁ δαί-
μῶν A 3 προστεταγ. P: προσταγμένα L, προσταχθέντα C | αὐτῷ HC
— LP | ἐποίει HP ἐνεργεῖν C ἐπάγει C
C. VIII. MSS HLPVW = Recc. ABC. (34) 4 κἀγὼ δὲ HP. κἀγὼ σολο-
μῶν L, καὶ ἐγὼ C | πάλιν — L | θεὸν τοῦ οὐρανοῦ H | μοι τὴν — C
5 καὶ ἐκέλευσα ... σκότους (l. 9) textum ex ms. W exscr. Gaulminius (Glm) in
notis ad Psellum, de oper. daem., Migne PG 122, 824 D, n. 11 | ἄλλον .. μοι
A. παρεῖναί μοι ἕτερον δαίμονα C (δαιμόνιον) P, add. rubric. περὶ τὸν ἑπτὰ
δαιμόνων H 6 * f. 12ᶻ H | ἑπτὰ πν(εύμ)ατα H | πν. ἑπ. θηλυκὰ P | συνδεδ
LPG. συνδεόμεθα H, ÷ ἀλλήλων L | κ. συμπεπλ P· κ. ἐμπεριπλεγμέν(εν)α H,
— LC 7 εὐμ. τ εἴδει HC εὐμ τὸ εἶδος P, ἄμορφα τὰ εἴδη L | κ. εὐσχ.
P: κ. ἄσχημα A, — C | § 2. ἐγὼ δὲ HP: κἀγὼ C, κἀγὼ δὲ L | ἰδὼν
αὐτὰ εἶδον αὐτὰ καὶ H, ἰδόντα τοῖτα L, ἰδὼν ταῦτα C | ἰδὼν — Glm | αὐτὰ
— P 8 ἐθαυμ. κ.· — P, ἐθαυμ τὰς ἐναλλαγὰς αὐτῶν καὶ L | ἐπερώ-
τουν L | αὐτά PC. αὐτὸν H, αὐτοὺς L, pr. ραὶ W, — Glm, ÷ λέγω V, ÷ λέ-
γων W | τίνες τίνος L, pr ὑμεῖς P, pr καὶ ὑμεῖς C | οἱ δὲ εἶπον H· καὶ
εἶπον μοι L, αἱ δὲ ὁμοθυμαδὸν μιᾷ φωνῇ ἔφησαν P, εἰ δὲ μοθημαδὼν φω-
ν(ὴν) ἐφησαν μιᾶ V, οἱ δὲ ὁμοθημαδ(ῶν) ἔφησαν μιᾶ φωνῇ καὶ εἴπων W |
ἡμεῖς ἐσμεν — L 9 στοιχ. κοσμ ς. σκοτ H τὰ λεγόμενα στοιχεῖα οἱ
κοσμ. τ. σκοτ. τούτου C, ἐκ τῶν τριάκοττα τριῶν στοιχείων τοῦ κοσμοκράτορος τοῦ σκοτ. P, στοιχία τοῦ κοσμοκράτορος τὸ ὄργανον τοῦ θη (l. θεοῦ?) L,
sequitur in textu character magicus luna similis radios habens septem parallelos
alio melius depicto in marg. rect. | add. nomina daemonum haec Gaulminius
Ἀπάτη, Ἔρις, Κλώθων, Ζάλη, Πλάνη, Δύναμις 9 § 3. καὶ   πρωτ. HV
× ὁ μὲν πρῶτος ἔφη W, ἔφησε δὲ ἡ πρώτη P | § 3. om. L 10 ὁ δευτ. HC
ἡ δευτέρα P, — H, ÷ εἶπεν C | ἡ Ἔρις PC. ὁ ἀὴρ H

ὁ τρίτος· »ἐγώ εἰμι ἡ Κλωθώ.« ὁ τέταρτος· ἐγώ εἰμι ἡ Ζάλη.«
ὁ πέμπτος· »ἐγώ εἰμι ἡ Πλάνη.« ὁ ἕκτος· »ἐγώ εἰμι ἡ Δύναμις.«
ὁ ἕβδομος· »ἐγώ εἰμι ἡ Κακίστη. 4. καὶ τὰ ἄστρα * ἡμῶν ἐν
οὐρανῷ * φαίνονται μικρὰ καὶ ὡς θεοὶ καλούμεθα· ὁμοῦ ἀλλασ-
5 σόμεθα καὶ ὁμοῦ οἰκοῦμεν ποτὲ μὲν τὴν Λυδίαν, ποτὲ δὲ τὸν
Ὄλυμπον, ποτὲ δὲ τὸ μέγα ὄρος.« 5. ἐπηρώτων δὲ αὐτοὺς ἐγὼ
Σολομῶν, ἀρξάμενος ἀπὸ τοῦ πρώτου· »λέγε μοι τίς σου ἡ ἐργασία.«
καὶ λέγει· »ἐγὼ Ἀπάτη· ἀπάτην πλέκω καὶ κακίστας αἱρέσεις ἐν-
θυμίζω. ἀλλ᾽ ἔχω τὸν καταργοῦντά με ἄγγελον Λαμεχιήλ.« 6. ὁ
10 δεύτερος λέγει· »ἐγώ εἰμι ἡ Ἔρις· ἐρίζω φέρων ξύλα λίθους ξίφη
τὰ ὅπλα μου τοῦ τόπου ἀλλ᾽ ἔχω ἄγγελον τὸν καταργοῦντά

MSS HLPVW = Recc ABC. 1 ὁ τριτ. HC ἡ τρίτη P, + υπ < (1 εἶ-
πεν) V | ἡ Κλωθώ ego ὁ κλοθῶ H, κλοθοῦ ὃ ἐστι μάχη P, ὁ κλόθον V,
ὁ κλῶθον W | ὁ (τέταρτ)ος HC· ἡ τετάρτη P, + ὑπι V | Ζάλη P: μάχη H,
supra δύναμις primum scriptum et postea deletum scr. ζάλη W, δύναμις V
2 ὁ (πέμπτ)ος HC· ἡ πέμπτη P, + ὑπ(εν) V | ἡ Πλάνη C· ζὰ H, ἡ δύνα-
μις P, cf. infra § 9 | ὁ (ἕκτ)ος HC· ἡ ἕκτη P, pr. καὶ V, + εἶπεν C | ἡ
Δύναμις C: ἡ πλάνη HP 3 ὁ (ἕβδομ)ος HC· ἡ ἑβδόμη P, pr. καὶ V, + εἶπεν C
ἡ Κακίστη P (-ην) H ὁ κάκιστος πάντων C | § 4. καὶ — C | ᵏ V f. 439ʳ |
ἡμῶν εἰσιν C | ἐν τῷ οὐρανῷ C 4 ᵏ P f. 8ʳ | φαιν. μικρὰ A· εἰσιν,
ἑπτὰ ἄστρα μικροφανῆ ἐν ὁμονοίᾳ, ἑπτὰ ἄστρα (— W) μικροφανῆ C |
καὶ .. καλουμ. A: κ ὡς θεὰς καλ. P, — C | ὁμοῦ PC — A | ἀλλασσ.
ἀλασσώμ. W, ἀλασῶμ V, ἀλλεσώμ. L. ἀλλασσοῦμ. P, — H 5 οἰκούμενα C
| ποτὲ μὲν C. ποτὲ P, παρὰ A | Λυδίαν: λύδαν H, λυδα L | δὲ HC·
— LP | τ Ὄλυμπ. P τ. ὄλυπον H, τὴν ὀλ C, τοῦ ἔμτον L 6 ποτὲ δὲ
HPC: καὶ ποτὲ L, + καὶ C | τὸ — PV | § 5 (35) ἐπηρώτησα P | ἐπ.
... Σολ.. — C | αὐτοὺς L. αὐτὰς P, αὐτὸν H 7 ἀρξ... πρώτου L: ἀρξ.
ἀπὸ τῆς πρότης H, ἀρξ. δὲ ἐγώ ἀπὸ τοῦ (πρώτ)ου εἶπον W, ἀρξ. δὲ ἐγώ ἀπὸ
τὸν (πρώτ)ον λεγώ V, μιᾷ ἑκάστῃ, ἠρξάμην δ᾽ ἀπὸ πρώτης ἕως τῆς ἑβδό-
μης P | ᵏ L f. 13ᵛⁱ | λέγε . ἔργασ. — L | μοι AV — W | σου HC:
— L 8 κ λέγει A: ἡ πρώτη ἔφη P, ὁ (πρώτ)ος λεγ- V, κ. ὁ μὲν πρῶτος
εἶπ(εν) W | Ἀπάτη· pr. ἡ W, + εἰμι P | ἀπάτην ego· ἀπατῶ PC, om per
haplographiam A | ᵏ H f. 12ᵛ | καὶ ... ἐνθυμ. H: αἱρέσεως κακίστις ἐνθυμ L,
ὧδε (ὥ in ras.) κἀκεῖ αἱρέσεις ἐρεθίζω P, πλεκολογῶ (πλοκ- V) τὸ δὲ καὶ
ἐρεθίζω C 9 τὸν ... ἄγγελον LPC ἀγγ τὸν κατ με H | Λαμεχιήλ C.
γλαμεχιήλ H, χλαμεὴλ L, λαμεχαλαλ P | § 6. (36) ὁ δευτ λέγει H: καὶ ὁ
δ. ἔφη C, ὁμοίως καὶ ἡ δευτέρα ἔφη P | sectionem om. L 10 εἰμι — W
| εἰμι ἡ Ἔρις PC: ἡμίρρης H | ἐρίζω . ξίφη C. ἔρις ἐρίδων (ad marg.
καὶ ἔρις τῶν)· φέρω ξύλα λίθους, ξίφει P, ἐρρίδων ξύλα φαίρων· λίθους δὲ
ξίφη H 11 μου PC: — H | τοῦ τόπου HP, τοιαῦτα C | ἀλλ᾽ ἔχω.
ἔχω δὲ H

με Βαρουχιήλ.« 7. ὁμοίως καὶ ὁ τρίτος ἔφη· »ἐγὼ Κλωθώ·
κυκλίσκομαι καὶ πάντα ποιῶ μάχεσθαι καὶ μὴ εἰρηνεύειν εὐσχημόνως περιέξουσιν ⌜καὶ τί πολλὰ λέγω;⌝ ἔχω ἄγγελον τὸν καταργοῦντά με Μαρμαρώθ.« 8. καὶ ὁ τέταρτος ἔφη· »ἐγὼ ποιῶ ἀνθρώπους μὴ σωφρονεῖν· μερίζω· χωρίζω· παρακολουθούσης μοι καὶ
τῆς Ἔριδος ἀποχωρίζω ⌜ἀδελφοὺς καὶ ἄλλα πολλὰ ὅμοια τούτοις
ποιῶ.⌝ ⌜καὶ τί πολλὰ λέγω;⌝ ἀλλ' ἔχω ἄγγελον τὸν καταργοῦντά
με τὸν μέγαν Βαλθιούλ « 9. ὁ πέμπτος ἔφη· »ἐγὼ Πλάνη εἰμί,
βασιλεῦ * Σολομῶν, καὶ σὲ πλανῶ καὶ ἐπλάνησά σε * καὶ ἐποίησα
ἀποκτῆναι τοὺς ἀδελφούς. ἐγὼ πλανῶ ὑμᾶς τάφους ἐρευνᾶν

MSS HLPVW = Recc. ABC.   1 Βαρουχιήλ C: βαρουχιαὴλ H, βαρουχια-
χὴλ P | § 7. (37) ὁμ καὶ HP — LC | ὁ τριτ. LC. ἡ τρίτη P, ἡ τρίτων H
| ἐγώ εἰμι C | Κλωθώ ego; κλοθῶ H, κλώθω L, κλωθοῦ (supra ω scr. o) P,
ὁ κλώθων W, ὁ κλοθ < V   2 κυκλίσκομαι (i. q. κυκλίζω) LC: καὶ ἀλίσκο-
μαι H, καλοῦμαι P, l fortasse κινήσκομαι | καὶ   μαχεσθ ∂ ἐστι μάχη P
| πάντα HC πάντας L | κ μὴ εἰρην. — P | εἰρην. C ἐρην. H, — L |
εὔσχημ περιεξ. ego· εὐσχημ πέξουσιν H, εὐχῆ μόνος περιέξουσι L, εὐσχη-
μόνους χύσαι (vel χόσαι) καὶ περισχηθῆναι (supra η — ι° — scr ε) ποιῶ P, οὐ
σχημόνους (falso) περισχεθῆναι ποιῶ Fl, — C   3 ⟋ τί πολ ⟍εγ PC — A
| ἔχω pr καὶ A, pr. εἰ μὴ V, pl. ἀλλ' W | τ. κατ με ἀγγ L   4 Μαρ-
μαρώθ V μπρμαρούθ W, μαρμαράθ P, μαρτυρώθ H, μετίρον L | § 8. (38)
⟋ ὁ τετ. C (— καὶ) L. ἡ δὲ τετάρτη H, ὁμοίως καὶ τετάρτη P | ἔφη εἰ-
πεν H | ἐγὼ ὁ χάλη C | τοὺς ἀνθρ. P   5 μὴ σωφρ PC· μισοκακεῖν A
| μερίζω A. μετρίζω P, — C | χωρίζω: + ἀπομερίζω P, + ἀποχωρίζω C
| παραχολ. μοι PC: παρακολουθοῦσιν H, — L | ⟋. τε Ἐρ — L   6 ἀπο-
χωρ ⟍ ποιῶ (— ἀποχωρ.) L: ἀποσχίζω (ad marg χωρί scr P_C, i. q. ἀποχωρίζω) ἄνδρα ἀπὸ τῆς συγκοίτου αὐτοῦ καὶ τέκνα ἀπὸ γονέων καὶ ἀδελφοὺς
ἀπὸ ἀδελφῶν P, ἀποσχίζω ἄνδρας ἀπὸ τοὺς συνκενοῖς (l συγγενεῖς, σονγκηι <
V, l. συγκοίτ⟨ους⟩) αὐτῶν (αὐτοῦ V) καὶ γονεῖς ἀπὸ τέκνων καὶ ἀδελφοὺς
ἀπὸ ἀδελφᾶς C   7 καὶ ⟍ λέγω PC· — A, + κατ' ἐμοῦ P | ἀλλ' HW.
καὶ L, — PV | τὸν scr bis L   8 τ. μέγα HP τ. μέγα L, — C | Βαλ-
θιούλ P· μαχιθιούμ C, μελχοῦ H, μελχουήλ L | § 9 (39) πειπτ. LC ἡ
πέμπτη HP, pr. ὁμοίως καὶ P, pr. καὶ C | ἔφη — W | Δύναμις operaque
illius (§ 10) pro quinto, at Πλάνη operaque huius pro sexto habet P | Πλάνη
PC· πλάνα H, πλάνος L, pl ἡ W, pr εἰμι P | εἰμι AV — PW   9 * P
f. 8^V | Σολ. + εἰμι C | σε — L, + δὲ P | σὲ ἐπλάνησά scripta et post
σὲ signo omissionis posito super ἐπλάνησά ad marg sup δὲ πλανῶ, ὡς καὶ
adscr. P^c | πλανῶ AP πλανήσω C | ⟋ ἐπλαν. σε — I | ⟍ ἐπλαν .
ἀδελφ ἐπ' ἐσχάτων τῶν ἡμερῶν τῆς ζωῆς σου C | * H f 13¹ | ἐποίησά
σε L   10 τὸν ἀδελφόν σου P | ὑμᾶς L ἡμᾶς HP, πάντας C | τάφους
... εὐσεβείας — A | ταφ ἐρειν P· καὶ τοὺς ταφ. ἐρευνῶ (-να V) C

καὶ διορυκτὰς διδάσκω, καὶ ἀποπλανῶ ψυχὰς ἀπὸ πάσης εὐσε-
βείας, καὶ ἕτερα πολλὰ φαῦλα * ποιῶ. ἔχω δὲ τὸν καταργοῦντά
με ἄγγελον Οὐριήλ.« 10. ὁμοίως δὲ ὁ ἕκτος ἔφη· »ἐγὼ Δύναμις·
τυράννους ἀνιστῶ, βασιλεῖς καθαιρῶ, * καὶ πᾶσι τοῖς ὑπεναντίοις
5 παρέχω δύναμιν. ἔχω ἄγγελον τὸν καταργοῦντά με Ἀστεραώθ.«
11. ὁμοίως καὶ ὁ ἕβδομος ἔφη· »ἐγώ εἰμι Κακίστη, καὶ σέ, βασιλεῦ, κακώσω ὅτε κελευθῶ Ἀρτέμιδος δεσμοῖς· ⌜διὰ ταῦτα γάρ
σε διαπρᾶξαι ἔχεις τὴν ἐπιθυμίαν ὡς φίλτατος, ἐμοὶ δὲ κατ᾽.
ἐμαυτὴν ἐπιθυμίαν τὴν σοφίαν.⌝ ἐὰν γάρ τις σοφός, οὐκ ἐπι-
10 στρέψει ἴχνος πρὸς μέ.« 12. κἀγὼ δὲ Σολομῶν ἀκούσας ταῦτα
ἐσφράγισα αὐτοὺς τῷ δακτυλιδίῳ τοῦ θεοῦ καὶ ἐκέλευσα αὐτοὺς
ὀρύσσειν τοὺς θεμελίους τοῦ ναοῦ· * καὶ ἐτάξατο τὸ μὲν μῆκος

MSS HLPVW = Recc. ABC. 1 κ. διορύκτας διδ P: κ. ριορείκτα διδάσκων,
V, — W　2 ἐτ. ποιῶ φαυλ πολ. Η ｜ πολλὰ — L ｜ φαῦλα ΑΡ φαντάσματα C
｜ * Mg 1329 ｜ ποιῶ. ἐν ἐμοὶ P ｜ ἔχω δὲ LPV. ἔχων δὲ Η, ἀλλ᾽ ἔχω W ｜
ἀγγ. τ. κατ. με C　3 Οὐριήλ P· οὐρουήλ Α, οὐρικά C ｜ § 10. (40) ὁμοίως
δὲ HP　καὶ C, — L, + καὶ Η ｜ ὁ ἕκτος LC　ἡ ἕκτη HP ｜ de inversione
sectionum 9 et 10 in ms. P v. supra ｜ ἐγὼ. + δὲ Η,ʼ+ δὲν L, + εἰμι P,
+ ἡ C ｜ Δυν. ... ἀνιστῶ ego: δύναμαι (— Η) τυρ. ἀνιστάναι Α, δύναμις·
δυνάμαι τυρ. ἀνιστῶ P, δίναμις· ὁμοῦ τυρ ἀνιστῶ C　4 καθαιρῶ P. καθαι-
ρεῖν L, — HC ｜ * L f. 13ᵛ ² ｜ κ. πᾶσι ... ἀγγ τὸν — Η ｜ τοὺς ὑπεναντίους
— C ｜ τοὺς ὑπεναντίους W　5 παρέχων W ｜ ἔχω δὲ C ｜ τὸν κατ. με
ἀγγ L ｜ καταργοῦντα μαι ὑπὸ ἀγγέλου Η ｜ Ἀστεραώθ W(?)P (-αἐθ) V
ἀσταρααθ(?) P, περαώθ H, περεώθ L　6 § 11. (41) ὁμοι. καὶ HPV καὶ W,
— L ｜ ὁ ἑβδ. LC: ἡ ἑβδόμη P, ζ̄ H ｜ εἰμι LP. ἡ Η, + βασιλεὺς L ｜
εἰμι .. πρὸς μέ (l 10)· ἡ (καλοῦμαι V) ζάλη· ζαλίζω· σκοτίζω πάντας
ἀνθρώπους ἀπὸ τῆς εὐθείας ὁδοῦ, καὶ ἑτέρας (ἔχω καὶ ἑτέρας ἐνεργείας καὶ
W) κακουργίας ἔχω οὐκ ὀλίγας. ἔχω δὲ τὸν ἄγγελον τὰν (— W) καταργοῦντά
με, μέγαν κανωνήλ (κανγουήλ W) C ｜ βασ. H βασιλεὺς L, αὐτὸν P　7 κακώσω A. κακῶ P ｜ ὅτε ... δεσμοῖς A. ὅτι κελευστῶ ἀρτέμιδος δεσμούς, ἡ
δὲ ἄκρις με λύσει P (cf. XXVI 4 ff.) ｜ κελευσῶ conj. FlCr ｜ διὰ ... φίλτα-
τος· δι᾽ αὐτῆς γάρ σε δεῖ πραξαι τὴν ἐπιθυμίαν P　8 διαπρᾶξαι (aor. inf.
act) ego: διὰ πράξαι H, διὰ πράξας L ｜ ἔχεις L ἔχων H ｜ ἐμοὶ ...τῆς
σοφίας H, ἐμοὶ ... ἐπιθυμῶμην τὴν σοφίαν L, ἐμὴ δὲ κατ᾽ ἐμαυτῆς τὴν σοφίαν P　9 σοφὸς τὶς H ｜ ἐπιστρίψη P, ἐπιστρέ L　10 ἴχνος αὐτῆς A ｜
§ 12. (42) κἀγὼ A· ἐγώ P ｜ κἀγὼ ... ταῦτα· καὶ C ｜ ταῦτα A καὶ θαυμάσας P　11 ἐσφραγ. AP: σφραγίσας C ｜ αὐτοὺς HC αὐτὰς LP ｜ τῷ
— L, pr ἐν P ｜ τοῦ θεοῦ A· — PC ｜ καὶ HP: — LC, + ἐπειδὴ σύντομαι
ἦσαν P ｜ αὐτοῖς L, αὐτὰς P　12 ὀρύσσειν PW: ὀρύσσαν H, ὀρείση V,
ὀρύην L ｜ τὸ θεμέλιον L, ἐν τοῖς θεμελίοις H ｜ ι. ναοῦ καὶ ὀρυσσον W,
κ. ὀρείσον V, + τοῦ θεοῦ P ｜ * H f. 13ᵛ ｜ καὶ ἐτ. τ. μὲν μηκ. H (— τὸ) L.
τὸ μὲν γὰρ μηκ C ｜ κ. ἐτ. ... πεντ.. ἐπεὶ διακ. πεντ. πηχ. ἦν τ. μηκ. P

πήχεις διακοσίους πεντήκοντα· καὶ πάντα τὰ κελευσθέντα αὐτοῖς
κατηργάζοντο.

IX. Καὶ πάλιν ᾔτησα περιελθεῖν ἕτερα δαιμόνια, καὶ προσ-
ενέχθη μοι δαιμόνιον, ἄνθρωπος μὲν πάντα τὰ μέλη αὐτοῦ,
ἀκέφαλος δέ. 2. καὶ εἶπον αὐτῷ »λέγε μοι σὺ τίς εἶ, καὶ πῶς
καλεῖσαι.« ὁ δὲ δαίμων ἔφη »Φόνος καλοῦμαι· ἐγὼ γὰρ κεφαλὰς
κατεσθίω, θέλων * ἐμαυτῷ κεφαλὴν ποιήσασθαι, καὶ οὐ χορτά-
ζομαι· * ἐπιθυμῶ κεφαλὴν ποιῆσαι οἵαν ὡς καὶ σύ, βασιλεῦ.«
3. ταῦτα ἀκούσας ἐγὼ ἐσφράγισα αὐτὸν ἐκτείνας τὴν χεῖρά μου
κατὰ τοῦ στήθους αὐτοῦ. καὶ ἀνεπήδησεν ὁ δαίμων καὶ ἔρρηξεν
ἑαυτὸν καὶ ἐγόγγυσεν εἰπών »οἴμοι· ποῦ ἐπέτυχον προδότην
Ὀρνίαν; οὐ βλέπω.« 4. κἀγὼ εἶπον αὐτῷ· »καὶ πόθεν βλέπεις;«

MSS HLPVW = Recc. ABC   1 πήχας διακοσίας πεντ H, πήξας ͞ον L,
πηχῶν ͞ν C | λ. παντ. . . . κατηργ.: ἔφησα δὲ αὐτὰς εὐτόνους εἶναι, καὶ κοι-
νῶς γογγύσασαι τελέσαι τὰ κελευσθέντα αὐταῖς κατηργάζοντο P | κελευ-
σθέντα A, κελεστέντα V | αὐτοῖς A· αὐτοῦ V, — W   2 κατηργ · ἐποίουν W
C. IX. (43) 3 Κ. πάλιν H: καὶ L, ἐγὼ δὲ σολομῶν δοξάσας τὸν θεὸν
(+ πάλιν C) CP, add. super θεὸν prim man κ(ύριο)ν P | ᾔτησα ego: αἴτησα L,
ᾐτισάμην W, ἐτισαμ V, ἔταξα H, ἐκέλευσα P | περιελθεῖν H· τοῦ ἐλθεῖν
καὶ L, παρεῖναι μοι P, παραστῆναι μοι καὶ C | ἕτ δαιμ. A: ἕτερον δαιμό-
νιον P, ἕτερον δαιμον < V, ἕτερος δαίμων W   4 δαιμόνιον P: δαιμόνια L,
— HC | μὲν A: ἔχων P, — C | πάντα τὰ H   ὅλα τὰ L, τὰ πάντα PC |
αὐτοῦ — P   5 ἀκεφ δὲ C | §2 καὶ κἀγὼ P | εἶπον αὐτῷ H (pr. ἰδὼν)
P ἰδὼν αὐτὸν εἶπον W, ἰδὼν αὐτῷ εἶπα V, λέγει τούτων L | λέγε μοι — L
| σὺ — H | κ. πῶς καλ. A   κ π. καλεῖ C, — P   6 δὲ — H | δαίμων
— PC | ἔφη LW: εἶπεν PV, λέγει L, + δαιμόνιον εἰμὶ PC, add. adhuc εἶπον
οὖν αὐτῷ· τίς. ὁ δὲ ἔφη P | Φόνος δὲ C | ἐγὼ καλοῦμαι φθόνος P |
γὰρ LP· δὲ H, — C | κεφαλ. + ἡδέως PC   7 θέλων HP. θέλον L, θέλω C
|· * L f 14ʳ¹ | ἐμαυτῷ HP: ἐμαυτοῦ L, ἐμαυτὸν W, ἐμαυτῶν V | ποιή-
σασθαι HC. ποιήσασθαι L, περιποιήσασθαι P | χορτάζω P   8 * P f. 9ʳ |
ἐπιθυμῶ· pr ὡς L, + δὲ PC | ποιῆσαι A: περιποιήσασθαι C, τοιαύτην
ἔχειν P, + μοι L | οἵαν ὡς: ἐὰν ὡς H, ἵνα ὡς L, οἵαν P, ἥνπερ C | καὶ
σύ: καὶ ἐσύ L | βασιλεῦ A — PC   9 §3. ταῦτα δὲ H | ἐγὼ σολομῶν
PC | ἐσφραγ. ἐσφάλησα L | τ χειρ.· τὰς χεῖρας H   10 κατὰ ἐκ H |
καὶ (1°) — H | ἔρρηξεν H. ῥήξας L, διέρηξεν C, ἔρριψεν P   11 ἑαυτὸν P·
αὐτὸν vel αὑτὸν HC, αὐτὴν L | ἐγογγ. P· γόγγυσαν H, ἐκό[κ]κυσεν αὐτῶ C,
— L | εἰπών PC εἶπον H, εἶπεν L, pr. αὐτῷ C | οἴμοι PL εἶμι C, ἡμὶν
H | ἐπέτυχον πρ. Ὀρν. L ἐνέτυχον πρ. Ὀρν H, πάρειμι, ὦ προδότα Ὀρν-
νία PC   12 οὐ — L | §4 κ εἶπον αὐτῷ H· (βλέπω) κἀγὼ καὶ εἶπον
αὐτὸν L, ἔφην δὲ αὐτῷ ἐγὼ σολομῶν P, εἶπον δὲ ἐγὼ σολ. C | καὶ Α· λέγε
μοι C (+ γὰρ) P | ⁴ H f 14ʳ

ὁ δὲ ἔφη »διὰ τῶν μαστῶν μου« * 5. κἀγὼ δὲ Σολομῶν τὴν
ἡδονὴν τῆς φωνῆς αὐτοῦ ἀκούσας καὶ θέλων μαθεῖν ἐπηρώτησα
αὐτόν· »πόθεν λαλεῖς;« ὁ δὲ ἔφη· »ἡ ἐμὴ φωνὴ πολλῶν ἀνθρώπων
φωνὰς ἐκληρονόμησεν· ὅσοι γὰρ ἐν ἀνθρώποις βωβοὶ καλοῦνται,
5 ⌜τούτων ἐγὼ κατέκλεισα τὰς κεφαλάς.⌝ ὅτε παιδία γίνονται δέκα
ἡμερῶν, τότε τῆς νυκτὸς κλαίοντος τοῦ παιδίου γίνομαι πνεῦμα
καὶ διὰ τῆς φωνῆς ἐπεισέρχομαι. 6. ἐν ἀωρίαις δὲ πλεῖον τὸ
συνάντημά μου βλαβερόν ἐστιν. * ἡ δὲ δύναμίς μου ἐν ταῖς
χερσί μου τυγχάνει καὶ ὡς ἐπὶ ξύλου λαβὼν ταῖς χερσί μου κε-
10 φαλὰς ἀποτέμνω καὶ προστίθημι ἐμαυτῷ, καὶ οὕτως ὑπὸ τοῦ
πυρὸς τοῦ ὄντος ἐν ἐμοὶ διὰ τοῦ τραχήλου καταδαπανῶ. ἐγώ
εἰμι ὁ πυρῶν τὰ μέλη καὶ τοῖς ποσὶν ἐπιπέμπω καὶ ἕλκη ἐμποιῶ.

MSS HLPVW = Recc ABC 1 μαστῶν LC μασθῶν V, παθῶν P ⫶
* W f 269ʳ | § 5. κἀγὼ AP ἐγὼ C | δὲ· οὖν P, γοῦν V | Σολ — C
2 ἀκούσας ante τὴν ἡδ ponit C | ἡδονὴν A ἄνοδον P, ἐδοδὴ (1 ἐδωδὴν?
sic) C, 1. fortasse αὐδὴν | αὐτοῦ PC τούτου L, — H, + ἀκούην V | κ.
θέλων P καὶ (— V) θέλω C, ἤθελον H, ἤθελα L | μαθεῖν ante αὐτὸν H,
εὐδηλότερον P | ἱπηρ αὐτὸν A.C ἐπηρ. (+ δὲ W) αὐτ. λέγων — L
3 λαλεῖ L | ὁ δὲ ἔφη H ἔφη δέ μοι PC, καὶ λέγει μοι | ἡ ἐμὴ φωνὴ H
(ἐμοὶ) L ἐγώ, σολομῶν, ἡμεὶ φωνὴν C, ἐγὼ βασιλεῦ σολομῶν ὅλως φωνὴ
εἰμὶ P | πολλῶν ἐκληρον H (-ησα) L ἡ πολλὰς φωνὰς κληρονομήσασα C,
πολλῶν γὰρ ἀνθρώπων φωνὰς κατεκληρονόμησα P 4 ἐν ἀνθρωπ. AC
ἄν(θρωπ)οι P | καὶ. βοβοὶ C, καὶ. κωφοὶ P 5 τούτων . . ἡμερῶν C
— A | τὰς κεφαλὰς κατεκλ P | γιν δ. ἡμ C γεννῶνται, καὶ ἡμερῶν ὀκτὼ
φθάσωσι P 6 τότε PC τό(τε?) L, οὗτος H, + ἐγὼ A | τῆς A — PC |
νυκτὸς post παιδίου ponit P | παιδὸς L | γένομαι A | φωνῆς αὐτοῦ P
7 ὑπεισέρχομαι C | § 6 ἀωρίαις ἀορίαις H, ὁρίαις P, ad marg ἐν
ἀωρι < Pc, ἀορία L, ἀορίας C | δὲ καὶ P | πλεῖον A πάνυ PC,
— διακονῶ· καὶ P 8 ἐστιν δὲ H | * L f.14ʳ2 | ἡ δὲ . . τυγχάνει C
(— τυγχ.) A om P per homoeoarcton, καὶ enim sci. in fine lineae (ἐστίν·
καὶ) et rursus in initio lineae alterae (καὶ εὐθέως λαβὼν) | δὲ — L 9 τυγ-
χάνει . . . χερσί μου C om. A per homoeoteleuton | ὡς . . . μου C
εὐθέως λαβὼν ταῖς χερσί μου ὡς ἐπὶ ξίφος P | τὴν κεφαλὴν P 10 προσ-
τίθημι (-ημοι) L πρὸς τέθημος H, προσιτθῶ PC | ἐμαυτῷ PV ἐμαυ-
τὸν W, ἐν αὐτῷ A | τοῦ — P 11 ὄντος — C | καταδαπανῶ L δα-
πανῶ L, καταδαπανᾶται PC 12 ὁ πυρ. . . . ἐπιπέμπω A ὁ τὰς πυρώσεις τὰς μεγάλας καὶ (τοὺς V, τὰς W) ἀθεραπεύτους ἐν τ ποσὶν ἐπιπέμπων
P (ἐπιπίμπω) C | ⸜ ἕλκη ἐμπ HP κ. ἔγκαι ἐπιῶ V, ⸜ ἕλκη ἐνεμπιῶ
L, — W

γ. καὶ διὰ τῆς ἐμπύρου ἀστραπῆς καταργοῦμαι.« 8. κἀγὼ ἐκέλευσα αὐτὸν εἶναι μετὰ τοῦ Βεελζεβοὺλ μέχρι καὶ τούτου φίλος παραγένηται.

Χ. Καὶ ἐκέλευσα παρεῖναί μοι ἕτερον δαιμόνιον. καὶ ἦλθε πρὸ προσώπου μου ἔχων τὸ σχῆμα * ὡς κύων μέγας, καὶ ἐλάλησέ μοι φωνὴν μεγάλην· »χαῖρε, ὦ βασιλεῦ Σολομῶν.« 2. καὶ ἐκπληκτικὸς ἐγενόμην καὶ εἶπον αὐτῷ· »τίς εἶ σύ, κύον;« ὁ δὲ λέγει· »κύων δοκεῖς εἶναί με· πρὸ γὰρ σοῦ, βασιλεῦ, ἤμην ἐγὼ ἄνθρωπος. κατηργασάμην δὲ ἐν τῷ * κόσμῳ ἔργα πολλὰ ἄθεσμα καὶ καθ' ὑπεροχὴν ἴσχυσα καὶ ἄστρα οὐρανῶν κατασχεῖν, καὶ

MSS HL = Rec. A. § 7. cum mss. HL textus legitur 1 ἐμπυρ. H ἠπείρου L

MS P interpolationem maiorem praebet pro § 7 hanc: κἀγὼ σολομῶν ἀκούσας ταῦτα, εἶπον αὐτῷ· λέγε μοι οὖν πῶς ἐπαφίης τὸ πῦρ, ἀφ' ὧν ἀποπέμπεις ἐξ αὐτῶν. ἔφη δέ μοι τὸ πνεῦμα ἀπὸ τῆς ἀνατολῆς· ὧδε γὰρ οὕτω supra τ scr. π ut in οὕτω corr.) εὑρέθη κἀκεῖνος ἐλβουρίων ὡς ἐπεύχων τὸ τόδ καὶ λυχναψίας) (-ίαν Fl falso)-αὐτῶ οἱ ἄνθρωποι ἐπιτελοῦσι, κἀκεῖνον ὁ οὔνομα ἐπικαλοῦνται (* f. 9ᵛ) οἱ ἑπτὰ δαίμονες ἐνώπιόν μου κἀκεῖνος θεραπεύει αὐτούς· εἶπον δὲ αὐτῷ εἰπέ μοι τὸ ὄνομα αὐτοῦ. ὁ δὲ ἔφη οὐ δύναμαι σοι εἰπεῖν· ἐὰν γὰρ εἴπω αὐτοῦ τὸ ὄνομα ἀθεράπευτον ἐμαυτὸν ποιῶ· ἀλλ' ἐκεῖνος ἐλθὼν ἐπὶ αὐτὸ (α ex τ corr.) τὸ ὄνομα. καὶ ταῦτα ἀκούσας ἐγὼ σολομῶν εἶπον αὐτῷ εἰπέ μοι οὖν ὑπὸ ποίου ἀγγέλου καταργῇ σύ. ὁ δὲ διὰ τῆς ἐμπύρου ἀστραπῆς ἔφη.

MSS VW (Rec C) textum praebent hunc: κἀγὼ σολομῶν ἀκούσας ταῦτα, εἶπον (εἶπα αὐτῷ V) λέγε μοι, οὖν, ἐν ποίῳ ἀγγέλῳ (ἐπὶ ποίου ἀγγέλου V) καταργεῖσαι. ὁ δὲ ἔφη· διὰ τοῦ ἐμπύρου ἀγγέλου

MSS HLP = Recc AB 1 § 8. hoc a loco mss. codd VW (i. q. recensio C) extum diversum habet, cf. infra, pp. 76ᵇ—87* κἀγὼ H καὶ ἐγὼ L, καὶ προσανήσας ἐγὼ κυρίῳ τῷ θεῷ τοῦ Ἰ(σρα)ὴλ P 2 εἶναι μετὰ τ. Βεελ. H. ἐν τηρήσει εἶναι ὑπὸ τοῦ βεελ P, διὰ τοῦ βεελζεβουὲλ ἐπιεῖναι L | μέχρι κ τ ριλ. A μέχρις ὅτου ἰαξ P 3 παραγ P ἐπιγίνεται L, παραγέγονεν H

C. Χ. (47) 4 ἐκέλευσα (ι -σε) L | ἕτερα δαιμόνια L 5 μου — L, + δαίμων L | ἔχων .. μέγας κίων· τὸ σχῆμα ἔχων (* Mg 1332) μέγα P τὸ — II | σχῆμα· + αὐτοῦ L | μοι — P 6 φωνῇ μεγάλῃ καὶ εἶπεν P | χαίροις L | ὦ L ὁ H, κύριε P | § 2. κ. ἐκπ. ἐγ. κ ἐκπλη-τος ἐγ. H, καὶ ἀκούσας ἐγὼ ἐκπληκτικὸς ἐγ. ι L, ἐκπληκτικὸς δὲ γεγονὼς ἐγὼ σολομῶν P 7 σύ — P | κύων P | ὁ δὲ λέγει H· καὶ εἶπεν μοι L, ὁ δέ μοι ἔφη P 8 κύων .. με H (μοι) L κὰι κύων σοι δοκῶ εἶναι P | πρὸ LP πρὸς II | βασιλεὺς A, βασιλεῖ σολομῶν P | ἐγὼ ἀνθρ. ἤμην P 9 κατηργ. ... ἴσχυσα A· κατεργασάμενος ἀθέμιτα ἐν τῷ κόσμῳ πολλὰ καθ' ὑπερβολὴν φιλολογήσας ὑπερίσχυσα P 10 οὐρανῶ L | κατασχῶν A

C. Χ 2 Rev XII 4, cf. Dieterich, Abraxas 118 ff

πλείονα κακὰ ἔργα κατασκευάζω. 3. ἐγὼ οὖν βλάπτω ἀνθρώπους
τοὺς τῷ ἐμῷ ἄστρῳ παρακολουθοῦντας καὶ εἰς ἐξηχείαν τρέπω,
καὶ τὰς * φρένας τῶν ἀνθρώπων διὰ τοῦ λάρυγγος κρατῶ καὶ
οὕτως ἀναιρῶ.« 4. καὶ εἶπον αὐτῷ· »τί σου τὸ ὄνομα;« ὁ δὲ
5 ἔφη· »Ῥάβδος.«

 5. Κἀγὼ εἶπον αὐτῷ· »τίς σου ἡ ἐργασία καὶ τί μοι δοκεῖς
κατορθῶσαι,« ὁ δαίμων ἔφη »δός μοι ἄνθρωπον σὸν καὶ ἀπαγάγω αὐτὸν ἐν τόπῳ ὄρους καὶ ἐπιδείξω αὐτῷ λίθον πράσινον
μετασαλευόμενον ἐν ᾧ * κοσμήσεις τὸν ναὸν τοῦ θεοῦ.« 6. κἀγὼ
10 δὲ ἀκούσας ταῦτα ἐπέταξα ⌜πορευθῆναι⌝ τὸν οἰκέτην μου ἅμα
αὐτῷ ἔχοντα τὸ δακτυλίδιον τῆς σφραγῖδος τοῦ θεοῦ * μετ᾽ αὐτοῦ καὶ εἶπον αὐτῷ· »ἄπελθε μετ᾽ αὐτοῦ καὶ οὗ δ᾽ ἂν ἐπιδείξει
σοι τὸν λίθον τὸν πράσινον, σφράγισον αὐτὸν τῷ δακτυλιδίῳ
κατασκόπευσον τὸν τόπον ἀκριβῶς, καὶ ἄγαγέ μοι ⌜τὸ δακτυλί-
15 διον⌝.« 7. ὁ δὲ ἀπελθὼν ἔδειξεν αὐτῷ τὸν λίθον τὸν πράσινον,
καὶ ἐσφράγισεν αὐτὸν τῷ δακτυλιδίῳ τοῦ θεοῦ, καὶ ἤγαγον τὸν
λίθον τὸν πράσινον πρὸς μέ. 8. καὶ ἔκρινα περισφραγίδας τὰ

 MSS HLP ═ Recc. AB. 1 πλείονα θεῶν ἔργα κατασκεύασα P | § 3.
οὖν A γὰρ P 2 τὸ ἐμὸν ἄστρῳ L | εἰς ἐξηχίαν τρ. LP, ἐξηχίαν πρέπω H
3 τὰς ... ἀνθρ A τοὺς φρενητιῶντας ἀνθρώπους P | * H f. 15ʳ 4 οὕ-
τως H οὗτος H | ἀναιρῶ αὐτὸν H | § 4 (48) κ. εἶπον αὐτ L. ἔφη δὲ
αὐτῷ ἐγὼ σολομῶν P 6 § 5. κἀγὼ καὶ P | αὐτῷ — P | τίς καὶ τί P
| καὶ — L | μοι (με L) δοκεῖς A δίνασαι P 7 δαίμων A δὲ P
8 ὄρους — H | δείξω P | αὐτῷ P, αὐτὸν H, — L 9 * P f. 10ʳ | κοσμεῖ
H | ναὸν + κυρίου P | § 6. (49) κἀγὼ P ἐγὼ P 10 δὲ — H, + σολο-
μῶν P | ἐπέταξα H: ὑποπροετάξα L, ὑπέταξα P | πορευθῆναι P — A |
ἅμα αὐτῷ HP ἅματο L 11 ἔχοντα P ἔχοντι H, κρατοῦντα L | τὸ
δακτ. A δακτύλιον P | * L f 14ᵛ² — μετ᾽ αὐτ. P μετὰ τούτ(ους) L, — H
12 κ. εἶπον αὐτ. — L | ἀπελ. ... καὶ — P | ἄπελθε H. ἀπέλθατε L |
μετ᾽ αὐτοῦ ego· μετ᾽ αὐτῶν H, μετὰ τούτων L | οὗ δ᾽ ἂν ego: οὐδὰν H, ᾧ
δ᾽ ἂν P, — L | ἐπιδείξει σοι P (σου) H· ἀποδεῖ ἡμῖν vel ἀποδείκμιν L
13 τὸν (1° et 2°) — L | αὐτὸν HP τούτου L | τῷ δακτ A μετὰ τοῦ
δακτυλιδίου τούτου P 14 τὸν τόπον ... αὐτὸν (1. 16) — H | ἀκριβ. τ
τοπ. P | τὸ δακτ. L τὸν δαίμονα ἐνθάδε P fortasse recte 15 § 7. ὁ δὲ
ἀπ L καὶ P | αὐτῶν P αὐτοῖς L | τὸν πρασ λιθ P 16 αὐτὸν P
αὐτῷ L | τ δάκτυλ. τ. θ. A — P | κ. ἤγαγον ... με H (—πρὸς μέ) L
κ. ἤναγκε τὸ δαιμόνιον πρὸς με P 17 § 8. ἔκρινα + αὐτὸν A, + ἐγὼ
σολομῶν P | περισφραγῆσαι L | ˣ H f 15ᵛ

 MS P pro textu τὰ δύο . . τεχνίταις (l. 17 ss.) praebet haec. τοὺς δύο τῇ
δεξιᾷ τὸν ἀκέφαλον, ὁμοίως καὶ τὸν κύνα προσδεδέσθαι ἐκεῖνον τὸν μέγαν,
καὶ τὸν μὲν κύνα τηρεῖν τὸν διάπυρον πνεῦμα ὡς λαμπάδας νυκτὸς καὶ ἡμέρας διὰ τοῦ λαιμοῦ παραπίπτειν τοῖς ἐργ. τεχνίταις

δύο δαιμόνια τὸν ἀκέφαλον καὶ τὸν κύνα δεθῆναι καὶ τὸν λίθον
ἡμέραν καὶ νύκτα ὥσπερ λαμπάδα περιφέρειν τοῖς ἐργαζομένοις
τεχνίταις. 9. Καὶ ἦρα ἐγὼ ἐκ τοῦ μετοικισμοῦ ἐκείνου τοῦ λίθου
διακοσίους σίκλους ἐν τοῖς ἀναφορεῦσι τοῦ θυσιαστηρίου· ἦν δὲ
5 ὁ λίθος ὡσεὶ πράσον τὸ εἶδος ὅμοιος. 10. κἀγὼ δὲ Σολομῶν
δοξάσας κύριον τὸν θεὸν καὶ περικλείσας τὸν θησαυρὸν τοῦ
λίθου ἐκέλευσα * τοὺς δαίμονας μάρμαρα κόπτειν εἰς τὴν οἰκοδομὴν τοῦ ναοῦ. 11. καὶ ἐπηρώτησα αὐτὸν τὸν κύνα· »διὰ
ποίου ἀγγέλου καταργεῖσαι;« ὁ δὲ ἔφη· »διὰ τοῦ μεγάλου Βριαθοῦ.«

XI. Καὶ ἐκέλευσα πάλιν παρελθεῖν ἐμοὶ ἕτερα δαιμόνια· καὶ
ἦλθε βρυχώμενος ὡς λέων ὀρθὸς καὶ σταθεὶς ἀπεκρίθη μοι λόγῳ
* »βασιλεῦ Σολομῶν, ἐγὼ καὶ τὸ σχῆμα ἔχω ** τούτου, πνεῦμα
δυνάμενον μηδόλως δεθῆναι. 2. ἐγὼ πᾶσι τοῖς ἀνθρώποις τοῖς

MSS HL § 8 l. 1 δύο — H | τὸν κύνα τε καὶ ἀκεφ. L   2 νύκταν κ
ἡμέραν L | ὥσπερ ... τεχνίταις H κρατοῦντες τὸν λίθον ἵνα τοῖς ἐργ. τεχν.
λάμπη ὡς λαμπάδα L
MSS HLP = Recc. AB. 8 § 9. ἦρα ... ἀναφορεῦσι cum dubio ego
l. fortasse εἶαρ ἐκ τ μετ. ἐκ. τ. λιθ. ἔτρεχεν ἐν τοῖς ἀναφεροῦσιν ἐπὶ τοῦ
θυσ? | ἐγὼ σολομῶν P | μετοικ. A μετάλλου P | τ. λιθ. ἐκ. L   4 διακ.
σικλ. P: ἔτρεχον A | ἀναφορ P ἀνωφέρεσιν H, ἀναφέρεσιν L | ἦν ..
πράσου — P   5 πράσον ego κερασίου A | ὅμοιος A ὁμοιούμενον P |
§ 10. καὶ ἐγὼ H   7 λίθου ἐκείνου P | κελεύσας L * L f. 15ʳ 1 |
ἐκέλευσα δὲ πάλιν P | εἰς τ. οἰκ. L· ἐν τοῖ οἰκοδομοῖ H, εἰς τὰς οἰκοδομὰς P
8 τ ναοῦ A τῶν ἔργων τοῦ θεοῦ P | § 11. καὶ εὐξάμενος τῷ κυρίῳ ἐγὼ
σολομῶν ἐπηρ. P | αὐτὸν — P | διὰ π ἀγγ. καταργ. L διὰ ποίου ἄγγε-
λον κατ. H, ποίῳ ἀγγέλῳ καταργῇ συ P   9 ὁ δὲ ἔφη — H | δὲ + δαί
μων P | διὰ τ. μεγ. Βριαθοῦ (l. Βριαρίου?) H διὰ τ. μεγ. βριαθαουηλ L,
τῷ μεγάλῳ βριεῶ P, Βριαρίῳ coniect Bn
C XI (51) 10 καὶ εὐλογήσας κύρι(ον) τὸν θεὸν τοῦ οὐρανοῦ καὶ τῆς
γῆς ἐκελ. P | πάλιν — P | παρελθεῖν ἐμοὶ ego: παρελθῆναι μοι H, ἀνελ-
θεῖναι μοι I, παρεῖται μοι P | ἕτερον δαίμονα P   11 βρυχ. · ὀρθὸς H
δαιμόνιον τὸ σχῆμα αὐτοῦ λέοντος ὀρθοβρυχόμενος L, πρὸ προσώπου μου
λέοντος σχῆμα βρυχόμενος P̄ | λόγῳ A λέγων P   12 * H f 16ʳ | Σολ.
— P | ἐγὼ .. τούτου H ἐγὼ δὲ τούτου τοῦ σχήματος (ad marg. sin. Marc.
5. 4 scr. man rec) L, τὸ μὲν σχῆμα τοῦτο ὃ ἔχω P | ** P f. 10ᵛ | πνεῦμα
... δεθῆναι ego· καὶ πνεῦμα δυνάμεως μηδόλως σθῆναι (l. στῆναι?) H, οὐδ'
ἄλλος δυνάμενος δεθῆναι I, πνεῦμα εἰμὶ μηδόλως δυνάμενον νοηθῆναι P
13 § 2. καὶ λέγει ἐγὼ L | πᾶσιν P, πάσῃ H, πάσης L | τοῖς (1°) H
— PL | τοῖς (2°) .. κατακειμ. H. τ ἐν νοσήμασι P, κατακ. ἐν νοσήμα-
τι L

ἐν νοσήματι κατακειμένοις ἐφορμῶμαι παρεισερχόμενον, καὶ ἀνέν-
δοτον ποιῶ τὸν ἄνθρωπον ὡς μὴ δυνηθῆναι ἰαθῆναι αὐτοῦ τὴν
αἰτίαν. 3. ἔχω καὶ ἑτέραν πρᾶξιν· ἐμβάλλω τοὺς δαίμονας τοὺς
ὑποτεταγμένους μοι λεγεῶνας, δυτικόν ⸢γάρ εἰμι τοῖς τόποις,⸣
5 ὄνομα δὲ πᾶσι δαίμοσι τοῖς ὑπ' ἐμὲ * ὃν λεγεῶνες.« 4. καὶ ἐπηρώτησα αὐτόν· »τί σου τὸ ὄνομα;« ὁ δὲ ἔφη· »Λεοντοφόρον,
Ἄραψ τῷ γένει.« 5. καὶ εἶπον αὐτῷ· »πῶς καταργεῖσαι μετὰ
τοῦ λεγεῶνός σου, ἢ ποῖον ἄγγελον ἔχεις;« * ὁ δαίμων εἶπεν·
»ἐὰν εἴπω σοι τὸ ὄνομα οὐκ ἐμαυτὸν δεσμεύω μόνον ἀλλὰ * καὶ
10 τὸν ὑπ' ἐμὲ λεγεῶνα τῶν δαιμόνων« 6. ἐγὼ δὲ εἶπον αὐτῷ·
»ἐγὼ ὁρκίζω σε τὸ ὄνομα τοῦ μεγάλου θεοῦ τοῦ ὑψίστου· ἐν
ποίῳ ὀνόματι καταργεῖσαι μετὰ τοῦ λεγεῶνός σου;« ὁ δαίμων
εἶπεν· »ἐν τῷ ὀνόματι τοῦ μετὰ πολλὰ παθεῖν ὑπομείναντος

MSS HLP = Recc AB **1** ἐφορμ P ἀφορμόμενος L, ἐμορφόμενος H |
παρεισερχόμενον P περιερχόμ(ενο) < H, περιεισερχόμενος L | ἀνειδ. A
ἀνενδότερον P **2** δυνηθῆ H | ἰαθῆναι L, ἰασθῆναι L, — HP | αὐτ τ
αιτιαν A αὐτῷ τὴν δίαιταν P, + ταύτην L **3** §3 καὶ pr δὲ P | πρᾶ-
ξιν A δόξαν ἐγὼ βασιλεῦ, P | εἰσβάλλω L | ἐμβ. τ. δαιμ. δαίμοιας ἐμ-
βάλλω (ἐκβάλλω Fl) ἔχω δὲ P **4** δυτικὸν A δεκτικὸν P | γάρ supplevi
— AP | εἰμι add inter εἰμι et τοῖς signum omissionis at super lineam com-
pendium mihi inodabile, fortasse l καὶ vel δὲ vel γὰρ P | τ τοπ P τοῖς
τόπους A, cf Cr, p. 28 **5** ὄνομα A ἅμα P | τοῖς πᾶσι P | τοῖς super
lineam adscr. τ(ῶν) P | * L f. 15ʳ² | ὃν λεγεῶνες ego: ὧν λεγεῶας H,
λεγεώνων P, οὗ λέγω L | §4. κ ἐπηρ αὐτ A + λέγω L, ἐγὼ δὲ σοι ο-
μὼν ἀκούσας ταῦτα ἐπηρ αὐτ P **6** τι ὃν. HP τὸ σὸν ὃν πῶς καλεῖ-
ται L | ἔφη μοι H | Λεοντοφόρον P: λεοντόφρον A, l fortasse Λεγεωνο-
φόρον, sed cf supra §1 **7** Ἄραψ A ῥᾶθ P, ῥαδινός conι. Bn | τῷ γένει P
ὦ γένη L, τὸ γένος H | §5. κ εἶπον A εἶπον δὲ P | καταργῇ συ P
8 τοῦ A τῆς P | ἢ HP καὶ εἰς L | ἔχεις H — L, τὸν καταργοῦντα
σε P | * Mg 1333 | ὁ δ εἶπεν H ἔφη δὲ μοι P, — L **9** ἐὰν δὲ L |
εἴπω σοι ego εἴπωσι P, ὑποσοι H, εἴποσοι L | ὄνομά μου A | ἐμαυτῶ L
| δεσμεύεις H, forte recte | * H f 16ᵛ **10** ὑπ' A · ἐπ' P | §6 ἐγὼ ὁ.
εἰπ A ἔφην δὲ P **11** ἐγὼ .. ὅν. ἐξορκίζω σε κατὰ L | μεγ .. ὑψί-
στου H: θεοῦ του (+ compendium = τῶν?) ὧντος τοῦ ὑψίστου L, θεοῦ
σαβαωθ P | ἐν A ἰδεῖν σε P **12** ὄνομα L | καταργῇ συ P | τοῦ
λεγ A τῆ δυνάμεως P | ὁ δ. εἶπεν A. εἶπε δέ μοι τὸ πνεῦμα P **13** ἐν
.. Ἐμμανουὴλ (p. 41*, l. 1) H· ὁ μεγάλοις (μέγας ἐν Crtr) ἀνθρώποις ἔχων
πολλαπαθεῖν ἱπ' ἀνθρώπων οὗ τὸ ὄνομα ψῆφος χμδ, ὅ ἐστιν ἐμμανουὴλ P |
ὑπομειν — L

§ 3. Mk V 13, Mt VIII 32, Lk. VIII 31 f
§ 6 Mk. IV 35—V 20, Mt. VIII 23 - 34, Lk. VIII 22—39.

ὑπὸ τῶν ἀνθρώπων, οὗ τὸ ὄνομα Ἐμμανουήλ, ὃς καὶ νῦν ἐδέ-
σμευσεν ἡμᾶς καὶ ἐλεύσεται κατὰ τοῦ ὕδατος κρημνῷ βασανίσαι
ἡμᾶς· ἐν δὲ τρισὶ χαρακτῆρσι κατάγεται περιηχούμενος.« 7. κἀγὼ
δὲ κατέκρινα αὐτοῦ τὸν λεγεῶνα φέρειν ἀπὸ τοῦ δρυμοῦ ξύλον,
τὸν δὲ Λεοντοφόρον καταπρίζειν αὐτὰ * λεπτὰ τοῖς ὄνυξι καὶ
ὑποκάτω τῆς καμίνου τῆς ἀσβέστου ῥίπτειν.

XII. Κἀγὼ προσκυνήσας τὸν θεὸν τοῦ Ἰσραὴλ ἐκέλευσα προ-
ελθεῖν ἕτερον * δαίμονα. καὶ ἦλθε πρὸ προσώπου μου δράκων
τρικέφαλος φοβερόχροος. 2. καὶ ἐπηρώτησα αὐτόν· »σὺ τίς
εἶ;« ὁ δὲ ἔφη· »πνεῦμα τρίβολον ἐν τρισὶ κατεργαζόμενον ἐγὼ
ἔργοις· ἐν κοιλίαις γυναικῶν τυφλῶ τὰ παιδία καὶ ὦτα ἐπιδινῶ
καὶ ποιῶ αὐτὰ βωβὰ καὶ κωφά, καὶ τύπτω τοὺς ἀνθρώπους
κατὰ τοῦ σώματος καὶ ποιῶ καταπίπτειν καὶ ἀφρίζειν καὶ τρι-

MSS HLP = Recc AB　1 οὗ ἐστὶν τὸ ὀν. αὐτοῦ ἐμμαν. L | νῦν — P
2 κ. ἐλευσ A ὃς καὶ τότε ἐλευσόμενος P | κρημ βασαν. L κριμμῷ βας H,
κρημνοβατίσει (l. -ήσει) P, κρημανοβαπτίσει Fl　3 δὲ P — A | τοῖς τρισὶ P
| καταγ. περιηχ H κατάγουσαι (-ούσαις Cr) περιηχούμενον P, εἰσὶν καταρ-
γούμεθα περιηγούμενος L | § 7 κἀγὼ δὲ H: ἐγὼ δ᾽. L, κἀγὼ σολομῶν
ἀκούσας ταῦτα καὶ δοξάσας τὸν θεὸν P　4 * P f 11ʳ | αὐτοῦ τ. λεγεῶνα
P αὐτὸν A | φέρειν .. ξύλον A ξυλοφορεῖν ἀπὸ δρυμοῦ P　5 τ. δὲ
Λεοντ ego· τὸν δὲ λεοντόφρον H (-τόφρων) L, αὐτὸν δὲ τὸν λεοντόμορ-
φον κατέκρινα P | καταπρ HP κύπτίζει L | αὐτὰ — P | * L f. 15ᵛ¹
ὄνυξι L, ἄνυξι H, ὀδοῦσιν P | κ ὑποκ A εἰς ὑπόκαυσιν P　6 ῥίπτειν A
εἰς τὸν ναὸν κυρίου τοῦ θεοῦ P

C XII. (54) I. 7 κἀγὼ A καὶ P | προσκυνν HP παρεκάλεσα L, + κύ-
ριον P | τοῦ — L | καὶ ἐκέλευσα L | προελθ. H. παρεῖναι μοι P, ἵνα
καὶ ἕτερα δαιμόνια ἐλθεῖν ἐν ἡμῖν L　8 * H f. 17ʳ | μου — P | δρακ
τρικεφ P δράκων τὸ κέφαλος L, δράκον τὸ κέφαλον H　9 φοβεροχ. LP
— H | § 2 δὲ δαίμων L, + μοι P　10 τρίβολον ego: τριόβολον A, τρι-
βόλαιον εἰμὶ P, τριβολαῖον (τρι et βολαῖος) conj Bncn | ἐν HP. | L
κατεργ ἐγὼ ἔργοις κατεργαζόμενος ἐγὼ ἔργοις H (— ἔργοις) L πράξεσι
κατεργαζόμενον ἐγὼ δὲ P　11 ἐν LP — H | κοιλίαις A κοιλίᾳ P,
+ τῶν L | τυφλώνω A | παιδία LP νήπια H | ἐπιδέτω A　12 αὐτὰ
— P | βωβὰ P ὀδοθῆ H (-δεῖ) L, λωβὰ conj. Fu | κωφά + καὶ ἐμοὶ
γ(ὰρ) πάλιν ἐν τῇ τρίτῃ μοι κεφαλῇ ὑπόδυνα P　13 κατὰ + τὸ εἰκῶδες P,
ἀκωδὸς in textu, »εἰκώδος — εἰκώδες« ad marg Fl, conj ἀληθές (unbewachten
Teilen) Fu, ἄκωλος (limbless part) Cr, l. fortasse τὸν εἰκόνα? | καὶ φρίζει καὶ
τρίζει L | κ τρίζ — H

C. XII 2. Mt XVII 15, Mk. IX 18

ζειν τοὺς ὀδόντας. 3. ἔχω δὲ τρόπον ἐν ᾧ καταργοῦμαι ὑπὸ τοῦ
σημειομένου τόπου ἐγκεφάλου, ἐκεῖ γὰρ προώρισεν ἄγγελος τῆς
μεγάλης βουλῆς με παθεῖν, καὶ νῦν φανερῶς ἐπὶ ξύλου οἰκήσει.
ἐκεῖνός με καταργήσει ἐν οἷς καὶ ὢν ὑποτέταγμαι. 4. ἐν δὲ τῷ
5 τόπῳ ἐν ᾧ ἤρθη, βασιλεῦ Σολομῶν, στήσει κίονα πορφυροῦν
* ἐπὶ τοῦ ἀέρος δῶρα μεμορφούμενον Ἐφιππᾶς ἀπὸ τῆς Ἐρυθρᾶς θαλάσσης ἀγαγὼν ἀπὸ τῆς ἔσω Ἀραβίας. ἐν δὲ τῇ ἀρχῇ
τοῦ ναοῦ ὅνπερ ἤρξω κτίζειν, βασιλεῦ Σολομῶν, ἀπόκειται χρυσίον πολύ, ὅπερ ὀρύξας ἆρον.‹ 5. κἀγὼ Σολομῶν ἀποστεί-
10 λας τὸν παῖδά μου εὗρον καθὼς εἶπέ μοι τὸ δαιμόνιον καὶ
σφραγίσας τὸ δακτυλίδιον ᾔνεσα τὸν θεόν. 6. εἶπον οὖν
αὐτῷ ›λέγε μοι πῶς καλεῖσαι.‹ καὶ ὁ δαίμων ἔφη· ›κορυφὴ
δρακόντων.‹ καὶ ἐκέλευσα αὐτὸν πλινθουργεῖν εἰς τὸν ναὸν
τοῦ θεοῦ

MSS HLP = Rec. AB.   1 ὀδόντ. LP· ὀδύν. H | § 3. ἐν ᾧ HP   ὡς L
| καταργοῦν H | τοῦ . . τόπου L (— τοῦ) H σημειουμένης τῆς ἱ(ερου-
σα)λήμ, εἰς τὸν λεγόμενον τόπον P   2 ἐγκεφάλου H· ἐν κεφάλῳ L, κεφά-
λαιον P | προόρισεν L, προόρισον H, προώριστο P | ὁ ἀγγελ. P |.
ἄγγελον H   3 με παθεῖν — P | φανερὸν L | τ᾽ ἐπὶ P | οἰκήσει
ἥμισι L   4 καταργήσει L   καταργήσε H, καταργεῖ P | ἐν οἷς καὶ ὢν L·
ἐν εἰς ὃν καὶ H, ἐν ᾧ P | ὑποτέταμαι H | § 4. (55) δὲ ᾧ L   5 ἤρθη
καθέξει P | βασ. Σολ   ὁ βασιλεὺς L | στήσῃ H, στήκει P, στήσῃς L |
κίονα . . μεμορφ   κίων ἐπὶ τοῦ ἀέρος πορφυροδανόμενος P | πορφυροῦν L
πορφύριον H | * H f. 17ᵛ   6 * L f. 15ᵛ ² | μεμορφούμενον ego· μεμορ-
φουμένου L, μαιμορφομένου H | ὁ δαίμων ὁ λεγόμενος ἐφιππᾶς P | ἐφοί-
ποις H, ἔφιππος L   7 ἀγαγῶ L, ἀναγὼν H, ἀναγαγὼν P | Ἀραβίας:
+ ὅστις καὶ εἰς ἀσκὸν κατακλεισθείς, κομισθήσεται ἔμπροσθέν σου P | δὲ
— A   8 ὅνπερ P. οὗ περ L, περ H | ἀπόκειται . Σολ — L | * P
f. 11ᵛ | χρυσίον . . ὅπερ P   χρόνον πολὴν ὅνπερ H   9 ἆρον P   φαῖρον H
§ 5. κἀγὼ δὲ H | ἀποστείλας . δαιμ. καὶ — P   10 τὸ παιδίον L |
καὶ εὗρεν L | εἶπε P· ᾔρηκε L | τὸ δαιμ P· ὁ δαίμων P | τὸ δακτ. A·
τῷ (forte ex τὸ corr.) δακτυλιδίῳ P   11 ᾔνεσα P   καὶ ἔνεσα H, καὶ ὕμνησα L
§ 6. (56) εἶπον . . αὖτ P   δὲ (vel κὲ, l καὶ) εἶπον αὐτ. H, ἔπειτα δὲ εἶπον
πρὸς τὸν δαίμον⟨α⟩ L   12 λέγε . καὶ· H· τί σὺ λέγεις P   σὺ τίς εἶ L
| κ. ὁ δ. ἔφη L (— καὶ) P   ὁ δὲ ἔφη H | κορ. δρακ. P (κορυφὴν) H.
κορυφὴν δρακόντος L, + εἰμι P   13 πλιν.θ. (ex πλιθ corr) P· λειτουρ-
γεῖν H, λεπτουργεῖν L | εἰς A· ἐν P   14 τ. θεοῦ A· εἶχεν χεῖρας ἀν-
(θρώπ)ων P

---

§ 3. Mk. XV 22, Mt. XXVII 33, Lk XXIII 33

XIII. Καὶ ἐκέλευσα παρεῖναί μοι ἕτερον δαίμονα. καὶ ἦλθε
πρὸ προσώπου μου γύνη μὲν τὸ εἶδος, ⌜τὴν δὲ μορφὴν κατέχουσα
ἅμα τοῖς μέλεσιν αὐτῆς λυσίτριχος⌝ ταῖς θριξίν. 2. καὶ εἶπον
πρὸς αὐτήν· »σὺ τίς εἶ;« ἡ δὲ ἔφη· »καὶ τίς σύ, ἢ τίνα χρείαν
ἔχεις μαθεῖν τὰ κατ' ἐμοῦ πράγματα ποῖά εἰσιν ὄντα, * ἀλλ' εἰ
θέλεις μαθεῖν, πορεύθητι ἐν τοῖς ταμείοις τοῖς βασιλικοῖς καὶ·
ψιφάμενος τὰς χεῖράς σου πάλιν καθέσθητι ἐπὶ τοῦ θρόνου σου
καὶ ἐρώτησαί με, καὶ τότε μαθεῖς, βασιλεῦ, τίς εἰμι ἐγώ« 3. καὶ
τοῦτο ποιήσας ἐγὼ Σολομῶν καὶ καθίσας ἐπὶ τοῦ θρόνου μου
ἠρώτησα αὐτὴν καὶ εἶπον· »τίς εἶ σύ;« ἡ δὲ ἔφη· * »Ὀβυζούθ,
ἥτις ἐν νυκτὶ οὐ καθεύδω, ἀλλὰ περιέρχομαι πάντα τὸν κόσμον
ἐπὶ ταῖς γυναιξί, καὶ ⌜στοχαζομένη τὴν ὥραν μαστεύω⌝ καὶ

MSS HLP = Recc. AB. ᴄ. XIII. (57) **14** Καὶ προσκυνήσας κύριον τὸν
θεὸν τοῦ Ἰ(σρα)ὴλ ἐκελ. P | δαιμόνιον L **2** γύνη . εἶδος ego. βοῦς μὲν
τῷ εἶδει H, βοῦς με τὸ ἔδος L, πνεῦμα γυναικοειδὲς P | τὴν δὲ ... λυσί-
τριχος ego: τῆς δὲ μορφῆς καταπέμπουσαν ἅπαν τοῖς μέλεσιν λίαν τρίχων H,
τὴν δὲυ μορφὴν καταπέμπουσαν ἅπ(αν) τοῖς μέλεσιν αὐτοῦ λυσιν τριχῶν L,
τὴν κορυφὴν κατέχουσα ἀπὸ παντὸς μέλους· καὶ τὰς λυσίτριχας P **8 § 2.**
εἶπον A. ἔφην P **4** αὐτήν P αὐτὸν A | λέγε μοι σὺ P | εἶ LP. εἰ-
σὶ H | ἡ δὲ ... χρείαν P. — A | καὶ τίς σύ P° ad marg. lat., ın textu
καὶ σὺ τίς εἰ prim man scrı subter σὺ τίς εἶ lınea fracta ducta **5** καὶ
ἔχεις A | μαθεῖν A ἀκοῦσαι P | τὰ — L | πραγ. π. εἰσιν ὄντα L
πραγ πεισηνόντα H, — P | * H f. 18ʳ | εἰ — L **6** μαθεῖν: + στήκω
γὰρ δεδεμ(έν)η πρὸ προσώπου σου P | πορεύου L | * L f. 16ᵣ¹ | τα-
μίοις σου L **7** σου — P | καὶ πάλιν H | καθεσθ A· καθήσας P, ad
marg. scr. σεις quod forte pro σας ın καθήσας legendum est | ἐπὶ τ. θρον. A:
πρὸ τοῦ βήματος P **8** καὶ ἐρώτησαί με ego· κ. ἐρώτησε ἡμῖν L, τότε
ἐρωτήσεις με P, — H | τότε — P | μαθεῖς H μαθεῖν L, μαθήση P |
βασιλεὺς σολομῶν L | τί τίς H **§ 3.** (58) **9** Σολομῶν. — L, καθὼς
συνέταξέ μοι, ἠνεσχόμην δὲ διὰ τὴν ἐνοῦσάν μοι σοφίαν, ἵνα δυνηθῶ ἀκοῦσαι
τὰς πράξεις αὐτῆς, καὶ ἐλέγξαι αὐτάς, καὶ φανερῶσαι τοῖς ἀνθρώποις P |
καθήσας LP | ἐπὶ ... εἶπον. ἔφησα πρὸς τὸν δαίμονα P **10** ἠρώτησα
ego ἐρώτησα L, ἐρωτῖσαι H | αὐτὴν ego. αὐτὸν H, ἐγώ L | λέγε μοι
τίς H | σύ — P | ἡ δὲ ἔφη H (δ) L. καὶ εἶπεν P | Ὀβυζούθ ἀβυζούθ L,
ἡ βυζοῦθ καὶ ἰδιοῦθ H, ἐγὼ (* Mg 1336) λέγομαι παρὰ ἀνθρώποις ὀβι-
ζοῦθ P, l. Ἀβυζοῦ? cf. Intro pp. 78 et 82 **11** ἥτις . . καθεύδω ego,
ἥτις ἐὰν ἐκτήσω καθεύδω H, καὶ τῆς ἐνυκτὶ οὐ καθ. L, ἥτις νυκτὸς οὐ
καθ. P | περιερχόμενος H | τὸν — L | * ἐπὶ HP ἐν L | τ.
τικτούσαις γυν. P | στοχαζ. | μαστεύω ego: μαστίζομ(έν)η τὴν ὥραν
μαστίζω H, στομαχηζόμην τὴν ὥραν μαστίζω L, τὴν μὲν ὥραν στοχαζομένη
σταματίζω (ın marg. Ἵσταμαι) P

πνίγω τὰ βρέφη, * καὶ καθ᾽ ἑκάστην νύκτα ἄπρακτος οὐκ ἐξέρχο-
μαι. σὺ δὲ οὐ δύνασαί με διατάξαι. καὶ εἰς τὰ δυσηκῆ μέρη περιέρχομαι. 4. καὶ οὐκ ἔστι μου τὸ ἔργον εἰ μὴ βρεφῶν ἀναίρεσις καὶ
ὀφθαλμῶν ἀδικία καὶ στομάτων καταδίκη καὶ φρενῶν ἀπώλεια
5 καὶ σωμάτων ἄλγησις.« 5. καὶ ταῦτα ἀκούσας ἐγὼ Σολομῶν
ἐθαύμασα, καὶ τὸ εἶδος αὐτῆς οὐκ ἐθεώρουν ἀλλὰ σκότος τὸ σῶμα
* αὐτῆς ὑπῆρχε καὶ αἱ τρίχες αὐτῆς ἠγριωμέναι. 6. κἀγὼ δὲ
Σολομῶν λέγω αὐτήν· »λέγε μοι, πονηρὸν πνεῦμα, ὑπὸ ποίου
ἀγγέλου καταργεῖσαι.« ἡ δὲ εἶπέ μοι· »ὑπὸ τοῦ ἀγγέλου Ῥαφαὴλ
10 καὶ ὅτε γεννῶσιν αἱ γυναῖκες, γράψαι τὸ ὄνομά μου ἐν χαρτίῳ
καὶ ἐγὼ φεύξομαι ἀπὸ τῶν ἐκεῖσε. 7. κἀγὼ ἀκούσας ταῦτα προσέταξε δεσμευθῆναι αὐτὴν ταῖς θριξὶ καὶ κρεμασθῆναι ἔμπροσθεν

τοῦ ναοῦ ἵνα πάντες οἱ διερχόμενοι υἱοὶ Ἰσραὴλ βλέποντες
δοξάσουσι τὸν θεὸν τὸν δόντα μοι τὴν ἐξουσίαν ταύτην.* * *

XIV. Καὶ πάλιν ἐκέλευσα παρεῖναί μοι ἕτερον δαίμονα· καὶ
ἦλθε πρός με τῷ εἴδει δράκων κυλινδούμενος, τὸ δὲ πρόσωπον
ἔχων καὶ τοὺς πόδας ἀνθρώπου καὶ τὰ μέλη αὐτοῦ δράκοντος
καὶ τὰ πτερὰ κατὰ νώτου. 2. καὶ ἰδὼν αὐτὸν ἔκθαμβος γενόμενος εἶπον αὐτῷ· »σὺ τίς εἶ καὶ πόθεν ἐλήλυθας;« καὶ εἶπέ μοι
τὸ πνεῦμα· ›τὸ μὲν πρῶτον παρέστηκά σοι, βασιλεῦ Σολομῶν,
πνεῦμα θεοποιούμενον ἐν ἀνθρώποις, * νῦν δὲ κατηργημένον
διὰ τῆς τοῦ θεοῦ δεδομένης σοι σφραγῖδος. 3 καὶ νῦν ἐγώ εἰμι
ὁ λεγόμενος Πτεροδράκων, οὐ συγγινόμενος πολλαῖς γυναιξίν,
ὀλίγαις δὲ καὶ εὐμόρφοις, αἵτινες ⌈τοῦ ξύλου⌉ τούτου τοῦ ἄστρου
ὄνομα κατέχουσι. 4 καὶ ἀπέρχομαι πρὸς αὐτὰς ὡσεὶ πνεῦμα
πτεροειδὲς συγγινόμενον διὰ γλουτῶν. καὶ ἡ μὲν βαστάζει ᾗ ἐφώρ-
μησα καὶ τὸ γεννηθὲν ἐξ αὐτῆς Ἔρω⟨ς⟩ γίνεται· ὑπ᾽ ἀνδρῶν δὲ
μὴ δυνηθὲν βασταχθῆναι ἐψόφησεν ἄρα καὶ ἡ γύνη ἐκείνη. αὕτη

MSS HLP = Recc. AB   **1** τ ναοῦ LP   μου καὶ τοῦ ναοῦ Η, + τοῦ
θεοῦ P | οἱ · Ἰσρ. ego οἱ ἐρχόμενοι υἱοὶ ἰ(σρα)ὴλ καὶ Η, οἱ διερχόμενοι
τῶν υἱῶν ἰ(σρα)ὴλ L, οἱ (supra lin adscr Pᶜ) υἱοὶ Ἰσραὴλ διερχόμενοι καὶ P
ἰι ἐβλίποντες αὐτὴν καὶ L   **2** δοξάσουσι ego — Η, δοξάζουσι LP | κύριον
τ. θεὸν ἰ(σρα)ὴλ P | ταύτην + καὶ σοφίαν καὶ δύναμιν παρὰ θεοῦ (⁴ f. 12ᵛ)
διὰ τῆς σφραγῖδος ταύτης P | ** ΙΙ f 19ʳ

C. XIV. (60)   **3** δαιμόνιον L   **4** πρός . κυλινδ Η πρ με τὸ ἶδος
ὡς δράκοντος κυλινδ L, πρὸ προσώπου δρακοντοειδὴς ἀνακυλινδ P | καὶ
τοὺς πόδας ἔχων P   **5** κ. τ μέλη αὐτ Η τὸ δὲ ἕτερον σῶμα L, τὰ δὲ μέλη
αὐτοῦ πάντα ἀπὸ τῶν ποδῶν P | δράκοντος ΗΡ κοντὸς L   **6** κατὰ νό-
τον Ρ, κατὰ νώτον Η, ἐκ τὰ νότατον L | § 2. ἰδὼν vel ἰδοὺ P | αὐτὸν Η
(ex -ος corr.) P τούτου L   **7** καὶ εἶπον L | αὐτῷ Η αὐτὸι L, — P | σὺ
— P | εἰ ὁ δαίμων· καὶ τίς λ(έ)γ(ει) καὶ P | ἐλήλυθας εἰπέ μοι P | καὶ
.. πνεῦμα Η κ ἀποκριθεὶς τὸ πνεῦμα λέγει Ρ, — L   **8** τὸν μὲν Η
θ πνεῦμά τε P | θεοποιημένον L | ἐν ἀνθρώποις δὲ νῦν καταργοῖμαι Η
* L f. 16ᵛ ι   **10** τῆς ... σοι P· τῆς σῆς δεδομένης Η, τοῦ θεοῦ δεδωμέι ου
τοι L | σφραγῖδος καὶ σοφίας P | §3 καὶ νῦν P νῦν δὲ A | ἐγὼ ...
δαιμόνιον (p 48*, l. 5), ι, ε, XIV 3—XVI 1) om. mss HL

MS P = Rec B   **12** ξύλου certe falsum est ξυλ ‹ (λ super ι posito)
MS, ξύλι Fl errore, ξιφίου vel Σειρίου conj Bn, stellae vel sideris nomen aut
compendium falso enodavit scriptor, l forte Τοξότου?   **14** γλουτῶν Crtr
(nates) πλοῦτον P | βαστάζει ego ἐβάσταζεν P | ᾗ Fl ἢ P | ἐφόρ-
μησα P   **15** Ἔρως Fl ἔρω punctis tribus incertum esse notatum P, ἥρως
·onj. Bn vix recte

μου ἡ πρᾶξίς ἐστιν. 5. θέσον οὖν μοι μόνον ἀρκεσθῆναι, τὰ δὲ
λοιπὰ τῶν δαιμονίων ἐνοχλούμενα ὑπό σου καταταρασσόμενα
πᾶσαν μὲν ἀλήθειαν εἴπωσι· τὰ δὲ διὰ πυρὸς ποιήσουσιν ἀναλω-
θῆναι τὴν μέλλουσαν ὕλην τῶν ξύλων ὑπό σου συνάγεσθαι εἰς
5 οἰκοδομὴν ἐν τῷ ναῷ.« 6. καὶ ὡς ταῦτα ἐλάλησεν ὁ δαίμων,
ἰδοὺ τὸ πνεῦμα ἀπὸ τοῦ στόματος αὐτοῦ ἐξελθὸν ἐνέπρησε τὸν
δρυμῶνα τοῦ Λιβάνου καὶ ἐνεπύρισε πάντα τὰ ξύλα ἅπερ εἰς τὸν
ναὸν τοῦ θεοῦ ἐθέμην. 7. καὶ εἶδον ἐγὼ Σολομῶν ὃ πεποίηκε
τὸ πνεῦμα καὶ ἐθαύμασα, καὶ δοξάσας τὸν θεὸν ἠρώτησα τὸν
10 δαίμονα τὸν δρακοντοειδῆ λέγων· »εἰπέ μοι ποίῳ ἀγγέλῳ καταργῇ
σύ.« ὁ δέ μοι ἔφη· »τῷ μεγάλῳ ἀγγέλῳ τῷ ἐν τῷ δευτέρῳ
οὐρανῷ καθεζομένῳ τῷ καλουμένῳ Ἑβραϊστὶ Βαζαζάθ.« 8. κἀγὼ
Σολομῶν ἀκούσας ταῦτα καὶ ἐπικαλεσάμενος τὸν ἄγγελον αὐτοῦ
κατέκρινα μάρμαρα πρίζειν εἰς οἰκοδομὴν τοῦ ναοῦ τοῦ θεοῦ.

15 XV. καὶ εὐλογήσας τὸν θεὸν ἐκέλευσα παρεῖναί μοι ἕτερον
δαίμονα. * καὶ ἦλθε πρὸ προσώπου μου ἕτερον πνεῦμα ὡς γύνη
μὲν τὸ εἶδος ἔχον, εἰς δὲ τοὺς ὤμους ἑτέρας δύο κεφαλὰς σὺν
χερσίν. 2. καὶ ἠρώτησα αὐτήν· »λέγε μοι σὺ τίς εἶ.« ἔφη δέ
μοι· »ἐγώ εἰμι Ἐνήφιγος, ἥτις καὶ μυριώνυμος καλοῦμαι.« 3. καὶ
20 εἶπον αὐτῇ· »ἐν ποίῳ ἀγγέλῳ καταργῇ σύ;« ἡ δέ μοι ἔφη· »τί
ζητεῖς; τί χρῄζεις; ἐγὼ μὲν μεταβάλλομαι ὡς θεὰ λεγομένη, καὶ
μεταβάλλομαι πάλιν καὶ γίνομαι ἕτερον εἶδος ἔχουσα. 4. καὶ μὴ
θελήσῃς κατὰ τοῦτο γνῶναι πάντα τὰ κατ' ἐμέ, ἀλλ' ἐπειδὴ
πάρει μοι, εἰς τοῦτο ἄκουσον· ἐγὼ παρακαθέζομαι τῇ σελήνῃ
25 καὶ διὰ τοῦτο τρεῖς μορφὰς κατέχω. 5. ὅτε μὲν μαγευομένη ὑπὸ
τῶν σοφῶν γίνομαι ὡς Κρόνος. ὅτε δὲ πάλιν περὶ τῶν κατα-
γόντων με κατέρχομαι καὶ φαίνομαι ἄλλῃ μορφῇ· τὸ μὲν τοῦ
στοιχείου μέτρον ἀήττητον καὶ ἀόριστον καὶ ἀκατάργητόν ἐστιν.
ἐγὼ γοῦν εἰς τὰς τρεῖς μορφὰς μεταβαλλομένη κατέρχομαι καὶ
30 γίνομαι τοιαύτη ἥνπερ βλέπεις. 6. καταργοῦμαι δὲ ὑπὸ ἀγγέλου

MS P = Rec. B. 1 § 5. θέσον θὲς Bn   2 καταρασσ καὶ ταρασσ.
ἵνα Bn   4 μέλλουσαν corr. Bn μέλουσαν P | σου ego τοῦ P, τούτων
conj. Bn § 6. (62) 6 ἰδοὺ corr. Bn ἴδον P | * Mg 1337 | ἐξελθὼν P
7 * f. 13ʳ
MS P = Rec. B   c. XV. 1 16 * (64)   17 ἔχοι ego ἔχουσα P
18 § 2. ἐρώτησα P   § 3. 20 αὐτῇ η incertum, αὐτῷ Fl   § 5. 28 ἀήττητον P ἀνίττητον Fl errore

Ῥαθαναὴλ τοῦ καθεζομένου εἰς τρίτον οὐρανόν. διὰ τοῦτο οὖν σοι λέγω· οὐ δύναταί με χωρῆσαι ὁ ναὸς οὗτος.«

7. κἀγὼ οὖν Σολομῶν εὐξάμενος τῷ θεῷ μου καὶ ἐπικαλεσάμενος τὸν ἄγγελον ὃν εἶπέ μοι, Ῥαθαναήλ, ἐποίησα τὴν σφραγῖδα καὶ κατεσφράγισα αὐτὴν ἁλύσει τριττῇ, καὶ κάτω δεσμῶν τῆς ἁλύσεως ἐποίησα τὴν σφραγῖδα τοῦ θεοῦ. 8. καὶ προεφήτευσέ μοι τὸ πνεῦμα λέγον· »ταῦτα μὲν σύ, βασιλεῦ Σολομῶν, ποιεῖς ἡμῖν. μετὰ δὲ χρόνον τινὰ ῥαγήσεταί σοι ἡ βασιλεία σου, καὶ πάλιν ἐν καιρῷ διαρραγήσεται ὁ ναὸς οὗτος καὶ συνλευσθήσεται πᾶσα Ἰερουσαλὴμ ἀπὸ βασιλέως Περσῶν καὶ Μήδων καὶ Χαλδαίων· καὶ τὰ σκεύη τούτου τοῦ ναοῦ οὗ σὺ ποιεῖς δουλεύσουσι θεοῖς. 9. μεθ' ὧν ἂν καὶ πάντα τὰ ἀγγεῖα ἐν οἷς ἡμᾶς κατακλείεις κλασθήσονται ὑπὸ χειρῶν ἀνθρώπων καὶ τότε ἡμεῖς ἐξελευσόμεθα ἐν πολλῇ δυνάμει ἔνθεν καὶ ἔνθεν καὶ εἰς τὸν κόσμον κατασπαρησόμεθα. 10. καὶ πλανήσομεν πᾶσαν τὴν οἰκουμένην μέχρι πολλοῦ καιροῦ ἕως τοῦ θεοῦ ὁ υἱὸς τανυσθῇ ἐπὶ ξύλου· καὶ οὐκέτι γὰρ γίνεται τοιοῦτος βασιλεὺς ὅμοιος αὐτῷ ὁ πάντας ἡμᾶς καταργῶν, οὗ ἡ μήτηρ ἀνδρὶ οὐ μιγήσεται. 11. καὶ τίς λάβῃ τοιαύτην ἐξουσίαν κατὰ πνευμάτων εἰ μὴ ἐκεῖνος; ὃν ὁ πρῶτος διάβολος πειρᾶσαι ζητήσει καὶ οὐκ ἰσχύσει πρὸς αὐτόν, οὗ ἡ ψῆφος τοῦ ὀνόματος χμδ̄, ὅ ἐστιν Ἐμμανουήλ. 12. διὰ τοῦτο, βασιλεῦ Σολομῶν, ὁ καιρός σου πονηρὸς καὶ τὰ ἔτη σου μικρὰ καὶ πονηρὰ καὶ τῷ δούλῳ σου δοθήσεται ἡ βασιλεία σου.‹

13. Κἀγὼ Σολομῶν * ἀκούσας ταῦτα ἐδόξασα τὸν θεὸν καὶ θαυμάσας τῶν δαιμόνων τὰς ἀπολογίας ἕως τῶν ἀποβάσεων ἠπίστουν αὐτοῖς καὶ οὐκ ἐπίστευον τοῖς λεγομένοις ὑπ' αὐτῶν. 14. ὅτε δὲ ἐγένοντο, τότε συνῆκα καὶ ἐν τῷ θανάτῳ μου ἔγραψα τὴν διαθήκην ταύτην πρὸς τοὺς υἱοὺς Ἰσραὴλ καὶ ἔδωκα αὐτοῖς ὥστε εἰδέναι τὰς δυνάμεις τῶν δαιμόνων καὶ τὰς μορφὰς αὐτῶν

MS P = Rec. B.   2 § 6 χωρῆσαι conj. Cr χωρίσαι P   3 § 7. (65) 5 δεσμῶν ego δεσμόν P   § 8. 9 συνλευσθ ego συνλευθ P, vox nihili cuius vis fortasse est 'congeries lapidum fiet', "shall be undone" = (συν)λυθήσεται Cr, συνλουθήσεται (sic) Fl errore   18 § 9. κατακλείεις ego κατακλύεις P 24 § 13. (66) * f. 14ʳ   27 § 14. * Mg 1340

C. XV 10. Apoc. XII 9 notat James
C. XV 11. Mt IV 1—11, Lk. IV 1—13
C XV 12. Gen. XVII 9 notat James

καὶ τὰ ὀνόματα αὐτῶν τῶν ἀγγέλων ἐν οἷς καταργοῦνται οἱ
δαίμονες. 15. καὶ δοξάσας κύριον τὸν θεὸν Ἰσραὴλ ἐκέλευσα
περιδεθῆναι τὸ πνεῦμα δεσμοῖς ἀλύτοις.

XVI. Καὶ εὐλογήσας τὸν θεὸν ἐκέλευσα παρεῖναι ἕτερον
5 πνεῦμα. καὶ ἦλθε πρὸ προσώπου μου ἕτερον δαιμόνιον * ἔχον
τὴν μορφὴν ἔμπροσθεν ἵππου, ὄπισθεν δὲ ἰχθύος. καὶ λέγει
μεγάλην τὴν φωνήν· »βασιλεῦ Σολομῶν, ἐγὼ θαλάσσιόν εἰμι
πνεῦμα χαλεπόν. ἐγείρομαι οὖν καὶ ἔρχομαι ἐπὶ τοὺς πελάγους
παρὰ * τῆς θαλάσσης καὶ ἐμποδίζω τοὺς ἐν αὐτῇ πλέοντας ἀν-
10 θρώπους. 2. διεγειρόμενος δὲ καὶ ἐμαυτὸν ὡς κῦμα καὶ μετα-
μορφούμενος ἐπεισέρχομαι τοῖς πλοίοις καὶ αὕτη μου ἡ ἐργασία
τοῦ ὑποδέχεσθαι τὰ χρήματα καὶ τοὺς ἀνθρώπους. ⌜λαμβάνω
γὰρ καὶ διεγείρομαι καὶ διαρρίπτω τοὺς ἀνθρώπους ὑπὸ τῆς
θαλάσσης, οὕτως εἰμὶ ἐπιθυμῶν σωμάτων, ἀλλ' ἐκρίπτω αὐτὰ
15 ἔξω τῆς θαλάσσης ἕως τοῦ δεῦρο⌝ 3. ἐπεὶ δὲ ὁ Βεελζεβοὺλ ὁ
τῶν ἀερίων καὶ ἐπιγείων καὶ καταχθονίων πνευμάτων δεσπότης
συμβουλεύει εἰς τὰς καθ' ἑνὸς ἑκάστου ἡμῶν πράξεις, διὰ τοῦτο
κἀγὼ ἀνέβην ἐκ τῆς * θαλάσσης σκέψιν τινὰ λαβεῖν παρ' αὐτῷ.

MS P = Rec B. **1** ante ἀγγέλων scriptum δαιμόν(ων) linea delevit
prim man

C XVI. (67) l. **5** * iursus inc. mss. HL

MSS HLP = Recc AB **6** μορφ ἔχω H, μορφ ἔχων L | ἔνπροστεν H
| ὄπιστεν L | κ. λ. μεγάλη τὴν φωνήν H, κ. λεγ(ει) μετὰ μεγάλης φωνῆς L,
κ. φωνῇ ἦν αὐτῷ μεγάλη καὶ ἔλεγε πρός με P **7** ἐγὼ πνεῦμα θαλάσσιον
εἰμι P | θαλάσσιος L **8** ἐγειρ. . θαλάσσης καὶ ἀποδέχομαι ἐν χρυσῷ
καὶ ἀργύρῳ. ἐγὼ τοιοῦτον εἰμι πνεῦμα διεγυρόμενον καὶ ἐρχόμενον ἐπὶ τὰ
ἁπλώματα τοῦ ὕδατος τῆς θαλ P | οὖν H δὲ L | ἐπὶ . θαλάσσης H
διὰ τῆς θαλάσσης ἐπὶ τὰ πλεῖα (l πλοῖα) L **9** + H ſ 19ᵛ | ἐν αὐτῇ πλ.
HP ἐν τῷ πλεῖω (l πλοίῳ) L **9** 2. διεγειρω . μεταμορφ. διεγύρω
γὰρ ἐμαυτὸν εἰς κῦμα καὶ μεταμορφοῦμαι· ἐπιρίπτω καὶ P | διεγυρόμενοι L
| καὶ — L | ἐμαυτὸν L ἐμαυτοὺς H | ὡς κῦμα L κεῖμαι H **11** ἐπεισ-
ερχ. P· περιέρχομαι L | ὑπεισέρχομαι τοῖ πλείοι H | μου ἐστὶν P
12 τοῖς ἀν(θρώπ)οις L

MS P = Rec. B **12** λαμβάνω ... δεῦρο (l 15) — A

MSS HLP = Recc. AB. § 3 l. **15** ἐπεὶ ego ἐπὶ Λ ἐπειδὴ P | ὁ τῶν
. δεσπότης A ἄρχων τῶν ἀερίων πνευμάτων ⁄ καταχθ. ⁊ ἐπιγ δεσπόζει
καὶ P **17** ἐυβουλεύει L | εἰς τὰς P τοῦ A | καθ' — P **18** ἀνέβη
LP ἀναβαίνω H | ἐκ A. ἀπὸ P | * P ſ. 14ʳ | σκέψιν· σκήψιν
conj Cr cum dubio | σκέψιν . . θαλάσσης (p 49, l 2) P om per homoeo-
teleuton A

4. ἔχω δὲ καὶ ἑτέραν δόξαν καὶ πρᾶξιν· μεταμορφοῦμαι εἰς κύματα καὶ ἀνέρχομαι ἀπὸ τῆς θαλάσσης καὶ δεικνύω ἐμαυτὸν τοῖς ἀνθρώποις καὶ καλοῦσί με Κυνόπηγον ┌ὅτι μεταμορφοῦμαι εἰς ἄνθρωπον· ἔστι μοι τὸ ὄνομα ἀληθές. ναυτίαν δὲ ἀποστέλλω τινὰ διὰ τῆς ἀνόδου μου εἰς τοὺς ἀνθρώπους. 5. ἦλθον οὖν εἰς τὴν συμβουλὴν τοῦ ἄρχοντος Βεελζεβοὺλ καὶ ἐδέσμευσέ με εἰς τὰς χεῖράς σου┐ νῦν δὲ παρέστηκά σοι καὶ διὰ τὸ μὴ ἔχειν ὕδωρ δύο ἢ τρεῖς ἡμέρας ἐκλείπει τὸ πνεῦμά μου τὸ λαλοῦν σοι.«* 6. κἀγὼ εἶπον αὐτῷ »λέγε μοι ποίῳ ἀγγέλῳ καταργεῖσαι.« ὁ δέ λέγει »διὰ τοῦ * Ἰαμέθ « 7 κἀγὼ ἐκέλευσα αὐτὸν βληθῆναι εἰς φιάλην καὶ ὕδατος θαλάσσης δοχὰς δέκα περιχύνεσθαι καὶ περιέφραξα ἐπάνω μαρμάρῳ καὶ περιήπλωσα τῇ ἀσφάλτῳ καὶ πίσσῃ καὶ στυπείῳ τὸ στόμα τοῦ ἀγγείου καὶ σφραγίσας τῷ δακτυλιδίῳ ἐκέλευσα ἀποτεθῆναι εἰς τὸν ναὸν τοῦ θεοῦ

XVII. Καὶ ἐκέλευσα παρεῖναί μοι ἕτερον πνεῦμα. * καὶ ἦλθε πνεῦμα ἀνθρώπου μορφὴν ἔχον σκοτεινὴν καὶ ὀφθαλμοὺς λάμ-

MSS HLP — Recc AB. § 4. 1 κύματα conj. Cr καύματα P   8 καὶ Α ὡς οἱ ἐπίγειοι P | Κυνόπηγον H κύνόπιγω L, 1 forte κυματόπηγον, κυνόπαστον P, l. κυνόσβατον, Κυνόσπαστον Cr cum Plin., *HN* XXIV 74

MS P — Rec B ll 3—9 habet P textum peculiarem. ὅτι . . . χεῖράς σου (l. 7) om. A   7—9 νῦν . σοι κἀγὼ παρέστιν ἐνώπιόν σου διὰ τῆς σφραγίδος ταύτης· καὶ σὺ νῦν βασανίζεις με, ἰδοὺ οὖν δύο καὶ τριῶν ἡμερῶν ἐκλείπει τὸ πν(εῦμ)α τὸ λαλοῦν διὰ τὸ μὴ ἔχειν με ὕδωρ P

MSS HL — Rec A. 4 δὲ + παρέχω L   7 σοι H σε L   8 ὅτι δύο τρεῖς ἡμέρας ponit post λαλοῦν σοι L   9 * L f. 16ᵛ2

MSS HLP — Recc AB. § 6. (69) 9 κἀγὼ   αὐτ HP λέγω δὲ τοῦτον L | λέγε μοι — L | ἀγγέλων A | καταργῇ συ P   10 λέγει ἔφη Pˣ | *H f 20ʳ | Ἰαμέθ LP λαβέθ H | § 7. κἀγὼ + δοξάσας τὸν θεὸν P | κελεύσας H | αὐτ βληθ H tr L | αὐτὸν — P   11 εἰς φιαλ. βληθ τὸ πνεῦμα P | φιάλιῳ P φυλακὴν A | περιχυν. A: ἀνὰ μετρητῶν β̄ P 12 ἐπάνω P ἐπάνωθεν L, — H | μαρμάρῳ H, μαρμάρων LP | περιήπλωσα A — P | τῇ ἀσφ A ἀσφάλτων — P   13 πίσσῃ ego πίσαν H, πίσα L, πίσσης P | κ στυπείῳ ego· κ στυπίων H, στιπίων L, — P | εἰς τὸ P | στόμα HP σόμα L | ἀγγείου APCι ἀγγέλου F1 errore | τὸ δακτυλίδιον H   14 ἐκέλ . . θεοῦ — H | ἐν τῷ ναῷ L

C XVII 15 ἐκέλευσαν H | πνεῦμα HP δαίμονα L | * (70) ἦλθε. + πρὸ προσώπου μου κατειδωλισμένον (καταλισμένον Mg, καταδουλισμένον Cι) ἕτερον P   16 ἔχον P ἔχων L, ἔλουσαν H | σκοτεινὴν L σκοτεινὴν H, σκοτεινὸν P | . λ. ὀφθ. λαμπ. A τοὺς ὀφθ ἔχον λαμπ. καὶ ἐν τῇ χειρὶ φέρον σπάθην P

πόντας. καὶ ἐπηρώτησα αὐτὸν λέγων· »σὺ τίς εἶ;« ⌈ὁ δὲ ἔφη·
»ἐγώ εἰμι ὀχεικὸν πνεῦμα ἀνθρώπου γίγαντος ἐν σφαγῇ τετελευ-
τηκότος ἐν τῷ καιρῷ τῶν γιγάντων.⌉« 2. καὶ εἶπον αὐτῷ·
»λέγε μοι τί διαπράττεις ἐπὶ τῆς γῆς καὶ ποῦ ἔχεις οἰκητήριον.«
5 ὁ δέ μοι ἔφη· »ἡ * κατοικία μου ἐν τόποις ἀβάτοις. ἡ ἐργασία
μου αὕτη παρακαθέζομαι τοῖς τεθνεόσιν ἀνθρώποις ἐν τοῖς μνη-
μείοις καὶ ἐν ἀωρίᾳ παραμορφῷ * τοῖς τεθνεόσι καὶ εἰ λήψομαί **
τινα εὐθέως * ἀναιρῶ αὐτὸν τῷ ξίφει. 3. εἰ δὲ μὴ δυνηθῶ ἀναιρεῖν, ποιῶ αὐτὸν δαιμονίζεσθαι καὶ τὰς σάρκας αὐτοῦ κατατρώ-
10 γειν καὶ σιάλους ἐκ τῶν γενείων αὐτοῦ καταρρεῖν.« 4. ἔφην δὲ
αὐτῷ· »φοβήθητι τὸν θεὸν τοῦ οὐρανοῦ καὶ τῆς γῆς καὶ εἰπέ
μοι ποίῳ ἀγγέλῳ καταργεῖσαι.« ὁ δὲ ἔφη μοι· »ἐμὲ καταργεῖ ὁ
μέλλων κατελθεῖν σωτήρ, οὗ τὸ στοιχεῖον ἐν τῷ μετώπῳ, εἴ τις
γράψει, καταργεῖ με καὶ ἐπιτιμηθεὶς ἀποστρέψω ἀπ’ αὐτοῦ τα-
15 χέως· τοῦτο δὲ τὸ σημεῖον σταυρός·« 5. ταῦτα δὲ ἀκούσας ἐγὼ
Σολομῶν κατέκλεισα τὸν δαίμονα ὥσπερ καὶ τἆλλα δαιμόνια

MSS HLP = Recc. AB. 1 αὐτὸν A. αὐτὸ P | λέγων — P
MS P = Rec B. 1—3 τὸ δὲ. . γιγάντων P, καὶ ὁ δαίμων ἔφη· τὸ ὄνομά
μου μαχθὸν L, — H | 1 ὁ δὲ cum rec. A infra. τὸ δὲ P   2 ὀχεικὸν ego,
1 q., ὀχεντικὸν ὀχικὸν P
MSS HLP = Recc. AB. 3 § ↲ καὶ — P   4 καὶ — L   5 ὁ δέ μοι
H. ὁ δαίμων L, τὸ δὲ P | ἡ κατοικία . . . ἐργασία ἡ κακοία (1. κακία) H |
ἡ μὲν κατ. P | * P f. 15ʳ | τόποις ἀβάτοις L: τοῖς κατακάρποις τόποις P
| ἡ δὲ ἐργ. P   6 αὕτη HP. ἐτούτη εἶναι L, + ἐστὶν H | παρακαθίζω
ἐμαυτὸν P | τεθνεόσιν A: παρερχομένοις P   7 καὶ ἀλλ’ ἐν H | παρα-
μορφῷ + ἐμ H | * H f. 20ᵛ | τεθν A τελευτῶσι P | εἰ P: ἡ H, ὁ L
| ** L f. 17ᴧ   8 εὐθέως post ξίφει ponit L | * Mg 1341 | ἀναιρῶ H
ἀνερῶ P, ἀερῶ L | τῷ H τὸ L, — P | § 3. μὴ L μοι H, οὐ P | ἀναι-
ρεῖν A: ἀναιρῆσαι P   9 ποιῶ· ποιὸν L | αὐτοῦ: αὐτῶν L | κατατρώ-
γειν A κατεσθίειν P   10 σιάλους ego: σὺ ἄλλοις H, σει ἄλλους L, τοὺς
σιέλους P | ἐκ A ἀπὸ P | γενείων P γονιῶν A | αὐτοῦ H αὐτ(ῶν) L,
— P | καταρέειν H, καταρέων L | § 4 ἔφη A   11 αὐτῷ + ὁ βασιλεὺς
σολομῶν φοβηθ οὖν P | τοῦ . τῆς HP πν(εῦμ)α πονηρὸν L   12 ἀγγέ-
λων H | καταργῇ συ P | ὁ δὲ A. τὸ δ’ P | μοι H — LP | ὁ ἐμὲ H |
ἐμὲ καταργή με L   13 κατελθ. σωτ. A σ(ωτ)ὴρ γενέσθαι ἄν(θρωπ)ος P |
καὶ εἰ A   14 γράψει. + αὐτῷ A, ἐπιγράψει P | καταργεῖ . . . αὐτοῦ A
ἡττήσει με καὶ φοβηθεὶς ἀποστραφήσομαι P   15 καὶ τοῦτο P | στ(αυ)-
ρ(ό)ς A· ἐάν τις ἐπιγράψῃ φοβηθήσομαι P | § 5. ταῦτα δὲ A: καὶ τοῦτο P,
+ αὐτοῦ H   16 κατεκλ A: καὶ δοξάσας κύριον τὸν θεὸν ἐπέκλεισα P |
τ δαιμ H αὐτὸν L, τὸ δαιμόνιον P | τὰ ἄλλα L | δαιμόνια A πν(εύμ)ατα P

XVIII. Καὶ ἐκέλευσα παρεῖναί μοι ἕτερον δαίμονα. καὶ ἦλθον πρός με τὰ τριάκοντα ἓξ στοιχεῖα, * αἱ κορυφαὶ αὐτῶν ὡς κύνες ἄμορφοι. ἐν αὐτοῖς δὲ ἦσαν ἀνθρωπόμορφα, ταυρόμορφα, θηριοπρόσωπα, δρακοντόμορφα, σφιγγοπρόσωπα, πτηνοπρόσωπα. 2. καὶ ταῦτα ἰδὼν ἐγὼ Σολομῶν ἐπηρώτησα αὐτὰ λέγων· »καὶ ἡμεῖς τίνες ἔστε;« αἱ δὲ ὁμοθυμαδὸν μιᾷ * φωνῇ εἶπον· »ἡμεῖς ἐσμεν τὰ τριάκοντα ἓξ στοιχεῖα, οἱ κοσμοκράτορες τοῦ σκότους τοῦ αἰῶνος τούτου. 3. ἀλλ᾽ οὐ δύνασαι ἡμᾶς, βασιλεῦ, ἀδικῆσαι οὐδὲ κατακλεῖσαι· ἀλλ᾽ ἐπειδὴ ἔδωκέ σοι ὁ θεὸς τὴν ἐξουσίαν ἐπὶ πάντων τῶν ἀερίων πνευμάτων καὶ ἐπιγείων καὶ καταχθονίων, ἰδοὺ παραστήκομεν ἔμπροσθέν σοι ὡς τὰ * λοιπὰ πνεύματα.«

4. Κἀγὼ δὲ Σολομῶν προσκαλεσάμενος τὸ ἓν πνεῦμα εἶπον

C. XVIII. MSS HLP = Recc. AB. **1** (72) παρεῖναί μοι LP. — H | ἕτεροι δαιμ. P ἕτερα δαιμόνια L, πν(εύμ)ατα H | καὶ ἦλθον π με: — L | ἦλθον P· ἤλθασιν H   **2** πρός με H πρὸ προσώπου μοι P | τὰ λς στοιχ. H, τὰ λεγόμενα στοιχ. L, τριάκοντα ἓξ πν(εῦμ)α P | * H f. 21ʳ | αἱ κορ. HP καὶ ἡ κορυφῆ L | ὡς LP ὡσεὶ H   **3** ἐν αὐτοῖς· ἦσαν δὲ H | ἦσαν καὶ L | ἀνώμορφα καὶ κατόμορφα· θηρ. δρακ. σφιγγ. πτερωτα· ἐν τὰ πρόσωπα H, ἀπὸ ἀνώμορφα· καὶ ταυρο. καὶ θηρ. L, ἀνθρωπόμορφοι, ὀνοπρόσωποι, βοοπρόσωποι, καὶ πτηνοπρόσωποι P   **5** § 2. καὶ ... Σολ. A· κἀγὼ σολομῶν ἀκοίσας καὶ ἰδὼν αὐτὰ ἐθαύμασα καὶ P | αὐτὰ — H | καὶ — P   **6** αἱ HP· εἱ L | ὁμοθ. HP· ὁμοῦ L | μίαν φωνὴν L | * L f. 17ʳ² εἶπαν μιᾷ φωνή L   **7** ἐσμεν HP ἐσταὶ L | τριακ. ἕξει δαιμόνια καὶ στοιχεῖα L | οἱ HP | τὸ σκότος L   **8** τοῦ αἰῶνος A — P | § 3 δυνήσῃ βασιλεῦ σολομῶν ἡμᾶς P | καὶ ἀδικεῖσαι L   **9** οὐδὲ κατακλ. — L, + οὐδὲ κελεῦσαι ἡμῖν P | ἐπειδὴ LP ἐπεὶ H | κύριος ὁ θεὸς P   **10** πάντων (+ ἡμῶν L) ... (καὶ — 1° — om H) ... καταχθ A παντὸς πν(εύμα)το)ς ἀερίου τὲ καὶ ἐπιγείου καὶ καταχθονίου P   **11** ἰδοὺ A διὰ τοῦτο καὶ ἡμεῖς P | παραστήκομεν H παραστίκαμέν σοι L, παριστάμεθα P | ἔμπροσθέν H pr. καὶ ἡμεῖς L, ἐνώπιον P | ὡς καὶ L | * P f. 15ᵛ   **12** πνεύματα· + ἀπὸ κριοῦ, καὶ ταύρου, διδύμου τὲ καὶ καρχίνου, λέοντος, καὶ παρθένου, ζυγοῦ τε καὶ σκΚορπίου (sic, κ = η?) τοξότου, αἰγωκέρωτος, ὑδροχόου, καὶ ἰχθύος P

MS P = Rec. B   § 4 ll. 13—p. 52*, 1 pro Κἀγὼ ... μοι praebet P haec· τότε ἐγὼ σολομῶν ἐπικαλεσάμενος τὸ ὄνομα κυρίου σαβαώθ, ἐπερώτησα αὐτὰ καθ᾽ ἕνα ὁποῖος τρόπος αὐτῶν τυγχάνει, καὶ ἐκέλευσα αὐτοὺς ἕνα ἕκαστον εἰς τὸ μέσον ἐλθόντα εἰπεῖν τὴν ἑαυτοῦ πρᾶξιν. τότε προσελθὼν ὁ πρῶτος εἶπεν P

MSS HL = Rec. A. § 4. l. 13 δὲ — L | τὸ — L

αὐτῷ· »σὺ τίς εἶ;« ὁ δὲ ἔφη μοι »ἐγὼ δεκανὸς α' τοῦ ζῳδιακοῦ
κύκλου, ὃς καλοῦμαι 'Ρύαξ.'⟩ 5. κεφαλὰς ἀνθρώπων ποιῶ ἀλγεῖν·
καὶ κροτάφους σαλεύω. ὡς μόνον ἀκούσω· »Μιχαήλ, ἔγκλεισον
'Ρύαξ‹, εὐθὺς ἀναχωρῶ.« 6. ὁ δεύτερος ἔφη· »ἐγὼ Βαρσαφαὴλ
5 καλοῦμαι. ἡμικράνους ποιῶ τοὺς ἀνθρώπους τοὺς ἐν τῇ ὥρᾳ
μου κειμένους. ὡς δὲ ἀκούσω· »Γαβριήλ, ἔγκλεισον Βαρσαφαήλ‹,
εὐθὺς ἀναχωρῶ.« 7. ὁ τρίτος ἔφη· »Ἀρτοσαὴλ καλοῦμαι. ὀφθαλμοὺς ἀδικῶ σφόδρα. ὡς δὲ ἀκούσω· »Οὐριήλ, ἔγκλεισον Ἀρτοσαήλ‹, εὐθὺς ἀναχωρῶ.«
10 8. Ὁ τέταρτος ἔφη· »ἐγὼ καλοῦμαι * Ὀροπέλ λαιμοὺς καὶ
συνάγχας καὶ σηπεδόνας ἐπιπέμπω ὡς δὲ ἀκούσω »Ραφαήλ,
┌Ἔγκλεισον Ὀροπελ,⟩┐ εὐθὺς ἀναχωρῶ.« 9. ὁ πέμπτος ἔφη »ἐγὼ
Καιρωξανονδάλον * καλοῦμαι. ἐμφράξεις ὠτίων ποιῶ. ἐὰν δὲ

MSS HL = Rec. A.   § 4 1 * H f 21ᵛ | μοι — L

MS P = Rec. B   § 4. ll. 1—2 pro ἐγὼ ... 'Ρίαξ praebet P textum interpolatum hunc ἐγώ εἰμι ὁ (πρῶτος) δεκανὸς τοῦ ζῳδιακοῦ κύκλου, ὃς καλοῦμαι
κριός, καὶ μετ' ἐμοῦ οἱ δύο οὗτοι. ἐπηρώτησα οὖν αὐτούς· τίνες καλεῖσθε;
§ 5. ὁ μὲν πρῶτος ἔφη· ἐγώ, κύριε, ῥύαξ καλοῦμαι
MS HL = Rec. A. § 4. ll 1—2 ἐγὼ ... 'Ρύαξ dubitanter propono ἐγω
δεκαδὰν (δεκάδων L) τοῦ ἐξοδίου (ἐξοδίδν L) κυκλῶνος (κακόκλονος — κο
supra lin. adscr. — H) καλοῦμαι καὶ κριὸς HL
MSS HLP = Recc AB § 5. 2 ποιεῖν H | ἀλγεῖν — A   3 καὶ
— L | σαλεύειν H | μόνον μὲν L | ἔγκλεισον ego. ἔκλυσον (forte recte,
sed in ms. tribus punctis dubii indicandi notatum) P, ἔγγεισον H, ἔγγισον L
4 'Ρύαξ P οὖ οὐρὸν H, οἰροήλ L | § 6. (74) δεύτερος· numeros constanter
per compendia scr. codd. omnes | ἔφη λέγ < L | βαρσαβαὴλ L   5 ἡμί-
κρανος L, ἢ μικρανοες Mg | τοὺς ἀνθρ. A ἀλγεῖν P   6 ὡς δὲ L ἕως
δὲ H, ἐὰν μόνον P | ἔγκλησον HP, ἔκλεισον (κ ex λ corr) L   7 εὐθὺς
semper scr. P, εὐθέως semper L, interdum εὐθὺς, interdum εὐθέως H |
§ 7. (75) καὶ ὁ L | Ἀρτοσαὴλ HL ἀρωτοσαὴλ P   8 ὡς δὲ H ὡς μόνον P,
καὶ ἐὰν L | ἀκοῖσαι P | οὐρουὶλ L | ἔγκλεισον P ἔκκλεισον H, ἔκλει-
σον L | ἀρατοσαὴλ P, ἀρσαὴλ L
§ 8. sectionem 8 om. Fl cum nota hac »Hic omisi quae v. in additam.
sub signo *),« quae additamenta reperire non potui   10 ἔφη HP εἶπεν L |
* L f 17ᵛ¹ | Ὀροπέλ P ὁροπόλος L, ἀροπόλον H | λαιμοὺς ... ἐπι-
πέμπω P λιμοὺς καὶ συμπεδώνας καὶ συν(εχὰς linea delet.) μπεδώνας καὶ
συνοχὰς ἐμποιῶ H, λιτ(οὺς) καὶ σιπεδώνας κ. συνοχὰς ἐμπιῶ L   11 ὡς δὲ
A ἐὰν P   12 ἔγκλεισον Ὀρ — A | § 9 (76) 13 καὶ ρωξανονδάλον H
καιριξενονδάλων L, ιουδὰλ P | ' H f. 22ʳ | ἔμφραξιν P | ὠτίων HP
ὅτι L | ποιῶ H ἐνμπιῶ L, καὶ σφήνωσιν ἀκοῶν ἐπιτελῶ P | δὲ — P

ἀκούσω· »Οὐρουήλ, ⌜ἔγκλεισον Καιρωξανονδάλον,⌝ εὐθὺς * ἀναχωρῶ«. 10. ὁ ἕκτος ἔφη· »ἐγὼ Σφενδοναὴλ καλοῦμαι. παρυ-
τίδας καὶ ὀπισθοτόνους ἐμποιῶ. ἐὰν ἀκούσω· »Σαβαήλ, ⌜ἔγκλει-
σον Σφενδοναήλ,⌝ εὐθὺς ἀναχωρῶ« 11. ὁ ἕβδομος ἔφη· »ἐγὼ
Σφανδῶρ καλοῦμαι. ὤμων δύναμιν ἐλαττῶ καὶ χειρῶν νεῦρα
παραλύω, καὶ μέλη κοπιάζω. ἐὰν ἀκούσω· »Ἀραήλ, ⌜ἔγκλεισον
Σφανδῶρ,⌝ εὐθὺς ἀναχωρῶ.« 12. ὁ ὄγδοος ἔφη· »ἐγὼ Βελβὲλ
καλοῦμαι. καρδίας ἀνθρώπων καὶ φρένας διαστρέφω . . ἐὰν
ἀκούσω· »Καραήλ, ⌜ἔγκλεισον Βελβέλ,⌝ εὐθὺς ἀναχωρῶ.«

13. Ὁ ἔννατος ἔφη· »ἐγὼ Κουρταήλ καλοῦμαι. στρόφους
ἐγκάτων * ἐπιπέμπω ἐὰν ἀκούσω· »Ἰαώθ, ⌜ἔγκλεισον Κουρταήλ,⌝
εὐθὺς ἀναχωρῶ.« 14. ὁ δέκατος ἔφη· »ἐγὼ Μεταθίαξ καλοῦμαι
νεφρῶν πόνους ποιῶ ἐὰν ἀκούσω· * Ἀδωναήλ, ⌜ἔγκλεισον
Μεταθίαξ,⌝ εὐθὺς ἀναχωρῶ.« 15. ὁ ἑνδέκατος ἔφη· »ἐγὼ Κατανικοταήλ καλοῦμαι μάχας καὶ αὐθαδείας κατ' οἴκους ἐπιπέμπω.
ἐάν τις θέλει εἰρηνεύειν, γραφάτω εἰς ἑπτὰ φύλλα δάφνης τὰ

MSS HLP — Recc AB. **1** οὐριὴλ H | ἔγκλεισον Καιρ. ego ἔγκλησον
ἰουδὰλ P, — A | * P f. 16ʳ   **2** § 10. Σφενδοναὴλ P σφενδεναὴλ H, φε-
δοναὴλ L | παρυτιδ· + ποιῶ· καὶ παρίσθμια P   **3** ὀπιστοτόνους H, ὀπι-
σ̄τονότους L, ὀπισθότονα P | ἐμποιῶ A· — P | Σαβαὴλ (β ex λ corr.) P·
Σαβραὴλ Mg errore, σαφαὴλ L, σφεβαὴλ H | ἐγκλ. Σφεν. — A   **4** σφαν-
δοναὴλ P | § 11. (78) ἔφη HP εἶπεν L   **5** Σφανδῶρ P δορὸν H, φαν-
δωρὸν L | ὤμων δυν. P ἀν(θρώπ)ων (ἀν̄ο̄ν̄ H) δυνάμεις A | ἐλαττῶ P
ἐλαττόνω H, ἐλαττῶν L, + καὶ σαλεύω P, + ἐὰν ἀκούει L | καὶ — H |
χειρῶν εὖρα H   **6** παραλύω HP   παρχύω L, + καὶ ὀστᾶ παλαμῶν συν-
τρίβω P | κ. μέλη κοπ. H κ. μυελοὺς ἐμπιπύζω (ἐκπιπύζω Fl, l. ἐκπιπίζω
= ἐκπίνω) P, — L | ἐγκλ Σφανδ. — A   **7** § 12. (79) βοκβέλ in βελβέλ
corr. L   **8** διαστρέφω HP ἀναστρέφω L   **9** Καραὴλ A ἀραὴλ P | ἐγκλ.
Βελβ. — A

   § 13. (80) **10** ἔφη HP εἶπεν L | Κουρταὴλ P κουρταὴλ vel κοφταὴλ H,
ἀκσιρταραὴλ L   **11** ἐγκάτων A ἐν κοιλίᾳ P | * Mg 1344 | ἐπιπέμπω A
ἀποπέμπω, πόνους ἐπάγω P | ἐὰν ... ἀναχωρῶ — I | Ἰαώθ P σα-
βαώθ H | ἐγκλ Κουρτ — H   **12** § 14 (81) ἔφη HP εἶπεν L | Μετα-
θίαξ P μεταθύαξ H, μετάθεαξ L   **13** νεφροὺς ποιῶ πονεῖν P | ἐὰν
δὲ H | * H f. 22ᵛ | Ἀδωναὴλ P ἀδωναῖ H, ἀδωνὰν L | ἐγκλ. Μεταθ.
— A   **14** § 15. (82) ἔφη HP εἶπεν L | Καταν. P· κανικοταὴλ L, νικο-
ταὴλ H   **15** αὐθαδείας A ἀδικίας P | οἴκους + ποιῶ καὶ σκληρίας P |
* L f 17ᵛ²   **16** εἰρηνεύειν εἰρηνεύει L, + εἰς τὸν οἴκον αὐτοῦ P | γρα-
φάτω γράψαι P, γράφη L | ...με H τὰ ἑπτὰ ὀνομ. τ. κατ. με
εἰς ἐπ. φύλα δάννης ἐτοῦτα L, εἰς ἐπ φύλλ < δάφνης τὸ ὄνομα τοῦ καταρ-
γοῦντος με ἀγγέλου, καὶ ταῦτα τὰ ὀνόματα P

ὀνόματα τὰ καταργοῦντά με· ›ἄγγελε· ἐαέ· ἰεώ· σαβαώθ· ἐγκλεί-
σατε Κατανικοταήλ,‹ καὶ πλύνας τὰ φύλλα τῆς δάφνης ῥανάτω
τὸν οἶκον αὐτοῦ τῷ ὕδατι, καὶ εὐθὺς ἀναχωρῶ.‹ 16. ὁ δωδέ-
κατος ἔφη· ›ἐγὼ Σαφθοραήλ καλοῦμαι. διχοστασίας ἐμβάλλω
5 τοῖς ἀνθρώποις καὶ εὐφραίνομαι αὐτοὺς σκανδαλίζων. ἐάν τις
γράψει ταῦτα· * ›ἰαέ· ἰεώ· υἱοὶ Σαβαώθ,‹ καὶ φορεῖ ἐν τῷ τραχήλῳ αὐτοῦ, εὐθὺς ἀναχωρῶ.‹

17. Ὁ τρίτος καὶ δέκατος ἔφη· ›ἐγὼ Φοβοθὴλ καλοῦμαι
νευρῶν χαλάσεις ποιῶ. ἐὰν ἀκούσω· ›Ἀδωναί,‹ εὐθὺς ἀναχωρῶ.‹
10 18. ὁ τέταρτος καὶ δέκατος ἔφη· ›ἐγὼ Λερωήλ * καλοῦμαι. ψῦχος
καὶ ῥῖγος καὶ στομάχου πόνον ἐπάγω. ἐὰν ἀκούσω· ›Ἰάζ, μὴ ἐμμείνῃς, ⌜μὴ θερμάνῃς, ὅτι καλλίον ἐστὶ Σολομῶν ἔνδεκα πατέρων,⌝‹ εὐθὺς ἀναχωρῶ.‹ 19. ὁ πέμπτος καὶ δέκατος ἔφη· ›ἐγὼ
Σουβελτὶ καλοῦμαι φρίκην καὶ νάρκην ἐπιπέμπω ἐὰν μόνον

MSS HLP = Recc AB. 1 ἄγγελε A — P | ἐαέ H ἰεαὲ L, ἰαὲ P |
ἰεώ LP· ἰωεώ H | σαβαώθ A· υἱοὶ σαβαώθ, διὰ τὸ ὄνομα τοῦ μεγάλου
θεοῦ P | ἐγκλήσαται H, ἐγκλησάτω P, ἐγγίσατε L, + τῷ Fl errore 2 καὶ
A πλύνα vel πλύνας P, πλύνων Fl | τ. φυλ. τ. δαφ. H. τὰς δάφας L, τὰ
δαφόφυλλα P, τὰ δαφνόφυλλα Fl, + ἐπὶ τοῦ ὕδατος P | ῥεννάτω (sic) Fl
errore 3 τὸν .. ὕδατι P τοῦ οἴκου μετὰ τὸ ὕδωρ ἐκείνω L, τὸ ὕδωρ ἐπὶ
τὸν οἶκον αὐτοῦ H, + ἀπὸ ἔσω ἕως ἔξω P | § 16. (83) 4 σαφαθωραήλ P
| ἐμβάλω P 5 εὐφρ. αὐτ. σκανδ. P φρένας σκανδαλίζω (-ζων H) A 6 γρά-
ψει ταῦτα A εἰς χάρτην ἐπιγράψη ταῦτα τὰ ὀνόματα τῶν (* f. 16ᵛ) ἀγγέ-
λων P | ἰαέ ἰεώ· (ἰαὼ L) υἱοὶ Σαβ. A ἰαεῶ· ἰειλῶ· (Ἰαελῶ Fl) ἰωελὲτ·
σαβαώθ· ἰθθθ· βαὲ P, cf. supra § 15, l. 1, textum cod ms. P | φορεῖ ...
αὐτοῦ H — L, πλίξας φορέση τῷ τραχήλῳ, ἢ καὶ τὰς (scil. χάρτας?) πρὸς
τὸ οὖς ἔθη (1 τιθῇ) P 7 ἀναχωρῶ + καὶ τὴν μέθην λύω P
§ 17. (84) 8 Φοβοθὴλ A βοθήλ P 9 νευρ χαλ. ego. νευρῶν κολάσ-
σης H, νευρ. χαλάσας L, νευροχαλάσης P, νευροχρίλασεις (sic) Fl errore |
ἐὰν ... Ἀδωναΐ H ἐὰν ἀκ αδ. δ . L, ἐὰν ἐφαπτόμενος ἀκ. τοῦ μεγάλου
ἀδοναήλ τὸ ὄνομα ἔγκλησαν βοθοθήλ P 10 § 18. (85) ἔφη P εἶπε L,
— H | ἐγὼ Λερωήλ ... ἀναχωρῶ (l. 13) et ἐγὼ Σουβελτι ... ἀναχωρῶ
(l 13—p. 55*, 1) tr. P | ⌝ερωήλ L, ῥοκλήδ P, ῾Ροηλήδ Fl | * H f. 23ᵣ |
ψῦχος LP· ψυχρὸς H 11 κ. στ. πόνον P κ. στόμαχον H, κ. στομαχὸν L
ἐπάγω A ἐποιῶ P | ἐὰν A ὡς μόνον P | Ἰάζ, μὴ ἐμμ. ego· ἰὰς μὴ ἐμ-
μενὴς H, ἰὰς μὴ ἐμμβείνῃς L, ἴας μὴ ἐμμείνῃς P 12 μὴ θερ. ὅτι κάλ-
λιον ... ἐν δέκα πατ P, — A 13 § 19. (86) ἔφοι ὁ ιε̄ H 14 Σουβελτὶ L
σουβελτὴ H, κουμελτήλ P, Κουμεατήλ Fl | φριχ κ ναρκ. ἐπιπ. P — L,
τὸν (ν)οῦν καὶ σάρκας ἐμποιῶ H | ἐὰν A ὡς P | μόνον — L

ἀκούσω· »Ῥιζωήλ, [ἔγκλεισον Σουβελτί,] εὐθὺς ἀναχωρῶ.« 20 ὁ
ἕκτος καὶ δέκατος ἔφη· »ἐγὼ Κατρὰξ καλοῦμαι. ἐπιφέρω τοῖς
ἀνθρώποις πυρετοὺς ἀνιάτους. * ὁ θέλων ὑγιὴς γενέσθαι τρι-
ψάτω κολίανδρον καὶ ἐπιχριέτω τὰ χείλη λέγων· »ὁρκίζω σε κατὰ
5 τοῦ Δάν, ἀναχώρησον ἀπὸ τοῦ πλάσματος τοῦ θεοῦ,« καὶ εὐθὺς
ἀναχωρῶ«

21. Ὁ ἕβδομος καὶ δέκατος ἔφη· »ἐγὼ Ἱεροπὰ καλοῦμαι ἐπὶ
τοῦ στομάχου τοῦ ἀνθρώπου καθέζομαι, καὶ ποιῶ ἀσπασμοὺς ἐν
βαλανείῳ· καὶ ἐν ὁδῷ εὑρίσκω τὸν ἄνθρωπον καὶ πτωματίζω.
10 ὃς δ' ἂν εἴπῃ εἰς τὸν δεξιὸν ὠτίον τοῦ πάσχοντος ἐκ τρίτου
»Ἰοῦδα ζιζαβοῦ« ἰδέ, ποιεῖ με ἀναχωρεῖν.« 22. * Ὁ ὄγδοος καὶ
δέκατος ἔφη· »ἐγὼ Μοδεβὴλ καλοῦμαι. γυναῖκα ἀπὸ ἀνδρὸς χω-

MSS HLP — Recc. AB.   1 Ῥιζωήλ Η· ριζωὲλ L, ζωρωὴλ P | ἔγκλει-
σον Σουβ. ego cum dubio. — A, ἔγκλησον κουμενταὴλ P, de Κουμενταὴλ
annotavit Fl »diversa genera scripturae in una enuntiatione.« | ἀναχωρῶ
ὅτι τὸν νοῦν καὶ σάρκας ἐμπιῶ L | § 20 (87)   2 ἐγώ — Η | Κατρὰξ
Η ἰατρὰξ L, ἀτρὰξ P | ἐπιφέρω Α   ἐγὼ καταστρέφω P | τοὺς ἀν(θρώ-
π)ους L   3 ἀνιατ. + καὶ βλαβεροὺς P | * L f. 18ʳ¹ | ὁ ... γενέσθαι Α
ἐὰν θέλῃς με ἐγκλῆσαι L | τριψ. κολ. τρ. κολύατρον Η, τρ. κολίαντρον L,
καὶ κόψας P   4 καὶ — Η | ἐπιχρ. τ χειλ. L ἐπίχριε τὰ χείλη αὐτοῦ Η,
ἐπίχριε τῶν χειλέ(ων) P | λέγων + οὗτος Η, + τὴν ἐπῳδὴν ταύτην P |
ὁρκίζω .. θεοῦ Η (— ἀπὸ .. θεοῦ) L   τὸ πύρεθρον τὸ ἀπὸ ῥυπαρί(ας),
ὁρκίζω σε κατὰ τοῦ θεοῦ τοῦ ὑψίστου τοῦ θρόνου, ἀναχώρει ἀπὸ ῥυπαρί(ας),
καὶ ἀναχώρει ἀπὸ τοῦ πλάσματος τοῦ θεοῦ P   5 καὶ — Η   6 ἀναχωρῶ
+ ἀπὸ τὸ πλάσμα τ. θεοῦ L

§ 21 (88)   7 Ἱεροπὰ ego ἱερωπὰ L, κεροπὰκ \ el ἡεροπάη Η, ἱεροπαὴλ P
| ἐπὶ ρι. ἐὰν L   8 τοῦ — Η | τ. ἀνθρ. Α τῶν ἀν(θρώπ)ων P | ποιῶ
ἀσπασμοὺς Η (i. q σπασμοὺς, cf Dieterich, Unters. p. 33, ἀσπασμένος) ποιώ-
σας σπασμοὺς L, ποιῶ ἀσπαρμοὺς (sub ϱ lineam posuit man. prim.?) P |
ἀσπ. ἐν βαλ. κ ἐν ὀδῷ scr. mss. omnes, sed ἐν ὁδῷ cum εὑρίσκω legendum
est   9 εὑρίσκω Η· εὕρω L, καὶ ὅπου δ' ἂν εὑρεθῶ καὶ εὕρω P | τὸν
— L | πτωματ. P παραστοματίζω Η, ἀποστοματίζω L   10 ὃς δ' ἂν P
ὡς δ' ἂν Η, καὶ ἐὰν L | εἴπῃ Η, εἴποι P, εἰπεῖ τις L | εἰς .. τρίτου L
εἰς ... ὠτίον (* f. 23ᵛ) τοῦ ἀν(θρώπ)ου ἐκ τρίτου Η, τοῖς πάσχουσιν εἰς τὸν
οὓς αὐτῶν, τὰ ὀνόματα ταῦτα ἐκ τρίτου εἰς τὸ δεξιὸν P   11 Ἰοῦδα ... με
ego ἰουδαζιζαβουιδέποι εἰ με Η, ἰούδαζειζαβονιδὲ· ποιοῦμαι L, ἰουδαριζῇ,
ζαβουνῇ· δούνῃ P, Fl falso legit | ἀναχωρεῖν Α εὐθὺς ἀναχωρῶ P |
§ 22. (89) * P f. 17ʳ   12 ἔφη ὁ ιη Η | Μοδ. και Η· μοδιὴλ καλ. L, καὶ
βουλδουμήχ P | γυναῖκα L γυναῖκας ΗP | ἀνδρὸς P ἄνδρα L, τοὺς ἑαυ-
τῶν ἄνδρας Η | χωρίζω P χωρήζωμαι L, χορίζων Η, + καὶ φθόνον ἐπι-
τελῶ P | γράψῃ P

ῥίζω. ἐάν τις γράψει τῶν ὀκτὼ πατέρων τὰ ὀνόματα καὶ θήσει
αὐτὰ ἐν προθύροις, εὐθὺς ἀναχωρῶ.« 23. ὁ ἔννατος καὶ δέκατος
ἔφη· »ἐγὼ καλοῦμαι Μαρδέρω. ἐπιφέρω πυρετοὺς ἀνιάτους; καὶ ἐν
οἵῳ δὲ οἴκῳ * γράψεις τὸ ὄνομά μου, εὐθὺς ἀναχωρῶ.« 24. ὁ εἰκο-
5 στὸς ἔφη· »ἐγὼ καλοῦμαι Ῥὺξ Ναθώθω   εἰς γόνατα καθέζομαι ⁝
τῶν ἀνθρώπων. ἐάν τις γράψει εἰς χάρτην· »Φνουνηβιήλ,« εὐθὺς
ἀναχωρῶ.« 25 ὁ πρῶτος καὶ εἰκοστὸς ἔφη· „ἐγὼ Ῥὺξ Ἀλὰθ
καλοῦμαι. δύσπνοιαν τοῖς νηπίοις ἐμποιῶ. ἐάν τις γράψει· »Ῥαρι-
δέρις,« καὶ * βαστάζει, εὐθὺς ἀναχωρῶ «
10   26. Ὁ δεύτερος καὶ εἰκοστὸς ἔφη· »ἐγὼ καλοῦμαι Ῥὺξ Αὐδαμεώθ   καρδιόπονον ἐπιπέμπω. ἐάν τις γράψει· »Ῥαιονώθ,« εὐθὺς ἀναχωρῶ « 27. ὁ τρίτος καὶ εἰκοστὸς ἔφη »ἐγὼ Ῥὺξ Μαν-

---

MSS HLP = Recc AB.   1 ὀκτὼ   η̄ vel fortasse ϛ̄ H, ἔξη L, σῶν P |
ὀνόματα + σολομῶν ἐν χάρτῃ P | θήσει LP θέσει H   2 αὐτὰ — H |
ἐν προθ. P ἐμπροσθέραι, H, ἐμπροσθύραις L, + τοῖ οἴκου αὐτοῦ P

MS P = Rec. B   pro εὐθὺς ἀναχωρῶ praebet textum hunc ἐκεῖθεν ἀναχωρῶ. ἡ δὲ ἐπιγραφή ἐστιν αὕτη· κελεύει σοι ὁ θεὸς ἀβραάμ, καὶ ὁ θ(εὸ)ς
ἰσαὰκ, καὶ ὁ θεὸς ἰακώβ, ἀναχώρησον ἀπὸ τοῦ οἴκου τούτου μετ᾽ εἰρήνης,
εὐθὺς ἀναχωρῶ

MSS HPL = Recc AB   § 23 (90) 3 ἔφη ὁ ιθ̄ H | Μαρδέρω . μου
(l 4) et Ναθάθω ... Φνουνηβιήλ (ll. 5—6) tr. P | ἐγὼ καλοῦμαι Μαρδέρω P
ἐγὼ ῥὺξ καλοῦμαι μαδούωρ H, ἐγὼ μανδραβουρουῦν καλοῦμαι δου L | ἐπιφ.
πυρ. ἀνιατ. H πυρ. ἀν. ἐπιφ L, πυρετὸν ἐπιπέμπω ἀνίατον τοῖς ἀν(θρώ)-
π)οις P | καὶ   μου H ἐνίω οἴκω γράψει τὸ ὀν. μου L, ἐάν τις (* Mg
1345) γράψη εἰς χάρτην βιβλίον· σφηνήρ, ῥαφαήλ, ἀναχώρημχν (ἀναχώρημεν
Fl), σύρον δούρον, καὶ τῷ τραχήλῳ περιάψῃ P   4 εὐθὺς P εὐθέως L,
— H | § 24. (91) 5 ἔφη — H | ἐγὼ ῥιξίνα θά· θω καλοῦμαι L |
Ῥὺξ Ναθώθω H ναωθ P | καὶ εἰς τὰ γόνατα P | τῶν ἀνθρ. P τῶν ἀν-
(θρώπ)ω L, τοῦ ἀν(θρώπ)ου H   6 ἐπιγράψῃ P | εἰς χάρτην H εἰς γαρ-
τίον L, ἐν χάρτῃ P | Φνουνηβ. H φνουνιφαήλ L, φνουνοβοηὸ), ἔξελθε
ναθάθ, καὶ τραχείλιν μὴ ἅψης P   7 § 25. (92) ἔφη ὁ κ̄ᾱ H | Ῥὺξ Ἀλὰθ
.. βαστάζει (l. 9) et Ῥὺξ Αὐδαμεώθ ... ῥαιονώθ (ll. 10—11) tr. H | Ῥὺξ
Ἀλὰθ ego ῥὴξ ὁ ἀλὰθ H, ῥὶξ ὀλὰθ L, ἀλὰθ P   8 δίσπνοιαν P δίσπιαα H,
δύσπνια L, pr. βήχα καὶ P | νηπίοις L παισὶν P, — H | γράψει . βα-
στάζει (+ αὐτῶ) H γραψ. καὶ βαστ· ῥαριδέρι, L, ἐπιγράψῃ εἰς χάρτην·
ῥορὴξ δίωξον σὺ ἀλὰθ, καὶ τῷ τραχήλῳ περιάψῃ P   9 * H f 24ʳ

MSS HL = Rec. A.   10 § 26. ὁ δευτ. ... ἀναχωρῶ — P, errore Mg ὁ
κβ´ pro ὁ κγ´ posito ὁ κγ´ (§ 27) omittere videtur | sectiones 26 et 25 tr. H,
cf. supra | Ῥὺξ Αὐδαμ H ῥὶξ αὐμαδεὼθ (ante καλοῦμαι) L   11 καρ-
διοπ .. ἀναχωρῶ H ἐὰν τις γράψει ῥαιζὼθ καλοῦμαι ἐὰν τῆς γράψει
ῥαιζὼθ καὶ βαστάζει ἀναχωρῶ ὅτι καρδιόπονος ἐπιμπέσει καὶ πέμπω L

MSS HLP = Recc. AB § 27. (93) 12 ἔφη ὁ κ̄γ̄ H | Ῥὺξ Μανθ. ῥὶξ
μανθαδῶ L, ῥὶξ αὐθάδης H, νεφθαδᾶ P

θαδῶ καλοῦμαι. νεφροὺς ἀλγεῖν ποιῶ. ἐάν τις γράψει· ›Ἰαώθ, Οὐριήλ,‹ εὐθὺς ἀναχωρῶ.‹ 28. ὁ τέταρτος καὶ εἰκοστὸς ἔφη· ›ἐγὼ ῾Ρὺξ Ἀκτονμὲ καλοῦμαι. πλευρὰς ἀλγεῖν ποιῶ. ἐάν τις γράψει ἐν ὕλῃ ἀπὸ πλοίου ἀστοχήσαντος· ›ἀερίου Μαρμαραώθ,‹ εὐθὺς ἀναχωρῶ.‹ * 29. ** ὁ πέμπτος καὶ εἰκοστὸς ἔφη· ›ἐγὼ ῾Ρὺξ Ἀνατρὲθ καλοῦμαι. ζέσεις καὶ πυρώσεις εἰς σπλάγχνα ἀναστέλλω. ἐὰν ἀκούσω· ›ἀραρὰ ἀραρή,‹ εὐθὺς ἀναχωρῶ‹ 30. ὁ ἕκτος καὶ εἰκοστὸς ἔφη· ›ἐγὼ ῾Ρὺξ ὁ Ἐναυθὰ καλοῦμαι. φρένας ἀποκλέπτω καὶ καρδίας ἀλλοιῶ. ἐάν τις γράψει· ›Καλαζαήλ,‹ εὐθὺς ἀναχωρῶ.‹ 31. ὁ ἕβδομος καὶ εἰκοστὸς ἔφη· ›ἐγὼ ῾Ρὺξ Ἀξησβὺθ καλοῦμαι. ὑπεκτικοὺς ποιῶ ἀνθρώπους καὶ αἱμορρόους. ἐάν τις ὁρκίσει με εἰς οἶνον * ἄκρατον καὶ δώσει τῷ πάσχοντι, εὐθὺς ἀναχωρῶ.‹

32. Ὁ ὄγδοος καὶ εἰκοστὸς ἔφη· ›ἐγὼ ῾Ρὺξ Ἀπὰξ καλοῦμαι. ἀγρυπνίας ἐπιπέμπω. ἐάν τις γράψει ›κὸκ· φνηδισμός,‹ καὶ περιάψει τοῖς κροτάφοις, εὐθὺς ἀναχωρῶ.‹ 33. ὁ ἔννατος καὶ εἰκοστὸς ἔφη· ›ἐγὼ ῾Ρὺξ Ἀνοστῆρ καλοῦμαι. μητρομανίας ἐπιπέμπω καὶ πόνους ἐν τῇ κύστει ποιῶ. ἐάν τις εἰς ἔλαιον καθαρὸν τρεῖς

MSS HLP = Recc. AB　**1** ποιῶ· + καὶ στραγγισμοῖς οὔρων ἐπιτελῶ P | Ἰαώθ, Οὐριήλ Η ἰαώθ ὀριήλ L, εἰς λαμνὸν (in maig dextr. πέταλ <) κασσιτήρινον, ἰαθώθ, οὐρουήλ, νεφθαδὰ καὶ περιάψῃ τῷ ἰσχίῳ P　**2** § 28. (94) ἔφη ὁ κδ Η　**3** ἐγὼ — L | ῥὴξ ἀκτονμὲ Η, ἐρὶξ κτονμὲ L, ἄκτον μὲν P, + δίωξον transversa linea deletum P | πλευρὰς καὶ ψόας P | ἐμποιῶ Η　**4** γράψει γλύψῃ P | ὕλῃ P οἷλο Η, ἡλίῳ L, + χαλκοῦ P | ἀπὸ .. εὐθὺς — L | ἀπὸ πλ. ἀστοχ. P ἀποπλοῦ. ου ἀστολίσαντος ΙΙ | ἀερίου Μαρμ. Η ἀρνίου μαρμαραώθ, σαβαώθ, ἄκτον μὲν δίωξον, καὶ περιάψῃ τῷ ἰσχίῳ P　**5** * hic explicit in media col. cod. ms L (f 18ʳ²)

MSS HP = Recc. AB　§ 29 (95) **5** ** P f 17ᵛ　**6** ῾Ρὺξ Η — P | ζέσεις κ. πυρέσεις Η, καύσεις κ. πυρώσεις P | εἰς τὰ σπλ ἀποστέλλω P　**7** ἄραρα χάραρα P | § 30. (96)　**8** ῾Ρὺξ ὁ Ἐν ἐνενοὺθ P　**9** ἀλλοιῶ καὶ νοδὸν (l. νωδὸν) ποιῶ P | Καλαζαὴλ Η ἀλλαζοωλ, δίωξον ἐνενουθ, καὶ περιάψῃ τὸν χάρτην P　**10** § 31. (97) ῾Ρὺξ Ἀξησβὺθ Η· φὴθ P　**11** αἱμορόους Η, αἱμορασίας (αἱμορραγίας conj. Βn) ποιῶ P　**12** τις γράψει ἢ Η | * Η f. 24ᵛ | οὖν εὐώδη ἄκρατον P | δώσει Η κατὰ τοῦ ἐνδεκάτου ἐῶν (l. αἰῶνος Crtr) λέγων· ὁρκίζω σε κατὰ τοῦ ἐνδεκάτου ἐῶν παῦσαι ἀξιωφθιθ, καὶ δὸς ποιεῖν (l. πιεῖν Crtr) P

§ 32. (98) **14** ῾Ρὶξ Ἀπὰξ Η· ἄρπαξ P　**15** ἀγρυπνοπνίας P | γράψῃ P | κὸr . . περιάψῃ P, — Η　**16** § 33. (99)　**17** ῾Ρὶξ — P | Ἀνοστῆρ P ἀστῆρ Η | ἐπιπέμπω· + ἐάν τις γράψῃ κὸκ· φνηδισμὸς· καὶ περιάψῃ transversa linea deleta P　**18** κύστει κήτη Η | εἰς: γράψει Η

κόκκους δάφνης λεάνας ἐπαλείψει λέγων· »ὁρκίζω σε κατὰ τοῦ
Μαρμαραώθ,‹ εὐθὺς ἀναχωρῶ.« 34. ὁ τριακοστὸς ἔφη· »ἐγὼ ῾Ρὺξ
Φυσικορὲθ καλοῦμαι. μακρονοσίαν ποιῶ. ἐάν τις βαλεῖ ἅλας εἰς
ἔλαιον καὶ ἐπαλείψει τὸν ἀσθενὴν λέγων· »χερουβίμ, σεραφίμ,
5 βοηθεῖτε,‹ εὐθὺς ἀναχωρῶ.« 35. ὁ πρῶτος καὶ τριακοστὸς ἔφη·
»ἐγὼ ῾Ρὺξ Ἀλευρὴθ καλοῦμαι. ὀστέα ἰχθύος καταπίνων, ἐάν τις
⟨τοῦ⟩ αὐτοῦ ἰχθύος ὀστέον ἐπιθήσει εἰς τὰ βύζια τοῦ πάσχοντος,
εὐθὺς * ἀναχωρῶ.« 36. ὁ δεύτερος καὶ τριακοστὸς ἔφη· »ἐγὼ
῾Ρὺξ Ἰχθύον καλοῦμαι. νεῦρα παραλύω. * ἐὰν δὲ ἀκούσω· »Ἀδω-
10 ναΐ, μάλθη,‹ εὐθὺς ἀναχωρῶ.« 37. ὁ τρίτος καὶ τριακοστὸς ἔφη·
»ἐγὼ καὶ ῾Ρὺξ Ἀχωνεὼθ καλοῦμαι ἐν τῷ φάρυγγι καὶ τοῖς
παρισθμίοις πόνον ποιῶ· ἐάν τις εἰς φύλλα κισσοῦ γράψει· »λει-
κουργός,‹ βοτρυδὸν ⌜ἀναχωρίς,⌝ εὐθὺς ἀναχωρῶ.«
38. Ὁ τέταρτος καὶ τριακοστὸς ἔφη· »ἐγὼ ῾Ρὺξ Αὐτὼθ κα-
15 λοῦμαι. φθόνους φίλων καὶ μάχας ποιῶ. καταργεῖ με δὲ τὸ α′
καὶ β′ γραφόμενον.« 39. ὁ πέμπτος καὶ τριακοστὸς ἔφη· »ἐγὼ
καὶ ῾Ρὺξ Φθηνεὼθ καλοῦμαι. βασκαίνω πάντα ἄνθρωπον.
καταργεῖ με δὲ ὁ πολυπαθὴς ὀφθαλμὸς ἐγχαραττόμενος. 40. ὁ

MSS HP = Recc. AB. 1 λεώνας δάφνης H | σε· ἀνοστὴρ P 2 Μαρ-
μαραώθ H μαρμαραῶ, παῦσον P | § 34. (100) ῾Ρὺξ Φυσικ. .. βοήθειτε
(l. 5) et ῾Ρὺξ Ἀλευρὴθ . πάσχοντος (ll 6—7) tr. P | ῾Ρὺξ Φυσικ H· ἡ
φησικιρὲθ P 3 βαλεῖ (βαλεῖν ms) ... ἀσθενὴν H εἰς ἔλαιον βαλὼν ἅλας
τριπτὸν ἐπαλείφη τὸν κάμνοντα P 4 σεραφὶμ· χερουβὶμ· βοηθήσατέ μοι P
5 § 35. (31) 6 ἐγὼ — H | ῾Ρὺξ Ἀλ. H ἀλλεβοριὴθ P | sectiones 35 et
34 tr. P, v. supra | καταπίνων ego. καταπίνειν H 7 ὀστέα ... πάσχον-
τος ἐάν τις νυκτοφαγήση (sub v linea brevi ducta supra eandem η ponit ms.,
in marg lat. ἰχθυο scr. man prim) ὀστέον κατατίθῃ, καὶ ἄρας ὀστέον ἀπὸ
τοῦ ἰχθίος βήσσει P | βήζια H 8 * H f. 25ʳ | § 36. (102) 9 ῾Ρὺξ
— P | ἰχθύος H | παραλύω P· παλίω H, + καὶ συντρίβω P | * P f 18ᵛ
| δὲ – P | Ἀδωναί, μάλθη H. ἀδοναὴθ βοήθει P 10 § 37. (103)
11 καὶ — P | ῾Ρὺξ Ἀχων. H ἀγχονίων P | ἐν ... ποιῶ ἐν τοῖς σπαρ-
γάνοις καὶ ἐν τῷ φάρυγγι κεῖμαι P | φάραγγι H | παρισθμίοις H 12 ἐὰν
.. ἀναχωρίς H καὶ ἐάν τις εἰς φύλλα συκῆς γράψῃ· λυκοῦργος, ἐν παρὰ ἐν
γράμμα (ἐνπαρὰ· ἐνγραμμὰ ms.), γράψῃ δὲ βοτρυδὸν (in marg. βο <) P
13 ἀναχωρῶ + λυκοῦργος ὑκοῦργος· κούργος· οὖργος· γὸς· ὃς P
§ 38. (104) 14 ῾Ρὺξ — P | Αὐτὼθ H αὐτοθιθ P 15 φθον. ποιῶ
κ. μάχας P | καταρ. με καταργοῦμαι H | δὲ . γραφ. H | ἡ οὖν τὸ ἄλφα
καὶ τὸ ὠμέγα γραφόμενα P 16 § 39. (105) 17 κ. ῾Ρὺξ Φθην. φθηνοθ P
| παντὶ ἀν(θρώπ)ῳ P 18 κατ με καταργοῦμαι H | δὲ ... ὀφθαλ.· οὖν
ὀφθαλμὸς πολυπαθῆς P | ἐνχαραττόμενον H | § 40. (106)

ἕκτος καὶ τριακοστὸς ἔφη· »ἐγὼ καὶ Ῥὺξ Μιανὲθ καλοῦμαι. τῷ
σώματι ἐπίφθονός εἰμι· οἴκους ἐρημῶ· σάρκας ἀφανίζω. ἐάν τις
γράψει ἐν τοῖς προθύροις τοῦ οἴκου οὕτως· * »μέλπω ἀρδὰδ
ἀναάθ,« φεύγω ἐγὼ τοῦ τόπου,« * 41. καὶ ταῦτα ἀκούσας ἐγὼ
5 Σολομῶν ἐδόξασα τὸν θεὸν τοῦ οὐρανοῦ καὶ τῆς γῆς καὶ ἐκέλευσα αὐτοὺς ὕδωρ φέρειν. 42 καὶ ηὐξάμην πρὸς τὸν θεὸν τοὺς
τριάκοντα ἓξ δαίμονας τοὺς ἐμποδίζοντας τῇ ἀνθρωπότητι προσέρχεσθαι εἰς τὸν ναὸν τοῦ θεοῦ.

XIX. Καὶ ἤμην ἐγὼ Σολομῶν τιμώμενος ὑπὸ πάντων τῶν
10 ἀνθρώπων τῶν ὑποκάτω τοῦ οὐρανοῦ. καὶ ᾠκοδόμουν τὸν ναὸν
τοῦ θεοῦ, καὶ ἡ βασιλεία μου ἦν εὐθύνουσα. 2. καὶ ἤρχοντο
πάντες οἱ βασιλεῖς πρός με θεωρῆσαι τὸν ναὸν τοῦ θεοῦ ὃν
ᾠκοδόμουν, καὶ χρυσίον καὶ ἀργύριον ἐκόμιζον πρός με, χαλκὸν

MSS HP = Recc. AB. 1 καὶ Ῥὺξ ego. χερὴξ H. — P | Μιανὲθ. βια-
ναλθ P | τοῦ σώματος P　　2 ἐπιφθ. ἐφθόμενον H | ἐρήμους H |
ἀφανίζω + καὶ ὅσα ἄλλα τοιαῦτα P　　3 τοῖς — P | οὕτως αὐτοῦ P |
* H f. 25ᵛ | μηλτω ἀρδοῦˑ ἀναάθ P　　4 ἐγὼ — P | * Mg 1348 | τό-
που ἐκείνου P | § 41. (107)　　5 κ. ἐκελ. ἐκελ. δὲ P　　6 φέρειν H κομί-
ζειν ἐν τῷ ναῷ τοῦ θεοῦ P

MS P = Rec B pro § 42 textum interpolatum praebet hunc § 42 καὶ
ἔτι προσηυξάμην πρὸς κύριον τὸν θεὸν ὥστε τοὺς ἔξω δαίμονας καὶ ἐμποδίζοντας τὴν ἀνθρωπότητα συμποδίζεσθαι καὶ προσέρχεσθαι εἰς τὸν ναὸν τοῦ
θεοῦ. § 43. ἐγὼ δὲ τοὺς μὲν τῶν δαιμόνων κατέκρινα ἐργάζεσθαι τὰ βαρέα
ἔργα τῆς οἰκοδομῆς τοῦ ναοῦ τοῦ θεοῦˑ τοὺς δὲ φρουραῖς (Fl, ex φρουροὺς
corr. ms.) κατέκλεισα § 44. ἑτέρους πυρομαχεῖν ἐκέλευσα χρυσίῳ καὶ ἀργυ-
ρίῳ καὶ μολύβδῳ καὶ φιάλῳ παρακαθέζεσθαι, καὶ τοῖς λοιποῖς δαίμοσι τρόπους ἡτοιμάσθαι ἐφ᾽ οἷς ὀφείλουσι κατακλεισθῆναι
MS H = Rec A in § 42 brevem textum praebet.

C. XIX. MS P = Rec B pro c XIX, ll. 9—p. 60ᵛ, 4, textum interpolatum
praebet hunc (108) Καὶ εἶχον πολλὴν ἡσυχίαν ἐγὼ σολομῶν (in marg. inf. add.
βασιλεὺς ms.) ἐν πάσῃ (f. 18ᵛ) τῇ γῇ καὶ ἐν εἰρήνῃ διῆγον πολλῇ, τιμώμενος
ὑπὸ πάντων ἀν(θρώπ)ων καὶ τῶν ὑπὸ τῶν οὐρανῶν, καὶ ᾠκοδόμουν τὸν ναὸν
ὅλον κυρίου τοῦ θεοῦ, καὶ ἡ βασιλεία μου ἦν εὐθύνουσα καὶ ὁ στρατός μου
ἦν μετ᾽ ἐμοῦ, καὶ λοιπὸν ἀνεπαύσατο ἡ πόλις Ἱ(ερουσα)λὴμ χαίρουσα καὶ ἀγαλ-
λιωμένη. § 2. καὶ ἅπαντες οἱ βασιλεῖς τῆς γῆς ἤρχοντο πρός με ἀπὸ τῶν
περάτων τῆς γῆς θεωρῆσαι τὸν ναὸν ὃν ᾠκοδόμουν κ(υρί)ῳ τῷ θ(ε)ῷ, καὶ
ἀκούσαντες τὴν σοφίαν τὴν δοθεῖσάν μοι προσεκύνουν μοι εἰς τὸν ναόνˑ
χρυσίον καὶ ἀργύριον, καὶ λίθους τιμίους πολλοὺς διαφόρους, καὶ χαλκὸν καὶ
σίδηρον, καὶ μόλιβδον, καὶ ξύλα κέδρινα, καὶ ξύλα ἄσηπτα προσέφερόν μοι
εἰς τὴν κατασκευὴν τοῦ ναοῦ τοῦ θεοῦ.

MS H. § 1. l. 10 ἐκοδώμουν ms

τε καὶ σίδηρον καὶ μόλυβδον καὶ ξύλα προσέφερον εἰς τὴν
κατασκευὴν τοῦ ναοῦ. 3. ἐν οἷς καὶ ἡ Σάβα βασίλισσα Νότου
γόης ὑπάρχουσα πολλῇ τῇ φρονήσει ἦλθε καὶ προσεκύνησεν ἐνώπιόν μου.

5　　XX. Καὶ ἰδοὺ εἷς τῶν τεχνιτῶν γηραιὸς ἔρριψεν αὑτὸν ἐνώπιόν μου λέγων· »βασιλεῦ Σολομῶν υἱὸς Δαυείδ, ἐλέησόν με τὸ
γέρας.« καὶ εἶπον αὐτῷ· »λέγε, γέρον, ὃ θέλεις.« 2. ὁ δὲ ἔφη·
»δέομαί σου, βασιλεῦ. υἱὸν ἔχω μονογενῆ, καὶ οὗτος καθ᾽ ἑκάστην * ὕβρεις ἐπάγει μοι χαλεπάς, ἔτυπτέ μου γὰρ τὸ πρόσωπον
10　καὶ τὴν κεφαλήν, ὅτι θάνατον πικρὸν ἐπαγγέλει μοι ποιῆσαι.
τούτου χάριν προσῆλθον ἵνα ἐκδικήσῃς μοι.« 3. ἐγὼ δὲ ταῦτα
ἀκούσας ἐκέλευσα ἀγαγεῖν ἐμοὶ τὸν υἱὸν αὐτοῦ· τούτου δὲ ἐλθόντος εἶπον * αὐτῷ· »οὕτως ἔχεις,« 4. ὁ δὲ ἔφη· »ἕως ἀπο-
νοίας ἐμπέπλησμαι, βασιλεῦ, ὥστε τὸν γεννήτορά μου παλάμῃ
15　τινάξαι. ἵλεώς μοι γενοῦ, ὦ βασιλεῦ· ἀθέμιτον γὰρ ἀκοῦσαι τοι-

---

MS P = Rec. B § 3. ἐν οἷς καὶ βασίλισσα νότου γοὴς ὑπάρχουσα ἐν
πολλῇ φρονήσει ἦλθεν καὶ προσεκύνησεν ἐνώπιόν μου ἐπὶ τὴν γῆν, καὶ ἀκού-
σασα τὴν σοφίαν μου ἐδόξασε τὸν θεὸν τοῦ Ἰ(σρα)ἠλ· ἐν οἷς καὶ ἐδοκίμασε
δοκιμασίαν τὰ τῆς σοφίας μου πάντα, ὅσα ἐσοφισάμην αἱτὴν κατὰ τὴν δο-
θεῖσαν μοι σοφίαν. καὶ πάντες υἱοὶ Ἰ(σρα)ἠλ ἐδόξασαν τὸν θεόν.

Parallela ad c. XX v. infra in ms D c. IV.
C XX　MSS HP = Recc. AB.　(110) 5 ἰδοὺ ἐν ταῖς ἡμέραις ἐκείναις P |
γηραιὸς τὴν ἡλικίαν P　6 υἱὸς Δ. — P | με μου conj. James | τὸ γερ.
ὅτι γηραιὸς ὑπάρχω P　7 κ. εἶπον αὐτ. ego· κ. εἶπον αὐτὸν Η, κελεύσας
οὖν αὐτὸν ἀναστῆναι καὶ φησὶν P | λίγε εἰπὲ P | § 2.　8 ἔχων Η |
οὕτως P | καθ᾽ ἑκ. (scil ἡμέραν) — P　9 * P f. 19ʳ | ἐπαγάγη μου Η |
ἔτυπτε ego· ἔτυπον Η, καὶ τύψας P | μου ... προσωπ · με κατὰ προσ P
10 κεφαλήν μου διέτιλλεν P | ὅτι καὶ P | πικρὸν πονηρὸν P | ἐπαγ-
γέλεται P | ποιῆσαι — P　11 τούτον Η | προσ. ... μοι· προεξίημοι (sic,
προσίημαι? Fl, l. πρόσειμι) ὑμῖν, ἐκδίκησόν με P | ἐκδικήσῃς conj James
ἐκδικῆς εἰς Η | § 3. (111) δὲ + σολομῶν P　12 ἀκούσας κατενύγην ἀπο-
βλέψας εἰς τὸ ἐκείνου γῆρας, καὶ P | ἀγαγεῖν ego· ἀγάγεν Η, ἀχθῆναι P
| τούτου ... ἔχεις· τοῦ δὲ ἀχθέντος ἐπερώτουν αὐτὸν εἰ οὕτως ἔχει P
13 § 4. ὁ δὲ ἔφην Η, ὁ δὲ νέος ἔφη P

MS P = Rec. B pro ἕως ... ταλαιπορίαν (ll. 13—p. 61*, 1) textum interpolatum praebet hunc οὐχ οὕτως ἀπονοίᾳ ἐγὼ ἐμπεπλησμένος ὥστε τὸν γεννήτορά μου π(ατέ)ρα παλάμῃ τύψαι. ἵλεως γενοῦ μοι βασιλεῦ (ς finali transversa linea deleta). οὐ γ(ὰρ) ἀθέμιτα τοιαῦτα τετόλμηκα ὁ ταλαίπορος ἐγώ
MS H = Rec. A. 15 ἀθέμιτον ego· ἀθές μοι τὸν Η

αὐτὴν παραβολὴν καὶ ταλαιπωρίαν.« 5. ἐγὼ οὖν Σολομῶν τοῦ
νέου ἀκούσας παρεκάλουν τὸν πρεσβύτην εἰς ἔννοιαν ἐλθεῖν. ὁ
δὲ οὐκ ἤθελεν ἀλλ᾽ εἶπε »θανατωσάτω αὐτόν.

6. Καὶ θεωρῶν τὸν δαίμονα Ὀρνίαν γελάσαντα ἐγὼ ἐθυμώ-
5 θην λίαν ἐν τῷ γελάσαι αὐτὸν ἐνώπιόν μου, καὶ τοῦτον μεταστή-
σας ἐκέλευσα τὸν Ὀρνίαν ἐλθεῖν καὶ εἶπον αὐτῷ· »κατηραμένε, ἐμὲ
προσεγέλασας;« 7. ὁ δὲ ἔφη· »δέομαί σου, βασιλεῦ· οὐ διὰ σὲ
ἐγέλασα, ἀλλὰ διὰ τὸν δύστηνον γέροντα καὶ τὸν ἄθλιον νέον,
* τὸν τούτου υἱόν ὅτι μετὰ τρεῖς ἡμέρας τεθνήξεται, καὶ ἰδοὺ
10 ὁ γέρων βούλεται αὐτὸν κακῶς ἀνελεῖν.« 8. καὶ ἐγὼ εἶπον· »ἢ
ἀληθῶς * οὕτως ἔχει;« ὁ δαίμων εἶπε· »ναί, βασιλεῦ.« 9. καὶ
ἐκέλευσα μεταστῆναι τὸν δαίμονα καὶ ἐλθεῖν τὸν γέροντα καὶ
τὸν τούτου υἱόν, καὶ ἐκέλευσα αὐτοὺς εἰς φιλίαν γενέσθαι.
10. * καὶ εἶπον τῷ πρεσβύτῃ »μεθ᾽ ἡμέρας τρεῖς ἄγαγέ μοι τὸν
15 υἱόν σου ὧδε.« οἱ δὲ προσκυνήσαντες ἀνεχώρησαν.

MSS HP — Recc. AB. 1 § 5. οὖν δὲ P | τ. νέον ἀκ ταῦτ᾽ ἀκ. παρὰ
τ, νέου P 2 πρεσβύτερον P | ἔννοιαν HP εὔνοιαν conj. James | ἐλθεῖν
καὶ δέχεσθαι τοῦ υἱοῦ τὴν ἀπολογίαν P 8 ἀλλ᾽ ... αὐτ. ἀλλὰ μᾶλλον
θανατωθήτω P

MS P — Rec B pro § 6 textum praebet hunc ἐν δὲ τῷ μὴ πειθεσθαι τὸν
πρεσβύτερον ἔμελλον τῷ νέῳ τιμωρίας ἀποφήνασθαι· καὶ θεωρήσας ὀρνίαν
τὸν δαίμονα γελῶντα· ἐθυμώθην μεγάλως διὰ τὸ γελάσαι τὸν δαίμονα ἐνώπιόν μου· καὶ τούτους μεταστῆσαι ἐκέλευσα ὀρνίαν εἰς μέσον ἀχθῆναι τοῦ
βήματος τοῦ δὲ ἀχθέντος (Mg 1349) ἔφην αὐτῷ· ἐπικατάρατε, τί με προσχῶν
ἐγέλασας,

MS H — Rec A. § 6. 4 θεωρῶ H | γελάσσαντα H 5 αὐτῷ ego
αὐτὸν H | κατηραμένε vel κατειρμένε ego κατερειμένε H

MSS HP — Recc. AB 6 § 7. δὲ δαίμων P 8 τοῦτον τὸν δυστ. P
9 * H f. 27ʳ | τ τουτ. υἱόν υἱὸν αὐτῶν H | μετὰ .. τεθνήξ. τρεῖς ἡμέρας
καὶ ἐν ἀωρίᾳ τετελευτήσει ὁ υἱὸς αὐτοῦ P 10 κακῶς ἀναιρεῖν αὐτόν P

MS P — Rec B in § 8 textum praebet hunc (112) ἐγὼ δὲ σολομῶν
ἀκούσας ταῦτα· ἔφην πρὸς δαιμόνιον ἀληθῆ εἰσιν (* t. 19ᵛ) ἃ λέγεις; ὁ δὲ
λέγει ἀληθῆ ταῦτα, βασιλεῦ
MS H — Rec A in § 8 textum breviorem praebet.

MSS HP — Recc. AB. 11 § 9. καὶ ἀκούσας ἐγὼ P 12 ἐλθεῖν πάλιν
τὸν γηραιὸν μετὰ καὶ τοῦ υἱοῦ αὐτοῦ P 18 καὶ — P | εἰς φιλ γεν. φιλίᾳ
τραπῆναι, καὶ τὰ εἰς τροφὴν αὐτοῖς παρασχόμενος P

MSS HPQ — Recc. AB. 14 * § 10. " post omissionem maximam hic rur-
sus incipit ms Q (cc. III—XX 9 omissis, v. supra p. 16*) | κ. εἶπον H· εἶπον
οὖν B | ὧδε τ. υἱόν σου B, + καὶ διατάξω αὐτόν Q, + καὶ ἐπινοοῦμαι
αὐτοῦ P 15 οἱ δὲ προσκυν. B καὶ προσσεκίνησαν H

11. Καὶ ἐκέλευσα πάλιν ἀγαγεῖν τὸν Ὀρνίαν πρός με καὶ εἶπον αὐτῷ· »λέγε μοι πόθεν τοῦτο σὺ οἶδας ὅτι μετὰ τρεῖς ἡμέρας τεθνήξεται ὁ νέος.« 12. ὁ δὲ ἔφη· »ἡμεῖς οἱ δαίμονες ἀνερχόμεθα ἐπὶ τοῦ στερεώματος τοῦ οὐρανοῦ καὶ μέσον τῶν ἄστρων
5 ἱπτάμεθα καὶ ἀκούομεν τὰς ἀποφάσεις ** τὰς ἐξερχομένας ἀπὸ
τοῦ θεοῦ ἐπὶ τὰς ψυχὰς τῶν ἀνθρώπων. 13 ⌜καὶ λοιπὸν ἐρχόμεθα καὶ εἴτε ἐν δυναστείᾳ, εἴτε ἐν πυρί, εἴτε ἐν ῥομφαίᾳ, εἴτε
ἐν συμπτώματι μετασχηματιζόμενοι ἀναιροῦμεν.«⌝ 14. καὶ ἐπηρώτησα αὐτόν· »λέγε μοι οὖν πῶς ὑμεῖς δύνασθε εἰς τὸν οὐρα-
10 νὸν ἀναβαίνειν δαίμονες ὄντες.« 15. ὁ δὲ ἔφη μοι· »ὅσα ἐν
οὐρανῷ ἐπιτελοῦντα, οὕτως καὶ ἐπὶ τῆς γῆς, αἱ γὰρ ἀρχαὶ καὶ
ἐξουσίαι * καὶ δυνάμεις ἄνω ἵπτανται καὶ τῆς εἰσόδου τοῦ οὐρανοῦ ἀξιοῦνται. 16. ἡμεῖς δὲ οἱ δαίμονες ἀτονοῦμεν μὴ ἔχοντες

MSS HPQ = Recc. AB. (113) 1 Καὶ Q — Η, τούτων δὲ ἀπελθόντων P
| ἐκελ ... με Η. πάλιν ἐκελ. ἐλθεῖν πρός με τὸν δαίμονα Ὀρνίαν Q, ἐκελ.
εἰς μέσον ἀχθῆναι τὸν ὀρνίαν P | εἶπον ˊαὐτ. HP λέγω πρὸς αὐτόν Q
2 τοῦτο ... νέος Η σὺ τὰ μέλλοντα γινώσκεις Q, σὺ ταῦτα οἶδας P 3 § 12.
ἔφη Η· εἶπεν P, λέγε μοι Q | ἀνερχόμενοι Η 4 ἐπὶ τ. στερ. Η κατὰ
τὸ στερέωμα B | ἀστέρων B 5 ἱπταμ. B ἀπτώμεθα Η | * Η f. 27ᵛ |
** Q f. 12ᵛ | ἀπὸ τ. θ. Η παρὰ θεοῦ Q, — P, + πρὸς τοὺς ἀγγέλους Q

MS Η = Rec. A pro § 13 textum praebet hunc καὶ ἐρχόμεθα μετὰ δυ-
ναστείας· εἴτε ῥομφαίᾳ εἴτε ἐν πυρί· καὶ ἀνεροῦμεν αὐτοὺς μετασχημ.

MSS PQ = Rec. B 6 § 13. ἐρχόμεθα εἰς τὴν γῆν Q | post ἀναιροῦ-
μεν add. PQ glossam hanc· καὶ ἐάν τις ἀποθάνῃ ἐν ἀωρίᾳ ἢ βίᾳ τινί (καὶ ...
τινί· καὶ ἐὰν μὴ ἐν ἀωρίᾳ τίς, ἢ βίᾳ τινὶ ἀποθ. P), μεταμορφούμεθα ἡμεῖς
οἱ δαίμονες (+ εἰς τὸ ὄνομα τοῦ τεθνεότος, Q) ὥστε παραφαίνεσθαι (φαιν. P)
τοῖς ἀνθρώποις καὶ σέβεσθαι ἡμᾶς (+ ἐπὶ τῆς — ex τοῖς corr. — ἀνθρω-
πίνης φύσεως P)

MSS HPQ = Recc AB 8 § 14. κ ἐπ αὐτόν Η (114) ἐγὼ δὲ (ἐγὼ
γοῦν P) ταῦτα ἀκούσας ἐδόξασα κύριον τὸν θεὸν καὶ ἐπ. πάλιν τὸν δαίμονα B
9 οὖν et ὑμεῖς — B 10 ἀναβῆναι B | ὄντες + καὶ μέσον τῶν ἀστέρων
καὶ τῶν ἁγίων ἀγγέλων μιγῆναι B | § 15. μοι B

MSS PQ = Rec. B pro οὕτως ... ἀναπαύσεως (p. 63*, l. 1) praebent haec.
οὕτως καὶ ἐπὶ τῆς γῆς (οἱ ἐπὶ γῆς Q) οἱ τύποι αὐτῶν εἰσὶν γὰρ ἀρχαί, ἐξουσίαι, κοσμοκράτορες (* P f 20ʳ). καὶ ἱπτάμεθα ἡμεῖς οἱ δαίμονες ἐν τῷ ἀέρι
καὶ ἀκούομεν τῶν ἐπουρανίων τὰς φωνὰς καὶ (+ πάσας P) τὰς (+ ἐπουρα-
νίας Q) δυνάμεις θεωροῦμεν (ἐπιθεωρ P)· καὶ ὡς μὴ ἔχοντες βάσιν ἀναπαύσεως ἀτονοῦμεν

MS Η = Rec. A. 12 ἵπτανται ego ἥτταντε Η 13 § 16 ἀτονοῦμεν
(cf Rec. B supra) αὐτὸν οὖν μὲν Η, forte l. ἀκούομεν. μὴ δὲ ἔχοντες

§ 15. Eph. I 21; II 2

βάσιν ⌈ἀναβάσεως ἢ⌉ ἀναπαύσεως, καὶ ἐκπίπτομεν ὥσπερ φύλλα
ἀπὸ τῶν δένδρων καὶ δοκοῦσιν οἱ θεωροῦντες ἄνθρωποι ὅτι
ἀστέρες εἰσὶν οἱ πίπτοντες ἀπὸ τοῦ οὐρανοῦ. 17. οὐχ οὕτως
ἐστί, * βασιλεῦ, ἀλλὰ πίπτομεν διὰ τὴν ἀσθένειαν ἡμῶν καὶ ἐν
5 τῷ μηδαμόθεν ἔχειν ἀντίληψιν καταπίπτομεν ὡς ἀστραπαὶ ἐπὶ
τὴν γῆν, καὶ πόλεις καταφλέγομεν καὶ ἀγροὺς ἐμπυρίζομεν. οἱ
δὲ ἀστέρες τοῦ οὐρανοῦ τεθεμελιωμένοι εἰσὶν ἐν τῷ στερεώματι.‹
18. καὶ ταῦτα ἀκούσας ἐγὼ Σολομῶν ἐκέλευσα τὸν δαίμονα τη-
ρεῖσθαι ἕως ἡμερῶν πέντε.

0   19. Μετὰ δὲ τὰς πέντε ἡμέρας μετακαλεσάμενος τὸν γέροντα
οὐκ ἤθελεν ἐλθεῖν. εἶτα ἐλθών, εἶδα αὐτὸν τεθλιμμένον καὶ
πενθοῦντα. 20. καὶ εἶπον αὐτῷ· ›ποῦ ἐστιν ὁ υἱός σου, γέρον,‹
ὁ δὲ ἔφη· ›ἄπαις ἐγενόμην, ὦ βασιλεῦ, καὶ ἀνέλπιστος τάφῳ
υἱοῦ παραφυλάττω.‹ 21. ἐγὼ δὲ Σολομῶν ἀκούσας ταῦτα καὶ
5 γνοὺς ὅτι ἀληθῆ εἰσι τὰ παρὰ τοῦ δαίμονος * λαληθέντα μοι
ἐδόξασα τὸν θεὸν τοῦ οὐρανοῦ καὶ τῆς γῆς. *

MSS HPQ = Recc. AB.   2 δοκοῦσιν ... πίπτοντες H. θεωρῦντες ἡμᾶς
οἱ ἄνθρωποι δοκοῦσιν ὅτι (+ οἱ P) ἀστέρες πίπτοισιν B   3 § 17. οὐχ
οὕτως ἐστί· οὐχ ὅτως ἔσται H, pr. ἀλλ᾿ B   4 * H f. 28ʳ | ὦ βασ P |
ἀλλ᾿ ἡμεῖς ἐσμέν. καὶ πίπτομεν ἐπὶ τὴν γῆν διὰ Q   5 μηδαμόθεν B· μὴ
δυνάμεθα H | ἔχειν HPIs· ἔχημεν Q | ἀντιλέγειν. ἀντιλέγεται HPIs· πιπτω-
μεν H | ἐπὶ τ. γῆν H ἐν ἀωρίᾳ (πολλῇ ex πολλῆς corr add P) καὶ ἐξά-
πινα (αἰφνηδίως Q) B   7 δὲ HQ· γὰρ P | τοῦ οὐρανοῦ — B | τεθεμελ.
HPIs· τε θέμελοι ὅμοιοι P | στερεωμ. H· οὐρανῷ ὥσπερ ὁ ἥλιος καὶ ἡ
σελήνη B   8 § 18. (115) τὸν .. πέντε. φρουρεῖσθαι τ. δαιμ. ἄχρι ἡμερῶν
ε΄ B   9 ἡμέραις H
    § 19.   10 μετὰ δὲ ἡμ. ε̄΄ H | ἐπεκαλεσάμην Q | γέροντα H· γηραιὸν B,
+ ἔμπροσθέν μου Q, + ἤμελλον ἐρωτᾶν P   11 οὐκ ἤθελ. . . πενθ. H·
ἐλθὼν δὲ ὁ γέρων πρός με κατὰ πένθος καὶ μελανῷ τῷ προσώπῳ P, καὶ
ἐλθὼν πρός με ὁ ἄνθρωπος κατὰ πένθος καὶ μεμελα⟨σ⟩μένῳ τῷ προσώπῳ
αὐτοῦ Q   12 § 20. καὶ — B | εἶπον P· εἶπα H, λέγω Q | αὐτῷ P· αὐ-
τὸν H, πρὸς αὐτὸν Q, + εἰπὲ πρεσβύτα B | γέρον H — B, + καὶ τί τό
σχῆμα (+ τοῦτο P, + τοῦ προσώπου σου Q) B   13 ἔφη H· ἔφην Q,
+ ἰδοὺ P, + ἰδού, κύριε, Q | ἄπαις· ἄπας H | ὦ βασ — B | ἀνέλπιστα B
14 παραφυλ. εg᾿ παραφυλάττειν H, παρακαθέζομαι Q, παρακαθεζόμενος P,
+ ἤδη γὰρ ἡμέρας (ἡμέραι P) δύο νεκροῦ γεγονότος B | § 21.   15 ἀλη-
θὲς H | εἰσι ... μοι· εἰσὶν ἃ ἔφη μοι ὁ δαίμων Ὀρνίας, καὶ Q, μοι ἔφησεν
ὁ δαίμων ὀρνί(ας) P | * H f 28ᵛ   16 τοῦ .. γῆς· Ἰσραὴλ Q, τοῦ
ἰ(σρα)ὴλ P | * Q f. 13ˣ

C. XX 17, 1 5 Lc X 18 notat James

XXI. Καὶ Σάβα ἡ βασίλισσα Νότου ἐθαύμασα καὶ εἶδε τὸν
ναὸν ὃν ᾠκοδόμουν καὶ ἔδωκε μυρίους * * σίγλους χαλκοῦς.
2. καὶ εἰσῆλθεν εἰς τὸν ναὸν καὶ εἶδε τὸ θυσιαστήριον καὶ τὰ
χερουβὶμ καὶ τὰ σεραφὶμ κατασκιάζοντα τὸ ἱλαστήριον καὶ τοὺς
5 διακοσίους λίθους τῶν λύχνων ἐξαστράπτοντας ἐκ διαφόρων
χρωμάτων, λύχνοι καὶ σμαράγδων καὶ ὑακίνθου τῶν λίθων καὶ
σαμφείρου. 3. καὶ εἶδε τὰ σκεύη τὰ ἀργυρᾶ καὶ χαλκᾶ καὶ χρυσᾶ
καὶ τὰς βάσεις τῶν κιόνων ὑπὸ χαλκοῦ ἀλυσιδωτοῦ πεπλεγμένας.
εἶδε καὶ τὴν θάλασσαν τὴν χαλκῆν ἔχουσαν ἐπισταθὸν καὶ τοὺς
10 τριάκοντα ἓξ ταύρους. 4. καὶ ἦσαν ἐν * τῷ ἱερῷ τοῦ θεοῦ ἐργαζόμενοι πάντες . . . . * μισθοῦ ταλάντου χρυσοῦ
ἑνὸς χωρὶς τῶν δαιμόνων.

Parallela ad c. XXI v. infra ms D c V

C. XXI. (116) MSS HPQ — Recc. AB. 1 Σάβα . . . ἐθαυμ. καὶ H
ἰδοῦσα ἡ βασ νότου ταῦτα πάντα ἐθαυμ δοξάζουσα τὸν θεὸν ἰ(σρα)ὴλ καὶ P,
— Q, supplevit ἡ βασ Νότου Is 2 ναὸν + κυρίου P, οἶκον κυρίου Q |
ὃν ᾠκοδ. H οἰκοδομούμενον B | * Mg 1352 | κ. ἔδωκε (δέδωκεν ms.) . . .
χαλκ. H κ ἔδωκεν (* * f. 20ᵛ) σίκλον χρυσίον καὶ ἀργυρίον μυριάδας ἑκατὸν, καὶ χαλκοῦ ἐκλεκτοῦ P, ἐχαρίσατο ἐν τῷ ναῷ κυρίου χρυσίον καὶ ἀρ-
γυρίον καὶ χαλκοῦ ἐκλεκτοῦ λίτρας μυριάδας ρ Q 3 § 2. εἶδε — P | κ.
τὰ χερ. . . . ἱλαστ. τοὺς ἀναφόρους τοὺς χαλκοὺς τοῦ θυσιαστηρίου B
4 κατασκιάζοντα H 5 διακοσίους H ἀναφόρους Q, — P | λύγχων H
6 χρημάτων Q | λύχνοι . . . σαμφείρου καὶ λύχνη (λυχνίου P) τοῦ (l.
λυχνίτου) λίθου καὶ σμαράγδου καὶ ὑακίνθου καὶ σαμφύρου (σαπφείρου P) B
7 § 3 εἶδε — Q | τ. ἀργ. . . . χρυσᾶ· τ. χρυσᾶ κ. (+ τὰ Q) ἀργυρᾶ κ.
χαλκᾶ κ. ξύλινα κ. ἐκ δερμάτων ἀπλώματα ἠρυθροδανομένα (ἠρυθρηδανο-
μένων Q) B | καὶ (2°) pr εἶδε Q, + ἴδε P 8 κιόνων + τοῦ ναοῦ
κυρίου B
MSS HQ = Recc AB. 8—10 ὑπὸ . . . θεοῦ — P 8 ἀλυσιδωτοῦ
βαισιδώτου Q | πεπλεγμ. πεπληγμένας H, πλοκῇ περιπεπλεγμένων Q 9 δὲ
καὶ Q | ἔχουσαν . . . ταύρους ἔχουσα στάδιον κ. τ. λϛ ταυρ. H, ἣν ἐποίησα
εἰς τὸ μῆκος ἔχουσα (ἔχουσα(ν) Is) σταδίους καὶ ἐπὶ στάδιον καὶ τοὺς ιϛ
ταύρους Q 10 § 4. ἦσαν . . . ἑνὸς (l. 12) ἦσαν οἱ ἐργαζόμενοι εἰς τὸν
ναὸν κυρίου (rursus ms P) οἱ πάντες χρυσίου ἑνὸς Q, οἱ παντ. χρ. ἑνὸς P |
* H f. 29ʳ 11 * textum depravatum enodari non potui οἱ μελησιοι (apographum incertum) H

MSS HPQ = Recc. AB. 12 δαιμόνων + ὧν κατέκρινα ἐργάζεσθαι
καὶ ἦν εἰρήνη κύκλῳ τῆς βασιλείας μου (+ καὶ P) ἐπὶ πάσης τῆς γῆς (πᾶσαν
τὴν γῆν Q) B

XXII. ¹Ἀπέστειλε δὲ ἐπιστολὴν ὁ βασιλεὺς Ἀράβων Ἀδάρκης,
(λέγων οὕτως· »Βασιλεὺς Ἀράβων Ἀδάρκης)¹ βασιλεῖ Σολομῶντι χαίρειν. ἰδοὺ ἠκούσαμεν τὴν δεδομένην σοι σοφίαν καὶ
ὅτι ἄνθρωπος ὢν παρὰ κυρίου ἐδόθη σοι σύνεσις ἐπὶ πάν-
5 των τῶν πνευμάτων ἀερίων τε καὶ ἐπιγείων καὶ καταχθονίων.
2. πνεῦμα δέ ἐστιν ἐν τῇ Ἀραβίᾳ· ἐν γὰρ τῇ ἑωθινῇ ἔρχεται
αὔρα ἀνέμου ἕως ὥραν τρίτην καὶ ἡ πνοὴ αὐτοῦ δεινὴ καὶ
ἀποκτείνει ἀνθρώπους καὶ κτήνη καὶ * οὐ δύναται ζῆσαι πνοὴ
οὐδεμία ἐναντίον τοῦ δαίμονος. 3. δέομαί σου οὖν, ἐπειδὴ ὡς
10 ἄνεμός ἐστι τὸ πνεῦμα, σόφισαί τι κατὰ τὴν δεδομένην σοι σοφίαν ὑπὸ κυρίου τοῦ θεοῦ σου καὶ καταξίωσον ἀποστεῖλαι δυνάμενον ἄνθρωπον συλλαβέσθαι αὐτό. 4. καὶ ἰδοὺ σοῦ * ἐσόμεθα,
βασιλεῦ Σολομῶν, ἐγώ τε καὶ πᾶς ὁ λαός μου καὶ πᾶσα ἡ γῆ
μου, καὶ εἰρηνεύσει πᾶσα Ἀραβία, ἐὰν τὴν ἐκδίκησιν ταύτην ποιή-

---

Parallela ad c XXII v. infra in ms. D, c. VI 1—9

C. XXII. (117) MSS HPQ = Recc. AB **1** Ἀπεστ.... Ἀδάρκης (1. 2) ego
ἀπέστειλεν δὲ βασιλεὺς αἰδάρκις περσῶν H, καὶ ἐγένετο ἐν τῷ εἶναι με ἐν τῇ
βασιλείᾳ μου ἀπέστειλέ μοι ἐπιστολὴν ὁ βασ. ἀράβων ἀδάρης P, ἐν ταύταις
δὲ ταῖς ἡμέραις ἀπέστειλέν με ἐπιστολὴν ὁ βασ. Ἀράβων Ἀδάρκης ὀνόματι Q,
+ ἡ δὲ γραφὴ τῆς ἐπιστολῆς ἔγραφεν οὕτως B **2** βασιλεῖ βασιλεῦ H,
+ τῷ Q **3** χαιρ. τὸ χαίρειν H | τὴν .. σοφίαν (+ παρὰ θεοῦ) H καὶ
ἀκουστὸν (ἀκουστὰ Q) γέγονεν εἰς (— εἰς Q) πάντα τὰ πέρατα τῆς γῆς τὴν
(τῇ Q) ἐν σοὶ δεδομένην (-μένη Q) σοφίαν (σοφίᾳ Q) B **4** ὢν π. κυρ. H ἐλεή-
μων παρὰ κυρίου (θεοῦ Q) εἰ σὺ B | ἐδόθη σοι συν. H· καὶ συν ἐδόθη
σοι P, — Q | πνευματ... καταχθ. B ἀερίων κ. καταχθ. H **6** § 2 πνεῦμα
... Ἀραβ. H ἐπειδὴ πν. πάρεστιν ἐν τῇ χώρᾳ τῆς Ἀραβίας τοιόνδε B | ἐν
τῷ ἑωθινῷ B **7** τις αὔρα B | ὡρῶν τριῶν P (ḡ) Q | δεινὴ καὶ χαλεπὴ B |
ἀποκτένει H **8** * P f 21ʳ | οὐ δυν. ... δαίμονος H. οὐ δυν. πνοὴ οὐδ.
ζῆσαι ἐπὶ τῆς γῆς ἐναντίον τ. δαιμ. ἐκείνου P, οὐ δυνάμεθα οὐδεμία πνοῇ
ζῶντες ἐπὶ τῆς γῆς ζῆσθαι ἀπὸ τὴν δύναμιν τοῦ πνεύματος ἐκείνου Q

MS H = Rec A pro § 3 textum mutilatum praebet hunc δέομαί σου οὖν
φήσασθαι ἐπ' ἐμοὶ ποῖος ἄνεμός ἐστιν τὸ πνεῦμα καὶ εἰπεῖν μοι

MSS PQ = Rec. B. **9** § 3 σου — P | οὖν — Q **10** σόφισαι Kurz
σόφισε PQIs | τι P δὴ Q | σοι — Q **11** δυνάμενον P· δύναμιν καὶ Q
12 αὐτό Q αὐτῷ P

MSS HPQ = Recc AB. **12** § 4. σοῦ ego· συ vel ου H, — B | * H
f 29ᵛ | ἐσόμεθα H, ἔσομαι B, pr. ἐγὼ Q **13** πᾶς — P | πᾶσα ..
μου H· ἡ γῆ μου ἅπασα (πᾶσα P) δοῦλοί (δούλη P) σου ἕως θανάτου B
14 ἐὰν δὲ H, ἐάνπερ P | ἐκδίκ H δικαιοσύνην B

σεις ἡμῖν. 5. διὸ δεόμεθά σου, μὴ παραβλέψῃς τὴν ἱκεσίαν ἡμῶν,
καὶ κύριος ἡμῶν γενοῦ ἀείδια πάντοτε. ⌈ἐρρῶσθαι τὸν ἐμὸν
κύριον ἀεὶ διὰ παντός.«⌉

6. Ἐγὼ δὲ Σολομῶν ἀναγνοὺς τὴν ἐπιστολὴν ταύτην καὶ
5 πτύξας ἀπέδωκα τῷ δούλῳ μου εἰπὼν αὐτῷ· »μετὰ ἑπτὰ ἡμέρας
ὑπομνήσεις μοι τὴν ἐπιστολὴν ταύτην.« 7. ⌈καὶ ἦν Ἰερουσαλὴμ
ᾠκοδομημένη καὶ ὁ ναὸς συνεπληροῦτο.⌉ καὶ ἦν λίθος ἀκρογω-
νιαῖος μέγας ὃν ἐβουλόμην θεῖναι εἰς κεφαλὴν γωνίας τῆς πλη-
ρώσεως τοῦ ναοῦ τοῦ θεοῦ. 8. καὶ πάντες οἱ τεχνῖται καὶ πάν-
10 τες οἱ δαίμονες οἱ συνυπουργοῦντες ἦλθον ἐπὶ τὸ αὐτὸ ἀγαγεῖν
τὸν λίθον καὶ θεῖναι εἰς τὸ πτερύγιον * τοῦ ναοῦ καὶ οὐκ
ἴσχυσαν σαλεῦσαι αὐτόν. * 9 μετὰ δὲ τὰς ἑπτὰ ἡμέρας μνησθεὶς
ἐγὼ τῆς ἐπιστολῆς τοῦ βασιλέως Ἀράβων ἐκάλεσα τὸ παιδάριόν
μου καὶ εἶπον αὐτῷ· »ἐπίσαξον τὴν κάμηλόν σου καὶ λάβε ἀσ-
15 κὸν καὶ τὴν σφραγῖδα ταύτην, 10. καὶ ἄπελθε εἰς Ἀραβίαν εἰς
τὸν τόπον ἐν ᾧ τὸ πονηρὸν πνεῦμα πνίει, καὶ κρατήσας τὸν
ἀσκὸν καὶ τὸ δακτυλίδιον ἔμπροσθεν * τοῦ στόματος τοῦ ἀσκοῦ.

MSS HPQ = Recc. AB. 1 § 5. διὸ — H | ἡμῶν: + καὶ μὴ ἐξου-
θενημένην τὴν σὴν ὑποτελεῖ καὶ ὑποτεταγμένην ἐπαρχίαν ἀποτελέσῃ P 2 καὶ
.. πάντοτε H: ὅτι σου οἰκέται (ἱκέται P) ἐσμέν, ἐγὼ (+ τε P) καὶ ὁ λαός
μου καὶ πᾶσα ἡ γῆ μου B | ἐρρῶσθαι . παντός B: — H 3 ἀεὶ Q — P
§ 6. (118) 4 ταύτην — P | ϰ. πτυξ. H: κ. ἀναπτυξ. P, — Q 5 ἀπέ-
δωκα B ἐπιδέδωκα H | δούλῳ H λαῷ B | εἰπὼν αὐτῷ HP εἰπόντες Q
6 ὑπομν. ... ταύτην H ὑπομνήσεις (ὑπομνήσατέ Q) με περὶ τῆς ἐπιστολῆς
ταύτης B | § 7. καὶ ἦν .. συνεπληρ. B — H 7 οἰκοδομουμένη Q |
ἀκρογων. κείμενος B 8 μέγας ἐκλεκτὸς P | ὃν H· ὅντινα B | εἰς τὴν
κεφαλὴν τῆς γωνίας τῆς συμπληρώσεως B   9 τ. ναοῦ τ. θ. αὐτοῦ P |
§ 8. 10 συνυπεργοῦντες Q | ἀγαγεῖν H ὥστε ἀναγαγεῖν B 11 θεῖναι
αὐτὸν B | εἰς H ἐπὶ P, ὑπὸ Q | * H f. 30ʳ | ναοῦ + τοῦ ἱεροῦ B
12 * P f. 21ᵛ | αὐτόν + καὶ θεῖναι πρὸς τὴν γωνίαν τὴν θεματισμένην
αὐτῷ P, + ἦν γὰρ ὁ λίθος ἐκεῖνος πάνυ μέγας καὶ χρήσιμος εἰς τὸ τεθῆναι
ἐπὶ τῆς γωνίας (τὸ ... γων. τὴν γωνίαν P) τοῦ ἱεροῦ B | § 9. (119) καὶ
μετὰ τὰς B | ἐμνήσθην Q 13 ἐγὼ — B | τοῦ H Ἀδάρκου Q, ἀδάρου P
| ἐκάλεσα P. ἐπεκαλεσάμην Q, ἐκέλευσα H | τ. παιδ. H· τὸν παῖδα P, τὸν
παιδί Q 14 τὴν H· τὸν B | λάβε· + μετὰ σου Q, σεαυτὸν P | λάβε
δὲ καὶ B 15 φραγῖδα P | § 10. εἰς τὴν Ἀρ. ἐπὶ τὸν B 16 πνέει B.
πνῆ H | κρατήσας B· κατάργησον H 17 ἀσκὸν B. αἰκὸν H | καὶ τὸ ..
ἀσκοῦ P· ϰ τ δακτ θὲς ἐμπρ. τὸν ἐκὸν H, ἐπιτηδείως εἰς τὸ τόπον, ὅθεν
ἐξέρχεται ἡ πνοὴ τοῦ δαίμονος, ὁμοίως δὲ τὸ δακτιλίδιον Q, + κατὰ τὴν
πνοὴν τοῦ πνεύματος P | * Mg 1353

§ 7. Is XXVIII 16, I Pt II 6

11. καὶ ἐν τῷ ἐμπνευσθῆναι τὸν ἀσκὸν εὑρήσεις ὅτι ὁ δαίμων
ἐστὶν ὁ ἐκεῖσε ἐμπνέων· τότε σπουδαίως μετὰ βίας δῆσον τὸν
ἀσκὸν καὶ σφραγίσας τὸ δακτυλίδιον ἐπίσαξον ἐπὶ τὴν κάμηλον
καὶ κόμισον αὐτὸν ἐνθάδε, καὶ ἄπελθε ὑγιαίνων.«

5   12. Τότε ὁ παῖς κατὰ * τὰ ἐνταλθέντα ἐποίησε καὶ ἐπο-
ρεύθη εἰς Ἀραβίαν. καὶ οἱ ἄνθρωποι τοῦ τόπου ἐκείνου ἠπίστουν εἰ ἄρα δυνήσεται τὸ πονηρὸν πνεῦμα συλλαβέσθαι. 13. καὶ
ὄρθρου * ἀναστὰς ὁ οἰκέτης ἔστη κατενώπιον τοῦ πνεύματος
τῆς πνοῆς καὶ ἔθηκε τὸν ἀσκὸν ἐπὶ τὸ ἔδαφος, ἐπέθηκε δὲ καὶ
10 τὸ δακτυλίδιον * καὶ εἰσῆλθεν εἰς τὸν ἀσκὸν καὶ ἐπνευμάτωσεν
αὐτόν. 14. ὁ δὲ παῖς σταθεὶς ἔσφιγξε τὸν ἀσκὸν ἐπὶ τῷ στόματι ἐν ὀνόματι κυρίου Σαβαὼθ καὶ ἔμεινεν ὁ δαίμων ἔσωθεν

MSS HPQ — Recc AB. **1** § 11. ἐμπνευσθ. Η   πνευματωθῆναι Β |
ἀσκὸν αἶκὸν Η | εὑρήσεις ego εὑρέσεις Η, τότε συνήσεις Β   **2** ὁ ἐκ.
ἐμπν. — Β | τότε σπουδ. Η   κμὶ σπουδῇ Β | μετὰ βίας — Β | δῆσον τ.
ἀσκ. (ἐκὸν) Η· περιδήσας τὸ στόμα τοῦ ἀσκοῦ Β   **3** κ. σφραγ. τ. δακτ. Η
κατασφράγισον αὐτὸν μετὰ τοῦ δακτυλιδίου καὶ Ρ, σφράγισον αὐτὸν μὲ τὸ
δακτ. καὶ Q | ἐπίσαξον αὐτὸν Β | τὴν HP τὸν Β   **4** κόμισον αὐτ. ἐνθ.
Η κομ. μοι ἐνθ. Ρ, ἐλθὲ πρὸς ἡμᾶς Q, + καὶ ἐὰν κατὰ τὴν ὁδὸν τάξει
[τάξεται Q) σοι χρυσίον ἢ ἀργύριον (ἄργυρον Q, + ἢ θησαυροὺς Ρ) ἵνα
(ὅπως Q) ἀπολύσῃς αὐτόν, βλέπε μὴ πεισθῇς (+ καὶ ἀπολύσῃς αὐτόν Q).
σύνταξον δὲ (ἀλλὰ σύνταξαι Ρ, + αὐτοῦ Q) ἄνευ ὅρκου (+ ἀπολῦσαι Ρ).
καὶ ἐὰν ἀποδείξῃ (ὑποδείξῃ Q) σοι τόπους (τόπον ἔχοντα Q) χρυσίου ἢ (καὶ Q)
ἀργυρίου, σημειωσάμενος τοὺς τόπους σφράγισαι τὴν σφραγίδα ταύτην (⟨σ⟩φρά-
γισαι τὸν τόπον τοῦ χρήματος Q) καὶ ἄγαγέ μοι αὐτὸν (αὐτ ἀγ μοι ὧδε Q) Β
| καὶ Η ἔθη Β

§ 12. (120) **5** κατὰ (* f 30ᵛ) τ. ἐνταλθ. Η   τ. ἐντελόμενα Q, τὰ ἐντε-
ταλμένα αὐτῷ Ρ, + παρὰ τοῦ βασιλέως σολομῶν < Η | ἐποίησε· + καὶ ἐπέ-
σαξε τὴν (τὸν Q) κάμηλον καὶ ἔθηκε τὸν ἀσκὸν (+ ἐπὶ τὸν κάμηλον Q) Β
6 εἰς τὴν Ἀρ. Β   **7** ἄρα … συλλαβ Ρ· ἄρα τὸ πνεῦμα τὸ πονηρὸν δυνή-
σεται συλλαβ. Q, δυνατὸν ἄν(θρωπ)ον συλλαβ. Η | § 13. κ. ὄρθρου ego κ.
ὀρθὸς Η, ὄρθρου δὲ γενομένου Β   **8** * Ρ f 22ᵛ | ὁ — Η   **9** ἐπέθηκε
.. δακτ. Η   καὶ τὸ δακτ. (* Q f. 14ʳ) ἐπὶ τὸ στόμα (τοῦ στόματος Ρ) τοῦ
ἀσκοῦ Β   **10** εἰσῆλθεν .. ἐπνευματ. αὐτ ego εἰσῆλθεν … ἐμπνευσμάτισεν
αὐτ. ἀπὸ τῆς πνοῆς τοῦ πονηροῦ πν(εύματο)ς Q, ἐπνευματώθη ὁ ἀσκὸς Q,
ἔπνευσεν ὁ δαίμων διὰ μέσον τοῦ δακτυλιδίου εἰς τὸ στόμα τοῦ ἀσκοῦ καὶ
εἰσελθὼν ἐπνευμάτωσε τὸν ἀσκὸν Ρ   **11** § 14 παῖς HQ ἄνθρωπος Ρ |
σταθεὶς Η ἐνσταθεὶς εὐθέως Ρ, συντόμως Q | ἔσφιγξε (ἔσφηξε ms.) …
στόματι Η ἔσφιγξεν τῇ χειρὶ τὸ στόμα τοῦ ἀσκοῦ Ρ, ἔδησεν τὸ στόμα τοῦ
ἀσκοῦ Q   **12** ἐν HP ἐπὶ τῷ Q | κυρίου τοῦ θεοῦ Ρ | ὁ δαιμ. ἔσωθ. Η
ἔσω ὁ δαιμ. Β

5 **

εἰς τὸν ἀσκόν 15. ἔμεινε δὲ καὶ ὁ παῖς εἰς ἀπόδειξιν ἡμέρας
τρεῖς, καὶ οὐκέτι ἔπνευσε τὸ πνεῦμα, καὶ ἐπέγνωσαν οἱ Ἄραβες
ὅτι ἀσφαλῶς συνέκλεισε τὸ πνεῦμα. 16. τότε ἐπέσαξε τὸν ἀσκὸν
εἰς τὴν κάμηλον. προσέπεμπον δὲ οἱ Ἄραβες τὸν παῖδα μετὰ
5 δώρων καὶ τιμῶν εὐφημοῦντες τὸν θεόν, ἔμειναν γὰρ ἐν εἰρήνῃ.
εἰσήγαγε ⟨δὲ⟩ τὸ πνεῦμα ὁ παῖς καὶ ἔθηκεν αὐτὸ εἰς κεφαλὴν
τοῦ ναοῦ.

  17. Τῇ δὲ ἐπαύριον εἰσῆλθον ἐγὼ Σολομῶν εἰς τὸν ναόν·
καὶ ἤμην ἐν λύπῃ περὶ τοῦ λίθου τοῦ ἀκρογωνιαίου καὶ ἀναστὰς
10 ὁ ἀσκὸς καὶ περιπατήσας βήματα ἑπτὰ ἔστη ἐπὶ τὸ στόμα καὶ
προσεκύνησέ μοι 18 καὶ θαυμάσας ἐγὼ ὅτι μετὰ τοῦ ἀσκοῦ δυνάμεις ἔσχε καὶ περιεπάτησεν, ἐκέλευσα αὐτὸ ἀναστῆναι καὶ ἀνέστη
ὁ ἀσκὸς καὶ ἔστη ἐν τοῖς ποσὶν πεφυσιωμένος. 19. καὶ ἐπηρώτησα αὐτὸν λέγων· »σὺ τίς εἶ;« λέγει ἔσω τὸ πνεῦμα· *
15 »ἐγώ εἰμι δαίμων λεγόμενος Ἐφιππᾶς, ὁ ἐν τῇ Ἀραβίᾳ.«

MSS HPQ = Recc AB. 1 ἐν τῷ ἀσκῷ Q | § 15 ἔμ δὲ κ. Η καὶ
μετὰ τοῦτο ἔμ Β | παῖς ἐν τῇ χώρᾳ ἐκείνῃ ἤμ τρεῖς εἰς ἐπίδειξιν Β
2 πνεῦμα + πλέον τῇ πόλει ἐκείνῃ Ρ, + πλέον ἐν τῇ χώρᾳ ἐκείνῃ Q |
ἔγνωσαν πάντες οἱ Β 3 § 16 (121) ἐπίσαξε Β | ἀσλὸν + ὁ παῖς Β |
τὴν ΗΡ τὸν Q 4 προσεπ δὲ Η καὶ προεπ Ρ, καὶ ἐξαπέστειλαν Q | τ
παιδ. οἱ Ἀρ Β | μετὰ ... τιμῶν Η· μετὰ τιμῆς πολλῆς καὶ δώρων πολυ-
τίμων Ρ, μ. τιμ. πολ. καὶ δῶρα πολλὰ ἐδωροφόρησαν τὸν παῖδα Q 5 εὐφ.
τ. θ. Η εὐφημ. καὶ δοξάζοντες τὸν θεὸν Ἰσραὴλ Ρ, ἐπαίνους καὶ δόξαν πεμ-
ψάμενοί μοι Q | ἔμειν.. εἰρ — Β 6 εἰσηγ .. παῖς Η ὁ δὲ παῖς
εἰσηγ τὸν ἀσκὸν Β | αὐτὸ ego αὐτῷ Η, αὐτὸν Q, — Ρ | κεφαλὴν Η
τὸ μέσον Β 8 § 17. εἰσῆλθον ἐλθὼν Β | ἐγὼ βασιλεὺς Ρ | ναὸν τοῦ
θεοῦ Β 9 καὶ — Β | λύπῃ πολλῇ Β | καὶ ἐν τῷ εἰσέρχεσθαί μοι εἰς
τὸν ναὸν (+ κυρίου Q) Β 10 κ. περιπ. βημ ἐπ Η πεφυσημένος (— Ρ)
ἐπεριεπάτησεν ἐπ. βημ. Β | ἔστη (ἔστι ms.) ... στόμα Η ἔπεσεν δὲ ἐπὶ
στόμα Ρ, καὶ ἐλθὼν ἔμπροσθέ μου ἔπεσεν ἔμπροσθέν μου κῆπον (l. κύπτον Is)
τὸ στόμα τοῦ ἀσκοῦ ἐπὶ τὴν γῆν Q 11 ἐπροσκύνησε Q | § 18. κ θαυμ.
ἐγὼ ΗΡ ἐγὼ δὲ ταῦτα θεωρήσας ἐθαύμασα Q | ὅτι καὶ Β | μετὰ τ.
ἀσκοῦ Η (— τοῦ) Ρ· ἐν ἀσκῷ δεδεμένος ὁ δαίμων Q | δύναμιν Β 12 ἔσχε
ὁ δαίμων Ρ | περιεπάτει Β | ἐγὼ δὲ ἐκέλευσα Q | αὐτὸν Ρ, 13 κ.
ἔστη — Η · ἐν — Ρ | πεφυσ. Η· πεφυσιωμένος Ρ, πεφυσημένος Q |
§ 19 14 σὺ pr. εἰπέ μοι Β, — Q | λέγει ἔσω Η. καὶ ἔφη ἔσωθεν Β |
* Ρ f. 22ᵛ | ὁ δαίμων ὁ λεγόμενος Β | ἐφιππὰς Ρ, ἐφίππας Q, Ἔφιππας Η,
cf supra VI 5, infra XXIV 1 | ὁ ὢν Ρ, ὃ ἤμην Q

20. καὶ εἶπον αὐτῷ· »ποίῳ ἀγγέλῳ καταργεῖσαι;« ὁ δὲ λέγει· »τῷ
διὰ παρθένου μέλλοντι γεννηθῆναι ἐπειδὴ αὐτὸν προσκυνοῦσι
ἄγγελοι, καὶ ὑπὸ Ἰουδαίων μέλλοντι σταυρωθῆναι.«

XXIII. Ἐγὼ δὲ λέγω πρὸς αὐτόν· »τί μοι δύνασαι ποιῆσαι;«
5 ὁ δὲ ἔφη· »ἐγὼ δυνατός εἰμι ὄρη μεταστῆναι καὶ μεταφέρειν
οἴκους καὶ βασιλεῖς καταβαλεῖν.« 2. καὶ εἶπον αὐτῷ· »εἰ δυνατός εἶ, ἔπαρον τὸν λίθον τοῦτον εἰς τὴν ἀρχὴν τῆς γωνίας τοῦ
ναοῦ.« ὁ δὲ ἔφη· »οὐ μόνον τοῦτον τὸν λίθον ἐπαρῶ, βασιλεῦ,
ἀλλὰ καὶ σὺν τῷ δαίμονι τῷ ἐν τῇ Ἐρυθρᾷ θαλάσσῃ τὸν ἐν τῇ
10 Ἐρυθρᾷ θαλάσσῃ κίονα τὸν ἀέριον, καὶ στήσεις αὐτὸν ὅπου
θέλεις.« 3 καὶ ταῦτα εἰπὼν ὑπεισῆλθεν ὑποκάτω τοῦ λίθου καὶ
ᾖρεν * αὐτὸν καὶ ἀνῆλθεν εἰς τὸν κλίμακα βαστάζων τὸν λίθον

MSS PQ = Rec. B pro § 20 praebent textum hunc καὶ (ἐγὼ δὲ Q) εἶπον
αὐτῷ· (+ τοῦτό σοι ἐστὶ τὸ ὄνομα; ὁ δὲ ἔφη· ναί· ὅπου γὰρ βούλομαι
ἐφίπταμαι καὶ ἐμπυρίζω καὶ θανατῶ καὶ εἶπον αὐτῷ· P) ποίῳ ἀγγέλῳ
καταργεῖσαι (καταργῇ σὺ P) ὁ δὲ εἶπεν· ὁ μονάρχης θεὸς ὁ ἔχων ἐξουσίαν
κατ' ἐμοῦ (+ καὶ ἀκούεσθαι P), ὁ διὰ παρθένου μέλλων γενᾶσθαι (ὁ καὶ
μέλλων ἐκ παρθ. τίκτεσθαι Q) καὶ ὑπὸ Ἰουδαίων (+ μέλλει Q) σταυρωθῆναι
ἐπὶ ξύλου, ὃν προσκυνοῦσι ἄγγελοι ἀρχάγγελοι, ἐκεῖνός με καταργεῖ καὶ
ἀτονεῖ με ἐκ τῆς πολλῆς μου δυνάμεως (ἀτονεῖ μου τὴν πολλήν μου δύναμιν Q) τῆς δοθείσης μοι (μου Q) ὑπὸ τοῦ πατρός μου τοῦ διαβόλου.
MS H = Rec. A. 1 § 20. τοῦ δ. π μέλλοντο < γεννηθ ms.   3 μελλ < ms

Parallela ad c XXIII v. infra in ms. D c. VI 10f
C. XXIII. MSS HPQ = Recc AB.   4 ἐγὼ . . αὐτόν Q   ὁ δὲ λέγει αὐ-
τῶν H, εἶπον δὲ αὐτῷ P | δύνασαί μοι Q | μοι — P   5 μεταστῆ-
ναι H μεταφέρειν P, σαλεῦσαι Q | κ μεταφ.   καταβ. (καταβαλῶ ms.) H
οἰκίας βασιλέων καταβαλ. (καταλαβεῖν Q), δένδρα ἀπέταλα (ἀπέταλλα Q, -αλα
Kurz) ξηραίνω (μαραίνω P) B   6 § 2 εἰ . . . τοῦτον H δύνασαι ἐπᾶραι
τὸν λίθον τοῦτον καὶ θέσαι (ex θέσθαι corr. P) αὐτὸν B   7 γωνίας ταύτης
τῆς οὔσης ἐν τῇ εὐπρεπείᾳ τ ναοῦ B   8 οὐ μόνον HP δύνομαι καὶ Q |
τὸν λίθον — B | ἐπάραι | βασιλεῦ, ἀλλὰ — Q   9 * Mg 1356 | σὺν
. . . θαλάσσῃ ego· σὺν τῷ δαίμονι τῷ ἐπὶ τῆς ἐρυθρᾶς θαλάσσης P, συντόμως
ἵνα H, — Q | τὸν ἐν . . . ἀέριον H ἀναγάγω τὸν κίονα τὸν ἀερίστην P,
τὸν κίοναν τὸν ἐν βύθῳ τῆς θαλάσσης (f. 14ᵛ) τῆς Ἐρυθρᾶς θαλάσσης, ὅνπερ
βαστάζει ἕτερος δαίμων φυλάττων αὐτὸ ἐκεῖ ἕως τὴν σήμερον Q   10 στήσεις . . θέλεις H. στήσω αὐτ. (αὐτ. θέσω Q) ὅπου βούλει (βούλῃ Q) ἐν Ἱε-
ρουσαλὴμ B   11 § 3. καὶ — B | ὑπεισῆλθεν   λίθου H ἠνάγκασα αὐτὸν,
καὶ ὡσεὶ ἐκφυσηθεὶς ὁ ἀσκὸς ἐγένετο καὶ ὑποδέδωκα τῷ λίθῳ καὶ διέζωσεν
ἑαυτὸν P, ἐπέδειξα αὐτοῦ τὸν λίθον. ὁ δὲ ἀσκὸς ἐγένετο ὡσεὶ ἐκφυσηθεὶς
καὶ διέζωσεν ἑαυτὸν Q   12 ᾖρεν αἰτ. H ἐπῆρεν (+ τὸν λίθον Q, * P
f. 23ʳ) ἐπάνω τοῦ ἀσκοῦ B | εἰς τ κλιμ. H ὁ ἀσκὸς τὰς κλίμακας P, ὁ
ἀσκὸς τὰς σκάλας Q | * H f. 32ʳ

καὶ ἔθετο αὐτὸν εἰς τὴν ἄκραν τῆς εἰσόδου τοῦ ναοῦ. 4. ἐγὼ δὲ
Σολομῶν ἐπαιρόμενος εἶπον· »ἀληθῶς νῦν ἐπληρώθη ἡ γραφὴ
ἡ λέγουσα· ›λίθον ὃν ἀπεδοκίμασαν οἱ οἰκοδομοῦντες οὗτος ἐγε-
νήθη μὲν εἰς κεφαλὴν γωνίας,‹ καὶ τὰ λοιπά.

5   XXIV. ⌈Καὶ πάλιν εἶπον αὐτῷ »ἄπελθε, ἄγαγέ μοι ὃν
εἶπας κίονα ἐν τῇ Ἐρυθρᾷ θαλάσσῃ. καὶ ἀπελθὼν ὁ Ἐφιππᾶς
ἀνήγαγεν τὸν δαίμονα καὶ τὸν κίονα ἀμφότεροι βαστάζοντες
ἀπὸ τῆς Ἀραβίας. 2. ἐγὼ δὲ κατασοφισάμενος⌉ ὅτι τὰ δύο πνεύματα ταῦτα ἐδύναντο πᾶσαν τὴν οἰκουμένην σαλεῦσαι ἐν μιᾷ
10 ῥοπῇ περιεσφράγισα ἔνθεν καὶ ἔνθεν τῷ δακτυλιδίῳ καὶ εἶπον·
»φυλάττεσθε ἀκριβῶς.« *   3. καὶ ἔμειναν βαστάζοντες τὸν κίονα

MSS HPQ = Recc. AB.   1 ἔθετο HP   ἔθηκεν Q | τῆς ... ναοῦ B
τοῦ ναοῦ τῆς ὁδοῦ H | § 4.   2 ἐπαιρόμενος H   ἰδὼν τὸν λίθον ἐπηρμέ-
νον καὶ τεθεμελιωμένον (+ ἐθαύμασα καὶ Q) B | νῦν ..   λέγουσα H
(— νῦν) P   ἡ γραφὴ εἶπεν Q   3 ὃν ἀπεδοκ. B   ἀναπεδοκ H   4 μὲν
— B | καὶ τὰ λοιπά H   ὅτι τοῦτο οὐκ ἔστιν ἐμὸν δοῦναι ἀλλὰ τοῦ θεοῦ τὸ
κατισχύσαι τὸν δαίμονα ἐπάραι τὸν λίθον τηλικοῦτον καὶ ἀποθέσθαι αὐτὸν
εἰς τόπον ὃν ἐβουλόμην P, ὅτι τοῦ θεοῦ τὸ θέλημά ἐστιν τῷ δώσαντι τὴν
ἰσχὺν δαίμονος ⟨ἐ⟩πάραι λίθον τοσοῦτον μέγεθος καὶ ἀποτεθῆναι εἰς τὸν τόπον ὃν ἐβουλόμην Q

Parallela ad c. XXIV v. in ms. D c. VI 12—14

C. XXIV   MSS HPQ = Recc. AB   (124) textum eius capitis depravatum
per conjecturam dubitanter emendavi   5 καὶ ... θαλάσσῃ H   — B   6—8 καὶ
.. Ἀραβίας Q   καὶ ἀπῆλθεν καὶ ᾖρεν αὐτῶν. ἐγὼ δὲ εἶδον αὐτὸν ἄφνω
ἐρχόμενον βαστάζοντα τὸν κίονα τὸν ἀέριον H, + ὡς δὲ ἐθεασάμην τὸν
κίοναν φέροντες εἰς ὕψος τοῦ ἀέρος βαστάζοντες πάντες οἱ θεωροῦντες τὰ
θαῦμα ἐξεπλάγησαν Q (l. fortasse ὡς δὲ εἶδον αὐτὰ ἀμφότερα ἐρχόμενα βαστάζοντα τὸν κίονα τὸν ἀέριον cum κατεσοφισάμην, v infra), καὶ ἤγαγεν
Ἐφιππᾶς τὸν δαίμονα τὸν ἐν τῇ Ἐρυθρᾷ θαλάσσῃ μετὰ τοῦ κίονος, καὶ λα-
βόντες ἀμφότεροι τὸν κίονα ὑψώθησαν ἀπὸ τῆς γῆς P   8 § 2 ἐγὼ δὲ
κατασ B   κατεσοφισάμην H   9 ἐδυν. ... οἰκουμ. H   ἠδύναντο τ. οἰκ. ὅλην
(ὅλ. τ. οἰκ. Q) B, pr. μὴ Cr   σαλεῦσαι B   σαλέσαι H | μιᾷ ῥοπῇ H   ῥυπῇ
(l. ῥιπῇ Kurz) Q, στιγμῇ χρόνου P   10 καὶ περιεσφράγισα αὐτὸν H |
μετὰ τοῦ δακτυλιδίου Q   11 φυλαττ. ἀκριβ H   φυλάσσου ἀκριβ. P, πρὸς
τοὺς δαίμονας· ἐπ᾽ ὀνόματος κυρίου Ἰσραὴλ θεοῦ Σαβαὼθ στῆτε, δαίμονες.
μετὰ τοῦ κιονίου εἰς τὸ ὕψος τοῦ ἀέρος ἐν τῷ τόπῳ τούτῳ, βαστάζοντες τὸν
κίονα ἕως τῆς συντελείας τοῦ αἰῶνος Q | * H f. 32ᵛ | § 3. ἔμειναν·
+ τὰ πνεύματα B, add. adhuc εἰς τὸν τόπον Q | βαστάζοντα P | τ.
κίονα — P

§ 4. Ps. CXVIII 22, Mk. XII 10, Mt. XXI 42, Lk. XX 17; I Pt II 6f.
Mt. XX 23; Mk. X 40

εἰς τὸν ἀέρα μέχρι τῆς σήμερον ⌈εἰς ἀπόδειξιν τῆς δεδομένης μοι
σοφίας. 4. καὶ ἦν κρεμάμενος ὁ κίων ὑπερμεγέθης διὰ τοῦ ἀέρος
ὑπὸ τῶν πνευμάτων βασταζόμενος καὶ οὕτως κάτωθεν τὰ πνεύματα ἐφαίνοντο ὥσπερ ἀὴρ βαστάζοντα   5. καὶ ἐν τῷ ἀτενίζειν
5 ἡμᾶς ⟨ὑπόλοξος⟩ ἐγένετο ἡ βάσις τοῦ κίονος καὶ ἔστιν ἕως τῆς
σήμερον.⌉ *

XXV. Καὶ ἐγὼ ἠρώτησα τὸν ἕτερον δαίμονα τὸν ἀνελθόντα
ἐκ τῆς θαλάσσης μετὰ τοῦ κίονος· ›σὺ τίς εἶ καὶ τί καλεῖσαι
καὶ τί σου ἡ ἐργασία; ὅτι πολλὰ ἀκούω περί σου ‹ 2. ὁ δὲ δαί-
ο μων ἔφη· ›ἐγώ, βασιλεῦ Σολομῶν, καλοῦμαι Ἀβεζεθιβοῦ· καὶ
ποτε ἐκαθεζόμην ἐν πρώτῳ οὐρανῷ, οὗ τὸ ὄνομα Ἀμελούθ.
3. ἐγὼ οὖν εἰμι * πνεῦμα χαλεπὸν καὶ πτερωτὸν καὶ μονόπτε-
ρον, ἐπίβουλον πάσης πνοῆς ὑπὸ τῶν οὐρανῶν. ἐγὼ παρήμην
ἡνίκα ὁ Μωϋσῆς εἰσήρχετο εἰς Φαραὼ βασιλέα Αἰγύπτου σκληρύ-
5 νων αὐτοῦ τὴν καρδίαν. 4. ἐγώ εἰμι ὃν ἐπικαλοῦντο Ἰαννῆς
καὶ Ἰαμβρῆς οἱ μαχόμενοι τῷ Μωϋσῇ ἐν Αἰγύπτῳ. ἐγώ εἰμι ὁ
ἀντιπαλαίων τῷ Μωϋσῇ ἐν τοῖς τέρασι καὶ τοῖς σημείοις.‹

MSS HPQ — Recc. AB. 1 εἰς τ. ἀέρα — B | μέχρι τ (τὴν H) σημ
HP ἕως καὶ τὴν σήμερον Q

MSS PQ — Rec. B. 1—6 εἰς ἀποδ ... σήμερον magnem partem om.
ms. H, v infra ll 4f   2 § 4, ὁ κίονας ἐν μεγέθει φρικτῷ εἰς τὸν ἀέρα Q
3 καὶ οὕτως . . βαστάζοντα om Q per homoeoteleuton   4 § 5 καὶ ἐν .
κίονος (ὑπόλοξος ex P supplevi) H· κ. ἐν τ. ἀτεν. τις ὁ κίων ὑπόλοξος βασταζόμενος ὑπὸ τῶν πνευμάτων P, φερόμενος ὡς ὑπὸ λοξήγον οὐχὶ ὀρθῶς Q
5 ἕως καὶ τὴν σήμερον Q   6 * P f. 23ᵛ

C. XXV. MSS HPQ — Recc. AB. (125) 7 ἠρώτησα H Σολομῶν ἐπη-
ρωτ. B | τὸν ἐτ. . . κίονος H τὸ ἕτερον τὸ ἐν τῇ ἐν Ἀραβίᾳ τῆς Ἐρυθρᾶς
θαλάσσης Q, τὸ πνεῦμα τὸ ἕτερον τὸ ἀνελθὸν μετὰ τοῦ κίονος ἀπὸ τοῦ βυθοῦ τῆς θαλάσσης τῆς ἐρυθρᾶς καὶ εἶπον αὐτῷ P

MSS PQ — Rec. B. §§ 1—5. ll. 8—p. 72*, 1 σὺ ... αὐτῷ — H | εἰ
καὶ τί — Q   9 περί P· παρά Q | § 2.   10 Σολ — Q | Ἀβεζεβιθοῦ Q |
καὶ ποτε ἐκαθεζ Q ἀπόγονός εἰμι ἀρχαγγέλου, καθεζομένου μου P 11 ὄνομα
+ τοῦ ἀγγέλου τοῦ καταργοῦντός με Q | Ἀβελούθ Q   12 § 3 οὖν — Q
| χαλεπὸν (* f 15ᵛ) πνεῦμα Q ·| καὶ (1°) — Q   18 ἐπιβουλ . . οὐρα-
νῶν P· πολλὰ κακὰ ἐνεργῶι Q | ἐγὼ παρ. ἡνίκα P ὅθεν ἐγὼ εἰμι, ὅταν Q
14 ὁ Μωϋσῆς Q μωσῆς P | βασιλέως mss   15 ἰανὶς καὶ ἰαμβρὶς P,
Ἰανῆς κ. Ἰαμβρὶς Q | οἱ μαχόμενοι Q οἱ καυχώμενοι P, οἰκουχώμενοι Fl
16 ἐν Αἰγ . Μωϋσῇ om Q per homoeoteleuton   17 τέρασι καὶ Q πέρασι P,
τέρασι conj. Cr

5. εἶπον οὖν αὐτῷ ⸣ »πῶς οὖν εὑρέθης ἐν τῇ Ἐρυθρᾷ θαλάσσῃ;«
ὁ δὲ ἔφη· Γ»ἐν τῇ ἐξόδου τῶν υἱῶν Ἰσραὴλ ἐγὼ ἐσκλήρυνα τὴν
καρδίαν Φαραὼ καὶ ἀνεπτέρωσα αὐτοῦ τὴν καρδίαν καὶ τῶν
θεραπόντων αὐτοῦ. 6. καὶ ἐποίησα αὐτοὺς ἵνα καταδιώξωσιν
5 ὀπίσω τῶν υἱῶν Ἰσραήλ, καὶ συνηκολούθησε Φαραὼ καὶ πάντες
οἱ Αἰγύπτιοι. τότε ἐγὼ παρήμην ἐκεῖ καὶ συνηκολουθήσαμεν,
καὶ ἀνήλθομεν ἅπαντες ἐν τῇ Ἐρυθρᾷ θαλάσσῃ. 7. καὶ ἐγένετο
ἡνίκα διεπέρασαν οἱ υἱοὶ Ἰσραήλ,⸣ ἐπαναστραφὲν τὸ ὕδωρ ἐκάλυψε
πᾶσαν τὴν παρεμβολὴν τῶν Αἰγυπτίων· τότε εὑρέθην ἐγὼ ἐκεῖ
10 καὶ συνεκαλύφθην ἐν τῷ ὕδατι Γκαὶ ἔμεινα ἐν τῇ θαλάσσῃ
τηρούμενος⸣ ὑποκάτω τοῦ κίονος Γμέχρι ἀνῆλθεν Ἐφιππᾶς.« *
8. κἀγὼ δὲ Σολομῶν ὥρκισα αὐτὸν βαστάζειν τὸν κίονα ἕως
τῆς συντελείας. 9. καὶ σὺν θεῷ ἐκόσμησα τὸν ναὸν αὐτοῦ ἐν
πάσῃ εὐπρεπείᾳ. καὶ ἤμην χαίρων καὶ δοξάζων αὐτόν.⸣

MSS PQ = Rec. B. 1 § 5. οὖν P δὲ ἐγὼ Q   2 ἔφη P· λέγει μοι Q
| ἐσκλήρουν Q   4 § 6. ἵνα καταὸ P ὅπως καταδιώξουσιν Q   5 συνε-
κολούθησεν Q   6 ἐσυνηκολούθησάν με Q | § 7.   7 ἡνίκα P ὅτε Q
MS H = Rec A   §§ 5—7. pro ll. 1—2 πῶς ... ἔφη, praebet H haec·
πῶς ἐν τη ἐριθρᾷ θαλάσσῃ οἰκῆς ὁ δαίμων ἔφη   2—8 ἐν τῇ . Ἰσραήλ — H

MSS HPQ = Recc AB   8 ἐπαναστραφὲν .. ἐκαλ. B· ὅταν ἐστράφη ὁ
ὕδωρ καὶ ἐκάλειψεν H   9 πᾶσαν — H | Αἰγυπτ. + καὶ πᾶσαν τὴν δύνα-
μιν αὐτῶν B | τότε εὑρ. H εὑρ οὖν B   10 συνεκ. ἐν τ. ὑδ. H· ἐκάλυψέν
με τὸ ὕδωρ B | κ. ἔμεινα . τηρούμενος B· — H   11 κίονος τούτου B

MS II = Rec. A   §§ 7—9, ll 11—14 μέχρι . αὐτόν textum brevem praebet
MSS PQ = Rec. B eiusdem sectionis textum interpolatum praebent hunc.
ὡς δὲ ἦλθεν Ἐφιππᾶς πεμφθεὶς παρὰ σοῦ ἰν ἀγγείῳ ἀσκοῦ (* P f. 24ʳ)
ἐγκλεισθεὶς καὶ ἀνεβίβασέ με πρὸς σέ. § 8 (127) κἀγὼ (+ οὖν P) Σολομῶν
ἀκούσας ταῦτα ἐδόξασα τὸν θεὸν καὶ ὥρκισα τοὺς δαίμονας ὥστε μὴ παρα-
κοῦσαί μου ἀλλὰ μεῖναι βαστάζοντας (-τες Q) τὸν (τὴν P) κίονα. καὶ ὤμοσαν ἀμφότεροι λέγοντες· ζῇ κύριος ὁ θεός (+ σου P, + ὃς παρέδωκεν ἡμᾶς
ὑποχειρίους σου Q), οὐ μὴ ἀποθώμεθα τὸν στύλον τοῦτον ἕως τῆς συντελείας
τοῦ αἰῶνος. ᾗ δ᾽ ἂν * ἡμέρᾳ (ego εἰ δ᾽ ἂν ἡμέραν P, εἰς δ᾽ ἂν ἡμέραν Q,
εἰς δ᾽ ἦν ἡμ. conj. Kurz, * Mg 1357) πέσῃ ὁ λίθος οὗτος, τότε ἔσται ἡ συντέλεια τοῦ αἰῶνος § 9. (128) ἐγὼ δὲ (κἀγὼ P) Σολομῶν ἐδόξασα τὸν θεὸν
καὶ (+ ἐδὸ linea deletum P) ἐκόσμησα τὸν ναὸν τοῦ κυρίου πάσῃ εὐπρεπεία,
καὶ ἤμην εὐτυμῶν ἐν τῇ βασιλείᾳ μου καὶ εἰρήνη ἐν ταῖς ἡμέραις μου

XXVI. Ἔλαβον δὲ γυναῖκας ἀπὸ πάσης χώρας * καὶ βασιλείας, ὧν οὐκ ἦν ἀριθμός. καὶ ἐπορεύθην πρὸς τῶν Ἰεβουσαίων βασιλέα καὶ εἶδον γυναῖκα ἐν τῇ βασιλείᾳ αὐτῶν καὶ ἠγάπησα αὐτὴν σφόδρα, καὶ ἠθέλησα αὐτὴν μῖξαι σὺν ταῖς γυναιξί μου. 2 καὶ εἶπον πρὸς τοὺς ἱερεῖς αὐτῶν »δότε μοι τὴν Σουμανίτην ταύτην, ὅτι ἠγάπησα αὐτὴν σφόδρα.« καὶ * εἶπον πρός με· »εἰ ἠγάπησας τὴν θυγατέρα ἡμῶν, προσκύνησον τοὺς θεοὺς ἡμῶν, τὸν μέγαν Ῥαφὰν καὶ Μολόχ, καὶ λάβε αὐτήν.« 3. ἐγὼ δὲ οὐκ ἠθέλησα προσκυνῆσαι, ἀλλ᾽ εἶπον αὐτοῖς· »ἐγὼ οὐ προσκυνῶ θεῷ ἀλλοτρίῳ.« 4. αὐτοὶ δὲ παρεβιάσαντο τὴν παρθένον λέγοντες ὅτι· »ἐὰν γένηταί σοι εἰσελθεῖν εἰς τὴν βασιλείαν Σολομῶν⟨τος⟩, * εἰπὲ αὐτῷ· »οὐ κοιμηθήσομαι μετά σου ἐὰν μὴ ὁμοιωθῇς τῷ λαῷ μου, καὶ λάβε ἀκρίδας πέντε καὶ σφάξαι

C. XXVI. MSS HPQ — Recc AB   1 Ἔλαβον δὲ H· καὶ ἔλαβ P, ἐγὼ δὲ ἐλ. Q | γυναῖκας: + ἐμαυτοῦ P, + εἰς ἀνάπαυσίν μου Q | πάσας Q | * H f. 33ʳ | κ. βασιλείας — B   2 ὧν B: οὐ H | ἐπορεύθη H | τ. Ἰεβους. βασ. ego τὸν ἰεβ. βασιλέων H, τοὺς Ἰεβουσαίους Q, τὸ ἰεβουσαῖον P 3 εἶδον HQ ἰδὼν P | γυναῖκα . . αὐτῶν H ἐκεῖ θυγατέρα ἀνθρώπου Ἰεβουσαίαν B | καὶ — P   4 σφόδρα + ὡς πολλὰ ὡραίαν οὖσαν Q | ἠθέλησα . . . μου H ἠβουλόμην δέξεσθαι αὐτὴν μετὰ ταῖς γυναιξί μου εἰς γυναῖκα P, ἐζήτησα αὐτὴν ἵνα μου γυναῖκαν μετὰ τῶν ἑτέρων γυναικῶν Q § 2.   5 αὐτῶν — κ. εἰπ. πρὸς τ. ἱερεῖς linea deleta P | μοι HQ μου P | Σουμανίτην P σονμανίτην Q, παῖδα Q   6 ὅτι . . . σφόδρα H εἰς γυναῖκα (+ μου Q) B | * Q f. 15ᵛ | με + οἱ (— Q) ἱερεῖς τοῦ Μολόχ B, add. etiam διότι εἴδωλα ἐσεβόντισαν Q | ἐὰν ἀγαπᾷς B   7 θυγατ. ἡμῶν H· παρθένον B, + εἴσελθε (+ δὲ Q) καὶ B   8 τὸν μέγαν τῷ μεγάλῳ θεῷ P (+ ἡμῶν) Q | ραφάμ H | Μολόχ pr. τῷ καλουμένῳ θεῷ P | καὶ λάβε αὐτ HQ· — P | § 3 δὲ οὖν B, + τοῦτο H, + φοβηθεὶς τὴν δόξαν τοῦ θεοῦ (+ ἡμῶν Q) B   6 ἤθελ HQ ἠκολούθησα P | προσκυνῆσαι . . . ἐγὼ P (κἀγὼ) Q. — H | οὐ οὐδὲ H

MSS PQ — Rec. B in fine sectionis 3 (post ἀλλοτρίῳ) et pro sectionibus 4 et 5 praebent textum hunc καὶ τίς δὲ (κ. τίς δὲ omisso spatioque puro relicto in marg scr. τίς αὕτη P) ἡ (— Q) ὑπόθεσις ὅτι τοσοῦτον (τοῦτο Q) με ἀναγκάζετε ποιῆσαι, § 4 οἱ δὲ εἶπον ἵνα ὁμοιωθῇς (ἵνα ὁμ. om. spatioque puro relicto ωθεὶς scr. P) τῶν πατέρων ἡμῶν. (129) ἐμοῦ δὲ πυθομένου ὅτι οὐδαμῶς (οὐδαμὴ Q) προσκυνήσω (προσθύσω Q) θεοῖς ἀλλοτρίοις, αὐτοὶ (καὶ P) παρήγγειλαν τὴν παρθένον τοῦ μὴ κοιμηθῆναί μοι, ἐὰν μὴ πεισθῶ θῦσαι τοῖς θεοῖς (+ αὐτῶν Q)

MS H — Rec. A   § 4. 12 αὐτῷ ego αὐτῶν H | ad σφάξαι (l. 13) et ἔθυσα (ἔθησα ms.; p. 74*, 4) cf. Dial. Tim. et Aquil., p. 70, et mss. PQ infra, v. Intro p. 38.

αὐτὰς εἰς τὸ ὄνομα Ῥαφὰν καὶ Μολόχ.«« 5. ἐγὼ δὲ διὰ τὸ ἀγαπᾶν με τὴν κόρην ὡς ὡραίαν οὖσαν πάνυ, καὶ ὡς ἀσύνετος ὤν,
οὐδὲν ἐνόμισα τῶν ἀκρίδων τὸ αἷμα καὶ ἔλαβον αὐτὰς ὑπὸ τὰς
χεῖράς μου καὶ ἔθυσα εἰς τὸ ὄνομα Ῥαφὰν καὶ Μολόχ τοῖς
5 εἰδώλοις, καὶ ἔλαβα τὴν παρθένον εἰς τὸν οἶκον τῆς βασιλείας μου.

6. Καὶ ἀπήρθη τὸ πνεῦμα τοῦ θεοῦ ἀπ᾽ ἐμοῦ, καὶ ἀπ᾽
ἐκείνης τῆς ἡμέρας ἐγένετο ὡς λῆρος τὰ ῥήματά μου. καὶ ἠνάγ-
κασέ με οἰκονομῆσαι ναοὺς τῶν εἰδώλων. 7. κἀγὼ οὖν ὁ δύστη-
10 νος ἐποίησα τὴν συμβουλὴν αὐτῆς καὶ τελείως ἀπέστη ἡ δόξα
τοῦ θεοῦ ἀπ᾽ ἐμοῦ καὶ ἐσκοτίσθη τὸ πνεῦμά μου, καὶ ἐγενόμην
γέλως τοῖς εἰδώλοις καὶ δαίμοσιν.

8 Διὰ τοῦτο ἀπέγραψα ταύτην μου τὴν διαθήκην ἵνα οἱ

MSS PQ = Rec. B. § 5. κἀγὼ οὖν ὁ δόλιος (+ καὶ πανάθλιος Q) κι-
νουμένου μου πικροῦ καὶ ἀσώτου βέλους τοῦ ἔρωτος τῆς κόρης, ἔδωκα ἐπί-
σχυσιν, καὶ (πικροῦ ... ἐπισχ. καὶ Q: ἔρως παρ᾽ αὐτῇ P) ἔφερέν μοι πέντε
ἀκρίδας (P f. 24ᵛ) λέγων (+ μοι Q)· λάβε ταύτας τὰς ἀκρίδας καὶ σύντριψον
αὐτὰς ἐπ᾽ ὀνόματος (·ατι Q) τοῦ θεοῦ Μολόχ (+ καὶ Ῥαφὰ Q), καὶ (+ νῦν P)
κοιμηθήσομαι μετὰ σου ὅπερ καὶ ἐτέλεσα (+ ἐγὼ τὴν ἀπώλειαν ταύτην Q)
MSS PQ = Rec. B pro § 6 textum praebent hunc καὶ (+ ταῦτα ποιήσας ὁ ἄθλιος Q) εὐθὺς ἀπέστη (+ ἀπ᾽ ἐμοῦ Q) τὸ πνεῦμα (+ τὸ ἅγιον Q)
τοῦ θεοῦ, (+ ἀπ᾽ ἐμοῦ P, + καὶ ἅπασα ἡ δόξα καὶ ἡ σοφία Q), καὶ ἐγενόμην
ἀσθενὴς ὡσεὶ λῆρος τοῖς ῥήμασί μου (καὶ τὰ ῥήματά μου ὡς ἡ — ὡσεὶ Kurz
— λῆρος Q)· ἐξ οὗ καὶ ἠναγκάσθην (-σθη P) παρ᾽ αὐτῆς (αὐτοῖς Q) κτίσαι
ναὸν τῶν εἰδώλων τῇ Βαὰλ (Τηβὰλ Q) καὶ τῷ (— Q) Ῥαφὰ καὶ τῷ (τὸν)
Μολὸχ καὶ τοῖς λοιποῖς εἰδώλοις (τῶν λοιπῶν εἰδώλων Q)
MS H = Rec. A. § 6. 7 ἀπήρθη ego· ἐπήρθη ms

MS H = Rec A pro sectione 7 textum, ut mihi videtur, interpolatum
praebet nunc ἐγὼ δὲ ὁ δύστινος ᾠκοδόμησα διὰ τὸ πάνυ ἀγαπᾶν αὐτήν. καὶ
διερράγη ἡ βασιλεία μου καὶ ὀλόλυξα μεγάλως, καὶ ἐσκορπίσθη τὸ πν(εῦ)μα
καὶ ἐδόθη εἰς δουλείαν τὸν ὄρθρου (* f. 34ʳ) σκῆπτρα ι᾽· τὸ συνη (sic) κατὰ
⟨τὰ⟩ ῥηθέντα μοι ὑπὸ τῶν δαιμόνων, ὅτι ἔφησάν μοι· ὑπὸ τὰς χεῖρεις ἡμῶν
μέλλεις τελευτῆσαι «
MSS PQ = Rec B a sectione 7 usque ad finem praebent breviorem et, ut
mihi videtur, meliorem textum. § 7 9 κἀγὼ οὖν P· ὅπερ ἐγὼ Q   10 ἐποίησα
... αὐτῆς P. κατηργασάμην ἅπαντα Q   11 ἀπ᾽ ἐμοῦ post ἀπέστη ponit Q
| 12 καὶ παίγνιον τοῖς δαίμοσιν Q

MS H = Rec. A pro § 8 textum interpolatum praebet hunc καὶ ἔγραψα
τὴν διαθήκην μου ταύτην τοῖς ιουδαίοις καὶ κατέλιπον ταύτην αὐτοῖς εἰς μνημόσυνον πρὸς τελευτῆς μου. ἡ διαθήκη μου φυλαττέσθω παρ᾽ ὑμῶν (ἡμῶν ms.)
MSS PQ = Rec. B § 8. 18 διὰ γὰρ Q

ἀκούοντες εὔχησθε καὶ προσέχητε τοῖς ἐσχάτοις καὶ μὴ τοῖς πρώτοις, ἵνα τελείως εὕρωσι χάριν εἰς τοὺς αἰῶνας· ἀμήν.

εἰς μυστήριον μέγαν κατὰ πνευμάτων ἀκαθάρτων ὥστε γνῶναι ὑμᾶς (ἡμῶν ms.) τῶν πονηρῶν δαιμόνων τὰς μηχανὰς καὶ τῶν ἁγίων (τὸν ἅγιον ms.) ἀγγέλων τὰς δυνάμεις ὅτι ἐνισχύει μέγας κύριος σαβαὼθ ὁ θεὸς τοῦ ἰσραὴλ καὶ ὑπέταξεν ἐπ᾽ ἐμοὶ πάντα τὰ δαιμόνια, ἐν ᾧ ἐδόθη μοι σφραγὶς διαθήκης αἰωνίου. ταῦτα οὖν ἔγραψον ἅπερ κατέλαβον μετὰ τῶν υἱῶν ἰσραὴλ ⌜πν(ευ-μάτ)ων τε πν(εύμ)α τὸ ἀκαθάρτων (f 34ᵛ) ὀνειδισμῶν προσφέρωσιν⌝ εἰς τὰ ἅγια τῶν ἁγίων. § 9. ἐγὼ οὖν σολομὼν υἱὸς δα(νεὶ)δ υἱοῦ ἰεσσαὶ ἔγραψα τὴν διαθήκην μου καὶ ἐσφράγισα αὐτὴν (αὐτῶν ms.) τῷ δακτυλιδίῳ τοῦ θεοῦ. καὶ ἀπέθανον ἐν τῇ βασιλείᾳ μου καὶ προσετέθην μετὰ τῶν π(ατέ)ρων μου ἐν εἰρήνῃ ἐν ἱ(ερουσα)λήμ. καὶ ἐπληρώθη ὁ ναὸς κυρίου τοῦ θεοῦ οὗ ὑπὸ θρόνου αὐτοῦ ποταμὸς (πυρὸς ex Dan. VII 10 suppl. James) ἕλκει· ᾧ παρει-στήκεισαν μυριάδες ἀγγέλων καὶ χιλιάδες ἀρχαγγέλων καὶ χερουβὶμ ἐπικρά-ζοντα σεραφὶμ κεκραγότα καὶ λέγοντα· ἅγιος, ἅγιος, ἅγιος κύριος σαβαὼθ καὶ εὐλογητὸς εἶ εἰς τοὺς αἰῶνας τῶν αἰώνων ἀμήν

§ 10. δόξα σοι, ὁ θεός μου, καὶ κ(ύριο)ς, δόξα σοι
σὺν τῇ ὑπ(ε)ρευκ(λεεῖ)(?) θ(εοτό)κῳ καὶ τῷ τιμίῳ
προδρόμῳ καὶ πάντας ἁγίους, δόξα σοι.

MSS PQ = Rec. B   **1** ἀκούοντες λαχόντες P | εὔχησθε Q εὔχεσθε P, + μοι ὅπερ ῥυσθῶ τοῦ σκότους καὶ τῆς κολάσεως τῆς πικρᾶς ὡς θεῷ παρή-κοος (Kurz. παρήκωος ms.) Q | προσέχητε Q προσέχετε P, + ὀφείλην τοῖς ἀνθρώποις Q | καὶ μὴ P τὰ μᾶλλον ἢ Q   **2** τελείως — Q

Lectiones novas et emendationes ex ms. N (Sancti Saba) v in App., infra p 112 ff.

ΔΙΑΘΗΚΗ ΣΟΛΟΜΩΝΤΟΣ

Recensio C

Prologus

1. Ἐγένετο μετὰ τὸ ἀποθανεῖν τὸν Δαυεὶδ τὸν βασιλέαν
5 προσευξαμένου τοῦ υἱοῦ αὐτοῦ οἰκοδομεῖν τὴν Σιών, προσευχο-
μένου δὲ αὐτοῦ ἦλθεν φωνὴ λέγουσα· »Σολομῶν υἱὸς Δαυείδ,
κύριος ὁ θεὸς τῶν πατέρων σου αὐτὸς εἰσακούσας τῆς προσευχῆς
σου δέδωκά σοι πᾶσαν τὴν ἰσχὺν, καὶ ἰδοὺ ἔσῃ βλέπων πᾶσαν
τὴν σοφίαν λελευκασμένην ὡς χιόναν ἐνώπιόν σου καὶ τῶν
10 ὀφθαλμῶν σου.« 2. Ταῦτα ἀκούσας καὶ ὥσπερ ὑπό τινος αὐγῆς
ἐλλαμφθεὶς καὶ ἐμπνευσθεὶς τὴν διάνοιαν ἣν παρακαλῶν καὶ
δεόμενος τοῦ θεοῦ λέγων οὕτως »θεὲ αἰώνιε«, ἔφη, »θεὲ ἀπε-
ρινόητε, ἄκτιστε καὶ ἀόρατε, ὁ πάντα κτίσας τῷ νεύματί σου
μόνῳ, ἔπιδε τοῦ δούλου σου δέησιν καὶ διασάφησον τὴν τῶν
15 χειρῶν σου ἐνέργειαν. 3. καὶ γὰρ ὅσα ἐποίησας σὺ ὁ θεός, πρὸς
σύστασιν πάντων τῶν ἡμετέρων σωμάτων ἐποίησας καὶ ὠφέλειαν,
τά τε καρποφόρα καὶ μὴ καρποφόρα δένδρα, θηρία τε καὶ πε-
τεινά, καὶ αὐτὸν δὴ τὸν θεῖον ἀέραν ὃν πᾶσα φύσις ἐπιπνέει.
4. τὸ μέγιστόν σε τοίνυν δυσωπῶ ἵνα διανοιχθῶσί μου οἱ ὀφθαλ-
20 μοὶ καὶ ὁρῶ τὴν ἀποκεκρυμμένην σοφίαν σου, ὅτι εὐλογητὸς εἶ
εἰς τοὺς αἰῶνας· ἀμήν.« 5. ταῦτα τοίνυν εὐξαμένου φωνῆς

MSS VW. conspectum titulorum vide infra, p. 99*. 4 τὸν (1°)· — V
6 αὐτοῦ αὐτὸν V | φωνή. φο(νὴν) V 7 ὁ — W | εἰσακούσει V
9 καὶ ἐν τοῖς ὀφθαλμοῖς σου W § 2 l. 11 ἐλαμφῆς ἐπνευσθῆς (— καὶ) V
| παρακαλῶ V 12 οὕτως — V | ἀπεῤιν. + θεὲ ἐών V 18 τὸν
εὔματι V 14 ἔπιδε· ἐπι ἐπι V § 3. l. 16 ὑμετέρων V § 4 l. 21 αἰῶ-
νας τῶν αἰώνων W | § 5. τοίνυι δεύτερον V

ἤκουσεν λεγούσης· »Σολομῶν, Σολομῶν, κύριος ὁ θεός σου ἐρεῖ·
·ἄρξαι κτίζειν μου οἶκον εἰς ὄνομα τῆς ἐπουρανίου μου Σιών.·
καὶ ἤρξατο οἰκοδομεῖν τὴν Σιών.

8. Καὶ ταῦτα εἰπὼν ἔφη μετὰ κλανθμοῦ * »δέομαί σου,
βασιλεῦ Σολομῶν, ἵνα μή με κατακαύσῃς ὑπὸ τῆς σφραγῖδος,
καὶ ὑπόσχομαί σοι ἐν ὅρκῳ ὅτι εἰς τὸ ὄνομα τοῦ Ὄντος προσ-
φέρω σοι πάντα τὰ δαιμόνια καὶ παραδώσω σοι ταῦτα ὑποχειρίους δι᾽ ἑνὸς ἑκάστου σημείων καὶ τῶν δυνατῶν καὶ τῶν δυνα-
μένων καὶ τῶν ἐξουσιαζόντων.« καὶ εἶπον ἐγὼ Σολομῶν· »εἰ
τοῦτο ποιήσεις, ἔσῃ ἐλεύθερος.« 9. καὶ λέγει μοι· »λάμβανε
ἐρίφους μελανοὺς ἀγεννήτους εἰς ἀριθμὸν ποσουμένων να´, καὶ
ἔνεγκέ μοι μάχαιραν καινὴν τρίκωλον μελανοκέρατον, καὶ ἐκδεί-
ραντες τὰς ἐρίφους.« 10. εἶτα προσέταξεν ἐναχθῆναι αἷμαν ἀν-
θρώπινον τοῦ δευθῆναι τὰ δέρματα καὶ ἔρραψεν αὐτὰ ἀνὰ δύο
φύλλων καὶ ἔρρυψεν αὐτὰ ἐν τριφδίῳ, καὶ εὗρεν γεγραμμένον
ἑνὸς ἑκάστου ὄνομα ἰδιοχείρως ἐν τοῖς δερματίοις καὶ τὸ ση-

MSS VW. 1 λεγούσης + αὐτὸν W, + πρὸς αἶτὸν U
   MSS UVW   πρὸς αὐτὸν· Σολομῶν   ἐρεῖ exscr editores ex MS U
cf supra, Introd p. 20 f. | ἐρεῖ U ἔρει V, ἐρεῖ W
   MSS VW   Textus recensionis C cc. I—IX 7 cum recc. A et B supra
pp. 5*—37* exhibitur.   4 § 8 κλανμοι W | * V f. 439ᵛ   5 βασ. Σολ
βασιλεύς V   7 παραδίδο V   8 ἑκάστοι αὐτοῦ V | σημείων + καὶ εἶπα
ἐγὼ σολομῶν καὶ V | τ(ὸν) δυνατ(ὸν) καὶ τ(ὸν) διναμενον καὶ τ(ὸν) ἐξουσιά-
ζοντα V   9 τοὺς ἐξουσιάζοντας W   10 ἔσῃ ἔστο V
   MSS TUVW. § 9 l 10 καὶ λέγει μοι VW\ Δαίμων σφραγισάμενος ὑπὸ
Σαλυμῶνος τάδε εἶπε δαιμονίων δυνάμεις καὶ ὀνόματα (ὀνομ. inter lineas sub
δαιμ. δυναμ. scr) hoc modo inc. fragmentum ms. U   §§ 9—10 l. 10—14 καὶ
.. δέρματα ἕτερα πρᾶξις τῆς αὐτῆς. ὁμοίως παιδίον παρθένον καθαρὸν·
κάθισον εἰς ἄμουλον (f 39b²) καὶ ξῦσον μετὸ ἔλαιον ἀπὸ τηγανίου κόλον εἰς
τὴν παλάμην τοῦ παιδίου, καὶ λέγε ταῦτα τὰ ὀνόματα ἕως ἑπτὰ φορές· Ναχπιέλ·
Ναχπιέλ· Χατμὴν Ἑρμὴν μελανοκέρατο τοῦ δευθῆναι τὰ δέρματα, καὶ μετὰ
τοῦ δευθῆναι τὰ δέρματα λαβὼν ὁ βεελζεβοὺλ τὰ να̅ δέρματα hoc modo inc
sectio in Clavicula — ms. T   § 9. 1 11 ἀγεννήτους· pr. καὶ + καὶ ἔλαβεν ἐκ
πάντων τῶν θρεμμάτων αὐτοῦ V | ποσουμένων UW ποσον V   12 τρίκωλον
ego· τρήκλον V, τρίκλον vel τρίηλον UW   § 10. l. 14 δευσῆναι V | καὶ
— TV | ἔρραψεν ... τριφδίῳ TV· ἐποίησα οὕτως καὶ ἔρρυψεν αὐτὰ ἐν
τριωδίῳ ἀνὰ δίο φύλλων UW | ἔρραψεν ἔραψεν V . ἔρρυψεν ἔραψεν .. ἔρηψεν T,
ἔρηψεν .. ἔρηψεν U, ἔρριψεν U, ἔρυψεν W   15 τριφδίῳ l. fortasse τριόδῳ,
pr. τῷ T | γεγραμμένα mss   16 ἐν ... αὐτοῦ (3°) p. 78*, 1· — T | ση-
μεῖον αὐτοῦ σιμάδη του V

μεῖον αὐτοῦ καὶ τὴν ἐνέργειαν αὐτοῦ καὶ τὴν δεσποτείαν αὐτοῦ
οὕτως·

X. Τζιανφιέλ· * δεσπόζει ϱμ´· ἐνεργεῖ δὲ εἰς τὸ ἀναγγεῖλαι
τὰ παρεληλυθότα καὶ τὰ ἐνεστῶτα καὶ τὰ μέλλοντα. 2. Φα-
5 ϱάν· * δεσπόζει ͺα´· ἐνεργεῖ δὲ εἰς τὸ πληρεῖν πάντα τὰ θελήματα. δύναται καὶ πῦρ ἀναβιβάζειν εἰς τὸν ἀέρα καὶ ὕδωρ
κατάγειν καὶ ἀστέρας ὑποδεικνύειν. 3. Μαχουμέτ· * δεσπόζει σ´·
ἐνεργεῖ εἰς τὸ γελᾶν ἀνθρώπους ἀλλήλων. ποιεῖ δὲ καὶ τετράποδα λαλεῖν ἀνθρωπίνως καὶ ἀναφαίνεσθαι τοὺς ἀνθρώπους
10 ἀκεφάλους. ποιεῖ δὲ τούτους * γυμνοὺς περιπατεῖν ἀλλὰ καὶ
τὰ ἄλογα κτήνη βλέπειν ἀλλήλα ὡς θηρία ἄγρια. 4. Ναπούρ· *
δεσπόζει ν´· δύναται ἐν μιᾷ ὥρᾳ παρέχειν χρυσίον καὶ ἀργύριον
ὅπερ διεπράξας πρὸς τῆς ἀπαντῆς σου τῆς ζωῆς καὶ τῆς γεν-
νήσεως μέχρι τότε, ὁμοίως καὶ στολὰς μὴ ῥηγνυμένας. 5. Ῥοάπτ·
15 * δεσπόζει υ´· ἐνεργεῖ δὲ εἰς τὸ γενέσθαι φρόνιμον καὶ νοῦν
ἐμφύειν. 6. Παρέλ * δεσπόζει κε´· ἐνεργεῖ δὲ εἰς τὸ ἀνθῆσαι
τὰ δένδρα παρὰ καιρόν, φῦναι δὲ καὶ βοτάνας εἰς ξηρὸν ξύλον.

MSS TUVW. **1** δεσπ. αὐτοῦ ἀρχὴν τον V   **2** οὕτως UW ταῦτα
T, — V

C. X 1. l. **3** Τζιανφιέλ TV Τζηαν. UW, pr. ā´ T, pr. ὁ πρῶτος ἔχει
ὄνομαν V. In hoc loco et in locis sequentibus asterisco denotatis mss. habent
post nomen sive ante nomen signum (σημεῖον) daemonis, in hoc loco signum
ante nomen ponunt UW, in marg. sin. apud nomina numeros ab α´ ad ις´ scr V,
in textu ante nomina numeros ab initio ad finem scr. T | δεσπ.· + ἐνερ-
γίαις T | ϱμ´ ϱ´ T | δὲ — V   **4** § 2. A secundo ad extremum ante nomen
scr. ὁ T | in locis XI (§§ 2, 3, 4, 5, 8, 11, 14, 17, 18, 29, 45) signum post δεσπόζει
ponit T, in locis V (§§ 12, 38 40, 42, 44) signum post numerum imperii (= δε-
σποτείας) ponit T   **5** ͺα´ η´ U | πληρεῖν UW· πληρῇ V, πληροῦν T |
πάντα — V   **6** δύναται· pr. καὶ V | εἰς. + τω transversis lineis delet. U
| ἀναβιβάζει V   **7** κατάγει UVW | ὑποδεικνήει V   § 3. l. **8** ἐνεργεῖ
δὲ T | εἰς τὸ — T | ἀνθρώποις UVW | ἀλλήλων τοῖς ἀνθρώποις T |
καὶ — T   **9** ἀναφαιν. Γ νὰ φαίνεται V, φαίνεσθαι UW | τοὺς ἀνθρ. ἀκεφ.
ego οἱ ἀν(θρωπ)οι ἀκέφαλοι mss.   **10** * L f. 40ᵀ1 | γυμνοὺς T — UVW
11 τὰ ἀλ. κτήνη ego· τοῖς ἀλόγοις κτήνεσιν mss. | ἐβλέπει T | ἀλλήλα
ego· ἀλλήλοις TUW, ἀλείης V | ὡς. ὁ V   § 4. l. **12** ἀργύριον καὶ χρυ-
σίον T | ἄργυρ < U   **13** τ. ἀπαντῆς U· τῆς ἀπαντῇ W, τὴν ἀπάντη V,
τὴν T | τῆς ζωῆς καὶ — T   **14** μέχρι τότε ὁμοίως V — UW, ὁμοίως
τότε μέχρι T | καὶ — T   § 5. l. **15** τινὰ ἀφρόνιμον T | φρόνιμον V,
κ. νοῦν ἐμφ. — T   **16** ἐμφυνῇ UVW | § 6. Παρελκοζίου (sine signo) κοζίου
pro signo scr Γ   **17** δένδρι παρὰ καιρῷ V | φῦναι· φόνε T | δὲ — T

7. Ἀσμοδεῶ· δεσπόζει ξ΄· δύναται ἐν τῷ θέρει παρέχειν χιόνας καὶ βρέχειν, ἀλλὰ καὶ κεράσια παρέχειν ἐν χειμῶνι.

8. Μπηλέτ· * δεσπόζει σ΄· δύναται εἴ τι θέλει ποιῆσαι ἐν τῷ μέρει τῆς Παλαιστίνης. 9. Λασαράκ· * δεσπόζει τ΄ δύναται ποιῆσαι πολέμους καὶ παρατάξεις καὶ νίκας καὶ ἀνδραγαθίας. 10. Ῥααμέτ * δεσπόζει σ΄ οὗτος προλέγει τὰ μέλλοντα καὶ πλουτοδοτεῖ. 11. Τζερεπόνες· * δεσπόζει ρν΄· δύναται ποιῆσαι καὶ συντύχωσιν ἱστορίαι καὶ τὰ εἴδολα, ἀκούειν δὲ καὶ ὀρνέων * φωνάς. 12. Νταρωγάν· * δεσπόζει τ΄ ἐνεργεῖ δὲ εἰς τὸ καθαρεῦσαι πᾶσαν ῥυπαρίαν καὶ τοὺς πτωχοὺς ὡς πλουσίους ποιῆσαι, καὶ εἰ ἔσται αὐτοῦ, βασιλεύει. 13. Πελών· * δεσπόζει ͵α ἐνεργεῖ δὲ εἰς τὸ παραδοῦναι κάστρα καὶ πόλεις καὶ χώρας. 14. Σουπιέλ· * δεσπόζει ͵α· ἐνεργεῖ δὲ εἰς τὸ ποιῆσαι ἐπανάστησιν κατὰ τοῦ δεσπότου καὶ παραδοῦναι ἑτέρῳ τῷ ἄρχοντι εἰς τὸ ἄρχειν καὶ ἐλευθερῶσαι δεσμίους ἐν ταῖς φυλακαῖς ὁμοίως καὶ αἰχμαλότους. 15. Ὀριένς * δεσπόζει φ΄ πνευμάτων τῶν ἀνατολικῶν δύναται καὶ αὐτὸς ὁμοίως ὅσα δύνανται οἱ πάντες. 16. Ἀμεμῶν· * δεσπόζει μεσημβρινῶν πνευμάτων φ΄· δύναται καὶ αὐτὸς ὁμοίως.

17. Ἐλτζήν· * δεσπόζει βορείων ** πνευμάτων φ΄· δύναται καὶ αὐτὸς ὁμοίως. 18. Πανῶν· * δεσπόζει καὶ οὗτος τῶν πνευμάτων τῶν θαλασσίων χ΄· ἐνεργεῖ δὲ καὶ αὐτὸς εἰς ἀνέμους

MSS TUVW. 1 § 7. ἀσμοδέος T, ἀσμοδεὼ U | ἐν τῷ ... δύναται (1 ͵3) — T | παρέχειν· κατεχ < V   2 βρέξει V | χειμωναν V

§ 8 1 4 Παλαιστίνης TU παλεστ. V, παληστ. W   § 9 1. 5 ἀντραγαθίας V   6 § 10. Ῥααμέτ· ῥαεμέτ V, ῥαιμὲτ T, + καὶ αὐτὸς UW | οὗτος .. πλουτοδ. δύναται τοῦ προλέγει⟨ν⟩ τὰ μελ. κ. πλουτοδοτεῖν T | πλουτωδωτή VW   7 § 11. τζεραπώνες UW | καὶ· — W, 1. fortasse ἵνα? 8 συντήχωσιν UW | συντειχόσην εστορίε V, συντιχοσιν ηδοριαι T | καὶ ἀκούην φωνᾶς ὀρνέων πετεινῶν T | δὲ — V | * explicit fragmentum ms. U

MSS TVW. 9 § 12. ἰτάρογαν T | ἐνεργεῖ δὲ δύναται T | καριεῦσαι πᾶσα T   § 13. 1. 12 κάστρα ... χώρας κάστοι κ. χώρας T   18 § 14 signum om. T | ͵α μ΄ T | ἐπανάστασι V   14 τῷ ἀρχ εἰς — T | 15 τὲς φυλακὲς W, τῆς φυλακῆς V   16 § 15. τῶν — V | ἀνατολικῶν τῶν πνευμάτων tr. V   17 δύναται καὶ tr. V | δύνανται δύνοντ⟨ο⟩ T 18 § 16. ἀμαιμῶν V   20 § 17. ἐλτζεῖν V, ἐλτζὶν T | * V f. 440ʳ | βορίην V | ** W f. 269ᵛ   21 ὁμοίως· οὗτως T   §§ 18—19 ll. 21-p. 80*, 1 καὶ οὗτως ... αὐτὸς — T   § 18. 1. 22 θαλασσίην V | καὶ — V

καὶ πλοῖα. 19. Βούλ· * δεσπόζει καὶ αὐτὸς πνευμάτων τῆς
δύσεως φ'· δύναται καὶ αὐτὸς ὁμοίως. 20. Ἀμπατζούτ· δεσπόζει καὶ αὐτὸς ‚α· ἐνεργεῖ δὲ εἰς πᾶσαν τέχνην καὶ μάθησιν
καὶ φρόνησιν καὶ γράμματα. 21. Ἀσταρώθ· * δεσπόζει ‚β·
5 ἐνεργεῖ δὲ εἰς τοὺς ἀπερχομένους καὶ ἐξερχομένους καὶ στήκον-
τας· ποιεῖ δὲ καὶ θησαυροὺς φανερωθῆναι. 22 Λουπῆτ· *
δεσπόζει ‚ε· ἐνεργεῖ δὲ εἰς τὸ ἀκούειν καὶ κράτειν καὶ πράττειν,
κτίζειν καὶ χαλᾶν καὶ βλέπειν καὶ μεταφέρειν ἀπὸ τόπου εἰς
τόπον. 23. Ἀπολῆν· * δεσπόζει ‚ϱ'· ἐνεργεῖ δὲ εἰς τὸ πλουτῆσαι
10 καὶ παρέχειν χρυσίον καὶ ἄργυροι πολύν. 24. Ἀστερώθ· * δεσπόζει ‚α'· ἐνεργεῖ δὲ εἰς βασιλείας καὶ πόλεις καὶ κάστρα καὶ
πύργους καὶ κτίσματα. 25 Λάτζηφερ· δεσπόζει ‚γ ἐνεργεῖ εἰς
πάντας τοὺς ἄρχοντας δηλαδὴ καὶ εἰς τοὺς βασιλεῖς, καὶ δύναται
καὶ ὅσα θέλει.. 26. Μαγώτ· δεσπόζει καὶ αὐτὸς ‚δ· ἐνεργεῖ *
15 δὲ εἰς τὸ λέγειν καὶ ποιεῖν. 27. Καράπ· * δεσπόζει ‚ζ ἐνεργεῖ
δὲ εἰς πόλεις καὶ κάστρα καὶ οἴκους. 28. Οὔλεος· * δεσπόζει
μιᾶς φυλῆς, ἤτοι ‚α. ποιεῖ δὲ μεγιστάνους καὶ στολὰς λαμπρὰς
καὶ παίγνια καὶ παροφθαλμίας, καὶ ποιεῖ ὄνους τοὺς ἀνθρώπους
καὶ ἄλλα ζῷα οἷα θέλεις. 29. Κρινέλ· * δεσπόζει ‚σ· ἐνεργεῖ
20 δὲ εἰς τὸ ἀναιρεῖν ἄνδρας τε καὶ γυναῖκας, ποιεῖ δὲ μάχας καὶ
ταραχὰς καὶ ὀχλήσεις. 30. Τουγέλ· * δεσπόζει ‚χ'· ποιεῖ δὲ ἀγά-

---

MSS TVW. 1 § 19. πνευμάτων . . ὁμοίως τῶν τ(ῆς) δύσεως πν(ευ-
μάτ)ων δύναντ(αι) καὶ αὐτὸς ὅσα δύναντ(αι) οἱ πάντες T | καὶ pr. δὲ W |
§ 20 1. 3 δὲ — W | κ. μάθησιν — T   4 κ γράμματα V· κ πρᾶγμα T,
— W   § 21 1. 5 δὲ καὶ αὐτὸς T | τοὺς — T | κ ἐξερχομ. — T
§ 22. 1 7 ε' T | ἐνεργεῖν W | δὲ καὶ αὐτὸς T | τὸ τοὺς T | καὶ (2°)
— VW   8 κ. χαλᾶν ... βλέπειν — W | χαλᾶν ego· χαλνᾶν T, χαλάτι V
| μεταφέρει VW | τόπου τόπον VW   9 § 23. Ἀπολήν V. ἀπόλην W,
ἀπολιῖ T | ϱ' φ' W   10 παρέχει TW | § 24. ἀστηρώϑ W, ὁ ἕτερος
ἀστηρώϑ Γ | καὶ οὗτος δεσπόζει V   11 ἐνεργεῖ   κάστρα δύναται δὲ
καὶ βασιλείαν πόλιν κάστρη T | κ. πύργους — W, πυργοὺς T   12 § 25. λατ-
ζιφέρ T | ‚γ ἐνεργεῖ εἰς — T   13 δηλαδὴ + δύνανται T | κ δύνανται
θέλει V δύναται ὅσα θέλει T, — W   14 § 26. μαγώτ W | καὶ αὐ-
τὸς — T | ἐνεργεῖ δύναται T | * f. 40ᵛ2   15 λέγειν· + ἐνεργεῖν T
§ 27. 1 16 πόλιν κάστροι T | § 28. οὐλατὸς T   17 ἤτοι ἤτι V, ἥτης T |
α' T | ἐνεργεῖ δὲ ποιεῖν μεγιστάνους T   18 παροφϑ. TW παρεροα (α,
ε, et ο supra lin) in fine lineae, ὀφθαλμίας in linea altera scr. V | ποιεῖ ego
ποιεῖν W, πιήν V, ἣν T   19 ἀλλα ζῶα οἱ καὶ θελ < V | θέλης T,
θελ < W | § 29. σ' T | ἐνεργεῖν W   20 καὶ ποιεῖ δὲ T   21 κ. ὀχ-
λησ. — T | § 30. τουγελ T | ἀγάπας καὶ φιλίας W

·πας, πόλεις πρὸς πόλεις καὶ ἀνθρώπους μετὰ ἀνθρώπων καὶ
ἄνδρας μετὰ γυναικῶν. 31. Σεταριέλ· * δεσπόζει κ´· φανερεῖ
θησαυρούς, ποιεῖ δὲ καὶ τὸν χρώμενον ἀθεώρητον, παρὰ μηδενὸς θεωρούμενον. παρέχει δὲ καὶ ταῖς γυναιξὶν γνώμας χρηστάς.
5 32. Φακανέλ· * δεσπόζει ζ· ἐνεργεῖ δὲ εἰς πάντα τὰ θελήματα
τοῦ βουλομένου.

33. Ὀέλ * δεσπόζει γ· δύναται δὲ καὶ αὐτὸς ὅσα δύνανται
οἱ πάντες αὐτὸς μόνος. 34. Δένελ· * δεσπόζει λ´· ἐνεργεῖ δὲ
εἰς τὸ παρέχειν χρυσίον καὶ ἀργύριον καὶ φέρει γυναῖκας παρὰ
10 μηδενὸς θεωρούμενος. 35. Σαρατιέλ· * δεσπόζει ρ´· ἐνεργεῖ δὲ
εἰς σεληνιαζομένους· δοκεῖ δὲ καὶ τὴν σελήνην καταβιβάζειν.
36. Μυρατζιέλ· * δεσπόζει β´ ἐνεργεῖ δὲ εἰς στρατείας καὶ πο-
λιορκίας καὶ πόλεων αἰχμαλωσίας. 37. Σανσωνιέλ· * δεσπόζει
ξτ´· ἐνεργεῖ δὲ εἰς τὸ ποιῆσαι κλύδωνας μεγίστους καὶ ἀνέμους
15 σφοδρούς. 38. Ἀσιέλ· * δεσπόζει ι´· ἐνεργεῖ εἰς τὸ φανερωθῆναι
τὰ κλεπτόμενα καὶ τοὺς κλέπτας καὶ θησαυρούς τινας, ἐπιγινω-
σκομένους μὲν εἰς τόπον, μὴ γινωσκομένους δὲ ἐν ποίῳ μέρει
κεῖνται τοῦ τόπου. 39. Καστιέλ * δεσπόζει σ´· ἐνεργεῖ δὲ εἰς
τὸ ὑγιᾶναι πᾶσαν ἀσθένειαν. 40 Μεινγέτ· * δεσπόζει ξ´· δύνα-

MSS TVW. 1 πόλεις ego πόλας V, πολλὰς TW | πόλεις (2°) W
πόλας V, πόλιν T | ἄνθρωπον μετὰ ἀνθρώπου T   2 γυναικὸς (-κος bis,
primum compendio, tum in linea altera scr) T | § 31. Σεταριέλ: σε in fine
lineae, εταριέλ in linea altera scr. V | φανερεῖ ... θεωρούμενον (l. 4) exscr
Gaulminius in notis ad Psellum, de oper. daem. (Migne, PG 122, col. 829, n. 25)
φανερεῖ· ἐμφαίνει Gaulmin   8 παρὰ ὑπὸ Gaulmin | οὐδενὸς T   4 δὲ
— T   5 § 32 καὶ ἐνεργει (ἐν. ex δύναμαι corr.) εἰς T
§ 33 l. 7 δύναται ... μόνος καὶ ὁδὰν (f. 41ʳ 1) ὁ δύναται οἱ πάντες
αὐτὸς μόνος ἐνεργεῖ, et ad marg sup in med col. scr. λα´ T | καὶ δύναται
αὐτὸς ὅσα δυν ἡ ὅλη (l. αἱ ὅλοι) αὐτὸς μόνος του V   7 § 34. Δένελ V
ὁ δελήήλ T, νένελ W | λ´ VW σ´ T   9 ἀργ. κ. χρυσ. T | κ. φόρει T
κ. φέρνει V, φέρει δὲ καὶ W   10 μηδεν. μιθεν < V   § 35. l. 11 σεληνι-
αζ. ἑλληνικὰ πάθη T   12 § 36. μιρατζηέλ W, μυρακιέλ T, + ὁ δαίμων
καὶ αὐτὸς (ante signum) W | β´ β T | εἰς· εἰ V | στρατείας ἀστραπὰς T
| καὶ πόλεων tr. W   13 § 37. σανσονιέλ T   14 ξτ´ ξ καὶ τ´ V |
κλύδωνας ς ex ν corr W | μεγίστους T μεγιστ < V, μεγάλους W   15 post
σφοδρούς signum scr V, post spatium purum parvulum relictum scr. * signum
W, tum ἐνεργεῖ δὲ (— V) καὶ αὐτὸς ὁμοίως add. VW | § 38. ι´ — T
καὶ ἐνεργεῖ T   16 ἐπιγιν. ... μὴ — T   17 μὲν δὲ V | ἐν ... τόπου.
ἐν ποίῳ τόπῳ κεῖται W   18 κεῖται V | § 39 ἀστιέλ T | ἐνεργεῖ ὀφε-
λεῖ V   19 ὑγιένε V | § 40 μεινγέτ W, μηνγέτ V, μινγότ T

ται ὄφεις καὶ δράκοντας ποιῆσαι. 41. Ἐνοδάς * δεσπόζει ν΄
δύναται * εἰς τὸν ἀέραν πῦρ ἀνάγειν καὶ ἅρματα ἐμφανῶς κα
τακαῦσαι. 42. Ἀτανιανούς· * δεσπόζει ,α΄ δύναται δοῦναι πᾶ
σαν τέχνην καὶ γνῶσιν καὶ φρόνησιν τοῖς ἀνθρώποις.

5　　43. Μυραγκούς· * δεσπόζει λ΄· δύναται κρατεῖν τὸν ἥλιον
τοῦ μὴ φαίνεσθαι. 44. Ποτζέτιες· * δεσπόζει σ΄· δύναται ποιῆ
σαι ἀνθρώπους καὶ ζῶα ἀνελθεῖν εἰς τὸν ἀέραν 45. Ἄνετ *
δεσπόζει ρ΄· γνωρίζει δὲ ὅλας τὰς πέτρας καὶ τοὺς μαργάρους
ποιεῖ καὶ τὰ ἄλλα μέταλλα. 46. Παλτάφωτε * δεσπόζει ι΄·
10　ποιεῖ γνωρίζειν πάντα τὰ βότανα καὶ ποῦ ἕκαστον ἐνεργεῖ καὶ
ὠφελεῖ. 47. Σαπαρατζήλ· * δεσπόζει ν΄· ποιεῖ γνωρίζειν τὰ
ὄρνεα πάντα καὶ ποῦ ἕκαστον ἐνεργεῖ. 48. Ταρσεύς· * δεσπόζει ξ΄·
ποιεῖ δὲ γνωρίζειν τὰ δένδρα καὶ ποῦ ἕκαστον ἐνέργεῖ. 49. Ναβέλ
* δεσπόζει μ΄· ποιεῖ δὲ γνωρίζει τὰ τετράποδα πάντα καὶ ποῦ
15　ἕκαστον ὠφελεῖ. 50. Σαταήλ· * δεσπόζει ε΄· ἐνεργεῖ εἰς τοὺς
κροκοδείλους καὶ παρέχει * τούτους εἰς ὑποταγήν. 51. Ναπα
λαικόν· * δεσπόζει ε΄ δύναται ποιῆσαι τὴν ἡμέραν νύκταν καὶ
τὴν νύκταν ἡμέραν. 52. Μαχατάχ· * δεσπόζει ε΄ ἐνεργεῖ δὲ εἰ
τὸ πληθῦναι τὰ ποίμνια καὶ τοὺς ἵππους.
20　　53. Ἐγὼ δὲ ἐν ἀποκρύφῳ θέμενος τόπῳ καταλιμπάνω τοῖς
τέχνοις μου ὅρκῳ παραδοὺς θεοῦ Σαβαὼθ ἁγίου ὀνόματος τοῦ

MSS TVW 1 § 41. * L f. 41ᴦ2　　2 ἀέραν VW· ἄρα T | ἀνάγειν
VW ἀναγαγῇ T　　3 § 42. Ἀτανιανούς· ἀντιναός T, + καὶ αὐτὸς W
4 τέχνην + δοῦναι T | τοὺς ἀνθρώπους T

§ 43. 1 5 μιραγκούς W, μύραχος T | καὶ δύναται T　　6 τοῦ W
— TV | § 44 ποτζέτιος T　7 ἀνελθεῖν T — VW | ἀέρα T, ut semper
§ 45. l. 8 δύναται γνωρίζειν ὅλας T | πέτρας + ποιεῖ T | τοὺς — W
9 ποιεῖ — T | § 46 παλταφάτε T | ι΄ T | V f. 440ᵛ 10 γνωρίζει V
| πάντα — T | ἐνεργεῖν T | ὠφελεῖ καὶ ἐνεργ. V | κ. ὠφελ — Γ
11 § 47. σαρατήλ T | ποιεῖ . . πάντα ἐνεργεῖ δὲ γνωρίζει πᾶν ὄρνεον T
| γνωρείζει V　12 ὄρνεα super βότανα, quod linea expunxit, scr. pr. man.
W | πάντα — W | ἐνεργεῖ καὶ ὠφελεῖ W | § 48 ταρσές V, — T
13 ποιεῖν T | δὲ — W | γνωρίζει T, γνον < (l. γνῶναι) V, + πάντα T
| ἐνεργεῖ· ὀφειλ(εῖν) T | § 49 ναβήλ Γ　14 δὲ — W | ποιεῖ δὲ … ὠφε
λεῖ — T | γνωρίζει W, γνων < V　15 § 50. τασαήλ T | ͵ε W | ἐνερ
γεῖ δὲ T　16 παρέχειν T | * T f. 41ᵛ1 | § 51. ναμπαλαικόν T　17 ͵ε W
| ποιῆσαι κατὰ φαντασίαν T　18 § 52. μακκατάκ W, μαχατάκ V | ε΄ V·
͵ε W, — T　　19 ἵππους + καὶ ἔστην οὕτως, βασιλεῦ σολομῶν V, + τέ
λος T, explicit sectio haec Claviculae cod. T (cod. Harl. f. 41ᵛ1)

μηκέτι τινὶ μεταδοῦναι τοῦτο τὸ μέγα καὶ θεῖον μυστήριον,
ἀλλ' ἐν ἀσφαλεῖ κατέχειν τόπῳ ὡς θησαυρὸν ἀδαπάνητον·
ταῦτα * τοῖς πολλοῖς ἀθεώρητα καὶ ἀπόκρυφα διὰ τοὺς φρικ-
τοὺς ἀπεχώρισα ὅρκους.

XI. Ἐρωτηθεὶς δὲ ὁ Βεελζεβοὺλ, ὃς Ἐντζιανφιὲλ καλεῖται
παρ' ἐμοῦ, εἰ ἔστιν καὶ θήλεα δαιμόνια, τοῦ δὲ φήσαντος εἶναι,
ἐβουλόμην ἰδεῖν. 2. καὶ ἀπελθὼν ὁ τοιοῦτος ἤνεγκεν ἔμπροσθέν
μου τὴν Ὀνοσκελοῦν καλουμένην μορφὴν ἔχουσαν περικαλλῆ καὶ
σῶμα γυναικὸς εὐχρώτου, κτήμας δὲ ἡμιόνου. 3. ἐλθούσης δὲ
αὐτῆς ἔφην αὐτὴν λέγων· »σὺ τίς εἶ,« ἡ δὲ ἔφη μοι· »ἐγώ Ὀνοσκε-
λοῦ καλοῦμαι, πνεῦμα σεσωματοποιημένον. φωλεύω δὲ ἐπὶ τῆς
γῆς· σπήλαιον οἰκῶ ἔνθα χρυσίον κεῖται. 4 ἔχω δὲ πολυποίκιλον τρόπον· ποτὲ μὲν ἀνθρώπους πνίγω ὡς δι' ἀγχόνης, ποτὲ
δὲ ἀπὸ τῆς φύσεως ⸢ἐπιεγκόνων⸣ σκολιάζω αὐτούς. * 5. πλεῖστά
μοι οἰκητήρια· πολλάκις δὲ καὶ συγγίνομαι τοῖς ἀνθρώποις ὡς
γυναῖκάν με εἶναι, πρὸ δὲ τῶν ἄλλων τοὺς μελιχροὺς, οὗτοι
γὰρ καὶ συνάστροί μού εἰσιν· καὶ γὰρ τὸ ἄστρο μου οὗτοι λάθρα
καὶ φανερῶς προσκυνοῦσιν.« 6. ἐπηρώτησα δὲ αὐτὴν ἐγὼ Σολο-
μῶν· »πόθεν γεννᾶσαι;« ἡ δὲ ἔφη· »ἀπὸ φωνῆς βηρσαβεὲ ἱππικῆς χρηματικῆς.«

MSS VW. § 53. 2 ἀσφαλια mss.   3 * W f. 170ᵣ | φρικτοὺς V πολοὺς W
C. XI. MSS Tᵒ (= T)VW. inc. narratio acephala de Onoskelou in cod
Harl. 5596 f. 7ᵣ¹ (= Tᵒ, vel T). 5 ἐπηρώτησα δὲ ἐγὼ τὸν βεελζεβοὺλ W |
ὃς ... ἐμοῦ· ὁ καὶ τζιανφιὲλ T | ἐλτζιανφηὲλ V, ἐντζιανφιὲλ W   6 εἰ
— T | ἔστιν W ἔστι T, εἰσι V | θήλεια W, θήλια V | τοῦ· τούτου T |
δὲ + μοι W | εἶναι T ἔνι W, ἦναι φῆ V   7 § 2. ὁ τοιοῦτος W ὅτι
οὗτος V, ὅτι οὗτος T | ἔμπροστέν μου W, ἐμπροστέ μου V, μοι (— ἔμπρ.) T
3 καλουμένη, ἔχουσα V | ἔχουσιν περικαλην W | περικαλῆ V, περιπερ-
καλῆ T   9 κνήμας· μνημος T | ἡμίονος T | § 3. δὲ — T   10 λέγων
λέγε μοι T | τίς εἶ σύ T | μοι — T | ὀνοσκελεῖς V   11 σεσωμα-
τοποιημένον W, σεσῶματοπηείμένω V, σεσωματωμένω T | φωλεύων W |
δὲ — W   12 σπήλαιον οἰκῶ· ἐν σπηλαίω T   § 4. 13 ὡς δι' ἀγχ — T
14 ἀπὸ ὑπὸ T | ἐπιεγκόνων ἐπιενγκόνων W, ἐπὶ ἐγκῶνα V, ἐπὶ ἐγκόναν T;
. ἐπιεγκονῶν, vel ἐπιεγχώνων (= ἐπὶ + ἐν + χώνω, pro χώννυμι)? |
σκολιάζω W, σκωλιάζω V | * T f 7ᵣ² | § 5 πλεῖστα ἔσται μὴ οἰκ. V
ἀλ. μοι δὲ ἔσται οἰκ. V   16 με· μὲν T | πρὸ πρὸς TW | τοὺς μελιχροὺς
VW τ. μελαχρους T, 1. τοῖς μελιχροῖς   17 γὰρ (1ᵒ) + μου V | καὶ
οἷς om T | τὸ γὰρ ἄστρο T | ἄστρον W | λαθ. προσκ. οὗτοι (— κ. φαν.) T
18 προσκ. λαθ. κ. ἐναργῶς W | § 6. ἐρώτησα T   19 γενάσθαι W, γεναστ <
V | ἔφη εἶπεν T, + μη (1. μοι) V | βειρσαβεὲ V, βηρφβεὲ T, βηρσαβεὲλ
W | ἱππ· + καὶ T

7. Καὶ κατέκλεισα αὐτὴν ὑποκάτωθεν τεσσάρων λίθων μεγάλων. ἡ δὲ ἐβόησεν »ἔξελέ με, ἔξελέ με, καὶ ἐνεγκῶ σοι τράπεζαν μετὰ φιάλου καὶ κύλικος, ἥντινα λαβὼν ἐπικρούσας μετὰ
ἱμάσθλης πάντα προσφέρει σοι τὰ ὑποτεταγμένα βρωτὰ καὶ
5 ποτά.« 8. καὶ κελεύσας ἀχθῆναι αὐτήν, ἤνεγκέ μοι τράπεζαν
λιθίνην ἐκ λίθου ἰάσπιδος· μῆκος αὐτῆς ὡς πηχῶν τεσσάρων
καὶ πλάτος πηχῶν τεσσάρων, ἔχουσα καὶ ἐν τοῖς κέρασιν μυρμη-
κολέοντας τέσσαρας λαλοῦντας ἀντ᾽ ἐμοῦ ὅσα ἤθελον. 9. καὶ
δὴ κελεύσας ὁμοῦ καὶ τὴν τράπεζαν ἐναχθῆναι ἐπεζήτουν καὶ
10 τὴν * κύλικαν, μέντοι καὶ λίθον λυχνίτην κύλικος, καὶ περιέχον
σχῆμα ἐπιδέδωκεν, καὶ ἡ μὲν τράπεζα ὅσα βρωτά, ἡ δὲ κύλιξ
ὅσα ποτὰ παρεῖχεν ἐπιζητούμενα.

XII. Ἀνεζήτησα γὰρ ἐκ τῆς σφραγῖδος τὸ Παλτιὲλ Τζαμάλ,
καὶ εὐθέως παραστὰς ἔφη μοι· »Σολομῶν, υἱὲ Δαυείδ, τί ἐκ-
15 πειράζεις τοὺς δούλους σου καὶ τὰς δούλας σου; ἡμεῖς πάντες
ἕως καιροῦ * σου καὶ δουλεύειν καὶ ὑπείκειν καθυποσχόμεθα καὶ
τὰ ὀνόματα ἡμῶν ⌈ἔχειν⌉ ἐν ἀσφαλείᾳ ἐγράψαμεν καὶ τὰς δυνάμεις ἀνηγγείλαμεν ἁπάσας. 2. ὅντινα προστάσσεις, τὸ κελευόμενον ἐκπληρεῖν προθυμότατα. καὶ δεόμεθά σου ἵνα μὴ ἐάσῃς
20 ἡμᾶς ἀπελθεῖν εἰς πέλαγος ἀχανές.«

3. Ἐγὼ δέ φησιν αὐτὸν εἰ ἔστιν ἀνάστασις τῶν τεθνεότων.

MSS ΓVW. 1 § 7. ὑποκάτω Τ	2 ἡ δὲ καὶ W | ἐνεγκῶ Τ· ἐνορ-
κομι (V, ἐν ὅρκῳ μοι W, 1. ἐνορκοῦμαι) δοῦναι VW	3 φιαλίου V | λα-
βὼν καὶ W	4 ἱμάσθλης Τ, ἰσησμάλης W, ἠσασμάλης V | περφέρει Τ
5 § 8 ἐκέλευσαν Τ | τράπεζα ληθήνη ἐκ ληθ < ἰασπίδος V	6 ἰάσπεως W
| ὁ μῖκος Τ | ὡς + ἀπὸ V	7 καὶ (1°) — W | μυρμηγκολέοντας VW,
μυρμυκωλευάντας Τ	8 ἀντ᾽ ἐμοῦ πάντας Τ	§ 9. 1 9 δὴ
— Τ | ἐκέλευσα Τ | ὁμοῦ καὶ — Τ | ἐναχθῆναι μοι ὁμοῦ Τ | ἐπεζή-
τουν W ἐπιζητῶν Τ, ἐπειζήτον V	10 ¹ Τ f. 7ᵛ¹ | μέντοι — Τ | λίθον
λυχνήτην κοίλοικος W, λίθον ληχνεῖτι κύλεικος V, λίθον λιχνύτ(ων) κύλικες Τ
| καὶ (2°) — Τ | περιέχοντα VW, ἐνπεριέχων Τ	11 ἐπιδέδοκεν W, ἐπι-
δώδεκα Γ | ὅσα + περιεῖχεν Τ	12 ποτὰ — Τ | παρεῖχεν περιεῖχεν Τ
C. XII. 1. 13 παλτιὲλ Τ	14 εὐθέως — Τ | υἱὸς Τ	15 σου (1°)
— Τ | ἡμεῖς· ἐμῆς V | πάντες πάντοτε Τ	16 * V f 441ʳ | σου — W
| καὶ τὰ πλὴν ἔπειτα V	17 ἡμῶν: εἰ μὴ V | ἔχειν Τ· ἔχων V, — W
| ἀσφαλείᾳ· κεφαλῇ Τ | ἐγράψαμεν· ἐνγραφῆναι Τ	18 ἐναγκείλαμεν
ΤV | ἁπάσας ex ἁπάσης corr V | § 2. ὅντινα ego ὅντι W, ἥντιναν V
εἶτινα Τ | προστάσσεις· + ἐκπληροῖ W	19 καὶ — Τ	20 ἀπελθεῖν — W
§ 3. 1. 21 φησιν Τ φήσας VW | τ. τεθνεότων: νικρῶν Τ

καὶ ἐφώνησεν φωνὴν μεγάλην λέγων· »ἔστιν, ἔστιν, μὰ τὸν
ἰσχυρὸν θεὸν καὶ ζῶντα. καὶ ἡμεῖς γὰρ οἴησιν περιφερόμενοι
ἐξοφώθημεν * φωτεινοὶ ὄντες τὸ πρότερον, καὶ ἔτι τῇ μετανοίᾳ
οὐ προσεκλίναμεν. 4 λέγω δέ σοι ταῦτα, ὦ βασιλεῦ, θεὸς μόνος εἷς ἐστιν, ὃς τριὰ ὑμνολογεῖται παρὰ τῶν φωτεινῶν ἀγγέλων. αὐτὸς οὕτως σε ἡμᾶς παρέδωκεν, ἡμεῖς δὲ οἰκειοχείρως
τὰ ὀνόματα ἡμῶν παρεδώκαμεν καὶ ἐπετάξαμεν καὶ ταῖς σφραγ-
ῖσιν ὁμοίως. 5. καὶ ὅστις, ὦ βασιλεῦ, γίνωσκε τ' ἀληθές, ἁγνίζει
ἑαυτὸν ἡμέρας τρεῖς καὶ ἐπικαλεῖται τῇ ἁφῇ τῆς χειρὸς ἕναν
ἡμῶν ὃν αἴρεται ἄρχοντα, ἐκπληροῖ τὸ κελευόμενον αὐτοῦ, καὶ
ὥσπερ οἰκέτης τῷ ἰδίῳ δεσπότῃ πειθαρχεῖ, οὕτως ὁμοίως καὶ
αὐτὸς τῷ κεκτημένῳ ἡμῶν τὰ ὀνόματα. 6. πρέπει οὖν ταῦτα
ἐπιλέγειν τὰ ὀνόματα διὰ λίθου Ἰάσπιδος ἐγγεγλυμμένης ζῳδίοις
τοῖς δώδεκα· μέσον δὲ ὁ ὄφις καὶ λύρα, ἱστὸς καὶ ἄρκος, καὶ
ὑπὲρ τὸν τύμπανον κυλικὴ φορὰ καὶ ἄνωθεν τούτου τὰ γράμματα ταῦτα· ZABARζHC, καὶ αὐτίκα ὑποτασσόμεθα τῷ κεκτημένῳ καὶ ἄκοντες.

XIII Πλὴν, ὦ βασιλεῦ, καὶ τούτῳ προσεκτέον σοι· ἄνθρωποι

MSS TVW. 1 ἐφώνησεν ἐβόησεν T | ἔστιν, ἔστιν ego· ἔστιν ἔστιν καὶ
ἔστιν T, ἔστι ἔστη V, ἔστιν W   2 θεὸν — T | καὶ (2°) — T | οἴησιν
ego εἴησιν W, ἤηση V, — T | περιφερόμενοι ego προσφεράμενοι T, περι-
φερόμεθα VW   8 ἐξοφώθημεν — πρότερον exscr. Gaulminius in notis ad
Psellum, *de oper daem.* (Migne, *PG* 122, 827, n. 19) | * L f. 7ᵛ² | ἔτι W |
εἰς W, — T   4 οὐκ ἐκλίναμεν W   § 4. 1. 5 ὃς ὡς T   6 αὐτὸς· οὗ-
τος T | οὕτως οὗτος TV | σε] σοι | παρέδωκεν· παραδωκὸς T | οἰ-
κειοχ. ego· εἰκηοχύρος V, οἰχειδχείρος W, — T   7 παρεδώκαμεν + ἰδιο-
χειρα T | ἐπεταξ. καὶ V ἐγράψαμεν ὁμοίως καὶ T, — W   8 ὁμοίως
ἡμῶν T | post ἡμῶν punct. magn. argent rubricumque ponit T, et posteaquam
sequuntur quae verba infra ad 1. 15 adducuntur   §§ 5—6. ll. 8—16 καὶ
ὅστις ... ταῦτα — T

MSS VW. § 5. 1. 12 τῷ κεκτ. ego τῶν κεκτημένων W, τὸν κεκτημέ-
νον V | § 6. πρέπει V· χρὴ W   13 ἐπιλέγι V | Ἰάσπιδος V, Ἰάσπεως W
| ἐγκεγλυμμ(ένως) W   14 ἱστὸς W· εἰστὸς V, l. fortasse οἰστὸς |
ὑπέρι VW

MSS T.   16 ZABARζHC (rubric) VW ταῦτα δὲ ὀφίλην (l. ὀφείλει)
βαστάζειν ἐπάνω σου, ἔστι γὰρ φύλαξ σου· ZABAPζHS T | explicit frag-
mentum MS T

MSS VW   16 ὑποτασσόμ(ενα) W   17 ἄκωντες W
C. XIII. 1. 18 τοῦτο W | προσ. σοι. προσεκτέοσην V

πολλοὶ μέλλουσιν ζητεῖν τὸ τοιοῦτον μέγα μυστήριον ἵνα ὑπο-
τασσώμεθα ὑπ᾽ αὐτῶν, καὶ εἰ ἀκούσεις ἡμῶν ἐροῦμεν.‹ καὶ
εἶπον· ›λέγε, ἀποστάτα καὶ ἀπατεών.‹ 2. ὁ δὲ ἔφη· ›σὺ καὶ
τοῖς τέκνοις σου μόνοις ἐγκατάλειπε τὴν θησαυρὸν καὶ μὴ τοῖς
5 πᾶσιν καὶ ἀφελεστέροις. ποίησον δὲ ἡμῖν σημεῖον ὅπως μετὰ τὸ
ἀποθανεῖν σε Ἐζεκείᾳ τῷ βασιλεῖ ποιήσεις ἑτέραν διαθήκην τῷ
κόσμῳ καὶ ἡ τοιαύτη ἔσται ἀποκεκρυμμένη καὶ μὴ φανερὰ τοῖς
κοινοῖς καὶ ἀφελεστέροις, ἵνα μὴ ὁ θησαυρὸς ἐκλείπῃ τοῖς οἰκου-
μένοις. 3. οὐδεὶς γὰρ ἀπ᾽ ἀρχῆς μέχρι τῆς σήμερον ἡμᾶς ἐδου-
10 λώσατο, καὶ μὴ παραχωρίσῃς ἡμᾶς θνητοῖς σώμασιν πειθαρχεῖν‹
4. ὁ γὰρ Ἐζεκείας, ὦ βασιλεῦ, πολλὰ μὲν καὶ πατροπαράδοτα
κατακαύσει καὶ ἄλλα πολλὰ μέν ἀφανίσει βιβλία, καὶ τὴν οἰκουμένην στηρίξει καὶ τὰ περιττὰ διακόψει.

5. Ἐγὼ δὲ Σολομῶν ἀκούσας εἶπον αὐτόν· ›ἐξορκίζω σε εἰς
15 τὸν θρόνον τοῦ θεοῦ τὸ ἀσάλευτον καὶ εἰς τὸ ὄρνεον τὸ περι-
πετόμενον ἐπάνω τῆς κεφαλῆς αὐτοῦ ἵνα με εἴπῃς ἐν ποίῳ ἀγγέλῳ οἱ πάντες καταργεῖσθε.‹ 6. καὶ εἶπέν μοι· ›βασιλεῦ Σολομῶν, ἡμεῖς πάντες ὑπὸ τοῦ θεοῦ δυνάμει καταργούμεθα καὶ ἐν
τῷ ὀνόματι Ἀγλά, ἀλλ᾽ ἐπειδὴ τῇ σφραγῖδι κατεδεσμεύσας ἡμᾶς
20 σὺ μόνος, ὑποτασσόμεθα μέχρι τινός. 7. ἐλεύσονται γὰρ ἡμέραι
ἐν αἷς πολλὰ δεηθήσῃ, καὶ διὰ τοῦτο ἱκετεύομέν σοι ὅπως ἐν
ταῖς ἑξῆς γενεαῖς ἕξομεν σημεῖον τῆς βασιλείας σου καὶ ὑπο-
δείξομεν τοῦτο Ἐζεκείᾳ τῷ βασιλεῖ ὅπως δειχθῇ καὶ πλατυνθῇ
εἰς τὴν οἰκουμένην ἣν δάσομεν αὐτῷ διαθήκην καινήν. 8. καὶ
25 ταύτην, ἐν ᾗ ἀληθινῶς τὰ ὀνόματα ἡμῶν ἐχαράξαμεν, κατακαύσει ἄνευ ἑνὸς μόνου ἥτις φυλαχθήσεται καὶ ἐν τῇ προσδοκου-

---

MSS VW   1 μέλλωσιν W, μέλοσην V   2 ει — V | ἡμῶν ego· ὑμῶν
VW | καὶ εἶπον W. ὁ δὲ ἔφη V   3 § 2 ὁ δὲ V   καὶ W   4 μόνοις V
— W   5 ἀφελεστέρης V, ἀσφελεσταίραις W   6 σε ση V, σοι W | ἐζεκία
τὸ βασιλεῖ VW | ποιήσῃ V | ἑτέρα διαθήκη V | τὸ κωσμ < V, — W
7 ἀποκεκρ. V: ἀποσφαλισμένη W   8 ἀσφαλεστέροις W   9 § 3 τη ση-
μερον V, τὴν σημ. W   10 θνητοῖς ego θικτοῖς W, θεικτεῖς V   11 § 4. μὲν
W δὲ V | πατροπαραδ. ego παιδοπ(ατρὸ)ς W, πεδοπ(ατρὸ)ς V   12 ἄλλα W
ἄλον V
§ 5. 1. 14 αὐτὸν VW· 1. αὐτῷ   15 καὶ ... αὐτοῦ V· — W   16 με
VW 1. μοι | ποίῳ ... πάντες W. πίω ἢ πάντες ἀγγέλων V   § 6. 1. 18 πάν-
τες pr ἢ (1. οἱ) V   20 σὺ μόν(ος) VW 1. σοὶ μόνῳ cum ὑποτασσ.⁹
§ 7 1 22 ἕξωμεν VW   23 πλατιθῇ V   24 αὐτὸ W, αὐτ < V

μένη τοῦ θεοῦ παρουσίᾳ πάλιν διαπλατυνθήσεται. 9. ἡ δὲ παρ'
ἡμῶν δοθεῖσα τῷ Ἐζεκείᾳ ἐν ὅλῳ τῷ κόσμῳ παραδοθήσεται
καὶ ὡς μέγα τι κειμήλιον παρὰ τοῖς σοφοῖς φυλαχθήσεται,
ἥντινα ὡς παίγνιον καὶ ἀπάτην ἐκδώσομεν ἐν τῷ κόσμῳ.

5   10. Ταῦτα ἀκούσας ἐγὼ Σολομῶν ἐδεήθην τοῦ θεοῦ καὶ
εἶπον· »θεὲ πατέρων, Ἀδωνάϊ μέγας, ὁ τὴν σοφίαν τῷ δούλῳ
σου χαρισάμενος, ἀποκάλυψόν μοι τί δεῖ ποιῆσαι.«   11. καὶ ἦλθεν
φωνὴ λέγουσα· »Σολομῶν, Σολομῶν, ἔασον γραμμάτιον τῷ Ἐζεκείᾳ τῇ σφραγῖδι ταύτῃ ἐκσφραγισάμενος.«   12. καὶ καθίσας
10 ἔγραψα· »τῷ Ἐζεκείᾳ τῷ μέλλοντι βασιλεῖ· Σολομῶν βασιλεύς,
υἱὸς Δαυείδ, ἀπέστειλά σοι τάδε. λάβε ἐκ τοῦ Παλτιὲλ Τζαμὰλ
διαθήκην ἣν δώσει σοι καὶ τῷ κόσμῳ παντὶ καταπλούτισον·
τὴν δὲ ἐμὴν παραδοὺς πυρὶ πλὴν ἑνὸς ἥτις καὶ ἐν λαϊνέοις ἐν-
τυπωθήσεται γράμμασιν ἕως ὁ μέγας καὶ ἰσχυρὸς θελήσαιεν.«

15   13. Ταῦτα γράψας παρέδωκα τῷ Τζαμάλ, καὶ πάλιν ἠρώτησα αὐτὸν εἰ ἔστιν καλὸν τοῦ ὑγιαίνειν ὁλοσώματον καὶ ἀτραυμάτιστον ἐν τῷ κόσμῳ ἐᾶσαι πλοῦτον. καὶ εἶπέν μοι· »ἓν μόνον ἔασον δι' οἰκείας γραφῆς σου τῇ μέσῃ τῆς γῆς γράμμασιν
ἀσημάντοις.«   14. καὶ δὴ καθίσας ἔγραψα χαλδαϊκοῖς γράμμασιν
20 χερσὶν οἰκείαις τοῦ ὑγιαίνειν ὁλοσώματον καὶ ἀτραυμάτιστον
(ἐᾶσαι) πλοῦτον, παραδοὺς μόνην τὴν Παλαιστίνην, ὡς, ὁπόταν
φανήσεται, οὐ μόνον κεκτημένον ἀλλὰ καὶ ἅπαντα κόσμον ὀνήσῃ
ὑγιαινὰ καὶ πλουτοποιὰ χαρίσματα παρέχῃ ἑκάστοτε, ἐπεὶ οὐρα-
νόθεν ταῦτα κατέβησαν χερσὶν Ὑψίστου, μεγάλων κυδῶν κατέ-
25 χουσι παλάμην, τοῦτο καὶ ἐπιδοῦσί μοι
15   Ὧδε ἐγὼ Σολομῶν. εἰς δὲ τὸ ἑξῆς θεὸς ἰσχυρός, Ὕψιστος Σαβαώθ· ἀμήν.

MSS VW. § 8 l 1 διαπλατιδεί(σεται) V   4 ἥντινα ego· ἣν τινὲς VW
5 § 10. ἐδεήθη V   6 εἶπον W ὕπαι (l εἶπε) V   § 12. l. 11 παλτιὲ W,
πατιὲλ V   13 λαϊνέοις ego λεανέες V, λεανὲς W   14 θελήσῃ(εν) W,
θελεισίΐεν V
§ 13 l. 16 τὸ εἰγίενί V | ὁλὸ σῶματον V   § 14. l. 19 ἔγραψεν V
20 ὑγίὴν ὁλὸ σῶματον V | ἀτραμάτιστον πλούτων V   21 ἐᾶσαι addo |
* V f 441ᵛ | μόνην τ. Παλ. l fortasse μόνῃ ἐν τῇ Παλαιστίνῃ᾿   22 ὀνήσῃ
ego ὃν εἰσί V, ὠνήσῃ W   24 κυδῶν V εἰδῶν W | κατέχουσι ego κατέ-
χουσα VW   25 τοῦτο .. μοι — W | ἐπιδοῦσι ego· ἐπιδούσαν V
§ 15. l. 26 Ὧδε W ὡς δὲ V | εἰς δὲ W καὶ εἰς V

ΠΕΡΙ ΤΟΥ ΣΟΛΟΜΩΝΤΟΣ

I. Ὁ Σολομῶν υἱὸς Δαυεὶδ ἐγένετο ἐκ τῆς τοῦ Οὐρίου γυναι-
κός· ἐγένετο δὲ οὕτως. ἐσκέψατο Δαυεὶδ ὁ βασιλεὺς τὴν τοῦ
Οὐρίου γυναῖκα ἐν τῷ βαλανείῳ γυμνήν. καὶ ἐμβατεύσας ὁ Σα-
5 τανᾶς εἰς τὴν καρδίαν αὐτοῦ ἔρωτα ἐπιθυμίας, ἐμοίχευσεν αὐτήν.
2 καὶ οὐ μόνον τὸ τῆς μοιχείας ἔργον εἰργάσατο, ἀλλὰ καὶ
φονεῦσαι προήχθη τὸν Οὐρίαν τὸν ἄνδρα τῆς μοιχευθείσης ὁ
ἀγαπητὸς τοῦ θεοῦ, ὁ μέγας προφήτης, ὁ ἐκλεκτὸς τοῦ θεοῦ, ὁ
μέγιστος τοῖς πᾶσιν, ὁ τῆς ψαλμῳδίας καλλωπισμός, ὁ τῆς πα-
10 λαιᾶς καὶ νέας διαθήκης σημειοφόρος, ὁ μεγαλώνυμος θεοπάτωρ.
ἠπατήθη γὰρ παρὰ τοῦ Βελίαρ καὶ ἀρχεκάκου ἐχθροῦ· ἠπατήθη
γὰρ ὡς ὁ πρωτόπλαστος ἐκεῖνος Ἀδάμ   3 ἐφονεύθη δὲ Οὐρίας
ἀποσταλεὶς παρὰ τοῦ Δαυεὶδ εἰς τὸν πόλεμον, καὶ ταχθεὶς βου-
λήσει αὐτοῦ καὶ θελήσει εἰς τὸ ἔμπροσθεν τοῦ πολέμου ὅπως
15 καταληφθεὶς μόνος καὶ μὴ ἔχων τὸν βοηθοῦντα φονευθῇ. ὅπερ
δὴ καὶ γέγονεν.

    4. Πρὸ δὲ τοῦ ταῦτα γενέσθαι ἦλθεν ἄγγελος Κυρίου εἰς
Νάθαν τὸν προφήτην λέγων αὐτῷ· »ἄπελθε εἰς τὸν Δαυεὶδ τὸν
βασιλέα τὸν προφήτην καὶ δίδαξον αὐτὸν τοῦ μὴ ποιῆσαι * τὰ
20 ἄθεσμα ἔργα τοῦ Σατανᾶ.«   5. ἐξελθὼν δὲ ὁ Νάθαν ἄπεισι
πρὸς τὸν Δαυεὶδ καὶ ἐνεμποδίσθη παρὰ τοῦ Βελίαρ   εὗρε γὰρ
ὁ διάβολος ἄνθρωπον ἐσφαγμένον γυμνὸν καὶ ἄρας αὐτὸν ἔθηκεν ἐν τῇ ὁδῷ τοῦ Νάθαν. 6. ἰδὼν δὲ τὸν νεκρὸν ἄνθρωπον
ὁ Νάθαν ἐβουλήθη θάψαι αὐτόν   καὶ ἐν τῷ θάπτειν ἐπλήρωσεν
25 ὁ Δαυεὶδ τὰ ἄθεσμα ἔργα τοῦ Σατανᾶ   καὶ ἐπιγνοὺς τοῦτο

MS D = codex 132 Monasterii Sancti Dionysii in Monte Atho (v. supra
p. 7), incipit f 367ᴸ
    10 ὁ μεγ θεοπάτωρ, ὁ τῆς . σημειοφόρος hoc ordine exscriptis, postea
super ὁ μεγαλων littera β, et super ὁ τῆς littera α scripta ordinem ut in textu
indicavit scriptor   19 * f 367ᵛ

Νάθαν ὁ προφήτης ἐθρήνει πικρῶς καὶ ἔλεγεν· »δι᾽ ἐμὲ γέγονε τοῦτο τὸ ἁμάρτημα.« 7. καὶ πάλιν ἐλθὼν ὁ ἄγγελος πρὸς αὐτὸν ἔλεγε· »διὰ σοῦ γέγονε τὸ πτῶμα, διὰ σοῦ ἔσται καὶ ἡ διόρθωσις. ἄπελθε τοίνυν καὶ ἔλεγξον αὐτὸν τὴν ἀνομίαν.« καὶ λέγει Νάθαν πρὸς τὸν ἄγγελον· »πῶς ἐγὼ πένης ὢν ἐλέγξω βασιλέα;« 8. ὁ δὲ ἄγγελός φησι πρὸς αὐτόν· »ἐγὼ ἔσομαι μετὰ σοῦ· σὺ ἀνάγγειλον, ἐγὼ δὲ τὸν φόβον φέρω εἰς αὐτόν.« 9. καὶ ἀπελθὼν Νάθαν πρὸς τὸν Δαυεὶδ προσεκύνησεν αὐτῷ καὶ εἶπε· »δέσποτα βασιλεῦ, δίκην ἔχω μετά τινος, καὶ ἦλθον τοῦ εἰπεῖν πρὸς σὲ ταύτην.« ὁ δὲ βασιλεὺς πρὸς αὐτὸν λέγει· »τίς ἐστιν ἡ δίκη αὕτη;« 10. ὁ δὲ Νάθαν παραβολικῶς ἔλεγε· »δεσπότην ἔχω τὸν δεσπόζοντά με, καὶ κέκτηται ἀμνάδας ἑκατόν· καὶ εὐφραίνεται μετ᾽ αὐτῶν. * ἐγὼ δὲ κέκτημαι ἀμνάδα μίαν. καὶ ἔλαβεν αὐτὴν ἀπ᾽ ἐμοῦ ὁ τὰς ἑκατὸν ἔχων καὶ κατέφαγεν αὐτήν.« 11. τότε ἔγνω ὁ Δαυεὶδ τὸ σκευασθὲν αὐτῷ δρᾶμα καὶ ἀναστὰς ἐκ τῆς κλίνης αὐτοῦ στενάξας πικρῶς μετὰ δακρύων ἔλεγεν· »ἐγώ εἰμι ὁ ταῦτα διαπραξάμενος.« καὶ ἤρξατο κατανυκτικῶς λέγειν τὸν πεντηκοστὸν ψαλμόν, καὶ ὁ Νάθαν πρὸς αὐτόν. καὶ ἀφείλατο λοιπὸν κύριος ὁ θεὸς τὸ ἁμάρτημα.

12 Ἔτεκε Δαυεὶδ τὸν Σολομῶντα ἐκ τῆς τοῦ Οὐρίου. καὶ ἔλαβε τὴν βασιλείαν τοῦ πατρὸς αὐτοῦ Δαυεὶδ καὶ ἦν ἐληλακὼς εἰς ἄκρον σοφίας καὶ φρονήσεως· καὶ ἡ σειρὰ τῆς γενεαλογίας αὐτοῦ κατήντησε μέχρι καὶ τῆς θείας σαρκώσεως τοῦ κυρίου ἡμῶν Ἰησοῦ Χριστοῦ, ἐπεί ἐστι καὶ αὐτὸς ἐκ φυλῆς, μᾶλλον δὲ ἐξ ὀσφύος τοῦ θεοπάτορος Δαυεὶδ ἵνα καὶ ἡ προφητικὴ ῥῆσις πληρωθῇ ἡ λέγουσα· »οὐκ ἐκλείψει ἄρχων ἐξ Ἰούδα οὐδὲ ἡγούμενος ἐκ τῶν μηρῶν αὐτοῦ ἕως οὗ ἔλθη ὃ ἀπόκειται.« 13. ἡ σοφία δὲ Σολομῶντος ὁμοία ἦν τῇ σοφίᾳ τοῦ πρώτου ἐκείνου ἀνθρώπου Ἀδάμ. ἐπαιδεύθη ταύτην τὴν σοφίαν τὴν μὲν παρὰ τοῦ θαυμασίου Σιράχ, τὴν δὲ παρὰ τῆς ἄνω προνοίας. τούτου δὲ τὴν σοφίαν ἐμφαίνων ὁ κύριος ἐν τοῖς εὐαγγελίοις ἔλεγεν, ὅτι »οὐδὲ σοφίαν * Σολομῶντος ὑψηλοτέραν οἶμαι τῶν ἄλλων,« ταύτην κρίνας ὥσπερ δῆτα καὶ ἦν.

---

4 αὐτὸν in αὐτῷ corr. prim. man. false   § 10. l 18 * f. 368ʳ
§ 12. l. 21 ἐληλακὼς ms   § 13. 31 σοφία ms.   32 * f. 368ᵛ

§ 12. ll. 26f. Gen. XLIX 10 — § 13. ll 32f. Mt XII 42, Lk. XI 31

II. Ταύτῃ τῇ σοφίᾳ θαρρήσας ὁ θαυμάσιος Σολομῶν ἐβουλήθη ἀνεγεῖραι οἶκον κυρίῳ τῷ θεῷ περικαλλῆ καὶ κρείττω
πάντων τῶν ἀναθημάτων τῶν ἐπὶ τῆς γῆς. ἐγένετο δὲ καὶ
ἀνηγείρετο ὁ οἶκος κυρίου τοῦ θεοῦ θελήσει καὶ σοφίᾳ καὶ δη-
5 μιουργίᾳ θεοῦ διὰ τοῦ σοφοῦ Σολομῶντος καὶ τῆς τούτου προθυ-
μίας. ἀνήγειρε τοίνυν μετὰ μεγάλης εὐπρεπείας τὸν τοιοῦτον
ναὸν αὐτός τε καὶ οἱ παῖδες αὐτοῦ. 2. ἔσχε δὲ ἕνα ἀπὸ τῶν
παίδων αὐτοῦ ποθεινότατον παρὰ πάντας, τὰ γὰρ σιτία καὶ τὰς
τροφὰς καὶ τὰ ἱμάτια ἐπὶ τὸ διπλοῦν παρεῖχεν αὐτῷ. ἦν δὲ
10 ὁ τοιοῦτος παῖς ἀηδὴς τῇ ὄψει καὶ τὸ πρόσωπον ἀκαλλώπιστος,
καὶ ἐλυπεῖτο βλέπων αὐτὸν οὕτως ἔχοντα ὁ Σολομῶν. 3. ἐν
μιᾷ δὲ τῶν ἡμερῶν φησι πρὸς αὐτόν· »πῶς οὕτως ἀηδὴς ἔχεις;
τί σε τῶν παρόντων λυπεῖ; μὴ οὐ λαμβάνεις τὰ πάντα διπλᾶ
παρ᾽ ἐμοῦ;« 4. καὶ ὁ παῖς φησι πρὸς τὸν βασιλέα· »τὰ μὲν σιτία,
15 δέσποτα βασιλεῦ, ἅπερ μοι παρέχεις πάντα καταναλίσκω. οὐκ
εὐφραίνει δὲ ἀπὸ τούτων οὐδέν, καταλαμβάνει γὰρ ἐπ᾽ ἐμὲ διὰ
τῆς νυκτὸς δαιμόνιον πονηρὸν καὶ ἀκάθαρτον καὶ ὑποπιάζει καὶ
ἐκθλίβει τὸ ἄκρον τοῦ δακτύλου μου. καὶ ἀπεργάζεται * τὴν
ὄψιν μου τοιαύτην οἵαν ὁρᾷς ἀηδῆ καὶ σκυθρωπήν.«
20   5. Ἀκούσας δὲ τὸ ῥῆμα τοῦτο ὁ Σολομῶν ἐποίησεν ὑπὲρ
τούτου ἔντευξιν καὶ παράκλησιν πρὸς κύριον τὸν θεόν. 6. καὶ
ἀπεστάλη πρὸς αὐτὸν Μιχαὴλ ὁ ἀρχάγγελος μετὰ σφραγῖδος
χαλκοῦ δακτυλίου, καὶ δέδωκε τὴν τοιαύτην σφραγῖδα πρὸς τὸν
Σολομῶντα. 7. καὶ φησι· »ἐπίδος τῷ παιδὶ τὴν τοιαύτην σφρα-
25 γῖδα καὶ κατεχέτω ταύτην ἐν τῇ κλίνῃ αὐτοῦ, καὶ ὁπόταν ἔλθῃ
πρὸς αὐτὸν ὁ διάβολος, κρουσάτω τοῦτον μετὰ τῆς σφραγῖδος
ἐπὶ τὸ στῆθος, καὶ δήσας ἀγαγέτω τοῦτον πρὸς σέ· μέλλεις γὰρ
ὑποτάξαι πᾶν δαιμόνιον μετ᾽ αὐτοῦ καὶ τῆς σφραγῖδος τοῦ θεοῦ,
καὶ οἰκοδομῆσαι τὸν οἶκον τοῦ θεοῦ μετὰ τοῦ πλήθους τῶν δαι-
30 μόνων σὺν τοῖς ἀνθρώποις.« 8. λαβὼν δὲ ὁ Σολομῶν τὴν
σφραγῖδα καὶ εὐχαριστήσας τῷ ἁγίῳ θεῷ, ἀπῆλθεν ἀπ᾽ αὐτοῦ ὁ
ἄγγελος. 9. καὶ προσκαλεσάμενος τὸν παῖδα δέδωκε τὴν σφραγῖδα, 10. ἀναγγείλας τὸ προσταχθὲν παρὰ τοῦ ἀγγέλου. 11. λαβὼν δὲ ὁ παῖς τὴν σφραγῖδα τοῦ θεοῦ, ἑσπέρας γενομένης ἀνε-

---

C. II. 1. 2 οἴκου ms. | κρείττοια Is   4 ἀνήγειρ. Kurz· ἀνεγ. ms.
§ 4. l. 18 * f 369ʳ   19 οκυθρωπήν ms., σκηπτώπην Is

κλίθη εἰς τὴν κοίτην αὐτοῦ, καὶ κατὰ τὸ εἰθισμένον παραγέγονε
πρὸς αὐτὸν ὁ διάβολος. 12. καὶ ἀθρόον ὁ παῖς παίει τὸν ἐχθρὸν
κατὰ τῆς καρδίας μετὰ τῆς τοῦ θεοῦ σφραγῖδος. * 13. ὁ δὲ
σατανᾶς ἐλεεινῇ τῇ φωνῇ ἐβόησεν· »οἴμοι, οἴμοι, πῶς καταδου-
λοῦμαι βασιλεῖ Σολομῶντι;« καὶ δήσας τοῦτον εἰσήγαγε πρὸς
τὸν βασιλέα Σολομῶντα.

III. Καὶ θεασάμενος αὐτόν φησι· »εἰπὲ ἡμῖν, πονηρὸν πνεῦμα
καὶ ἀκάθαρτον, τίς ἐστιν ἡ κλῆσίς σου καὶ τίς σου ἡ ἐργασία.«
καὶ ὁ διάβολος ἔφη τῷ βασιλεῖ »Ὀρνίας καλοῦμαι ἡ δὲ ἐργασία
μου εἰς πάντα ἐπιτήδεια.« 2. καὶ λέγει ὁ βασιλεύς »τίς ὁ καταργῶν τὴν δύναμίν σου ἄγγελος;« καὶ ὁ διάβολος· »ὑπὸ τοῦ
μεγάλου ἀρχαγγέλου Μιχαὴλ καταργοῦμαι αὐτός τε καὶ ἡ ἐμὴ
δύναμις.« 3 καὶ ὁ βασιλεύς φησι· »δύνασαι ποιῆσαί τι εἰς τὸν
ναὸν κυρίου καὶ εἰς τὴν οἰκοδομὴν αὐτοῦ χρησιμόν,« καὶ ὁ διά-
βολος· »δύναμαι μετὰ τῆς σφραγῖδος ταύτης ἐπισυνάξαι πᾶν δαιμόνιον ἔμπροσθέν σου καὶ ὑποτάξαι τῷ σῷ θελήματι καὶ οἰκοδομῆσαι, καὶ ἀνεγερεῖς μετὰ τῆς δουλείας καὶ ὑποταγῆς ἐκείνων
τὸν ναὸν κυρίου παντοκράτορος.« 4 ταῦτα ἀκούσας ὁ Σολομῶν εὐχαρίστησε κυρίῳ τῷ θεῷ καὶ προέτρεψε τὸν Ὀρνίαν
δαίμονα μετὰ τῆς σφραγῖδος καὶ τοῦ παιδίου ἀπελθεῖν καὶ ἐπισυνάξαι πᾶν δαιμόνιον. 5. καὶ ἀπῆλθον καὶ ἐπισυνήγαγον πάντα
καὶ εἰσῆγον ταῦτα εἰς * τὸν βασιλέα Σολομῶντα ἅμα δὲ τὸ
πλησιάσαι ταῦτα εἰς τὸν βασιλέα προσεκύνουν αὐτῷ. 6 καὶ
ἠρώτα ἓν ἕκαστον ὁ βασιλεὺς τῶν δαιμόνων τό τε ὄνομα καὶ
15 τὴν ἐργασίαν καὶ ὑπὸ ποίου τῶν ἁγίων ἀγγέλων καταργεῖται.
καὶ ὡμολόγουν τήν τε ἐργασίαν αὐτοῦ καὶ τὴν κλῆσιν καὶ τὸν
καταργοῦντα ἄγγελον 7. ἐπέτρεπε δὲ αὐτὰ ἐργάζεσθαι εἰς τὴν
τοῦ ναοῦ οἰκοδομήν. καὶ ἐνήργει ἓν ἕκαστον τὴν δουλείαν εἰς
ἣν δὴ καὶ ἐτάχθη παρὰ τοῦ σοφοῦ Σολομῶντος. 8. καὶ οὕτως
 p ἦν ἰδεῖν θαῦμα ἐξαίσιον ἄνδρας μετὰ πλήθους δαιμόνων θελήσει
κυρίου ἀνοικοδομοῦντας καὶ ἐκπληροῦντας τὸν ναὸν κυρίου εἰρηνι-
κῶς μετὰ πάσης ἐπιμελείας τε καὶ σπουδῆς, μὴ τολμώντων τῶν

---

§ 12. l. 2 ἀθρόον ms. ἀθρόων Is   8 * f. 369ᵛ
C. III 1 l. 10 ἐπιτήδεια Is· ἐπιτήδειος ms.   § 2. l. 12 ἡ — Is | ε
in voce ἐμή primum omissum postea supra ἡ scr ms   13 § 3 δύνασε ms.
§ 5. l. 22 * f. 370ʳ   23 πλησιάσαι Is πλησιᾶσαι ms., l πλησιᾶσθαι?

δαιμόνων μηδὲ τὸ τυχὸν σκανδαλίσαι ἢ ἀδικῆσαι τοὺς ἀνθρώπους.

    IV. Ἀπὸ δὲ τῶν ἀνδρῶν τῶν ἐχόντων ἀκριβῆ εἴδησιν εἰς
τὴν τοῦ ναοῦ οἰκοδομὴν ἦλθεν εἷς εἰς φιλονεικίαν καὶ ἔριν μετὰ
5 τοῦ υἱοῦ αὐτοῦ, καὶ ἐμάχοντο ἀλλήλοις θυμοῦ πνέοντες ἀλλή-
λους διασπαράξαι βουλόμενοι. 2. ὅλος δὲ τοῦ θυμοῦ ὁ πατὴρ
γεγονὼς ἀπῆλθε πρὸς τὸν βασιλέα Σολομῶντα μετὰ δακρύων
καὶ ὀδυρμῶν λέγων αὐτῷ· »δέσποτα βασιλεῦ· ἢ θανάτῳ τὸν
ἐμὸν καταδίκασον * παῖδα ὡς ἐνυβρίσαντα παρανόμως εἰς ἐμὲ
10 τὸν πατέρα, ἢ σαφῶς ἴσθι ὡς οὐδέποτε κινήσω τὴν χεῖρά μου
εἰς τὴν τοῦ ναοῦ οἰκοδομήν « 3. ἀκούων δὲ ταῦτα ὁ βασιλεὺς
καὶ βουλευόμενος, ἦλθε καὶ ὁ υἱὸς ἐκείνου πρὸς τὸν βασιλέα
ταῦτα ἐγκαλῶν καὶ λέγων τῷ πατρί. 4. διαλογιζόμενος δὲ περὶ
τούτου ὁ βασιλεὺς καὶ διαπορῶν τί ἄρα ἀποκρίνοιτο, στραφεὶς
15 βλέπει τὸν Ὀρνίαν δαίμονα ἐργαζόμενον καὶ μειδιῶντα· καὶ λέγει
πρὸς τοὺς κρινομένους· »ἀπόστητε μικρὸν ἀπ᾽ ἐμοῦ.« 5. καὶ ἀπο-
στάντων τὸν Ὀρνίαν μετακαλεῖται καὶ φησι πρὸς αὐτόν· »τί
γελᾷς, ὦ Ὀρνία; τὴν βασιλείαν μου κατεγέλας, ἢ τὴν κρίσιν μου,
ἢ τὸν ναὸν κυρίου,« 6. καὶ ὁ Ὀρνίας πρὸς τὸν βασιλέα λέγει·
20 »δέσποτα βασιλεῦ· σοφώτατε καὶ δικαιότατε Σολομῶν· οὔτε τὴν
βασιλείαν σου κατεγέλασα, οὔτε τὴν κρίσιν σου, οὔτε τὸν ναὸν
κυρίου, ἀλλὰ τούτους τοὺς ἀθλίους τοὺς κρινομένους, τὸν δύστηνον λέγω γέροντα καὶ τὸν τούτου υἱόν. οὐ μὴ γὰρ παρέλθωσι
τρεῖς ἡμέραι καὶ τὸ τέλος διαδέξεται τὸν νέον.« 7. καὶ ὁ βασι-
25 λεὺς πρὸς τὸν Ὀρνίαν λέγει· »ἄπελθε καὶ ἐργάζου μετὰ σπουδῆς
καὶ εἰρήνης καὶ ὑποταγῆς εἰς τὸν ναὸν κυρίου θεοῦ παντοκράτορος.« καὶ ἀπῆλθεν ἀπὸ τοῦ τόπου ἐκείνου ὁ Ὀρνίας καὶ *
εἰργάζετο 8. μετεκαλέσατο δὲ ὁ βασιλεὺς τοὺς δύο κρινομένους
καὶ φησι πρὸς αὐτούς· »ἀπέλθατε καὶ ἐργάζεσθε τὸ ἔργον ὑμῶν
30 ἄχρι πέντε ἡμέρας, καὶ μετὰ ταῦτα ποιήσομαι ἀπόφασιν καὶ τέλος τῆς κρίσεως ὑμῶν.« προσέταξε δὲ ὁ βασιλεὺς διορίσασθαι τὴν
ἡμέραν καθ᾽ ἣν ἔλεγε ταῦτα.

C. IV 1. l. 4 εἰς supplevi τις conj. Is   6 § ⟨. ὅλος Is ὅλως ms
9 * f. 370ᵛ   § 6 l. 22 δύστηνον· δύστυνον ms., δύστυχον Is errore
24 διαδέξεται conj Is· διαδέξονται ms.   § 7. l. 25 πρὸς supplevi
27 ' f. 371ʳ

9. Παρελθουσῶν οὖν τῶν πέντε ἡμερῶν, ἦλθεν ὁ γέρων πρὸς τὸν βασιλέα κατηφὴς καὶ σπυθρωπὸς καὶ δάκρυα πρὸ τῶν ὀμμάτων ἀφεὶς φησι· »τέθνηκεν ὁ ἐμὸς υἱός, τέθνηκεν, καὶ οὐκ ἔτι ἴδῃς αὐτόν. ἐμὲ δὲ ἀπέλιπεν ἐν πένθει βαρυτάτῳ καὶ ὀδύνῃ
5 καρδίας καὶ ἀφορήτῳ στεναγμῷ· οὐκ ἔτι γὰρ βλέψω αὐτόν· οὐκ ἔτι τὸ πρόσωπον ἐκείνου θεάσομαι κατεκρύβη γὰρ ἐν τόπῳ ἀφεγγεῖ, ἐν τῇ σκοτεινῇ, ἐν τῇ ζοφερᾷ.« 10. ἐκπλαγεὶς οὖν ταῦτα ὁ βασιλεύς φησι· »ποίαν ἡμέραν τέθνηκεν;« καὶ φησι ὁ γέρων· »μετὰ τρίτην ἡμέραν ἀπέθανεν ἀφ᾽ ὅτου πρὸς τὸ σὸν κράτος
10 ἤλθαμεν.« 11. καὶ λέγει ὁ βασιλεύς· »ἄπελθε ἐν εἰρήνῃ, ὁ γέρων, κύριος δὲ ὁ θεὸς ὁ πάτηρ τῆς παρακλήσεως καὶ παραμυθία τῶν θλιβομένων παρακαλέσαι σου τὴν καρδίαν εἰς τὸ μηκέτι λυπεῖσθαι μνήσθητι γὰρ ὅτι ὁ σὸς υἱὸς ἄνθρωπος ἦν, πᾶς δὲ ἄνθρωπος θνητὸς ἦν. * μὴ τοίνυν λυποῦ, οὐ γὰρ ἀνύσεις οὐδὲν
15 ὧν βούλεσαι.« ταῦτα ἀκούσας ὁ γέρων ἀπῆλθεν ἀναψυχθεὶς τὴν καρδίαν.

12. Καὶ μετακαλεσάμενος τὸν Ὀρνίαν φησίν· »εἰπὲ ἡμῖν πῶς ἐπιγινώσκεις τὸν θάνατον τοῦ ἀνθρώπου, πνεῦμα ἀκάθαρτον ὄν.« 13. Ὁ δὲ Ὀρνίας λέγει· »ἡμεῖς, δέσποτα, ἐκ τοῦ οὐρανοῦ
20 ἐρρίφημεν κάτω, καὶ ἄγγελοι θεοῦ ὄντες καὶ φῶς περικείμενοι, νῦν δαίμονες καὶ ἀκάθαρτα πνεύματα καὶ σκότος, ὡς ὁρᾷς, ἐγενόμεθα, καὶ λειτουργοὶ θεοῦ τυγχάνοντες. νῦν σοῦ θεράποντες καὶ ὑπουργοί, θεοῦ κελεύοντος, γεγενήμεθα. 14. κάτω τοίνυν ἐξ οὐρανοῦ πεσόντες καὶ εἰς ᾄδην ῥιφέντες δεινῶς, πάλιν ἀνερχό-
25 μεθα εἰς τὸ κάτω τοῦ οὐρανοῦ πέταλον, καὶ τὰς τῶν ἀγγέλων ὁμιλίας ἀκούομεν, καὶ ἐξ αὐτῶν μανθάνομεν τὸν τοῦ ἀνθρώπου θάνατον πρὸ τεσσαράκοντα ἡμερῶν. 15. καὶ ἀκούσαντες τούτων ἐπιμελούμεθα καὶ ἀγωνιζόμεθα ἵνα τὸν τοῦ ἀνθρώπου θάνατον ἢ διὰ πυρὸς ἢ δι᾽ ὕδατος ἢ διὰ κρημνοῦ οἰκονομήσωμεν, ὅπως
30 λάβωμέν τινα ἐξ αὐτοῦ μερίδα. 16. καὶ ἐν τῷ μὴ ἔχειν ἡμᾶς βάσιν ἀναπαύσεως ἐν τῷ πετάλῳ τοῦ οὐρανοῦ πίπτομεν ὥσπερ φύλλα ἀπὸ τῶν δένδρων, καὶ δοκοῦμεν τοῖς ἀνθρώποις ὡς

---

§ 9 l. 2 σκυθρωπὸς ms· σκυτρ. Is, corr Kurz   4 ἔτι ms. ἔστι Is, corr. Kurz | ἴδῃς conj Is ἴδοις ms.   § 10. l 9 ἀφ᾽ ὅτου Is ἀφότου ms.   § 11 l 14 * f. 371ᵛ   § 15. l. 28 τοῦ supra lineam adscr. prim. man.

ἀστέρες χυνόμενοι, * ἵνα δοξαζώμεθα παρὰ τῶν ἀνθρώπων.‹
17. καὶ ὁ βασιλεύς· ›καὶ οἱ χυνόμενοι ἀστέρες, καὶ δοκοῦντες
ἀστέρες, οὔκ εἰσιν ὄντες ἀστέρες;‹ καὶ ὁ Ὀρνίας· ›οὐχὶ, βασιλεῦ·
οἱ γὰρ τοῦ οὐρανοῦ ἀστέρες ἀθάνατοί εἰσι καὶ ἐστηριγμένοι καὶ
5 οὐ κινοῦνται.‹ 18. καὶ ἀκούσας ταῦτα ὁ βασιλεὺς ἀπέλυσε τὸν
Ὀρνίαν εἰς ἔργον αὐτοῦ ἐργάζεσθαι.

V. Ὠικοδομεῖτο δὲ ὁ ναός· καὶ πάντες οἱ βασιλεῖς τῆς γῆς
καὶ οἱ ἄρχοντες τῶν τιμίων καὶ βασίλισσα Νότου ἡ σοφὴ Σιβύλλα καὶ αὐτὴ ἦλθε θεάσασθαι τὸν ναὸν κυρίου, καὶ εἰσέφερε
10 καὶ αὐτὴ εἰς τὴν οἰκοδομὴν τοῦ ναοῦ ξύλα πολυτελῆ καὶ
ἀξιόλογα.

VI. Ἀπέστειλε δὲ ὁ βασιλεὺς Ἀράβων ἐπιστολὴν πρὸς τὸν
βασιλέα Σολομῶντα καὶ διελάμβανεν οὕτως· ›βασιλεῦ Σολομῶν,
χαίροις γινωσκέτω ἡ βασιλεία σου ὅτι εἰς τὴν ἡμῶν χώραν
15 οἰκεῖ χαλεπὸν δαιμόνιον δυνατόν, καὶ κατὰ τρεῖς ἡμέρας ἀνεγείρει
ἄνεμον ἰσχυρόν, καὶ ἐκριζοῖ οἰκίας καὶ δένδρα καὶ βουνοὺς καὶ
ἀνθρώπους ἀπόλλυσι, ῥίπτων τούτους εἰς κρημνοὺς καὶ εἰς ὕδωρ
καὶ εἰς πῦρ. 2. εἰ οὖν βούλει τὸ σὸν κράτος, ἀπόστειλον καὶ
ἐξάλειψον καὶ ἐξολόθρευσον τοῦτον * ἀπὸ τῆς τοιαύτης χώρας.
20 εἰ οὖν τοῦτο ποιήσει ἡ βασιλεία σου, εἰσενέγκομεν εἰς τὴν τοῦ
ναοῦ οἰκοδομὴν τάλαντα χρυσίου καὶ ἀργυρίου καὶ χαλκοῦ ἑκατὸν εἴκοσι πέντε.‹

3. Ἀναγνοὺς οὖν τὴν ἐπιστολὴν ὁ βασιλεὺς ἐνετείλατο τῷ
παιδαρίῳ τῷ ἔχοντι τὴν σφραγίδα τάχιστα καταλαβεῖν πρὸς αὐ-
25 τόν καὶ ἐλθόντος φησὶν ὅτι· ›τάχιστα ἄπελθε εἰς τὸν τῶν
Ἀράβων βασιλέα, καὶ λάβε μετά σου τὴν σφραγῖδα καὶ κάμηλον
μίαν τὴν ταχίστην καὶ ἀσκὸν καινόν. 4. καὶ δειξάτω σοι τὸν
τόπον ἔνθα πνεῖ τὸ πονηρὸν πνεῦμα· καὶ καταλαβὼν τὸν τόπον
ἐκεῖνον ἐπίθες τὸν ἀσκὸν ἀνεῳγμένον ἔχοντα τὸ στόμα αὐτοῦ
30 πρὸς τῇ ὀπῇ τοῦ φωλεοῦ, καὶ παρατήρει τὴν ἡμέραν ἐν ᾗ ἐξέρχε-

§ 16. l. 1 * f. 374ʳ
C. V. l 7 Ὠικοδομεῖτο ego οἰκοδόμητο ms., -μεῖτο Is   8 σιβύλλα ms.,
(Σι-) Is, l. Σιβύλλα?
C. VI l. l. 16 ἐκριζοῖ Is ἐκριζεῖ ms.   18 § 2. βούλει l. βούλεται?
19 * f. 374ᵛ   20 εἰσενέγκομεν Is εἰσενέγκωμεν ms.   § 3. l. 26 ἀρά-
βων ms.   27 § 4. σοι ego σε ms.   28 ἔχοντα ego ἔχον ms.

ται τὸ πονηρὸν πνεῦμα. 5. καὶ ὅταν ἴδῃς τὸν ἀσκὸν πλησθέντα
δίκην ἀνέμου, ἀσφάλισαι μετὰ τοῦ δακτυλίου τὸ στόμα αὐτοῦ
τοῦ ἀσκοῦ, καὶ ἐπίθες αὐτὸν εἰς τὴν κάμηλον καὶ κατάλαβε
ταχέως πρὸς ἡμᾶς.‹

6. Καὶ ἀπῆλθε τὸ παιδάριον καὶ ἐποίησε πάντα κατὰ τὴν
θέλησιν τοῦ βασιλέως Σολομῶντος. 7. ἐπαναστρέφοντος δὲ αὐτοῦ λέγει τὸ δαιμόνιον· ›ἄνοιξόν μοι, ὦ παιδίον, καὶ ἐπιδείξω
σοι τόπον ἐν ᾧ κέκρυπται πράσινος λίθος καὶ τὸ χρυσίον τὸ
τίμιον.‹ τὸ δὲ παιδίον λέγει· ›ἀπέλθωμεν πρῶτον πρὸς τὸν
βασιλέα, καὶ μετὰ ταῦτα αὐτοῦ κελεύοντος ποιήσομεν.‹ 8. ὡς δὲ
τὴν ὁδὸν ἤνυσαν καὶ τὸν τόπον κατέλαβον ἐν ᾧ ἦν, πεσὼν ἐκ τῆς κα-
μήλου προσεκύνει ἄνω καὶ κάτω φερόμενος τὸν Σολομῶντα. 9. ὁ
δὲ βασιλεὺς φησι· ›τίς εἶ καὶ τίς σου τὸ ὄνομα;‹ ὁ δέ φησι·
›δαιμόνιόν εἰμι, Ἐφίππας καλούμενος.‹ 10. καὶ λέγει αὐτῷ·
›δύνασαι ποιῆσαί μοι τι χρήσιμον;‹ καὶ ὁ Ἐφίππας· ›δύναμαι
ἆραι τὸν λίθον τὸν ἀκρογωνιαῖον ὃν ἀπεδοκίμασαν ἄνθρωποί
τε καὶ δαίμονες καὶ θεῖναι τοῦτον εἰς κεφαλὴν γωνίας·‹ 11. καὶ
ὁ βασιλεὺς προέτρεψε τὸν Ἐφίππαν πονῆσαι ταῦτα. καὶ ἐποίησε
τοῦτο ὁρώντων πάντων τοῦ τε βασιλέως καὶ τῶν περιεστηκότων
ἀνδρῶν. 12. ἔκθαμβος δὲ γενόμενος ὁ βασιλεὺς ἤρετο τὸ Ἐφίππαν εἰ γινώσκοι καὶ ἕτερον πνεῦμα ὅμοιον αὐτῷ. καὶ λέγει ὁ
Ἐφίππας ›ἔστι, βασιλεῦ, καὶ ἕτερον πνεῦμα * ἐν τῇ Ἐρυθρᾷ
θαλάσσῃ καθήμενον καὶ ἔχον ἐν ἑαυτῷ τὸν πορφυροῦν κίονα.‹
13. καὶ λέγει ὁ βασιλεύς· ›ἄπελθε μετὰ τῆς σφραγῖδος καὶ ἄγαγέ
μοι αὐτὸν ὧδε.‹ ἀπελθὼν δὲ ὁ Ἐφίππας μετὰ τῆς σφραγῖδος
καὶ ἀνασπάσας αὐτὸν ἤγαγεν αὐτόν τε καὶ δαίμονας δύο βαστάζοντας τὸν κίονα καὶ φέροντας τοῦτον εἰς τὸν ἀέρα. 14. ἰδὼν
δὲ ταῦτα ὁ βασιλεὺς καὶ ἔκθαμβος γενόμενος ἐκέλευσεν αὐτοῖς βαστάζειν τὸν κίονα καὶ κρέμασθαι εἰς τὸν ἀέρα μέχρι τῆς συντελείας τοῦ αἰῶνος καὶ μὴ ῥῖψαι τοῦτον ἐπὶ τῆς γῆς ποτε, μήπως
λύμην τῷ τῶν ἀνθρώπων προξενήσωσι γένει.

§ 6 l. 6 * f. 373ʳ § 7. l. 7 ἐπιδείξω Is. ἐπεδείξω ms. § 8. l. 12 προσεκύνει ego. προσεκύνη ms., προσεκύνη σε Is § 9. l 14 Ἐφίππας Is· ἐφ'
Ἵππας ms. § 11 l 18 πονῆσαι· ποιῆσαι Is § 12. l. 21 γινώσκοι ego
γινώσκεις ms. 22 * f. 373ᵛ 23 ἔχων ms.

VII. *Πάλιν οὖν ὁ βασιλεὺς πρὸς τὸν Ὀρνίαν λέγει·* »ἔστι
καὶ ἕτερον δαιμόνιον;« καὶ ὁ Ὀρνίας λέγει· »εἰσὶ μὲν πολλά, ὦ
*βασιλεῦ· ὑπάρχει δὲ ἀπὸ τούτων ἓν μεγίστην κεκτημένον τὴν
δύναμιν.«* 2 *»ποῖον δὲ τοῦτο,« φησὶν ὁ βασιλεύς, »καὶ τίνα με-
5 γίστην ἔχει τὴν δύναμιν καὶ τί τούτῳ τὸ ὄνομα,«* Ὁ Ὀρνίας
λέγει· »Σαμαὴλ τὸ ὄνομα, ὦ βασιλεῦ, ἄρχων δὲ τοῦ τῶν δαι-
*μόνων ὑπάρχει συστήματος· καὶ συμφέρον σοι ὑπάρχει, ὦ βασι-
λεῦ, τοῦ μὴ ἰδεῖν αὐτόν.« 3. *καὶ ὁ βασιλεύς·* »μηδέν σοι * περὶ
τούτου μελέτω, πονηρὸν καὶ ἀκάθαρτον πνεῦμα, ἀλλὰ λαβὼν
10 *τὴν σφραγῖδα ἄγαγέ μοι αὐτὸν ὧδε κατὰ τάχος«* λαβὼν δὲ ὁ
Ὀρνίας *τὴν σφραγῖδα τοῦ θεοῦ ἀπῆλθε τὸ τοῦ βασιλέως πληρώ-
σων θέλημα. 4. *ὁ δὲ Σολομῶν ἐπὶ θρόνου καθήμενος ἦν τῷ
τῆς βασιλείας κεκοσμημένος στέμματί τε καὶ διαδήματι καὶ τὸν
Ὀρνίαν *μετὰ τοῦ Σαμαὴλ ἐκδεχόμενος, σκῆπτρόν τε τὸ βασιλι-
15 κὸν ἀνὰ χεῖρα εἶχεν.* 5 *ἐλθόντων δὲ τοῦ τε Σαμαὴλ καὶ τοῦ*
Ὀρνία *πρὸς τὸν βασιλέα, φησὶν ὁ βασιλεὺς πρὸς τὸν Σαμαήλ·
*»τίς εἶ, καὶ τί σου τὸ ὄνομα;« ὁ δέ φησι· »Σαμαὴλ κέκλημαι·
ἄρχων δὲ τοῦ τῶν δαιμόνων ὑπάρχω συστήματος. 6. *καὶ ὁ
βασιλεύς· »δύνασαι ποιῆσαί μέ τι;« *ὁ δέ φησι·* »δύναμαι ἐμ-
20 *φυσῆσαί σοι καὶ ἀπαγαγεῖν σε εἰς τὸ ἔσχατον τῆς γῆς.« καὶ
*ἅμα τῷ λόγῳ ἐνεφύσησεν αὐτὸν καὶ ἀπήγαγεν εἰς τὰ ἔσχατα
τῆς γῆς.

VIII. *Διεφημίζετο δὲ ἡ φήμη τοῦ βασιλέως εἰς πάντα τὰ
*πέρατα τῆς γῆς, καὶ προσκυνοῦντες ἦσαν αὐτῷ πάντες οἱ βασι-
25 *λεῖς τῆς γῆς καὶ οἱ ἄρχοντες, καὶ χορηγοῦντες εἰς τὴν τοῦ
ναοῦ οἰκοδομήν. 2. *τῷ δὲ καιρῷ ἐκείνῳ * ἐρρητόρευσε τὸ
ᾆσμα τῶν ᾀσμάτων. καὶ ἔλεγεν οὕτως· »ἐκτησάμην βασιλείαν·
*ἐκτησάμην ᾄδοντας καὶ ᾀδούσας.« καὶ καταλέξας τὰ πάντα τέ-
λος ἐπάγει· »τὰ πάντα δὲ ματαιότης ματαιοτήτων· τὰ πάντα

---

§ 3. l. 8 * f. 372ʳ   § 6. l. 22 In hoc loco add. c. VIII 4 James
forte c. VIII 1 post 2—7 ponendum
     C VIII. § 2 l 26 ἐκείνῳ in marg. inf. scr man. prim. | * f. 372ᵛ

§ 2. 27 cf. Ec. 2 7 *ἐκτησάμην δούλους καὶ παιδίσκας,* 2 8 *ἐποίησά μοι*
ᾄδοντας καὶ ᾀδούσας   29 Ec. 1·2, 12·8f.

ματαιότης.« 3. ἔλεγε δὲ καὶ τοῦτο· »πάντων τῶν γραμμάτων
ἄρχει τὸ x̄ 4. εὐδοκίᾳ δὲ θεοῦ διεσώθη Σολομῶν εἰς τὰ αὐτοῦ
βασίλεια. 5. καὶ ᾠκοδομεῖτο ὁ πάνσεπτος ναὸς τοῦ θεοῦ. ᾠκοδομεῖτο δὲ πάντα κατὰ μίμησιν τῆς ἀνατάξεως. 6. ὑπῆρχον τὰ
χερουβὶμ καὶ τὰ σεραφὶμ καὶ τὰ ἑξαπτέρουγα· ὄπισθεν δὲ τοῦ
θυσιαστηρίου τὰ πολυόμματα καὶ οἱ θρόνοι καὶ αἱ κυριότητες.
7. ἄρρητον δὲ τὸ κάλλος τοῦ τοιούτου ναοῦ καὶ ἀνερμήνευτον,
καὶ τοιοῦτον οἷον οὔτε ἐγένετο οὔτε γενήσεται.

---

5. ll. **3—4** οἰκοδομεῖτο ms. (bis)   § 7. l. 7 κάλλος Is κάλλους ms.

CONSPECTUS TITULORUM

Tituli Codicum Manu Scriptorum Recensionum A, B, et C
Titulus Codicum MSS PQ

Διαθήκη Σολομῶντος υἱοῦ Δαυείδ, ὃς ἐβασίλευσεν ἐν Ἱερου-
5 σαλὴμ καὶ ἐκράτησεν καὶ ὑπέταξεν πάντων ἀερίων, ἐπιγείων, καὶ
καταχθονίων πνευμάτων· δι᾽ ὧν καὶ πάντα τὰ ἔργα τοῦ ναοῦ τὰ
ὑπερβάλλοντα πεποίηκεν· καὶ τίνες αἱ ἐξουσίαι αὐτῶν κατὰ ἀνθρώπων, καὶ παρὰ ποίων ἀγγέλων οὗτοι οἱ δαίμονες καταργοῦνται. τοῦ σοφοῦ Σολομῶντος.

10 ### Titulus Codicis MS I

⟨Διαθήκη τ⟨οῦ⟩⟩ Σολομῶντος υἱοῦ Δαυείδ, ὃς ἐβασίλευσεν ἐν
Ἱερουσαλήμ, καὶ περὶ τῶν δαιμόνων οὓς ἐκράτησε, καὶ τίνες εἰσὶν αἱ ἐξουσίαι δοθεῖσαι αὐτῷ ὑπὸ θεοῦ κατὰ τῶν δαιμόνων καὶ
παρὰ τίνων ἀγγέλων καταργοῦνται οἱ δαίμονες, καὶ τὰ ἔργα τοῦ
15 ναοῦ ἃ ὑπερβαλλόντως πεποίηκεν.

Titulus Codicis MS H

Διήγησις περὶ τῆς διαθήκης Σολομῶντος καὶ περὶ τῆς ἐλεύ-
σεως τῶν δαιμόνων καὶ περὶ τῆς τοῦ ναοῦ οἰκοδομῆς.

MSS PQ. Du C(angius in *Notae ad Zonorae Annalia*, p. 83), Fab(ricius,
Cod. Pseudepigr. Vet. Test. I 1036 sq.) **4** Διαθήκη P· ἡ διήγησις Q | δς.
ὡς Q **5—6** πάντων . . πνευμ. om. Q | ἐπιγείων om DuC. **7** αἱ om. Q
| ἀνθρ. pr. τῶν Q **8** οὗτοι PQ· εἶτοι DuC, αὐτοὶ conj. Fab | καταρ-
γοῦνται P καταρχθῦνται DuC, καταργάζονται Q **9** τοῦ σ. Σολ. P om. Q
DuC Fab | Hic sequitur benedictio, cf. infra p. 99* l. 1 s.

MS I. l. **11** Διαθήκη τοῦ· in marg sup. negligenter exaratis litteris scr
man. alt. διαθήκη τ **14** οἱ εἱ ms. | Sequitur benedictio

MS H. l **17** Sequitur benedictio, cf. infra

Benedictio Codicum MSS HIPQ

Εὐλογητὸς εἶ, κύριε ὁ Θεός, ὁ δοὺς τῷ Σολομῶντι τὴν ἐξουσίαν ταύτην. σοὶ δόξα καὶ κράτος εἰς τοὺς αἰῶνας· ἀμήν.

Titulus Codicum MSS VW

Διαθήκη τοῦ σοφωτάτου Σολομῶντος μετὰ τῶν παραλλήλων αὐτῆς ὀνομάτων ἅτινα ὡς μυστήρια ὑπὸ τοῦ Ἐζεκίου μετὰ τὸ ἀποθανεῖν τὸν Δαυεὶδ τὸν βασιλέαν ἐφυλάχθησαν.

Subscriptio Codicis MS V

Τέλος τῆς διαθήκης τοῦ σοφωτάτου Σολομῶν²τος υἱοῦ Δαβίδ, ὅπερ ἐγράφη μετὰ τὸ ³ἀποθανεῖν Δα(βὶ)δ τὸν βασιλέαν ὃς ⁴ἐφυλάχθη ὑπὸ Ἐζεκίου τοῦ βασιλέως. ⁵ἐγράφη παρ᾽ ἐμοῦ Ἰω(άννου) ἰατροῦ τοῦ αρο(?)· ἐν ἔτει ͵ϛϠμθ´ ⁶(ἰνδικτιόνος) δ´ ἐν μηνὶ Δεκε(μ)βρίῳ ιδ´. ⁷καὶ ὁ θεός ἐστι μεθ᾽ ἡμῶν καὶ οὐδεὶς καθ᾽ ἡμῶν.

MSS HIPQ. 1. 2 εἶ om. H | κύριε om. HQ | ὁ Θεός om. IQ | τ. ἐξους. ταυτ.· τοιαύτην ἐξουσίαν PQ   3 σοὶ .. ἀμήν PQ om. I

MSS VW. 1. 5 παραλλ. add. π̅ν̅ο̅ύ̅ (1 πνευμάτων) V   6 ἅτινα ὡς W· εἷος (1. ἃ ὡς) V | μυστ. add. ἐφυλάχθη V   7 ἀποθανὸν W | τὸν om. V ἐφυλάχθησαν om V | In πίνακι MS V scr. man. alt. titulum hunc ἡ διαθήκη τοῦ σολομῶντος περὶ τ(οὺς) δαίμονας πῶς ἐπίασ(εν) αὐτοὺς καὶ ἔκτισεν τὴν ἁγί(αν) σι(όν).

MS V. ll. 9—13 Numeri superiores ad lineas textus referunt. Τέλος αρο in notis Tironianis scriptum est   9 Δαβίδ· δαβηθ ms.   10 ὅπερ 1. ἥπερ | δϛ· 1. ἡ   12 Δεκεμβ. δεκενρίω ms.

SIGILLA ANULI SALOMONIS

PQ Ἡ δὲ γλυφὴ τῆς σφραγίδος τοῦ δακτυλιδίου τῆς πεμφθεί-
σεις ἐστὶν πεντάλφα αὕτη.

L Ἡ δὲ σφραγὶς ταῦτα ἔλεγεν· ἰδοὺ αὕτη ἐστὶν ἡ σφραγίς|
5 κ̄ ō θ̄ ρ̄ σ̄ β̄ ῑ ω̄ ν̄ κ̄ ᾱ ω̄ ᾱ ω̄ ε̄ λ̄ ῑ γ̄ ω̄ ῑ ō σ̄ γ̄ ω̄ ā ε̄ σ̄ ρ̄ ου ρ̄ +

HL Ἦν δὲ ἡ γλυφὶς αὐτοῦ* λέγων οὕτως· κ(ύρι)ε ὁ θεὸς ἡμῶν·
λέων· λέων· σαβαώθ· βιωνίκ· ἀωᾶ· ἐλωΐ· αιαῶ· αιῶ· ιωασέ· σου-
γεωά· αιέ· ἀενίου· οὐ· οὐνίου· ἠρώ.

T Περὶ τοῦ δακτυλιδίου· Λαβὼν κηρὸν παρθένον, ποίησον
10 δακτυλίδιον ὥσπερ ὁρᾷς φορεῖν ἐν τῷ δεξιῷ σου δακτύλῳ τῆς
χειρός σου. περιενδύσας αὐτῷ χαρτίον παρθένον ἐπίγραφε πᾶν
μετὰ κονδυλίου τῆς τέχνης ταῦτα τὰ ιβ' ὀνόματα· λέων· σαβαώθ·
βιωνιά· ἐλωΐ· ἀωά· λαώ· ιασού· σουιεωά· ἀενιού· οὐ· οὐνιού·
ιού· ιρώ.

15 Vʳ. Τοῦ Σολομῶντος μεγάλου· λθλθῑ | μ̄ κ(ύρι)ε ὁ θ(εὸ)ς
ἡμ|ῶν· λεων· σαβα|ωθ· αιαῶ· βιονη|κα· ωαελοῑ· ιωα|σε· σουγεῶ·
α|αιε· αε· νιουφυ|ουνη· ιαησ|ω

MSS PQ = Rec B. ll. 2—3. l. 3 in mss. pentalpha non est

MS L. ll. 4—5. 1 4 ταῦτα αὐτὰ ms. | αὕτη ἐστὶν οὕτη εἰσὶν ms.

MSS HI. ll. 6—8. l. 6 αὐτοῖ HIs· αὕτη I | * H f. 2ᵛ | λέγων
λέγοντος(?) Diels, l. fortasse λέγουσα   7 λέων. om. H, λέγων Is | post
σαβαώθ scripta ἀωᾶ· ἐλωΐ· αιαῶ· ἐλωΐ transversis lineis delevit I | βιο-
νίκ H | ἀωᾶ I ᾱ· ω̄· ᾱ· H | αιαῶ I ἐαὼ H, add. ἐλωΐ· I | αιῶ om. H
8 αιὰ H, ἀγέ I | οὐ om. I | οὐνίου: οὐρανίου Is | ἠρα H

MS T. ll. 9—14 vide *Introductionem* p. 19 s   10 δρ(ας) ms. | χει-
ρας ms.

MS Vʳ. ll. 15—17 vide *Introductionem* p. 24 s.

Rec. C. *Ἦν δὲ ἡ ἐπιγραφὴ τῆς σφραγῖδος τοῦ δακτυλίου αὕτη·* . . . . . * *καὶ ἔδωκεν τῷ Σολομῶντι· αὗταί εἰσιν αἱ ἔνδεκα σφραγῖδαι ἃς ἔδωκεν ὁ ἄγγελος μετὰ τῶν δώδεκα λίθων· ἐξ ὧν ἡ μία σφραγῖδα ἔχει τῶν χαρισμάτων τὸ μέγεθος.*

Sigilla Salomonis ex ms. L.

MSS VW. ll. 1—2 *Ἦν . . . Σολομῶντι*   2 *αὕτη: ταύτης αὕτη ἡ σφραγ(ῖδα) τοῦ δακτυληδίου* V | hic, sequuntur duodecim sigilla | * V f. 437ᵛ, W f. 267ᵛ | *Σολομῶντι τὸν υἱὸν δᾱδ* V

MSS VVˢW. ll. 2—4 *αἷται . . . μέγεθος*   3 *μετὰ . . . λίθων: τὸν σολομῶντα* Vˢ, add. *τὸν τὰ προτία ἔχων τὸν ιβ' λιθ* <. *Μετὰ (δὲ) τὸ λαβ(εῖν) τ(ὴν) ᾱ σφραγήδ(αν). ἐδόθισαν καὶ αὗται αἱ ἔνδεκα* V | *ἐξ ὧν* VW: *ἐξ οὗ* Vˢ 4 *σφραγ.* om. Vˢ | *τῶν .. μεγ.: τὸ χαρισμ* < *καὶ τὴν χάριδ* < *καὶ ιβ' λειθ* < *με* (l. *μετ'*) *αὐτ(ῶν)* Vˢ

ΔΙΗΓΗΣΙΣ ΠΕΡΙ ΤΟΥ ΠΡΟΦΗΤΟΥ ΚΑΙ
ΣΟΦΩΤΑΤΟΥ ΤΟΥ ΒΑΣΙΛΕΩΣ ΣΟΛΟΜΩΝΤΟΣ

Ι. *Διήγησις περὶ τοῦ σοφωτάτου βασιλέως Σολομῶντος πολὺ ὠφέλιμος, ὅπου ἦτον υἱὸς τοῦ προφήτου Δαυεὶδ τοῦ βασιλέως·*
5 *καὶ ἀκούσατε πῶς τὸν ἐγέννησεν τὸν Σολομῶν⟨τα⟩ ἀπὸ τοῦ Οὐρία τὴν γυναῖκα τὴν ὁποίαν τὴν εἶδεν ὁ προφήτης Δαυείδ.* 2. *ἀγναντεύοντες εἶδεν αὐτὴν ἀπὸ τὰ παραθύρια τοῦ παλατίου του καὶ τὴν ἠγάπησεν καὶ ἔστειλεν καὶ τὴν ἐπῆρεν καὶ ἔπεσεν μετ' αὐτῆς. καὶ ἐγγαστρώθη καὶ ἐγέννησεν αὐτὸν τὸν σοφώτα-*
10 *τον Σολομῶν⟨τα⟩.* 3. *καὶ ὄχι μόνον πῶς ἔκαμεν τὴν μοιχείαν ἀλλὰ καὶ τὸν ταλαίπωρον τὸν ἄνδρα της ἔστειλεν καὶ τὸν ἐφόνευσεν.*

4. *Καὶ ἰδὼν ὁ μεγαλοδύναμος θεὸς τὸ κακὸν ὁπού ἐποίησεν ὁ Δαυεὶδ καὶ θέλοντας νὰ τὸν γυρίσῃ εἰς ἐπιστρόφην καὶ εἰς με-*
15 *τάνοιαν ἵνα μὴν κολασθῇ αἰωνίως, ἔστειλεν τὸν ἀρχάγγελον αὐ- τοῦ Μιχαὴλ βαστῶντας εἰς τὰς χεῖρας αὐτοῦ ἕνα μαχαίρι δίστο- μον.* 5. *καὶ ἐπῆγεν εἰς τὸν προφήτην Νάθαν καὶ εἶπεν αὐτόν· »ὕπαγε ἔλεγχον τὸν προφήτην Δαυεὶδ τὸν βασιλέαν εἰς * τὴν μεγάλην ἁμαρτίαν ὁπού ἔκαμεν. καὶ ἐσὺ μὴν φοβᾶσαι τίποτες*
20 *ὅτι ἐγὼ θέλω στέκεσθαι εἰς τοὺς νόμους ὀπίσω μὲ τοῦτο τὸ δίστομον σπαθὶ τὸ ξεγυμνωμένον. καὶ ἐσὺ Νάθαν θέλεις με βλέπειν καὶ ὁ Δαυεὶδ δὲν θέλει με βλέπειν οὐδὲ ποσῶς.*

6. *Καὶ οὕτως ἐγερθεὶς ὁ Νάθαν κατὰ τὸν λόγον τοῦ ἀρχ- αγγέλου καὶ ἐπῆγεν εἰς τὸν προφήτην Δαυεὶδ καὶ ἔλεγξεν αὐτὸν*
25 *καὶ του ἔλεγεν παραβολικῶς· »βασιλέα καὶ προφήτη Δαυεὶδ, ἄν- θρωπος εἶχεν ἐννενήκοντα ἐννέα προβατίνες. καὶ εἶχεν καὶ ἕνα δοῦλον, καὶ ὁ δοῦλός του ἐκεῖνος εἶχεν μόνον μίαν προβατίναν.*

MS E = codex Monasterii Sancti Saba 290; inc. f. 177ᵛ. Ad. c. I cf. D
I 1—11. Tit.· add. λόγ⟨ος⟩ β   C. I § 1 l. 8 πολλὶ   18 ἔλεξον | * f. 178ᵛ
20 στέκεστε   24 ἔλεξον   25 βασιλέαν   26 ἐνέαν

καὶ ἐξήλευσέν του καὶ του τὴν ἐπῆρεν καὶ εἰς τὸ τέλος ἔστειλεν
καὶ τὸν ἐφόνευσεν καὶ ἐπῆρεν καὶ τὴν προβατίναν του. καὶ ὡς
δικαιοκρίτης ὁποῦ εἶσαι, ἀπόφασισον τί μέλλει γενέσθαι ὁ ἄνθρωπος ἐκεῖνος;« 7. Καὶ ἀπεκρίθη ὁ προφήτης Δαυεὶδ καὶ εἶπεν
5 ὅτι· »ἐκεῖνος ὁ ἄνθρωπος πρέπει νὰ σκάψουν ἕνα λάκκον καὶ
τὸν ἐβάλουν μέσα ἕως τὴν μέσην καὶ νὰ τὸν ἐχώσουν μὲ τὸ χῶμα
καὶ οὕτως νὰ τὸν λιθοβολήσουν«. 8. καὶ λέγει ὁ προφήτης
Νάθαν· »ὦ βασιλεῦ, ἐσὺ εἶσαι ἐκεῖνος ὁποῦ ἔκαμες τὸν φόνον
καὶ τὴν μοιχείαν«. 9. καὶ τότες ὁ Δαυεὶδ ὡσὰν ἄκουσεν, ἔτζι
10 ἔμεινεν ὡσὰν νεκρὸς καὶ ἄλλαξεν ἡ ὄψις τοῦ προσώπου του.
καὶ ἐγνώρισεν τὴν ἁμαρτίαν του ὁποῦ ἔκαμεν τὸ πῶς ἦτον μεγάλη. ὅμως * δὲν ὑπερηφανεύθηκεν ὡς βασιλέας ὁποῦ ἦτον ἵνα
ὀργισθῇ κατὰ τοῦ προφήτου Νάθαν ὁποῦ τὸν ἔλεγξεν μεγάλως,
ἀμὴ παρευθὺς ἐσηκώθη ἀπὸ τὸν θρόνον του καὶ ἐπροσεκύνησεν
15 τὸν προφήτην Νάθαν μετὰ δακρύων καὶ ἀναστεναγμῶν ἐξ ὅλης
τῆς καρδίας καὶ εἶπεν· »ἀληθῶς ἐγὼ εἶμαι ὁποῦ ἥμαρτον ἐνώπιον τοῦ θεοῦ καὶ ἀνθρώπων«. 10. καὶ εὐθὺς ἔβγαλεν τὰ βα-
σιλικὰ φορέματα ὁποῦ ἐβάσταζεν καὶ ἔβαλεν σάκκον τρίχινον καὶ
εἰσέβη εἰς ἕνα λάκκον καὶ ἔλεγεν καὶ ἐθρήνει ὡς καθὼς ἔκαμεν
20 τὴν ἀπόφασιν μὲ τὴν κρίσιν του καὶ ἐκεῖ ἥρμοσεν τὸ ψαλτήριον
αὐτὸ ὁποῦ διαβάζομεν ἡμεῖς τὴν σήμερον ἡμέραν. καὶ μετ᾽ ἐκείνην τὴν μετάνοιαν ἐσυνχώρεσέν τον ὁ θεὸς καὶ ἐκοιμήθη ἐν
Κυρίῳ ἅγιος καὶ προφήτης καὶ βασιλέας.

II. Τὸ λοιπὸν ἃς ἔλθωμεν καὶ εἰς τὸν υἱόν του τὸν βασιλέαν
25 Σολομῶντα ὁποῦ ἦτον μέγας καὶ σοφὸς καὶ ἦτον υἱὸς τοῦ προφήτου Δαυεὶδ καὶ ἐπαρέλαβεν τὸν θρόνον τοῦ πατρός του καὶ
ἡ σοφία του ὑπὲρ πᾶσαν τὴν σοφίαν τοῦ κόσμου. καὶ ἐζήτησεν
σοφίαν ἀπὸ τὸν θεὸν καὶ οὐχὶ πλοῦτον καὶ δόξαν καὶ τιμήν.
ὅμως ὁ θεὸς ἔδωσέν του ὅλα τὰ καλά, τὴν σοφίαν, τὸν πλοῦτον
30 καὶ τὴν δόξαν καὶ τὴν τιμήν. 2. καὶ ὅμως θαρρόντας εἰς τὴν
σοφίαν τὴν πολλὴν ὁποῦ του ἔδωσεν ὁ θεὸς ἐβουλήθη νὰ κτίσῃ
ἐκεῖνον τὸν ναὸν τοῦ θεοῦ ὁποῦ ἠθέλησεν νὰ τὸν ἀρχίσῃ ὁ πα-

---

9 l 9 l. ἔτσι   10 ἄλαξεν   11 * f. 178ᵛ   13 ἔλεξεν   14 ἀμὴ
= εἰ μὴ   17 § 10. εὔγαλεν   19 ἐσέβη   21 ἐκύνον   22 τὸν: του
C. II. v. parallela in ms. D I 12—II   24 τοῦ υἱοῦ | τοῦ βασιλέως
Σολομῶντος   30 § 2. θαρῶντας   31 πολλὴν. τηνλλυν scripto supra τὴν
scr. no man. prim.

τέρας του ὁ Δαυείδ. καὶ ὁ Σολομῶν ἐβουλήθη νὰ τὸν ἀνακτίσῃ
ἀπὸ θεμελίων ἐκλεκτὸν καὶ περίφημον ἵνα μὴ εὑρίσκεται κάτωθεν
τοῦ οὐρανοῦ εἰς τὴν γῆν ἀπάνω ὡσὰν ἐκεῖνον τὸν ναόν. 3. ὅμως
ἐσύναξεν τὴν κατασκευὴν ἅπασαν. λοιπὸν ἐσύναξεν τεχνίτας καὶ
5 μαΐστόρους ἐπιτηδείους τὸν ἀριθμὸν χιλιάδες τέσσαρις δίχως τῶν
ἐργατῶν. καὶ ἄρχισαν νὰ κτίζουν τὸν ναὸν τοῦ θεοῦ εἰς ὄνομα
τῆς ἁγίας Σιών.

3. Λοιπὸν ὁ βασιλεὺς Σολομῶν εἶχεν ἕνα παιδίον πολλὰ
ὡραιότατον καὶ ποθεινότατον ἀπὸ ὅλα τὰ παιδία τοῦ παλατίου
10 του καὶ ἦτον σῶφρον καὶ γνωστικὸν καὶ ἐπιτήδειον εἰς πᾶσα
τέχνην, καὶ ἐχαίρετον ὁ βασιλεὺς βλέποντάς το καὶ τὸ ἔκαμεν
ἐπίτροπον καὶ ἐπιτηρητὴν εἰς πᾶσαν του θέλησιν καὶ ἀγάπα το
ὁ βασιλεὺς καὶ εἶχεν το ὡσὰν ἴδιον υἱόν. λοιπὸν τὸ ἔβαλεν ὁ
βασιλεὺς τὸ παιδίον ἐκεῖνο ἀπάνω εἰς τοὺς μαΐστόρους ὅπου
15 ἐδούλευαν τὸν ναὸν τοῦ θεοῦ ἐπίτροπον καὶ ἐπιτηρητὴν καὶ
ἑρμήνευεν τοὺς μαΐστόρους ὅπου ἐδούλευαν τὸν ναὸν τοῦ θεοῦ.
καὶ ἔβλεπαν ὅλοι τὸ παιδίον καὶ αὐτὸς ὁ βασιλεὺς καὶ ἐθαύμαζαν
εἰς τὴν γνῶσιν ὅπου εἶχεν 4. ὅμως βλέποντας ὁ διάβολος ὁ
ἐχθρὸς τῆς ἀληθείας δὲν ἠμπόριεν ὁ μιαρὸς νὰ βλέπῃ τὸ ἔργον
20 ὅπου ἐκαταπιάστηκεν ὁ βασιλεὺς Σολομῶν ὅπου οἰκοδόμα τὸν
ναὸν τοῦ θεοῦ καὶ ἤθελεν νὰ κάμῃ καὶ τὸν βασιλέαν νὰ λυπηθῇ
διὰ νὰ ἀμελήσῃ τὸ ἔργον τοῦ θεοῦ ἐκεῖνο διὰ νὰ μὴν φτειαστῇ
τελείαν

5. Ἀλλὰ θέλετε τὸ * ἀκούσῃ παρέμπροσθεν τί ἔπαθεν ὁ
25 μιαρὸς καὶ ἐγελάσθη καὶ ἐπιάσθη καὶ αἰσχύνθη. λοιπὸν εἰς
ἐκεῖνες τὲς ἡμέρες ἄρχισεν ἐκεῖνο τὸ ὡραιότατον παιδίον καὶ
ἔχανεν τὴν ὄψιν του καὶ τὸν νοῦν του καὶ ἔγινεν ὡσὰν ἐξεστη-
κόν. λοιπὸν ἤρχετον ἀοράτως ἀπὸ τὸν ἀέρα ἕνα πονηρὸν πνεῦμα
καὶ ἀκάθαρτον δαιμόνιον καὶ ἐπείραζε τὸ παιδίον ὅποτε ἤθελεν
30 νὰ κοιμηθῇ εἰς τὴν κλίνην του καὶ τοῦ ἔδειχνεν ὁ μιαρὸς δαίμων λογιῶν φαντασίες. 6. καὶ βλέποντας ὁ βασιλεὺς τὸ παιδίον
ἐκεῖνο ἐθαύμαξεν καὶ ἐλυπᾶτον πολὺ καὶ ἔδιδέν του ὁ βασιλεὺς
διπλὸν τὸ φαγητὸν καὶ τὰ φορέματά του παρὰ τῶν ἄλλων παι-

---

1 * f. 179ʳ | νὰ ... θεμελίων per dittographiam bis scr.   5 τέσαρης
9 παιδίαν   12 πᾶσα του θέλημα corr. Pr. Bessarion   15 ἐδούλευεν
§ 4. 1. 20 οἰκοδόμαν   § 5. 1. 24 * f 179ᵛ   25 ἐπηάσθην | αἰσχύνθην
§ 6. 1 32 πολλὶ

ὅλων ὁποῦ εἶχεν εἰς τὸ παλάτιόν του ὅπως νὰ ἔλθῃ εἰς τὴν
προτέραν του κατάστασιν καὶ εἰς τὴν τάξιν ὁποῦ εἶχεν, ἀλλὰ ἡ
ὄψις τοῦ προσώπου του δὲν ἄλλαξεν ἀλλὰ μᾶλλον εἰς τὸ χει-
ρότερον.

6. Καὶ μίαν τῶν ἡμερῶν ἐρώτησεν ὁ βασιλεὺς τὸ παιδίον
καὶ ἔλεγεν του· »εἰπέ μου, τέκνον μου, διὰ τί εἶσαι κίτρινος καὶ
σκυθρωπὸς εἰς τὴν ὄψιν καὶ ὁ νοῦς σου δὲν εἶναι μετὰ σοῦ μόνον εἶσαι παρηλλαγμένος«. 7. καὶ τὸ παιδίον δὲν ἤθελεν νὰ
εἰπῇ τοῦ βασιλέως τί ἔπάθενε καὶ βλέποντας τοῦτο ὁ βασιλεὺς πῶς
δὲν τοῦ ἀπηλογᾶτον ἐθαύμαζε καὶ ἐλυπᾶτον πολὺ τὸ τί νὰ κάμῃ
καὶ ἄρχισεν ὁ βασιλεὺς μετὰ ὀργῆς καὶ θυμοῦ καὶ ἔλεγεν πρὸς τὸ
παιδίον »νὰ μοῦ εἰπῇς τὴν ἀλήθειαν ἀπὸ τί ἐκαταστάθεις ἔτζι
εἰς τέτοιαν * θεωρίαν καὶ πῶς ἐβγῆκες ἔξαφνα ἀπὸ τὸν νοῦν
σου, ἀμμὴ νὰ ἠξεύρῃς ὅτι πολλὰ βάσανα μέλλεις νὰ πάθῃς καὶ
νὰ χάσῃς καὶ τὴν ζωήν σου. 8. ταῦτα ὡς ἤκουσεν τὸ παιδὶ
ἐκεῖνο ἔλεγεν πρὸς τὸν βασιλέαν μετὰ δακρύων καὶ φόβου καὶ
τρόμου· »αὐθέντη μου πολυχρονημένε, ἐμένα ὅλα τὰ καλά μου
τὰ ἔχει ἡ βασιλεία σου δομένα καὶ τίποτες δέν μου λείπει. ἀπὸ
τὰ καλὰ ὅλα αὐτὰ δὲν εὐφραίνεται ἡ καρδία μου, ἀλλὰ ἄκουσόν
μου, αὐθέντη, νὰ σοῦ διηγηθῶ τί παθαίνω. ἐκεῖ ὁποῦ κοιμοῦμαι
εἰς τὴν κλίνην μου ἔρχεται ἕνας ἄνθρωπος μαῦρος κατὰ πολλὰ
ὡσὰν Ἀράπης καὶ μὲ πλακώνει εἰς τὴν καρδίαν καὶ πιάνει τὴν
ἄκρην τοῦ δακτύλου μου τοῦ μικροῦ καὶ βυζάνει καὶ πίνει τὸ
αἷμα μου καὶ πάλιν μοῦ φαίνεται τὴν ἡμέραν καὶ ἔρχεται ὡς
ἄγγελος καὶ μοῦ λέγει ὅτι νὰ μὴν τὸ εἰπῶ τῆς βασιλείας σου
αὐτὰ ὁποῦ παθαίνω καὶ ἐκεῖνος θέλει με ἐγλυτώσει ἀπὸ τὸν
μαῦρον καὶ μοῦ εἶπεν ὅτι ἂν σοῦ τὸ εἰπῶ γλυτωμὸν δὲν ἔχω«.

9. Ταῦτα ἀκούσας ὁ βασιλεὺς ἐθαύμασεν καὶ εὐχαρίστησεν
κύριον τὸν θεὸν καὶ ἐνόησεν ὁ βασιλεὺς ὅτι ἐκεῖνος ὁμοῦ ἐπείρα-
ζεν τὸ παιδίον μὲ τοιαῦτες φαντασίες εἶναι πνεῦμα πονηρὸν καὶ
ἀκάθαρτον δαιμόνιον καὶ παρευθὺς ἔκαμεν ὁ βασιλεὺς δέησιν
πρὸς τὸν θεὸν μετὰ δακρύων καὶ μετὰ συντετριμμένης καρδίας
ἡμέραν καὶ νύκταν διὰ νὰ τοῦ ἀποκαλύψῃ ὁ θεὸς μὲ τί μόδον

---

§ 7. l. 8 ἤθελε   12 l. ἔτσι   13 * f. 180ʳ | εὐγῆκες | ἔξαφνα ego
ἔξα   14 ἀμὴ   § 8. l. 25 λέγει: λέῃ mss.   27 ὅτι ἂν ex ὁ ἂν   § 9.
l 32 καρδίαις

νὰ καταραθῇ τὸ δαιμόνιον ἐκεῖνο ὁποῦ ἐπείραξε τὸ παιδίον.
10. καὶ ἰδὼν ὁ θεὸς τὰ δάκρυα καὶ τοὺς κόπους του εἰσή-
κουσεν ὁ θεὸς τῆς δεήσεως Σολομῶν⟨τος⟩ καὶ παρευθὺς
ἔστειλεν τὸν ἀρχάγγελον αὐτοῦ Μιχαὴλ μὲ μίαν βοῦλλαν ἤγουν
5 σφραγῖδα καὶ τὴν ἔδωκεν τοῦ βασιλέως καὶ τοῦ εἶπεν ὅτι ἐκεῖνος ὁ Ἀράπης ἦτον πονηρὸν δαιμόνιον καὶ ἔρχεται ἀοράτως καὶ
πειράζει τὸ παιδίον καὶ ὁ βασιλεὺς νὰ τὴν δώσῃ τοῦ παιδίου
καὶ ᾿ὅταν ὑπάγῃ πάλιν τὸ δαιμόνιον εἰς τὴν κλίνην νὰ τὸν
πειράξῃ, νὰ τὸν κρούσῃ εἰς τὸ στῆθος μὲ τὴν σφραγῖδα τοῦ
10 θεοῦ καὶ νὰ τὸν δέσῃ καὶ νὰ τὸν φέρῃ ἔμπροσθέν σου καὶ ἐσὺ
Σολομῶν ἐξέταξον αὐτὸν ἵνα σου δείξῃ ὅλες τον τὲς ἐπιβουλὲς
καὶ ἐσὺ μετ᾽ αὐτῆς τῆς σφραγῖδος θέλεις πατάξῃ πάντα διάβολον
καὶ τὴν δύναμίν του καὶ νὰ τοὺς συνάξῃ ὅλους τοῦ ἀέρος καὶ
τῆς γῆς καὶ τῆς θαλάσσης καὶ τῶν καταχθονίων καὶ νὰ οἰκοδομήσῃς
15 τὸν ναὸν τοῦ θεοῦ μετ᾽ αὐτῶν τῶν πονηρῶν δαιμόνων καὶ νὰ
εἶνε ἐργάτες εἰς τοὺς τεχνίτας». 11. καὶ ἐπῆρεν ὁ βασιλεὺς τὴν
σφραγῖδα ἀπὸ τὸν ἀρχάγγελον Μιχαὴλ καὶ εὐχαρίστησεν τὸν θεὸν
καὶ ἀπ᾽ ἐκείνης τῆς σφραγῖδος ἔφτειασεν ὁ Σόλομῶν ἕνα δακτυλίδιον παρόμοιον ἀπὸ λίθου τιμῆς πολλῆς. καὶ ἔκραξεν τὸ παι-
20 δίον καὶ ἔδωκέν τοῦ τὴν βοῦλλαν τοῦ θεοῦ καὶ τοῦ εἶπεν ὡς
καθὼς τοῦ ἐπαρήγγειλεν ὁ ἄγγελος.

 12. Ἑσπέρας δὲ γενομένης ἔπεσεν τὸ παιδίον νὰ κοιμηθῇ εἰς
τὴν κλίνην του· καὶ ἰδοὺ ἔφθασεν καὶ ὁ διάβολος κατὰ τὴν συνήθειαν ὁποῦ εἶχεν διὰ νὰ περικυκλώσῃ τὸ παιδίον. καὶ εἶχεν
25 * τὴν ἔννοιαν κατὰ τὴν παραγγελίαν ὁποῦ τοῦ εἶπεν ὁ αὐθέντης
του ὁ Σολομῶν καὶ ἐβούλλωσεν τὸν διάβολο⟨ν⟩ ἐπὶ τὸ στῆθος
μὲ τὴν βοῦλλαν τοῦ θεοῦ. 13 ὁ δὲ σατανᾶς ἐβόησε φωνῇ μεγάλῃ καὶ εἶπεν· ᾿οὐαί μοι τῷ ἀθλίῳ, πῶς ἐκαταδουλώθην καὶ
ἔγινα ὑπόδουλος ὑπὸ τοῦ Σολομῶντος». καὶ παρευθὺς ἐσηκώθη
30 τὸ παιδίον ἀπὸ τὴν κλίνην του καὶ ἔδεσεν τὸν διάβολον καὶ τὸν
ὑπῆγεν ἔμπροσθεν τοῦ βασιλέως.

 III. Καὶ ὡς τὸν εἶδεν ὁ Σολομῶν ἐθαύμασεν καὶ εὐχαρίστησεν
Κύριον τὸν θεόν, καὶ εἶπεν ὁ Σολομῶν πρὸς τὸ διάβολον· ᾿εἰπέ

---

 1 * f. 180ᵛ § 10. l. 12 πάντα ex πᾶσα corr. Pr. Bessarion 13 δύναμιν ex δυν. corr. prim. man. § 12 l. 23 εὔθασεν 25 * f. 181ʳ
 C. III. cf parallele ın *Test. Sal* II et ms. D. III l. 32 εὐχαρίσθησεν

μοι, πνεῦμα πονηρὸν καὶ ἀκάθαρτον, τί σοῦ ἐστιν ὄνομα καὶ
τί⟨ς⟩ σου ἡ ἐργασία πρὶν μή σε τιμωρήσω εἰς τὸν τόπον τῆς
γεέννης;« 2. καὶ ὁ δαίμων εἶπεν· »τὸ ὄνομά μου καλοῦμαι Ὀρνίας καὶ εἶμαι ὑπὸ ἀέρος τελώνιον καὶ ἡ ἐργασία μου εἶναι αὐτη·
5 σκανδαλίζω τοὺς ἀνθρώπους καὶ τὰς καρδίας των καὶ ἁμαρτάνουν καὶ λησμονοῦν τὸν ἐπουράνιον θεόν. καὶ πότε ὡσὰν γυναῖκα ἔμορφη φαντάζομαι εἰς τὸν ὕπνον τους καὶ ἁμαρτάνουν
καὶ πότε ὡσὰν σκύλος γίνομαι καὶ πότε ὡσὰν γάιδαρος καὶ πότε
ὡσὰν ἀετὸς μετὰ πτέρα γίνομαι, καὶ πότε ὡσὰν λεοντάρι μὲ
10 ἄλλους δαίμονας γινόμεσθεν, καὶ πότε ἄλλων λογιῶν φαντασίες
φανταζόμεσθεν εἰς τοὺς ἀνθρώπους. καὶ ὁπότε ἰδοῦμεν τὸν
ἀρχάγγελον Μιχαὴλ καὶ τὸν Γαβριὴλ μᾶς ἐπιτιμοῦν μὲ τὴν δύναμιν τοῦ θεοῦ, καταργιζόμεσθεν«. 3. καὶ ταῦτα ἀκούσας ὁ βασιλεὺς Σολομῶν ἐδόξασε τὸν θεὸν καὶ * ἐπικαλέσθηκεν τοὺς
15 ἀρχαγγέλους τὸν Μιχαὴλ καὶ τὸν Γαβριήλ. καὶ εὐθὺς ἐφάνηκαν
οἱ ἀρχάγγελοι ἀπὸ τὸν οὐρανὸν καὶ ἁλυσιδέσαντες τὸν Ὀρνίαν
τὸν σατανᾶν μὲ τὸ τάγμα του ὅλον ὁρισᾶν τους οἱ ἀρχάγγελοι
ὅτι νὰ ὑπάγουν ἀπὸ ἄκρον τῆς γῆς ἕως ἄκρον καὶ ἀπὸ θαλάσσης νὰ κουβαλήσουν μάρμαρα βαρύτατα. καὶ πάλιν ὡσὰν ἦλθαν
20 οἱ δαίμονες ἀπὸ ἐκείνην τὴν ὑπηρεσίαν τοὺς ἔβαλεν πάλιν ὁ βασιλεὺς καὶ ἔκοπταν μάρμαρα καὶ σίδερον διὰ τὴν οἰκοδομὴν τοῦ
ναοῦ τοῦ θεοῦ.

IV. Καὶ πάλιν ὁ βασιλεὺς ἔκραξεν ἐκεῖνο τὸ ἐκλεκτὸν παιδίον καὶ εἶπεν του· »ἔπαρε, τέκνον, τὴν σφραγῖδα τοῦ θεοῦ καὶ
25 τὸν Ὀρνίαν τὸν σατανᾶν καὶ ὑπάγετε κατὰ τοὺς ἐρήμους τόπους
καὶ ὅπου ἂν εὕρετε δαίμονας μὲ τὸ τάγμα του νὰ τοὺς βουλλώ-
σετε ὅλους καὶ νὰ τοὺς φέρετε ἐδῶ εἰς ἡμᾶς« 2. καὶ ἐπῆρεν τὸ
παιδίον τὴν σφραγῖδα τοῦ θεοῦ καὶ τὸν Ὀρνίαν τὸν Σατανᾶν
καὶ ὑπῆγεν κατὰ τοὺς ἐρήμους τόπους καὶ ἐκεῖ ηὗραν τὸν ἄρ-
30 χοντα τῶν δαιμόνων τὸν Βεελζεβοὺλ καὶ λέγει ὁ Ὀρνίας ὁ σατανᾶς πρὸς τὸν Βεελζεβοὺλ τὸν ἄρχοντα τῶν δαιμόνων καὶ τοῦ
λέγει· »καλεῖ σε ὁ βασιλεὺς Σολομῶν μὲ τὸν ὁρισμὸν τοῦ θεοῦ
τοῦ σαβαώθ«. 3. καὶ λέγει ὁ Βεελζεβούλ· »καὶ ποῖος εἶναι αὐτὸς
ὁ Σολομῶν ὁποῦ λέγεις;« καὶ τὸ παιδίον παρευθὺς ἔριξεν τὴ⟨ν⟩

σφραγῖδα καὶ ἐκόλλησεν εἰς τὸν Βεελζεβούλ, καὶ εὐθὺς ἐσηκώθη
μετὰ βίας μὲ ἕξι χιλιάδες δαιμόνια. καὶ ἐπῆγαν ἔμπροσθεν τοῦ
βασιλέως * Σολομῶν⟨τος⟩ καὶ τὸν ἐπροσκύνησαν ὅλοι οἱ δαίμονες
καὶ ὁ βασιλεὺς εὐχαρίστησεν τὸν θεὸν τοῦ οὐρανοῦ καὶ τῆς γῆς
5 ὅπου τὸν ἠξίωσεν τοιαύτης χάριτος καὶ τιμῆς καὶ τὸν ἐπροσκυ-
νούσαν οἱ δαίμονες 4. καὶ ἐπαράστησεν ὁ βασιλεὺς Σολομῶν
τὸν Βεελζεβοὺλ τὸν σατανᾶν μὲ τὸ τάγμα του ὅλον σιδεροδε-
μένους καὶ βουλλωμένους ὅλους μὲ τοῦ θεοῦ τὸ ὄνομα. εἶτα
λέγει πρὸς τὸν Βεελζεβοὺλ τὸν πρῶτον διάβολον· »τί σού ἐστι
10 τὸ ὄνομα καὶ ἡ ἐργασία σου ἡ μιαρὰ ὁποῦ πράττεις;« 5. καὶ ὁ
δαίμων εἶπεν· »ἐγὼ εἶμαι ὁποῦ ὀνομάζομαι Βεελζεβοὺλ καὶ εἶμαι
ἄρχων ἕξι χιλιάδων δαιμόνων καὶ λέγομαι γαστὴρ θηλυμανίας,
καὶ ἐγὼ ἤμουν ὁ πρῶτος ἄγγελος τοῦ οὐρανοῦ ὁ λεγόμενος Βεελζεβούλ. καὶ ἦτον μετ᾽ ἐμοῦ καὶ ἄλλος πρῶτος σατανᾶς ὁ λεγό-
15 μενος Ἑωσφόρος, πλὴν ἐπετίμησέν τον ὁ θεὸς καὶ ἐκατακλείσθη
ἐν ταρτάρῳ δεσμῷ. 6 καὶ ἐγὼ εἶμαι ὁποῦ κάμνω τοὺς δαίμονας
καὶ εἶνε εἰς τὴν ἐξουσίαν μου. ἐγὼ εἶμαι ὁ ἄρχων τοῦ ἀέρος εἰς
τὰ πονηρὰ καὶ ἀκάθαρτα πνεύματα. καὶ μετασχηματίζουνται καὶ
γίνουνται ὡς ἄνθρωποι καὶ φαίνουνται εἰς ὄνειρα καὶ εἰς φαν-
20 τασίες κακὲς καὶ ἁμαρτάνουν καὶ μικρὰ παιδία πνίγω σιμὰ εἰς
τὲς μάνες των κοντά. 7. καὶ ὅποιος ἄνθρωπος κἂν ἄνδρας κἂν
γυναῖκα καὶ εἶναι ἀπὸ ἐνεργείας ἐδικῆς μας καὶ νὰ καπνισθῇ μὲ
χολὴν ὀψαρίου γλιανοῦ ὁποῦ εἶναι εἰς τὰ γλυκὰ τὰ νερὰ καὶ νὰ
λέγῃ ἔτζι· »πρόφθασον Ῥαφαὴλ ὁ παρεστηκὼς ἐνώπιον τοῦ θεοῦ«,
25 εὐθὺς ἀναιροῦμαι ἀπὸ ἐκεῖ. 8. ἐγὼ εἶμαι ὁποῦ ἀναγκάζω τοὺς
βασιλεῖς καὶ πολεμοῦν ἕνας μὲ τὸν ἄλλον καὶ κάμνουν αἰχμαλω-
σίες πολλὲς κἂν τε εἰς θάλασσαν κἂν τε εἰς ξηρὰν γῆν. καὶ ποτὲ
καλὸν τοῦ ἀνθρώπου δὲν θέλω«

9. Καὶ ὁ βασιλεὺς Σολομῶν εἶπεν πρὸς αὐτούς· »ὑπὸ τίνος
30 ἀγγέλου καταργεῖται ἡ δύναμίς σας«; καὶ εἶπεν ὁ Βεελζεβούλ·
»ἀπὸ τοῦ παντοκράτορος θεοῦ κυρίου σαβαὼθ καταργεῖται ἡ
δύναμίς μας καὶ ἀπὸ τοῦ ἀρχαγγέλου Ῥαφαήλ«. καὶ οἱ δαίμονες
ἔτρεμαν μήπως καὶ ὁ βασιλεὺς τοὺς ἐπιτιμήσῃ καὶ τοὺς ὀργισθῇ

---

§ 3 l 2 βίαν 3 * f. 182ʳ § 4 l 10 μιαρὰ ex μιχρὰ corr. man. alt
§ 5. l. 12 ἄρχον ex ἄρσον corr. man. alt. | χιλιάδων ex χιάδων corr. man. alt.
§ 6 l. 20 παιδίαν 21 ἦτες μάναις τους § 7. l. 24 * f. 182ᵛ

μὲ τοῦ θεοῦ τὸ ὄνομα. 10. εἶτα τοὺς ὅρισεν ὁ βασιλεὺς νὰ πριο-
νίζουν μάρμαρα καὶ λίθους ὅλοι οἱ δαίμονες σιδεροδεμένοι. καὶ
ὁ καθεὶς δαίμων ἐτάχθη νὰ δουλεύῃ εἰς τὸν ναὸν τοῦ θεοῦ ὅπου
ἔκτιζεν ὁ Σολομῶν. 11. καὶ ἐκεῖ ὅπου ἐργάζουνταν οἱ δαίμονες
5 πρᾶγμα ἦτον ἀνεκδιήγητον καὶ εἰς θαῦμα πολὺ τότες. ποῖος νὰ
ἔβλεπεν καὶ νὰ μὴν ἐθαύμαζεν τοὺς ἀνθρώπους τοὺς τεχνίτας
μὲ τόσον πλῆθος δαιμόνων νὰ ἐργάζουνται εἰς τὸν ναὸν τοῦ
θεοῦ εἰρηνεμένα μετὰ πάσης ἐπιμελείας καὶ σπουδῆς. καὶ οὐδ'
ὅλως ἐτολμοῦσαν οἱ δαίμονες νὰ πειράξουν ἵνα ἀδικήσουν κανέ-
10 ναν ἀπὸ τοὺς ἀνθρώπους. 12. καὶ τόσον τοὺς εἶχεν ὁ Σολομῶν
ὅλους τοὺς δαίμονας βουλλωμένους μὲ τὴν σφραγίδα ἐκείνην ὅπου
' τοῦ ἔστειλεν ὁ θεὸς μὲ τὸν ἀρχάγγελον αὐτοῦ Μιχαὴλ καὶ τόσον
τοὺς ἐκατάστησεν ὅλους ὅτι ὡσὰν σκλάβους. ἔτζι ἔκοπταν μάρμαρα * καὶ λίθους καὶ ἀσβέστην, καὶ τὸ νερὸν τὸ ἐκουβαλοῦσαν
15 μὲ κάδους βαρυτάτους. ὅλοι των ἀλυσοδεμένοι ἐδούλευαν τὸν
ναὸν τοῦ θεοῦ.

V. Λοιπὸν ἐκεῖ εἰς τὸ κτίσιμον ὅπου ἔκτιζαν οἱ μαΐστόροι
καὶ οἱ δαίμονες ἐργάζουνταν, ἕνας ἀπὸ τοὺς μαΐστόρους ἦλθεν
εἰς φιλονεικίαν μὲ τὸν υἱὸν αὐτοῦ. ὁ δὲ πατέρας τοῦ παιδίου
20 ἐπῆγεν εἰς τὸν βασιλέαν μετὰ πολλῶν δακρύων καὶ ἐγκάλεσεν
τὸν υἱὸν αὐτοῦ τὸ πῶς τὸν ἀτίμησεν καὶ τὸν ὕβρισεν καὶ ἔλεγεν
πρὸς τὸν Σολομῶν⟨τα⟩· »βασιλεῦ πολυχρονημένε, θανάτωσαι
τὸν υἱόν μου ὅτι ἐμένα τὸν πατέρα του μὲ ἀσχήμισεν καὶ μὲ
ὕβρισεν καὶ μὲ ἀτίμησεν. καὶ ἐὰν δὲν τὸν θανατώσῃς ἐγὼ πλέον
25 δὲν βάνω τὸ χέριν μου νὰ δουλεύσω εἰς τὸν ναὸν τοῦ θεοῦ«.
Καὶ ἰδοὺ μετὰ ὥραν ἱκανὴν ἐπῆγεν ὁ υἱὸς τοῦ μαΐστορος εἰς τὸν
βασιλέαν Σολομῶν⟨τα⟩ καὶ ἐγκάλειε τὸν πατέρα του. 2. καὶ διαλογιζόμενος ὁ βασιλεὺς καὶ ἀπορῶντας τί ἀπόκρισιν νὰ δώσῃ
καὶ τοὺς δύο νὰ τοὺς εἰρηνεύσῃ ἐστράφη εἰς τὸν ναὸν καὶ ἔβλε-
30 πεν καὶ εἶδεν τὸν Ὀρνίαν τὸν διάβολον καὶ δὲν ἐργάζατον νὰ
δουλεύῃ ὡσὰν καὶ τοὺς ἄλλους δαίμονας, μόνον ἔστεκεν καὶ ἐγέ-
λαν. καὶ λέγει ὁ βασιλεὺς πρὸς τοὺς δύο τὸν πατέρα καὶ τὸν

§ 10 l. 3 καθεεῖς § 11. l.5 πολλὺν   6 εὔλεπεν   § 12. l. 11 ἐκεῖ-
νον   12 τοῦ: τους   13 ἐκατάσησεν   14 * f 183ᵛ   15 κάδδους |
των· τους

C V. Parallele in ms. D c. IV. l. 18 ἦλθαν   22 Βασιλεὺς   § 2. l. 29 τοὺς:
τὸν | ἐστράφην

υἱὸν ὁποῦ ἐκρένουνταν· »ἀναχωρήσατε ὀλίγον ἀπ᾽ ἐμοῦ« καὶ
οὕτως ἀνεχώρησαν καὶ οἱ δύο καὶ τότες ὁ βασιλεὺς ἔστειλεν
ἐκεῖνο τὸ ἐκλεκτὸν παιδίον νὰ φέρῃ τὸν Ὀρνίαν τὸν σατανᾶν*
μὲ τοὺς ἄλλους δαίμονας καὶ νὰ τοὺς φέρῃ ἔμπροσθέν του. καὶ
5 ἐπῆγεν τὸ παιδίον καὶ τοὺς ἤφ⟨ερ⟩εν. 3. καὶ λέγει ὁ Σολομῶν
πρὸς τὸν Ὀρνίαν· »ὦ πνεῦμα ἀκάθαρτον δαιμόνιον, διὰ τί γελᾷς
τὴν βασιλείαν μου καὶ τὴν κρίσιν μου καὶ τὸν ναὸν τοῦ θεοῦ
ὁποῦ οἰκοδομῶ«; 4. καὶ ὁ Ὀρνίας ὁ διάβολος ἔλεγεν πρὸς τὸν
βασιλέαν· »οὐχί, δέσποτα βασιλεῦ, σοφώτατε καὶ δικαιότατε, οὔτε
10 τὴν κρίσιν σου. ἐγέλασα ποτέ μου, οὔτε τὴν βασιλείαν σου, οὔτε
τὸν ναὸν τοῦ θεοῦ ὁποῦ οἰκοδομᾶς, ἀλλὰ αὐτουνοὺς τοὺς δύο
ἀθλίους ὁποῦ ἦλθαν καὶ κρίνουνται εἰς τὴν βασιλείαν σου αὐτὸν
τὸν γέροντα μὲ τὸν υἱόν του ὁποῦ μαλώνουν καὶ φιλονεικοῦν
καὶ ὑβρίζουνται. ἀκόμη νὰ μὴν περάσουν τρεῖς ἡμέρες καὶ αὐ-
15 τουνοῦ τοῦ γέροντος ὁ υἱὸς μέλλει νὰ ἀποθάνῃ«. 5. ταῦτα
ἀκούσας ὁ βασιλεὺς παρὰ τοῦ Ὀρνίου τοῦ εἶπεν· »σύρε ἐργάζου
εἰς τὸν ναὸν τοῦ θεοῦ μετὰ σπουδῆς καὶ εἰρήνης«. καὶ ἀπῆλθεν
ὁ Ὀρνίας καὶ ἐργάζετον μετὰ φόβου καὶ τρόμου εἰς τὸν ναὸν
τοῦ θεοῦ. καὶ πάλιν ὁ βασιλεὺς ἐκάλεσεν τοὺς δύο κρινομένους
20 τὸν πατέρα καὶ τὸν υἱὸν ὁποῦ ἐφιλονεικοῦσαν καὶ ἐμάλωναν καὶ
τοὺς ἔδωσεν διορίαν νὰ ἀναμείνουν ἡμέρας πέντε καὶ οὕτως νὰ
κάμῃ τὴν κρίσιν τους. καὶ τοῦτο τὸ ἔκαμεν ὁ Σολομῶν διὰ τὸν
λόγον ὁποῦ τοῦ εἶπεν ὁ Ὀρνίας ὅτι νὰ μὴν περάσουν τρεῖς ἡμέρες καὶ νὰ ἀποθάνῃ ὁ υἱὸς τοῦ γέροντος.
25 6. Καὶ ὡσὰν ἐπέρασαν αἱ πέντε ἡμέρες ἦλθεν ὁ πατὴρ τοῦ
παιδίου ἐκείνου εἰς τὸν Σολομῶν⟨τα⟩ καὶ μετὰ δακρύων καὶ
ὀδυρόμενος ἔλεγεν· »βασιλεῦ πολυχρονημένε, ἀπόθανεν ὁ υἱός μου
καὶ πλέον δὲν θέλω ἰδεῖν αὐτόν«. λέγει του ὁ βασιλεύς »καὶ
πότε ἀπόθανεν ὁ υἱός σου, γέροντά μου«; λέγει του ὁ μαΐστορας·
30 »ἀφότης ἐδικαστήκαμεν καὶ ἐμαλώσαμεν δὲν ἐπέρασαν τρεῖς ἡμέρες καὶ ἀπόθανεν«. λέγει τοῦ ὁ βασιλεύς· »ἄπελθε, γέροντά μου,
εἰς τὸν καλὸν καὶ δόξαζε τὸν θεόν, καὶ ὁ κύριος νὰ σοῦ δώσῃ
ὑπομονὴν εἰς τὴν θλίψιν τῆς καρδίας σου«. καὶ ταῦτα παρη-

1 ἀπ᾽ ἐμοῦ· ὁπονεμοῦ   3 * f. 183ᵛ   § 4. 1 12 ἀθλιγί | εἰς: ἡ
13 γέροντα: γέρων m τόων corr. man. alt. errore   § 5. l. 16 ἐργάζου
§ 6. l. 25 αἱ: ἡ   27 * f. 184ʳ

γορήσας τὸν γέροντα ἐκεῖνον, ἀπῆλθεν. 7 καὶ πάλιν ἔστειλεν ὁ
βασιλεὺς τὸ παιδίον νὰ φέρῃ τὸν Ὀρνίαν τὸν δαίμονα. καὶ εὐθὺς
τὸν ἤφερεν καὶ τὸν ἐπαράστησεν ἔμπροσθέν του. εἶτα λέγει ὁ
Σολομῶν πρὸς ἐκεῖνον· »εἰπέ μοι, πνεῦμα πονηρὸν καὶ ἀκάθαρ-
5 τον, πόθεν ἐγνωρίζεις τὸν θάνατον τοῦ ἀνθρώπου,« 8. καὶ ὁ
διάβολος εἶπεν μετὰ φόβου καὶ τρόμου· »καὶ ἡμεῖς, δέσποτα βασιλεῦ, ἤμεσθεν πρῶτα ἄγγελοι καὶ ἀπὸ τὴν ὑπερηφάνειάν μας
ὀργίστηκέν μας ὁ θεὸς ἀπὸ τοῦ οὐρανοῦ τὸν πρῶτον μας τὸν
Ἑωσφόρον τὸν σατανᾶν καὶ ἐκεῖ ἔπεσεν κάτω εἰς τὴν ἄβυσσον.
10 καὶ ὅταν ἐφώ(νη)σεν ὁ ἀρχάγγελος Μιχαὴλ καὶ εἶπεν τὸ· »στῶ-
μεν καλῶς«, καὶ καθὼς ὁ θεὸς ὥρισεν ἔτζι ἐσταθήκαμεν, καὶ ἡμεῖς
ἤμεσθεν ἐναέρια τελώνια τῶν ψυχῶν, καὶ ἀπὸ φῶς θεοῦ ὁποῦ
ἤμεσθεν καὶ ἄγγελοι ἐγίνημεν σκότος καὶ μαυρισμένοι ὡς καθὼς
μᾶς ἐβλέπεις καὶ θεωρεῖς. 9. καὶ ἡμεῖς ἀνερχόμεθα εἰς τὸ κά-
15 τωθεν μέρος τοῦ οὐρανοῦ ὑμνοῦμεν καὶ δοξάζομεν τὸν θεὸν τὸ
ἡμερόνυχτον, καὶ ἡμεῖς πετῶντας ἀκούομεν τῶν ἀγγέλων * τὲς
ὁμιλίες καὶ τὰ γράμματα τοῦ καθενὸς ἀνθρώπου, καὶ μανθάνομεν τὸν θάνατοι τοῦ ἀνθρώπου ἀπὸ σαράντα ἡμέρες καὶ πρω-
τύτερα, καὶ διὰ τοῦτο πάσχομεν καὶ ἡμεῖς νὰ τὸν κολάσωμεν
20 καὶ νὰ πέσῃ εἰς κακὲς καὶ ἄτυχες πράξες ἕως ὁποῦ νὰ ἔλθῃ ἡ
ζωὴ τοῦ ἀνθρώπου ἐκείνου εἰς ζημίαν θανάτου καὶ νὰ κολασθῇ
νὰ τὸν κερδέσωμεν. 10. καὶ πετόμενοι τὸ κάτωθεν μέρος τοῦ
οὐρανοῦ καὶ ὡς φύλλα ἀπὸ δένδρου ὁποῦ πέφτουν ὑπὸ ἀνέμου
μεγάλου εἰς τὴν γῆν, οὕτῳ καὶ ἡμεῖς πέφτομεν ὑπὸ θεοῦ ῥοπῆς
25 καὶ δὲν δυνάμεσθεν διὰ νὰ σταθοῦμεν. καὶ βλέποντάς μας οἱ
ἄνθρωποι νομίζουν ὅτι εἶναι ἀστέρες τοῦ οὐρανοῦ χυνόμενοι καὶ
μᾶς δοξάζουν οἱ ἄνθρωποι καὶ λέγουν ὅτι αἰχμάλοτος ἐλευθε-
ρώθη, καὶ ὁ θεὸς νὰ τὸν γλυτώσῃ«. 11. ὁ βασιλεὺς Σολομῶν
ἔλεγεν πρὸς τὸν Ὀρνίαν »αἲ γὰρ τοῦ οὐρανοῦ ἀστέρες χύνονται
30 ποτὲ κάτω;« καὶ ὁ δαίμων ἔλεγεν· »οὐχί, δέσποτα, αἱ γὰρ ἀστέρες
ἀνατέλουν καὶ βασιλεύουν καὶ περιπατοῦν μαζὶ μὲ τὸν οὐρανὸν
καὶ εἶνε ἀσάλευτοι καὶ στερομένοι ὡσὰν τὸν ἥλιον καὶ τὴν σελήνην ἕως τὸν μέλλοντα αἰῶνα«.

---

§ 8 l. 8 ὀργίθηκεν　　14 εἰλέπεις　§ 9. ἀνέρχομαι　　16 * f. 184ᵛ
§ 10. l. 23 ἀπὸ ὑπὸ |　πέφτουν πέμπτουν　24 πέφτομεν. πέμπτομεν
26 χυνόμενοι· χιόμενοι　§ 11. l. 29. 30 αἱ ἡ, οἱ

12. Ταῦτα ἀκούσας ὁ βασιλεὺς Σολομῶν εὐχαρίστησεν τὸν
θεὸν καὶ πάλιν ὅρισεν τὸν Ὁρνίαν νὰ δουλεύῃ εἰς τὸν ναὸν τοῦ
θεοῦ μὲ τοὺς ἄλλους δαίμονας.   ¶

VI. Καὶ πάντες οἱ βασιλεῖς τῆς γῆς καὶ ἡ σοφὴ Σιβύλλα
5 ἦλθαν καὶ αὐτὴ μετ' αὐτοὺς νὰ ἰδοῦν τὸν ναὸν τοῦ θεοῦ καὶ
ἐπήγασι καὶ κανίσκια μεγάλα τοῦ * βασιλέως Σολομῶν⟨τος⟩. καὶ
ἤφεραν οἰκοδομὴν διὰ τὸν ναὸν τὴν ἁγίαν Σιών, καὶ πολυτελῆ
καὶ ἀξιόλογον ὕλην καὶ σκεύη πολλὰ καὶ πολύτιμα καὶ τὰ
ἀφιέρωσαν εἰς τὸν ναὸν τοῦ θεοῦ.

10 VII. Καὶ ὁ βασιλεὺς τῶν Ἀσσυρίων τῆς Ἀραβίας ἔστειλεν
ἐπιστολὴν εἰς τὸν βασιλέαν Σολομῶν⟨τα⟩ καὶ ἔγραφεν οὕτως
›εἰς τὸν βασιλέαν τὸν Σολομῶν⟨τα⟩ τὸν σοφώτατον καὶ τιμώ-
τατον παρὰ ὅλους τοὺς βασιλεῖς τῆς γῆς χαίροις ἐν κυρίῳ τῷ
θεῷ, ὑγίαινε κατὰ βασιλείαν Σόλυμα τῆς Ἰουδαίας καὶ Παλαι-
15 στίνης. νὰ τὸ ἐγνωρίζῃς καλὰ ἡ βασιλεία σου κατὰ Σόλυμα ὅτι
ἐδῶ εἰς τὸν ἐδικόν μου τόπον καὶ τὴν χώραν κατοικεῖ ἕνα δαιμόνιον πονηρὸν καὶ δυνατὸν καὶ εἰς καθὲ τρεῖς ἡμέρας σηκώνει
ἄνεμον δυνατὸν καὶ ῥίπτουνται σπίτια καὶ δένδρα καὶ βουνὰ καὶ
τοὺς ἀνθρώπους τοὺς ῥίχνει εἰς τὸ πῦρ καὶ εἰς τὸ νερὸν τοὺς
20 ἐγκρεμνίζει. καὶ ἤκουσα ὅτι μὲ τῆς σφραγίδος ὁποῦ σου ἔστειλεν
ὁ θεὸς ἀπὸ τοῦ οὐρανοῦ μὲ τὸν ἀρχάγγελόν του καὶ ἐπάταξες
πᾶσαν τὴν δύναμιν τῶν δαιμόνων. καὶ σὲ παρακαλῶ πολλὰ
στεῖλε καὶ εἰς ἐμᾶς καὶ πέμψον νὰ τὸ ἐξολοθρεύσῃς τὸ πνεῦμα
τὸ πονηρόν. καὶ ἐὰν τὸ κάμεις αὐτὸ ἡ βασιλεία σου, νὰ σοῦ
25 στείλω ἔξοδον εἰς τὴν οἰκοδομὴν τοῦ ναοῦ τοῦ θεοῦ τάλαντα
τριάντα χρυσίου καὶ ἀργυρίου· τὸ ἕνα τάλαντον κάμνει ἑκατὸν
πενήντα λίτρες‹.

2. Λαβὼν δὲ τὴν ἐπιστολὴν ὁ βασιλεὺς καὶ ἀναγνοὺς αὐτὴν
εἶπεν τοῦ παιδίου νὰ πάρῃ * τὴν σφραγῖδα τοῦ θεοῦ καὶ νὰ
30 παγαίνῃ εἰς τὸν βασιλέαν τῆς Ἀραβίας τὸ γληγορότερον, καὶ
ἔδωκέν του καὶ γραφὴν ὁποῦ τὸν ἐχαρέτα, καὶ εἶπεν τοῦ παιδίου
ὅτι νὰ πάρῃ μαζί του καὶ ἕνα δερμάτι καινούριον καὶ ἕνα γοργοκάμηλον, καὶ ἔστειλεν τὸ παιδίον ὁ βασιλεὺς Σολομῶν μὲ

C. VI. l. 7 ˣ f. 185ʳ
C. VII l. 10 Ἀσσυρίων: ἀσσάριον ms., l. Ἀραβίων?   14 βασιλέαν
σολομὲ   15 σολομὲ   16 δαιμόνον   23 νὰ τὸ: νὰ τον   § 2. l. 29 * f. 185ᵛ

συνοδίαν ἀνθρώπων πολλῶν. καὶ ἐπαρήγγειλέν του· »κύτταξε,
τέκνον μου, νὰ εὕρῃς τὸν τόπον ὅπου κατοικεῖ ὁ δαίμων καὶ
ἰδὲ τὴν ὥραν καὶ τὴν ἡμέραν ὅπου μέλλει διὰ νὰ πνεύσῃ τὸν
ἄνεμον. καὶ οὕτως ἔχε ἐσὺ τὸ δερμάτιον ἀνοικτὸν πρὸς τὴν
πέτραν τῆς φωλεᾶς ὅπου κατοικεῖ ὁ δαίμων καὶ ὅταν ἰδῇς τὸν
ἀσκὸν καὶ φουσκώσῃ ἄνεμον, ἐσὺ νὰ εἶσαι ἕτοιμος, ὀγλήγορα νὰ
δέσῃς τὸ στόμα του τοῦ ἀσχοῦ καὶ νὰ τὸ βουλλώσῃς μὲ τὴν
σφραγῖδα τοῦ θεοῦ καλούτσικα καὶ οὕτως βάλε τὸν ἀσκὸν ὅπου
ἔχει τὸν δαίμονα ἀπάνω εἰς τὸν γοργοκάμηλον καὶ νὰ τὸν φέρῃς
ἐδῶ εἰς ἡμᾶς.

3. Καὶ ἀπῆλθεν τὸ παιδίον εἰς τὸν βασιλέαν τῆς Ἀραβίας
καὶ ἔκαμεν ὡς καθὼς τοῦ ἐπαρήγγειλεν ὁ Σολομῶν. καὶ ἔτζι
ἔφερεν τὸ παιδίον βουλλωμένον τὸν ἀσκὸν εἰς τὸν βασιλέαν.
καὶ εἰς τὴν στράταν ὅπου ἤρχετον τὸ παιδίον μετὰ τοῦ δαίμονος
ἔλεγεν ὁ δαίμων· »δέομαι, ὦ παιδίον, μήν με ὑπάγῃς εἰς τὸν βασιλέαν καὶ ἐγὼ νὰ σοῦ δείξω ποῦ εἶναι ὁ πράσινος ὁ λίθος καὶ
τὸ χρυσίον τὸ τιμημένον καὶ κεκρυμμένον«. καὶ τὸ παιδίον ἔλεγεν πρὸς τὸν δαίμονα· »εἰς τὸν βασιλέαν τὸν Σολομῶν⟨τα⟩ καὶ
εἴ τι ὁρίσῃ ἐκεῖνος, ἂς ποιήσῃ«. 4. καὶ ὡς * ἦλθαν ἔμπροσθεν
εἰς τὸν βασιλέαν εὐθὺς ἔπεσεν ὁ ἀσκὸς κάτω ἀπὸ τὸ καμήλιον
καὶ ἐκυλίετον ἄνω καὶ κάτω. καὶ πάντες ὅσοι ἦσαν ἐκεῖ ἐθαύμασαν. καὶ ἔλυσεν τὸ παιδίον τὸν ἀσκὸν καὶ εὐθὺς ἐβγῆκεν ὁ
δαίμων ἔξω. 5. καὶ ἐβούλλωσεν αὐτὸν ὁ βασιλεὺς ἐπὶ τὸ στῆθος
καὶ τὸν τράχηλον καὶ ἔδεσεν αὐτὸν καὶ ἔλεγεν ὁ βασιλεύς· »πῶς
ὀνομάζεσαι;« καὶ ὁ δαίμων εἶπεν· »Ἐφίππας τὸ ὄνομά μου καλοῦμαι«. 6. λέγει ὁ βασιλεύς· »τί εἶναι ἡ ἐργασία σου ἡ μιαρά;«
καὶ ὁ δαίμων εἶπεν »ἡ ἐργασία μου εἶναι εἰς μύρια κακὰ ποιήματα. καὶ παρακαλῶ σε, ὦ βασιλεῦ, νὰ μήν με ἐπιτιμήσῃς μὲ
τοῦ θεοῦ τὸ ὄνομα, καὶ ἐγὼ νὰ σοῦ φέρω τὸν λίθον τὸν ἀκρογωνιαῖον ὅπου φέγγει εἰς τὸ βάθος τῆς θαλάσσης ὑπὲρ τὸν
ἥλιον τὸν ὁποῖον ἀπεδοκίμασαν οἱ ἄνθρωποι καὶ οἱ δαίμονες καὶ
ἐγὼ νὰ σοῦ τὸν στήσω αὐτὸν εἰς τὴν πρώτην κεφαλαίαν τοῦ
ναοῦ«.

8 l. διὰ νὰ πνεύσῃ Pr. Bessarion· διαναπεύσῃ   5 φωλεᾶς· φολεὰν
8 καλούτζικα   § 3. l. 14 ἤρχετον ex ἤχετον cor. prim. man   17 τεμη-
μένον   18 πρὸς bis scr.   § 4. l. 19 * f. 186ʳ   § 5. l. 23 στῆθι
UNT   9   McCown   8*

7. Καὶ εὐθὺς ὅρισεν ὁ βασιλεὺς ἐκεῖνον τὸν Ἐφίππαν τὸν
δαίμονα μὲ ἄλλους ἑτέρους δαίμονας. καὶ ὑπῆγεν καὶ ἤφεραν τὸν
λίθον ἐκεῖνον τὸν ἀκρογωνιαῖον καὶ ἔστησάν τον εἰς τὴν μέσην
τοῦ ναοῦ, καὶ οἱ πάντες ὅσοι ἦσαν ἐκεῖ ἐθαύμασαν ἰδόντες τὸ
5 παράδοξον θαῦμα. 8. ἀλλὰ ἀφότης ἐκατέβη ὁ κύριος ἡμῶν Ἰησοῦς Χριστὸς ὁ υἱὸς καὶ λόγος τοῦ θεοῦ, τὸ φῶς τὸ ἀληθινὸν
τὸ φῶς τῆς οἰκουμένης, ὁ ἥλιος ὁ ἀνέσπερος, ἐκεῖνος ὁ λίθος
ἐσκοτίσθη ὅπου ἦτον ὑπὸ τοῦ βασιλέως Σολομῶν⟨τος⟩. καὶ
ἀφότης ἔκτισεν ἐκεῖνον τὸν ναὸν τοῦ θεοῦ, ἤγουν τὴν ἁγίαν Σιών,
10 ἕως ὅπου ἐγεννήθη ὁ κύριος ἡμῶν Ἰησοῦς Χριστός, ἐπέρασαν
χρόνοι ψκζ, ἤγουν ἑπτακόσιοι εἴκοσι ἑπτά. ἀλλὰ ἂς ἐλθοῦμεν
πάλιν ὅθεν ἀφήσαμεν τὸν λόγον μας.

VIII. Καί πάλιν εἶπεν ὁ βασιλεὺς τὸν Ἐφίππαν τὸν δαίμονα·
»ὦ Ἐφίππα, ἠξεύρης καὶ ἕτερον δαιμόνιον ὡσὰν καὶ τοῦ λόγου
15 σου«; καὶ ὁ δαίμων εἶπεν »ἠξεύρω, ὦ δέσποτα, καὶ ἕτερον δαιμόνιον ἐν τῇ Ἐρυθρᾷ θαλάσσῃ καὶ καθοῦνται καὶ φυλάγουν τὸν
στύλον τὸν πορφυρόν«. 2. καὶ ὡσὰν ἤκουσεν ἔτζι ὁ βασιλεὺς
εἶπεν τοῦ παιδίου· »τέκνον μου, ἔπαρε τὴν σφραγῖδα τοῦ θεοῦ
καὶ τὸν Ἐφίππαν τὸν δαίμονα καὶ νὰ ὑπᾶτε εἰς τὴν Ἐρυθρὰν
20 θάλασσαν, καὶ ὅσους δαίμονας καὶ ἂν εὕρης ἐκεῖ ὅπου φυλάγουν
τὸν στύλον τὸν πορφυρόν, σφράγισε τοὺς ὅλους ἀπάνω εἰς τὸ
στῆθος καὶ ἂς πάρουν ἐκεῖνον τὸν κίονα τὸν πορφυρὸν ἀπάνω
τους καὶ ἂς τὸν φέρουν ἐδῶ εἰς ἐμᾶς«. 3. καὶ οὕτως ὑπῆγεν
ἐκεῖνο τὸ παιδίον μὲ τὸν Ἐφίππαν εἰς τὴν Ἐρυθρὰν θάλασσαν
25 καὶ ἐπλήρωσεν τοῦ βασιλέως τὸ θέλημα, καὶ ἐκεῖνο τὸ παιδίον
ἐσφράγισεν ὅλους τοὺς δαίμονας μὲ τὴν σφραγῖδα τοῦ θεοῦ καὶ
εἶπεν τους· »ἐπάρετε τὸν κίονα αὐτὸν καὶ ἐλᾶτε νὰ ὑπᾶμεν εἰς
τὸν βασιλέαν τὸν Σολομῶν⟨τα⟩«. καὶ εὐθὺς οἱ δαίμονες ἐκεῖνοι
ἐπῆραν τὸν κίονα τὸν πορφυρὸν ἀπάνω τους καὶ τὸν ἐβαστοῦσαν
30 καὶ φέρνοντάς τον ἀπάνω εἰς τὸν ἀέρα. 4. καὶ ὁ βασιλεὺς ἰδὼν
τοὺς δαίμονας τὸ πῶς φέρνουν ἐκεῖνον τὸν κίονα * ἐθαύμασεν
καὶ ὅσοι ἦσαν ἐκεῖ ἔφριξαν ἰδόντες τὸ παράδοξαν τοῦ θαύματος.
εἶτα ὅρισεν ὁ βασιλεὺς ἐκείνους τοὺς δαίμονας νὰ βαστοῦν ἐκεῖνον

§ 8 1 5 ἐκατεύη   7 τῆς τῆς   9 * f. 186ᵛ
C. VIII. cf. parallela in *Test. Sal* c. XXIV. § 2. 1. 20 ἀνεευρης ms., l.
forte ἀνεύρεις   § 4 1 31 * f 187ʳ

τὸν κίονα ἀπάνω τους εἰς τὸν ἀέρα καὶ νὰ μὴν τὸν ἐρίξουν
ποτὲ κάτω ἕως τὸν μέλλοντα αἰῶνα.

IX. Καὶ πάλιν ὥρισεν ὁ βασιλεὺς Σολομῶν, καὶ ἤφεραν τὸν
Ὀρνίαν τὸν διάβολον ὁποῦ τὸν ἐπίασεν ἀπὸ τὴν ἀρχὴν ὁποῦ
5 ἐδούλευεν καὶ ἐπαρέστησαν αὐτὸν ἔμπροσθεν τοῦ βασιλέως· καὶ
λέγει τοῦ Ὀρνία· »εἶναι καὶ ἄλλα δαιμόνια καὶ πνεύματα πονηρὰ
ὡσὰν καὶ αὐτά,« καὶ εἶπεν ὁ Ὀρνίας· »εἶνε, δέσποτα βασιλεῦ,
πλὴν εἶναι ἕνα δαιμόνιον καὶ ἔχει δύναμιν περισσήν«. 2. καὶ ὁ
βασιλεὺς εἶπεν· »καὶ ποῦ εἶναι αὐτὸ ὁποῦ κατοικεῖ;« καὶ ὁ Ὀρ-
10 νίας εἶπεν· »εἶναι εἰς τοὺς τάφους τῶν ἀπεθαμμένων καὶ εἰς τόπους κρημνώδεις ἡ κατοικία, καὶ ἀφανίζει πολλοὺς τῶν ἀνθρώπων, καὶ ὀνομάζεται Σαμαήλ, καὶ εἶναι καὶ αὐτὸς ἄρχων εἰς ἕνα
τάγμα τῶν δαιμόνων· καὶ δὲν εἶναι κανεὶς νὰ τοῦ ἀντισταθῇ ὅτε
διασείει τὴν γῆν«. 3. καὶ ὁ βασιλεὺς λέγει πρὸ⟨ς⟩ τὸν Ὀρνίαν·
15 »δέν σε μέλει ἐσένα, πνεῦμα πονηρόν, διὰ τὴν δύναμιν ἐκείνου,
μόνον σῦρε μὲ τὸ παιδίον καὶ μὲ τοῦ θεοῦ τὴν πρόσταξιν ὅπου
καὶ ἂν εἶναι νὰ τὸν εὑρῆτε νὰ τὸν φέρετε ἐδῶ εἰς ἐμᾶς«. 4. εἶτα
ἔκραξεν ὁ βασιλεὺς τὸ εὔμορφον παιδίον καὶ λέγει αὐτό· »ἔπαρε,
τέκνον μου, τὴν σφραγῖδα τοῦ θεοῦ καὶ τὸν Ὀρνίαν καὶ σῦρτε
20 νὰ εὑρῆτε τὸν σατανᾶν τὸν Σαμαὴλ * καὶ νὰ τὸν βουλλώσῃς καὶ
νὰ τὸν δέσῃς καὶ νὰ τὸν φέρετε ἐδῶ«. 5. λαβών τε τὸ παιδίον
τὴν σφραγῖδα τοῦ θεοῦ καὶ τὸν Ὀρνίαν καὶ ὑπῆγαν καὶ ηὗραν
τὸν Σαμαὴλ τὸν δαίμονα μὲ τὸ τάγμα του. εἶτα εἶπεν τὸ παι-
δίον· »ἐν ὀνόματι κυρίου τοῦ θεοῦ τοῦ ὑψίστου νὰ σταθῆτε, ὅλα
25 τὰ πονηρὰ καὶ ἀκάθαρ⟨τα⟩ πνεύματα, ⌈καὶ νὰ μὴν συσταθῆτε,
ὅλα τὰ πονηρὰ καὶ ἀκάρθατα πνεύματα,⌉ καὶ νὰ μὴν συστῆτε ἀπὸ
τὸν τόπον σας«, καὶ πλέον δὲν ἐσπάραξαν ἀπὸ τὸν τόπον τους.
καὶ ὑπῆγεν τὸ παιδίον μὲ τὴν βούλλαν τοῦ θεοῦ καὶ τοὺς ἐβούλλωσεν ὅλους καὶ ἔδεσέν τους καὶ τοὺς ὑπῆγεν εἰς τὸν βασιλέαν
30 6. Ὁ δὲ βασιλεὺς ἐκάθετον ἐπὶ θρόνου ὑψιλοῦ καὶ ἐνδυμένος
μὲ βασιληκὸν στέμμα, καὶ εἶχεν εἰς τὸ χέριν του τὸ σκῆπτρον καὶ
βίτζαν καὶ ἐβίγλιζαν εἰς τὸν ναὸν· τοῦ θεοῦ τὸ πῶς ἐδούλευαν
οἱ μαΐστοροι καὶ οἱ δαίμονες ἐδούλευαν ὡσὰν ἐργάται καὶ ἐπριώ-

---

C. IV. cf. parallele in ms. D VII   l. 5 ἐπαρέστησεν   § 2. l. 11 κατ-
οικίαν   § 4. l. 20 * f 187ᵛ   § 5. l. 25 ⌈ ⌉ certe dittogr.   29 ὑπῆγεν
ex ὑπῆγαν cor prim. man

νιζαν λίθους καὶ μάμαρα. καὶ ἀπαντείχενεν ὁ βασιλεὺς τὸ παιδίον νὰ φέρῃ καὶ τοὺς δαίμονας. 7. καὶ ἰδοὺ μετὰ ὥραν ἱκανὴν
ἔφθασεν καὶ τὸ παιδίον σύρνοντας καὶ τοὺς δαίμονας, καὶ τοὺς
ἤφερεν ἔμπροσθεν τοῦ βασιλέως. καὶ ὁ βασιλεὺς ἰδὼν τοὺς δαί-
5 μονας ἐθαύμασεν καὶ εὐχαρί⟨στη⟩σεν τὸν θεὸν τοῦ οὐρανοῦ καὶ
τῆς γῆς ὁποῦ τὸν ἠξίωσεν τοιαύτης χάριτος καὶ ἐκατίσχυνεν ὅλους
τοὺς δαίμονας. καὶ ἦτον τὰ δαιμόνια ἐκεῖνα τὰ πρόσωπά τους
μαῦρα. καὶ ἐρώτησεν τὸν * πρῶτον τους καὶ εἶπεν· »εἰπέ μοι,
πνεῦμα πονηρὸν καὶ μιαρόν, τί τὸ σὸν ὄνομα καὶ τί εἶναι ἡ μιαρά
10 σου ἐργασία;« 8. καὶ ὁ δαίμων εἶπεν· »τὸ ὄνομά μου λέγεται
Χάθρου Σαμαήλ. ἥ τε ἐργασία μου εἶναι αὕτη· καθεζόμεσθεν
εἰς τόπους τῶν διαβατῶν καὶ ⟨ἐ⟩γκρεμνίζομεν αὐτοὺς καὶ τοὺς
πνίγομεν, καὶ ἔμπροσθεν εἰς τὰ κουφάρια τῶν ἀποθαμμένων καὶ
εἰς τὰ μνήματα τῶν ἀποθαμμένων σεβαίνομεν καὶ σχηματιζό-
15 μεσθεν εἰς ἐκείνου τοῦ ἀνθρώπου τὴν μορφήν· καὶ κατατρόγομεν
τὰς σάρκας τῶν ἀνθρώπων· ἕως ὁποῦ καὶ ἔρχωνται εἰς θάνατον.
καὶ πάλιν ἐρχόμεσθεν ἐν τῷ ἀέρι καὶ κάμνομεν τοὺς ἀνθρώπους
καὶ σεληνιάζουνται καὶ κατατρόγουν τὰς σάρκα⟨ς⟩ των, καὶ ἀφρί-
ζουν καὶ τρίζουν τοὺς ὀδόντας τους. καὶ ἄλλους πάλιν πνίγομεν
20 εἰς γωνίες καὶ εἰς ⟨τὲς⟩ φάραγγες καὶ εἰς τοὺς ἐγκρεμνοὺς τοὺς
ἐγκρεμνίζομεν καὶ θανατώνουνται αἰφνίδιον θάνατον καὶ κολά-
ζομεν αὐτοὺς καὶ τοὺς κερδαίνομεν«. 9. καὶ εἶπεν ὁ βασιλεὺς
πρὸς τὸν δαίμονα· »ἀμμὴ δὲν φοβᾶσαι τὸν θεὸν τοῦ οὐρανοῦ
καὶ τῆς γῆς; ἀμμὴ ὑπὸ τίνος ἀγγέλου καταργεῖται ἡ δύναμίς σας;«
25 καὶ εἶπον οἱ δαίμονες· »ὁπότε μέλλει νὰ ἔλθῃ ὁ σωτὴρ τοῦ κόσμου
ὁ υἱὸς καὶ λόγος τοῦ θεοῦ ἐπὶ τῆς γῆς καὶ θέλει κάμνειν ἕνα
στοιχεῖον εἰς ὅσους ἀνθρώπους θέλουν τὸν πιστεύσῃ εἰς ἐκεῖνον
τὸν βασιλέα⟨ν⟩ καὶ θέλουν ποιῇ οἱ ἄνθρωποι ἐκεῖνο τὸ στοιχεῖον
εἰς * τὸ μέτωπον καὶ εἰς τὸ στῆθος μὲ τὴν δεξιάν τους τὴν
30 χεῖρα«. τουτέστιν ἐπροέλεγεν ψ̅ξ̅ χρόνους προτύτερα ἀπὸ τοῦ
Χριστοῦ, τουτέστιν τὸν τίμιον σταυρόν. καὶ ἔλεγον οἱ δαίμονες·
»τότε ἐμεῖς, δέσποτα, καταργεῖται ἡ δύναμίς μας, καὶ ἀναχωρί-
ζομεν γοργὰ ἀπὸ τὸν ἄνθρωπον ἐκεῖνον«.

---

§ 7. l. 3 ἔφθασεν εὔθασεν   8 * f. 188ʳ   10 ἐργασίαν   § 8. l. 20 φάραγγες   ἐγκρεμμοὺς ms., l. f. κρημνοὺς   § 9. l. 23 ἀμὴ (bis)   29 * f. 188ᵛ

Cf. parallela ad §§ 8f in *Test.* ι. ΧVII 2—4.

10. Καὶ ταῦτα ἀκούσας ὁ βασιλεὺς εὐχαρίστησεν τὸν κύριον. εἶτα ἐπετίμησεν τὸν Σαμαὴλ καὶ τὸ τάγμα του ὅλον ὑπὸ κυρίου τοῦ θεοῦ καὶ ἐκατηργήθηκαν. καὶ ἐκατασιδέρωσεν τὸν Σαμαὴλ τὸν δαίμονα ἐπὶ τὸν τράχηλον καὶ ἐπριόνιζεν λίθους καὶ μάρ-
5 μαρα καὶ ἐκουβαλοῦσαν καὶ ἀσβέστην εἰς τὸν ναὸν τοῦ θεοῦ.

X. Καὶ εὐφημίσθη ὁ βασιλεὺς Σολομῶν καὶ πάντες οἱ βασι-λεῖς καὶ οἱ ἄρχοντες καὶ οἱ μεγιστάνοι ὅλοι τους τὸν ἐπροσκυ-νοῦσαν ὡς βασιλέαν καὶ τιμημένον ἀπὸ ὅλους τοὺς βασιλεῖς τῆς γῆς καὶ τὸν εἶχαν εἰς μεγάλην φήμην εἰς ὅλον τὸν κόσμον καὶ
10 ἐθαύμαζαν ὅλοι τους καὶ εὐχαριστοῦσαν καὶ ἐδόξαζαν τὸν θεὸν τοῦ οὐρανοῦ καὶ τῆς γῆς ὅπου τὸν ἔδωσεν τοιαύτην ἐξουσίαν καὶ ὅρισεν ὅλους τοὺς δαίμονας τῆς γῆς καὶ τοῦ ἀέρος καὶ τῆς θα-λάσσης καὶ τῶν καταχθονίων. 2. καὶ μετὰ τὴν συμπλήρωσιν τοῦ ναοῦ τοῦ θεοῦ ἐμάζωξεν ὁ βασιλεὺς Σολομῶν ὅλα τὰ δαιμόνια
15 καὶ ἀκάθαρτα πνεύματα καὶ ἐπαράστησεν ἔμπροσθέν του ἀμέτρη-τον πλῆθος δαιμόνων καὶ ὅρισεν νὰ ἔλθουν ἄνθρωποι τεχνῖτες καὶ καλοὶ ὅπου ἐδούλευαν τὰ * χαλκώματα καὶ ὅρισεν ὁ βασιλεὺς νὰ φτειάσουν ἀγγεῖα χαλκωματένια. καὶ τότες ἐπίασεν καὶ τὰ ἔκαμεν παρόμοια ὡσὰν πιθάρια κάδους τρανοὺς καὶ μὲ τοῦ θεοῦ
20 τὸ ὄνομα ὅρισεν ὁ βασιλεὺς ὅλους τοὺς δαίμονας καὶ ἐσέβησαν μέσα εἰς ἐκεῖνα τὰ ἀγγεῖα τὰ χαλκωματένια. καὶ τότες ἐπίασεν ὁ βασιλεὺς ἀτός του καὶ τοὺς ἐσφάλισεν καὶ ἐβούλλωσεν τὰ ἀγ-γεῖα μὲ τὴν βούλλαν τοῦ θεοῦ καὶ ἦταν αἱ βούλλες ἀργυρὲς καὶ ἦταν οἱ δαίμονες μέσα. καὶ πλέον δὲν ἐτολμοῦσαν διὰ νὰ ἔβ-
25 γουν ἔξω.

3. Καὶ ἐχαίρετον ὁ βασιλεὺς Σολομῶν εἰς τὴν πλήρωσιν τῆς οἰκοδομῆς τῆς ἁγίας Σιών, καὶ τὸν καιρὸν ἐκεῖνον ἐρητόρευσε τὸ ᾆσμα τῶν ᾀσμάτων. καὶ ἐκατοίκησεν ἡ χάρις τοῦ ἁγίου πνεύ-ματος εἰς τὸν ναὸν ἐκεῖνον τὸν ἱερόν. καὶ ἦτον τὸ μῆκος του
30 πήχες ο̅β̅ καὶ τὸ πλάτος κ̅δ̅, καὶ ὁ πῆχυς ἐκεῖνος θέλουν νὰ εἰ-ποῦν το πῶς ἦτον δέκα ἑπτὰ ποδάρια. καὶ ἀπὸ τοῦ γύρου τοῦ ναοῦ ἔκαμεν πολλὰ κελλία διὰ νὰ κατοικοῦν οἱ ἱερεῖς καὶ διὰ νὰ βάνουν καὶ τὰ ἱερὰ σκεύη ὅπου τὰ εἶχαν οἱ προπάτορες ἀρχιερεῖς

C. X. cf. parallele in Test Sal. XVIII 42—44 (ms. P) —XIX. l. 6 εὐ-φημίσθην   8 τιμημένοι   § 2. l. 17 τὰ bis scr. | * f. 189ʳ   18 ἀγγείαν
19 κάδδους   24 ἦταν ταν bis scr et postea primum eras.   § 3. l. 30 πῆχας
32 κελλιᾶν (sic)

ὁποῦ ἐλειτουργοῦσαν ἐκεῖ εἰς τὰ ἅγια τῶν ἁγίων. 4. καὶ ἐκεῖ εἰς
τὸ βῆμα τοῦ ναοῦ ἦταν ἡ πλάκες ὁποῦ εἶχαν τὸν θεόγραφον
νόμον ὁποῦ ἔδωκεν ὁ θεὸς τοῦ προφήτου Μωυσέως. ἦτον ἡ
στάμνος ὁποῦ εἶχεν τὸ μάννα μέσα. ἦτον καὶ ἡ κιβωτός, ἦτον
5 καὶ ἡ ῥάβδος τοῦ Ἀαρών, τὸ χρυσοῦν * θυμιατήριον, ἡ λυχνία,
ἡ ἁγία τράπεζος, καὶ ἄλλα πολλὰ ἦσαν ἀφιερωμένα τῷ θεῷ τῷ
ὑψίστῳ. καὶ ἐκεῖ εἰς τὸ ἅγιον βῆμα δὲν ἐσέβαινεν κανεὶς μόνον
ὁ ἀρχιερεὺς καὶ ἐκεῖνος μίαν φορὰν τὸν χρόνον μὲ τοὺς ἱερεῖς
του ὡς καθὼς τὸ εἶχαν συνήθειαν. 5. τὸν καιρὸν ἐκεῖνον καὶ
10 ἦτον ὁ ναὸς ἐκεῖνος ὑψηλὸς ἕως ρκδ πῆχες καὶ τὸν ἐσκέπασεν
ὁ βασιλεὺς τὸν ναὸν ἀπὸ πάνω ὅλον μὲ χρυσάφι καθαρὸν καὶ
ἁγνὸν μάλαγμα καὶ ἦτον κτισμένος μὲ δέκα λογιῶν μάμαρα
πελεκητά. καὶ ἔφεγγεν ὁ ναὸς ἐκεῖνος ὡσὰν τὸν οὐρανὸν ὡς
καθὼς φαίνεται εἰς τὴν ἐξαστερίαν μὲ τὸν ἥλιον καὶ μὲ τὴν
15 σελήνην.

6. Καὶ ὁ Σολομῶν ὡσὰν ἐτελείωσεν τὸν ναὸν ἐκεῖνον τὴν
ὀνομαζομένην ἁγίαν Σιὼν ἐστάθη καὶ ἔκαμεν προσευχὴν εἰς τὸν
θεὸν μὲ ὕμνους καὶ δοξολογίας καὶ νηστεύων καὶ ἀγρυπνιζόμενος
καὶ παρακαλῶν διὰ τὰ ἁγιάσῃ τὸν ναὸν ὁποῦ ἔκτισεν. καὶ ἤκου-
20 σεν ὁ θεὸς τὴν δέησιν τοῦ Σολομῶν⟨τος⟩ καὶ ἐφάνη ὁ θεὸς καὶ
εἶπεν του ὅτι· »ἤκουσα τῆς φωνῆς τῆς δεήσεώς σου καὶ ἡγίασα
τὸν ναὸν ἐτοῦτον καὶ ὑπάρχοντα χερουβὶμ καὶ τὰ σεραφὶμ καὶ
τὰ ἐξαπτέρυγα καὶ οἱ θρόνοι καὶ αἱ κυριότητες ὄπισθεν τοῦ θυσιαστηρίου τοῦ ναοῦ ἔσωθεν καὶ ἔξωθεν« τό τε κάλλος τοῦ
25 ναοῦ ἐκείνου οὔτε ἔγινεν εἰς τὴν γῆν οὔτε θέλει γένῃ εἰς τὸν
αἰῶνα

XI. Καὶ ἐπέρασαν ἀπὸ τὸν καιρὸν τοῦ Σολομῶν⟨τος⟩ τοῦ *
υἱοῦ Δαυεὶδ ἕως τοῦ Σεδεκίου τοῦ βασιλέως τῆς Ἰερουσαλὴμ χρόνοι 425. καὶ εἰς ἐκεῖνον τὸν καιρὸν ἦτον καὶ ὁ προφήτης Ἰερε-
30 μίας ἱερεὺς τοῦ θεοῦ τοῦ ὑψίστου μὲ τὸν Βαροὺχ καὶ τὸν Ἀβι-
μέλεχ, καὶ ἦσαν εἰς τὸν ναὸν τοῦ θεοῦ ἐκεῖνον ὁποῦ ἔκαμεν ὁ
βασιλεὺς Σολομῶν καὶ ἔκαμαν προσευχὲς καὶ δεήσεις πρὸς τὸν
θεὸν καὶ ὑμνοῦσαν καὶ ἐδοξολογοῦσαν τὸν θεὸν νύκταν καὶ ἡμέ-

---

5 * f. 189ᵛ | λυχνίαν 8 τῶν χρόνων § 6 l. 17 προσευχήθη
23 οἱ: αἱ
C XI. l. 27 * f. 190ʳ

ραν   2. ὅμως βλέποντας ὁ θεὸς τὴν ὑπερηφάνειαν καὶ τὴν σκλη-
ροκαρδίαν τοῦ Σεδεκίου τοῦ βασιλέως εἶπεν τὸν Ἰερεμίαν τὸν
προφήτην ὅτι νὰ ὑπάγῃ εἰς τὸν ναὸν καὶ πάρῃ τὰ ἅγια σκεύη
τοῦ ναοῦ καὶ νὰ παραδώσῃ τὴν γῆν. καὶ τότες ὁ προφήτης
5 Ἰερεμίας ἐπῆγεν εἰς τὸν ναὸν τοῦ θεοῦ καὶ ἐπῆρεν τὰ ἅγια σκεύη
τῆς ἁγίας Σιὼν καὶ ἐπαρέδωκεν αὐτὰ τὴν γῆν καθὼς τὸν ἐπαρήγγειλεν ὁ θεὸς καὶ ἐπῆρεν καὶ τὰ κλειδία ἀπὸ τὸ ἅγιον θυσιαστήριον τοῦ ναοῦ καὶ τὰ ἔριψεν κάτω εἰς τὴν γῆν ἔμπροσθεν τοῦ
ἡλίου καὶ εἶπεν ὁ προφήτης· »Ἔπαρε αὐτὰ καὶ φύλαξέ τα ἕως
10 ὅπου νὰ ἐξετάσῃ κύριος ὁ θεὸς δι᾽ αὐτά, ὅτι ἡμεῖς δὲν εὑρεθή-
καμεν ἄξιοι διὰ νὰ τὰ φυλάξωμεν«.

     3. Καὶ τότες ἦλθεν καὶ ὁ βασιλεὺς ὁ Ναβουχοδονόσωρ ἀπὸ
τὴν Βαβυλῶνα καὶ ἐπαρέλαβε τὴν Ἱερουσαλὴμ καὶ ἐκούρσευσεν
αὐτὴν καὶ τότες ἐκάει τὸ σκέπασμα τοῦ ναοῦ ὅπου ἔκτισεν ὁ
15 βασιλεὺς Σολομῶν ὅπου τὸν εἶχεν σκεπασμένον τὸν ναὸν ὅλον μὲ
ἁγνὸν μάλαμα, καὶ καίοντας ἔτρεχεν * τὸ μάλαμα ὡσὰν ποτάμι
μεγάλον. καὶ τὸν Σεδεκίαν τὸν βασιλέαν τῆς Ἱερουσαλὴμ ἔκοψεν
τὴν γυναῖκα του καὶ τὰ παιδία του ἔμπροσθεν εἰς τ᾽ ἀμμάτιά
του καὶ αὐτὸν τὸν ἐτύφλωσεν καὶ τὸν ἐπῆρεν αἰχμάλωτον μὲ
20 τὸν λαὸν ὅλον τῆς Ἱερουσαλὴμ εἰς τὴν Βαβυλῶνα.   4. οἱ δὲ Χαλδαῖοι ὅπου ἐκούρσευσαν τὴν Ἱερουσαλὴμ καὶ κουρσεύοντας ηὗραν
ἐκεῖνα τὰ ἀγγεῖα τὰ χαλκωματένια ὅπου εἶχεν ὁ βασιλεὺς Σολομῶν τοὺς δαίμονας σφαλισμένους καὶ βουλλωμένους μὲ τὴν σφραγίδα ὅπου τοῦ ἔστειλεν ὁ θεὸς ἀπὸ τοὺς οὐρανοὺς μετὰ τοῦ ἀρχ-
25 αγγέλου Μιχαήλ. καὶ βλέποντας οἱ Χαλδαῖοι τὲς βοῦλλες τὲς
χρυσὲς καὶ τὰ ἀγγεῖα ἐκεῖνα τὰ χαλκωματένια ὅπου ἦτον εἰς τὴν
γῆν χωσμένα, καὶ ἐφαίνουνταν ὡσὰν πηγάδια βουλλωμένα ἐθάρ-
ρεψαν οἱ Χαλδαῖοι ὅτι εἶναι θησαυρὸς κεκρυμμένος ⟨καὶ⟩ ἐπῆγαν
καὶ ἐξεβούλλωσαν ἀπὸ ἐκεῖνα τὲς βοῦλλες τὲς χρυσὲς καὶ τὲς
30 ἐξεβούλλωσαν καὶ ἔφυγον οἱ δαίμονες ἀπὸ ἐκεῖ πάλιν καὶ ἐπῆγαν
πάλιν εἰς τὲς πρῶτες ὀργισμένες κατοικίες καὶ πάλιν πειράζουν
τοὺς ἀνθρώπους.

     XII. Λοιπὸν αὐτὰ τὰ κατορθώματα ὅπου ἔκαμεν ὁ βασιλεὺς
Σολομῶν δὲν ἦτον ἀπὸ ἐδικήν του δύναμιν οὐδὲ ἀπὸ τὴν σοφίαν

---

§ 2 l. 7 κλυδίαν   § 3. l. 16 ποταμὴν   § 4. l. 21 ε pro κουρσεύοντας
scr. postea eras.   **22. 26** ἀγγίαν

του τὴν πολλὴν ἀλλὰ ἡ δύναμις ἦτον τοῦ μεγάλου θεοῦ τοῦ
ὑψίστου τοῦ μονογενοῦς υἱοῦ τοῦ θεοῦ ὁποῦ ἔμελλεν ἀπὸ τοῦ
Σολομῶντος τοῦ βασιλέως τὴν φυλὴν νὰ σαρκωθῇ καὶ ἕως τὸν
καιρὸν ὁποῦ ἦλθεν καὶ ἐσαρκώθη ὁ κύριος ἡμῶν Ἰησοῦς Χριστὸς
5 χρόνοι 726 καὶ ἔκαμεν εἰς τὴν γῆν σωματικῶς χρόνους λγ, καὶ
ἐσταυρώθη καὶ ἐτάφη καὶ ἀνέστη ἐκ τῶν νεκρῶν. καὶ ἡμᾶς
ἐχάρισεν ζωὴν τὴν αἰώνιον καὶ μὲ τὴν ἐνέργειαν τοῦ τιμίου καὶ
ζωοποιοῦ σταυροῦ ἐκατίσχυνεν τὸν μέγαν διάβολον τὸν ἐχθρὸν
τῆς ψυχῆς μας. 2. λοιπὸν καὶ ἐκείνη ἡ σφραγῖδα εἶχεν τὸν τύ-
10 πον τοῦ τιμίου καὶ ζωοποιοῦ σταυροῦ καὶ ἐπάταξεν ὅλους τοὺς
δαίμονας καὶ ὄχι μόνον τοὺς ἔδεσεν ἀλλὰ καὶ ἐπάταξέν τους καὶ
τὸ ἐν ὑστέροις πάλιν ὡσὰν ἐτελείωσεν τὸν ναὸν τοῦ θεοῦ πάλιν
τοὺς ἐσφάλισεν καὶ τοὺς ἐφυλάκωσεν ὅλους εἰς ἐκεῖνα τ⟨α⟩ ἀγγεῖα τὰ χαλκοματένια. 3. λοιπὸν εἰς ἐτοῦτον τὸν καιρὸν ὅσοι
15 πιστεύουν τὸν κύριον ἡμῶν Ἰησοῦν Χριστὸν τὸν δι᾽ ἡμᾶς σταυ-
ρωθέντα καταδεξάμενον μὲ καλὴν πίστιν καὶ μὲ καλὰ ἔργα μὲ τὸ
σημεῖον τοῦ τιμίου καὶ ζωοποιοῦ σταυροῦ τοὺς δένει καὶ τοὺς
καταργεῖ διότι μεγάλη ἁλυσίδα εἶναι ὁ τίμιος καὶ ζωοποιὸς σταυ-
ρὸς ὁποῦ μᾶς ἀφῆκεν νὰ κάμνομεν νὰ τὸν ὑμνοῦμεν καὶ νὰ τὸ
20 δοξάζομεν διὰ νὰ μᾶς γλυτώνῃ ἀπὸ ἐχθροὺς ψυχικοὺς καὶ σω-
ματικοὺς καὶ νὰ μᾶς ἀξιώσῃ ἐν τῇ βασιλείᾳ τῶν οὐρανῶν ἧς
γένοιτο πάντας ἡμᾶς ἐν Χριστῷ τῷ θεῷ, ᾧ ἡ δόξα καὶ κράτος
τοῦ πατρὸς καὶ τοῦ υἱοῦ καὶ τοῦ ἁγίου πνεύματος νῦν καὶ ἀεὶ
καὶ εἰς τοὺς αἰῶνας τῶν αἰώνων. ἀμήν.

C. XII. I 8 * f. 191ʳ § 2. l. 18 *ἀγγεῖαν* § 3. l. 21 *βασιλείαν*

Emendationes in Textum.

8. Καὶ ἔγραψα τὴν διαθήκην μου ταύτην ⌜τοῖς Ἰουδαίοις⌝ καὶ
κατέλιπον ταύτην αὐτοῖς εἰς μνημόσυνον πρὸ τελευτῆς μου. ἡ διαθήκη
μου φυλαττέσθω παρ᾽ ὑμῶν εἰς μυστήριον μέγα κατὰ πνευμάτων
ἀκαθάρτων ὥστε γνῶναι ὑμᾶς τῶν πονηρῶν δαιμόνων τὰς μηχανὰς
καὶ τῶν ἁγίων ἀγγέλων τὰς δυνάμεις· ὅτι ἐνισχύει μέγας κύριος
Σαβαὼθ ὁ θεὸς Ἰσραὴλ καὶ ὑπέταξεν ἐπ᾽ ἐμοὶ πάντα τὰ δαιμόνια,
ἐν ᾧ ἐδόθη μοι σφραγὶς διαθήκης αἰωνίου 9. καὶ ἀπέθανον ἐν τῇ
βασιλείᾳ μου καὶ προσετέθην μετὰ τῶν πατέρων μου ἐν εἰρήνῃ, καὶ
ἐπληρώθη ὁ ναὸς κυρίου τοῦ θεοῦ, ᾧ πρέπει τιμὴ καὶ προσκύνησις
εἰς τοὺς αἰῶνας τῶν αἰώνων· ἀμήν.

Corrigenda.

P. L
48   5 *L.* a nail *pro* wood
7*   5 ἐπεδίδοντο, *app* ἐπεδίδον τὸ
9*   2 *App.* ὁ δυνόμενος *in* ὀδυνώμενος *cor.* Windisch
9*   7 *App.* φόβου
22* 6 πρόσκαιρός
26*   *App.* § 4, *l* 4 ἀπόλωνται
27*   *App.* § 7, *l* 4 Ῥωμαίων
28* 11 *App.* εἴγειρεν H. *L.* 13 *App.* εἶπεν P
32* 7 *App* ἐγὼ W
36* 6 τότε
39*   3 *App.* § 9, *l.* 2 ἀναφέρουσιν
40*   3 ἑτέραν
44* Head Ὀβυζοίθ
46*   *App.* καταταρασσ.
64* 11 *L. fortasse* ὡς μέλισσαι
67*   2 *App.* καὶ *pro* κμὶ
85* 14 *Ante* ὑπερι *pr* 15
86* 15 δρᾶμα (MS δράμα)
92*   1 ἤ
96* 27 ᾆσμα τῶν ᾀσμάτων
100* 6 *Pro* HL *l.* HI
103* Head Σολομῶντος
118*   1 *Post* αὐτὸς *add.* ἀναγογεῖν

INDEXES

References in Indexes I to IV are to chapter and section of text, in Indexes V and VI to pages of Introduction. * Hapax legomena, † conjecturally restored, (?) Probable copyist's errors

I. Index of Grammar and Syntax

A complete exhibit is not attempted

Adverbs and conjunctions

Ἀλλά I 2 C, V 3 PC, VIII 5, 6, 8, IX 7, XI 5, XIII 2, 3, 5, XV 4 P, XVI 2 P, XVIII 3 (*bis*), XX 5, 7, 17, XXV 8 B, XXVI 3, C V 3, XIII 6; D VII 3; cf. οὐ μόνον

ἄν *c. ind.* X 6, *c. subj.* I 9, XVIII 21, XXV 8 P

ἄρα I 2 L, XIV 4, XXII 12 B, D IV 4

Γάρ IV 7, VIII 12 (*bis*), IX 2, X 2, 3†, XII 3, XVI 2 P, XX 2 H, C IV 6, V 3 (PC), VIII 12, XI 5, D I 2 (*bis*), 5, II 1, *et pas.*; cf. καὶ γάρ

γέ XIII 3 P

γοῦν IX 5 V, XV 5

δέ I 1 L, C, 2 AL, C (*bis*), 3, 4, 11, 12, II 4, 5, 6, C X 1, 2, 3, D I 1, 3, 4, 5, 6, 8, 9, 10, *et pas.*

δὲ καί II 3, IV 6, V 9, XIV 3, C I 3, 4, 11, IV 5, VII 2, VIII 5, X 3, 6, 11, 21, D II 1, VIII 3, *et pas.*, cf. ὁ δέ under Article, and μὲν . δέ

δή I 3 C. 4 Q, C Pro 3, XI 9, XIII 14, D I 3, III 7

δηλαδή C X 25

δῆτα D I 13

διό I 1 L, XXII 5 P, διότι IV 9, V 10 P, 12, VII 6, XXVI 2 Q

Ἐάν *c. ind.* VIII 11, XVIII 15 (?), 35, *c. subj.* I 12 W, 13, VI 8, 10 (*bis*), VII 5, XI 5, XVII 4 P, XXVI 4 (*bis*), *c. ind. vel subj* XVIII 9, 10, 11, 12 *et pas*

εἰ == *whether* IV 1, XXII 12; C XI 1, XII 3, XIII 13, D VI 12, == *if, c. ind. praes.* VI 10, XIII 2, XXIII 2, C X 8, *c. ind aor* XXVI 2, *c. ind. fut.* XVII 2, 4, C IX 8, X 12, XIII 1, D VI 2, *c. subj.* XVII 3

εἰ μή XIII 3 P, 4, XV 11 P

εἶτα XVIII 15 P, XX 19 H, L I : (*bis*), II 1, 5, III 4, IV 1, 12, V 12 (*pas.*), VII 8 (*bis*), C IX 10

εἴτε XX 13 (*pas.*)

ἔνθα IV 4 PCC°, C XI 3, D VI 4

ἐπεί XVI 3 A, XVIII 3 H, C XIII 14, D I 12

ἐπειδή XV 4 P, XVI 3 P, XVIII 3 LP, XXII 3 B, 20, C XIII 6

Τέ D VII 4, τί . . καί I 3 P, 7 A, XIX 2H, XXII 1 B, 4, C Pro 3 (*bis*), X 29, D II 1, III 2, 6 (*bis*), 8, VI 10, 11, 13, VII 4, 5

τοίνυν C Pro 4, 5; D I 7, II 1, IV 11, 14

Ως — *like, as* I 10, II 3, III 4, V 5, VI 11 P, VII 1 LC, VIII 4, IX 2 A, 6, X 1, 8 LP, XI 1 H, XV (P) 1, 3, 5, XVI 2, XVIII 1, 3, 18 P, 19 P, XX 17 H, XXII 3 B, XXVI 1, 5 (*bis*), Tit C, D I 2, IV 2, 16, *c. inf.* C XI 5, — *about* C XI 8; — *when* III 5, XIV 6, XXIV 1 Q, XXV 7 B, D IV 13, VI 8, *c. subj. vel ind. fut.* XVIII 5, 6, 7, 8, — ἵνα *c. subj.* XIII 14, — ὅτι D IV 2

ὡσεί *c. gen.* VII 1 HP, X 9, *c. nom.* XIV 4, XVIII 1 H, XXIII 3 P, XXVI 6 B

ὥσπερ V 12, X 8 H, XX 16, 17 B, C Pro 2, D IV 16, *c. ind* C XII 5, D I 13, Sig T

ὥστε *c. inf.* I 1 H, 2 C (τοσοῦτον), I 10, IV 12, V 5, 8 P, XV 14, XVIII 8 H

Anacoluthia H II 4, 7, V 9, VII 3, VIII 7, *et pas.*; I II 4, 7, V 9, L I 1, 2, 3, 4, 5, 6, 9, 10, V 9, VII 7, VIII 1—3, *et pas.*, P I 4, II 3, 4, 6, IV 8, V 13, VI 2, 8, 10, VII 2, 3, 6, VIII 11, XI 5, 6, XIII 3, *et pas.*, Q II 9; C Pro 1, I 4, II 7, IV 1, 7, IX 9, XI 1, 5, 6, XII 6, XIII 8, 12, see Cases-solecism

Article

Demonstrative — ὁ δέ, ἡ δέ, etc. IV 4, 8, 9, 10, 11, V 2, 3, 8, 10, etc., VIII 2, XIV 5, XVIII 2, XX 10, *et pas*, ὁ μέν, ἡ μέν, VIII 12, XIV 4, XVIII 5 P With infinitive, see Verbs — Inf.

Omitted In prepositional phrases I 2, 3 C, 4, II 5, 6, 7, III 4, IV 9, *et pas.*; with infinitive XI 6, with θεός C XII 4, cf. IX 8 (φίλος)

Asyndeta I 4, 12, II 1 AQ, III 6, IV 5, V 4 A, VIII 6, IX 2 C, A, 3, 6, C X 3,

7, 8, 9, 10, *et pas.*, XI 7, 8, XII 1, 2, 4, XIII 10, 13, D I 2, 7, 8, 12, 13, IV 9, VII 2, VIII 2, 6

Attic forms διαπράττω, ἐλλέω, ἐλαττῶ, ἡττάω, κρείττω, περιττός, τριττός, ὑποτάττω, φρίττω, φυλάττω (XXIV 2 H, XXVI 8 H), see Index III

Cases

Nom pendens I 1 L, 2 L, 3 W, 4 B, XII 4, XVIII 1, XX 19 H, C XI 1; D IV 3

Gen absolute I 1, 2 A, 4, II 3, 4 L, 6, 7, IV 1, 3, V 5, VI 3, VIII 8, IX 5, XX 3, XXII 13 B, C Pro 1 (*bis*), XI 1, 3, D II 11, III 8, IV 9, 13, VI 7 (*bis*), 11, VII 5, noun om C Pro 5, II 7, D IV 5, VI 3

Gen. of time, age, etc I 5 B, VI 5 (*errore*), IX 3, 5, XVI 5 P (*errore*), XXII 13 H, C VII 5, XI 8

Gen. with adj. III 5, V 13; D IV 2, with comparative XVIII 18 P, D I 13, II 1, see preps. παρά, ὑπέρ

Gen., possessive, in predicate VI 8, XXII 4, XXIII 4 H†, C X 12

Gen. with verbs I 2 L, 4, 9 C, II 6, IV 1, V 10, VI 2, 8, VII 6, XVIII 40, XX 2, 5, 7, 15, XXII 3, 5, 9, (cf acc. XXII 6), C Pro 1, 2, 5, IX 8, X 15 —19, 38, XII 2, 5, XIII 10, D IV 1

Dative, indirect object I 1, 3, 3 C, 5—10, 12—14, II 1, 2, 6, 9, III 1, 2, 5, 6, 7, IV 2, 3, V 3, *et pas.*, C Pro 1, IX 8, 9, X 42, 53, XII 1, 5, XIII 2, 3, 8—13, D I 4, II 7, 8, III 1, 4, IV 16, VI 3, 4, 7, VII 3

Dat of advantage and disadvantage I 9(?), II 7, VIII 4, IX 2, XV 8, XVIII 44 P, C X 53, D I 11, II 1

Dat., possessive in predicate I 1, IV 5, XI 3, XVI 4 P, XXVI 4, C XI 5, D VII 2

Dat., associative III 4, VIII 8, XXV 4, XXVI 4, D IV 1; *c. adj.* VIII 8, XV 10; D I 13, IV 3, VI 12

μελανοκέρατος IX 9 C
νευροχάλασις XVIII 17 P
νυκτοφαγήση(?) XVIII 35 P
ξυλοφορέω XI 7 P
ὀνοπρόσωπος XVIII 1 P
πλινθουργέω XII 6 P
πορφυροδανόμενος XII 4 P
προεπιστρέφω V 2 L
πρωτομαίστωρ I 2 B
πτηνοπρόσωπος XVIII 1 P
στραγγισμός XVIII 27 P
ὑπογινώσκω V 13 L
ὑποπροτάσσω X 6 L
φοβερόχροος XII 1
χαλινόδεσμα XIII 4 P

Crasis κἀγώ pas., κἀκεῖ VIII 5 P, κἀκεῖνος IX 7 P, -ως II 8; τἄλλα XVII 5,
τἀληθές C XII 5, ταὐτά D IV 3

Elision, cf. ἀλλά, ἀντί, ἀπό, ἐπί, κατά,
μετά, παρά; not observed VII 1 (ταῦτα
ἀκούσας); IX 7 P (ἐπί αὐτό)

Gender—solecisms I 1 HI, 14 CQ, II 2;
C IX 8, XII 2

Hebraismus ἐγένετο, καὶ ἐγένετο, etc.
I 6, XXII 1 P, XXV 7 B, C Pro 1; D
II 1, εἰς χεῖρας I 5; ζῇ κύριος ὁ θεός
I 13, V 12, XXV 8 B, πρὸ προσώπου
cf. πρό under Prepositions

Hiatus P VI 11, IX 7, C XIII 10, 12

Indirect Discourse—Questions IV 1,
XXII 12; cf. Inf. with subj. Acc.

Latinisms κάστρον C X 13, 24, 27, Λε-
γεών XI 3, 5, 6, 7; λίτρα XXI 1 Q,
ὃ ἐστιν P XI 6, XV 11, πρὸ τεσσ.
ἡμερῶν D IV 14

Nouns — case endings
ἄνδρες — Acc I 1 L
ν in Acc. Third Declension 1 5 HL,

X 8 L; C I 3, 4, 6, 8, 9, 11, 14, II 9,
IX 8, 10, X 51, XII 5
σφραγῖδα, -δαι Sig C
φάραγγει C III 5

Prepositions
Ἅμα c. dat X 6, XIII 1, D VII 6; c. acc.
D III 5, VII 4
ἀνά c. gen. C IX 10, c. acc. D VII 4
ἄνευ XXII 11 B, C XIII 8
ἀντί C XI 8
ἄνωθεν C XII 6
ἀπό c. gen. I 1 L (= ὑπό), C, 2 P, 4, 4 B,
II 1, III 4, IV 8 et pas., — contrary
to IV 5, C XI 5, c. dat. II 5 L, c. acc.
XVIII 20 L, XXII 2 Q
ἄχρι c. gen. XX 18 B, c. acc. D IV 8
Διά c. gen. agent, means, etc., I 6, 7,
IV 7, V 3, 8, 11, VI 4, et pas., C IV 5,
IX 8, XI 4, XIII 13; D I 7, II 1, IV
15, place, I 5, IX 6, X 3, XIV 4,
XXIV 4; C XII 6, time, D II 4, c.
acc. cause, II 2, V 4, 13. VI 1, 2, 6, 9,
VII 6, et pas, C I 1, 3, XIII 2, D I 6,
means C X 53, δ. παντός XXII 5 B
δίκην D VI 5
Ἔγγιστα C, ἔγγιστεν P, ἐγγύθεν A
III 7
εἰς I 1, 3 C, 4, 9, II 3, 5, 7, 8, 9, III 3,
5, et pas., C Pro 4, IX 9, X 2, 6, 18,
20, 21, 24, 25, et pas., D I 1, 3, 4, 8,
12, II 11, et pas.; ἐνεργεῖν εἰς C X 1,
2, 3, 5, 6, 12, 13, 14 (bis), 22, 23, 26,
29, 34, 35, 36, 37, 38, 39, 52, εἰς τὸ
ὄνομα XXVI 4, 5; C IX 8, εἰς ὄνομα
C Pro 5, εἰς = ἐν XV 6, XXII 14;
XXIV 3 (?), D VI 1
ἐκ I 2 L, 4, 4 L, 5, 6 L, II 8, VI 5, X 9,
XIV 4, XVI 3, XXVI 3, XXI 2, XXV
1 H, C IV 11, XI 8, XII 1, XIII 12,
D I 1, 11, 12 (5), IV 13, 14 (bis), 15,
VI 8, ἐκ τρίτου 1 2 L, XVIII 21
ἔμπροσθεν c. gen. IV 2 C, VI 1, XIII 7,
XX 19 Q, XXII 10, D III 3, C IV 2,
XI 2
ἐν 1 1, 3 (tris), II 1 (bis), IV 4, 5, 8, 9
(tris), 10, et pas, C IX 10, X 8, 14,

Σύν V 4P, XV 1P, XXIII 2, XXV 9H,
  D II 7
Ὑπέρ c. gen. D II 5; c. acc. I 1L, 3A;
  C XII 6
ὑπό c. gen. I 1H, 2, 6L, 9P, II 4, IV
  11, VI 8 (bis), IX 6, 7P, XI 6, XII 3,
  XIII 6 (bis), XIV 4, 5 (bis), XV 5, 6, 9,
  13, XIX 1, XXI 3, XXII 3B, 20, XXIV
  4, XXV 3, XXVI 7H, 9H, C Pro 2,
  IX 8, D III 2, 6, c. dat. C XIII 6,
  c. acc. XI 3, 5, XXII 8Q, XXVI 5H,
  7H
ὑποκάτω XI 7, XIX 1, XXIII 3H, XXV 7
ὑποκάτωθεν C XI 7
Χάριν XX 2
χωρίς XXI 4
Ὡς VII 1 C
ὡσεί VII 1

Pronouns

αὐτός Third Person, passim, = idem
  V 3, XVIII 35H, XXII 8, C IX 9T,
  D IV 3, = ipse VII 6, IX 7P, C Pro
  1, 3, X 15—20, XII 5, D I 12, II 1,
  III 2, V 1 (bis)
ἐγώ passim
εἷς as indef. pron. I 1A, 3, XX 1, C
  XII 5
ἐμαυτοῦ, ἑαυτοῦ IV 6, VI 3P, IX 2, 3P,
  6, 7P, XI 5, XVI 2, 4, XVIII 4P, C
  XII 5, D VI 12, cf. VI 3
ἐμός V 4, VI 4P, IX 5, X 3, XXIII 4P,
  C XIII 12; D III 2, IV 2, 9
ἡμέτερος C Pro 3
σός I 4Q, III 5, X 5, D IV 10, 11, VI 2
σύ passim
τις, τίς passim

Verbs — Inflexion

Augment ἠνεσχόμην XIII 3P, προεφή-
  τευσε XV 8

Future from Subjunctive (Aor.)
  ἀγαγῶ II 6, VI 5, X 5
  εἴπωσι XIV 5P
  ἐνέγκω VI 5H, C XI 7Y, D VI 2
  εὕρωμεν V 5C
  ἔχωμεν V 5A
  ἴδῃς D IV 9
  μαθεῖς XIII 2H
  παρέλθωσι D IV 6
Periphrastic tenses I 1, 2, XVI 2P, XX
  17, XXI 4, XXII 7B, XXV 9H, XXIV
  4B, C Pro 1, 2, D I 12, VII 4, VIII 1
Reduplication σεσωματοπεποιημένον
  IV 4P

Verbs — Syntax

Infinitive with Art. in oblique cases
Gen. I 14, II 5, 7C, 8, V 6L, VII 4,
  C IX 10, X 43, 53, XIII 13, 14, D
  I 4 (bis), 9; = Nom. XVI 2, D VII 2
Dat. I 4, 7, VI 9, XX 17, XXII 1P, 11,
  17B, XXIV 5, D I 6, IV 16
Acc. I 1, 2L, 4, V 13, VI 2, VII 2,
  XVI 5, XX 6P, XXVI 5, 7H, C Pro 1,
  X 1, 2, 3, et pas, XIII 2, D III 5 (?),
  IV 11
As noun without Art XI 6
Optative C XIII 12 θελήσαιεν, D IV 4
  ἀποκρίνοιτο, VI 1 χαίροις, 12 γινώ-
  σκοι
Participle
  Unnecessary XI 3 ὄν, XIII 2 ὄντα
  Future of purpose D VII 3
Perfect for Aorist II 9CL, D I 3, II 6,
  8, 9, 11
Subjunctive
  With ἄν, ἐάν, εἰ, ἕως, ἵνα, ὅπως, ὡς
    cf supra Adverbs
  Hortatory D VI 7
  In oath P XXV 8
  Prohibitions I 12, 13, V 10, 11, VI 6,
    XV 4P, XVIII 18 (bis), XXII 5, C
    XIII 3

II. Index of Angelology, Astrology, Demonology, Magic

ἃ καὶ β´ XVIII 38
Ἀβεζεθιβοῦ XXV 2 HP, -εβιθου Q
Ἀβελούθ XXV 2 Q, cf. Ἀμελούθ
Ἀβραάμ XVIII 22 P
Ἀβυζοί(θ) XIII 2 L
ἄγγελος v. XVIII 15 and Index III
Ἄγλα C XIII 6
Ἀγχονίων XVIII 37 P, cf. Ἀχωνεώθ
Ἀδωναήλ P XVIII 14, 17, cf. Ἀδωναί
Ἀδωναί XVIII 14 H, ἀδωιάν L, XVIII
17 A, Ἀδωναήλ P, XVIII 36 H, ἀδο-
ναήθ P
ἀενιου Sig A, T, Vʳ
ἀερίου XVIII 28 H, ἀρνίου P
Ἀζαήλ VII 7
αιαώ Sig A, T (ιαώ), Vʳ
Αἰγώκερας XVIII 3 P
διέ Sig A, Vʳ
ἀιώ Sig A
Ἀκέφαλος δαίμων IX 1, X 8
Ἀκουρταραήλ XVIII 13 L
Ἀκτονμέ XVIII 28 H, κτονμέ L, ἄκτον
μέν P
Ἀλάθ XVIII 25 HP, ὀλάθ L
ἀλακαρτανακ I 9 C
Ἀλενρήθ XVIII 35 H, ἀλλεβοριθ P
Ἀλλαζοώλ XVIII 30 P, cf. Καλαζαήλ
Ἀλλεβοριθ XVIII 35 P, cf Ἀλενρήθ
ἄμαξα V 4
Ἀμελούθ XXV 2, cf. Ἀβελούθ
Ἀμεμῶν C X 16, ἀμαιμῶν V
Ἀμπατζούτ C X 20
ἀναάθ XVIII 40
Ἀνατρέθ XVIII 29
Ἄνετ C X 45
Ἀνοστήρ XVIII 33 P, ἀστήρ H
Ἀντιναός C X 42 T, cf Ἀτανιανούς
Ἀξησβύθ XVIII 31 H, φήθ, ἀξιωφθιθ P
Ἁπάξ XVIII 32 H, ἅρπαξ P
Ἀπάτη VIII 3, 5
Ἀπολήν C X 23
Ἀραήλ XVIII 11
ἀραρὰ ἀραρή XVIII 29 H, ἄραρα χά-
ραρα P

Ἄραψ XI 4, ῥάθ P
ἀρδάδ XVIII 40 H, ἀρδοῦ P
ἀρνίου XVIII 28 P, cf. ἀερίου
Ἅρπαξ XVIII 32 P, cf. Ἁπάξ
Ἀρτοσαήλ XVIII 7 A (bis), L, ἀρωτο-
σαήλ, ἀρατοσαήλ P, ἀρσαήλ L
Ἀσιέλ C X 38
Ἀσμοδαῖος V 1, 7, 9, 11, 12, 13, Ἀσ-
μοδεῶ C X 7 UVW. ἀσμοδέος T
Ἀσταρώθ C X 21, 24 T, cf. Ἀστερώθ
Ἀστεραώθ VIII 10 PW, ἀστεραέθ V,
cf. περαωθ
Ἀστερώθ C X 24 V, ὁ ἕτερος Ἀσταρώθ
T, ἀστηρώθ W
Ἀτανιανούς C X 42 VW, cf. Ἀντιναός
Ἀτραξ XVIII 20 P, cf. Κατράξ
Αὐδαμεώθ XVIII 26 H, αὐμαδεώθ L
Αὐθάδης XVIII 27 H, cf. Μανθαδώ
Αὐτοθίθ P, αὐτώθ H, XVIII 38
Ἀφαρώφ XIII 6 P
Ἀχωνεώθ XVIII 37 H, ἀγχονίων P
ἀωᾶ Sig A, L (αωαω), T

βαέ XVIII 16 P
Βαζαζάθ XIV 7
Βαλθιούλ VIII 9 P
Βαρονχιήλ VIII 6 C, -χιαήλ H, -χια-
χήλ P
Βαρσαφαήλ XVIII 6 (bis), -σαβαήλ L
Βεελζεβούλ III 1, 3, 4, 5 C, 6, IV 2,
VII 1, 2, 4 P, 9, 10, IX 8, XVI 3 A,
5 P; C IX 9 T, X 1; βελζεβουήλ H
III 1, etc, V III 3, βεελζεβουέλ L
saepe, βελζεβούλ W III 3
βειρσαβεέ IV 8 V°, C XI 6, cf. βηροσαβεέ, -βεέλ
Βελβέλ XVIII 12
βηροσαβεέ C XI 6, -βεέλ IV 8 W°, C XI
6 W, βειρσαβεέ V, βηρφβεέ T
βιαναχιθ XVIII 40 P, cf. Μιανέθ
βιωνίχ Sig L(?), A (βιωνιά), V¹ (βιο-
νηχα)
Βοθήλ, Βοθοθήλ XVIII 17 P, cf. Φο-
βοθήλ

III. Index of Greek words

6, XIV 3, 4, XV 1, XVIII 22, XXVI 1,
C X 29, 30, 31, 34, XI 2, 5, D I 1
γυπότερος? (= ὑπόπτερος) II 3 C
γωνία V 12 L, VII 5, XXII 7, 8 B, XXIII
2, 4   D VI 10

Δαβίδ, cf. Δαυείδ, Sub V
δαιμονίζομαι XVII 3
δαιμονικός I 2
δαιμόνιον saepe
δαίμων saepe
δάκρυ D I 11, IV 2, 9
δακτυλίδιον I 6, 8 B, 9, 9 B, 10 L, 11, 12,
12 W, II 5 L, III 1, 4, VII 3, VIII 12,
X 6, XIII 3 P, XVI 7, XXII 10, 11, 13,
XXIV 2, XXVI 9 H, Sig BT
δακτύλιος I 6 C, 8 C, 12 W, III 1 C, 3 C,
X 6 P, D II 6, VI 5, Sig C
δάκτυλος I 2 C, D II 4, Sig T
Δαυείδ I 1, 7, V 10, XX 1, XXVI 9 H;
C Pro 1, C XII 1, XIII 12, D I 1, 3,
4, 5, 6, 9, 11, 12, Tit BIC, cf Δαβίδ
δάφνη XVIII 15, 33
δαφνόφυλλον ⊢ XVIII 15 P
δέ cf. Index I
δέησις C Pro 2
δεῖ I 7 P, C XIII 10
δείδω VI 8
δείκνυμι IV 2, X 7; C XIII 7, D VI 4
δεικνύω XVI 3
δειλιάω I 9 P (δειλιάζω?) Q
δεινός XXII 2
δεινῶς V 12, D IV 14
δεῖπνον I 1 C
δέκα V 12, IX 5, XVI 7, XXVI 7 H
δεκανός XVIII 4
δέκατος XVIII 14
Δεκέμβριος Sub V
δεκτικός XI 3 P
δέμας† IV 2
δένδρον XX 16, XXIII 1 B, C Pro 3, C
X 6, 48, D IV 16, VI 1
δεξιός I 2, 3, 4, XVIII 21, Sig T
δέομαι I 4, 5, 14 BC, II 7, V 11 P, XX
2, 7, XXII 3, C Pro 2, IX 8, XII 2,
XIII 7, 10

δέρμα IV 2 W, XXI 2 B, C IX 9
δερμάτιον C IX 10
δεσμεύω V 6, 11, VI 5, XI 5, 6, XIII 7,
XVI 5 P
δέσμιος III 7; C X 14
δεσμός IV 2 P, V 11, VI 3, VIII 11, XV
7, 15
δεσμόω Fleck (errore) V 6, 11, cf. δεσμεύω
δεσπόζω cf. Index II
δεσποτεία cf. Index II
δεσπότης I 4 L, 14 BC, XVI 3 A, C X 14,
XII 5; D I 9, 10, II 4, IV 2, 6, 13
δεσποτικός V 12 L
δεῦρο I 9, 11, 13 B, III 1, 3 HI, XVI 2 P
δεύτερος VI 3, VIII 3, XIV 8, XVIII 6
δεύω C IX 10
δέχομαι XX 5 P, XXVI 1 P
δέω I 14, II 6 L, III 7 I, IV 12 L, 12, V 1,
X 8, XI 1, XIII 2 P, XXII 11, 14 Q,
D II 7
δή cf. Index I
δηλαδή cf. Index I
δημιουργία D II 1
δῆτα cf. Index I
διά cf. Index I
διάβολος cf. Index II
διάγω I 1 H, XIX 1 P
διαδέχομαι D IV 6
διάδημα D VII 4
διαζώννυμι XXIII 3 B
διαθήκη V 9 L, 12 L, XV 14, XXVI 8,
9 H, C XIII 2, 9, 12, D I 2, Tit B, I(?),
H, C, Sub V
δίαιτα XI 2 P
διακονέω IX 6 P
διάκονος VI 10 L
διακόπτω C XIII 4
διακόσιοι VIII 12, X 9, XXI 2 H
διαλαμβάνω D VI 1
διαλογίζομαι I 9 I, D IV 4
διάνοια C Pro 2
διανοίγω C Pro 4
διαπεράω XXV 7
διαπλατύνω C XIII 8
διαπορέω D IV 4

εὐδηλότερον IX 5 P
εὐδοκία D VIII 4
εὐθέως II 7, V 1 P, XVII 2, XXII 14 P,
  C XII 1, cf. εὐθύς
εὐθυμέω XXV 9 B
εὐθύνω XIX 1
εὐθύς VIII 11 C
εὐθύς or εὐθέως XVIII 5—37
εὔκοσμος II 3 AB
εὐλογέω I 1 A, VII 1, XI 1 P, XV 1 P,
  XVI 1 P
εὐλογητός I 1 AP, III 5, XXVI 9 H;
  C Pro 4
εὔμορφος VIII 1, XIV 3
εὐπρέπεια XXIII 2 B, XXV 9, D II 1
εὑρίσκω V 5 C, 10, VII 5, 6, IX 7 P,
  XII 5, XVIII 21, XXII 11, XXV 5, 7,
  XXVI 8 B, C IX 10, D I 5
εὐσέβεια VIII 9
εὐσχημόνως VIII 7
εὔσχημος VIII 1
εὔτονος VIII 12 P
εὐφημέω XXII 16
εὐφραίνω I 1 A, XVIII 16, D I 10, II 4
εὐχαριστέω II 1, III 6, VII 4; D II 8,
  III 4
εὔχομαι II 5, 7, VII 7, X 11 P, XV 7,
  XVIII 42, XXVI 8 B, C Pro 5
εὔχρωτος* IV 2; C XI 2
εὐώδης XVIII 31 P
ἐφάπτω XVIII 17 P
ἐφίπταμαι XXII 20 P
ἐφίστημι I 9
ἐφοράω XI 2 P
ἐφορμάω XIV 4
ἐχθρός D I 2, II 10
ἔχω I 1, 3 C, 4, 4 P, 6, II 3, et pas.
ἑωθινός XXII 2
ἕως V 8, VI 11, VII 2, XV 10, XVIII
  15 P, C XIII 12, cf. also Index I

Ζάω XXII 2, XXV 8 B, C XII 3
ζέσις XVIII 29 H
ζητέω XV 3, 11, XXVI 1, C XIII 1
ζοθερός D IV 9
ζοφόω C XII 3
UNT 9 McCown

ζωδιακός XVIII 4 P
ζῴδιον II 2, C XII 6
ζωή C λ 4
ζῷον C X 28, 44

Ἡγέομαι D I 12
ἡδέως IX 2 PC
ἡδονή IX 5 A
ἡλικία XX 1 P
ἥλιος I 2, 4, VI 10, 10 HP, C X 43
ἧλος XVIII 28
ἡμέρα I 2, 2 A, 3, 5 et pas.
ἡμικρανος* XVIII 6 (= ἡμικρανικός)
ἡμίονος IV 2, C XI 2
ἡμιπρόσωπον* VII 1 C
ἥμισυς I 2, 4
ἡμιτριταῖος VII 6
ἧπαρ V 9, 13
ἥσυχος I 4
ἡττάω XVII 4 P
ἦχος IV 8

Θάλασσα II 5, 8, VI 3, 5, 6, 10, XII 4,
  XVI 1, 2, 3, 4, 7, XXI 3, XXIII 2,
  XXIV 1, 1 P, XXV 1, 5, 6, 7, D VI 12
θαλάσσιος XVI 1, C X 18
θαμβέω VII 2
θάνατος XV 14, XX 2, 4, D IV 2, 12, 14,
  15
θανατόω XX 5, XXII 20 P
θάπτω D I 6
θαρρέω D II 1
θαῦμα D III 8
θαυμάζω VIII 2, XIII 5, XIV 7, λVIII
  2 P, XXI 1, 18
θαυμάσιος D I 13
θεά VIII 4 P, XV 3
θεάομαι XXIV 1 Q, D III 1, IV 9, V 1
θεῖος I 1, 4 C, 10 L, C Pro 3, C X 53,
  D I 12
θέλημα C X 2, 32, D III 3, VII 3
θέλησις D I 3, II 1, III 8, VI 6
θέλω II 6, IV 7, VII 3, 4, 7, et pas
θεματίζω XXII 8 P
θεμέλιος VIII 12

10*

θεμελιόω XX 17, XXIII 4 B
θεοπάτωρ D I 2, 12
θεοποιέω XIV 2
θεός I 4, 5, 6, 7, 8 *et saepe*
θεοτόκος XXVI 10 H
θεραπεύω IX 7 P
θεράπων XXV 5, D IV 13
θερμαίνω XVIII 18 P
θέρος VII 5, C X 7
θεωρέω II 1 P, XIII 5, XIX 2, XX 6, 15, 16, XXIV 1 Q, C X 31, 34
Θηβαῖος VI 9
θηλάζω I 2, 4
θηλυκός I 7, II 3, VIII 1 P
θηλυμανία V 8
θῆλυς IV 1, C XI 1
θηρίον C Pro 3, C X 3
θηριοπρόσωπος XVIII 1
θησαυρός I 14 V, X 10, XXII 11 P, C X 21, 31, 38, 53, XIII 2
θικτός(?) C XIII 3, cf θνητός
θλίβω I 4, XX 19 H, D IV 11
θνήσκω XVII 2, XX 7 H, 11, 13 Q, C XII 3, D IV 9, 10
θνητός C XIII 3† (MSS θικτός), D IV 11
θρασύς II 8 B
θρέμμα C IX 9 V
θρηνέω D I 6
θρίαμβος(?) VI 3
θρίξ XIII 1, 5, 7
θρόνος II 1, III 5, V 4, 9 P, XIII 2, 3, XVIII 20, XXVI 9 H, C XIII 5, D VII 4, VIII 6
θυγάτηρ V 3, XXVI 1 B, XXVI 2
θυμιάω VI 10
θυμός V 2 P, D IV 1, 2
θυμόω XX 6
θύρα I 14 BC
θυσιαστήριον X 9, XXI 2, D VIII 6
θύω XXVI 4 B, 5 H

Ἰαμβρῆς XXV 4
Ἰαννῆς XXV 4
ἰάομαι VII 6, XI 2
ἰασαφῆτην*(?) I 3 C
ἴασπις† I 3 C, C XI 8, XII 6

ἰατρός Sub V
ἴδιος VI 3, C XII 5
ἰδιοχείρως C IX 10
ἰδού I 11
ἰδού I 1, 4, 10, 14, XIV 6, XVIII 3, XX 1, 7, XXII 1, 4, C Pro 1, Sig L
Ἰεβουσαῖοι XXVI 1
ἱερεύς VI 4
ἱερόν XXI 4, XXII 8 B
Ἱεροσόλυμα I 1 P
Ἱερουσαλημ (*fere compendio scr sic,* ιλημ I 1, 7, XV 8, XIX 1 P, XXII 7, XXIII 2 B, XXVI 9 H, Trt B I
Ἰεσσαί XXVI 9 H
Ἰησοῦς Χριστός D I 12
ἱκεσία XXII 5
ἱκετεύω C XIII 7
ἱλαστήριον XXI 2 H
ἵλεως XX 4
ἱμάσθλη C XI 7
ἱμάτιον D II 2
ἰνδικτιών Sub V
Ἰουδαῖος XXII 20, XXVI 8 H
Ἰούδα D I 12
ἱππικῆς? IV 8 C°, C XI 6
ἵππος XVI 1, C X 52
ἵπταμαι XX 12, 15
Ἰσραήλ IV 12 A, XII 1, XIII 1 P, XIX 3 P, XX 21 B, XXII 16 P, XXIV 2 Q, XXVI 8 H
ἵστημι VII 3, XII 4, XXII 13, 17, *et pas.*
ἱστορία C X 11
ἱστός C XII 6
ἰσχίον XVIII 27 P, 28 P
ἰσχυρός C XII 3, XIII 12, D VI 1
ἰσχύς C Pro 1
ἰσχύω X 2, XV 11, XXII 8
ἰχθύς V 9, 10, 13, XVI 1, XVIII 35
ἴχνος VIII 11
Ἰωάννης Sub V

Καθαιρέω VI 4, VIII 10
καθαριεύω C X 12
καθαρός VI 10, XVIII 33, C IX 9 T
καθέζομαι XII 4 P, XIII 2, XIV 7, XV 6, XVIII 21, 24, XXV 2
καθεύδω XIII 3

κατεργάζομαι V 12, VIII 12, IX 2, XII
	2, XXVI 7 Q
κατέρχομαι II 7, VI 2 P, 8, XV 5, XVII 4
κατεσθίω IX 2, XVII 3 P
κατέχω X 2, XIII 1, XIV 3, XV 4, C
	X 53, D II 7
κατηφής D IV 9
κατισχύω XXIII 4 P
κατισχύω XXIII 4 P
κατοίκησις IV 4
κατοικία I 10 L, XVII 2
κατορθόω X 5
κάτω D IV 13, 14, VI 8
κάτωθεν XXIV 4
καῦμα (?) XVI 4 P
καῦσις XVIII 29 P
κέδρινος XIX 2
κεῖμαι II 2, 5, IV 4 PCC°, VII 6, XVIII 6,
	C X 38, XI 3
κειμήλιον C XIII 9
κέλευσμα VI 6 P
κελεύω I 1, 8, 14 B, et pas.
κέρας VII 6, C XI 8
κεράσιον X 9, C X 7
κερατίζω IV 2 P
κεφάλαιον XII 3 P
κεφαλή IV 2, V 6 L, IX 2, 5, 6, XV 1,
	XVIII 5, XX 2, XXII 7, 16, XXIII 4;
	C XIII 5; D VI 10
κηρός Sig T
κῆτος II 8
κικλήσκω† VIII 7
κινέω XXVI 5 B, D IV 2, 17
κιόνιον XXIV 2 Q
κισσός I 3 C†, XVIII 37
κίων XII 4, XXI 3, XXIII 2, XXIV 1,
	2 Q, 3, 4, 5, XXV 1, 7, 8; D VI 12,
	13, 14
κλάζω XV 9
κλαίω IX 5
κλάσμα V 13
κλαυθμός C IX 8
κλέπτης C X 38
κλέπτω C X 38
κληρονομέω IX 5
κλῆσις II 1, D III 1, 6
κλῖμαξ XXIII 3 HP

κλίνη D I 11, II 7
κλίνω C XII 4 W
κλύδων C X 36
κνήμη IV 2, C XI 2
κοιλία XII 2, XVIII 13 P
κοιμάω XXVI 4
κοινός C XIII 2
κοίτη D II 9
κόκκος XVIII 33
κοκκύζω IX 3 C
κολαπτός I 6 I
κολίανδρον XVIII 20
κόλον C IX 9 T
κόλπος II 3 W
κόμη? V 12
κομίζω XVIII 41 P, XIX 2 H, XXII 11
κονιορτός VII 2, 3
κοπιάζω XVIII 11 H
κόπτω II 5 Q, 8, X 10
κόρη XXVI 5
κορυφή XII 6, XIII 1 P, XVIII 1
κοσμέω X 5, XXV 9, D VII 4
κοσμοκράτωρ VIII 2, XVIII 2, XX 14 B
κόσμος V 7, VI 4 P, X 2, XIII 3, XV 9;
	C XIII 2, 12, 13, 14
κοχλίας VII 1
κόχλος VII 1 H
κράζω I 14, III 4 L, XXVI 9 H
κρατέω X 3, 8 L, XXII 10, C X 21, 43,
	Tit B I
κράτος I 1 AB, D IV 10, VI 2
κραυγάζω I 12, 14 QC
κρείττων D II 1
κρεμάννυμι XIII 7, XXIV 4; D VI 14
κρημνοβατέω XI 6 P
κρημνός IV 5, XI 6, D IV 15, VI 1
κρίνω X 8, D I 13, IV 4, 6, 8
κρίσις D IV 5, 6, 8
κρόκινος V 9
κροκόδειλος C X 50
κρόκος VI 10
κρόταφος XVIII 5, 32
κρούω IV 11, D II 7
κρύπτω V 10, D VI 7
κτάομαι C XII 5, 6, XIII 14, D I 10,
	VII 1, VIII 2
κτῆμα II 1 L

Νάθαν D I 4, 5, 6, 7, 9, 10, 11

ναί XX 8 H, XXII 20 P

ναός I 1, 3, 4, 5, 8, II 5, IV 12, *et pas.*

νάρδος VI 10 H, νάρδιν L, νάρσιν P

νάρκη XVIII 19

ναυτία XVI 4 P

νεανίας I 10 L, 13 L

νεκρός XX 20 B, D I 6

νεόνυμφος V 7

νεός I 1, 10 L, XX 5, 6, 7, 11, D I 2

νεώτερος I 2 L, 3 L, 4 L

νεῦμα C Pro 2

νευρά XVIII 17 A

νεῦρον XVIII 11, 36

νευροχάλασις * XVIII 17 P

νεφρός XVIII 14, 27

νήθω IV 12

νήπιος XVIII 25 L

νίκη C X 9

νίπτω XIII 2

νοέω XI 1 P

νομή V 5

νομίζω IV 6, XXVI 5 H

νόσημα XI 2

νότος VII 6, XIX 3, XXI 1, D V 1

νοῦς XVIII 19 A, C X 5

νυκτοφαγήση * XVIII 35 P

νύξ I 3, C, 5, IV 12, V 8, VII 5, IX 5, *et pas.*

νωδός XVIII 30 P

νῶτον XIV 1

Ξηραίνω II 8, XXIII 1 Q

ξηρός C X 6

ξίφος VIII 6, XVII 2

ξύλινος XXI 3 B

ξύλον VIII 6, IX 6, XI 7, XII 3, XIV 3, 6, XV 10, XIX 2, C X 6, D V 1

ξυλοφορέω XI 7 P

ξύω C IX 9 T

Ὅδε I 3 C, C IX 9 U

ὁδεύω IV 9

ὁδοιή(?) XII 2 Λ

ὁδός VIII 11 C, XVIII 21, XXII 11 B; D I 5, VI 8

ὁδούς V 13 †, XI 7 P, XII 2

ὀδύνη D IV 9

ὀδυρμός D IV 2

οἶδα IV 1 A P, 6, V 13, XX 11, D IV 2

οἰδαίνω V 7

οἴησις † C XII 3

οἰκεῖος C XIII 13, 14

οἰκειοχείρως C XII 4

οἰκέτης X 6, XXII 13, C XII 5

οἰκέω IV 4 CC°, VIII 4, XII 3, C XI 3, XIII 2, D VI 1

οἰκητήριον IV 5, XVII 2, C XI 5

οἰκία I 14 L, VI 10, D VI 1

οἰκοδομέω I 1, 7, XIX 1, 2, XXI 1, XXII 6, XXIII 4, XXVI 7 H, C Pro 1, 5, D II 7, III 3, V 1, VIII 5

οἰκοδομή I 1, 1 A, II 8, X 10, XIV 5, 8 XVIII 43 P, D III 3, 7, IV 1, 2, V 1, VI 2, VIII 1, Tit H

οἰκονομέω I 1 P, XXVI 6, D IV 15

οἶκος I 5 L, VII 5, XVIII 15, *et pas*

οἰκουμένη XV 10, XXIV 2, C XIII 4, 7

οἶμαι D I 13

οἴμοι IX 3, D II 10

οἶνος XVIII 31

οἷος IX 2 H P, XVIII 23, C X 23, D II 4 VIII 7

οἰστός † C XII 6

ὀλίγος IV 7, V 5, VII 2, VIII 11 C, XIV 3

ὀλολύζω XXVI 7 H

ὅλος I 5, V 7, 12, VI 9, XIII 5 P, XIX 1 P, C X 45, XIII 9, D IV 2

ὁλοσώματος C XIII 13, 14

Ὄλυμπος VIII 4

ὅλως IX 5 P

ὁμιλία D IV 14

ὄμμα V 2 C, D IV 9

ὄμνυμι XXV 8 B

ὁμοθυμαδόν VIII 2 PC, XVIII 2

ὅμοιος VIII 8, X 9, XV 10, D I 13, VI 12

ὁμοιόω XXVI 4

ὁμοίως VIII 7, 10, 11, X 8 P, C IX 9, X 4, 14—19, XII 4, 5

ὁμολογέω D III 6

ὁμόνοια VIII 4 P

ὁμοῦ VIII 4, 11 C, C XI 9

ὑπεναντίος VIII 10
ὑπερβάλλω Tit B, ὑπερβαλλόντως Tit I
ὑπερβολή X 2P
ὑπερευκλεής†* XXVI 10H
ὑπερήφανος V 3
ὑπερί C XII 6
ὑπερισχύω X 2P
ὑπερμεγέθης XXIV 4
ὑπεροχή X 2
ὕπνος II 3B
ὑπνωτικός II 3
ὑπογινώσκω* V 13L
ὑποδείκνυμι XXII 11Q, C XIII 7
ὑποδεικνύω C X 2
ὑποδέχομαι XVI 2
ὑποδέω XXIII 3P
ὑπόδυνα(?) XII 2P
ὑποδύνω VII 5
ὑπόθεσις XXVI 3B
ὑποκαίω V 13
ὑποκαπνίζω I 3C
ὑποκάτωθεν C XI 7
ὑπόκαυσις XI 7P
ὑπολαμβάνω I 4L
ὑπολείπω VI 2, VII 1
ὑπόλοιπος VII 1P
ὑπόλοξος XXIV 5
ὑπομένω XI 6
ὑπομιμνήσκω XXII 6
ὑποπιάζω D II 4
ὑποπροτάσσω* X 6L
ὑπόπτερος II 3
ὑπόσχομαι C IX 8
ὑποταγή C X 50, D III 3, IV 6
ὑποτάσσω II 5L, 7, 8, III 5, et pas.
ὑποτελέω XXII 5P
ὑποτελής XXIII 5P
ὑπουργός D IV 13
ὑποχείριος XXV 8B, C IX 8
ὑψηλός VII 1, 8, comp. D I 13
ὕψιστος I 7, XI 6, XVIII 20P
ὕψος VI 8, XXIV 1Q
ὑψόω XXIV 1P

Φαίνω II 3B, VIII 4, XV 5, et pas
φανερέω* C X 31

φανερός C XIII 2
φανερόω XIII 3P, C X 21, 38
φανερῶς IV 6, VI 6P, XII 3, C XI 5
φαντασία III 7, C X 51T
φάντασμα VIII 9C
φάραγξ IV 5
Φαραώ XXV 3, 5, 6
φάρυγξ XVIII 37
φαῦλος VIII 9
φέρω I 7, VI 4P, VIII 6, XI 7, et pas.
φεύγω XIII 6A, XVIII 40
φήμη D VIII 1
φημί passim
φθάνω IX 5P
φθονέω I 2A
φθόνος VI 4, XVIII 38
φιάλη XVI 7P
φίαλος* XVIII 44P, C XI 7
φιλία XX 9
φιλολογέω X 2P
φιλονεικία D IV 1
φίλος VIII 11, IX 8, XVIII 38
φλέγω I 10
φλόξ III 4
φοβερός I 3C
φοβερόχροος* XII 1
φοβέω II 6, V 9, VI 10L, XVII 4
φόβος I 4L, D I 8
φονεύω V 8, D I 2, 3
φόνος V 8P, VI 4
φορά C IX 9T, XII 6
φορέω V 12, XVIII 16, Sig T
φράζω VI 8L
φρένιμος (cf. φρόνιμος)* I 1C, C X 5\
φρενιτιάω X 3P
φρήν X 3, XIII 4, XVIII 12, 30
φρίκη XVIII 19P
φρικτός XXIV 4Q, C X 53
φρίσσω II 1
φρόνησις XIX 3, C X 20, 41, D I 12
φρόνιμος (cf φρένιμος) C X 5UW
φρουρά XVIII 43P
φρουρέω XX 18B
φυλακή XVI 7A, C X 14
φυλάσσω XXIII 2Q, XXIV 2HP, XXVI
    8H, C XIII 8, 9, Tit C, Sub V
φυλή C X 28, D I 12

IV. Index of Modern Greek

(Not including MS E)

V. Index of Subjects and Persons

Hezekiah 36, 92, 96 ff., 99, 102
Hippolytus 96 f
Holkham Hall, Library 11
Hygromanteia, *see* Solomon, apocryphal books

Iblis 81
Incantations 90
Inventiones Nominum 73
Iranian influences 54 ff.
Isidor (pseudo-), de muneris 103
Isis 4
Istrin, V. M. 10, 12, 17, 18, 29, 105
Italy, Greek manuscripts 14 n 1, 15 n. 1, 19, 20, 25, 26 f.; *see also* Bologna, University Library, Milan, Ambrosian Library, and Manuscripts U, V, and W

James, Montague Rhodes 11 n 3, 29, 49, 60, 91
Jantsch, Heinrich 10 n 1, 20 n. 3
Jerusalem, manuscripts, *see* Appendix, manuscripts E and N pp. 112—115
Jesus Christ 2, 50 f., 74, 83
Jeu, First Book of 85, Second Book of 70
Jewish elements in Testament 59—66
Jinn 78 ff., *see also* Solomon, jinn of
Johannes Canabutzes 12
John of Aron (Aro?) 23
Judaism 59—66

Key of Solomon, *see* Solomon, apocryphal books, Clavicula
Kohler, Kaufman 3 n 1, 30, 65, 106, 108
κοσμοκράτορες 45, 60, *see also* Elements
Kurz, E. 29
Kynopeges 44, 45

Language of Testament 38—43
Legend, *see* Folklore, Solomon
Leicester, Earl of 11
Letter formulae 40 ff.
Lix Tetrax 67
Locusts as sacrifice 49, 64, 72, 81
Lucifer 45

Magianism 54 f., 85
Magic 47 f., Arabian 78 f., Christian 2 f., 74, Egyptian 56 f, Ethiopian 72, Hel-

lenistic 67 f., Jewish-Aramaic 65 f; materials used 48, mediaeval 84 f., medicine and magic 4, 13, 32, 47 f, 90, *see also* Cup, Demonology, Incantations, Table
Maimonides 93
Manuscripts consulted, Austrian, *see* Vienna, English, *see* England, French, *see* France, German, *see* Munich, Italian, *see* Italy, Russia, *see* Moscow, *see also* Jerusalem, Mount Athos; relationships 5—9, 30—33, manuscript D 10 f., 29, 31, 32 f., 38 f., 85 f., 111, E, *see* Appendix, H 11 f., 31, 37, I 12 f., 29, 31, 37, L 13 ff., 31, 86; N, *see* Appendix; P 15 ff., 28, 31, 37, 50, Q 18 ff., 29, 31, S 15, 18, 31 f., T 18 f., 23, 31 f, U 20 f., 23, V 14 ns. 2, 3, 15, 18, 20, 21—25, 26, 31 f., W 14 and n. 1, 18, 20, 25—27, 31 f.
Marcus Aurelius 1 f.
Mastema 61
Mazdaism, *see* Magianism
Mediates, George 25, 27
Mesmes, de, Henri and Jean Jacques, 16, 17 and n. 5
Michael 46, 49, 54, 72
Middle Ages, science 22, 26
Migne, Abbé 15, 29
Milan, Ambrosian Library 20
Minas, Minoides 12 f.
Montgomery, James A. 65
Moscow 27, 58
Moses as magician 93
Mount Athos 14 n. 1, 27
Munich 14 n 1, 20
Mysticism, cosmic 71
Myths, motifs, *see* Folklore

Name, power of 4, 47, 74
Names, magic, *see* Angels, Demons, Re
Nathan 85
New Testament 68 f
Nino, *see* St. Nino
Notaricon 82, 84

Obsequies of the Virgin (Syriac) 73
Obyzuth 78, 82

11**

.

VI. Index of Quotations from Ancient Authors

Druck von August Pries in Leipzig.

Milton Keynes UK
Ingram Content Group UK Ltd.
UKHW020958240124
436589UK00004B/87

9 781015 503748